What fun to belon[g]
or should I s[ay]

Intellectual and social, babies
and all.   With appreciation —

[signature] Ellen

Emma Teng   [signature]

[signature]

Joanna Handlin Smith

with much gratitude — [signature]

[signature]   with love.

[signature]

cheers! [signature]

Writing and *Materiality*
in *China*

Essays in Honor of Patrick Hanan

Harvard-Yenching Institute Monograph Series 58

Essays in Honor of Patrick Hanan

edited by

Judith T. Zeitlin & Lydia H. Liu

with Ellen Widmer

Published by the Harvard University Asia Center

for the Harvard-Yenching Institute

and distributed by Harvard University Press

Cambridge, Massachusetts, and London 2003

Writing and

Materiality

in China

Printed in the United States of America

The Harvard-Yenching Institute, founded in 1928 and headquartered at Harvard University, is a foundation dedicated to the advancement of higher education in the humanities and social sciences in East and Southeast Asia. The Institute supports advanced research at Harvard by faculty members of certain Asian universities and doctoral studies at Harvard and other universities by junior faculty at the same universities. It also supports East Asian studies at Harvard through contributions to the Harvard-Yenching Library and publication of the *Harvard Journal of Asiatic Studies* and books on premodern East Asian history and literature.

Library of Congress Cataloging-in-Publication Data

Writing and materiality in China : essays in honor of Patrick Hanan / edited by Judith T. Zeitlin & Lydia H. Liu, with Ellen Widmer.

    p. cm. -- (Harvard-Yenching Institute monograph series ; 58)

    Includes bibliographical references and index.

    ISBN 0-674-01098-1 (alk. paper)

    1. Chinese literature--History and criticism. 2. Mass media and culture. I. Hanan, Patrick. II. Zeitlin, Judith T., 1958– III. Liu Lydia He. IV. Widmer, Ellen. V. Series.

    PL2262.W74 2003

    895.1'09--dc21   2002038714

Index by Mary Mortensen

♾ Printed on acid-free paper

Last number below indicates year of this printing

13 12 11 10 09 08 07 06 05 04 03

Title page: Li Zhuqi (19th c.), Painted fan (verso) decorated with inscribed pages and fragments of rubbings and printed pages. Courtesy of the Arthur M. Sackler Museum, Harvard University Art Museums, Bequest of the Hofer Collection of the Arts of Asia. Photograph by Junius Beebe and Katya Kallsen; © President and Fellows of Harvard College.

Contents

Illustrations

Preface

Many of these papers were first presented at a three-day symposium held on December 12–14, 1997, to mark the retirement of Professor Patrick Hanan from Harvard University. Hosted by the Department of East Asian Languages and Civilizations, the symposium brought together Professor Hanan's students, colleagues, friends, and family from around the world.

Unlike more generic conference volumes, this one is not a simple selection of papers presented at a particular event. From the outset, a number of talks coalesced around a set of thematic clusters relating to publishing, readership, illustration, and the media. In the years since the symposium, editors Lydia Liu and Judith Zeitlin have subsumed these themes under the larger rubric of writing and materiality and solicited other essays to fill out the volume. Their efforts have helped us contributors to see our work in a different light and have challenged us to expand our perspectives on texts and images in China. Contributions from outside Hanan's immediate circle of students, too, have created new resonances and expanded the volume's thematic range. In considering writing and materiality, the authors in this volume take their cues from such fields as anthropology, art history, and history of the book, where traditional literary studies are decentered, and the focus moves away from the author and his or her work. In such fields, publishing, perishability, illustration, and visuality interact with the written text in ways that could not have been imagined twenty, or even ten, years ago.

This volume would not exist were it not for Patrick Hanan's long devotion to the study of Chinese fiction and his faculty for inspiring a similar devotion in his students. Even more, the diverse contents of this volume reflect his ability to encourage others to pursue their own, varied research interests. His distinctiveness as a teacher, mentor, and colleague are his generosity of spirit and his gift for seeing the implications of others' work and commenting constructively on them. His major literary studies on the vernacular novel and short fiction, with their insights into language, form, and historical context, are foundational to the efforts of anyone coming after him in the field. Among these, *The Chinese Short Story, The Chinese Vernacular Story, The Invention of Li Yu*, and the articles on *Jin Ping Mei, Pingyao zhuan*, the classical tale, court case fiction, and Lu Xun come most readily to mind. They are models of the scholarly accuracy, felicity of expression, and discernment to which we all aspire. We are further inspired by his activities as a translator. Writers as diverse in time and mood as Li Yu, Wu Jianren, and Chen Diexian have obtained a new life in English, thanks to his precise yet lively prose.

One of the most tantalizing aspects of Professor Hanan's work has been his excavation of the anonymous writer, variously known as "X" or "Langxian," from the fiction of the first half of the seventeenth century. It seems fitting that one of the contributors to this volume himself prefers to remain anonymous, a rare incidence of opaqueness in our information age. Remarkably, more than any other essay in the volume, Anonymous's work lives up to the high standards set by Professor Hanan, in terms of both scholarly quality and writing style. Moreover, in showing how a newspaper contest became a catalyst for the "new" novel in China, this piece exemplifies the volume's focus on extra-authorial issues and the power of the press. For these two reasons, the editors have chosen to include it, despite their misgivings about any confusion to which it might lead.

Most recently, Professor Hanan's post-retirement activities have brought to light another outstanding quality, the spirit of adventure that carries him ever forward into new research frontiers. His writings on late Qing and missionary publications were not foreshadowed in the milestones of his career before retirement, yet they are no less seminal than the scholarship we came to celebrate when we gathered in December 1997.

Those of us who were Professor Hanan's students share an acquaintance with his methodology and a long history of collaboration with one another. These range from jointly published research to panels at professional meetings to more informal critical readings of one another's writings to mutual citation. Those of us who never studied under Professor Hanan, too, are indebted to his insights, whether through interactions with his students and their students or through direct contact with his ideas. Such interrelations are part of what bind this volume into a single whole. Less a festschrift than an outgrowth of shared scholarly affinities, *Writing and Materiality in China* joins sinological positivism to a wide range of contemporary concerns.

The collaboration underlying this volume draws on support of another, more practical but no less important kind. As the primary source of funding for the symposium, Harvard's Department of East Asian Languages and Literatures cannot go unmentioned. Peter Bol, Leo Ou-fan Lee, and Stephen Owen, in particular, deserve thanks for their help and vision in steering it toward a workable schedule, given the large number of scholars who wanted to attend. From the same department, Susan Kashiwa and Frankie Hoff must be thanked for their unstinting staff support when there were many competing claims on their time. Those present at the symposium and who contributed so much to its success include Victor Mair, Meir Shahar, Paul Clark, Yenna Wu, Angelina Yee, Sally Church, Tina Lu, Laura Hua Wu, Paul Clark, Alice Cheang, Sally Church, Margaret Wan, Daisy Ng, George Hayden, Ron Egan, Jeff Kinkley, Perry Link, David Wang, Wang Ch'iu-kuei, Li-li Chen, Graham Sanders, Nancy Hodes, Eva Chou Shan, Jeanne Tai, and Lin Hua. Finally, John Ziemer, director of the Asia Center Publications Program, was the first to encourage us to translate our oral presentations into something more permanent. His active involvement and intellectual engagement throughout the project continuously reinforced one of the volume's main points: that the editor's role in making a book is as fundamental as that of its authors.

The importance of these contributions does not diminish Professor Hanan's role as progenitor of this volume, and it is to him that it is dedicated. We thank him for his wise and good-humored counsel over many years.

Ellen Widmer
Wesleyan University

Contributors

RANIA HUNTINGTON is assistant professor of Chinese language and literature at the University of Illinois at Urbana-Champaign. Her primary research interests are classical language narrative (*wenyan xiaoshuo*) and the supernatural in literature. Her book, *Alien Kind: Foxes and Late Imperial Chinese Narrative*, is forthcoming from this press in 2003. She is presently working on a project on memories of ages of chaos and rebellion as preserved in classical narrative.

LYDIA H. LIU is Helmut F. Stern Professor of Chinese Studies and Professor of Comparative Literature and Asian Languages and Cultures at the University of Michigan. She is the author of *Translingual Practice* (1995) and the editor of *Tokens of Exchange* (1999). Her new book, *Desire and Sovereign Thinking*, is forthcoming from Harvard University Press.

KATHRYN LOWRY is Assistant Professor of East Asian Languages and Cultural Studies at the University of California at Santa Barbara. She is author of the forthcoming book *A Tapestry for the Eyes* on printed performance texts and readerships from the 1550s on, as well as several articles including "The Space of Reading" on letter writing and fictions of the self.

SHANG WEI is Associate Professor of Chinese literature at Columbia University. He is the author of *"Rulin waishi" and Cultural Transformation in Late Imperial China*, forthcoming from this press in 2003. He is currently writing a book on *Jin Ping Mei cihua* and late Ming culture.

EMMA J. TENG is Associate Professor of Chinese Studies at the Massachusetts Institute of Technology, where she currently holds the Class of 1956 Career Development Chair. Her previous publications include "Taiwan as a Living Museum: Tropes of Anachronism in Late-Imperial Chinese Travel Writing" (1999); "An Island of Women: The Discourse of Gender in Qing Travel Accounts of Taiwan" (1998); and "The Construction of the 'Traditional Chinese Woman' in the Western Academy: A Critical Review" (1996). Her book, *A "Savage Island" Becomes "Chinese Province": Taiwan in the Imagined Geography of the Qing Empire*, is forthcoming from this press in 2003.

SOPHIE VOLPP is an Assistant Professor at the University of California at Davis. Her research interests include the literature of connoisseurship, autobiographical literature, the history of sexuality, and the drama of the late imperial period. Publications include a translation of the nineteenth-century woman playwright Wu Zao's "Qiao Ying" (A reflection in disguise) (2001); "Classifying Lust: The Seventeenth-Century Vogue for Male Love" (2001); and "Texts, Tutors and Fathers: Pedagogy and Pedants in Tang Xianzu's *Mudanting*" in *From Ming to Qing: Dynastic Decline and Transition*, forthcoming from this press in 2004.

EUGENE Y. WANG is Gardner Cowles Associate Professor of History of Art and Architecture at Harvard University. His numerous articles have appeared in *Critical Inquiry*, *The Art Bulletin*, and elsewhere; their subjects range from ancient bronze mirrors, Buddhist wall paintings, sculpture, architecture, to modern Chinese art and cinema. His book *Shape of the Visual: Imaginary Topography in Medieval Chinese Buddhist Art* , forthcoming in 2004, is on medieval Chinese visuality and world-making.

ELLEN WIDMER is Professor of Asian Languages and Literatures at Wesleyan University. She is the author of *The Margins of Utopia: "Shui-hu hou chuan" and the Literature of Ming Loyalism*, published by this press in 1987, and co-editor (with David Der-Wei Wang) of *From May Fourth to June Fourth: Fiction and Film in Twentieth-Century China* (Harvard University Press, 1994) and (with Kang-i Sun Chang) of *Writing Women in Late Imperial China* (1997). She is currently completing a book on women and fiction in the nineteenth century.

Wu Hung is Harrie A. Vanderstappen Distinguished Service Professor in Chinese Art History and Director of the Center for the Art of East Asia at the University of Chicago. He has published widely on both traditional and contemporary Chinese art. His major works on traditional Chinese art include *The Wu Liang Shrine: The Ideology of Early Chinese Pictorial Art* (1989), *Monumentality in Early Chinese Art and Architecture* (1995), *The Double Screen: Medium and Representation in Chinese Painting* (1996), and *Three Thousand Years of Chinese Painting* (co-author; 1997). His major books and edited volumes on contemporary Chinese art include *Transience: Chinese Experimental Art at the End of the Twentieth Century* (1999), *Exhibiting Experimental Art in China* (2000), *Chinese Art at the Crossroads: Between Past and Future, Between East and West* (editor; 2001), and *Reinterpretation: A Decade of Experimental Art in China* (1990–2000) (chief editor, 2002).

Catherine Vance Yeh is a scholar working in the field of Chinese literature and culture of the late Qing and Republican periods. After studying with Patrick Hanan, she received her Ph.D. from Harvard University in 1990. Her new book, *City, Courtesan, and Intellectual: The Rise of Shanghai Entertainment Culture, 1850–1910*, is about to be published. She is a Research Associate at the Institute for Chinese Studies, University of Heidelberg, Germany.

Judith T. Zeitlin is Professor of Chinese Literature at the University of Chicago. The author of *Historian of the Strange: Pu Songling and the Chinese Classical Tale* (1993), she has published widely on ghosts and gender in late imperial China and is completing a book-length study on this subject. Her current research focuses on the history of Chinese drama, performance, and vocal music as well as medicine.

Writing *and* Materiality *in* China

Essays in Honor of Patrick Hanan

Introduction

Lydia H. Liu and Judith T. Zeitlin

Speaking about writing, especially Chinese writing, entails thinking about the ways in which writing speaks to us through a variety of media and forms. Whether it be a consideration of the written character or its imprints, traces, or ruins, writing always appears in its multifarious guises to be much more than an embodiment of textuality. To reflect on this and related features of writing is the goal of this volume, as we consider a fundamental problem: What is the relationship of writing to materiality over the course of China's literary history? In some manner or other, all the chapters in this volume ponder the physical aspects of the production and circulation of writing as a dynamic process—something that can be collected and exchanged, bought and sold, bestowed as a gift or entered in a contest; something that can be cut up, pieced together and recycled, borrowed, copied, or appropriated; something that can be stolen, ruined, lost, or destroyed. To speak of the thing-ness of writing is to understand it not as an artifact inert and complete unto itself but as something in a constant state of motion and flux, which is continually transported from one place or time to another, one genre or me-dium to another, one person or public to another.

To put it yet another way: How does thinking about writing as the mate-rial product of a culture affect the way we do Chinese literary history? For one thing, it shifts the emphasis from the author as the main creator and ul-timate arbiter of a text's meaning to the editors and publishers, collectors and readers, producers and viewers, through whose hands a text, genre, or legend is reshaped, disseminated, and given new meanings. For another, it means taking seriously the arguments of recent European historians of the book and print culture such as D. F. McKenzie and Roger Chartier, that the form—or more precisely, the format, location, and technical medium—of a work and the meanings it generates at a particular moment are inseparable. Yoking writing and materiality, this volume aims to bypass the commonplace tendency to oppose form and content, words and things, documents and artifacts, to rethink key issues in the interpretation of Chinese literary and visual culture.

How, for example, does taking into account the physical properties of an inscription and rubbings of it expand our definition of the sign, of that which constitutes meaning? What effects have technical developments in China's particular experience of print had on the ways different literary and visual genres have been produced and perceived? How did the continual process of exchanging, copying, and commenting on manuscripts not necessarily meant for publication serve to build literary networks among the elite and open a space for elite "wanna-bes" to join existing networks or create their own? In what respects are maps, diagrams, and charts—words arranged in a spatial structure—simply another form of "writing"—and in what respects do they demand alternative ways of looking? How does physical writing—inscriptions present both *in situ* and in books—literally turn a natural site into "landscape" or "empire"? What role do modern forms of media play in the process of transcribing oral culture into tangible products whose ownership can then be contested and controlled?

Emphasizing writing as a mode of material production is hardly new to contemporary theorists or scholars of Chinese literature. Pierre Bourdieu's extensive work on language, symbolic exchange, cultural fields, and *habitus* has taught us a great deal about how symbolic capital functions at different social levels and how the production of knowledge forms an integral part of material production.[1] Walter Benjamin's earlier work on the Baroque allegory, material artifacts, memory, and ruins has been revived in recent years to generate a vast amount of scholarship and a whole new range of interpretations.[2] Others, such as Jacques Derrida, tackle writing as a mode of reading and thinking that would effectively obstruct or put under "erasure" the self-evidence or truth of metaphysical knowledge.[3] As scholars and teachers of Chinese literature, art history, and culture, we are interested in the new developments in poststructuralist theory but are fully aware of the self-imposed limits in the works of European theorists due to their lack of intimate engagement with cultures and societies other than their own. We ask, therefore: Can our own knowledge and research bring about a less Eurocentric understanding of writing and materiality?

In calling attention to the cultural and cognitive processes by which things become or stop being commodities, the anthropologist Igor Koptyff has noted that "commodities must be not only produced materially as things but also culturally marked as being a certain kind of thing."[4] Of course, even when writing is explicitly produced and marked as a commodity (as in the book trade), writing is never simply an ordinary thing. This is particularly true of imperial China, where incredible emphasis was placed on skill in writing in order to define elite status. The examination system and the culture it spawned, most recently studied by Benjamin Elman, is the most obvious and important example, but exchanges of poetry and participation in literary party games could also help determine who "belonged."[5] The fact that writing has tended to be culturally marked as a privileged thing different from all other things has tended to overwhelm an awareness of the thingness of writing even as we have analyzed how writing was produced, exchanged, and apprehended.

Taken collectively, the studies in this book span almost a millennium. They are loosely arranged in chronological order, with the first chapter (Wu Hung's) extending back to the antiquarian movement of the eleventh century and the last chapter (Lydia Liu's) extending forward into the intellectual copyright disputes of the 1990s. One of our major intentions in this volume is to help break down the vestiges of an absolute division in the Chinese literary field between "modern" (read: the twentieth century) and "traditional" (everything prior to that). Fortunately, under the onslaught of new research and new political realities, along with the waning of the twentieth century, this divide has been crumbling for some time. Rather than attempting broad sweeps or explicit comparisons between different ages, however, we have sought specific and focused historical studies, many of them on little known genres or works. Few of them focus on a history of the book *per se*. To represent the range of cultural production, we deliberately encouraged contributions on a wide variety of literary modes and formats: letters, popular encyclopedias and manuals, maps, poetry anthologies, inscriptions, rubbings, novels, full-length prosimetric fiction (*tanci*), accounts of the strange, advertisements, newspaper articles, local opera, and film. These run the gamut from the most prestigious and valued of cultural products to the decidedly lowbrow stuff of everyday life.

As the table of contents shows, this book is organized into four major thematic and temporal clusters. These rubrics are designed as signposts to orient the reader and to suggest some concrete ways in which the central topic of the book can be addressed. The opening section, "The Circulation of Writing," examines elite practices though which the written word continued to circulate apart from the mechanism of publishing in an age of print. Part II, "Print Culture and Networks of Reading," looks at how the format of printed books shaped reading and writing practices and explores the interactions between the editors, authors, and reading publics of popular forms associated with fiction in late Ming and Qing publishing. Print culture and publishing continue to be the focus of the third section, "The Late Qing Periodical Press: New Images, New Fiction," but the papers here are concerned more with the impact of a mass periodical press on literary and visual production in the late nineteenth century than with the printed book. Part IV, "Ethnography, Media, and Ideology," expands the scope of the volume beyond the written word to investigate the interplay of writing with visual modes and other nonprint media, from the maps of the Qing empire to the popular operas and films of the early 1960s.

In the discussion of the individual chapters below, we are not necessarily summarizing the main thrust of each; rather, we are trying to bring to bear on them perspectives that might not be apparent when the chapters are read in isolation. Our aim is to make the papers speak to one another, to bring about productive and surprising encounters among them, so that what happens between or among the essays becomes as interesting and important as what is in them. A major theme of this volume is how much the location of written works—for instance, the transplantation and juxtaposition of individually authored manuscripts within the physical pages of a collectively edited printed book—actively affects the ways in which we read and understand them. This collection of essays is, of course, no exception.

However, the thematic rubrics laid out in the organization of the chapters cannot substitute for an elucidation of what the notions of "writing" and "materiality" should be doing for this book. In the pages that follow, we explore a set of overarching concerns that may offer fruitful connections among individual essays as well as make the logic of the entire volume visible. We do so by considering central aspects of writing to determine the theoretical and historical parameters of each in relation to three of the primary physical constraints of the world in which we live: technology, space, and time.

Writing As Technology

China, as is well known, invented paper and printing. By at least the mid-ninth century, some Buddhist texts were being reproduced through the technology of woodblock printing.[6] The uses and spread of publishing grew over the next centuries; already by the twelfth century, in addition to extensive state-sponsored publishing projects, we find a flourishing commercial publishing industry and an established print culture.[7] It would be fascinating to explore to what extent the rise of what Benedict Anderson calls "print capitalism" in Europe and elsewhere was indebted or linked to this situation, since China was one of the leading economies of the world in the sixteenth through the eighteenth centuries.[8]

For the immediate purpose of this book, however, we are concerned mainly with the relationship of literary forms to technology, understood both in a technical sense, as the means for producing and reproducing writing, and in a social sense, as the ways in which these forms of writing were distributed, consumed, and apprehended. As such, the chapters in this volume should be seen as part of a growing body of new scholarship in the China field on the history of the book, the impact of print culture, and the effects of modern media such as the newspaper and cinema. As students of literature and art history, our goal is not to provide empirical studies of the publishing or film industries but to explore how a heightened awareness of the technological aspects of writing, reading, and viewing can make a difference in interpreting *specific* works, genres, or movements.

Recent scholarship on China has made much of the publishing boom of the mid-sixteenth century, which resulted in a huge outpouring of imprints of varying quality and price produced by a broad mix of commercial, private family, and state publishing houses for multiple reading publics. The late Ming is generally considered the apex of woodblock illustration as a technically sophisticated art form, both interspersed within a literary text and printed independently in deluxe monochrome or even multicolored editions.[9] Many different trends could be noted in this complex period, but we basically agree with Shang Wei's observation in his chapter, that during the late Ming "commercial publishing played a greater role than either private or official publishing in determining the overall orientation of print culture. Second, the late Ming witnessed a further growth in what is called 'quantity printing.'" Robert Hegel has suggested that increased standardization in the printing trade and the spread of the new, easier to read string-binding format could have been factors stimulating the boom, but no dramatic technological or organizational breakthroughs within the printing trade have been discovered that adequately explain this surge in publishing.[10] Scholars have therefore tended to stress broader economic, social, and intellectual factors such as the increase in commercialization and urbanization and the philosophical and literary ferment of the late Ming, especially in the cities of Jiangnan, where the publishing industry was concentrated.[11]

To understand more precisely what this new print culture involved, consider the encyclopedias for daily use (*riyong leishu*) and the literary miscellanies that were mainstays of commercial printing in this period. These popular compendia included diverse materials, both practical and entertaining, and freely copied from existing books and one another with no concern for provenance or integrity. These collections were more than how-to manuals or repositories of information or entertainment, however. As Shang Wei argues in his provocative study of the anonymous novel *Jin Ping Mei* (*The Plum in the Golden Vase*), these heterogeneous publications inculcated new modes of writing and reading. The puzzling habit of the *Jin Ping Mei*'s author of incorporating so many miscellaneous texts lifted from other books, can, in Shang's view, be seen as an extension of the promiscuous editing practices found in the encyclopedias and miscellanies. Likewise, the juxtaposition of fragmented and unrelated texts in such compendia facilitated random reading and fostered the ability to jump quickly from one subject to another, skills, he contends, that helped familiarize readers with the "recycling of the readymade" and the polyglot text world they would find in the novel.

Another important issue that emerges in this discussion is the relationship between printed text and illustration. It has frequently been remarked that one reason block printing was traditionally preferred over movable type in China was that block printing allowed for the reproduction of different calligraphic handwriting styles and facilitated the combination of pictures and text.[12] Indeed one of the most striking features of block-printed books is the range of images and styles of illustration they include—both pictorial representations and the abstract maps, charts, and diagrams known as *tu*. It is, in part, the quantity and scope of printed pictures produced during the

Ming, for instance, that prompts Craig Clunas to see the visual culture of the period as extending far beyond the paintings that art historians usually study.[13] Other scholars such as Hegel, Anne McLaren, Katherine Carlitz, and Hsiao Li-ling have discussed the multiple possible uses for pictures in printed fiction and drama, ranging from storytelling aids for readers with limited literacy to objects of connoisseurship for an elite audience.[14] Pictures were also important in the production of knowledge and abound in technical and informational books, such as geographical works. Emma Teng's chapter in this volume explores the role that visual materials, particularly maps and ethnographic illustrations, played in the travel literature on the Taiwan frontier and shows how such pictures furthered the Qing colonizing of the island.

The new lithographic and photolithographic printing processes introduced from the West in the nineteenth century may have been adopted with such speed and enthusiasm in China in part because they made the reproduction of complex pictures so easy.[15] Accompanying these technological and social changes in the publishing industry was an explosion of visual images in print. These mechanized printing techniques spearheaded the rise of new literary and social forms of print, such as the newspaper and the pictorial magazine, with new audiences and markets. Beginning with early missionary enterprises, book publication was closely intertwined with this periodical press through serialization and advertisement. Books and newspapers were produced by the same publishing houses, such as the almighty *Shenbao*, in the cosmopolitan city of Shanghai.[16] Pictorial magazines, such as the *Dianshizhai huabao*, issued by these publishing houses, initiated a new phase in the relationship between illustration and text involving modern forms of spectatorship. Rania Huntington's chapter shows how the old elite literary genre of *zhiguai* (reports of anomalies and accounts of the strange) became reborn as "news" in newspapers such as *Shenbao* and as "spectacle" in the pictorial *Dianshizhai huabao*. In her chapter, Catherine Yeh explores the ways in which a new image of a "modern" courtesan, created and publicized in newspapers and illustrated magazines, became a crucial part of a new urban identity in the emerging metropolis of Shanghai.

Although books continued to be produced through the old block-printing process into the twentieth century, the new lithographic technology "quickly came to dominate all book publication" before itself being eclipsed by offset printing.[17] During the 1920s and 1930s, the now old-fashioned technology of block printing could be reimagined under the influence of the European proletarian woodblock movement and put to a radically new use in the creation of illustrated book covers for leftist authors such as Lu Xun, where it carried a powerful *modernist* visual message.[18]

The new print media introduced at the end of the nineteenth century combined news and entertainment with the promotion of specific ideological, political platforms such as self-strengthening, cultural critique, reform, and revolution. Eugene Wang takes up the case of the Leifeng Pagoda, whose ruins had towered over the landscape at West Lake for centuries until their sudden collapse in 1924. This event received considerable press; since the pagoda played an important role in the ancient legend of the White Snake, this icon's collapse lent itself to metaphorical interpretation in the publications of the day. Wang reconstructs the rich visual, literary, and theatrical traditions for representing the pagoda and the folklore surrounding it to show how the monument's demise could become such a potent symbol for iconoclastic authors like Lu Xun, who championed its destruction as a liberatory act, releasing creative, demonic energies long imprisoned within.

As the twentieth century progressed, in China as elsewhere, many of the periodical press's functions were also taken over by new nonprint media such as film. Lydia Liu's chapter on the remaking of a folk goddess from Guangxi in the twentieth century demonstrates how a centralized state media industry, such as China's after 1949, borrowed popular theatrical performances to reinvent the meaning of local folklore for a national audience. Taking a 1990s copyright controversy over the "authorship" of the early 1960s hit film *Liu Sanjie* as her point of departure, Liu analyzes the contradictions involved in disputing the ownership of a folk legend that is not only part of oral literature but also a legacy of state-mandated official popular culture. She traces the making of this popular film to the rise of modern folklore studies in the May Fourth period and examines the appropriation of marginal, minority cultures by the Han, which has been so central to China's self-representation as a modern nation. The technologies of mass media enabled oral legends and local performing arts to be reproduced and disseminated with unprecedented speed across the vast geographical areas of China and Southeast Asia.

The place of oral literature and folklore in Chinese mass media that Wang and Liu address raises some key issues with regard to what the German folklorist Hermann Bausinger has dubbed "folk culture in a world of technology."[19] Bausinger's work "challenged the notion of folk culture as an isolated part within a cultural whole untouched by modernity," as something embalmed in an unchanging tradition.[20] In this view, new technologies of communication, rather than killing off folk culture, are what keep folklore going in the modern world. As Konrad Köstlin, a folklorist associated with Bausinger, asserted: "Technology allows for an unlimited reproduction of folk cultural goods . . . the technique for reproducing takes reproduced items out of the realm of any traditionality."[21] From the turn of the twentieth century, the modern inventions of photography, the gramophone, and film fed on folk culture in manufacturing mass entertainment in China, as in other parts of the world.[22] The domain of folklore does not exist in some sort of temporal and spatial opposition to the modern but constitutes a vital part of urban and political life.

This emphasis on printing technology and the rise of mass media allows us to trace the changing sphere of literary production from the late Ming publishing boom in the mid-sixteenth century (Parts I and II) to the introduction of lithographic printing, the periodical press in the last decade of the nineteenth century, and a modern mass culture based on print as well as other media, such as photography and film (Parts III and IV). This trajectory need not, however, be yoked to a teleological narrative of technological change and progress. In a recent study of technology and gender in late imperial China, the anthropologist Francesca Bray critiques conventional histories of technology for focusing too narrowly "on the production of commodities and the development of scientific knowledge." Instead, she advocates looking at how "everyday technologies shape material worlds"; this in turn leads her to conceptualize technology "as a form of communication," one that "contributes to producing people and relationships between people."[23]

Bray's insight helps us identify an alternative approach to the relationship between literature and technology adopted by several contributors to this book, who not only look at how technical modes of production have shaped conventions of writing and reading but, more fundamentally, consider how writing and reading can themselves be understood as technologies shaping everyday experience and social relations in the material world. Ultimately, however, their studies show that technology and writing cannot be uncoupled from the literary. Shang Wei, for example, posits a process through which sixteenth-century encyclopedias of daily use, which provided practical know-how on matters from drinking games to ritual protocol, are transported piecemeal into the novel to evoke the texture of everyday life. It is precisely because these household reference books are part of the technology of everyday life that passages lifted from them are able to evoke quotidian experience in the literary context of the novel.[24]

The personal letter provides an even clearer case of how writing and reading should be understood as technologies directly shaping social relations and subjectivity, but which turn out also to be highly mediated by literary concerns and by the workings of print. To take the late Ming again, for example, as Kathryn Lowry does in her chapter on the love letter, quantities of model letters were published in commercial compilations in this period: in sections on correspondence in household encyclopedias, in independent epistolary guides, and in letter miscellanies. The topics that this correspondence addresses run the gamut of ordinary life: contracts, requests to borrow things, notes accompanying gifts, thank-you notes, arrangements pertaining to the ritual occasions of birth, marriage, and death. As templates for scribes hired by the illiterate or as primers for the beginning writer to emulate, the model letters served a clearly pedagogical role and helped standardize and codify the texture of social relations; the same letters, however, when reprinted in letter miscellanies with narrativizing frames and commentary, lent themselves to reading as fiction. In either case, Lowry argues, the ubiquity of these printed letter-writing collections and the highly conventionalized literary form the letters exhibit belie our modern notion of personal correspondence as an inherently private mode of expression. On this basis, Lowry's research indicates that the love letter in Ming China was a technology that people used to order and fabricate subjectivity, rather than a free expression reflecting the sensibility of the individual.

The Space of Writing

In the introduction to *The Order of Books*, Chartier champions the need to pay historical attention to the "technical, visual, and physical devices that organize the reading of writing."[25] In the case of early modern China, however, we might do better to reverse his dictum and consider the technical, visual, and physical devices that organized the *writing* of *reading*. Chinese textual practices fostered a particularly close connection between reading and writing by valorizing the *written* response of educated readers to what they read, often incorporated into print alongside the original text. From early on, the correct response to reading certain poems was to write a new poem matching the rhymes of the original. When verse was encountered on the wall of a public building, for instance, readers passing by might write a matching verse alongside it, producing a potentially infinite chain of responses as new readers responded not only to the original poem but to the later ones. Some of these poems might eventually be published, inspiring a now larger community of readers to coin their own matching verses. We know that within the space of the printed text, readers could match poems with their favorite dead poet or even with a fictional character in a play or a novel, often written in the margin of their own copies, but then perhaps collected and reprinted elsewhere.

The habit of writing responses as part of the reading process can be detected in the typographical format of many woodblock books, particularly novels and plays, whose selling point was often the addition of printed commentaries by famous readers (or spuriously attributed to famous readers). Many imprints had extra-large "eyebrow" margins running along the top margins of the page so that readers could make notes or comments of their own. Some surviving late imperial imprints even contain two sets of margins: the lower margin is occupied by a printed commentary and the upper margin is filled with an even more copious handwritten one (Fig I.1). Readers' notes were not limited to margins or to the ends of chapters but were even jotted between the lines, again a habit visible in extant copies of books that include both printed interlinear comments and handwritten ones. Occasionally handwritten comments were even erroneously incorporated into a later printed version of a book as part of the text.[26] At least in the case of fiction, Ellen Widmer and David Rolston have demonstrated that published commentaries not only directly influenced how old novels were read but also how new novels were written.[27]

Even more ubiquitous in Ming and Qing book publishing was the practice of including multiple prefaces and dedicatory poems by the author's or editor's friends and acquaintances. Such prefaces and poems generally served as endorsements designed to introduce the author and his or her work to a reading public. But it also meant that a book went out into the world already embedded in a textual community of specific readers, whose printed responses were likely to color the responses and expectations of subsequent readers. Such prefaces and poems tended to be the most changeable part of a book, and new ones were added or old ones dropped in subsequent editions, reflecting changes in the market, the status of the book, or its

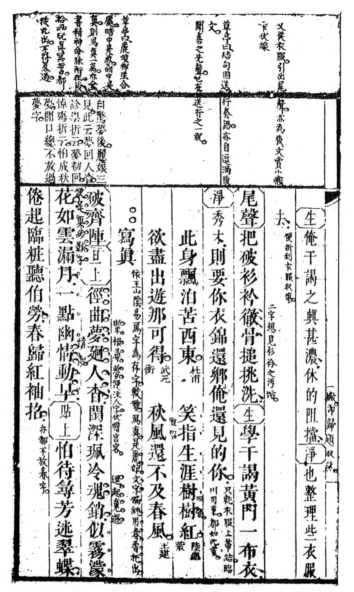

Fig. I.1 Leaf from a Qing edition (after 1694) of *Wu Wushan's Three Wives' Combined Commentary to The Peony Pavilion* (in the hands of a Chinese collector who wishes to remain anonymous). The middle tier margin reproduces the printed commentary of the Three Wives with handwritten punctuation; the upper tier margin contains the handwritten comments of the book's unidentified owner (spilling down into the middle tier on the right), who also copied in comments by famous figures printed in other books. Interlinear handwritten comments and punctuation marks are interspersed in the body of the text.

intended readership. These prefatorial materials are important tools in the attempt to gather evidence for the existence of different sorts of reading publics at different times as filtered through the experience of specific readers. Widmer's chapter in this volume, for example, masterfully uses this sort of material to trace the contours of a female reading public for narrative literature some one hundred years before the modern woman's self-conscious involvement in the writing of fiction. Taking two disparate works published in 1828, *Jinghua yuan*, a now-famous novel by Li Ruzhen, a male author, and *Zaisheng tian*, a now-obscure prosimetric novel by Hou Zhi, a female author, Widmer shows how readers treated these texts as physical objects to be written on as part of a dialogue with their authors. She explores the potential of audiences to influence the creation and publication of specific literary works and succeeds in reconstructing a rhetorical, social, and commercial context for female readers in the first decades of the nineteenth cenAlthough the center of gravity in this volume tends toward printed forms of writing, several of the contributors are concerned with the persistence of parallel channels for disseminating, consuming, and reproducing writing outside the mechanism of publishing, even after a strong print culture had taken root. These include inscriptions engraved on stone steles and the rubbings taken from them (Wu Hung), poetry written on the walls of public buildings and collected through transcription and memory (Judith Zeitlin), and poem texts written as gifts on social occasions and passed around a select private group of friends (Sophie Volpp). In the majority of these cases, writings that first circulated outside the medium of print are known today because they were eventually published and preserved in books. Thus although engraved inscriptions, rubbings, writings on walls, and occasional verse are all practices that predate the dominance of print in Chinese society, these contributors demonstrate that once publishing becomes the norm, even though alternative modes of writing continue to circulate outside print, they are continually absorbed into it.

"No site in China is without an overlay of writing," writes Eugene Wang in his chapter for this volume. This statement has a double meaning: on the one hand, the geographical landscape was textualized through displays of writing engraved on steles, carved on placards, or written in ink on cliffs and walls; on the other hand, these inscriptions were continuously gathered and redisplayed in the pages of printed books: in local gazetteers, travel guides, maps, and miscellanies.[28] The traffic in inscriptions went both ways—not only from place to book but from book to place. Famous inscriptions that had long disappeared *in situ* but were preserved in books, for example, could then be re-engraved and reinstalled in the original site. This recycling process is, as we have seen, typical of the workings of print culture, but Wu Hung's chapter for this volume shows how even much earlier in Chinese history, it was the practice to replace worn-out steles with re-engraved replicas, installed at the same spot. Connoisseurs avidly collected rubbings taken over the ages from the replica as a way of studying the inscription on the vanished original; over time, as scholars competed to date and rank old rubbings of the inscription available on the market, the actual stele languishing by itself in the landscape came to matter less and less.

Engraved words on steles and public walls, illustrations in printed books and local gazetteers, maps, travel guides, and the like constitute the landmarks of a textual landscape studied by Wang, Zeitlin, Wu Hung, and Teng in this volume. But the boundaries of writing cannot exist without invoking otherness. Teng's chapter demonstrates that the Qing empire interpellated Taiwan into its spatial order by encouraging mapmaking and ethnographic illustration, and she argues that whereas ethnic difference was relatively downplayed in Qing ethnographic *writings*, it was clearly visualized in Qing ethnographic *illustrations*. In many ways, the geographical other parallels the otherness of ethnicity, gender, and metaphysical beings, such as ghosts and spirits, that used to populate Chinese literature. The interesting connection between *tibishi*, or writing on walls, and ghost literature that Zeitlin analyzes in her chapter shows that foreignness and illegibility mark the boundaries of writing just as much as they define the worlds of the living and the dead. The material attributes of ghost-writing in Chinese literature—instability and evanescence—share in this precise sense of otherness or metaphysical heterogeneity of space and time. In the late nineteenth-century context, the anxiety to control the influx of foreign images and objects is expressed in illustrated publications that emphasize the monstrosity of exotic beings and suggest the need for them to be tamed, in part by being held up for display. Huntington's discussion of accounts of anomalies and Wang's of the White Snake legend show how some of these same processes and issues were worked out in new forms of media such as the newspaper and the pictorial magazine.

Further complicating the spatial consideration of writing is the extraordinary mobility of tales and legends, bits of news and gossip, which circu-

lated orally, both through casual conversation and through various performing arts. Subsequently these oral stories could be approximated or rein-
vented in some written form and published. Once in print, such tales and
legends could be copied into other books or transformed into new stories by
authors in search of material, but they also frequently re-entered the oral
domain of the performing arts once more.[29]

Shang Wei's chapter suggests how even during the late Ming, reports of
sensational events in the *dibao*, the official gazette published and distributed
by the state, made their way into other books, such as collections of strange
tales and jokebooks. Huntington's chapter shows that this process was still
ongoing during the Qing but underwent major changes in the late nineteenth century with the introduction of Western printing processes. The
creation of modern newspapers and magazines greatly increased the speed
with which weird stories traveled in and out of print, expanding and
facilitating the possibilities for incorporating reader response and dialogue
within the new textual community of the periodical press. Lydia Liu's study
of the legend of Liu Sanjie takes up some of the same issues, examining the
role new technologies such as film play in the age-old but futile attempt to
"fix" an oral legend in one set form and to stabilize its meanings.

Writing in Time

Cultures have an investment in thinking of writing as something that transcends a particular form at a particular time because writing can then become something that outlasts the death of its author, holding out the promise of individual immortality on the one hand and the preservation and
transmission of a cultural legacy on the other.[30] This myth of transcendence
had enormous currency and power in premodern Chinese thought, but it
also made writing a source of acute anxiety: what happens if writing, too, is
bound by time and, therefore, like any living thing, is fated to die and disappear? Such anxiety is bound to emerge whenever attention is called to the
material dimensions of writing, particularly its physical vulnerability to the
ravages of time and human destruction. Cultural anxiety about the death of
writing comes nakedly to the surface, for instance, in a seventeenth-century
play by You Tong, loosely based on events and fantasies from his own life,
which goes so far as to stage a scene that literally acts out the death of his
writing. After committing symbolic suicide by burning his poems in despair,
the protagonist Shen Bai (the playwright's alter ego) gathers up the burnt

scraps of paper and buries them, composing a funerary elegy on their behalf and ordering that a placard be erected at the tomb that reads: "Here lie the remains of Shen Bai's writing."[31] Through this act, You Tong's fictional protagonist takes his writings permanently out of circulation, thereby forestalling access to them, even as he attempts to give his writings eternal life through the commemorative funerary rite he stages.

The scenario You Tong imagines is predicated on a fundamental precept of Chinese poetics, that a poem is a metonym for the poet and can therefore serve as a material substitute for his or her body. Such a notion lies at the heart of Sophie Volpp's study of the exchange of poems within a circle of elite male writers to celebrate the wedding of an actor, who "belonged" to one of its members, and how this contributed to what she calls "the instantiation of sociality." Volpp explores the ways in which poems as material objects were exchanged in what we may call an "economy of the literary gift." She is particularly interested in the eroticized figure of the actor, who occupied an ambiguous status somewhere between person and luxury good during this period. It is the body of the actor that leads to the creation of these poems, which become, in part, imaginary substitutes for physical contact with him. Precisely because a poem is considered "an extension of the author that circulates in his or her stead," the exchange of poems, even in absentia, has the power to create membership in an exclusive community. In the case of occasional poetry, it is not so much that the exchange of verse brings together members of this community across space as that it creates the moment in time around which the community can constitute itself. The assertion of contemporaneity rather than the expectation of immortality is what primarily is at stake in the production of a textual event of this sort.

The problem of writing's vexed relationship to time is taken up with great sophistication in Wu Hung's chapter on rubbings. In contrast to block printing, which aims to produce multiple identical copies, making a rubbing from an engraved stone stele always results in a unique imprint, which attests to the physical condition of the stele at the time it is taken. Since the act of rubbing-making damages the engraving and necessarily hastens its erosion, each rubbing bears witness to a definitive moment of decay in the history of the stele. Seen in this light, a heavy stone stele is paradoxically more elusive and ephemeral than any of the ink rubbings of it on paper. This is why, argues Wu Hung, the objecthood of a stele cannot be represented by a single imprint but can be reconstructed only through a paper trail of prior rubbings, which simultaneously tell the story of the stele's successive ruin as an object. And this is also why a scorched remnant of an early rubbing can still be regarded today as a national treasure, becoming in effect a ruin on paper that supersedes the ruined stele itself.

Wu Hung's insight suggests a fruitful notion of the written character as the traces of *writing in time*. The materiality of writing must be experienced through its ruins, absences, and memories, out of which arises the familiar desire for the original and for the authentic. But what constitutes an original in the face of such a multiplicity of fragments and traces? The desire for the original, which has traditionally prompted study of the material aspects of books and documents, usually translates in our scholarly fields into the impulse to establish the most authentic and authoritative text. But isn't this desire burdened, at the same time, by a sense of futility? The very idea of authenticity is called into question by a number of the studies in this volume in which the authors follow the traces of a text and attempt to hear the echoes of lost words. Zeitlin's chapter, for instance, on poems left on walls, particularly those attributed to obscure dead women, shows that the appreciation of this poetry was bound up with the assumption that it was all that remained of the writer's passage in the world. One of the attractions of this verse form, she argues, was that it required readers to confront (or imagine) writing as material traces in real space and time; in practice, however, she shows that authenticating such writing in terms of authorship and originality becomes nearly impossible. In the end, however, what may have mattered most was not the poem's content but simply the notion that at a particular time, someone who is no more once wrote something in this place, the realization, as one Tang poet put it, that "on the old placard, the words of the poem have dissolved."

The writing of the future and for the future presents us with a new set of issues about time and the imagining of subjectivity in the nineteenth and twentieth centuries. The rise of the "new" Chinese novel, as our author who prefers to remain anonymous discovers, predates its avowed origins in Liang Qichao's call for the new novel and had an even closer relationship to the daily newspaper of the late nineteenth century than has previously been known. It turns out that the earliest "new" novels were actually created in response to a contest advertised in the *Shenbao* by the British missionary and translator John Fryer, as part of a larger effort to reform the ills of Chinese society. The serialization of traditional-type fiction had become standard practice in the nineteenth-century Chinese newspaper, as was the immediate publication of the work in book form upon the serial's completion. Both the size of this audience for fiction and the speed with which it could be reached were in part what enabled Fryer to envisage fiction as an agent of social change in China. The opening of Fryer's Chinese-language advertisement for the contest suggests just how intertwined his idea of the new novel and the power of the newspaper were: "With its wide and rapid circulation, fiction can, within a short period of time, become known to one and all, making it possible without difficulty to reform current practices." What was so novel about serialized fiction in the daily newspaper was that it conjured up a homogenous readership across the vast expanse of China as existing in the same clocked, calendrical time, thus providing what Benedict Anderson calls the basic "technical means of 're-presenting' the *kind* of imagined community that is the nation."[32] It is in the sense of ensuring the simultaneity or "the meanwhile" of a nation's experience of time that the new novel envisions a new kind of future for China.

Notes

1. See Bourdieu, *The Logic of Practice*, trans. Richard Nice (Stanford: Stanford University Press), 1990; and idem, *Language and Symbolic Power*, trans. Gino Raymond and Matthew Adamson (Cambridge, Mass.: Harvard University Press, 1991).

2. For the most interesting and exhaustive treatment of Benjamin in the recent flurry of published works, see Susan Buck-Morss, *The Dialectics of Seeing: Walter Benjamin and the Arcades Project* (Cambridge, Mass.: MIT University Press, 1989), a study of Benjamin's *Charles Baudelaire: A Lyric Poet in the Era of High Capitalism* and his other published and unpublished works.

3. Of some relevance to our concerns here is Derrida's discussion of the concept of Chinese writing in the West as a European hallucination in *Of Grammatology*, trans. Gayatri Chakravorty Spivak (Baltimore: Johns Hopkins University Press, 1976), pt. 1, chap. 3.

4. Igor Koptyff, "The Cultural Biography of Things," in *The Social Life of Things*, ed. Arjun Appadurai (Cambridge, Eng.: Cambridge University Press, 1986). p. 64.

5. Benjamin A. Elman, *A Cultural History of Civil Examinations in Late Imperial China* (Berkeley: University of California Press, 2000); see also Kai-wing Chow, "Writing for Success: Printing, Examinations, and Intellectual Change in Late Ming China," *Late Imperial China* 17, no. 1 (June 1996): 120–57, on the vast publishing industry for examination essays.

6. A woodblock text of the Diamond Sutra dated to 847 was found at Dunhuang, but the vast majority of the texts found there were manuscripts not imprints.

7. The most comprehensive account in English of the history of publishing in China remains Tsuen-hsuin Tsien, *Paper and Printing*, vol. 5, pt. I, of *Science and Civilization in China*, ed. Joseph Needham (Cambridge, Eng.: Cambridge University Press, 1985); on late imperial China in particular, the special June 1996 issue of *Late Imperial China* on publishing and print culture is especially helpful. For commercial publishing during the Song period, see Lucille Chia, "Printing for Profit: The Commercial Printers of Jianyang, Fujian (Song-Ming)" (Ph.D. diss., Columbia University, 1996); on state publishing in this period, see Susan Cherniack, "Book Culture and Textual Transmission in Sung China," *Harvard Journal of Asiatic Studies* 54 (1994): 5–125. On the publishing industry for fiction during the Ming, see, among others, Ellen Widmer, "The Huangduzhai of Hangzhou and Suzhou: A Study in Seventeenth-Century Publishing," *Harvard Journal of Asiatic Studies* 56, no. 1 (1996): 77–122; and Chen Dakang's 陳大康 comprehensive study, *Mingdai xiaoshuo shi* 明代小說史 (A history of Ming fiction) (Shanghai: Shanghai wenyi chubanshe, 2000).

8. For recent studies of the silver trade revolving around China and Asia in the early global economy, see André Gunder Frank, *ReOrient: Global Economy in the Asian Age* (Berkeley: University of California Press, 2000); Kenneth Pomeranz, *The Great Divergence: China, Europe, and the Making of the Modern World Economy* (Princeton: Princeton University Press, 2000); and R. Bin Wong, *China Transformed: Historical Change and the Limits of European Experience* (Ithaca: Cornell University Press, 1997).

9. For example, the amazing set of color illustrations by Min Qiji (1580–after 1661) for the play *Story of the Western Wing* (*Xixiang ji*) now in the Museum für Ostasiatische Kunst in Cologne, reprinted in facsimile in Edith Dittrich, *Hsi-hsiang chi: Chinesische Farbholzschnitte von Min Ch'i-chi, 1640* (Cologne, 1977); and discussed in Wu Hung, *The Double Screen: Medium and Representation in Chinese Painting* (London: Reaktion Books, 1996), pp. 246–59.

10. Robert E. Hegel, *Reading Illustrated Fiction in Late Imperial China* (Stanford: Stanford University Press, 1998), pp. 102–5; see also Ōki Yasushi 大木康, "Min-matsu Kōnan ni okeru shuppan bunka no kenkyū" 明末江南における出版文化の研究, *Hiroshima daigaku bungakubu kiyō* 50, special issue no. 1 (1991): 1–176.

11. See, e.g., Timothy Brook, "Communications and Commerce," in *The Cambridge History of China*, vol. 8, *The Ming Dynasty*, pt. 2, ed. Denis Twitchett and Frederick W. Mote (Cambridge, Eng.: Cambridge University Press, 1998), pp. 579–707; Dorothy Ko, *Teachers of the Inner Chambers* (Stanford: Stanford University Press, 1994); Ōki, "Minmatsu Kōnan"; Zhang Xiumin 張秀民, *Zhongguo yinshua shi* 中國印刷史 (The history of printing in China) (Shanghai: Shanghai renmin wenxue chubanshe, 1989); and Cynthia Brokaw and Kai-wing Chow, eds., *Printing and Book Culture in Late Imperial China* (Berkeley: University of California Press, forthcoming 2003).

12. For the latest instantiation of this view, see Hegel, *Reading Illustrated Fiction*.

13. Craig Clunas, *Pictures and Visuality in Early Modern China* (Princeton: Princeton University Press, 1997).

14. Hegel, *Reading Illustrated Fiction*; Anne E. McLaren, *Chinese Popular Culture and Ming Chantefables* (Leiden: Brill, 1998); Katherine Carlitz, "Printing as Performance: Literati Playwright-Publishers of the Late Ming," in *Printing and Book Culture in Late Imperial China*, ed. Cynthia Brokaw and Kai-wing Chow (Berkeley: University of California Press, forthcoming 2003); Xiao Liling (Hsiao Li-ling) 蕭麗玲, "Banhua yu juchang: cong Shide tang kanben *Pipa ji* kan Wanli chuqi banhua zhi tese" 版畫與劇場: 從世德堂刊本琵琶記看萬歷初期版畫之特色 (Woodblock prints and theater: characteristics of drama illustrations of the early Wanli period as revealed in the Shide tang edition of *Pipa ji*), *Yishu xue* 5 (1991): 133–84.

15. Meng Yue, "The Invention of Shanghai: Cultural Passages and Their Transformation, 1860–1920" (Ph.D. diss., University of California, Los Angeles, 2000), emphasizes that technology imported from Southeast Asia and Japan, not

simply the "West," played an important role in establishing Shanghai as a center of lithographic and photolithographic publishing.

16. On the *Shenbao*, see Rudolf G. Wagner, "The *Shenbao* in Crisis: The International Environment and the Conflict Between Guo Songtao and the *Shenbao*," *Late Imperial China* 20, no. 1 (June 1999): 107–38. For a study of the Shanghai-based Liangyou publishing house and the important role it played in the making of modern literary history, see chap. 8 of Lydia H. Liu, *Translingual Practice* (Stanford: Stanford University Press, 1995). On *Dianshizhai huabao*, see Christopher A. Reed, "Gutenberg in Shanghai: Mechanized Printing, Modern Publishing, and Their Effects on the City, 1876–1937" (Ph.D. diss., University of California, Berkeley, 1996). On print culture in Republican period Shanghai, see Leo Oufan Lee, *Shanghai Modern* (Cambridge, Mass.: Harvard University Press, 1999).

17. Hegel, *Reading Illustrated Fiction*, p. 135. As of 2000, there was still one traditional block-printing house operating in China, in Yangzhou.

18. Lu Xun was interested in visuality and woodcuts in general and German and Russian woodcut works in particular.

19. Hermann Bausinger, *Folk Culture in a World of Technology*, trans. Elke Dettmer (Bloomington: Indiana University Press, 1990).

20. Renata Bendix, *In Search of Authenticity: The Formation of Folklore Studies* (Madison: University of Wisconsin Press, 1997), p. 159.

21. Cited in ibid., p. 181.

22. On the appropriation of folksongs by the record industries, see Andrew Jones, "The Gramophone in China," in *Tokens of Exchange: The Problem of Translation in Global Circulations*, ed. Lydia H. Liu (Durham: Duke University Press, 1999), pp. 214–36.

23. Francesca Bray, *Technology and Gender: Fabrics of Power in Late Imperial China* (Berkeley: University of California Press, 1997), pp. 2–3.

24. Shang Wei enumerates this point more thoroughly in another essay, "*Jin Ping Mei* and the Making of Everyday Life," in *From Ming to Qing: Dynastic Decline and Cultural Innovation*, ed. David Der-wei Wang and Shang Wei (Cambridge, Mass.: Harvard University Asia Center, forthcoming).

25. Roger Chartier, *The Order of Books: Readers, Authors, and Libraries in Europe Between the Fourteenth and Eighteenth Centuries*, trans. Lydia G. Cochrane (Stanford: Stanford University Press, 1994), p. ix.

26. All these practices are detailed in David Rolston, *Traditional Chinese Fiction and Fiction Commentary* (Stanford: Stanford University Press, 1997).

27. Ellen Widmer, *Margins of Utopia* (Cambridge, Mass.: Harvard University, Council on East Asian Studies, 1987); and Rolston, *Traditional Chinese Fiction*.

28. For studies of writing and place that address these issues, see Stephen Owen, *Remembrances* (Cambridge, Mass.: Harvard University Press, 1986); Strassberg, "In-

troduction," in idem, *Inscribed Landscapes* (Berkeley: University of California Press, 1994); Robert Harrist, Jr., "Reading Chinese Mountains," *Orientations*, Dec. 2000, pp. 46–54; and Marion Eggert, *Deutungen des Unterwegsseins in chinesischen Reiseschriften vom 16. bis zum frühen 19. Jarhhundert* (Weisbaden: Harrassovitz, forthcoming).

29. Good examples are the vernacular novels recently studied by Meir Shahar in *Crazy Ji: Chinese Religion and Popular Literature* (Cambridge, Mass.: Harvard University Asia Center, 1998); or Pu Songling's seventeenth-century book of tales, *Liaozhai zhiyi*, which retold certain stories based on casual conversations or legend; the book then became subject matter for a famous professional storyteller in Tianjin.

30. Chartier ("Gutenberg Revisited from the East," *Late Imperial China* 17, no. 1 [June 1996]: 4) notes that one commonality between "discourses on written culture" in China and Europe is the obsessional concern with loss.

31. You Tong 尤侗, *Juntian yue* 鈞天樂 (Celestial court music), in idem, *Xitang quanji* 西堂全集 (Qing ed. in the Regenstein Library, University of Chicago); for an analysis of this scene in the context of You Tong's life and work, see Judith T. Zeitlin, "Spirit Writing and Performance in the Work of You Tong (1618–1704)," *T'oung Pao* 84 (1998): 132–33.

32. Benedict Anderson, *Imagined Communities* (London: Verso, 1983).

Works Cited

Anderson, Benedict. *Imagined Communities*. London: Verso, 1983.

Bausinger, Hermann. *Folk Culture in a World of Technology*. Trans. Elke Dettmer. Bloomington: Indiana University Press, 1990.

Bendix, Renata. *In Search of Authenticity: The Formation of Folklore Studies*. Madison: University of Wisconsin Press, 1997.

Bourdieu, Pierre. *Language and Symbolic Power*. Trans. Gino Raymond and Matthew Adamson. Cambridge, Mass.: Harvard University Press, 1991.

———. *The Logic of Practice*. Trans. Richard Nice. Stanford: Stanford University Press, 1990.

Bray, Francesca. *Technology and Gender: Fabrics of Power in Late Imperial China*. Berkeley: University of California Press, 1997.

Brokaw, Cynthia, and Kai-wing Chow, eds. *Printing and Book Culture in Late Imperial China*. Berkeley: University of California Press, forthcoming 2003.

Brook, Timothy. "Communications and Commerce." In *The Cambridge History of China*, vol. 8, *The Ming Dynasty*, pt. 2, ed. Denis Twitchett and Frederick W. Mote. Cambridge, Eng.: Cambridge University Press, 1998, pp. 579–707.

Buck-Morss, Susan. *The Dialectics of Seeing: Walter Benjamin and the Arcades Project*. Cambridge, Mass.: MIT University Press, 1989.

Carlitz, Katherine. "Printing as Performance: Literati Playwright-Publishers of the Late Ming." In *Printing and Book Culture in Late Imperial China*, ed. Cynthia Brokaw and Kai-wing Chow. (Berkeley: University of California Press, forthcoming, 2003).

Chartier, Roger. *Forms and Meaning: Texts, Performances, and Audiences from Codex to Computer*. Philadelphia: University of Pennsylvania Press, 1995.

———. "Gutenberg Revisited from the East." Special Issue: Publishing and the Print Culture in Late Imperial China. *Late Imperial China* 17, no. 1 (June 1996): 1–9.

———. *The Order of Books: Readers, Authors, and Libraries in Europe Between the Fourteenth and Eighteenth Centuries*. Trans. Lydia G. Cochrane. Stanford: Stanford University Press, 1994.

Chen Dakang 陳大康. *Mingdai xiaoshuo shi* 明代小說史 (A history of Ming fiction). Shanghai: Shanghai wenyi chubanshe, 2000.

Cherniack, Susan. "Book Culture and Textual Transmission in Sung China." *Harvard Journal of Asiatic Studies* 54 (1994): 5–125.

Chia, Lucille. "The Development of the Jianyang Book Trade, Song-Yuan." Special Issue: Publishing and the Print Culture in Late Imperial China. *Late Imperial China* 17, no. 1 (June 1996): 10–48.

————. "Printing for Profit: The Commercial Printers of Jianyang, Fujian (Song-Ming)." Ph.D. diss., Columbia University, 1996.

Chow, Kai-wing. "Writing for Success: Printing, Examinations, and Intellectual Change in Late Ming China." Special Issue: Publishing and the Print Culture in Late Imperial China. *Late Imperial China* 17, no. 1 (June 1996): 120–57.

Clunas, Craig. *Pictures and Visuality in Early Modern China.* Princeton: Princeton University Press, 1997.

Derrida, Jacques. *Of Grammatology.* Trans. Gayatri Chakravorty Spivak. Baltimore: Johns Hopkins University Press, 1976.

Dittrich, Edith. *Hsi-hsiang chi: Chinesische Farbholzschnitte von Min Ch'i-chi, 1640.* Monographien des Museums für Ostasiatische Kuntst 1, Museen der Stadt Köln. Cologne, 1977.

Eggert, Marion. *Deutungen des Unterwegsseins in chinesischen Reiseschriften vom 16. bis zum frühen 19. Jarhhundert.* Sinologica colonensia series. Weisbaden: Harrassovitz, forthcoming.

Elman, Benjamin A. *A Cultural History of Civil Examinations in Late Imperial China.* Berkeley: University of California Press, 2000.

Frank, André Gunder. *ReOrient: Global Economy in the Asian Age.* Berkeley: University of California Press, 2000.

Harrist, Robert, Jr. "Reading Chinese Mountains." *Orientations*, Dec. 2000, pp. 46–54.

Hegel, Robert E. *Reading Illustrated Fiction in Late Imperial China.* Stanford: Stanford University Press, 1998.

Jones, Andrew. "The Gramophone in China." In *Tokens of Exchange: The Problem of Translation in Global Circulations*, ed. Lydia H. Liu. Durham: Duke University Press, 1999, pp. 214–36.

Ko, Dorothy. *Teachers of the Inner Chambers.* Stanford: Stanford University Press, 1994.

Koptyff, Igor. "The Cultural Biography of Things." In *The Social Life of Things*, ed. Arjun Appadurai. Cambridge, Eng.: Cambridge University Press, 1986, pp. 64–94.

Lee, Leo Oufan. *Shanghai Modern.* Cambridge, Mass.: Harvard University Press, 1999.

Liu, Lydia H. *Translingual Practice.* Stanford: Stanford University Press, 1995.

McLaren, Anne E. *Chinese Popular Culture and Ming Chantefables.* Leiden: Brill, 1998.

McKenzie, D. F. *Bibliography and the Sociology of Texts.* Cambridge, Eng.: Cambridge University Press, 1999.

Meng Yue. "The Invention of Shanghai: Cultural Passages and Their Transformation, 1860–1920." Ph.D. diss., University of California, Los Angeles, 2000.

Ōki, Yasushi 大木康. "Minmatsu Kōnan ni okeru shuppan bunka no kenkyū" 明末江南における出版文化の研究. *Hiroshima daigaku bungakubu kiyō 50*, special issue no. 1 (1991): 1–176.

Owen, Stephen. *Remembrances*. Cambridge, Mass.: Harvard University Press, 1986.

Pomeranz, Kenneth. *The Great Divergence: China, Europe, and the Making of the Modern World Economy*. Princeton: Princeton University Press, 2000.

Reed, Christopher A. "Gutenberg in Shanghai: Mechanized Printing, Modern Publishing, and Their Effects on the City, 1876–1937." Ph.D. diss., University of California, Berkeley, 1996.

Rolston, David. *Traditional Chinese Fiction and Fiction Commentary*. Stanford: Stanford University Press, 1997.

Shahar, Meir. *Crazy Ji: Chinese Religion and Popular Literature*. Cambridge, Mass.: Harvard University Asia Center, 1998.

Shang Wei. "*Jin Ping Mei* and the Making of Everyday Life." In *From Ming to Qing: Dynastic Decline and Cultural Innovation*, ed. David Der-wei Wang and Shang Wei. Cambridge, Mass.: Harvard University Asia Center, forthcoming.

Strassberg, Richard. *Inscribed Landscapes*. Berkeley: University of California Press, 1994.

Tsien, Tsuen-hsuin. *Paper and Printing*, vol. 5, pt. I, of *Science and Civilization in China*, ed. Joseph Needham. Cambridge, Eng.: Cambridge University Press, 1985.

Wagner, Rudolf G. "The *Shenbao* in Crisis: The International Environment and the Conflict Between Guo Songtao and the *Shenbao*." *Late Imperial China* 20, no. 1 (June 1999): 107–38.

Widmer, Ellen. "The Huangduzhai of Hangzhou and Suzhou: A Study in Seventeenth-Century Publishing." *Harvard Journal of Asiatic Studies* 56, no. 1 (1996): 77–122.

————. *Margins of Utopia*. Cambridge, Mass.: Harvard University, Council on East Asian Studies, 1987.

Wong, R. Bin. *China Transformed: Historical Change and the Limits of European Experience*. Ithaca: Cornell University Press, 1997.

Wu Hung. *The Double Screen: Medium and Representation in Chinese Painting*. London: Reaktion Books, 1996.

Xiao Liling (Hsiao Li-ling) 蕭麗玲. "Banhua yu juchang: cong Shide tang kanben *Pipa ji* kan Wanli chuqi banhua zhi tese" 版畫與劇場: 從世德堂刊本琵琶記看萬歷初期版畫之特色 (Woodblock prints and theater: characteristics of drama illustrations of the early Wanli period as revealed in the Shide tang edition of *Pipa ji*). *Yishu xue* 5 (1991): 133–84.

You Tong. 尤侗. *Juntian yue* 鈞天樂. In idem, *Xitang quanji* 西堂全集. Qing ed. in the Regenstein Library, University of Chicago.

Zeitlin, Judith T. "Shared Dreams: The Story of the Three Wives' Commentary on *The Peony Pavilion*." *Harvard Journal of Asiatic Studies* 54, no. 1 (1994): 127–79.

———. "Spirit Writing and Performance in the Work of You Tong (1618–1704)." *T'oung Pao* 84 (1998): 102–35.

Zhang Xiumin 張秀民. *Zhongguo yinshua shi* 中國印刷史 (The history of printing in China). Shanghai: Shanghai renmin wenxue chubanshe, 1989.

Part I
The Circulation of Writing

On Rubbings

Their Materiality and Historicity

Wu Hung

What is a rubbing? Like a block print, a rubbing is made by directly transferring a sign—be it a text or a picture—from a sign-bearing object to a piece of paper. Unlike a block print, however, what is imprinted in a rubbing is *not* a mirror image. When a print is made, ink is applied to a block, and the paper is then placed face down on it. The reversed writing or image carved on the block is thus reversed again and appears as a black imprint on a white background. When a rubbing is made, however, the paper is laid face up over an engraved object, and the ink is then applied to the paper to register the entire surface of the object; the sunken inscription or image shows up as white against a black background. No reversing of images is involved. If a print duplicates carved signs, a rubbing duplicates a sign-bearing object and converts the object from a three-dimensional entity into a two-dimensional representation.

As a two-dimensional representation, a rubbing is connected to the object through physical contact, not through an imaginary resemblance in the rubbing maker's mind. It does not "depict" an object in the way a realistic painting does. A rubbing is closer to a photograph—a metonym that draws its image directly from the object. Indeed, Roland Barthes's well-known rumination on photography can serve to characterize a rubbing:

From the object to its image, there is of course a reduction: in proportion, in per-spective, in color. But this reduction is at no point a *transformation* (in the mathe-matical sense of the term); to shift from reality to its photograph[/rubbing], it is not at all necessary to break down this reality into units and to constitute these units into signs substantially different from the object they represent; between this object and its image, it is not all necessary to arrange a relay, i.e., a code; of course, the im-age is not the reality, but it is its perfect *analogon*, and it is just this analogical perfec-tion which, to common sense, defines the photograph[/rubbing].[1]

As we will see, the analogical function of a rubbing is crucial to its use as a substitute for the "real"—it freezes a moment of historical time in a still im-age. In contrast to a photograph, however, a rubbing minimizes the physical distance between an object and its image: it is akin to a manufactured skin peeled off the object. A photograph, on the other hand, is never completed *in situ*; it emerges mysteriously in a darkroom devoid of the reality the pho-tograph depicts. Moreover, contrary to the idea of mechanical reproduction (which photography typifies), the making of a rubbing is labor intensive and is supposed to produce images of inconsistent appearance. To a rubbing connoisseur, "even those [rubbings] made from the same blocks are never identical, their manual production making each an original work of art."[2] We can thus connect *rubbing* with *printing* and *photography* in a conceptual triangle. Rubbing overlaps with the other two to a certain extent, but it can never be equated with them.

Most research on rubbings has concentrated on their role in advancing traditional knowledge—classical learning, historical research, antiquarian studies, and especially the art of calligraphy. In this chapter, I focus on the materiality and historicity of rubbings themselves.

Two Kinds of Rubbings: Bei *and* Tie

The technique of rubbing gained wide currency in the West no earlier than the nineteenth century, when antiquarians began to use a crayon-like agent to record inscriptions and designs on tombstones and other ancient remains. But in China, ink squeezes made from engraved words and images appeared at least by the sixth century. During the following centuries, this technique gradually developed into a major means of preserving ancient engravings and transmitting famous examples of calligraphy. In the process, it gave rise to an independent art form. Rubbings were made with great care and eagerly collected, and a large body of literature on the historical values and artistic merit of these works accumulated. Commenting on the significance of rubbings for understanding traditional Chinese culture, the early twentieth-century antiquarian Zhao Ruzhen 趙汝珍 drew this analogy: "A gentleman not knowing or understanding rubbings is like a farmer being unable to differentiate the five grains or a carpenter being unable to use a line maker."[3]

Knowledge about rubbings starts from nomenclature: the traditional term for rubbings, *bei tie* 碑帖, signifies a twofold classification.[4] The character *bei* normally means "stone stele," but here it pertains to rubbings made from pre-existing engravings. *Tie* has the more specific meaning of rubbings made from blocks carved specifically for transmitting famous calligraphy (Figs. 1.1a–b).[5] These basic definitions of *bei* and *tie* imply many differences between these two types of rubbings in terms of origins, development, purpose, and readership. *Tie* appeared much later than *bei*, and the invention of *tie* in the tenth century may be explained as a possible influence from printing. As copies of calligraphic masterpieces, *tie* became indispensable to students of calligraphy; *bei*, on the other hand, were appreciated more by antiquarians and epigraphers. A *tie*-rubbing often registers only the calligraphic brushwork carved on a block; a *bei*-rubbing is much more sensitive to marks, intentional as well as unintentional, on an object. A *tie* can be easily reprinted in a book format, but it is difficult, if not impossible, to duplicate through printing all traces of damage and decay found in a *bei*-rubbing. These differences provide valuable clues for speculating on the relationship between *bei* and *tie*, but a full discussion of this relationship would require a separate study. My discussion here focuses more narrowly on the relationship between a rubbing and a sign-bearing object, a relationship that differs markedly in *bei* and *tie*.

Beginning in the Southern Tang (923–35) or the early Song, *tie* were made in large quantities through organized efforts. Emperor Taizong 太宗 (r. 976–97) of the Northern Song (960–1126), for example, ordered 419 famous pieces of calligraphy in the imperial collection engraved on wood blocks; rubbings made from them were bestowed on high-ranking officials. These blocks became cracked and unusable even before the dynasty perished;[6] in their place, the rubbings, called "Chunhua ge tie" 淳化閣帖 or "Ge tie" 閣帖 for short, became sources for new engravings. Among the several dozen such engravings made during the Song, some copied the "Ge tie"

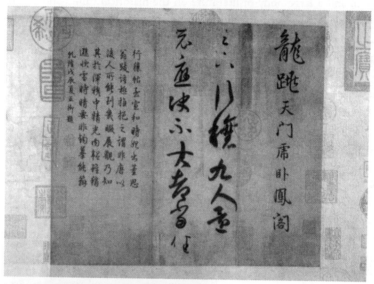

Fig. 1.1 Wang Xizhi, "Ritual to Pray for Good Harvest," Tang dynasty. (*a, above*) tracing copy, ink on paper, 24.4 x 8.9 cm, Princeton University Museum; (*b, left*) rubbing, from *Model Calligraphies from the Yuqing Studio* (*Yuqing zhai fatie*), 1614.

and inherited the title; others incorporated additional pieces and were given new names, such as Pan Sidan's 潘思旦 "Jiang tie" 絳帖 or Liu Cizhuang's 劉次莊 "Xiyu tang tie" 戲魚堂帖. These "second generation" rubbings again became blueprints for new engravings, from which further rubbings were made.[7] This chain of reproduction for the "Chunhua ge tie" has continued to the present day.

The history of a famous *tie* is characterized therefore, not by producing new sets of rubbings from the original engraving, but by the constant recreation of engravings based on older rubbings. The lack of authenticity of *tie*-engravings is coupled with a lack of materiality. Made of wood or stone, a *tie*-block is often rectangular in shape and of limited thickness; its plain form serves the purpose of transmitting the engraved calligraphy, but the block can hardly be appreciated as a work of art in itself.[8] In fact, traditional connoisseurs rarely described these blocks as three-dimensional objects; rather, they were interested only in the quality of the engraving as represented by their rubbings. In the reproduction of *tie*-calligraphy, therefore, these engraved blocks were shadowy transmitters between the original calligraphy and the *tie*-rubbings, and again between earlier *tie*-rubbings and later *tie*-rubbings. Their lack of materiality also explains why they never became a category of collected objects, even though by Ming (1368–1644) and Qing (1644–1911) times Song *tie*-blocks were extremely rare. People diligently collected *tie*-rubbings, not blocks. The Qing scholar Wu Yun 吳雲 (1811–83), for example, owned more than two hundred rubbings of different *tie*-versions of the "Preface to the Orchid Pavilion Collection" ("Lanting xu" 蘭亭序) by the master calligrapher Wang Xizhi 王羲之 (ca. 303–ca. 361); he thus proudly named his studio The Studio of Two Hundred Lanting (Erbai Lanting zhai 二百蘭亭齋). Commenting on this name, Qianshen Bai notes that Wu did not bother to specify that his "two hundred Lanting" were all rubbings: "for to Wu Yun, each rubbing was a work of art that could substitute for the original work, by then lost in the distant past."[9] These rubbings constituted a collective history of their own. They were of course made from two hundred different engraved blocks, but the condition and whereabouts of these blocks remained largely unmentioned.

We must therefore distinguish *tie*-engravings from other sources of rubbings—bronze vessels, ancient mirrors, carved jades, lacquerwares, inkstones, and especially stone steles. The only point shared by these diverse objects

Fig. 1.2 The Forest of Steles, Xi'an. (*a, above*) a section of the exhibition hall; (*b, opposite page*) rubbing of the Meng Xianda Stele.

is that they existed before they became sources of rubbings: unlike *tie*-engravings, these objects were not created for the purpose of making rubbings, and their creation often predated the earliest rubbings by a considerable time span. Also unlike *tie*-engravings, the materiality of these objects remained strong even after they became sources of rubbings; in fact their reputation as important monuments and ritual objects was not weakened but enhanced by the circulation of rubbings. At the same time, the rubbings became their counterparts. Because a rubbing "freezes" an object at a particular moment whereas the object itself continues to deteriorate, an older rubbing is always more "authentic" than the real object. In this sense, a rubbing also becomes the nemesis of the object, constantly challenging the historical authenticity of the object by juxtaposing the present with a more reliable past.

Although any pre-existing engraving can become a source for this type of rubbing, the most typical example is a *bei*—a stele (Figs. 1.2a, b). From their invention in the first century CE, stone steles were a major means for

commemoration and standardization.[10] A stele for a deceased individual commemorated his meritorious conduct in public service or, more frequently, presented a concise biography composed as the "last words" about the deceased from posterity's point of view.[11] The government might erect a stele to provide authoritative versions of Confucian classics or to record an event of extraordinary historical significance.[12] In short, the stele defined a legitimate site where a *consensual history*, albeit embodying a partisan view, was constructed for and presented to the public. For historians, the stele served as a major source of historical knowledge; their inscriptions provided evidence for reconstructing bygone eras.

Historical reconstruction became an important component of antiquarianism, which emerged as an influential intellectual movement during the Northern Song.[13] Also around this time, research on ancient objects became known as *jin shi xue* 金石學, or "the study of metal and stone," because *jin* (bronzes) and *shi* (stone carvings) constituted nearly the entire corpus of materials for antiquarian scholarship. Modern scholars have paid much attention to the historical significance of *jin shi xue*, especially to its relationship with new trends in Song historiography, archaeology, epigraphy, and literati arts.[14] But these discussions have generally neglected an aspect of Song antiquarianism—namely, the collection, transformation, and manipulation of historical evidence. These activities are especially important for understanding the Song notion of the stele, because, although antiquarians greatly valued steles, they did not collect them as they did ancient bronzes, jades, paintings, or books. What antiquarians sought out were the inscribed texts (and later, carved pictorial images) in the form of rubbings.

Northern Song writers mention rubbings as important commercial items.[15] In the Southern Song (1127–1279), according to the *Qingbo zazhi* 清波雜志 (Qingbo miscellaneous records), rubbings of ancient steles—most of which were located in northern territories under Jin control—were in great demand and were sold by traveling merchants south of the Yangzi River at high prices.[16] Through this and other channels, antiquarians could build huge collections of rubbings of ancient inscriptions. It is said that Ouyang Xiu 歐陽修 (1007–72), the first major Song collector and cataloguer of stele inscriptions, collected some 1,000 "rolls" (*juan* 卷) of ink rubbings.[17] His catalogue of 1060, the *Jigu lu* 集古錄 (Record of collecting antiques), contains his comments on more than 400 rubbings, most of which were stone inscriptions. The slightly later *Jin shi lu* 金石錄 (Records of bronze and stone inscriptions) by Zhao Mingcheng 趙明誠 (1081–1129) was even more extensive: it contained rubbings of 1,900 stone inscriptions, plus Zhao's comments on 502 of them. Antiquarians like Ouyang Xiu and Zhao Mingcheng did sometimes visit steles *in situ*; but such visits were relatively rare and often limited to steles located near the places where they held office. Their real passion was finding rubbings of unknown steles in the market. Li Qingzhao 李清照, the wife of Zhao Mingcheng and a famous poet in her own right, recalled the joy of collecting such items during the early days of her marriage:

On the first and fifteenth day of every month, my husband would get a short vacation from the Academy: he would "pawn some clothes" for five hundred cash and go to the market at Xiangguo Temple 相國寺, where he would buy fruit and rubbings of inscriptions. When he brought these home, we would sit facing one another, rolling them out before us, examining and munching. And we thought ourselves persons of the age of Getian 葛天.[18]

The consequence of these collecting activities was profound. Each rubbing faithfully reproduced a stele inscription, but it did so by transforming the stele into a material form analogous to a printed text. When hundreds of ink rubbings were brought together in a single collection, the separate localities and physical contexts of the originals were further erased. Made from steles in different parts of China, in temples or graveyards, these rubbings were now put side by side in a catalogue, often arranged chronologically. One such floating stele would be "The Stele at the Temple of the Western Marchmount Hua" ("Xiyu Huashan miao bei" 西嶽華山廟碑; hereafter, Stele of Mount Hua), whose inscription was recorded by at least three prominent Song antiquarians—Ouyang Xiu, Zhao Mingcheng, and Hong Kuo 洪适 (1117–84)—in their respective catalogues. All three wrote comments on this stele. Ouyang Xiu's comment was the earliest and provided a basis for further cataloguing and discussion of the stele. The historical information in the comment is also indispensable for my discussion of this particular stele in the second part of this chapter.

The first part of Ouyang Xiu's comment summarizes the inscription and introduces the history of the Temple of the Western Marchmount Hua and the establishment of the stele. According to the inscription, after Emperor Gaozu 高祖 (r. 206–195 BCE) founded the Western Han dynasty (206 BCE–8 CE), he established a new sacrificial system under state patronage. His efforts were continued by Emperor Hui 惠 (r. 194–187 BCE), who ordered local princes to offer seasonal sacrifices to mountains and rivers in the areas under their jurisdiction. Emperor Wu 武 (r. 140–87 BCE) constructed temples at the foot of the Five Sacred Marchmounts and sent officials to offer seasonal sacrifices there. But this ritual became lax toward the end of the Western Han, and when Wang Mang 王莽 (r. 9–23 CE) took power, he abolished this ritual altogether. The worship to Mount Hua was restored when the Eastern Han (24–220 CE) was established. Stone steles were erected in the temple, but their inscriptions had disappeared by the mid-second century. In the fourth year of Yanxi 延熹 (165 CE), the governor of Hongnong 弘農, Yuan Feng 袁逢, decided to repair the abandoned structures and restore the disrupted rituals in the temple. But before he could finish this project, he was promoted to the governorship of the Capital District. His project was completed by the new governor, Sun Qiu 孫璆.

In the second and much shorter part of his comment, Ouyang Xiu praised the value of the inscription as historical evidence. As an example, he pointed out that only this document records the name of the temple established by Emperor Wu at Mount Hua, which is absent in printed texts. For Ouyang, the conclusion was obvious: "From this instance one recognizes the importance of collecting bronze and stone [inscriptions]."[19] This comment is typical of Song scholarship on ancient steles. It is essentially a textual study: the writer single-mindedly focused on the inscription and disregarded other aspects of the stele such as its material, shape, decoration, and condition. The historical information contained in the inscription was carefully summarized and became the subject of additional remarks. Ouyang Xiu's views on the Stele of Mount Hua initiated a lively scholarly discussion. Zhao Mingcheng, for example, argued that, contrary to Ouyang's statements, the temple's name was in fact recorded by Li Daoyuan 酈道元 (d. 537) in his *Shui jing zhu* 水經注 (Commentaries on the *Classic of Waterways*); what could not be found in transmitted texts were the names of the temple's gate and main hall.[20] Hong Kuo, on the other hand, focused on the author of the inscription.[21] Scholars of later ages continued to debate these points and introduced new arguments. Almost all the comments written before the 1820s were collected by Ruan Yuan 阮元 (1764–1849) in a lengthy article entitled "An Examination of the Han Dynasty Stele of the Western Marchmount Hua Established in the Yanxi Reign" ("Han Yanxi Xiyu Huashan bei kao" 漢延熹西嶽華山碑考).[22]

What was the impact of antiquarian scholarship on the relationship between a rubbing and the original object? Ironically, the fame of a stele derived largely from the scholarly attention paid to rubbings of it, but making these rubbings unavoidably damaged the stele, because the continuous tapping by rubbing makers gradually eroded the inscription. This consequence has been the lament of almost every traditional connoisseur of ancient stone carvings. Because rubbing makers always focused on the engraved characters, the area surrounding a character is often undamaged, whereas the character itself has worn away, leaving behind a smooth depression. On a rubbing made from one such worn stele, as Ye Changchi 葉昌熾 (1849–1917) put it poetically, the words "look like a flight of white herons or flocks of white butterflies. Even if one studies the rubbing with concentrated attention, not a single brush stroke can be distinguished and not a single character can be recognized."[23]

Ye Changchi summarized the "seven calamities" (*qi e* 七厄) that can afflict a stele in addition to the damage caused by war, the elements, and animals: (1) floods and earthquakes, (2) the use of steles as building materials, (3) the practice of inscribing over old inscriptions, (4) the polishing of old steles to prepare a surface for new texts, (5) the destruction of steles established by one's political enemies, (6) the making of rubbings from famous steles for social relations and superiors, and (7) the collecting of rubbings by officials and connoisseurs. Of these seven, the last two were the most serious because these were widely practiced and unavoidable: "A friend came from the Region Within the Pass (Guanzhong 關中) [i.e., the Xi'an area, where many ancient dynasties established their capitals] and told me that the loud sound of making rubbings in the Forest of Steles (Bei lin 碑林) continues day and night. How could a stele not perish (*bu wang* 不亡) [under such torture]? Although the virtuous stone [of a stele] is unyielding, how can it resist this way of making rubbings!"[24]

Rather than a sudden event, the "death" of a stele was a long process. Ye Changchi left his poignant description:

At the beginning, only the edges of engraved characters become flat and blurred; the sharp edges of the original engraving are gone. When a stele is rubbed continuously day after day, it eventually becomes wordless, sometimes even losing its entire surface like a cicada shedding its skin. If one tries to read such a stele, even by shining a strong light on it, one finds nothing more than the stele's posthumous soul (*yi hun* 遺魂), lingering and faintly recognizable.[25]

The irony, however, is that Ye Changchi was himself a major collector of rubbings. He began his *Yu shi* 語石 (Talking about stone) by recalling his early interest in the subject: "Whenever I found a blurry rubbing, I would try hard to figure out the damaged characters; even my students secretly criticized and openly ridiculed my obsession." Later he passed the *jinshi* 進士 examination and became an official in Beijing, but his real passion remained finding rare rubbings. In his words, "After more than twenty years of persistent searching, my collection eventually reached more than 8,000 pieces. Handling and fondling them day and night, I forget that I have become an old man."[26] It is difficult to believe that he did not realize the contradiction between this passion for rubbings and the "death" of steles brought about by making these rubbings. Rather, this dilemma was irreconcilable for a person like him who worried about both.

As attested by Ye Changchi and other scholars, from the Song to the Qing, most ancient steles were left in their original locations. Even though an increasing number were removed to public places such as Confucian academies in cities and towns, these examples were hugely outnumbered by the unprotected ones. This situation was especially true during the Song. Scholars have traced the beginning of the famous Forest of Steles to the late Northern Song, when Lü Dazhong 呂大忠 (d. ca. 1066) moved a set of Tang "stone classics" and other ancient steles to the Confucian Academy in Xi'an in 1087.[27] But at that point the forest contained only 43 items, and most of them were concerned with Confucian learning and the academy itself.[28] In other words, this collection began not for the general purpose of preserving ancient steles but for the particular agenda of promoting Confucian scholarship in a specific institution. We can therefore understand why only 6 of the 400 stone inscriptions recorded in Ouyang Xiu's *Jigu lu* and only 22 of the 1,900 stone carvings collected by Zhao Mingcheng derived from the Forest of Steles.[29]

As mentioned above, in contrast to a *tie*-engraving, an ancient stele already had a long history before it attracted the attention of antiquarians, and it retained a strong sense of materiality even after it became a source of making rubbings. But a stele's history is by no means straightforward, and its materiality, as demonstrated by Ye Changchi, must serve as the precondition for its unavoidable decay and destruction. It seems unthinkable that a heavy stone stele is more ephemeral than an ink rubbing on paper. But this is true. A rubbing has a definite temporality: its imprint attests to a single moment in the history of a stele—a particular condition of the stele that can never be repeated.[30] An extant rubbing is always more authentic than the stele because it has outlived the stele that existed when the rubbing was made. Connoisseurs always try to find an earlier and thus more truthful appearance of the stele in an old rubbing.[31]

The objecthood of a stele can therefore never be embodied by a single image; rather, it must be realized in the struggle between its survival and its destruction as an object. The final destruction of a stele does not necessarily stop this struggle, however, because its objecthood can be transferred to a replacement. Many steles were made to replace older ones, which had finally vanished into oblivion.[32] What a new stele perpetuated was not only the material existence of the old stele but also the cycles of its birth, death, and rebirth. This aspect of a stele's objecthood can again be demonstrated by the Stele of Mount Hua. According to its inscription (as summarized in Ouyang Xiu's comment), this stele was created in 165 CE to replace older ones, whose "inscriptions had all worn away and disappeared" by the mid-second century. Some 900 years later, this second-century stele was rediscovered by Song antiquarians. Natural elements and human defacement must have left their mark on this stele, although the rubbing in Ouyang Xiu's collection still allowed "a complete reading of the inscription." As I discuss in the next section, one such rubbing still exists, but two other extant rubbings point to different—and later—moments of the stele.

This stele was finally destroyed by an earthquake in the thirty-fourth year of the Jiajing 嘉靖 era (1555) during the Ming dynasty.[33] This tragedy did not terminate the stele's life cycle, however: a number of replacements were made on the basis of the surviving rubbings. After one of these rubbings, the "Siming" 四明 version (Fig. 1.3), entered the collection of Ruan Yuan in the early nineteenth century, for example, Ruan Yuan fashioned his own Stele of Mount Hua based on this rubbing and placed the stele in his clan's school, along with two other "replacement" steles based on two other rare rubbings in his collection.[34] Ruan Yuan's new Mount Hua stele faithfully duplicated the "Siming" rubbing, including all the damage this rubbing registers. Ouyang Xiu's comments on this stele were also inscribed on this new stele in a different script (Fig. 1.4). At Ruan Yuan's encouragement, two of his former students, Lu Kun 盧坤 and Qian Baofu 錢寶甫, erected another Mount Hua stele in the Temple of the Western Marchmount Hua in Shaanxi (Fig. 1.5).

Fig. 1.3 The "Siming" rubbing of the Stele of the Western Marchmount Hua. 175 x 84.8 cm. The stele was made in 165 CE. The rubbing dates to the mid-Ming dynasty.

Fig. 1.4 Rubbing of a reconstructed Stele of the Western Marchmount Hua, established by Ruan Yuan in 1809 in his clan school in
Yangzhou.

Fig. 1.5 Rubbing of a reconstructed Stele of the Western March-mount Hua, established by Lu Kun and Qian Baofu in the early nine-teenth century in the Temple of the Western Marchmount Hua.

This stele omitted all later damage and reconstructed the second-century original. Standing in the temple, this nineteenth-century stele functioned as a surrogate or impersonator. Visitors went to visit it "as if" they were going to visit the second-century stele. Without exception, these visitors recalled the vanished original when commenting on the stele they saw. One of these visitors was Ruan Yuan himself, who visited the site in 1834 with some well-known official/scholars. He ordered an additional inscription to be engraved on the stele. This inscription included a couplet composed by his fellow visitors Jin Zhao 金釗 and Liang Zhangju 梁章鉅: "[Seeing] this 'stele within a stele,' / we realize what past and present means" (*beizhongbei, zhigujin*; 碑中碑, 知古今).

It is difficult to form a stable image of the Stele of Mount Hua: a number of steles have shared this name, and even the one erected in 165—commonly considered the "original"—was itself a replacement and is known only through three different rubbings. The Stele of Mount Hua highlights a series of contradictions or paradoxes shared by ancient steles as sources of rubbings. A stele is made of durable stone and has an imposing, monumental appearance; yet a stele is ever-changing, vulnerable to natural elements and human destruction. A stele can be defined as an object made of a specific material, but its objecthood is often constructed by multiple events, including the notion of an elusive original and the creation of later replacements. A stele is an important source of historical knowledge because of its inscription; however, the practice of reproducing the inscription in rubbings inevitably destroys the stele's physical integrity and undermines its historical authority. These paradoxes contradict the "punctuation function" of a rubbing, which, as mentioned earlier, always registers a particular and precise moment of a stele. As we shall see below, it is precisely this punctuation that has made rubbings a unique subject of historical scholarship. As a background for that discussion, I first inventory the physical properties of a rubbing. In so doing, my focus shifts from the materiality and historicity of the stele to the materiality and historicity of the rubbing.

Properties of a Rubbing

The material and visual properties of a rubbing include not only the imprint it bears but also its material, its mounting style, its colophons and seals, and, if the rubbing is an old one, the physical changes it undergoes during trans-

Fig. 1.6 Workers in the Lintong Museum, Shaanxi, making a rubbing from an ancient stele. 2000. Photograph by the author.

mission. To investigate these properties, we must know precisely how a rubbing is made. Generally speaking, the production of a rubbing consists of four basic steps.[35] The first is to prepare the object from which the rubbing is to be made. For an old stone stele, the rubbing maker would first rid the surface of dirt and moss and pay special attention to the engraved words and decoration, using a pointed bamboo pick to clean every sunken line. He or she should, however, never leave marks on the stone with the cleaning tools and should avoid excessive restoration. The idea is to preserve the stone's present and "natural" condition as much as possible, including damage and traces of age.

After the stele is washed and dried, the rubbing maker affixes a piece of paper to the stele, often with a light, water-based adhesive.[36] The rubbing maker either applies the adhesive on the stele and then spreads the paper over it or wets the paper with the adhesive and then spreads it on the stele. In either case, he uses a large "palm brush" (*zong shua* 棕刷) to spread the paper smoothly, eliminating wrinkles and folds (Fig. 1.6). Once this is done, the rubbing maker uses smaller brushes to tap the paper-covered surface over and over, forcing the damp paper to "sink" into every sunken part, whether it is a carved line or a fissure. To avoid damage to the paper, the tapping movement should be gentle and persistent. Ideally, the paper will register the minutest rise and fall of the stone's surface.

The next step is *shang mo* 上墨— "to apply ink" to the paper. The rubbing maker moistens large and small *mo bao* 墨包, or "ink pads," with wet ink and lightly taps the paper with them, gradually accumulating layers of ink till the desired darkness is reached. He normally starts from the edge of the stele or other empty areas, and gradually moves to the engraved parts. A careful rubbing maker never rushes the process, because excessive ink on a pad is destined to create an ugly mark and blur the outline of a character or an image. After *shang mo* is completed, the rubbing is immediately removed from the object. Since the paper becomes wrinkled and stiff when it dries, the last step in making a rubbing is to mount it into a presentable form, either on a scroll, in an album, or as a single sheet with a thin paper backing.

Although these four steps are mandatory, they can be done carefully or rushed. Consequently the quality of rubbings varies enormously. As Ye Changchi wrote in *Yu shi*:

In Shaanxi and Henan one finds all sorts of temple steles and tomb tablets exposed in the wilderness. They are mottled by moss and lichen, blown by strong wind, and baked under the sun. Using rough paper and coal-ink, several dozen rubbings are made from one stele in a single day; the thud of pounding can be heard nonstop. How can a rubbing made this way be any good? But if one washes the stele so that it is sparklingly clean and uses paper of superb quality, and if one spreads the paper smoothly on the stele with a cotton pad and lightly taps it over and over with a brush, then all the characters and carvings, even the most delicate, are easily registered on the rise and fall of the paper. A rubbing made this way naturally captures the spirit of the stele.[37]

For Ye Changchi and other traditional scholars of stone carvings, rubbings were distinguished by their material and technique, but most important by the quality of their imprints, which should be precise and delicate, capable of conveying the "spirit" of the engraved object. As collectors and connoisseurs, they often wrote next to or even on a rubbing, commenting on its origin, history, condition, and significance. Like the colophons accompanying a traditional handscroll or hanging scroll painting, such messages would become part of a rubbing: they changed the rubbing's physical appearance and supplied a layer of exegesis bridging the rubbing and the onlooker.[38] In addition to this premeditated human intervention, a rubbing can also be altered by natural elements and accidental events. An old rubbing thus often shows not only the erosion of the original stone but also damage to the rubbing itself over its long transmission.

All these signs and marks—those derived from the original stele and those accumulated later—seem to be intermingled in a rubbing in an undifferentiated manner. But to a rubbing connoisseur, these elements appear in clearly defined historical strata and interact with one another in specific ways. To demonstrate this, I will focus on a single work: the "Siming" version of the Stele at Mount Hua (Fig. 1.7).[39] As noted above, rubbings of this stele were collected and studied by Song antiquarians, and this particular rubbing was owned by Ruan Yuan in the nineteenth century and became the model for a number of new Mount Hua steles.

Well known to calligraphers and antique connoisseurs for the past three hundred years, this rubbing is rectangular in shape, fairly large (174 cm long by 85 cm wide), and mounted on a hanging scroll. Numerous colophons are written on the silk mounting surrounding the rubbing. The rubbing itself is a "negative" of the stele; the characters of the inscriptions appear in white against an inked ground. There are two kinds of inscriptions: those from the original stele and those added to the scroll. The original inscription includes the stele's title and a lengthy text underneath it. The title consists of six large "seal script" (zhuan shu 篆書) characters; the main text is written in an elegant "clerical script" (li shu 隸書). The inscription tells that the stele was erected in the eighth year of the Yanxi reign during the Eastern Han, or 165 CE. The inscription is unique among Han steles in identifying several individuals responsible for the making of the monument: an official purchased the stone, a secretary wrote the inscription or supervised its compilation, and one or two masons engraved the inscription.[40] Beside this second-century text, the rubbing also has several inscriptions written in "standard script" (kai shu 楷書), a calligraphic style invented after the Han. These include the short passages on either side of the stele's title, which record the visits of some prominent Tang officials in 829 and 830. Another passage, squeezed between the first two paragraphs of the original inscription, was added to the stele in 1085 by a Song courtier, who represented the emperor at a sacrifice to the sacred mountain that year.

These inscriptions, whether original or later, are texts with definite literary meaning. They are distinguished from other marks on the rubbing,

Fig. 1.7 The present appearance of the "Siming" rubbing of the Stele of the Western Marchmount Hua, with seal impressions and colophons. Palace Museum, Beijing.

which show damage that the stele suffered over its long history and hence register the passage of time. Some irregular "empty" areas on the rubbing reveal that by the time the rubbing was made in the mid-Ming dynasty, the stele had lost a large piece on the right and several smaller pieces in the middle.[41] Chips and scratches are everywhere, especially around the edges. But again, damage *in* the rubbing should be distinguished from damage *to* the rubbing. This second kind of damage is exemplified by the six white spots spaced evenly in two vertical rows. Clearly, before the rubbing was mounted, it had been folded for a long time into a rectangular shape of about 60 by 40 centimeters; the corners of this rectangle were subject to wear over these years. Interestingly, some of these white spots (as well as other "empty" areas in the rubbing) are "filled in" by red impressions of collectors' seals. The placement of these marks was intentional: stamped in these locations, the seal impressions would, it was hoped, prevent possible "restorations"—a common practice of forgery designed to give the rubbing an earlier date (and hence higher commercial value). The stamps thus protect the historical integrity of the rubbing; but in so doing they also changed the rubbing's appearance.

Finally, more than thirty collectors, connoisseurs, and scholars wrote colophons and stamped their seals on the silk mounting that frames the rubbing. To read these colophons in sequence is to reconstruct a history of the rubbing's collecting and viewing. These texts reveal that the rubbing changed hands frequently from the mid-Ming onward.[42] Ruan Yuan acquired the rubbing in Hangzhou in 1808 and mounted it as a hanging scroll. This explains why the colophons on the scroll are dated from 1810 to 1814: they resulted from the occasions on which Ruan showed this newly acquired treasure to important scholars and connoisseurs of his day and invited them to inscribe the scroll.[43] These early colophons are found close to the rubbing, on a piece of silk mounting that has darkened considerably. Fresher pieces of silk have been added to the top and the two long sides of the scroll, and all bear colophons written after 1826. The scroll was therefore remounted not long after its first mounting. A colophon by Ruan Yuan explains the reason for this seemingly unnecessary act. In 1826 he took this precious rubbing with him when he traveled to the southwest. During the journey the rubbing fell into a river and became mildewed; so he had to hire local craftsmen to restore the scroll immediately.

To summarize, the signs and marks that this rubbing bears register six kinds of information in two general categories, *inscription* and *damage*:

Inscription:
    Original stele inscription dated to 165 CE;
    Additional inscriptions on the stele dated to 829, 830, and 1085;
    Colophons and seals that have been added to the rubbing (and on its mounting)
        on various datable occasions since 1810.
Damage
    Damage to the stele from the time of its establishment to the time when the
        rubbing was made (mid-Ming);
    Damage occurring to the unmounted rubbing before it was first mounted in 1810;
    Damage and aging of the mounted rubbing after 1810.

As mentioned above, *inscriptions* result from intentional human acts; most *damage* results from unpremeditated natural causes and signifies the passage of time. What we find in the rubbing is therefore a twofold process: on the one hand, the layers of *inscriptions* testify to a continuous effort to bring the stele into the present—to revitalize its meaning and to reframe it within current intellectual trends; on the other, the layers of *damage* always point to the past and always blur inscriptions—hence they qualify the stele as a historical relic. The branch of historical scholarship that takes both *inscription* and *damage* as its subject is rubbing connoisseurship.

Rubbing Connoisseurship

This section elaborates on a point made above: compared with a stele that is both timeless and ever changing, a rubbing has a definite temporality because it registers a single moment in the history of a stele that can never be repeated. This historical punctuation constitutes the basis of *bei tie jianding* 碑帖鑒定, or rubbing connoisseurship. The degree of familiarity with the materiality and historicity of a particular rubbing determines the expertise of a rubbing connoisseur.

But what is rubbing connoisseurship? First, it is related to, but differs fundamentally from, three other intellectual practices, all of which deal with rubbings but emphasize them as sources of information. Initiated during the Song with the rise of *jin shi xue*, these three practices are concerned with (1) history, (2) epigraphy, and (3) calligraphy. Ouyang Xiu's comments on the Stele of Mount Hua demonstrate a strong interest in history; his detailed narrative deals with the worship of this sacred mountain and the value of this inscription as a unique source for historical research. Epigraphic studies of rubbings investigate the various styles and forms of written characters.

Zhao Mingcheng's remarks on the Stele of Mount Hua, for example, discuss the interchangeability of three characters, *zhi* 職, *zhi* 識, and *zhi* 誌, in ancient writings.[44] A similar discussion of "loan characters" (*jiajie zi* 假借字) can also be found in Hong Kuo's comment on this stele.[45] In other cases, these Song antiquarians remarked on the aesthetic value of ancient inscriptions. One such example is Zhao Mingcheng's views on the Wu Liang Shrine 武梁祠: while declaring the shrine's famous bas-relief carvings to be "simple and unadorned," he judged that their accompanying inscriptions were "exquisite and elegant and could serve as models [for practicing calligraphy.]"[46] The lofty position of the Stele of Mount Hua in the history of calligraphy was firmly established by the early Qing scholar Zhu Yizun 朱彝尊 (1629–1709), who concluded in 1700 after comparing various Han dynasty calligraphic styles:

> Only the inscription of the Stele of Mount Hua of the Yanxi era is characterized by both regularity and flexibility and shows deviation as well as unison. It incorporates the strength of all three styles and should be judged the first among all Han clerical writings. Until today I had only seen a single rubbing of this stele, but it was blurry and much damaged. Now this rubbing in the collection of Mr. Xipi 西陂 is unusually complete. Reading it over and over, I am completely overwhelmed by its extraordinary power.[47]

It is easy to see how these various discussions of rubbings could enrich broader disciplinary inquiries—general historical studies, the style of epigraphic research known as *xiao xue* 小學, and the history of calligraphy. But rubbing connoisseurship is different, and its specific goals and agendas should not be dismissed because of its usefulness for these disciplinary inquiries.[48] Simply stated, the purest form of this scholarship is the study of rubbings alone, freed from the original stones on the one hand and from the content of imprinted words or images on the other. In other words, rubbing connoisseurship is a branch of scholarship that takes rubbings as its sole subject as well as its enclosure.

The self-inclusiveness of rubbing connoisseurship implies that the history it discovers or constructs has little to do with a broader, external reality, whether this reality is about society, religion, language, or art. Nor does a rubbing connoisseur attempt a general history of the rubbing—what he constructs are numerous "micro-histories," each focusing on a series of rubbings that are ultimately linked to a single, original, and often elusive object. He arranges these rubbings into a chronological sequence by determining their relative positions. (In the process he also eliminates copies and fakes.) This purpose requires him to derive evidence from a rubbing itself—from its paper, ink, seals, and colophons, but most important from its imprint, whose minute differences from other related rubbings reveal the changing physical condition of the original object. In these differences he sees gradual erosion or decay or a sudden splitting or collapse of the object. His findings thus provide the sense of "events" or "happenings" necessary for a historical narrative. Perhaps unique to all scholarly practices, therefore, the principal technique of rubbing connoisseurship is to detect traces of ruination, and its chief accomplishment is to construct a sequence of ruins.

I first formulated this notion of rubbing connoisseurship while watching Mr. Ma Ziyun 馬子雲 (1903–86), a colleague 42 years senior to me, working in our shared office in the Division of Bronze and Stone in Beijing's Palace Museum. At that time—it was around the end of the Cultural Revolution in the mid-1970s—Mr. Ma was regarded as the finest surviving rubbing maker and the most knowledgeable connoisseur of old rubbings in the country. As a rubbing maker, he was particularly well known for making *quanxing ta* 全形拓 or a "rubbing of a complete shape," in which a three-dimensional image of a bronze vessel or a stone sculpture is achieved not through painting or photography but through the painstaking effort of making a rubbing from a round object.[49] As a connoisseur of old rubbings, Mr. Ma's main method was to diagnose minute but finite physical changes in an inscribed object by comparing rubbings made from it at different times. Among the changes he looked for were a peeling surface, a missing character or stroke, a widening crack or cleavage, any signs of wear and tear, and the changing shape and increasing dimensions of a *shi hua* 石花 (literally "stone flowers"; a *shi hua* is the patterned substance of a calcium compound that grows slowly on the surface of a stone monument). One day he pointed to the impression of a *shi hua* on a Qianlong rubbing of the "Stele of Sacrificing to Mount Sangong" ("Si Sangongshan bei" 祀三公山碑), and told us that it was absent in another rubbing of the same stele with a Kangxi period seal on it; the stone flower must therefore have grown to about two *cun* wide over some ninety years from the 1680s to the 1770s. This and other observations became the basis for a book called *Bei tie jianding* (Rubbing connoisseurship), which his student Shi Anchang 施安昌 compiled and published seven years after his death. In this massive compilation of 1,200 entries, each entry provides a micro-history of a sequence of rubbings.[50]

Considered a milestone in his scholarship, Mr. Ma's discussion of the Stele of Mount Hua is a detailed comparison of three surviving rubbings of the stele.[51] The first is known as the "Changyuan" 長垣 version because its earliest recorded collector was Wang Wensun 王文蓀 from Changyuan (present-day Shangqiu 商丘 in Henan). The second is called the "Huayin" 華陰 or "Guanzhong" 關中 version because it was first owned by Dong Yunju 東雲駒 and Dong Yunchu 東雲雛, two brothers from Huayin in Shaanxi. The third version is the "Siming" version, which we have studied in detail (see Fig. 1.7). The "Changyuan" rubbing is unquestionably the earliest, because it shows the complete text of the 165 CE inscription as transcribed by Hong Kuo in his 1166 Li shi 隸釋 (Interpreting clerical writings). Mr. Ma found 58 characters in this rubbing that show traces of damage. Possibly made in the mid-twelfth century, this rubbing thus registers the consequence of the stele's physical changes during the millennium since the mid-second century (Fig. 1.8a).

A more important discovery by Mr. Ma concerns the relationship between the "Huayin" version (Fig. 1.8b) and the "Siming" version (Fig. 1.8c). Arguing against the popular opinion that these two rubbings were made around the same time, he demonstrated convincingly that they are very different in date. Compared to the "Changyuan" version, both rubbings show major damage to the stele in the middle-right portion, a damage which caused more than a hundred characters of the inscription to be lost (see Fig. 1.7). But Mr. Ma also found at least 60 characters in the "Siming" version that show additional damage in comparison to their equivalents in the "Huayin" version. For example, in the imprints of the stele's title (Xi Yu Hua Shan Miao Bei 西嶽華山廟碑) in the two rubbings:

"Huayin" version: The characters are intact.

"Siming" version: The character "xi" 西 is damaged on the left; the crack continues to the space below the character. The "quan" 犬 radical at the right side of the character "yu" 嶽 shows slight damage in its last stroke. Further damages are found in the strokes of the character "shan" 山, the left diagonal stroke of the character "miao" 廟, and the upper right and left corners of the character "bei" 碑.[52]

These and other discrepancies between the two rubbings convinced Ma Ziyun that they must have been made at different times and represent two widely separated moments in the history of the stele. Neither had been made during the Song as Ruan Yuan insisted. Instead, the "Huayin" version

Fig. 1.8 Sections of three
early rubbings of the Stele
of the Western March-
mount Hua:
(*a, above left*) "Changyuan"
rubbing, Song dynasty;
(*b, above right*) "Huayin"
rubbing, late Yuan
or early Ming;
(*c, to left*) "Siming"
rubbing, mid-Ming.

should be dated to "some time from the Yuan to the Ming," and the "Siming" version was most likely made in the mid-Ming.[53] These new dates were not the only consequence of this exercise of rubbing connoisseurship, however. Mr. Ma's purely technical study raises questions about the intention behind the original dating. Checking historical records, we find that this dating was first proposed by Ruan Yuan, the owner of the "Siming" version in the early nineteenth century, and was agreed to by Zhu Xigeng 朱錫庚, the then owner of the "Huayin" version.[54] It seems clear that Ruan was motivated by the desire to promote the "Siming" rubbing in his collection, and that Zhu Xigeng did not dare to disagree because of Ruan's political power and status.

This case challenges the purely technical nature of rubbing connoisseurship and suggests the need for a sociological investigation of this scholarly tradition. But for the purposes of this section, let us focus on some general practices of a rubbing connoisseur. One thing striking about Mr. Ma's discussion of a rubbing is his total lack of interest in the content of the inscription. In fact, he never perceived and described an inscription as a readable text; what he saw were always individual characters and strokes. Moreover, his interest in characters and strokes had nothing to do with their original forms, not to mention their literal meaning or aesthetic value. His microscopic vision was instantaneously attracted by the *damaged* parts of a character or a stroke. The subject of his reading was therefore never the cultural phenomenon of writing, but only nonliterary signs—fissures, cracks, fractures—that displayed human agency or Nature at work to destroy writing.

But when he shifted his eyes to the colophons accompanying a rubbing, he changed his reading method abruptly and treated them as historical documents with intrinsic meaning. These colophons, written by successive collectors and viewers of a precious rubbing over a long period, often contain valuable information about the rubbing's production and transmission. Some colophons provide lengthy comparisons of a rubbing to related ones. Thus, although antiquarian catalogues since the Song have regularly inventoried and discussed stone carvings, these colophons are more directly concerned with rubbings themselves; they constitute a large body of texts on rubbing connoisseurship. The three rubbings of the Stele of Mount Hua, for example, are accompanied by a total of 145 colophons (64 on the "Changyuan" version, 48 on the "Huayin" version, and 33 on the "Siming" version). The book-like album format of the first two rubbings especially allowed various connoisseurs from the early Ming to the late Qing to append their writings—some of them full-length handwritten articles—to the rubbings. Mr. Ma's reconstruction of each rubbing's history was largely based on these texts, and his arguments about a rubbing's date also responded to previous proposals made by the colophon writers. To him, therefore, these colophons both provided historical information and constituted a scholarly tradition which he followed and reacted to.

It is possible to summarize Ma Ziyun's scholarship as a simultaneous construction of three separate histories: (1) a history of a decaying object, (2) a history of making rubbings from this object as a process of cultural production, and (3) a history of rubbing connoisseurship as the continuation of an intellectual tradition. The first kind of history, however, was not his purpose and only implied in the other two. A close reading of his writings reveals that he was, in fact, uninterested in any real object as the source material of rubbings. He was preoccupied only by what he could find in a rubbing. This is also what I remember of him: day after day, he surrounded himself with piles and piles of mounted and unmounted rubbings. I cannot recall a single occasion on which he visited an ancient site as a rubbing connoisseur—he visited ancient monuments only as a rubbing maker.

This is puzzling, because, as mentioned earlier, the practice of rubbing connoisseurship rests entirely on an acute awareness of the changing physicality of an object. But to Mr. Ma, such changes served only as an unspoken premise for his evaluation of rubbings; he could never bring himself to turn a precious rubbing into a piece of evidence for studying an object. All 1,200 case studies in his *Bei tie jianding* are micro-histories of rubbings, not micro-histories of carvings. We may thus borrow the concept of the "archive" to characterize the three principal roles of rubbings in the making of these micro-histories. First, like archives, a series of rubbings designates "an organized body of documents" structured and preserved by a person or an institution. Second, a series of rubbings provides material proof or evidence for a "history, a narrative, or an argument." Third, like archives, rubbings have detached themselves from the original object to gain an independent objectivity.[55] For this last point, which implies the separation of documents from monuments, Paul Ricoeur has noted a parallel situation in European history:

The development of positivist history at the end of the 19th and the beginning of the 20th century marked the triumph of the document over the monument. What makes a monument suspect, even though it often is found *in situ*, is its obvious final-ity, its commemoration of events that its contemporaries—especially the most powerful among them—judged worthy of being integrated into the collective memory. Conversely, the document, even though it is collected and not simply inherited, seems to possess an objectivity opposed to the intention of the monument, which is meant to be edifying. The writings in archives were thus thought to be more like documents than like monuments.[56]

Although differing in intention and historical situation, a similar "triumph of the document over the monument" started in China with the rise of antiquarianism during the Song and is best realized in rubbing connoisseurship. Ricoeur's analysis of the "objectivity" of archives independent from monuments also helps us understand a seemingly strange feature of Mr. Ma's writings on rubbings: they give no account of the stone carvings from which these rubbings were made, even though many still exist, sometimes right in the Palace Museum where Mr. Ma worked. The reason is simple: compared to its rubbings, a stone carving is always both too old and too new. It is too old because it has long lost its original appearance and is no longer useful for an empirical, scientific observation. It is too new because it is still changing: one must always assume that it has deteriorated further since the last rubbing was taken from it. A carving is therefore always "inferior" to its rubbings as historical evidence.

Predictably, this notion of a rubbing's objectivity encourages the construction of its objecthood. Earlier in this chapter, I discussed the physical features of a rubbing: made of a particular type of paper and ink, it is also mounted into a specific format for viewing and preservation. These physical features of a rubbing formed an alternative focus of Mr. Ma's observation in addition to his interest in a rubbing's imprint. His eyes shone when he saw a rubbing of superb quality. He touched it lightly here and there and occasionally brought it close to his face to smell it. He would praise the texture of its paper, the quality of its ink, and the artistry of its mounting; and would sum up his observation with a single defining phrase. It was then I heard, along with a dozen or so other such definitions, "cicada-wing rubbing" (*chanyi ta* 蟬翼拓) and "black-gold rubbing" (*wujin ta* 烏金拓). Later I learned that these terms come from a standard vocabulary of rubbing connoisseurship, each pertaining to a particular style, technique, and tradition in rubbing making. A "cicada-wing rubbing," for example, is a type of rubbing in which light ink is applied evenly to an extremely thin, silk-like, and slightly yellowish piece of paper; its delicate material and imagery reveal a refined, literati sensibility. The "black-gold rubbing" was invented in the early Qing court. Imprinted on a piece of pure white "peach-blossom" paper (*taohua zhi* 桃花紙), the shining, black-ink impression generates a visual effect that is at once striking and commanding.

A rubbing is therefore not simply a shadowy "reference" to an inscribed object or a conventional "document" offering a textual proof; rather, it has acquired its own material substance, artistic style, and aesthetic tradition. A rubbing's materiality is further substantiated by the practice of mounting it in a particular format. Among the three surviving rubbings of the Stele of Mount Hua, for example, only the "Siming" rubbing is an "uncut version" (*zhengzhuang ben* 整裝本), which shows the entire inscription on the surface of the stele (see Fig. 1.7). The other two are "cut versions" (*jianzhuang ben* 剪裝本), a rearrangement of the inscription into a book-like album (Figs. 1.8a, b). To transform an uncut rubbing into such an album, the mounter first adds a thin backing to the rubbing and then cuts it up into vertical strips, each containing one column of the text. He then cuts these strips into shorter ones and arranges them on each page of the album, omitting the "empty" part left by the damaged sections on a stele.[57] A "cut version" thus results from re-editing and redesigning and conveys even less of the original object. Confronting the "Huayin" rubbing, a viewer would have no idea that the stele was severely damaged and the text is incomplete, because all the missing spaces on the stele have been omitted and the characters are connected smoothly in continuous columns. In other words, this rubbing presents an incomplete text in the form of a complete literary composition. But it is this version that won the highest praise from Mr. Ma (and other connoisseurs) for its "most exquisite" visual effect.[58]

Having acquired its own materiality and objecthood, a rubbing is conceived as a *wu* 物, or a "thing," and is further associated with the concept *yi wu* 遺物, or "leftover thing." In ancient Chinese, the term *yi wu* often refers to possessions left behind by either a dead person or a defunct dynasty. But generally speaking, any object that points to the past is an *yi wu* because it is a surviving portion of a vanished whole; by arrangement or accident, it has been severed from its original context to become part of contemporary culture. An *yi wu* is thus characterized both by pastness and contemporaneity: it originated in the past, but it belongs to the here and now. An *yi wu* often shows signs of damage: its incompleteness guarantees its authenticity and becomes a stimulus for either poetic lamentation or historical reconstruction.

Rubbings not only constitute a particular kind of *yi wu* but also epitomize the essence of *yi wu*. A rubbing can be a "leftover thing" of (1) an object, (2) a rubbing collection, and (3) a former self; it can therefore confirm its potential as an *yi wu* three times. First, every rubbing of a stele is by definition a "leftover thing" of the stele: it is the skin of an object that has been pulled off the object's body. As such, it always registers a vanished past; yet at the same time it generates ongoing artistic and intellectual activities and interests. Second, a large group of rubbings accumulated by a devoted antiquarian was always considered a collective body of objects. None of the large collections of rubbings established from the Song to Qing has survived intact. All have suffered from personal or national tragedies. The rubbings were dispersed and destroyed; the leftover ones have become *yi wu* of the collectors and their collections. This transformation of rubbings from collectable *wu* to posthumous *yi wu* is the subject of accounts by a number of rubbing collectors, who watched their beloved collections disappear before their own eyes. Ye Changchi, for example, described his despair in abandoning the 8,000 rubbings he had spent twenty years accumulating, a decision he had to make when he fled the capital during the Boxer Rebellion in 1900.[59] But the most moving account of such an experience is found in Li Qingzhao's "Afterword" to her husband Zhao Mingcheng's rubbing catalogue.

Above I cite a paragraph from this text, which describes the joy Li Qingzhao and Zhao Mingcheng shared when they began to collect rubbings of ancient inscriptions and other texts. The joy of gathering soon gave way to the burden of *things* having been gathered, however. The collection demanded great care; consequently "there was no longer the same ease and casualness as before." Then the war between the Song and the Jin broke out. When Zhao Mingcheng heard it, "he was in a daze, realizing that all those full trunks and overflowing chests, which he regarded so lovingly and mournfully, would surely soon be his possessions no longer." But he died before the collection completely dissolved. Li Qingzhao was entrusted to watch over the remaining items, which still included, among other things, two thousand rubbings of bronze and stone inscriptions. Her effort to protect them was in vain: the bulk of the collection was reduced by burning, plundering, and robbery, until all that remained were "a few volumes from three or so sets, none complete, and some very ordinary pieces of calligraphy." These were indeed the ruins of a once great collection of historical data.

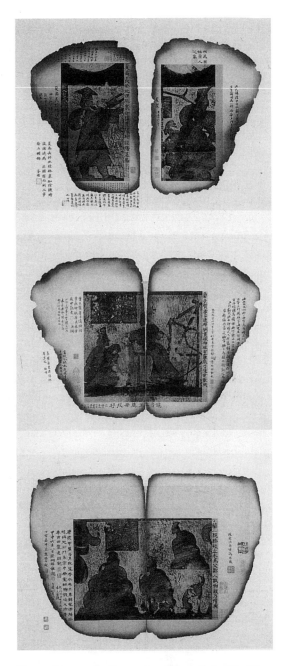

Fig. 1.9 Fragments of an early rubbing of the Wu Liang Shrine carvings. The carvings were made in 151 CE. The rubbing dates to the Song dynasty. Palace Museum, Beijing.

And as ruins they invoked memory and melancholy, as Li Qingzhao wrote toward the end of the "Afterword":

Nowadays, when I chance to look over these books, it's like meeting old friends. And I recall when my husband was in the hall called "Calm Governance" in Laizhou, . . . every day in the evening when the office clerks would go home, he would do editorial collations on two *juan* and write a colophon for one inscription. Of those two thousand items, colophons were written on five hundred and two. It is so sad—today the ink of his writing seems still fresh, yet the trees by his grave have grown to an armspan in girth.[60]

Not a single rubbing from Zhao's collection still exists. The few surviving Song rubbings have become ruins of their former selves. Hence lies the third significance of a rubbing as an *yi wu*. The burned pieces in Fig. 1.9, which are what is left of the only Song rubbing of the famous Wu Liang Shrine carvings, register multiple layers of history—the image created in the Han, the imprint made in the Song, the burning in the late Qing, and numerous colophons written before and after the fire. This history is the article that Ma Ziyun published in 1960.[61] This time, he studied not only the damage to the carvings (as demonstrated by the rubbing's imprint) but also the damage to the rubbing itself (as documented by the traces of burning). Based on the last colophon written before the burning (because it was partially destroyed by fire), he was able to date this accident to some time after 1849.[62] Today, this rubbing is ranked a national treasure, although even in its undamaged state it only represented a very small portion of the Wu Liang Shrine images, and even though this small portion of the images has been severely damaged.[63]

Made of thin and fragile paper, a rubbing could easily be destroyed or ruined—torn, scratched, mildewed, burned, or eaten by insects. The materiality of a rubbing thus enables it to display most sensitively the vulnerability of a manufactured object to natural or human destruction: in a "ruined" rubbing, an eroded carving is damaged for a second time.

Notes

1. Roland Barthes, *The Responsibility of Form*, trans. Richard Howard (New York: Hill and Wang, 1986), p. 5.

2. Qianshen Bai, "The Artistic and Intellectual Dimensions of Chinese Calligraphy Rubbings: Some Examples from the Collection of Robert Hatfield Ellsworth," *Orientations* 30, no. 3 (Mar. 1999): 83.

3. Zhao Ruzhen 趙汝珍, *Guwan zhinan* 古玩指南 (A guide to antiques) (Beijing: Zhongguo shudian, 1984), chap. 12, p. 6.

4. For example, Zhao Ruzhen (ibid., chap. 12, p. 1) explains: " The term *bei tie* people use nowadays does not mean an original stone stele or a stone carved with a piece of calligraphy but pertains to the rubbings from such stones."

5. For recent discussions of *tie*, see Amy MacNair, "The Engraved Model-Letters Compendia of the Song Dynasty," *Journal of the American Oriental Society* 114, no. 2 (Apr.–June 1994): 209–25; idem, "Engraved Calligraphy in China: Recession and Reception," *Art Bulletin* 160, no. 1 (Mar. 1995): 106–14; and Bai, "Artistic and Intellectual Dimensions of Chinese Calligraphy Rubbings."

6. It is said that Emperor Huizong (r. 1101–26) made a set of new rubbings of famous calligraphy in the imperial collection because the old blocks had cracked. A story relates that the original blocks resurfaced in the Ming court and were smuggled out by a certain Sun Zhonghan, who then made a few sets of rubbings from the blocks. See Zhao Ruzhen 趙汝珍, *Gudong bianyi* 古董辯疑 (Clarifying doubts about antiques) (Beijing: Zhongguo shudian, 1989), chap. 3, pp. 8b–9a. But this story is full of holes. It is more likely an invention of later forgers of "Chunhua ge" rubbings, who could thus claim that their rubbings were made from the "rediscovered" original blocks.

7. For these and other copies of the "Chunhua ge tie," see Zhao Ruzhen, *Gudong bianyi*, chap. 3.

8. Even when on occasion engraved blocks were built into a wall for display, they appear as flat pages from a book. What is displayed is not the blocks as independent art objects but the engraved calligraphy.

9. Bai, "Artistic and Intellectual Dimensions of Chinese Calligraphy Rubbings," p. 83.

10. Traditional scholars hold different opinions about the origin of the stele. Based on abundant archaeological evidence, however, we can safely date the earliest steles to the first century CE and link their appearance to the beginning of stone monuments in China. See Wu Hung, *Monumentality in Early Chinese Art and Architecture* (Stanford: Stanford University Press, 1995), pp. 121–42; and Zhao Chao 趙超, *Zhongguo gudai shike gailun* 中國古代石刻概論 (A general discussion of stone carvings from ancient China) (Beijing: Wenwu chubanshe, 1997), pp. 11–13.

11. For a brief introduction to this type of stele inscriptions, which are called *ming lei* 銘耒, see Wu, *Monumentality in Early Chinese Art and Architecture*, p. 222. For analyses of actual stele inscriptions and their social roles, see ibid., pp. 217–23; and Patricia B. Ebrey, "Later Han Stone Inscriptions," *Harvard Journal of Asiatic Studies* 40, no. 2 (1980): 325–53.

12. The most important examples of this kind of steles are those engraved with standardized versions of Confucian classics issued by the governments of different dynasties. A large body of scholarship is devoted to these "stone classics." For a concise introduction, see Zhao Chao, *Zhongguo gudai shike gailun*, pp. 20–25.

13. Even before the Northern Song, there had long existed a tradition of using stele inscriptions as valuable sources for historical information. Li Daoyuan, for example, recorded more than 100 Han dynasty stone carvings and close to 20 Northern Wei steles in his *Shui jing zhu* (Commentaries on the Classic of Waterways). Yang Xuanzhi cited more than 20 Buddhist steles at Luoyang in his *Luoyang qielan ji* (Records of Buddhist monasteries at Luoyang). A number of other scholars in the Northern and Southern dynasties, such as Yan Zhitui, Jiang Shi, and Liu Yao, also derived information from stele inscriptions in their historical writings. The systematic study of stone inscriptions began only in the Northern Song, however.

14. For examples, see R. C. Rudolph, "Preliminary Notes on Sung Archaeology," *Journal of Asian Studies* 22 (1963): 169–77; Kwang-chih Chang, "Archaeology and Chinese Historiography," *World Archaeology* 13, no. 2 (1968): 156–69; Wu Hung, *The Wu Liang Shrine: The Ideology of Early Chinese Pictorial Art* (Stanford: Stanford University Press, 1989), pp. 38–49; Xia Chaoxiong 夏超雄, "Song dai jin shi xue de zhuyao gongxian jiqi xingqi de yuanyin" 宋代金石學的主要貢獻及其興起的原因 (The rise of Song antiquarianism and its major contributions), *Beijing daxue xuebao* 北京大學學報 1982, no. 1: 66–76; and Robert E. Harrist, Jr., "The Artist as Antiquarian: Li Gonglin and His Study of Early Chinese Art," *Artibus Asiae* 55, no. 3/4 (1995): 237–80.

15. See Quan Hansheng 全漢升, "Bei Song Bianliang de shuchu maoyi" 北宋汴梁的輸出貿易 (Imports and exports in Bianliang during the Northern Song), *Bulletin of the Institute of History and Philology, Academia Sinica* 8, no. 2 (1939): 189–301.

16. Zhou Hui, *Qingbo zazhi* (1192). See Rudolph, "Preliminary Notes on Sung Archaeology," p. 175.

17. The effort to collect and compile stone inscriptions began long before the Song. Emperor Yuan of the Liang 梁元帝 (r. 552–54), for example, compiled a large work called *Bei ying* 碑英 (Gems of steles). During the Five Dynasties period, a person named Wang Fu collected rubbings of more than 3,000 stone inscriptions and compiled a catalogue of them. Both books, however, were lost long ago, and we know little about their contents.

18. Translation from Stephen Owen, *Remembrances: The Experience of the Past in Classical Chinese Literature* (Cambridge, Mass.: Harvard University Press, 1985), p. 82. See ibid. for a complete translation and an excellent discussion of this important document. "The age of Getian" refers to a mythical utopian period in China's prehistory.

19. Ouyang Xiu 歐陽修, *Jigu lu bawei* 集古錄跋尾 (Colophons from the *Records on Collecting Antiques*), in *Shike shiliao xinbian* 石刻史料新編 (A new compilation of historical materials on stone carvings) (Taibei: Xinwenfeng chuban, 1957), Mount Hua.

20. Zhao Mingcheng 趙明誠, *Jin shi lu* 金石錄 (Records of bronze and stone inscriptions), in *Congshu jicheng* 叢書集成 (Collected collectanea), no. 212 (Changsha: Shangwu yinshuguan, 1937), Mount Hua.

21. Hong was addressing a point made earlier by Ouyang Xiu's son, Ouyang Fei 歐陽棐, that the inscription states that it was written by Guo Xiangcha 郭香察. Hong cited other sources to prove that the person's name was Guo Xiang 郭香, and he did not write but only "supervised" (cha 察) the text's compilation. A comparison of the inscription and the standard history also led Hong Kuo to discover some discrepancies with regard to Yuan Feng's official career.

22. *Congshu jicheng xinbian* 52, pp. 113–29. Hong Kuo 洪适, *Li xu, Li shi* 隸續, 隸釋 (Beijing: Zhonghua shuju, 1985), pp. 25–27.

23. Ye Changchi 葉昌熾, *Yu shi* 語石 (Talking about the stone) (Shenyang: Liaoning jiaoyu chubanshe, 1999), p. 264; translation based on R. H. van Gulik, *Chinese Pictorial Art as Viewed by the Connoisseur* (Rome: Is. M. E. O., 1958), pp. 92–93.

24. Ye, *Yu shi*, p. 251.

25. Ibid., p. 251.

26. Ibid., p. 11.

27. As Lu Yuan 路远 (*Xi'an Beilin shi* 西安碑林史 [A history of the Forest of Steles in Xi'an] [Xi'an: Xi'an chubanshe, 1998], pp. 67–69) discusses in great detail, the Forest of Steles actually started much earlier.

28. Ibid., pp. 67–106.

29. See ibid., p. 71.

30. One possible exception is the carvings of the Wu Liang Shrine. These carvings were studied by Song antiquarians based on rubbings made from them. But the carvings were buried again and only rediscovered by Huang Yi 黃易 in 1786. When Huang made rubbings from the rediscovered stones, he claimed that because the stones had remained unchanged during these years, "these new rubbings are Song rubbings" (see Huang Yi, *Xiaopenglai ge jin shi wenzi* 小蓬萊閣金石文字 [Bronze and stone inscriptions from the Xiaopenglai Pavilion] [Shimoxuan, 1834]). But as Ma Ziyun 馬子雲 ("Tan Wu Liang Ci huaxiang de Song ta yu Huang Yi taben" 談武梁祠畫像的宋拓 與黃易拓本 [On the Song rubbings and Huang Yi's

rubbings of the pictorial carvings on the Wu Liang Shrine], *Gugong bowuyuan yuankan* 故宮博物院院刊, no. 2 [1960]: 170–77) has argued, the imprints in Huang Yi's rubbings differ from those in a Song rubbing of the shrine preserved in the Palace Museum. It is possible that the stones were not reburied till the Yuan dynasty, because it is recorded that in 1344, a flood destroyed the shrine and other stone monuments in the Wu family cemetery (see Wu, *The Wu Liang Shrine*, p. 329).

31. This relationship between a rubbing and a stele reminds me of Roland Barthes's (*Camera Lucida: Reflections on Photography*, trans. R. Howard [New York: Hill and Wang, 1981], p. 12) discussion of the relationship between his photographic portrait and himself: "What I want, in short, is that my (mobile) image, buffeted among a thousand shifting photographs, altering with situation and age, should always coincide with my (profound) 'self'; but it is the contrary that must be said: 'myself' never coincides with my image; for it is the image which is heavy, motionless, stubborn (which is why society sustains it), and 'myself' which is light, divided, dispersed; like a bottle-imp, 'myself' doesn't hold still, giggling in my jar: if only photography could give me a neutral, anatomic body, a body which signifies nothing!" It is interesting to imagine oneself in the place of a stele, as the source of "motionless" and "stubborn" rubbings.

32. For a useful list of famous steles "reproduced" in later ages, see Ma Ziyun 馬子雲 and Shi Anchang 施安昌, *Beitie jianding* 碑帖鑒定 (Connoisseurship of rubbings) (Guilin: Guangxi shifan daxue chubanshe, 1993), app. 2, pp. 477–82.

33. There are different theories about the destruction of the stele. Here I follow a record by Gu Yanwu 顧炎武. For these theories, see Shi Anchang 施安昌, *Han Huashan bei tiba nianbiao* 漢華山碑題跋年表 (A chronicle of colophons on rubbings of the Mount Hua stele) (Beijing: Wenwu chubanshe, 1997), p. 37.

34. One day Ruan Yuan found a hundred-year-old landscape painting by Wang Yuanqi 王元祁 (1642–1715) and thought that the painted scenery looked like the site of the steles. Inspired by this resemblance, he commissioned a painter to add the images of the three steles in the painting and wrote a long poem on the painting to record the event; see Ruan Yuan 阮元, "Han Yanxi Xiyu Huashan bei kao" 漢延熹西嶽華山廟碑考 (An examination of the Han dynasty stele of the Western Marchmount Hua established in the Yanxi reign); reprinted in *Congshu jicheng xinbian* 叢書集成新編 (A new edition of collected collectanea) (Taibei: Xinwenfeng chuban, 1985), 52: 121.

35. For the most detailed introduction in English to the techniques of rubbing, see Gulik, *Chinese Pictorial Art*, pp. 86–101.

36. Traditionally the two major ways of making a rubbing were called the "wet method" and the "dry method." But most rubbing makers in China today employ only the wet method. The most popular adhesive is made by soaking *baiji* 白芨 root

(*Hyacinth bletilla* tuber) in clean water. For an introduction to the "dry method," see Gulik, *Chinese Pictorial Art*.

37. Ye, *Yu shi*, p. 264.

38. See Wu Hung, *Double Screen: Medium and Representation in Chinese Painting* (London: Reaktion Books, 1996), pp. 29–48, for a discussion of the relationship between textual references and a painting and the suggestion that colophons in a painting constitute an "internal textual enclosure" for interpreting the painting.

39. See Palace Museum, *Gugong bowuyuan 50 nian rucang wenwu jingpinji* 故宮博物院 50 年入藏文物精品集 (Selected gems of cultural relics—collected in the Palace Museum in the past 50 years) (Beijing: Forbidden City Press, 1999), pl. 390, p. 342.

40. About the writer of the inscription, there are two different opinions based on different readings of a phrase in the inscription: "Guo Xiangcha shu" ("Guo Xiangcha wrote [the inscription]") or "Guo Xiang cha shu" 郭香察書 (Guo Xiang supervised the writing [of the inscription]); see note 21 to this chapter. For a detailed study of this inscription, see Ma Ziyun 馬子雲, "Tan Xiyue Huashan miao bei de sanben Song ta" 談西嶽華山廟碑的三 本宋拓 (On three Song rubbings of the stele at the Temple of the Western Marchmount Hua), *Wenwu* 1961, no. 8: 31–35; and idem, *Xiyue Huashan miao bei* 西嶽華山廟碑 (The stele at the Temple of the Western Marchmount Hua) (Beijing: Zhongguo shudian, 1992).

41. The rubbing has been dated variously to the Southern Song, Yuan, and Ming. Ma Ziyuan first dated it to the end of Southern Song or the early Yuan, but changed his opinion later to the middle Ming. Here I follow his later dating. See Ma, "Tan Xiyue Huashan miao bei de sanben Song ta," p. 31; and Ma and Shi, *Beitie jianding*, p. 50.

42. This rubbing earlier belonged consecutively to three Ningpo 寧波 collectors: Feng Xi 豐熙, Quan Xieshan 全謝山, and the Tianyi Pavilion 天一閣 of the Fan 范 family. Qian Dongbi 錢東璧, a son of the famous official and scholar Qian Daxin 錢大昕, obtained it in 1787.

43. For a summary of these events, see Shi, *Han Huashan bei tibao nianbiao*.

44. Zhao Mingcheng, *Jin shi lu*.

45. Hong, *Li xu, Li shi*, pp. 25–27.

46. Zhao Mingcheng, *Jin shi lu*, cited in Shi, *Xuezhai zhanbi*, pp. 47–48.

47. Zhu Yizun's colophon on the "Changyuan" rubbing of the stele.

48. The most important contribution of rubbing connoisseurship to these disciplinary inquiries is the dating and authentication of old rubbings.

49. This conversion of a three-dimensional object into a two-dimensional image must have had special appeal to him. It was said that as a young man he traveled several hundred *li* alone to visit those stone sculptures at the tomb of Huo Qubing 霍去病, from which he made eleven monumental "rubbings of complete shapes."

Later, he recalled that when he first entered the trade, no one would disclose to him how to make such rubbings. So he taught himself and demonstrated his mastery of this technique with a rubbing of Guo Ji Zi Bo pan 虢季子伯盘—a five-feet-long bronze basin that a modern scholar has declared to be an eighth-century BCE bathtub. This rubbing took Mr. Ma two years to complete. See Ma and Shi, *Beitie jianding*, "Preface," p. 1.

50. An example of this kind of micro-history is his study of the Kong Zhou stele dated to the Eastern Han. I translate this short article here in full because it best demonstrates the style of Ma Ziyun's scholarship.

> *The Stele of the Kong Zhou* 孔宙, *the Commandant of Taishan* 泰山: [The main inscription on this stele is] written in the style of clerical script. Those on the front side are arranged in 15 columns, each consisting of 28 characters. On the back, five characters written in the style of seal script appear above 21 columns [of names] arranged in three horizontal rows. On the stele's "forehead" [bei'e 碑額] are nine sunken characters in the style of seal script, which reads "An Eulogy to Kong Zhou, the Han Chief Commandant of Taishian." It is dated to the seventh month, the seventh year of the Yanxi reign (164), and is now in Qufu, Shandong.
>
> In an early Ming rubbing of the inscription, the last stroke of the "kou" 口 radical in the lower part of the character "gao" 高—a character in the phrase "fan bai yang gao"凡百仰高—is undamaged, and a space about half an inch wide still remains between the character and the [lower] edge of the stele. In a late Ming rubbing, more than half of the character "ci" 辭 in the phrase "qi ci yue" 其辭曰 in the tenth column still remains, and the upper-right part of the character "㕛," in the phrase "shu mo" 㕛殁 in the fourteenth column is still visible. Down to the Kangxi and Qianlong periods during the Qing, the character "xun" 訓 in the phrase "jia xun" 家訓 in the first column is still separated from a nearby *shi hua*, the character "ci" 辭 still has its upper part, and the character "mo" 殁 is only slightly damaged on the left half. In rubbings made after the Jiaqing and Daoguang periods, however, not only are all these characters seriously damaged, but other characters have become blurred and lost their spirit. (Ibid., p. 46)

This passage contains a mistake: the title of the stele consists of ten characters, not nine; and its wording differs from that cited by Ma Ziyun.

51. Ma, "Tan Xiyue Huashan miao bei de sanben Song ta." An abridged version of the article can be found in Ma and Shi, *Beitie jianding*, pp. 49–52, but here the rubbings are given different dates. There is another old rubbing of the stele, conventionally known as the Shunde 順德 version. Mr. Ma did not pay much attention to this version.

52. Ma, "Tan Xiyue Huashan miao bei de sanben Song ta," p. 33.

53. Ma and Shi, *Beitie jianding*, p. 50. But in an earlier article on the three rubbings, he dated the "Siming" version to "the end of the Southern Song or the beginning of the Yuan"; see "Tan Xiyue Huashan miao bei de sanben Song ta," p. 32.

54. After Ruan Yuan acquired the "Siming" version in 1808, he made an appointment in 1810 with Zhu Xigeng, the owner of the "Huayin" version, to compare the two rubbings in Beijing's Dragon Spring Monastery (Longquan si 龍泉寺). According to a colophon Ruan wrote afterward on his "Siming" version, he and Zhu "spent a whole day comparing the two rubbings [and concluded that] they were made at the same time [during the Song]." His opinion was shared by Zhu Xigeng, who confirmed it in a long colophon he inscribed in 1811 on his own "Huayin" rubbing. This conclusion was then repeated by all rubbing connoisseurs for the next 150 years. This view is suspicious, however, because the two rubbings differ considerably, as Mr. Ma convincingly demonstrated in his 1961 article. Nevertheless, the two men's comparison of the rubbings allowed Ruan Yuan to rank the "Siming" version the second among the three surviving rubbings of the stele. This ranking then provided a basis for his lengthy essay "An Examination of the Han Dynasty Stele of the Western Marchmount Hua of the Yanxi Era."

55. See Paul Ricoeur, *Time and Narrative*, trans. K. Blamey and D. Pellauer (Chicago: University of Chicago Press, 1985), 3: 116–19. All the quotations in this paragraph are from this part of Ricoeur's highly original book.

56. Ibid., p. 118.

57. For a detailed introduction to these two methods, see Gulik, *Chinese Pictorial Art*, pp. 94–95.

58. Ma, "Tan Xiyue Huashan miao bei de sanben Song ta," p. 32.

59. Ye, *Yu shi*, "Preface," p. 11.

60. Li, "*Jin shi lu* houxu"; trans. from Owen, *Remembrances*, p. 82.

61. Ma, "Tan Wu Liang Ci huaxiang di Song ta yu Huang Yi taben."

62. Ibid., p. 171.

63. The Wu Liang Shrine was rediscovered by Huang Yi in the late eighteenth century, but Huang never published images of the excavated stones. Instead he published, with great excitement, his tracing copy of the Song rubbing (which he willingly called a Tang version). This rubbing was prominently displayed in an exhibition in the Palace Museum in conjunction with the fiftieth anniversary of the People's Republic of China.

Works Cited

Bai, Qianshen. "The Artistic and Intellectual Dimensions of Chinese Calligraphy Rubbings: Some Examples from the Collection of Robert Hatfield Ellsworth." *Orientations* 30, no. 3 (Mar. 1999): 82–88.

Barthes, Roland. *Camera Lucida: Reflections on Photography.* Trans. R. Howard. New York: Hill and Wang, 1981.

———. *The Responsibility of Form.* Trans. Richard Howard. New York: Hill and Wang, 1986.

Chang, Kwang-chih. "Archaeology and Chinese Historiography." *World Archaeology* 13, no. 2 (1968): 156–69.

Ebrey, Patricia B. "Later Han Stone Inscriptions." *Harvard Journal of Asiatic Studies* 40, no. 2 (1980): 325–53.

Gulik, R. H. van. *Chinese Pictorial Art as Viewed by the Connoisseur.* Rome: Is. M.E.O., 1958.

Harrist, Robert E., Jr. "The Artist as Antiquarian: Li Gonglin and His Study of Early Chinese Art." *Artibus Asiae* 55, no. 3/4 (1995): 237–80.

Hong Kuo 洪适. *Li xu, Li shi* 隸續, 隸釋. Reprinted—Beijing: Zhonghua shuju, 1985.

Huang Yi 黃易. *Xiaopenglai ge jin shi wenzi* 小蓬萊閣金石文字 (Bronze and stone inscriptions from the Xiaopenglai Pavilion). Reprinted—Shimoxuan, 1834.

Lu Yuan 路远. *Xi'an Beilin shi* 西安碑林史 (A history of the Forest of Steles in Xi'an). Xi'an: Xi'an chubanshe, 1998.

Ma Ziyun 馬子雲. "Tan Wu Liang Ci huaxiang de Song ta yu Huang Yi taben" 談武梁祠畫像的宋拓 與黃易拓本 (On the Song rubbings and Huang Yi's rubbings of the pictorial carvings on the Wu Liang Shrine). *Gugong bowuyuan yuankan* 故宮博物院院刊, no. 2 (1960): 170–77.

———. "Tan Xiyue Huashan miao bei de sanben Song ta" 談西嶽華山廟碑的 三本宋拓 (On three Song rubbings of the stele at the Temple of the Western Marchmount Hua). *Wenwu* 1961, no. 8: 31–35.

———. *Xiyue Huashan miao bei* 西嶽華山廟碑 (The stele at the Temple of the Western Marchmount Hua). Beijing: Zhongguo shudian, 1992.

Ma Ziyun 馬子雲 and Shi Anchang 施安昌. *Beitie jianding* 碑帖鑒定 (Connoisseurship of rubbings). Guilin: Guangxi shifan daxue chubanshe, 1993.

MacNair, Amy. "Engraved Calligraphy in China: Recession and Reception." *Art Bulletin* 160, no. 1 (Mar. 1995): 106–14.

———. "The Engraved Model-Letters Compendia of the Song Dynasty." *Journal of the American Oriental Society* 114, no. 2 (Apr.–June 1994): 209–25.

Ouyang Xiu 歐陽修. *Jigu lu bawei* 集古錄跋尾 (Colophons from the *Records on Collecting Antiques*). In *Shike shiliao xinbian* 石刻史料新編 (A new compilation of historical materials on stone carvings). Taibei: Xinwenfeng chuban, 1957.

Owen, Stephen. *Remembrances: The Experience of the Past in Classical Chinese Literature.* Cambridge, Mass.: Harvard University Press, 1985.

Palace Museum. *Gugong bowuyuan 50 nian rucang wenwu jingpinji* 故宮博物院 50 年入藏文物精品集 (Selected gems of cultural relics—collected in the Palace Museum in the past 50 years). Beijing: Forbidden City Press, 1999.

Quan Hansheng 全漢升. "Bei Song Bianliang de shuchu maoyi" 北宋汴梁的輸出貿易 (Imports and exports in Bianliang during the Northern Song). *Bulletin of the Institute of History and Philology, Academia Sinica* 8, no. 2 (1939): 189–301.

Ricoeur, Paul. *Time and Narrative*, vol. 3. Trans. K. Blamey and D. Pellauer. Chicago: University of Chicago Press, 1985.

Ruan Yuan 阮元. "Han Yanxi Xiyu Huashan bei kao" 漢延熹西嶽華山廟碑考 (An examination of the Han dynasty stele of the Western Marchmount Hua established in the Yanxi reign). Reprinted in *Congshu jicheng xinbian* 叢書集成新編 (A new edition of collected collectanea). Taibei: Xinwenfeng chuban, 1985, vol. 52, 113–29.

Rudolph, R. C. "Preliminary Notes on Sung Archaeology." *Journal of Asian Studies* 22 (1963): 169–77.

Shi Anchang 施安昌. *Han Huashan bei tiba nianbiao* 漢華山碑題跋年表 (A chronicle of colophons on rubbings of the Mount Hua stele). Beijing: Wenwu chubanshe, 1997.

Wu Hung. *Double Screen: Medium and Representation in Chinese Painting.* London: Reaktion Books, 1996.

———. *Monumentality in Early Chinese Art and Architecture.* Stanford: Stanford University Press, 1995.

———. *The Wu Liang Shrine: The Ideology of Early Chinese Pictorial Art.* Stanford: Stanford University Press, 1989.

Xia Chaoxiong 夏超雄. "Song dai jin shi xue de zhuyao gongxian jiqi xingqi de yuanyin" 宋代金石學的主要貢獻及其興起的原因 (The rise of Song antiquarianism and its major contributions). *Beijing daxue xuebao* 北京大學學報 1982, no. 1: 66–76.

Ye Changchi 葉昌熾. *Yu shi* 語石 (Talking about the stone). Shenyang: Liaoning jiaoyu chubanshe, 1999.

Zhao Chao 趙超. *Zhongguo gudai shike gailun* 中國古代石刻概論 (A general discussion of stone carvings from ancient China). Beijing: Wenwu chubanshe, 1997.

Zhao Mingcheng 趙明誠. *Jin shi lu* 金石錄 (Records of bronze and stone inscriptions). In *Congshu jicheng* 叢書集成 (Collected collectanea), no. 212. Changsha: Shangwu yinshuguan, 1937.

Zhao Ruzhen 趙汝珍. *Gudong bianyi* 古董辯疑 (Clarifying doubts about antiques). Reprinted—Beijing: Zhongguo shudian, 1989.

———. *Guwan zhinan* 古玩指南 (A guide to antiques). Reprinted—Beijing: Zhongguo shudian, 1984.

Disappearing Verses
Writing on Walls and Anxieties of Loss

Judith T. Zeitlin

Ink traces beside the courier station dissolve in the mountain rain; tearstains on the wall are obscured by clouds over the pass. If we say, "This is none of your business," or "What has this got to do with me?" and make no effort to collect this verse, then we will have allowed it to perish forever.

—Wu Qi 吳琪 (1619–94)

What Are Tibishi?

This chapter is about a category of traditional Chinese poetry called *tibishi* 題壁詩—poems written on walls. Although it is tempting to translate *tibishi* as "graffiti poetry," in fact, the two are essentially different. Graffiti are generally understood to be a form of defacement, to compromise the integrity and value of the public surfaces on which they appear. For this reason, Susan Stewart has argued in an essay on graffiti as crime and art, "It is interesting to see how graffiti becomes dirt once we consider, in the mode of much recent cognitive anthropology, that dirt is something in the wrong place or the wrong time."[1] To use Mary Douglas's famous definition of dirt as "matter out of place,"[2] graffiti might then be defined as "writing out of place"—as inappropriate scrawls, trivial and destructive. There is some support for this view in Chinese sources as well. A Han dynasty inscription on the An Guo 安國 shrine (151 CE) appeals to passing herdboys not to scribble on the shrine, threatening them with curses if they do so, and almost a millennium later a Ming essay entitled "How to Kill Scenery" ("Sha feng-jing" 殺風景) lists "inscribing poems on walls at famous mountain sites" alongside other crimes such as "using a pine grove as a toilet."[3] Under the influence of such advocates of naturalness as Yuan Hongdao 袁宏道 (1568–1610), it became fashionable to bemoan "the scraping and gouging of ignorant monks and vulgar scholars inflicted on the landscape,"[4] but this concern with keeping natural surfaces intact did not necessarily extend to walls of manufactured structures. In the anecdotal literature, someone who complains about a poem spoiling his nice clean wall is almost sure to be ridiculed as a philistine.[5]

Instead, *tibishi* can best be defined as "writing *in* place"—a legitimate cultural practice in which individuals left inscriptions on the walls of public buildings (mainly temples, inns, taverns, courier stations, and government offices)—written mementos, which sometimes could not only enhance the cultural value of a spot but even put it on the map.[6] In his influential essay "What Is an Author?" Foucault singles out "an anonymous text posted on a wall" as an example of discourses that lack "an author function" in European culture.[7] But, as I will show, *tibishi* were emphatically sites for the attribution of authorship in traditional China, even if a given poem were unidentified and the actual author unknown.[8]

Like many artistic forms in Chinese culture, *tibishi* first emerged as a subgenre during the Six Dynasties but really only came into vogue during the Tang dynasty. Poems written on walls are well represented in the work of both major and minor Tang poets. "Inscriptions left behind" (*liuti* 留題, another term for writing on walls) are first classified as a separate category of verse, however, in the large thematic *shihua* 詩話 (anecdotal and critical discussions of poetry) compiled in the twelfth century.[9] Writing on walls remained a standard part of poetic practice during subsequent dynasties, and scattered examples of *tibishi* can be found in the literary works of most, if not all, late imperial figures. It is no accident, then, that the Han example I gave above, which predates the rise of *tibishi*, prohibited random scribbling (by herdboys), whereas the Ming example derided the ubiquity of poems inscribed in scenic spots (by tourists).

The writings on walls that attracted the most attention during the Ming and Qing are found mainly in anecdotal literature and anthologies, rather than in the individual literary collections of well-known writers. The authors

題壁圖

Fig. 2.1 Album leaf from
Sancai tuhui 三才圖會 (1610):
Inscription on a "rock wall."
Source: *Heaven and Earth:
120 Album Leaves from a Ming
Encyclopedia*, selected and
annotated by John A. Goodall
(London: Lund Humphries,
1979), p. 90.

of these *tibishi* tend to be obscure poets, an overwhelming proportion of them women. In the first half of this chapter, I provide a general overview of writing on walls as a social practice, literary genre, and mode of textual production. This survey establishes a base for the historical case study in the second half, in which I explore the seventeenth-century enthusiasm for *tibishi* written by women (or purportedly written by women). Although the fashion for collecting such verses arose during the late Ming, it took on a new urgency and significance after the fall of the dynasty in 1644. Throughout the chapter, I argue that a persistent undercurrent linking *tibishi* with death, ghosts, and the vanishing of the past is detectable in the literary responses these "inscriptions left behind" evoked.

    Tibishi were generally written with ink and brush on plaster walls or, sometimes, cliff faces, which were called "rock walls" (*shi bi* 石壁) (Fig 2.1). But they could also be given a less ephemeral existence by being copied onto wooden placards (or first written on specially prepared wooden placards at a famous spot); better yet, such poems might eventually be engraved directly on stone to give them a more permanent status at the site.[10] Walls and cliffs were not the only surfaces for inscriptions: other architectural components of buildings, such as pillars, windows, and screens, or natural objects, such as bamboo, trees, leaves, or rocks, could be used as well. But *tibishi* are defined less by their location than by their production and reception. As Luo Zong-tao and Wu Chengxue, two contemporary Chinese scholars who have studied *tibishi* during the Tang, have argued, what defines poetry written on walls as a poetic subgenre is not content or theme or location but the mode in which such verse was produced, read, and collected.

Both Luo and Wu emphasize the public nature of this poetry. They argue that the practice of *tibishi* was a kind of publishing since it was a way of displaying and disseminating one's work publicly, especially important during the Tang before publishing took off in China.[11] Once a poem had been transferred to stone, rubbings could even be taken from it, making it *de facto* a printing agent of sorts. Luo contends that Tang *tibishi* were generally written in plainer language and employed fewer allusions than other poems to make them intelligible at a glance to a wider public. And in keeping with this simplicity, I have found the dominant form of *tibishi* to be the quatrain, the *jueju* 絕句 (literally, "broken off lines"), the briefest form of Chinese verse. But unlike an ordinary published poem, whose point of spatial origin is largely irrelevant and blurred by the promiscuous circulation of print, a *tibishi* always remains at least theoretically defined by a specific location in space. Even when a later transcription of a *tibishi* is encountered in the printed pages of a book, the reader must imagine it located in a specific site; the experience is still one of stumbling across an inscription, of spying a private declaration in a public space. The presumed private and spontaneous nature of a *tibishi* is also an essential part of the subgenre. Poems written on walls were not the premodern equivalent of the big-character posters (*dazibao* 大字報) of the Cultural Revolution and should be distinguished from the many other kinds of exhortatory or commemorative placards that "textualized the social landscape" and served as public proclamations during the Ming and Qing.[12] The presumption was that *tibishi*, as a species of topographical verse, recorded someone's personal feelings and experience at (and toward) a place, which could then be witnessed by a later observer. The initial *tibishi* then itself became part of the place and thus part of the next visitor's experience there; it might even elicit a new poem written in the same spot in response to the old one, producing a potentially infinite chain of responses[13] (thus the phenomenon described in anecdotal literature and poetry of surfaces crammed to overflowing with inscriptions; see Fig. 2.2).[14] Accordingly, the real subject of this chapter is the literary response to *tibishi*.

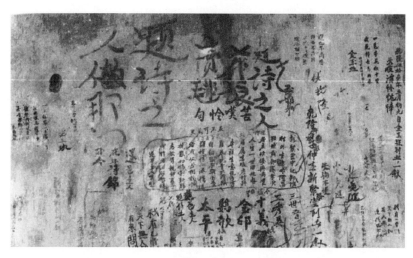

Fig. 2.2 Photograph of a rare instance of Qing dynasty *tibishi* written in ink preserved intact on a wall. The wall is part of a tunnel leading to a stage attached to the Xiang clan ancestral temple in Suichang 遂昌 county in Zhejiang province. The inscriptions, many of them dated, were left by the actors of itinerant troupes who performed on the stage here. Some of the inscriptions are simply scrawls such as "In Qianlong 54 [1790] the Celebrating Reunion Troupe was here" or lists of the titles of the plays the troupe performed. The longest inscription is a poem lamenting the sad lot of an actor's life. Source: *Zhongguo xiqu zhi* 中國戲曲志: *Zhejiang juan* 浙江卷 (Beijing: Zhongguo ISBN zhongxin chubanshe, 1997), p. 667.

What *tibishi* share with graffiti is the quality of being the opposite of a souvenir. If a souvenir is something one *takes away* to preserve one's personal memories of a place, graffiti and *tibishi* are things one *leaves behind* to mark one's presence at a place on a particular occasion (hence the locution *liuti*). What this means is that *tibishi* have not only a built-in spatial dimension but also a temporal dimension. As poems meant to be encountered by a later visitor, *tibishi* amount to visual displays of time. And as graphic testimony to the fact that someone else once stood in the exact spot the viewer stands now, *tibishi*, perhaps more forcefully than any other form of writing, point up the absence of the original writer(s). The man who discovers a poem he wrote on a wall many years earlier confronts the temporal disappearance of that younger self; the traveler who stumbles across a poem by an exiled friend experiences anew the physical separation caused by geographical distance. Of course, the most common reason for the absence of the original author of a *tibishi* is death.[15] As a couplet inscribed at a temple by the famous Tang poet Bai Juyi 白居易 (772–846) put it:

If you want to recognize an ancient pine tree,
  look at the dusty wall beside it—
How many of those who left poems there
  are dead now? [16]

Or this quatrain by the Tang poet Dou Gong 竇鞏 (772?–831?), written on seeing inscriptions by two officials from the previous dynasty in the guest hall of a government office:

Two hundred years between their time of Renshou [601–4] and
  mine of Yuanhe [806–20].
The ink is blurry, faint as mist or smoke.
That day they signed their names in distress,
The Tang founder was still a hidden dragon and had not yet
  ascended the throne. [17]

Visible traces of the past surviving in spatial form; the contrast between the longevity of nature and the brevity of human life; the concrete register of the passage of history—in the contemplation of writing on walls we arrive at something very close to "ruin-sentiment," to *huaigu* 懷古 or "lamenting the past," a poetic theme that has long roots in the Chinese literary tradition but that also solidified during the Tang. To differentiate *huaigu* from the many kinds of ruminations on history and the past in Chinese literature, let us reserve the term for poetic reflections "stimulated by visits to historic sites," to borrow Hans Frankel's formulation of this particular sort of "past-oriented poetry."[18] Such visits could be imaginary as well as real, but the premise of a visit somewhere is important: what most distinguishes the *huaigu* mode is the spatialization of time, the *mise-en-scène* of memory and history envisaged in a specific place.

In a poem written on the wall of the Donglin Monastery 東林精舍 by another famous Tang poet, Wei Yingwu 韋應物 (eighth c.), the confrontation with the past is more personal, folded into a chance encounter with a poem on a wall penned in a dead friend's calligraphy. Mourning a person one once knew shades imperceptibly into mourning the past in general here:

In mid-season the scenery is lovely,
  and so I make an excursion to Donglin.
There I find the poem of a dead friend,
  Sad and forlorn on a high wall.
He thought deeply, always cared about the age,
  But his voice and looks are stilled now.

Leftover splashes of his ink are here,
    But his handwritten traces are wearing away.
Life suddenly is like a dream,
    And everything in this world has become the past. . . .[19]

This, then, is one of the biggest differences between contemporary urban graffiti and *tibishi*: whereas graffiti tend to evoke a sense of immediacy, the present, forced confrontation, *tibishi* tend to elicit a melancholy response of pastness and loss. The quintessential graffiti (whether as dirt or art) are freshly painted and vivid; the quintessential *tibishi* are dust-covered and fading.

As ink traces exposed to the elements, *tibishi* are seen as particularly vulnerable to the ravages of time. Tang dynasty responses to writing on walls describe layers of dust obscuring the poem,[20] surfaces overgrown by moss,[21] mildew obliterating the poet's signature.[22] So vulnerable are inscriptions left behind, in fact, that they are in constant danger of disappearing, of vanishing without a trace, as expressed in this couplet written by the Tang poet Zhang Hu 張祜 (ninth c.) on a waterside pavilion:

    The water stains from the billowing waves still remain,
    But on the old placard, the words of the poem have dissolved.[23]

At stake in these examples is the ambiguity of writing's material status. Writing as literature is intended to survive independently of its original material form, by being memorized and passed down orally, or by being copied, circulated in manuscript, and, after the Tang dynasty, eventually published. This is how literature is supposed to grant immortality to a writer, to exist after a writer's physical death. But writing *in situ* possesses a uniqueness that other literary forms do not have because the emphasis is on the idea of the beholder confronting material traces occupying real space and time. The contemplation of ruined or faded *tibishi* thus registers anxiety over the failure of writing's ability (and with it the writer) to perdure after all—on the old placard, there's only a blank where words once were.

Tibishi *and Ghosts*

The materiality of writing consists not only of the graphic signs made by brush, chisel, or printing but also of the surface on which these marks are placed. Thus the material an inscription is written on may affect the identity and even the meaning of the inscription. Wu Chengxue has demonstrated that, in keeping with this logic, poems incised on bamboos acquire some of the cultural associations of this plant with the recluse; verses penned on leaves take on the fragile and romantic attributes of being blown by the wind; and poems written on rocks assume an air of wildness and naturalness.[24] As the normative place for "inscriptions left behind" (at least before inscribing paintings became popular), a wall may be the most neutral and hence most "unmarked" surface, but the meaning and reception of the inscriptions may be affected if the wall shows signs of neglect and ruin. What is interesting in these cases is how a poem becomes imbued with the symbolic properties of the medium on which it is written. A Tang anecdote about reading a mysterious verse written on a worn sheet of paper epitomizes this associative logic. As soon as the reader touches the paper, it crumbles to ashes, proof for him that the author of the poem must have been a ghost.[25]

It is not surprising that, as conventional signifiers for the vanishing of the past and the eerie absence of the writer, *tibishi* developed a close connection to ghost writing, that is, writing attributed to the spirits of the dead. As a major mode of lending form and image to phantoms, written communications from the spirit world, particularly poems, came to play an important role in Chinese ghost stories. In anecdotal literature, poems discovered on walls or received as spirit writing during planchette (*fuji* 扶乩) sessions are two common modes for otherworldly messages.[26] (For an anthology of stories and anecdotes up through the late Ming involving "ghost poetry," see Mei Dingzuo's 梅鼎祚 *Records of Talented Ghosts* [*Caigui ji* 才鬼記; author's preface dated 1605].) To be sure, not all such verse is portrayed as having been committed to writing by ghosts (ghost poems were also frequently chanted aloud and overheard); and of course content, mood, and imagery were also crucial for establishing the ghostly provenance of such poems. Still, it is striking that in any number of tales, it is the visual display of the writing rather than the information conveyed by the words that most clearly registers a ghostly effect. In these instances, the distance between signifier and signified collapses since the writing signifies not something else but itself. Writing has become both a thing and the message it imparts. In such ghost writing, we see the kind of "ontological border crossing" that Brigitte Peuker identifies in the European context as an "aim shared by trompe l'oeil in the visual arts" and those "moments in which writing aspires to invade, incorporate, or be a thing."[27]

Communications from the spirit world could be represented as foreign and illegible, as in two early Tang anecdotes in which occult messages are "written horizontally in the manner of barbarian script."[28] The more common attributes of ghost writing, however, are instability and evanescence, as in the example of crumbling paper noted above. In another Tang anecdote, a Buddhist mass is held for the soul of a female suicide who has not received a proper burial. During the ceremony, her ghost pens a poem on paper expressing her pent-up grievances. The man supervising the ritual takes the precaution of having the poem transcribed immediately, because, he cautions, "ghost writing doesn't last long and will gradually disappear."[29] Sure enough, the next day the original piece of paper has turned coal-black, blotting out the characters on it altogether.

Some of the examples of *tibishi* given above illustrate these points. It was conventional in mourning poems to index "leftover traces of brush and ink" as personal possessions of the deceased, things that remain when the person is gone and that painfully evoke his or her memory.[30] The poems by Wei Yingwu and Dou Gong are responses to discovering posthumous inscriptions on the wall. Particularly in Wei Yingwu's case, where the death was relatively recent and the poet was a personal friend, unexpectedly coming across his poem "sad and forlorn on a high wall" produces something of an uncanny shock. In both cases, the description of aging ink in the process of disappearing conveys the impression of ghostliness: "Leftover splashes of ink are here / but his handwritten traces are wearing away" (Wei); "The ink is blurry, faint as mist or smoke" (Du). Indeed a ghost is sometimes depicted in Chinese narrative as "vanishing like smoke or mist."[31]

In these two Tang examples, *tibishi* may be portrayed in ghost-like terms, but they are clearly not presented as ghost-written. By the time of Zhu Xi 朱熹, the great twelfth-century philosopher, however, the association of writing on walls with the returned spirits of the dead is firmly established. Indeed it is a piece of accepted lore in his discussion of ghosts and spirits. In *Conversations of Master Zhu, Topically Arranged* (*Zhuzi yulei* 朱子語類), Zhu Xi tells the story of a Daoist whose spirit used to leave his body whenever he burned cinnabar in the mountains. This Daoist once instructed someone to cremate his body if he had not come back in seven days, but the person disobeyed him and burned his corpse before the allotted time was up. "Afterwards, when the Daoist returned, he roundly cursed the wretch and took his body. This Daoist was also able to write characters on the wall, but the ink was rather faint, and before long it disappeared altogether."[32]

In Zhu Xi's discussion, this example of writing on the wall serves as an analogy for his overall theory of the phenomenology of revenants. For Zhu

Xi, death is ordinarily defined as the dispersion of *qi* 氣, the vital force within the body. But in certain extraordinary cases of violent, unjust death, such as murder, execution, or suicide, the *qi* may not have a chance to disperse fully; this enables the victim to return as a ghost. On his roster of those whose *qi* may not immediately disperse are certain monks who are able to nourish their "essence and spirit" (*jingshen* 精神) so that their *qi* continues to coalesce after death.[33] But even in such instances, Zhu Xi insists, the *qi* will *always eventually* disperse and the ghost cease to exist. The case of the cinnabar-burning Daoist is a perfect illustration. Because his *qi* had not dispersed, it could become visible in the form of writing on the wall, but eventually the ink (which is faded to register its ghostly, disembodied status) dissolved altogether, just as his *qi* was destined to do. Here the vanishing of written traces of the past is rationalized as part of the normal workings of the body and the cosmos.

The image of writing on a wall fading away became a conventional trope for signaling a ghostly presence in Chinese literature. In *Jiao Hong zhuan* 嬌紅傳, an important Yuan dynasty romance, the heroine of the tale starves herself to death after her parents oppose her marriage to a handsome scholar to whom she has pledged her love. The scholar, in his grief, soon follows her in death. Some time later, her maid glimpses the spectral apparitions of the pair strolling together in the garden. Upon the ghosts' disappearance, she discovers written on the wall a song-lyric commemorating their love. She notices that "the traces of the characters they had left behind were partly dark and partly faded, and before long they, too, vanished."[34]

In the 1630s, when Meng Chengshun 孟稱舜 adapted the tale into a long southern drama (*chuanqi* 傳奇), he kept the posthumous writing on the wall episode, including the tale's exact description of the ink traces and their disappearance.[35] Another southern drama from the same decade, Fan Wenruo's 范文若 *An Intoxicating Dream of Flowers* (*Menghua han* 夢花酣; preface dated 1632), also employs the trope of a mysteriously fading song-lyric to suggest the ghostly status of its writer, but in this case the inscription has been penned on paper rather than on the wall. Otherwise, the signifying techniques are the same.

OLDER WOMAN: (with an expression of surprise):

How is it that the marks of ink on the paper look as though they're not from a human hand?

SECOND FEMALE LEAD:
   At the end there are a couple of words that you can still faintly read.
MALE LEAD (with an expression of surprise):
   How could her song-lyric have been rubbed out like this?
   (sings, to the tune "Dahe fo") The characters are
   Thin like traces of a dragon in autumn;
   Leached of color, as though engraved by a ghost.[36]

In "Scholar Chu" ("Chu sheng" 褚生), a tale in Pu Songling's 蒲松齡 late seventeenth-century collection *Liaozhai's Records of the Strange* (*Liaozhai zhiyi* 聊齋誌異), this device crops up again. In this story, a man is taken for an excursion on a pleasure barge, ignorant of the fact that his soul has left his body and that his fellow revelers are all ghosts. After disembarking, he takes a moment on his way home to inscribe the lyrics sung by a courtesan at the party on a garden wall. Only afterward, when his soul has rejoined his body, does he learn the truth about his experience. Still skeptical, he returns the next morning to the garden wall for further corroboration. To his shock, he finds that "the lines he had inscribed were still there, but the ink was faint and almost illegible, as though the words were about to be rubbed out entirely. Only at that moment did he realize that the inscriber of the lines had actually been a disembodied soul and the composer of the lyrics a ghost."[37] The material marks of the ink on the wall have uncannily assumed the status of their writer—disembodied, elusive, in the process of dissolving entirely. What marks this most of all as phantom writing, however, is the miraculously accelerated speed of the aging process. Overnight, the freshly inscribed ink has faded to the point of near transparency, momentarily suspending the words between life and death, past and present, before passing into oblivion.

   As visual displays of time, *tibishi*, as I have shown, most frequently register pastness and vanishing. But occasionally in ghost stories, *tibishi* are deliberately used to do the opposite, to signal the manifestation of a recent presence rather than a distant past. In such instances, it is the contrast between a ruined setting and a fresh inscription that produces the shock of the ghostly. In one such Tang story, a man puts up for the night at an old inn, unaware that one wing of the inn is haunted and has been locked up for ten years. That night he hears snatches of conversation and the mournful sound of verse being chanted coming from that wing, but he cannot make out the exact words of the poem. The next morning he decides to investigate and makes the innkeeper open the courtyard of the deserted building. "The ground was overgrown with autumn grass and the steps were buried in green moss. . . . When the rooms were opened, he found that they were clean and completely bare except that in the front room on the pillar facing east was a poem, whose ink looked extremely fresh."[38] The text of the poem quickly confirms its ghostly provenance. In this case it is the newness of the ink registering "last night" against ten years of overgrowth and neglect at the site that provides evidence of a ghostly manifestation.

The most memorable instance of this device appears in "Yiniang of Taiyuan" (Taiyuan Yiniang 太原意娘), a famous ghost story about the fall of the Northern Song in Hong Mai's 洪邁 twelfth-century collection of tales, the *Yijian zhi* 夷堅志.[39] In this nostalgic story about refugees from the fallen capital, Kaifeng, meeting by chance in the new capital, Yanshan (Beijing), a man stumbles across a poem written on a wall that bears the signature of his cousin's wife. He has had no contact with either his cousin's wife or his cousin since the conquest. Because the ink of the inscription is not yet dry, he realizes his cousin's wife must still be in the vicinity; he succeeds in catching up with her and converses with her. He remains unaware that she had committed suicide and is actually a ghost until he later coincidentally runs into his cousin, who relates the tragic story of his wife's death. In the vernacular retelling of this tale included in Feng Menglong's 馮夢龍 early seventeenth-century anthology *Stories Old and New* (*Gujin xiaoshuo* 古今小說), discovering a poem inscribed on a wall is still the mechanism that leads the protagonist to a reunion with the ghost of his cousin's wife, but the motif of the still-wet ink on the wall is transferred to a supplementary *tibishi*, now written by his cousin, who is alive. When the two reunited kinsmen trace the ghost to a commemorative shrine in an abandoned mansion, they find another poem signed by the ghost dated that very day on the ruined wall of the neglected garden.[40] As in the Tang tale about the haunted inn, a freshly written poem is juxtaposed with a deserted, overgrown setting as evidence of a ghostly presence. But in the vernacular story, the number of *tibishi* has proliferated. The protagonist's repeated experience of unexpectedly coming across a poem written on a wall by a lost relative, uncertain whether the inscriber is dead or alive, contributes to the extreme uncanniness of this story. In each case, a *tibishi* works to destabilize the borders of life and death.

Collecting Female-Authored Tibishi *in the Seventeenth Century*

Tibishi in the late imperial period have not been well studied. Above I note that to judge from scattered examples in the published record, writing on walls remained a standard part of poetic social practice during Ming and Qing times. In the section on interior design in *Casual Expressions of Idle Feeling* (*Xianqing ouji* 閑情偶記), for instance, Li Yu 李漁 (1611–80) recommends using plain wallpaper in the study so that one section can be reserved for writing poems or painting pictures.[41] Quite a few stories and plays of the period feature poems written on walls as a pivotal plot device. The discovery of a *tibishi* may, for example, promote a match between lovers who have never met, reunite couples separated by war, present a prophecy, or solve a crime.[42] The most elaborate example is Wu Bing's 吳炳 romantic comedy of 1630, the aptly named *Love at a Courier Station* (*Qingyou ji* 情郵記). The plot revolves around three travelers (one man and two women) writing, reading, and matching one another's poems on the wall of a Shandong courier station as they travel to and from the capital. (There are no less than seven such scenes in this 43-act play). The initial *tibishi* is penned by the hero in loneliness and despair; it is partly matched by one talented woman and then completed by a second. In the end, it proves to be the felicitous medium through which he finds and marries both women (Figs. 2.3–6).

My general impression is that, particularly in comparison to the Tang and Song, the literary merit of *tibishi* as *poetry* is considered to have declined in later periods. As Kong Shangren 孔尚任 (1648–1718) quipped in a poem he wrote on the wall of a Yangzhou garden in 1686:

> How could lines of mine inscribed on a wall be any good?
> Their being passed on to posterity depends on the fame of this garden.[43]

Although Kong (whose poetic works include several *tibishi*) was undoubtedly being modest to flatter the garden's owner, his couplet frankly acknowledges that what matters most for a *tibishi* are the social circumstances of its production: place, occasion, and civility rather than literary quality are primary.

The impromptu and perishable nature of *tibishi* led some early Qing poets to regard the genre as a kind of throwaway verse form, tossed off for fun to

Fig. 2.3 Wu Bing, *Love at a Courier Station*: Scene 7: "Inscribing the Station" ("Tiyi" 題驛). Spending the night at the courier station en route to the capital to take the examinations, the male lead writes a quatrain expressing his loneliness on the wall of one of the pavilions.

while away the monotony of a journey, for instance, but not necessarily worth the trouble of preserving. Thus the famous poet and official Wang Shizhen 王士禎 (1634–1711) reminisces about traveling to the capital in his youth to take the examinations with his late elder brother Wang Shilu 王士祿 (1626–73): "Whenever the carriage stopped en route, we would always compose matching poems and write them on the walls of taverns and courier stations, but generally speaking, we never bothered to keep a draft ourselves. Our associates would see them; then later when we were in the capital, they would recite them for me; my memory of these lines was as hazy as yesterday's dreams." Wang Shizhen clearly regarded his youthful production of *tibishi* as ephemera, but he was pleased to discover "remnants" (*yiju* 遺句) from these forgotten poems in other people's anecdotes and copied some of the better ones into his own notation books (*biji* 筆記) as curiosities.[44] Even Zha Shenxing 查慎行 (1650–1728), a well-traveled early Qing poet whose poetic oeuvre stands out *because* of its abundance of *tibishi*, adopts a similar stance. Zha entitled one cluster of poems he composed over four months in 1690 "The Written on Walls Collection" (*Tibi ji* 題壁集)

Fig. 2.4 Wu Bing, *Love at a Courier Station*: Scene 13: "Completing the Matching Poem" ("Bu he" 補和). The second female lead arrives at the courier station and completes the half-written matching poem she finds on the wall alongside the male lead's original quatrain. In the previous scene, "The Half-Matched Poem" ("Banhe" 半和), the play's other female lead had stopped at the courier station, found the quatrain on the wall, and begun a poem in response but was called away before she could finish it.

because, he explains in a deprecatory preface,[45] he had spent two days during this period seeing off a friend and matching poems with him and other companions on the way. "We scribbled these verses on walls at taverns and courier station inns. They were mainly composed extemporaneously and were not really worth keeping, but I decided to keep them as a record of the events on our trip."[46]

The diffidence these prolific authors profess toward their own *tibishi* must have been something of a pose, since they nonetheless included examples of this form in their own work, and specimens by the celebrated Wang brothers, in particular, were avidly sought by their contemporaries.[47] But in the case of writing genuinely perceived as imperiled in the late Ming and early Qing, *tibishi* remained a focus for intense concern about the disappearance of the past. Nowhere does this phenomenon emerge more clearly than in the seventeenth-century vogue for collecting and matching female-authored *tibishi*.

The volume of such poems in early Qing anthologies and anecdotal collections is remarkably large; in the course of an unsystematic survey of likely

Fig. 2.5 Wu Bing, *Love at a Courier Station*: Scene 14: "Seeing the Poem" ("Jian he" 見和). En route home, the male lead passes through the courier station again and, to his delight, sees the now complete matching poem on the wall next to his quatrain.

sources, I turned up some forty different examples attributed to individual women.[48] When poems written matching these *tibishi* (by both sexes) are included, the figures are considerably higher. In addition, the same *tibishi* are frequently found in more than one source. In some cases, there is considerable textual variation in the poems, suggesting oral transmission, transcription from memory, and embellishment; in others, the text is essentially stable, a sign that a dominant published (or possibly a manuscript) version was circulating at the time.

Dorothy Ko has linked the kind of attention paid to accounts of female-authored *tibishi* "to the rise of a 'connoisseurship of women'" in seventeenth-century publishing.[49] One hallmark of *tibishi* attributed to women is the incorporation of self-conscious allusions to the contemporary practice of collecting writing of this sort. Most such *tibishi* are accompanied by author's prefaces said to have been discovered on the wall alongside the poems. These prefaces often incorporate a direct appeal to an idealized reader expressing the author's hope that after her death her poems may be found and appreciated. In the case of someone who signed herself simply "A Girl from Xiang-

Fig. 2.6 Wu Bing, *Love at a Courier Station*: Scene 35: "Matching the Poem Again" ("San he" 三和). The following year, the male lead, who has just passed the examinations in first place, and the second female lead, who is now his wife, spend the night at the courier station on their way home from the capital. They re-read their poems on the wall together, and she is inspired to pen another matching poem, reflecting the happiness of their present circumstances, beside it.

yang" (Xiangyang nüzi 湘揚女子), for example, whose poems and preface were reportedly seen by Deng Hanyi 鄧漢儀 (1617–89) on the wall of a Shandong inn in 1654 and published in his anthology of early Qing poetry in the 1670s, the preface expresses the girl's wish that her work will be anthologized: "I hope that some gentleman will take pity on me, but I also wonder whether some poet will have the heart to collect these inferior verses of mine to include in an anthology of women's poetry."[50]

Anthologists in turn were conscious of the need to document where, when, how, and by whom a given *tibishi* had been collected. Take Wang Duanshu 王端淑 (1621–ca. 1706), the pre-eminent female anthologist of women's poetry in the period of dynastic transition. Her enormous collection of Ming and Qing poets, *Classic Poetry by Renowned Women* (*Mingyuan shiwei* 名媛詩緯; begun in 1639, but not completed until 1664 and published in 1667), includes many examples of women's poems recovered from walls as part of her mission to rescue women writers from oblivion.[51] As a gentry woman, her own mobility was limited, and she reported no personal discoveries of *tibishi*, but she was meticulous in recording who had written down or sent her the poem. Only once or twice does she name a female traveler as the eyewitness who discovered and matched a poem *in situ*. Zhu Zhongmei's 朱中湄 preface to her "Matching a Poem by A Girl from Xiangjiang" is one of these rare examples. As Zhu describes her discovery:

In the summer of 1641, I was accompanying my husband to take up a post in the north. Our road passed through Xincheng [in Shandong], where we stopped for the night at an inn. I noticed that on a patch of wall, where some dust had been rubbed away, were several lines of writing in small *kai*-style calligraphy. I brushed off the inscription and read it, and it turned out to be a poem written in distress and resentment by A Girl from Xiangjiang.[52]

In early Qing literature, *tibishi* attributed to women in distress are occasionally discovered on the walls of abandoned palaces, but by far the most common location for such poems is on the buildings that serviced travelers: courier stations, inns, and temples (which doubled as hostels on the road). These itinerant sites had always been prime targets for "inscriptions left behind," of course, and are partly why we can consider *tibishi* essentially a subspecies of travel literature. As temporary way stations along a journey, however, travel buildings also had an inherent metaphorical as well as practical significance. In the opening lines of *Love at a Courier Station*, the playwright draws an analogy between the brevity of human life and the time spent at a courier station: "In the passage from life to death, human existence is like a courier station. How little time we get for the stopover!"[53] As early as the fourth century CE, the poet Tao Yuanming 陶淵明 had employed this metaphor in a funerary elegy he wrote for himself: "Master T'ao is about to take leave of 'the traveler's inn' [life] and return to 'his eternal home' [death]."[54] Life is like a traveler's inn because it is transient, a temporary stopping point on a longer itinerary; dying is like departing from an inn because it means that the journey is ending and one is on the way home, to one's place of origin.[55]

Most later writers failed to reach such a lofty level of resignation in the face of death. Dying on the road and being buried away from home were universally considered horrible, a fate destined to turn the deceased into a resentful ghost. Nonetheless, the association of the traveler's inn as a liminal way station between life and death might particularly come into play when *tibishi*, as the material traces of someone's passage, were discovered posthumously on the walls of hostels or courier stations.[56] In the seventeenth-century political context, the topos of passing by a ruined courier station also recurs in early Qing poems to describe the devastation wrought by the recent violence of dynastic fall and conquest.[57]

Dorothy Ko has argued that even though men were forced from home and subjected to travails during the Ming-Qing transition, the subgenre of *tibishi* left in inns or courier stations "seems to have been reserved for women in captivity, perhaps a testimony to the fact that their exile was longer and involuntary, and that they had few other options."[58] Ko maintains that although a few of these *tibishi* were proved to be forgeries, "the contextual information . . . contained in some of these works . . . was so specific and the existence of the poems so readily verifiable to anyone who traveled to the inn or temple in question, that their authenticity cannot be questioned."[59] Ko is right that very few *tibishi* are reportedly written by male loyalists or captives, but her confidence in the reliability of these poems as women's testimony may be misplaced. Wai-yee Li has noted how readily this image of the displaced woman, "authenticated by victimhood," was "a fictive or allegorical mask" for male poets in this period.[60] And the opinion of Jiang Yin, a specialist on Qing poetry, is clear from a notice entitled simply "Most Poems on Walls by Women Are Not Credible."[61] The question I pursue here, however, is not whether real women left these inscriptions (I lean toward skepticism on this question), but why their testimony was so often represented in the form of *tibishi*, how news of these poems circulated, and why their discovery evoked such a powerful contemporary response.

Case 1: The Girl from Kuaiji

Although it is possible to find *tibishi* attributed to women in distress from the Song, Yuan, and early Ming dynasties[62] (Fig. 2.7), especially in hagiographies of virtuous women, the early Qing vogue for collecting examples of this genre can quite securely be pegged to a celebrated case from the late Ming. Three quatrains by "A Girl from Kuaiji" (Kuaiji nüzi 會稽女子) were first discovered on the wall of the Xinjia 新嘉 courier station in southern Shandong around 1618.[63] (The prominence of courier stations in Shandong as a location for *tibishi* in Ming and Qing literature is due in part to the province's pivotal position on the route between north and south. In the seventeenth century at least, Shandong also seemed to be the point at which travelers from the south to the capital would shift from water to land

Fig. 2.7 The virtuous wife of
Xu Junbao (Xu Junbao qi 徐
君寶妻), who has been cap-
tured by soldiers after the fall
of Yuezhou 岳州, inscribes a
song-lyric on the wall of the
city's most famous building,
prior to drowning herself. The
side cartouche reads: "Looking
up at the wall to inscribe a
song-lyric, with tears in her
eyes, she stoically holds her
brush and writes." Source: *Gujin lienü zhuan pinglin*, p. 393.

transport and hence begin staying overnight in inns and courier stations instead of on boats.)[64] To judge from the outpouring of matching poems, news
of the inscription's discovery spread quickly through elite circles. A crucial
feature of these *tibishi*, which set the standard for future stories in this vein,
was that the quatrains were framed by a highly dramatic, confessional preface, in which the writer related her tragic life history and declared her intent
to commit suicide. The preface revealed that she had been born south of the
Yangtze and educated in her youth. When she came of age, she was married
off as a concubine to an unfeeling merchant from the north, whose principal
wife was a vicious shrew who beat and humiliated her. The preface concluded on this passionate note:

Alas! I'm just someone in a cage—what is worth regretting about my death? It's just
that I'm afraid to abandon my body to wasteland and vanish without being heard of.
And so I have postponed my death a little while. I waited till all my companions
were sound asleep and then stole out behind this pavilion, where, my tears mixing
with ink, I have written three quatrains upon the wall and this preface explaining
their provenance. I hope a sympathetic reader will read them and grieve for my unfortunate life; then though I die, I will not have perished!

The last couplet conveys the gist of the quatrains:

> You mustn't read my poems as ordinary verse:
> Each line is composed of the thousand tears I've shed.[65]

In this powerful notion of a *tibishi* composed of ink and tears, writing is once again portrayed not just as the *means* of representation but as the *content* of representation. This is no ordinary writing precisely because it is self-signifying: the writer's distress is materially present in the bodily fluids that spell out its message.

Readers, both men and women, leaped at the chance to answer this girl's appeal and declare their sympathy by penning matching quatrains. As a line from one such verse by Zhou Zhibiao 周之標 (fl. 1616–47) put it:

> For a time, a craze for matching these poems swept the land.
> Brilliance flowered from brushes and drops of ink rained down.[66]

The evidence in the published record emphatically confirms this assessment: the number of matching poems for these verses far exceeds those responding to any other *tibishi*.

The basic outlines of the Girl from Kuaiji's story bear a close resemblance to the more famous and detailed story of Xiaoqing 小青. Both stories involve a talented girl taken as a concubine by a man who neglected her and let her be tormented by his shrewish principal wife. In both cases, the girl's plight is discovered by the world only after her tragic death through the fortuitous discovery of a few of her poems. Both stories stimulated a torrent of writing from men and women who identified with the heroine and read their own fates allegorically into her history.[67] These two stories emerged at exactly the same time and from the same milieu. Both aroused suspicions that they were fabrications, and both served as literary prototypes for later imitations. The two figures are even yoked together in the preface to the early Qing *tibishi* attributed to the "Girl from Xiangyang" as precursors from which the writer is disingenuously trying to distance herself. As the Girl from Xiangyang's preface put it: "I am far from being a preposterous invention like Xiaoqing, but closer to home, I am still put to shame by the grievances expressed by the Girl from Kuaiji."[68] Or as the female traveler Zhu Zhongmei wrote after her discovery of the *tibishi* signed by "A Girl from Xiangjiang" on the wall of an inn: "Alas! The world competed to match the poems of Xiaoqing and A Girl from Kuaiji but because *this* girl and *these* poems were at a hostel in a desolate and uninhabited region, no one came to find them. This is especially sad."[69]

Xiaoqing and the Girl from Kuaiji also appear together in Zhou Zhibiao's anthology of women poets, *The Seven Talented Women's Orchid Verse Collection* (*Nüzhong qi caizi Lanke ji* 女中七才子蘭咳集; henceforth *Lanke ji*), published in the very late Ming or very early Qing.[70] Zhou Zhibiao, a self-avowed "slave to sentiment" (*qing zhi nu* 情之奴), whose couplet on the Girl from Kuaiji craze is cited above, contributed to this trend by including her *tibishi*, along with a series of matching poems by himself and six other writers (five men, one woman), in his *Lanke ji* anthology. One of these men, Wang Danian 汪大年 (字: 未央), was so carried away that he composed ten sets of matching poems, 30 quatrains in all, and appended a lengthy preface explaining how he came to write them.[71] This preface is a remarkable document in the history of the informal, casual storytelling that formed an important part of elite social conversation from at least the Tang dynasty on.[72] Dated 1619, this preface offers the most detailed account we possess of any individual's response to *tibishi*; the opening sections not only chart Wang Danian's changing reaction to the girl's story and her poems but provide a precise chronology of how and where he became acquainted with them.

How did I come to match the Girl from Kuaiji's poems? I first heard a guest relate a general outline of the story in the summer of 1618. I said, "This sounds like a quasi-real, quasi-fictional tale that some busybody made up to have something to talk about. Someone must have just forged this inscription on the wall of the courier station to amuse travelers stopping their horses there. Once it can be lumped with made-up cases of the 'No-Such Person' variety, there's no need to bother any further about it."[73]

On the thirteenth day of the twelfth month, I heard the poems and preface recited for the first time at my friend Bo Ping's 博平 place, but I still held fast to my original opinion about them. Two days later, on the fifteenth, I was having a drink at Mr. Zhongzhao's (Zhongzhao xiansheng 仲詔先生) Weishe Studio (Weishezhai 委蛇齋) when Song Xianru 宋獻孺 from Liyang 溧陽 asked for paper to make a copy of the verses, but I didn't have time to read them on that occasion. Then, on the nineteenth, I was perusing Yuan Zhongdao's 袁中道 literary collection from Xin'an (*Xin'an ji* 新安集), and I found the three poems right there in the book! Only then did I have the opportunity to trim a piece of paper to size and copy them down.

On the twenty-eighth day, I attended another gathering at the Weishe Studio, this time for peony viewing. I borrowed the previous manuscript and corrected two of the characters in the first quatrain, changing "don't turn to spring" (*bucheng chun* 不成春) to "the spring of former times" (*jiushi chun* 舊時春) to conform to Yuan Zhongdao's wording.

I then reflected that this fated chain of coincidences (*jiyuan* 機緣) had been going on for more than half a year now, yet I had still never taken the thing to heart. For a time, the experiences of encountering this girl's poems—hearing them with my ears, and seeing them with my eyes, recording them manually, and discussing them orally—have kept coming in succession. Could it be that some previous literary debt of sorrow I owe has been vaguely stirring the whole business up? In which case, I have no choice but to take it to heart in the end. And so I drafted ten sets of matching poems to atone for the error of my previous opinion.[74]

Wang Danian's account allows us to reconstruct the complex and prolonged process through which his initial skepticism and scorn toward the story became passionate support of its veracity and power. He first hears about the incident from an unnamed visitor in the course of conversation; four or five months later he hears the actual text of the poems and preface recited at a social gathering; two days later he witnesses someone else copying them down at another friend's studio; a week later he comes across the text of the poems and preface in the published collection of the famous writer Yuan Zhongdao (1570–1624); finally he copies them out for himself. A few months later, he gets hold of the "previous manuscript" version of the poems at his friend's studio (presumably a transcription of the poems from some oral recitation). He makes a few corrections to it so that it conforms to the wording in Yuan Zhongdao's published account. Only at that point does he finally succumb to "this fated chain of coincidences" and match the poems. Indeed, he goes to the other extreme to become one of the Girl's most fervent (and maudlin) supporters, composing not just one set of matching quatrains but ten of them. Upon completing this opus, he is stricken with a debilitating cough, which he suspects may indicate that he is being haunted by the dead girl's spirit. If my reconstruction is correct, then Wang Danian's saga of the story's circulation charts a progression from less acceptable to more acceptable forms of evidence, that is, from oral accounts to manuscript and finally to print. Wang's real moment of conversion comes when he beholds the poems in a published book by a famous author.

Yuan Zhongdao was indeed the first person to publish the Girl from Kuaiji's poems and preface. They appear in his *Kexuezhai qianji* 珂雪齋前集 along with a brief account of how he came across these inscriptions on the wall of the Xinjia courier station, accompanied by the text of the matching quatrains he inscribed in response at the spot. Yuan's account strikes a rare note of compassion in the general glorification of female suicide in this period by expressing the hope that the Girl might not have died, but the verdict in his final quatrain is pessimistic: "Who can avenge the wrongs suffered by this female ghost?"[75]

Yuan Zhongdao's *qianji* was published in Xin'an with the author's preface dated 1618, and we may assume "the collection from Xin'an" that Wang Danian read in 1619 refers to this publication.[76] Yuan's younger friend Qian Qianyi 錢謙益 (1582–1664) corroborated Yuan's account of seeing the poems *in situ*. Qian's own quatrains, entitled "Matching the Girl from Kuaiji's poems with Yuan Zhongdao at Xinjia," were published much later, in 1643, without any anecdotal preface.[77] More informative is Qian's note on the Girl's poems in the women's section of his *Anthology of Ming Poetry* (*Liechao shiji* 列朝詩集; 1652). He mentions that on a trip to the north around 1620, Yuan Zhongdao and he saw her inscription at the Xinjia courier station, and each left matching quatrains. Confirming for us once again the material ephemerality of *tibishi*, Qian adds: "But when I passed by there again, the wall had already been whitewashed, and it was impossible to find any further traces."[78]

To return to Wang Danian, in an addendum Wang mentions that the Girl from Kuaiji's handwritten characters were said to be "graceful and charming."[79] He had planned to make the three-day journey to the Xinjia courier station to trace the inscription on thin paper and have it carved in stone at the spot, with a gauze net placed over it for protection. But before his plans could be realized, he heard, to his shock, that some mischief-maker had scratched out most of the inscription, and consequently he never went. This deliberate defacement shook him to the core, prompting reflections on the malice the world directs against talented men and women, and it took him many days to recover. His preface concludes with the news that an unfinished poem signed by another woman calling herself A Girl from Kuaiji had been recently found at another courier station; Wang expresses reservations about the veracity of the claim.

In the intensity of its response to the Girl from Kuaiji, Wang Danian's preface provides a perfect example of the now all-too-familiar phenomenon of the seventeenth-century literatus frustrated in his ambitions pairing himself with the talented woman who dies young and unrecognized.[80] What is reassuring to men like Wang Danian about the Girl from Kuaiji (and subsequent *tibishi* writers of her type) is that ultimately she does succeed against all odds in leaving a trace of herself and in having that trace found and perpetuated in collective memory, so that, in the clichéd words of her preface, "Though I die, I will not have perished." She is in effect writing her own epitaph, and her death is both the prerequisite and the guarantor of her poetry's value. But even after the verses have been reproduced and published, the original inscription, as a substitute for her physical remains and their final resting place, continues to matter. If the posthumous discovery of her inscription amounts to a resurrection of sorts, the malicious obliteration of her handwritten traces amounts to a double blow, a second death, which is partly why it affects Wang Danian so deeply.

Some forty years later, in 1660, Shi Runzhang 施閏章 (1619–83), another important early Qing writer, made a pilgrimage to the Xinjia courier station to seek the original location of the Girl from Kuaiji's famous poems. Naturally, he found that not a single character of the inscription remained. He was, however, able to verify the spot precisely and add further details to the story by recording the testimony of an elderly guard at the courier station, who could recite the Girl's poems and preface by heart and claimed to have been the first to discover them.[81] In the manner of someone restoring the tomb of a famous person that has fallen into disrepair, Shi Runzhang proudly has the Girl from Kuaiji's words carved on a stone placard and affixed to the very spot said to be the site of the original inscription.[82]

The Shi Runzhang anecdote suggests the extent to which the Girl from Kuaiji was part of early Qing literati culture; so do the three quatrains Wang Shizhen and a friend found inscribed on the wall of an inn in Ande, Shandong, circa 1655, that bore the signature "Another Girl from Kuaiji" and the title "Matching the Girl from Kuaiji's Quatrains on the Xinjia Courier station." Both men were sufficiently moved that they left matching poems on the wall beside this inscription.[83] But the strongest evidence of the Girl's legacy in the early Qing are the quantities of *tibishi* reportedly left by the literate women killed or taken captive during the conquest, which were avidly collected in anthologies of this period. These poems in turn testified to the widely held sentiment, as Deng Hanyi put it, that "although countless beauties perished in the recent violence of the fall, the cases of talented women are the most pitiful."[84]

The discovery of a *tibishi* left by one of these women aroused such pathos in part because this meager inscription was deemed not only the sole scrap of her written output to survive but also the sole trace of her passage in the world. As Wang Duanshu explained, commenting on a *tibishi* of this sort in her *Classic Poetry by Renowned Women*:

After the havoc and turmoil of the war was over, how many girls of the scholar class had disappeared into wasteland mist and withered grass! Without such a poem, how could her person be passed on to posterity? There's a saying, "A person may be transmitted to posterity through a place," but from a case like this, we can understand how a person will be transmitted to posterity through a poem.[85]

Case 2: Furenji—A Collection of Fragments

There is always the possibility that the narrative of discovery that frames a *tibishi* will overshadow the content of the inscription unearthed. To rephrase this idea, sometimes what matters is not the thing found but the process (or multiple processes) of loss and recovery. Often the sense of process is accentuated by showing how what was found with such difficulty is shortly thereafter lost once more. A case in point is the following account by Wang Shilu of an incident involving his brother Wang Shizhen some ten years after the Qing conquest:

A girl from Changsha named Wang Suyin 王素音 was abducted by marauding soldiers. She wrote a poem on the wall of an old courier station, which included the lines "How pitiful my soul with no home to return to / I should alight on a branch and turn into a nightjar."[86] All who saw it pitied her.

In 1655, my little brother A-yi [an intimate appellation for Wang Shizhen] and Censor Fu from our hometown were on a journey north when they stopped at Baigouhe.[87] They saw that written on the wall of the inn were verses matching Suyin's poem. They looked for Suyin's original poem, but when they could not find it, they asked the innkeeper for help. He pointed to a woodpile five or six feet high heaped beside the wall, saying "It's on the wall under there." It happened to be the middle of winter, but A-yi and the Censor really wanted to read her poem. So with help from the servants they started moving the wood. They had to move half the pile before the poem was completely visible. The Censor held the candle, with A-yi blowing on his frozen brush to record the poem. When they were done, they chanted it aloud together, and then each composed a matching poem and inscribed it on the wall. When they had finished writing, they called for some liquor and drank their fill. Only then did they realize that their hands and wrists were almost frozen stiff. Each of them burst out laughing and, looking at the other, called himself a "perfect fool." This anecdote is really worth passing on.

Afterwards I went to the same inn and also matched the poems. My final line was "I, too, should learn to lower my head and bow to the nightjar."[88] Suyin's original poem consisted of three quatrains with a short preface in parallel couplets running to some 200 characters. Its exquisiteness was on par with the Girl from Langgan's *tibishi*. I have recorded Suyin's verses and preface in their entirety in my *Lamp Oil Collection*.[89]

Is the fear here not only that this particular poem but with it cultural memory will vanish, a concern particularly acute in the decades immediately following the Manchu conquest? This would explain the need to commemorate Suyin's poem on the spot by writing new poems on the wall alongside it. But even these are no bulwarks against loss since they, too, quickly disappear. Only transcription and publication can truly extend the life of a *tibishi*, but they come at a price: this transplantation stripped the poem of its original meaning *in situ*. Hence the emphasis here on the physical work and hardship of discovery. This framing is necessary not simply to authenticate the inscription but to allow the reader to experience vicariously the crucial process of loss and recovery that makes the verses precious. Even so, the unusual length of the frame here, coupled with the radical abridgement of Suyin's "exquisite" quatrains and preface to a single couplet, should give us pause. One effect is certainly to exalt the naive idealism and passion of the men involved in the quixotic attempt to save such writings.[90] But an equally important effect is to highlight the inherently fragmentary nature of any *tibishi* when it becomes in effect the writer's (only) remains. Even when the full text is in fact recovered, as in this case, the inscription signifies the incompleteness of the writer's life and output, cut short so unfairly.

Wang Shilu tells us that he recorded the full text of Suyin's poems and preface in his *Lamp Oil Collection (Ranzhi ji* 燃脂集). This massive, scholarly anthology of women's writings, which eventually totaled some 235 chapters on its completion in 1665, established him as the leading historian of the subject in this period.[91] Wang had begun compiling materials for the project as early as 1641, but most of what he had was lost during the collapse of the Ming. Thereafter he redoubled his efforts, enlisting his younger brothers' assistance, and by 1649 he had a sizable manuscript amounting to twenty large folders, which acquired its final organization in 1655. He continued to add to it until his death in 1673.[92] Still plagued by the fear that his anthology might have omissions, some time around 1655 he drafted "A Call for Contributions of Women's Poetry" ("Zheng guixiu shiwen shu" 徵閨秀詩文書), soliciting his fellow literati's help in gathering materials, exhorting them to scour old books and family manuscripts, broken steles, and courier station walls and to send him whatever they could find, complete works and fragments alike. (He specifically mentions Suyin's *tibishi* as an example of the treasures recoverable in this fashion.)[93] He elevated the enterprise of rescuing women's poetry from disappearance by drawing a parallel to the great discoveries of lost ancient writings in earlier times and implores: "Take all your materials . . . whether they're like the broken bamboo slips excavated from the tomb in Ji or like the old texts recovered from the walls of Confucius' house,[94] and put them in the mail to me."[95]

Wang Shilu contributed the story about the discovery of Suyin's inscription to a Ming loyalist work called *A Collection of Writings by and About Women* (*Furenji* 婦人集), a miscellany in the spirit of a *shihua*, rather than a full-fledged anthology. Suyin is one of thirteen women whose *tibishi* are the subjects of entries in *Furenji*. This understudied collection is particularly helpful for understanding the cultural meanings attributed to women's writings on walls in the early Qing because of the specific thematic and aesthetic contexts in which it embeds them.

The authorship of the collection is credited to the brilliant lyricist Chen Weisong 陳維崧 (1628–82), who came from Jiangsu and compiled *Furenji* in the vicinity of this southern province's cities of Nanjing and Yangzhou, the two centers of nostalgic *yimin* 遺民 (Ming loyalist) culture in the early Qing.[96] His good friend Wang Shilu is billed simply as the commentator on the title page, but swatches are internally acknowledged to have come from his pen (including about half the *tibishi* in the collection), and Wang is also named as the informant for additional entries, such as the note on his poetic exchanges with his own talented wife. Wang Shilu's brother, Shizhen, who was also close to Chen Weisong, is featured as a source for several items, including the ghost story "Lin Siniang" 林四娘, the best-known entry in the collection today; his verse is also lavishly quoted throughout.[97] Taken together, the Wang brothers are a dominant voice in the collection and, as natives of Shandong, lend a strong northern presence to what is otherwise primarily a southern endeavor. Finally, Mao Xiang 冒襄 (1611–93), Chen Weisong's patron and, like Chen's father, a former member of the late Ming Revivalist Society (Fushe 復社), is given the courtesy of being listed as the annotator.[98] Mao is mentioned in several entries, including one involving Dong Xiaowan 董小宛, the talented courtesan who became his concubine and compiled her own anthology of women's verse. His main literary contribution to *Furenji*, however, was to author a supplement, *Furenji bu* 婦人集補, which contains ten entries attached as an appendix, none of which involves *tibishi*.

The earliest extant edition of *Furenji* appears in a manuscript of the third supplement to *A Collectanea of Contemporary Writings* (*Zhaodai congshu guangbian* 昭代叢書廣編), which was assembled in the 1790s by the noted bibliographer Yang Fuji 楊復吉 (1747–1820) but not published until the 1830s.[99] Yang's colophon to *Furenji* describes his delight at finally obtaining a copy of this work after a twenty-year search, but there is evidence that manuscripts of *Furenji* were in circulation by 1673, and the work was certainly available during the earlier part of the eighteenth century.[100] There is unfortunately no preface, colophon, or list of editorial principles by Chen Weisong or any of his collaborators or contemporaries to shed explicit light on the dating, motivations, methods, or significance of the compilation.[101] But by and large these can be deduced from internal evidence in the collection itself. This kind of composite, disjointed, anecdotal collection is exactly the sort that would lend itself to cumulative composition over a period of fifteen to twenty years. My best guess is that it was compiled primarily from the very late 1640s to the mid-1660s, a time frame that also coincides well with the nostalgic mood of literati anthologies generally in this period.[102]

The *tibishi* included in *Furenji* epitomize this collection's desire to gather things surviving from the Ming related to women that are in danger of being overlooked and lost. The largest category of such relics are poems, but also included are gossip, tidbits about customs and dress in the palace, accounts of famous courtesans and talented gentry women, and the travails of women taken captive during the conquest. Any of these topics can also serve as the subject for a commemorative poem by a male poet, and *Furenji* is copiously supplied with these. The emphasis is certainly on assembling testimony on the fall of the Ming, but this is by no means the only concern of the collection. The operant logic fueling the work seems to have been a version of a statement made by the prominent Ming loyalist Huang Zongxi 黃宗羲 (1610–95): "Our dynasty may have passed, but its history should not disappear."[103]

And yet, in my opinion, *Furenji* is not the sort of history a conservative thinker like Huang Zongxi would have had in mind. Its seemingly frivolous focus on women and trivia to represent what was lost when the dynasty perished is close in spirit to a better-known work from the same period and milieu, *Banqiao zaji* 板橋雜記, Yu Huai's 余懷 (1616–96) nostalgic memoir of the former pleasure quarters in Nanjing. Although *Furenji* encompasses women of virtually every status, whereas *Banqiao zaji* showcases courtesans and entertainers, a number of figures appear in both works.[104] As private attempts to conserve elite memories of life under the previous dynasty, both works can be considered as occupying the fringes of unofficial historiography. But the methods of the two works differ considerably. In an effort to reconstruct the vanished world of the pleasure quarters in words, *Banqiao zaji* mainly takes a *descriptive* approach to its subject. By contrast, *Furenji*'s approach is primarily *documentary*, in that it attempts to collect textual "traces left by the past" as material evidence for history.[105] The remnants of poems collected from walls provide the clearest illustration of this documentary impulse in *Furenji*, of the work's unstated ambition to compile an archive of fragments and relics.[106]

The aesthetic of the fragment is traditionally strong in the anecdotal genres of *shihua* and *biji*, which tend to be composed of independent snippets and bits of quotations embedded in a narrative or commentary. But in *Furenji* this formal reliance on the fragment as a mode of composition is coupled with an awareness of the fragment's strong thematic association with ruins and remembrance of the past.

Two of the opening entries in the collection exemplify the notion of the fragment as remnant—as the sole surviving piece of an ensemble, the part standing for the whole, as in the trope of metonymy. Both entries concern former Ming palace ladies, themselves remnants of what was once a vast corps of palace women. In the first case, a former palace lady of the last Ming emperor, now a nun, who "often spoke of former events in the palace," recounts how in that fateful month in 1644 before the emperor hanged himself, he called all his ladies together and ordered them to leave the palace to escape the rebels who had already taken the capital. Each lady was issued a length of black gauze to protect her hair. In the ensuing turmoil, this palace-lady-turned-nun was robbed of every ornament; the only tokens of her former life still in her possession were "a couple of pieces of black gauze."[107] In the second case, the woman is a former palace lady in the entourage of a Ming prince, who ends up falling into the hands of a fisherman. She would sit fishing barefoot, wearing a light red undergarment on her head, saying

"This belonged to the former concubine of Prince Xiang 項 of the Ming."[108] In this incongruous gesture, we detect the literalization of metaphor. What was formerly worn on the lower body and hidden inside clothes is proudly draped on the head and exposed for all to see. The image is powerful as a self-conscious symbol of the palace lady's own plight, the pathos of her degradation, and her futile attempt to protest it, but it also signals the value and meaning that can be invested in something trivial and worthless when it is all that remains.

The palace lady was a natural magnet for ruin sentiment in China. As the embodiment of both the splendor and the fall of dynasties, the ruined palace came to be signified by a set of standardized ghostly images in *huaigu*: vegetation running rampant over collapsed buildings, moss creeping over and eroding every surface, will-o'-the-wisps, wild beasts and nocturnal birds scampering in and out. The powdered bones and buried fragrances of the ladies who once inhabited this space are as much staple fixtures of the *huaigu* as these other images of defilement, decay, and abandonment. *Huaigu*-inspired ghost stories typically imagine an encounter between a present-day seeker of the past and a spectral palace lady chanting her own laments for the past amid the ruins of her former abode. Ghost and mortal subsequently enter into a close friendship, sometimes becoming lovers, but the tantalizing gap between past and present can be bridged only temporarily, and such liaisons usually come to an abrupt end. In what is a standard feature of such stories, the palace lady "tells of past events in the palace" to her mortal audience. As a result, the palace lady becomes a synecdoche for what is being mourned and remembered, yet by venting her own feelings of loss in poetry and reminiscence, she also becomes both its chief mourner and the custodian of its memory.

This pattern strongly underlies the story of Lin Siniang, the ghost of a palace lady in the entourage of a Ming prince in Shandong who perished some time during the overthrow of the dynasty and returns to haunt an early Qing official serving in the vicinity. Several versions of this story can be found in seventeenth-century sources; the best known appears in *Liaozhai*.[109] The *Furenji* version of the tale enhances the theme of displacement by removing the site of the ghostly encounter between Ming past and Qing present from the ruined palace of the former dynasty to an official compound representing the new government. Lin Siniang tells the official that she had returned temporarily only to find the halls and towers of the old palace destroyed and the gardens buried beneath a thick "outgrowth of millet."[110] She asks if she may borrow his official residence for a banquet because she and her former companions from the palace have nowhere to go, nowhere they may gather to reminisce about the past. The official gives his consent and is rewarded by her willingness to entertain his own visitors by matching poems with them at social gatherings. We learn that "the poems she composed were mainly laments for the former palace"; the entry in *Furenji* concludes with the text of one such quatrain, which she gave to the official at their final parting.[111]

In the *huaigu*-inspired ghost story, the palace lady revenant is clearly a stand-in for an eyewitness to history, someone who experienced past events and can provide "inside information" to others with no firsthand memory of what happened. The white-haired palace lady, who, as a living relic of the past, chatted about the intimate affairs of an emperor after his deposal or death was a stock figure in Chinese poetry.[112] The advantage of casting a ghost in this role is that she does not age or lose her youthful beauty and so also satisfies, albeit briefly, the fantasy of encountering intact the glamour of the past. Within its pages, *Furenji* contextualizes Lin Siniang's ghost, however, by situating her in the company of living palace ladies; like her, they are displaced survivors of the *ancien régime*, but, unlike her, they are living ruins subject to the cruel pressures of time and debasement.

The poems on walls attributed to palace ladies in *Furenji* tend to reinforce the fragment's close affiliation to the ruin, something once whole and complete that is now broken or marred, pieces decayed or effaced by time. This logic is exemplified in the twelfth entry, which consists of two quatrains that "someone had seen inside the ruins of the Forbidden City in Nanjing" criticizing and lamenting the decadence of the Southern Ming court on the eve of its destruction. Here is my translation of the second quatrain:

> Outside Spring Belvedere Pavilion, the waters stretch on,
>   no trace of the horizon;
> Beacon fires of war day after day
>   jolt my woman's heart.
> Tonight ten thousand miles of enemy circles
>   will close in,
> And my Lord Emperor is still here
>   amid the Qin and Huai rivers.

Chen Weisong takes pains not only to record the words of the quatrains but to describe their visual appearance: "Since some character strokes had been eroded by moss, the person who saw the poems supplied what was missing from context. The meaning of the verses was sad and plaintive. Most likely these were the words of a palace lady in the Southern Ming court."[113] The juxtaposition of temporalities this *tibishi* creates is decipherable only through the hindsight available to the present: the imminence of the dynasty's collapse vividly conveyed through the content of the poem; the pastness and irrevocability of the events materially represented through the evidence of the ruined wall on which the verses were written.

Not only are these verses located on a ruin but they have literally become a ruin themselves. Applicable here is Anne Jankowitz's characterization of the fragment poem in English romanticism as a "a ruin for whose central category of temporal decline has been substituted an equally important assertion of spatial incompletion."[114] Or, as she puts it a moment later, "with the fragment, spatialization usurps temporality."[115] The art historian Bai Qianshen has written of the archaizing interest in broken steles and marred seals during the late Ming and early Qing and the influence of this aesthetics of the ruin on calligraphy. He notes contemporary accounts of people deliberately hurling their seal stones on the ground to chip them, to "distress" them (in the parlance of the modern furniture industry), and to achieve the antique look (*gu se* 古色) of rubbings from old steles whose characters have missing strokes.[116] And yet Chen Weisong does not attempt to reproduce the fragmented appearance of the original moss-eaten quatrains in *Furenji*. Although elsewhere in the collection *tibishi* are not always quoted in their entirety, because the informant has forgotten certain lines or because only certain lines are worth preserving, here the visual pleasure of imagining the look of a fragment is simultaneously tempered by the literary satisfaction of meaning completed.

Alternatively, the imperfections to the verse caused by moss in this anecdote may also register as "distress marks" of an emotional kind. If so, there is a striking affinity between this entry and the forty-fifth entry in the collection. In this anecdote, set in 1651, an official on his way north sees some lines of a poem written on the wall of an inn in Shandong, which describe the plight of a palace lady from the Southern Ming court who has been taken captive. The poem is signed Ye Zimei of Yangzhou (Guangling Ye Zimei 廣陵葉子眉) and dated to the previous year, 1650.

Dust from the horse's pounding hoofs settles on the hair at
    my temples;
In my misery, I'm too ashamed to set my old filigreed pins right.
I turn my head back but it's so hard to remember things in
    the palace:
The thinning willows must trail there in vain as the evening
    mist rises.

It bears this preface: "Composing this as my tears moisten my brush, I'm in a
hurry and my heart is in tumult so I'm unable to fashion my words into stanzas."[117] Here the inability to finish a stanza and polish the poem registers the
extreme duress of its author, reinforced by the putative mix of tears with ink.

The device of a former palace lady explaining the faults in her composition as a sign of uncontrollable emotion and haste is also employed in the
Liaozhai version of the Lin Siniang story. On the eve of her final leave-taking,
the ghost of Lin Siniang requests pen and paper and composes a poem on
the spot for the official as a parting keepsake. She tearfully cautions him:
"I am sick at heart, and my thoughts are jumbled. I cannot properly craft
this poem. The rhyme is wrong, and the meter is off. Please don't show it
to anyone."[118] Here, as in *Furenji* and the other well-known seventeenth-
century accounts, Lin Siniang writes her verse on paper and in the presence
of a human observer, but in another version of the story recently discovered
by Allan Barr in an obscure seventeenth-century manuscript, Lin Siniang's
poem is in fact represented as a *tibishi* discovered on the wall of a locked
room in Prince Heng's ruined palace, the ink still fresh and dripping wet.[119]
The discovery of a freshly written inscription in an abandoned setting is one
recurrent means, as we have seen, of registering "a ghostly autograph." The
device suggests the fundamental affinity between *tibishi* and ghost writing generally. Here it is taken one step further—the ink is not just fresh but dripping
wet, evoking not only ink but tears or even blood. (In certain hagiographic
tales, *tibishi* are sometimes even penned in blood.)[120] The juxtaposition of conflicting temporal orders in a single architectural space produces something of
the shock of a violent protest against the vanishing of the past.

I have written elsewhere about the frequent attribution of fragility and
vulnerability to women's writings during the seventeenth century as evidence
of a symbolic conflation of woman's body and text.[121] But there were real
grounds for the anxiety detectable in this trope: women's writings *were* less

likely to be published than men's and were more at risk of being lost. This is one reason why the challenge of collecting them appealed so much to the connoisseur, why a writer like You Tong 尤侗 (1618–1704) claimed that "we prize and cherish these fragments of powder and ceruse, these bits of pearl and jade, ten times more than ordinary writings."[122] The historical record of the past provided strong evidence for how much of this written record had been lost; indeed, the paucity of early poets in the anthologies of women's verse published in the sixteenth and seventeenth centuries made this only too clear to the reading public. The recent violent events of the Qing conquest and the wholesale destruction of so much of the Ming cultural heritage emphatically reconfirmed both the precariousness of the past's material legacy and the moral necessity to rescue the most perishable aspects of it from oblivion. *Tibishi*, as I argue throughout this chapter, were traditionally imagined to be the kind of writing most prone to disappear. Taken together, poems written on walls by women carried a double weight and were a particularly powerful way to figure what Marilyn Ivy has termed "a discourse of the vanishing."[123]

To conclude, the title *Furenji* furnishes an important clue to the significance of this compilation and sheds light more generally on the phenomenon of collecting *tibishi* attributed to women in the early Qing. Yang Fuji, who included this collection in his sequel to *Zhaodai congshu*, writes that he thought the use of the word *furen* for women in the title lacked refinement; he changed his mind after discovering a Six Dynasties work with the same title in the bibliographic treatise of the official *Tang History*.[124] In fact, *Furenji* is the title of all three of the earliest recorded anthologies of women's writing, none of which survives.[125] Wang Shilu, who was the leading historian of women's writings in the period, and who, I have suggested, was the key figure behind the seventeenth-century *Furenji*, was only too aware of the fate of its medieval predecessors. In the preface to his *Lamp Oil Collection*, he deplores the fact that although many of the books listed in the bibliographic sections of the dynastic histories over the ages have been lost, only in the case of writings by women have nearly *all* of them perished.[126] At least five times in the various critical documents he drafted to accompany his *Lamp Oil Collection*, he cites by name two of the compilers of the medieval *Furenji* and laments the irrevocable disappearance of their manuscripts. In reusing the title of these earliest collections from the past, Chen Weisong was signaling that *Furenji* was meant to be read as an attempt to staunch loss, to arrest the vanishing of a fallen dynasty by paradoxically testifying to its disappearance.

Publishing, of course, turns out to have been the key. Chen Weisong's *Furenji* was eventually published and has indeed survived; ironically Wang Shilu's enormous *Lamp Oil Collection* never found its way into print and was lost some time after the conclusion of the Sino-Japanese war in 1945.[127] All that remains are fragments: some scattered manuscript volumes preserved in a few Chinese libraries and museums and the supporting critical materials that were transcribed into other books and published.

Notes

The earliest version of this paper was presented at the symposium "Ruins in Chinese Visual Culture" held in 1997 at the University of Chicago. My particular thanks to Ma Tai-loi, Shang Wei, Stephen Owen, Bai Qianshen, Marion Eggert, Jonathan Hay, and Kim Rorschach for suggesting important sources; to Zheng Yan, Ellen Widmer, and Tobie Meyer-Fong for helping me obtain reproductions of rare materials; to Christian de Pee for his careful reading of an earlier draft of this paper; and to Lam Ling-hon for his assistance and suggestions.

EPIGRAPH: Wu Qi, preface to *Zhongxiang ci* 眾香詞, a collection of song-lyrics by women; reprinted in Hu Wenkai 胡文楷, *Lidai funü zhuzuo kao* 歷代婦女著作考 (Shanghai: Shanghai guji chubanshe, 1985), p. 899. For my complete translation of this preface, see Kang-i Sun Chang and Haun Saussy, eds., *Women Writers of Traditional China: An Anthology of Poetry and Criticism* (Stanford: Stanford University Press, 1999), pp. 772–74.

1. Susan Stewart, *Crimes of Writing: Problems in the Containment of Representation* (Durham, N.C.: Duke University Press, 1994), p. 216.

2. Mary Douglas, *Purity and Danger* (London: Routledge, 1984), p. 35.

3. For the An Guo shrine inscription, see Wu Hung, *Monumentality in Early Chinese Art and Architecture* (Stanford: Stanford University Press, 1995), p. 184. Huang Yunjiao 黃允交, "Sha fengjing" 殺風景, in *Zacuan sanxu* 雜纂三緒 1.b (in *Shuofu* 說郛; facsimile reprint of 1647 ed.); also cited in Wu Chengxue 吳承學, "Lun tibishi—jianji xiangguan de shige zhizuo yu chuanbo xingshi" 論題壁詩—兼即相關的詩歌製作與傳播形式, *Wenxue yichan* 1994, no. 4: 13.

4. Robert Harrist, Jr., "The Eulogy on Burying a Crane: A Ruined Inscription and Its Restoration," *Oriental Art*, Autumn 1998, p. 9, citing Richard Strassberg's translation of Fang Bao's 1743 travelogue in *Inscribed Landscapes: Travel Writing from Imperial China* (Berkeley: University of California Press, 1994), p. 401. Yuan Hongdao's essay "Qiyun" 齊雲 (*Yuan Hongdao ji jianjiao* 袁宏道集箋校, ed. Qian Bocheng 錢伯城 [Shanghai: Shanghai guji chubanshe, 1981], 10.457–59) is a diatribe against the vulgar scholars of Anhui for cluttering the mountainside with an excessive number of inscriptions. He jokingly wonders why innocent stones and mountains should be tortured by having their faces blackened and their skin flayed in such a manner and advocates that the defacement of the landscape be declared a capital crime on par with robbery and looting. Both Yuan Hongdao and his younger brother Yuan Zhongdao's works include poems written on walls.

5. Wu Chengxue, "Lun tibishi," p. 13.

6. Poems by famous people or particularly moving or unusual poems could turn a place into a tourist spot or pilgrimage site. For a complete list of sites and surfaces where poems were inscribed during the Tang, based on a survey of *Quan Tangshi*

全唐詩, see Luo Zongtao 羅宗濤, "Tangren tibishi chutan" 唐人題壁詩初探, *Zhonghua wenshi luncong* 47 (1991): 155–58. Luo concludes that poems could be written on any wall during the Tang, including those of private residences, but that the most frequently used surfaces were the walls of temples, courier stations, inns, and public offices.

7. Michel Foucault, "What Is an Author?" trans. Josué V. Harari, in *The Foucault Reader*, ed. Paul Rabinow (New York: Pantheon, 1984), pp. 107–8.

8. *Tibishi* without a known author become classified as *wuming shi* 無名詩 (anonymous poems) with "anonymous" as a placeholder for the author. The assumption is always that there was an author whose name has been lost or suppressed. As the preface to a *tibishi* attributed simply to a "Virtuous Woman from Shanxi" (Shanxi jiefu 山西節婦) puts it: "It isn't as if I simply neglected to leave my name; it's rather that I couldn't bear to leave it, I dared not leave it, and furthermore, there was no need to leave it" (Wang Duanshu 王端淑, *Mingyuan shiwei* 名媛詩緯 [1667 ed. in the Peking University Library], 15.23b–24b). In the celebrated case of the Girl from Kuaiji discussed below, the author's missing name was later miraculously detected on the wall; although the claim was that the name had been there all along and overlooked, what this episode most reveals is the intensity of the cultural desire to have a signature for an anonymous *tibishi*.

9. Wu Chengxue, "Lun tibishi," p. 5. See the early thirteenth-century *[Zengxiu] Shihua zonggui* 增修詩話總龜 (Shanghai: Sibu congkan ed., first series), compiled by Ruan Yue, *juan* 15 and 16. See also the second series, compiled by an anonymous author, *juan* 21. On the complex history of this book, which does not retain its original form, see Yves Hervouet, ed., *A Song Bibliography* (Hong Kong: Chinese University Press, 1978), p. 449.

10. For the practice of engraving inscriptions in stone on mountain cliffs, see Robert Harrist, Jr., "Reading Chinese Mountains," *Orientations*, Dec. 2000, pp. 46–54.

11. Hou Kaijia 侯開嘉 ("Tibi shufa xingfei shishu" 題壁書法興廢史述, *Shufa* 1997, no. 5 [no. 116]: 5–8) argues that writing on walls was important for calligraphy in the Six Dynasties and Tang because of technological limits on paper size and the cost of paper. He suggests that only walls afforded the calligrapher a large enough surface to practice certain styles and that once larger types of paper were developed and paper became cheaper, the importance of walls for the practice of calligraphy declined.

12. As in the Cultural Revolution, anonymous placards were used to lodge accusations against individuals in power during the Ming, too; see Timothy Brook, "Communications and Commerce," in *The Cambridge History of China*, vol. 8, ed. Denis Twitchett and Frederick W. Mote (New York: Cambridge University Press, 1998), pp. 645–46.

13. This holds true for Chinese poetic practice generally, and the encounter and response mode can take place entirely through printed books. But *tibishi* spell out this practice most clearly by situating it in geographical space. Cf. Strassberg, *Inscribed Landscapes*, pp. 5–6, on the implications of this practice in travel writing.

14. See, e.g., Kong Pingzhong 孔平仲, "Shu yishe bi" 書驛舍壁 (Written on the wall of a courier station inn), in *Songshi chao* 宋詩抄, comp. Wu Zhizhen 吳之振 (Shanghai: Shangwu yinshuguan, 1935), 1: 454. The poet, one of the "Three Kongs" of the Northern Song, bemoans that on a visit to this spot the previous year, the wall had been covered with inscriptions, but this year they were all gone, whitewashed by the official in charge of the courier station. The loss prompts a lament on the impermanence of writing, naturally written on the wall of the same courier station.

15. For examples of the first two in Bai Juyi's poetry, see Luo Zongtao, "Tangren tibishi," pp. 161–62, 164; see also Wu Chengxue, "Lun tibishi," p. 11. For a Qing example of coming across one's own *tibishi* on a later occasion, see Wang Shilu 王士祿, "Yiju fu de yiwei jiudi furan tibi" 移居復得乙未舊邸撫然題壁, in idem, *Shihu caotang ji* 十笏草堂集 (in *Guochu shi dajia shichao* 國初十大家詩抄 [Xin Fangge kanben 信芳閣刊本, 1830], 1.25a). For Ming and Qing examples of coming across a *tibishi* by a dead friend, see Yuan Zhongdao袁中道, "Youting jian wangyou Bai Erheng bijian shi ganfu" 郵亭見亡友白爾亨壁間詩感賦, in idem, *Kexuezhai ji* 珂雪齋集, ed. Qian Bocheng 錢伯城 (Shanghai: Shanghai guji chubanshe, 1989), 1: 8.395; Wang Shilu, "Fu jing Dingzhou ci Julu Bibu bijian yun; shi Bibu yi mo" 復經定州次菊廬比部壁間韻; 時比部已沒, in idem, *Shihu caotang xinjia ji* 十笏草堂辛甲集 (Kangxi ed. in the Academy of Sciences Library, Beijing); and Zha Shenxing 查慎行, "Baigou lüdian jian wangyou Zheng Panpu jiuti cangran yougan . . ." 白溝旅店見亡友鄭攀圃舊題愴然有感, in idem, *Jingye tang shiji* 敬業堂詩集 (Shanghai: Shanghai guji chubanshe, 1986), 11.306.

16. Bai Juyi, "Ti Liugou si gusong" 題流溝寺古松, in *Quan Tangshi* 全唐詩 (Beijing: Zhonghua shuju, 1960), 436.4838; quoted in both Luo Zongtao, "Tangren tibishi," p. 162; and Wu Chengxue, "Lun tibishi," p. 10. Luo uses this poem as evidence that poems entitled "inscribed on trees" were probably often not written on trees but on the walls beside them.

17. Dou Gong, "Shan'an fu bintang lan Fang Du ergong Renshou nianzhong tiji shouji" 陝安府賓堂覽房杜二公仁壽年中題紀手跡, in *Quan Tangshi* 271.3051; cited in Luo Zongtao, "Tangren tibishi," p. 170.

18. Hans Frankel, *The Flowering Plum and the Palace Lady* (New Haven: Yale University Press, 1976), p. 108.

19. Wei Yingwu, "Donglin jingshe jian gudian zhong Zheng Shiyu tishi" 東林精舍見故殿中鄭侍御題詩, in *Quan Tangshi* 191.1967; cited in Luo Zongtao, "Tangren tibishi," p. 164.

20. Bai Juyi, "Chongguo mishu jiufang yin ti changju" 重過秘書舊房因題 長句, in *Quan Tangshi* 438.4862; cited in Luo Zongtao, "Tangren tibishi," pp. 164–65.

21. Wu Yuanheng 武元衡, "Jian Guo shilang tibi" 見郭侍朗題壁, in *Quan Tangshi* 317.3578; cited in Luo Zongtao, "Tangren tibishi," p. 170.

22. Li Qunyu 李群玉, "Changsha Kaiyuan si yu gu Changlin Xu Shiyu ti song shi lianju" 長沙開元寺與故長林徐侍御題松石聯句, in *Quan Tangshi*, 569.6592; cited in Luo Zongtao, "Tangren tibishi," p. 170.

23. Zhang Hu, "Ti yu yueting" 題於越亭, in *Quan Tangshi* 511.5829; cited in Wu Chengxue, "Lun tibishi," p. 6.

24. Wu Chengxue, "Lun tibishi," pp. 6–8.

25. See "Jiewei gui" 介胄鬼, in *Quan Tangshi* 865.9778, and, under the title "Wulin jieweizhe" 武林介胄者, in Mei Dingzuo 梅鼎祚, *Caigui ji* 才鬼記, ed. Tian Pu 田璞 and Cha Hongde 查洪德 (Zhengzhou: Zhongzhou guji chubanshe, 1989), 3.46. The poem is mysteriously delivered by an armored sentry and augurs death for the man who receives it. In "Zhu xiucai" 朱秀才, another Tang story about a ghost poem, the paper it is written on is described as being "old and tattered"; see Mei Dingzuo, *Caigui ji* 3.48.

26. On poetry, ghosts, and the planchette in Chinese literature, see my "Spirit Writing and Performance in the Work of You Tong (1618–1704)," *T'oung Pao* 84 (1998): 102–35.

27. Brigitte Peucker, *Incorporating Images: Film and the Rival Arts* (Princeton: Princeton University Press, 1995), p. 105. There are significant differences from the Chinese situation since Peucker consistently glosses the signifier as the represented and the signified as the real. Thus for her, trompe l'oeil, and by extension, those moments when writing becomes a thing are expressions of "the drive to bring the real into the space of representation," to deny that what is seen is a representation at all. This part of her argument appears not to be applicable to my examples, but the idea of writing signifying itself when attention is paid to visual display rather than content is, I think, a kind of ontological border crossing. Of course, this also characterizes the entire premise of calligraphy; writing generally was a standard part of visual display in Chinese painting, architecture, and landscape.

28. "Su Shao" 蘇韶, in *Taiping guangji* 太平廣記, comp. Li Fang 李昉 (Beijing: Zhonghua shuju, 1981), 319.2528; "Guo Fanwen" 郭翻文, in *Taiping guangji* 321.2542. Both are also included in Mei Dingzuo, *Caigui ji* 1.10–12.

29. "Zheng Qiongluo" 鄭瓊羅, in Mei Dingzuo, *Caigui ji*, p. 78.

30. The *locus classicus* for this trope is Pan Yue's 潘岳 "Daowang shi" 悼亡詩. In these poems mourning a dead wife, posthumous writing and the belongings of the dead wife hanging on the wall are treated as separate things, but both contribute to the husband's pain.

31. For examples, see "Ziyu" 紫玉 in Gan Bao 干寶, *Soushen ji* 搜神記, ed. Wang Shaoying 汪紹楹 (Beijing: Zhonghua shuju, 1979), #394, 16.200; and "Pang'e" 龐阿 in *Taiping guangji* 358.2830.

32. "Guishen pian" 鬼神篇, in Zhu Xi 朱熹, *Zhuzi yulei* 朱子語類 (Beijing: Zhonghua shuju, 1986), 3.44. Daniel Gardner translates excerpts from this chapter (in Donald S. Lopez, Jr., comp., *Religions of China in Practice* [Princeton: Princeton University Press, 1996], pp. 108–19), but omits this anecdote from his translation of the relevant passage. For a discussion of Zhu Xi's theories about spirit beings, see also Gardner, "Ghosts and Spirits in the Sung Neo-Confucian World: Chu Hsi on Kuei-shen," *Journal of the American Oriental Society* 115, no. 4 (1995): 598–611.

33. *Zhuzi yulei* 3.43, 3.39.

34. "Jiao Hong zhuan" in Cheng Boquan 成柏泉, ed., *Gudai wenyan duanpian xiaoshuo xuan* 古代文言短片小說選 (Shanghai: Shanghai guji chubanshe, 1984), 2: 317.

35. Meng Chengshun孟稱舜, *Jiao Hong ji* 嬌紅記, ed. Ouyang Guang 歐陽光 (Shanghai: Shanghai guji chubanshe, 1988), scene 50 ("Xianyuan" 仙圓), p. 256. In keeping with dramatic method, Meng transposes the tale's narration of how the writing looked into the maid's direct speech. The main difference is that in the play the lovers are reunited as immortals rather than as ghosts after their death, and the maid takes the miraculous disappearance of their writing as proof of their transcendence. For a translation of this scene by Cyril Birch, see Meng Chengshun, *Mistress and Maid* (New York: Columbia University Press, 2001), pp. 344–46.

36. Fan Wenruo 范文若, *Menghua han* 夢花酣, scene 18 ("suo nü" 索女) (reprint of late Ming ed. in *Guben xiqu congkan* 古本戲曲叢刊, 3d series), 2: 4a–b.

37. Pu Songling 蒲松齡, *Liaozhai zhiyi [huijiao huizhu huiping ben]* 聊齋誌異會校會注會評本, ed. Zhang Youhe 張友鶴 (Shanghai: Shanghai guji chubanshe, 1983), 8.1084. For a fuller discussion of this story, see my *Historian of the Strange* (Stanford: Stanford University Press, 1993), pp. 8–10.

38. "Balingguan guishi" 巴陵館鬼詩, in Mei Dingzuo, *Caigui ji* 5.86 (*Taiping guangji* 345.2731).

39. Hong Mai 洪邁, *Yijian zhi* 夷堅志, ed. He Zhuo 何卓 (Beijing: Zhonghua shuju, 1981), "dingzhi" 丁志 9. 608–9. For other versions of this tale, see Tan Zhengbi 譚正璧, *Sanyan Liangpai ziliao* 三言兩拍資料 (Shanghai: Shanghai guji chubanshe, 1980).

40. "Yang Siwen Yanshan feng guren" 楊思溫燕山逢故人, in Feng Menglong 馮夢龍, comp., *Gujin xiaoshuo* 古今小說, ed. Xu Zhengyang 許政揚 (Beijing: Renmin wenxue chubanshe, 1981), #24, pp. 366–83. For a translation of the story, see Feng Menglong, *Stories Old and New*, trans. Shuhui Yang and Yunqin Yang (Seattle: University of Washington Press, 2000), pp. 430–49.

41. Li Yu 李漁, "Shufang bi" 書房壁, in idem, *Xianqing ouji* 閑情偶記, ed. Shan Jinheng 單錦珩 (Hangzhou: Zhejiang guji chubanshe, 1985), 4.170.

42. For making a match, see Wu Bing 吳炳, *Qingyou ji* 情郵記, in *Canhua zhai wuzhong* 粲花齋五種 (Nuanhongshi huike chuanqi 暖紅室彙刻傳奇 ed.; facsimile reprint—Yangzhou: Jiangsu guangling guji kanyinshe, 1982) (discussed below); for reuniting couples separated by war, see Ding Yaokang 丁耀亢, *Xihu shan* 西湖扇, scene 16 ("Shuangti" 雙題), scene 18 ("Yu shi" 遇詩), in *Ding Yaokang quanji* 丁耀亢全集, ed. Li Zengpo 李增坡 and Zhang Qingji 張清吉, vol. 1 (Zhengzhou: Zhongzhou guji chubanshe, 1999); for presenting a prophecy, see Hong Sheng 洪昇, *Changsheng dian* 長生殿, ed. Xu Shuofang 徐朔方 (Beijing: Renmin wenxue chubanshe, 1986), scene 10 ("Yi chen" 疑讖); for solving a crime, see "Shi yan" 詩讞, in Pu Songling, *Liaozhai zhiyi* 8:1135–37.

43. Kong Shangren 孔尚任, "Chusui tong Li Houyu Huang Xianshang yin Tianshi Banyuan tibi" 除歲同李厚餘黃仙裳飲田氏半園題壁, in *Kong Shangren shi* 孔尚任詩, ed. Wang Weilin 汪蔚林 (Beijing: Kexue chubanshe, 1958), 1.18. The last line contains an allusion to Han dynasty intellectual Yang Xiong's 楊雄 Ziyun ting 紫雲亭. For an unusual example of Kong Shangren using *tibishi* to preserve the cultural legacy of the past, see his "Ti gebi ting" 題閣逼亭 on a pavilion connected with Li Bai, in *Kong Shangren shi*, p. 235.

44. See Wang Shizhen 王士禛, *Xiangzu biji* 香祖筆記 (published 1706; Shanghai: Shanghai guji chubanshe, 1982), 2.40. The term *gong che* 公車 Wang Shizhen uses here refers to the official carriage used to convey provincial degree holders to the capital to sit for the metropolitan examinations. The two brothers traveled together to the capital to attend these exams in the winter of 1651. See Wang Shizhen 王士禛, "Yuyang Shanren zizhuan nianpu" 漁洋山人自轉年譜, in *Wang Shizhen nianpu* 王士禛年譜, ed. Sun Yancheng 孫言誠 (Beijing: Zhonghua shu-ju, 1992), pp. 10–11, which reprints an anecdote from Wang Zhuo 王晫, *Jin shishuo* 今世說 (Shanghai: Gudian wenxue chubanshe, 1957) about the brothers' *tibishi* activities on this journey. An entry in Wang Shizhen's 王士禛 *Chibei outan* 池北偶談 (published by 1690; Beijing: Zhonghua shuju, 1982), 18.44, records other of his forgotten *tibishi* later recited to him by friends. See also *Wang Shizhen nianpu*, p. 25.

45. Zha Shenxing's poetic work is divided into chronologically arranged clusters, each dated with the year and months covered, and each given a specific title relating to events in his life and treated as a "collection." On this work, see Yuan Xingyun 袁行雲, *Qingren shiji xulu* 清人詩集敍錄 (Beijing: Wenhua yishu chubanshe, 1994), p. 493.

46. Zha Shenxing, *Jingyetang shiji* 11.304.

47. All the examples I have given from Kong Shangren, Wang Shizhen, and Cha Jingye's poetry are taken from collections they themselves compiled rather than from posthumous collections of their work assembled by later editors.

48. The principal anthologies I consulted are Qian Qianyi 錢謙益, comp., *Liechao shiji* 列朝詩集, *runji* 閏集 (early Qing ed., Peking University Library); Chen Weisong 陳維崧, comp., *Furenji* 婦人集, in *Zhaodai congshu guangbian* 昭代叢書廣編, ed. Yang Fuji 楊復吉 (1919 facsimile reprint of 1876 ed.); Deng Hanyi 鄧漢儀, *Shiguan chuji* 詩觀初集 (1672; Kangxi Shenmotang 慎墨堂 ed. in the Library of Congress) and *Shiguan sanji* 詩觀三集 (1689; Qianlong ed. in Beijing Library); Wang Duanshu, *Mingyuan shiwei*; Xu Gui 徐軌, *Xu Benshi shi* 續本詩事, in *Benshi shi* 本詩事 (Shanghai: Shanghai guji chubanshe, 1991); Ji Liuqi 計六奇, *Mingji nanlüe* 明季南略, ed. Wei Deliang 魏得良 and Ren Daobin 任道斌 (Beijing: Zhonghua shuju, 1984); and Qian Zhonglian's 錢仲聯 indispensable modern compilation, *Qingshi jishi* 清人紀詩 (Nanjing: Jiangsu guji chubanshe, 1989), vol. 20.

49. Dorothy Ko, "The Complicity of Women in the Good Woman Cult," in *Family Process and Political Process in Modern Chinese History*, pt. I (Taipei: Academia Sinica, Institute of Modern History, 1992), pp. 464–65.

50. Deng Hanyi, *Shiguan chuji* 12. The women's *tibishi* in Deng Hanyi's *Shiguan* have clearly been embellished and differ considerably from extant versions in other sources. For studies of this anthology, see Tobie Meyer-Fong, "Site and Sentiment: Building Culture in Seventeenth-Century Yangzhou" (Ph.D. diss., Stanford University, 1998), chap. 3; and idem, "Packaging the 'Men of Our Times': Literary Anthologies and Political Accommodation in the Early Qing" (unpublished paper).

51. Kang-i Sun Chang's study shows that Wang Duanshu felt it incumbent upon herself "to preserve women's works for later generations and to make sure that she herself was not guilty of failing to rescue poems from obscurity." Chang cites the foreword by Wang's husband, which declares: "Why did my wife . . . compile *Mingyuan shiwei*? It is because she cannot bear to see the excellent poems of women of our times vanishing like mist and grass" ("Ming and Qing Anthologies of Women's Poetry and Their Selection Strategies," in *Writing Women in Late Imperial China*, ed. Ellen Widmer and Kang-i Sun Chang [Stanford: Stanford University Press, 1997], p. 158). On Wang Duanshu and her anthology, see also Widmer, "Ming Loyalism and the Woman's Voice in Fiction After *Honglou meng*," in *Writing Women in Late Imperial China*, pp. 368–73.

52. Zhu Zhongmei, preface to "Ci Xiangjiang nuzi" 次湘江女子, in Wang Duanshu, *Mingyuan shiwei* 4.11a.

53. Wu Bing, *Qingyou ji*, scene 1 ("Yue yan" 約言), 1.1a.

54. "Ziji wen" 自祭文, in Tao Qian 陶潛, *Tao Yuanming ji* 陶淵明集, ed. Lu Qinli 逯欽立 (Beijing: Zhonghua shuju, 1979), pp. 196–97; trans. by A. R. Davis, *T'ao Yüan-ming: His Works and Their Meaning* (Cambridge, Eng.: Cambridge Univer-

sity Press, 1983), 1: 240–41; for a discussion of this text, see Wu Hung, *Monumentality in Early Chinese Art*, pp. 257–59.

55. In classical Chinese, the word *gui* 歸 means "to die" as well as "to return home"; it is frequently punned on in early definitions of a ghost (also pronounced *gui* 鬼).

56. I have in mind Paul Ricoeur's observations on the trace: "'Passage' is a better way of speaking about the dynamics of a trace, 'mark' is a better way of indicating its static aspect" (*Time and Narrative*, trans. Kathleen Blarney and David Pellauer [Chicago: University of Chicago Press, 1988], 3: 119). In Chinese, *ji* 跡, one of the main terms for "trace," originally meant "footprint," and hence it nicely incorporates both of Ricoeur's senses of the trace, as visible in the present as a vestige and as a sign that someone or something once passed through.

57. For examples, see Zhou Lianggong 周亮工, "Bailian yi" 白蓮驛, in Deng Hanyi, *Shiguan chuji:*, 1.14b; and Wu Zhaoqian 吳兆騫, "Huangyi su" 荒驛宿, in Deng Hanyi 鄧漢儀, *Shiguan erji* 詩觀二集 (1678; Qianlong ed. in Beijing Library), 3.26a or 36a. Timothy Brook (*Cambridge History of China*, vol. 8, pp. 582–96) describes the Ming courier system as a system designed by law to service personnel traveling on government business. Because of the courier system's official function, poems on ruined stations in the early Qing can be read as laments on the breakdown in government order and the fall of the dynasty.

58. Ko, "The Complicity of Women," p. 462.

59. Ibid., p. 463. One famous fraud of the period was the *tibishi* secretly left by Wu Zhaoqian one night at Tiger Mound Temple, which he wrote in a woman's voice and signed with a woman's name. See "Huqiu si tibi ershi jueju" 虎丘寺題壁二十絕句, in *Qingshi jishi*, 4: 1958–60.

60. Wai-yee Li, "Heroic Transformations: Women and National Trauma in Early Qing Literature," *Harvard Journal of Asiatic Studies* 59, no. 2 (Dec. 1999): 423.

61. Jiang Yin 蔣寅 (Jinling sheng 金陵生, pseud.), "Nüzi tibishi duo bu kexin" 女子題壁詩多不可信, *Wenxue yichan* 1998, no. 3: 75.

62. For some of these early examples, see Zhang Jiahe 張嘉和, *Mingshu wencan* 名姝文燦 (late Ming ed. in the Peking University Library), *juan* 7 and 8; Wang Duanshu, *Mingyuan shiwei*, 4.8b–9a; and Zhong Xing 惺鍾, comp., *Mingyuan shigui* 名媛詩歸 (late Ming ed. in the Peking University Library), *juan* 21 and 26.

63. Kuaiji 會稽 (also pronounced Guiji) is modern Shaoxing 紹興 in Zhejiang province; the courier station was located in Ziyang 滋陽 county in Gundong 袞東 prefecture in southern Shandong. Evidence for this dating is given below.

64. Wu Bing's *Love at a Courier Station* develops this theme at some length. The courier station in the play is situated on the eastern banks of the Yellow River at the beginning of the road to Qingzhou, running northeast across the province to Beijing. All the main characters in the play, like the playwright himself, are southerners, who register their dismay at entering the alien terrain of the north in their reactions

to the "depressing and forlorn station," continually battered by the waves of the Yellow River. See scene 7 ("Ti yi" 題驛), 1. 19a-b, and scene 13 ("Bu he"), 1.45a.

65. My translation is based on the text in Yuan Zhongdao 袁中道, *Kexuezhai qianji* 珂雪齋前集 (facsimile of the 1624 reprint of the 1618 ed. in the Taiwan National Library—Taibei: Weiwen tushu chubanshe, 1976). Other important seventeenth-century sources for this text (with minor variations) include Zhou Zhibiao 周之標, *Nüzhong qi caizi Lanke ji* 女中七才子蘭咳集 (damaged ed. in Beijing Library; complete ed. in Nanjing Library), appendix to *juan* 5; and Qian Qianyi, comp., *Liechao shiji, runji, juan* 4. Ronald Egan translates the preface and poems in full (erroneously dated to the sixteenth century) in Chang and Saussy, *Women Writers of Traditional China*, pp. 200–201.

66. Zhou Zhibiao, "He Kuaiji nüzi shi bing wei jiechao" 和會稽女子詩並為解嘲, in his *Lanke ji*. On dates for Zhou Zhibiao, see Zhang Huijian 張慧劍, *Ming Qing Jiangsu wenren nianbiao* 明清江蘇文人年表 (Shanghai: Shanghai guji chubanshe, 1986), pp. 436, 620. Wang Duanshu, *Mingyuan shiwei, juan* 5, also notes the multitude of matching poems and includes a sizable number of them in her anthology.

67. See Ellen Widmer, "Xiaoqing's Literary Legacy and the Place of the Woman Writer in Late Imperial China," *Late Imperial China* 13, no. 1 (June 1992): 111–55; and Dorothy Ko, *Teachers of the Inner Chambers* (Stanford: Stanford University Press, 1994), pp. 91–110.

68. Deng Hanyi, *Shiguan chuji*, 12.38b; reportedly seen in 1651.

69. Zhu Zhongmei, preface to "Matching a Girl from Xiangjiang's *Tibishi*," in Wang Duanshu, *Mingyuan shiwei* 4.11a.

70. The Beijing Library catalogue dates this work to the late Ming; Hu Wenkai 胡文楷 (*Lidai funü zhuzuo kao*, p. 844) dates this edition to the early Qing, but neither gives reasons. Since Zhou Zhibiao dates his discovery of another woman's *tibishi* in *Lanke ji* to 1643 (appendix to *juan* 5), the collection could not have been published before then. Zhou Zhibiao is best known for having edited two anthologies of arias, *Yuefu shanshan ji* 樂府珊珊集 and *Wuyu cuiya* 吳歈萃雅. He also compiled a second installment to his anthology of women's poetry entitled *Nüzhong qi caizi Lanke erji* 女中七才子蘭咳二集 (Kangxi ed. in the Shanghai Library).

71. Wang Daniang's courtesy name is Weiyang 未央; all that I have been able to discover is that he wrote a preface dated 1642 to a collection of *zaju* 雜劇 by a Hangzhou-based playwright, Fu Yichen 傅一臣, *Sumenxiao ji* 蘇門嘯集, signed "An old commoner from Shandong" (Shandong lao buyi 山東老布衣). In the preface, Wang Danian mentions his good friend Wang Jide 王驥德 (d. 1623) as the playwright of *Nan huanghou* 男皇后 [*sic*]. See Cai Yi 蔡毅, comp., *Zhongguo gudian xiqu xuba huibian* 中國古典戲曲序跋匯編 (Ji'nan: Qilu shushe, 1989), pp. 889–90.

72. On this phenomenon and its influence on Chinese fiction, see Patrick Hanan, *The Chinese Short Story: Studies in Dating, Authorship, and Composition* (Cambridge,

Mass.: Harvard University Press, 1973), pp. 186–87; and Leo Tak-hung Chan, *The Discourse on Foxes and Ghosts: Ji Yun and Eighteenth-Century Literati Storytelling* (Honolulu: Hawai'i University Press, 1998), chap. 2.

73. This is "Wushi gong" 無是公, an allusion to an allegorized figure in Sima Xiangru's 司馬相如 prose poem "Zixu fu" 子虛賦. Like "Wuyou xiansheng" 無有先生, the expression means "fictional character" in late imperial usage.

74. *Lanke ji, juan 5.* The Beijing Library's copy is missing six characters, which I have filled in based on the copy of the same edition in the Nanjing Library. Wang Danian's text seems to have him viewing peonies at the end of the twelfth month, which is clearly impossible. He must have left out the month for the twenty-eighth day, presumably the fourth or fifth month, when peonies bloom in Jiangnan.

75. Yuan Zhongdao, "Ti Kuaiji nüzi shi ba" 題會稽女子詩跋, in *Kexuezhai qianji, juan 8.* Also included in *Kexuezhai ji* 8.393–94.

76. Yuan's original preface is dated 1618. See Qian Bocheng's discussion of editions of Yuan Zhongdao's work to confirm the 1618 publication of this collection (*Kexuezhai ji*, pp. 15–17). In 1616 Yuan Zhongdao was appointed an instructor in the prefectural school in Huizhou (Anhui, where Xin'an was located) (L. Carrington Goodrich and Chaoying Fang, eds., *Dictionary of Ming Biography, 1368–1644* [New York: Columbia University Press, 1976], p. 1638). Yuan's preface to his next collection, *Kexuezhai xuanji* 珂雪齋選集, which is dated 1622, specifically says that his earlier *Kexuezhai qianji* had been published in Xin'an. Although it is remotely possible that a subsection of the poems is entitled "Xin'an ji," no independent work with this title survives, and we can be reasonably confident that the work Wang Danian read was Yuan's *qianji*.

Another entry in Zhou Zhibiao's *Lanke ji* (appendix to *juan 5*) corroborates the 1618–19 time frame for the Girl from Kuaiji's inscription. The preface to another of the matching poems by Shen Shaofang 申紹芳 (字: 青門) mentions spending the night at the Xinjia station in the autumn of 1619 and matching her poems with a friend on that occasion.

77. Qian Qianyi 錢謙益, "Xinjia yibi he Yuan Xiaoxiu ti Kuaiji nüzi shi" 新嘉驛壁和袁小修題會稽女子詩, in idem, *Muzhai chuxue ji* 牧齋初學集, ed. Qian Zhonglian 錢仲聯 (Shanghai: Shanghai guji chubanshe, 1985), 2.94. Qian's quatrains are also included in Xu Gui, *Xu benshi shi, houji* 7.225–26 with the Girl's original poems and preface appended.

78. Qian Qianyi, *Liechao shiji, runji* 4.62a. Qian dates his trip with Yuan Zhongdao to the early Tianqi period (1620–21), but, writing some years later, must have misremembered the date.

79. The feminine quality of the calligraphy of an inscription was sometimes adduced in a (futile) effort to muster definitive proof for the feminine authorship of a *tibishi*. The best example is Zhou Zhibiao's comment on a *tibishi* attributed to Du

Qiongzhi 杜瓊枝: "Her characters were nicely formed but a bit on the weak side. It's really true that they were written by a member of the fair sex and are not a fabrication!" ("Ji Pucheng bijian nüzi tishi shi" 紀浦城壁間女子題詩事, *Lanke ji*, appendix to *juan* 5, p. 10b, Nanjing Library copy only).

80. This topic has received a lot of attention in recent scholarship. See particularly Widmer, "Xiaoqing's Literary Legacy"; Kang-i Sun Chang, *The Late Ming Loyalist Poet, Ch'en Tzu-lung* (New Haven: Yale University Press, 1995); and Martin Huang, *Literati and Self-Re/Presentation: Autobiographical Sensibility in the Eighteenth-Century Chinese Novel* (Stanford: Stanford University Press, 1995).

81. The guard's complete name and his age are given as guarantees of his existence, to corroborate the evidence. The guard said he had discovered the inscription by accident while hunting for a missing candlestick the morning after the Girl's party had left the station. He found the candlestick on a stone placard protruding from a wall at the rear of the station; he then noticed the writing on the wall. Shi therefore deduces the girl must have penned the inscription the night before by candlelight, using this very candlestick to hold her taper.

82. Shi Runzhang 施閏章, *Huozhai shihua* 蠖齋詩話, in *Qing shihua* 清詩話, vol. 1 (Shanghai: Shanghai guji chubanshe, 1978), 1: 404–5.

83. Wang Shizhen, "Ande dishe you Kuaiji nüzi Lanxue he Kuaiji nüzi xinjia yi sanjue. Tongchen zuo he he Kuaiji nüzi shi. Manti yi jue yu hou" 安德邸舍有會稽女子蘭雪和會稽女子新嘉驛三絕。 彤臣作和和會稽女子詩。 漫題一絕於後, in a joint edition of Wang Shizhen and Wang Shilu's poetry, *Langye erzi jinshi hexuan* 瑯琊二子近詩合選 (Kangxi ed. in Beijing Library, microfilm #11688), 10.21a. Prefaces include one by Gao Heng 高珩 dated 1656 and one by Wu Weiye 吳偉業 dated 1659. This collection provides strong evidence that Wang Shizhen was especially interested in women's poetry during the 1650s. It includes a poem about purchasing a copy of *Wumeng tang ji* 午夢堂集 at the Baoguo Temple and grieving for Ye Xiaoluan 葉小鸞 and another poem on Yu Niang 俞娘, a woman said to have composed a commentary on *The Peony Pavilion* before her early death and whom Tang Xianzu 湯顯祖 commemorated in two mourning poems (see 10.25a and 10.12b–13a, respectively).

There is another Kangxi edition in the Beijing Library of this work, entitled *Langye erzi shixuan chuji* 瑯琊二子詩選初集 (microfilm #1900). It is substantially the same but lacks the prefaces and is missing some pages of poems; however, it has a *fanli* 凡例, which the other edition does not have.

84. *Shiguan chuji* 12.3b–4a, comment on the female poet Wu Qi's response to a *tibishi* left by such a woman: "He nülang Wu Fanghua tibishi" 和女朗吳芳華題壁詩. *Shiguan* includes several of Wu Qi's poems responding to *tibishi* by women.

85. Wang Duanshu, *Mingyuan shiwei* 22.10b, comment after a *tibishi* attributed to a Miss Yi (Yishi 易氏). This sentiment corresponds to a guiding principle of her

anthology: "In the case of someone who had only a single poem or fragment surviving, I went ahead and recorded it regardless of flaws or imperfections. My rationale was to preserve the person." Although other anthologists of women's verse also adopted such a policy, Wang Duanshu carried this position to extremes by creating a "Section of Remains" ("Yiji" 遺集) to list the names of women who wrote poetry, even if not a single word of theirs survived.

86. Legend has it that an ancient king of Su metamorphosed into a nightjar (*dujuan* 杜鵑, also translated "cuckoo"). In some versions of the story, the nightjar was said to shed tears of blood, linking it to the azalea, also called *dujuan*. The nightjar was a popular poetic allusion, particularly useful in lamentations over a sovereign's death, and it was common in poems on dynastic fall in this period.

87. *Langye erzi shi hexuan* enables us to identify Censor Fu as Fu Yi 傅扆 (字: 彤臣), the same friend who matched the poems at the Ande inn with Wang Shizhen. Poems in the *Langye* collection show that Fu Yi was also a good friend of Wang Shilu's. An early Qing poem by Wang Duo 王鐸 (1592–1652) entitled "Baigou he" 白溝河 included in Deng Hanyi, *Shiguan chuji* 1.14a–b, suggests this particular place was the site of violence and devastation during the Qing.

88. My thanks to Lam Ling-hon for his interpretation of this difficult passage.

89. Chen Weisong, *Furenji* 29a–b (hereafter cited by title only). For the Girl from Langgan's *tibishi*, see ibid., 28a–b. For the parallel-prose preface and the three quatrains omitted from *Furenji*, see Chu Renhuo 褚人獲, *Jianhu ji* 堅瓠集 (facsimile reprint of 1926 ed.—Hangzhou: Zhejiang renmin chubanshe, 1986); or *Qingshi jishi*, 22: 15637–38.

90. The *Furenji* entry omits not only Suyin's preface and quatrains but also Wang Shizhen's matching poems. Instead the entry appends "Jianzi mulanhua" 減字木蘭花, a song-lyric by Wang Shizhen written in Suyin's voice. His matching quatrains, entitled "Liulihe ciyun Hunan nüzi Wang Suyin sanjue" 琉璃河次韻 湖南女子王素音三絕, were published in *Langye erzi shi xuan* 10.21b.

91. *Siku quanshu zongmu tiyao* 四庫全書總目提要 acknowledges Wang Shilu's contribution as a leading *kaozheng* scholar of women's writings in the entry on his essay "Editorial Principles for *Ranzhi ji*" ("Ranzhi ji li" 燃脂集例; see Hu Wenkai, *Lidai funü zhuzuo kao*, p. 910). Zhang Chao 張潮 published this essay in the second installment of *Zhaodai congshu, yiji* 昭代叢書 (乙集), vol. 28. Hu Wenkai acknowledged his indebtedness to Wang Shilu's scholarship by publishing the entire text of "Ranzhi ji li" in the original 1957 edition of *Lidai funü zhuzuo kao*, but it is omitted from the 1985 reprint of this work.

Wang Duanshu is the only other anthologist of women's writing in this period whose commitment to the subject equaled his, but she was more a critic than a historian. Wang Shilu was familiar with Wang Duanshu's anthology *Mingyuan shiwei* and used it as a source for *Ranzhi ji*. He wrote a poem upon her request after she showed him the manuscript. (See Wang Shilu, "Yingranzi chi cezi suo shi fuzeng" 映然子持冊子索詩賦贈 in idem, *Shihu caotang shangfu ji* 十笏草堂上浮集 2.1a–b, the collection of Wang Shilu's verse written from 1664 to mid-1666). He also copied Wang Duanshu's discussions of poetry from *Mingyuan shiwei* into the prose chapters of *Ranzhi ji*, a manuscript copy of which survives in Peking University Library.

92. Wang Shilu, "*Ranzhi ji xu*" 燃脂集序 (see Hu Wenkai, *Lidai funü zhuzuo kao*, p. 909). Wang Shizhen gives 1649 as the date his brother began compiling *Ranzhi ji* in earnest and 1665 as its completion date, with corrections and additions being made until his death in 1673 ("Wang Kaogong nianpu" 王考功年譜, in *Wang Shizhen nianpu*, entry for 1649, pp. 69–70).

93. Wang Shilu 王士祿, "Zheng guixiu shiwen shu" 徵閨秀詩文書, in *Xincheng Wangshi zawen shici shiyizhong* 新城王氏雜文詩詞十一種 (Kangxi ed. in Beijing Library). This is a collectanea cobbled together of various works by Wang Shizhen with one *juan* of the prefatory materials to Wang Shilu's *Ranzhi ji* included. (From the contents and tone of this collectanea, it had to have been published before Wang Shilu's death in 1673; since it includes Wang Shizhen's annual poetry collections for 1662 and 1663, it was probably published in 1663 or 1664.) It seems reasonable that "A Call for Contributions" could have been published earlier (in pamphlet form, for instance? inserted in a book by someone else?), but no earlier printed version of it survives. There is, however, a copy of it in the manuscript of the prefatory materials to *Ranzhi ji* in the Shandong Provincial Museum.

The "Call for Contributions" is undated, but since it mentions that *Ranzhi ji* numbered 170 *juan* at the time, it must have been written prior to the reorganization of the manuscript in 1655, described in Wang's preface to *Ranzhi ji*, after which the manuscript had over 230 juan. (This preface was originally written in 1658 but revised in 1672.) The "Call for Contributions" also mentions Suyin's *tibishi*, whose discovery Wang Shilu dates to 1655 in the *Furenji* entry, suggesting that the "Call for Contributions" could not have been written before then. Thus my best guess is that it was drafted in 1655 before Wang Shilu reorganized his manuscript; it is also possible that he added the reference to Suyin some time after he had circulated this document and before its publication in *Xincheng Wangshi zawen*; or more likely, that he changed the final number of *juan* from 170 to over 230 when he revised the preface in 1672.

94. First allusion: during the Six Dynasties the texts of several lost pre-Qin books written on bamboo slips came to light when a tomb in Ji was robbed. The find created a great stir. Second allusion: after the burning of the books by the first Qin emperor, manuscripts of some of the destroyed books were allegedly discovered hidden in the walls of Confucius's house.

95. Wang Shilu, "Zheng guixiu shiwen shu." At the end of this document, Wang appends mailing addresses for three cities: Beijing, Yangzhou, and Suzhou. On the practice of soliciting contributions for anthologies to be sent to the compiler by mail in the early Qing, see Meyer-Fong, "Site and Sentiment," chap. 3.

96. Most of *Furenji* was probably compiled when Chen Weisong was living in Rugao, on Mao Xiang's estate in the vicinity of Nanjing, but later parts could well have been assembled in Yangzhou in the first half of the 1660s when Chen and Wang Shilu together visited Wang Shizhen, who was serving as police commissioner there. See "Yuyang shanren zizhuan nianpu," entry for 1661, p. 20; and "Wang kaogong nianpu," entries for 1664, pp. 78, 81, 166. Chen Weisong wrote an elegy mourning Wang Shilu's death in 1673. See the cursory "Chen Weisong nianbiao" 陳維崧年表 included in Chen Weisong 陳維崧, *Chen Weisong xuanji* 陳維崧選集, ed. Zhou Shaojiu 周韶九 (Shanghai: Shanghai guji chubanshe, 1994), p. 411. Neither this chronology nor any biographical entry on Chen Weisong I have seen mentions *Furenji*. These sources include Arthur W. Hummel, *Eminent Chinese of the Ch'ing Period* (Taipei: Ch'eng-wen, 1967), pp. 103–4; and the entry in *Zhongguo wenxuejia dacidian* 中國文學家大辭典, ed. Qian Zhonglian 錢仲聯 (Beijing: Zhonghua shuju, 1996), Qing dynasty volume, pp. 466–67. For a study of seventeenth-century Yangzhou and Wang Shizhen's circle there, see Meyer-Fong, "Site and Sentiment," particularly chap. 2; and idem, "Making a Place for Meaning in Early Qing Yangzhou," *Late Imperial China* 20, no. 1 (June 1999): 49–84.

97. Wang Shizhen also authored a later, different version of the Lin Siniang story, which he included in his *Chibei outan*. For an argument that he nonetheless contributed the *Furenji* version of Lin Siniang, see my "The Return of the Palace Lady: The Chinese Historical Ghost Story," in *From the Late Ming to the Late Qing: Dynastic Decline and Cultural Innovation*, ed. David Der-wei Wang and Shang Wei (Cambridge, Mass.: Harvard University Asia Center, forthcoming).

98. For further details of Chen Weisong's relationship with Mao Xiang and their involvement with Jiangnan literary circles, see Volpp's chapter in this volume, pp. 138–42.

99. A manuscript copy of Yang Fuji's five supplements to *Zhaodai congshu* is preserved in the Academy of Sciences Library in Beijing. Yang Fuji says in his preface to the *guangji*, the installment in which *Furenji* appears, that he compiled it from 1787 to 1797. According to a note he appended to *Furenji*, Yang Fuji acquired a copy of this work in 1791 (*Furenji* 38b).

The manuscript of the five supplements to *Zhaodai congshu*, which I have seen, contains corrections marked in red and was clearly prepared under Yang Fuji's supervision because the prefaces and lists of editorial principles bear his original seals in red. In addition, the 1876 printed version must have been based on this manuscript, or a copy of it, because at least in the case of *Furenji*, the division into page numbers and the number of characters per line match up exactly and follow the corrections written into the manuscript. Finally, although Yang Fuji did not succeed in publishing his mammoth collectanea during his lifetime, he did publish his inscriptions and colophons from the work separately in 1818, two years before his death (see *Zhaodai congshu wubian tiba* 昭代叢書五編題跋 [Qing edition in the Academy of Sciences Library, Beijing]). For Shen Maode's 沈懋德 publication in the 1830s of these five supplements of *Zhaodai congshu*, along with Zhang Chao's original three installments, see *Zhongguo congshu zonglu* 中國叢書綜錄, comp. Shanghai Library (Shanghai: Shanghai guji chubanshe, 1986).

100. Yang Fuji's colophon to *Furenji* (p. 41a) mentions that several items were transcribed in *Xu Benshi shi*. This collection was compiled by Xu Gui (1636–1708), who was also a figure in Wang Shizhen and Chen Weisong's circle. *Xu Benshi shi* was completed in 1673 but not published until 1705. *Furenji* is also cited as a source in another of Xu Gui's compilations, *Ciyuan congtan* (see *Ciyuan congtan jiaojian* 詞苑叢談校箋, ed. Wang Baili 王百里 [Beijing: Renmin wenxue chubanshe, 1988]), which was published in 1689. It is also used as a source in Wang Qishu 汪啟淑, *Jiefangji* 擷芳集 (published 1773; photocopy of Qing ed. in the Fudan University Library, Regenstein Library, University of Chicago).

101. In his list of editorial principles for *Zhaodai congshu guangbian*, Yang Fuji explicitly stated that he was faithfully copying the complete text of the originals, including prefaces, colophons, and annotations. This implies that if there were any original prefaces or colophons to *Furenji*, they were missing from the manuscript Yang acquired in 1791.

102. *Furenji* had to have been compiled after the fall of the Ming proper in 1644 and the destruction of the Southern Ming in 1645; there are several references to items being collected in the 1650s; and the Lin Siniang story, the latest datable item in the collection, could not have been in circulation before 1662 and was most likely recorded by Chen Weisong a few years later, perhaps in 1666. The work must have been largely complete then by this last date; certainly it was finished before Wang Shilu's death in 1673. For further evidence on dating the collection, see my "Return of the Palace Lady." On anthologies in the early Qing, see Meyer-Fong, "Packaging the 'Men of Our Times'"; and Xie Zhengguang 謝正光 (Andrew Hsieh) and Yu Rufeng 余汝豐, *Qingchuren xuan Qingchushi huikao* 清初人選清初詩匯考 (Nanjing: Nanjing daxue chubanshe, 1998).

103. Huang Zongxi 黃宗羲, *Nanlei wending* 南雷文定 (Shanghai: Shangwu yinshuguan, 1937), *qianji* 6.101; quoted and translated in Bai, "Fu Shan and the Transformation of Chinese Calligraphy," p. 76.

104. These include Dong Xiaowan, Liu Rushi 柳如是, Li Xiangjun 李香君, Chen Yuanyuan 陳圓圓, and Kou Baimen 寇百門.

105. "Traces of the past" is Ricoeur's characterization of the document, which he discusses in terms of the commonsense notion of being "a warrant" for history, of "constituting material proof." "The accent is placed on the support, the warrant a document provides for a history, a narrative, or an argument. This role of being a warrant constitutes material proof, of what in English is called 'evidence,' for the relationship drawn from a course of events" (*Time and Narrative*, vol. 3, p. 117).

106. Again I am inspired by Ricoeur here: "The source of authority of the document, as an instrument of this memory, is the significance attached to the trace. If archives can be said to be instituted, and their documents are collected and conserved, this is so on the basis of the presupposition that the past has left a trace, which has become the monuments and documents that bear witness to the past" (ibid., p. 119).

107. *Furenji* 1b.

108. Ibid., 2a.

109. Convenient modern reprints of the different Lin Siniang versions include Zhu Yixuan 朱一玄, comp., *Liaozhai zhiyi ziliao huibian* 聊齋誌資料匯編 (Zhengzhou: Zhongzhou guji chubanshe, 1986), pp. 91–98; and *Qingshi jishi*, vol. 22, pp. 16299–36, but neither is complete.

110. An outgrowth of millet alludes to a poem in *The Book of Odes*, which was traditionally interpreted as a lament for the fallen Zhou capital.

111. *Furenji* 33a–b.

112. This figure was made famous in the Tang poet Yuan Zhen's 元積 quatrain "Xinggong" 行宮. See the translation and discussion of it in Chi-hung Yim, "The Poetics of Historical Memory in the Ming-Qing Transition: A Study of Qian Qianyi's Later Poetry" (Ph.D. diss., Yale University, 1998), p. 119. This poem and ballads about former palace ladies had particular currency during the early Qing. *Furenji* 1b–2a appends one by Wu Zhaoqian entitled "Baitou gongnü xing" 白頭宮女行.

113. *Furenji* 14b–15a.

114. Anne Jankowitz, *England's Ruins* (London: Basil Blackwell, 1990), p. 7.

115. Ibid.

116. Bai Qianshen, "Fu Shan and the Transformation of Chinese Calligraphy" (Ph.D. diss., Yale University, 1996), pp. 44–45. For the clever idea of calling imitations of folkloric or primitive literature "distressed genres," see Stewart, *Crimes of Writing*, pp. 66–101.

117. *Furenji* 18b–19a.

118. Pu Songling, *Liaozhai zhiyi* 2.288.

119. See Allan Barr, "The Early Qing Mystery of the Governor's Silver," *Harvard Journal of Asiatic Studies* 60, no. 2 (Dec. 2000): 385–12. The ideas in this paragraph are developed further in my "Return of the Palace Lady."

120. Examples of this trope can be found in *Gujin lienü zhuan pinglin* 古今列女傳評林, expanded by Mao Kun 茅坤 (facsimile reprint of Wanli ed., in *Zhongguo gudai banhua congkan erbian* 中國古代版畫叢刊二編 [Shanghai: Shanghai guji chubanshe, 1994]), pp. 400–403, 416–19.

121. See my "Shared Dreams: The Story of the Three Wives' Commentary on *The Peony Pavilion*," *Harvard Journal of Asiatic Studies* 54, no. 1 (July 1994): 127–79; and "Spirit Writing and Performance."

122. You Tong, "*Linxia cixuan xu*" 林下詞選序, in Hu Wenkai, *Lidai funü zhuzuo kao*, p. 897. In the preface, You Tong refers to his friend Wang Shilu's *Lamp Oil Collection*. I translate this preface in full in Chang and Saussy, *Women Writers of Traditional China*, pp. 768–72.

123. Marilyn Ivy, *Discourses of the Vanishing: Modernity, Japan, Phantasm* (Chicago: University of Chicago Press, 1995), pp. 20–21.

124. Yang Fuji, in *Furenji*, 39a. In fact, the title is also listed in the earlier bibliographic treatise in the *Sui History*.

125. Hu Wenkai, *Lidai funü zhuzhuo kao*, p. 875, lists two separate works with the title *Furenji*, respectively compiled by Yin Chun 殷淳 and Xu Mian 徐勉, along with a third work entitled *Furen shiji* 婦人詩集 compiled by Yan Jun 顏竣.

126. Wang Shilu, "*Ranzhi ji xu*," in Hu Wenkai, *Lidai funü zhuzuo kao*, p. 907. Concurrently to *Ranzhi ji*, Wang Shilu was compiling another anthology of women's writings, probably closer to the anecdotal style of *Furenji*, entitled *Zhuniao yishi* 朱鳥遺史 (also written *Zhuniao yishi* 朱鳥逸史). The manuscript was never completed, and no portion of it survives other than a few fragmentary *tibishi* copied into *Furenji* (p. 16a). In *Langye erzi jinshi hexuan*, *chuji* 2.2b–3a, in a note on one of his poems about receiving the posthumous poems of a friend's wife, he identifies *Zhuniao yishi* as "a compilation of mine designed to encompass women's lost writing."

127. Hu Wenkai, *Zhongguo funü zhuzuo*, p. 906. Wang Shilu's "Call for Contributions" says that he is refraining from publishing his *Ranzhi ji* at this time because there were provinces he had not yet scoured for women's writings ("Zheng guixiu shiwen shu").

Works Cited

Bai Qianshen. "Fu Shan and the Transformation of Chinese Calligraphy in the Seventeenth Century." Ph.D. diss., Yale University, 1996.

Barr, Allan. "The Early Qing Mystery of the Governor's Silver." *Harvard Journal of Asiatic Studies* 60, no. 2 (Dec. 2000): 385–12.

Brook, Timothy. "Communications and Commerce." In *The Cambridge History of China*, vol. 8, ed. Denis Twitchett and Frederick W. Mote. New York: Cambridge University Press, 1998, pp. 579–707.

Cai Yi 蔡毅, comp. *Zhongguo gudian xiqu xuba huibian* 中國古典戲曲序跋匯編. Ji'nan: Qilu shushe, 1989.

Chan, Leo Tak-hung. *The Discourse on Foxes and Ghosts: Ji Yun and Eighteenth-Century Literati Storytelling.* Honolulu: Hawai'i University Press, 1998.

Chang, Kang-i Sun. *The Late Ming Loyalist Poet, Ch'en Tzu-lung.* New Haven: Yale University Press, 1995.

———. "Ming and Qing Anthologies of Women's Poetry and Their Selection Strategies." In *Writing Women in Late Imperial China*, ed. Ellen Widmer and Kang-i Sun Chang. Stanford: Stanford University Press, 1997, pp. 147–70.

Chang, Kang-i Sun, and Haun Saussy, eds. *Women Writers of Traditional China: An Anthology of Poetry and Criticism.* Stanford: Stanford University Press, 1999.

Chen Weisong 陳維崧. *Chen Weisong xuanji* 陳維崧選集, ed. Zhou Shaojiu 周韶九. Shanghai: Shanghai guji chubanshe, 1994.

Chen Weisong 陳維崧, comp. *Furenji* 婦人集. In *Zhaodai congshu guangbian* 昭代叢書廣編, ed. Yang Fuji 楊復吉. 1919 facsimile reprint of 1876 ed.

Cheng Boquan 成柏泉, ed. *Gudai wenyan duanpian xiaoshuo xuan* 古代文言短片小說選. Shanghai: Shanghai guji chubanshe, 1984.

Chu Renhuo 褚人獲. *Jianhu ji* 堅瓠集. Prefaces dated 1690–1703. Facsimile reprint of 1926 ed. Hangzhou: Zhejiang renmin chubanshe, 1986.

Davis, A. R. *T'ao Yüan-ming: His Works and Their Meaning.* Cambridge, Eng.: Cambridge University Press, 1983.

Deng Hanyi 鄧漢儀. *Shiguan chuji* 詩觀初集. 1672. Kangxi Shenmotang 慎墨堂 ed. in the Library of Congress.

———. *Shiguan erji* 詩觀二集. 1678. Qianlong ed. in Beijing Library.

———. *Shiguan sanji* 詩觀三集. 1689. Qianlong ed. in Beijing Library.

Ding Yaokang 丁耀亢. *Xihu shan* 西湖扇. In *Ding Yaokang quanji* 丁耀亢全集, ed. Li Zengpo 李增坡 and Zhang Qingji 張清吉, vol. 1. Zhengzhou: Zhongzhou guji chubanshe, 1999.

Douglas, Mary. *Purity and Danger.* London: Routledge, 1984.

Fan Wenruo 范文若. *Menghua han* 夢花酣. Preface dated 1632. Facsimile reprint of late Ming ed. in *Guben xiqu congkan* 古本戲曲叢刊, 3d series.

Feng Menglong 馮夢龍, comp. *Gujin xiaoshuo* 古今小說. Ed. Xu Zhengyang 許政揚. Beijing: Renmin wenxue chubanshe, 1981.

———. *Stories Old and New*. Trans. Shuhui Yang and Yunqin Yang. Seattle: University of Washington Press, 2000.

Foucault, Michel. "What Is an Author?" Trans. Josué V. Harari. In *The Foucault Reader*, ed. Paul Rabinow. New York: Pantheon, 1984, pp. 101–20.

Frankel, Hans. *The Flowering Plum and the Palace Lady*. New Haven: Yale University Press, 1976.

Fu Yichen 傅一臣. *Sumen xiao ji* 蘇門嘯集. Dated 1642. Facsimile reprint.

Gan Bao 干寶. *Soushen ji* 搜神記. Ed. Wang Shaoying 汪紹楹. Beijing: Zhonghua shuju, 1979.

Gardner, Daniel. "Ghosts and Spirits in the Sung Neo-Confucian World: Chu Hsi on *Kuei-shen*." *Journal of the American Oriental Society* 115, no. 4 (1995): 598–611.

Goodrich, L. Carrington, and Chaoying Fang, eds. *Dictionary of Ming Biography, 1368–1644*. New York: Columbia University Press, 1976.

Gujin lienü zhuan pinglin 古今列女傳評林. Expanded by Mao Kun 茅坤. Facsimile reprint of Wanli ed. In *Zhongguo gudai banhua congkan erbian* 中國古代版畫叢刊二編. Shanghai: Shanghai guji chubanshe, 1994.

Hanan, Patrick. *The Chinese Short Story: Studies in Dating, Authorship, and Composition*. Cambridge, Mass.: Harvard University Press, 1973.

Harrist, Robert, Jr. "The Eulogy on Burying a Crane: A Ruined Inscription and Its Restoration." *Oriental Art*, Autumn 1998, pp. 2–10.

———. "Reading Chinese Mountains." *Orientations*, Dec. 2000, pp. 46–54.

Heaven and Earth: 120 Album Leaves from a Ming Encyclopedia. Selected and annotated by John A. Goodall. London: Lund Humphries, 1979.

Hervouet, Yves, ed. *A Song Bibliography*. Hong Kong: Chinese University Press, 1978.

Hong Mai 洪邁. *Yijian zhi* 夷堅志. Ed. He Zhuo 何卓. Beijing: Zhonghua shuju, 1981.

Hong Sheng 洪昇. *Changsheng dian* 長生殿. Ed. Xu Shuofang 徐朔方. Beijing: Renmin wenxue chubanshe, 1986.

Hou Kaijia 侯開嘉. "Tibi shufa xingfei shishu" 題壁書法興廢史述. *Shufa* 1997, no. 5 (no. 116): 5–8.

Hu Wenkai 胡文楷. *Lidai funü zhuzuo kao* 歷代婦女著作考. Shanghai: Shanghai guji chubanshe, 1985.

Huang, Martin. *Literati and Self-Re/Presentation: Autobiographical Sensibility in the Eighteenth-Century Chinese Novel*. Stanford: Stanford University Press, 1995.

Huang Yunjiao 黃允交. *Zacuan sanxu* 雜纂三續. In *Shuofu* 說郛. Facsimile reprint of 1647 ed.

Huang Zongxi 黃宗羲. *Nanlei wending* 南雷文定. Shanghai: Shangwu yinshuguan, 1937.

Hummel, Arthur W. *Eminent Chinese of the Ch'ing Period*. Taipei: Ch'eng-wen, 1967.

Ivy, Marilyn. *Discourses of the Vanishing: Modernity, Japan, Phantasm*. Chicago: University of Chicago Press, 1995.

Jankowitz, Anne. *England's Ruins*. London: Basil Blackwell, 1990.

Ji Liuqi 計六奇. *Mingji nanlüe* 明季南略. Preface dated 1672. Ed. Wei Deliang 魏得良 and Ren Daobin 任道斌. Beijing: Zhonghua shuju, 1984.

Jiang Yin 蔣寅 (Jinling sheng 金陵生, pseud.). "Nüzi tibishi duo bu kexin" 女子題壁詩多不可信. *Wenxue yichan* 1998, no. 3: 75.

Ko, Dorothy. "The Complicity of Women in the Good Woman Cult." In *Family Process and Political Process in Modern Chinese History*. Taipei: Academia Sinica, Institute of Modern History, 1992, pt. I, pp. 453–87.

———. *Teachers of the Inner Chambers*. Stanford: Stanford University Press, 1994.

Kong Shangren 孔尚任. *Kong Shangren shi* 孔尚任詩. Ed. Wang Weilin 汪蔚林. Beijing: Kexue chubanshe, 1958.

Li, Wai-yee. "Heroic Transformations: Women and National Trauma in Early Qing Literature." *Harvard Journal of Asiatic Studies* 59, no. 2 (Dec. 1999): 363–443.

Li Yu 李漁. *Xianqing ouji* 閑情偶記. Ed. Shan Jinheng 單錦珩. Hangzhou: Zhejiang guji chubanshe, 1985.

Lopez, Donald S., Jr., comp. *Religions of China in Practice*. Princeton: Princeton University Press, 1996.

Luo Zongtao 羅宗濤. "Tangren tibishi chutan" 唐人題壁詩初探. *Zhonghua wenshi luncong* 47 (1991): 153–86.

Mei Dingzuo 梅鼎祚. *Caigui ji* 才鬼記. Ed. Tian Pu 田璞 and Cha Hongde 查洪德. Zhengzhou: Zhongzhou guji chubanshe, 1989.

———. *Caigui ji*. Preface dated 1605. Photocopy of late Ming ed. from a microfilm at the Library of Congress.

Meng Chengshun 孟稱舜. *Jiao Hong ji* 嬌紅記. Ed. Ouyang Guang 歐陽光. Shanghai: Shanghai guji chubanshe, 1988.

———. *Mistress and Maid*. Trans. Cyril Birch. New York: Columbia University Press, 2001.

Meyer-Fong, Tobie. "Making a Place for Meaning in Early Qing Yangzhou." *Late Imperial China* 20, no. 1 (June 1999): 49–84.

———. "Packaging the 'Men of Our Times': Literary Anthologies and Political Accommodation in the Early Qing." Unpublished paper.

———. "Site and Sentiment: Building Culture in Seventeenth-Century Yangzhou." Ph.D. diss., Stanford University, 1998.

Peucker, Brigitte. *Incorporating Images: Film and the Rival Arts*. Princeton: Princeton University Press, 1995.

Pu Songling 蒲松齡. *Liaozhai zhiyi [huijiao huizhu huiping ben]* 聊齋誌異會校會注會評本. Ed. Zhang Youhe 張友鶴. Shanghai: Shanghai guji chubanshe, 1983.

Qian Qianyi 錢謙益, comp. *Liechao shiji* 列朝詩集, *runji* 閏集. Early Qing ed., Peking University Library.

———. *Muzhai chuxue ji* 牧齋初學集, ed. Qian Zhonglian 錢仲聯. Shanghai: Shanghai guji chubanshe, 1985.

Qingshi jishi 清人紀詩. Comp. Qian Zhonglian 錢仲聯. Nanjing: Jiangsu guji chubanshe, 1989.

Quan Tangshi 全唐詩. Beijing: Zhonghua shuju, 1960.

Ricoeur, Paul. *Time and Narrative*, vol. 3. Trans. Kathleen Blarney and David Pellauer. Chicago: University of Chicago Press, 1988.

Shi Runzhang 施閏章. *Huozhai shihua* 蠖齋詩話. In *Qing shihua* 清詩話, vol. 1. Shanghai: Shanghai guji chubanshe, 1978.

[Zengxiu] Shihua zonggui 增修詩話總龜. Shanghai: Sibu congkan ed.

Songshi chao 宋詩抄. Comp. Wu Zhizhen 吳之振. Shanghai: Shangwu yinshuguan, 1935.

Stewart, Susan. *Crimes of Writing: Problems in the Containment of Representation*. Durham, N.C.: Duke University Press, 1994.

Strassberg, Richard. *Inscribed Landscapes: Travel Writing from Imperial China*. Berkeley: University of California Press, 1994.

Taiping guangji 太平廣記. Comp. Li Fang 李昉. Beijing: Zhonghua shuju, 1981.

Tan Zhengbi 譚正璧. *Sanyan Liangpai ziliao* 三言兩拍資料. Shanghai: Shanghai guji chubanshe, 1980.

Tao Qian 陶潛. *Tao Yuanming ji* 陶淵明集. Ed. Lu Qinli 逯欽立. Beijing: Zhonghua shuju, 1979.

Wang Duanshu 王端淑. *Mingyuan shiwei* 名媛詩緯. 1667 ed. in the Peking University Library.

Wang Qishu 汪啟淑. *Jiefangji* 擷芳集. Published 1773. Photocopy of Qing ed. in the Fudan University Library. Regenstein Library, University of Chicago.

Wang Shilu 王士禄. *Ranzhi ji* 燃脂集. Manuscript copy of prefatory materials. Shandong Provincial Museum.

———. *Ranzhi ji*. Author's manuscript with corrections of several *juan*. Shanghai Library.

———. *Ranzhi ji*. Manuscript of several *juan* of the prose section. Peking University Library.

———. *Shihu caotang ji* 十笏草堂集. Included in *Guochu shi dajia shichao* 國初十大家詩抄. Xin Fangge kanben 信芳閣刊本, 1830.

———. *Shihu caotang shangfu ji* 十笏草堂上浮集. Kangxi ed. in the Academy of Sciences Library, Beijing.

———. *Shihu caotang xinjia ji* 十笏草堂辛甲集. Kangxi ed. in the Academy of Sciences Library, Beijing.

———. "Zheng guixiu shiwen shu" 徵閨秀詩文書. In *Xincheng Wangshi zawen shici shiyizhong* 新城王氏雜文詩詞十一種. Kangxi ed. in Beijing Library. Also in the *Ranzhi ji* materials in the Shandong Provincial Museum.

Wang Shizhen 王士禛. *Chibei outan.* 池北偶談. Published by 1690. Beijing: Zhonghua shuju, 1982.

———. "Wang Kaogong nianpu" 王考功年譜. In *Wang Shizhen nianpu* 王士禛年譜, ed. Sun Yancheng 孫言誠. Beijing: Zhonghua shuju, 1992.

———. *Xiangzu biji* 香祖筆記. Published 1706. Shanghai: Shanghai guji chubanshe, 1982.

———. "Yuyang Shanren zizhuan nianpu" 漁洋山人自轉年譜. In *Wang Shizhen nianpu* 王士禛年譜, ed. Sun Yancheng 孫言誠. Beijing: Zhonghua shuju, 1992.

Wang Shizhen 王士禛 and Wang Shilu 王士祿. *Langye erzi jinshi hexuan* 瑯琊二子近詩合選. Kangxi ed. in Beijing Library. Microfilm #11688.

———. *Langye erzi shixuan chuji* 瑯琊二子詩選初集. Kangxi ed. in Beijing Library. Microfilm #1900.

Wang Shizhen nianpu 王士禛年譜. Ed. Sun Yancheng 孫言誠. Beijing: Zhonghua shuju, 1992.

Wang Zhuo 王啅. *Jin shishuo* 今世說. Shanghai: Gudian wenxue chubanshe, 1957.

Widmer, Ellen. "Ming Loyalism and the Woman's Voice in Fiction After *Honglou meng*." In *Writing Women in Late Imperial China*, ed. Ellen Widmer and Kang-i Sun Chang. Stanford: Stanford University Press, 1997, pp. 366–96.

———. "Xiaoqing's Literary Legacy and the Place of the Woman Writer in Late Imperial China." *Late Imperial China* 13, no. 1 (June 1992): 111–55.

Widmer, Ellen, and Kang-i Sun Chang, eds. *Writing Women in Late Imperial China.* Stanford: Stanford University Press, 1997.

Wu Bing 吳炳. *Qingyou ji* 情郵記. In *Canhua zhai wuzhong* 粲花齋五種. Nuanhongshi huike chuanqi 暖紅室彙刻傳奇 ed. Facsimile reprint. Yangzhou: Jiangsu guangling guji kanyinshe, 1982.

Wu Chengxue. 吳承學. "Lun tibishi—jianji xiangguan de shige zhizuo yu chuanbo xingshi" 論題壁詩—兼即相關的詩歌製作與傳播形式. *Wenxue yichan* 1994, no. 4: 4–13.

Wu Hung. *Monumentality in Early Chinese Art and Architecture.* Stanford: Stanford University Press, 1995.

Xie Zhengguang 謝正光 (Andrew Hsieh) and Yu Rufeng 余汝豐. *Qingchuren xuan Qingchushi huikao* 清初人選清初詩匯考. Nanjing: Nanjing daxue chubanshe, 1998.

Xu Gui 徐軌. *Ciyuan congtan jiaojian* 詞苑叢談校箋. 1689. Ed. Wang Baili 王百里. Beijing: Renmin wenxue chubanshe, 1988.

———. *Xu Benshi shi* 續本詩事. In *Benshi shi* 本詩事. Shanghai: Shanghai guji chubanshe, 1991.

Yang Fuji 楊復吉, comp. *Zhaodai congshu* 昭代叢書. Qing manuscript in the Academy of Sciences Library, Beijing.

———. *Zhaodai congshu wubian tiba* 昭代叢書五編題跋. Qing ed. in the Academy of Sciences Library, Beijing.

Yim, Chi-hung. "The Poetics of Historical Memory in the Ming-Qing Transition: A Study of Qian Qianyi's Later Poetry." Ph.D. diss., Yale University, 1998.

Yuan Hongdao 袁宏道. *Yuan Hongdao ji jianjiao* 袁宏道集箋校. Ed. Qian Bocheng 錢伯城. Shanghai: Shanghai guji chubanshe, 1981.

Yuan Xingyun 袁行雲. *Qingren shiji xulu* 清人詩集敘錄. Beijing: Wenhua yishu chubanshe, 1994.

Yuan Zhongdao 袁中道. *Kexuezhai ji* 珂雪齋集. Ed. Qian Bocheng 錢伯城. Shanghai: Shanghai guji chubanshe, 1989.

———. *Kexuezhai qianji* 珂雪齋前集. Facsimile of the 1624 reprint of the 1618 ed. in the Taiwan National Library. Taibei: Weiwen tushu chubanshe, 1976.

Zeitlin, Judith T. *Historian of the Strange*. Stanford: Stanford University Press, 1993.

———. "The Return of the Palace Lady: The Chinese Historical Ghost Story." In *From the Late Ming to the Late Qing: Dynastic Decline and Cultural Innovation*, ed. David Der-wei Wang and Shang Wei. Cambridge, Mass.: Harvard University Asia Center, forthcoming.

———. "Shared Dreams: The Story of the Three Wives' Commentary on *The Peony Pavilion*." *Harvard Journal of Asiatic Studies* 54, no. 1 (July 1994): 127–79.

———. "Spirit Writing and Performance in the Work of You Tong (1618–1704)." *T'oung Pao* 84 (1998): 102–35.

Zha Shenxing 查慎行. *Jingye tang shiji* 敬業堂詩集. Shanghai: Shanghai guji chubanshe, 1986.

Zhang Huijian 張慧劍. *Ming Qing Jiangsu wenren nianbiao* 明清江蘇文人年表. Shanghai: Shanghai guji chubanshe, 1986.

Zhang Jiahe 張嘉和. *Mingshu wencan* 名姝文燦. Late Ming ed. in the Peking University Library.

Zhongguo congshu zonglu 中國叢書綜錄. Comp. Shanghai Library. Shanghai: Shanghai guji chubanshe, 1986.

Zhongguo wenxuejia dacidian 中國文學家大辭典. Qing dynasty. Ed. Qian Zhonglian 錢仲聯. Beijing: Zhonghua shuju, 1996.

Zhongguo xiqu zhi 中國戲曲志: *Zhejiang juan* 浙江卷. Beijing: Zhongguo ISBN zhongxin chuban, 1997.

Zhong Xing 惺鍾, comp. *Mingyuan shigui* 名媛詩歸. Late Ming ed. in the Peking University Library.

Zhou Zhibiao 周之標. *Nüzhong qi caizi Lanke ji* 女中七才子蘭咳集. Damaged ed. in Beijing Library. Complete ed. in Nanjing Library.

———. *Nüzhong qi caizi Lanke erji* 女中七才子蘭咳二集. Kangxi ed. in the Shanghai Library.

Zhu Xi 朱熹. *Zhuzi yulei* 朱子語類. Beijing: Zhonghua shuju, 1986.

Zhu Yixuan 朱一玄, comp. *Liaozhai zhiyi ziliao huibian* 聊齋誌異資料匯編. Zhengzhou: Zhongzhou guji chubanshe, 1986.

The Literary Consumption of Actors in Seventeenth-Century China

Sophie Volpp

Among the luxury goods traded by the elite during the late Ming and early Qing were actors.[1] Not only individual actors but entire troupes were bestowed on friends, bequeathed to relatives, or sold. Their circulation served to create and maintain networks of social exchange, in much the same manner as did gifts of fine ceramic wares, calligraphic scrolls, and ancient bronzes. The cultural prestige of the actor as a luxury good was, in turn, predicated on a highly refined discourse of connoisseurship, typified by the theater aficionado Pan Zhiheng's 潘之恒 (1556–1622) disquisitions on the art of acting, which were collected in a volume entitled *Chongding xinshang pian* 重定欣賞篇 (Recompiled texts on connoisseurship; published between 1600 and 1640).[2] In this chapter, I discuss the social significance of the connoisseurship of the actor and examine the exchange of actors and poems among a rarified stratum of the mid-seventeenth-century elite.

My analysis focuses on poems in praise of the actor Xu Ziyun 徐紫雲 (?–1675?) written by a number of high-ranking officials and literary luminaries, such as Gong Dingzi 龔鼎孳 (1616–73), Wang Shizhen 王士禎 (1634–1711), and Mao Xiang 冒襄 (1609–92).[3] Xu Ziyun, a servant in the home of Mao Xiang, was for seventeen years romantically involved with the poet

Chen Weisong 陳維崧 (1626–82), one of the most famed lyricists of the Qing.[4] Chen's privileged status contrasts sharply with that of Xu, who under Qing law was not a commoner but a "base person" (*jian min* 賤民).[5] Yet their romantic attachment was feted by some of the most eminent statesmen and literary luminaries of the early Qing. Their poems in praise of Xu declare both their desire to emulate Chen and the impossibility of fulfilling that desire. These poems are of particular interest because their authors employ a homoerotic discourse to identify themselves as members of an elite circle of aesthetes.

The men who frequented the salon of Mao Xiang were from the highest stratum of the national elite, in terms of both political and literary status. Wu Weiye 吳偉業 (1609–72), for example, took first place in the metropolitan examinations of 1631 and was one of the most famed men of letters of his day. Gong Dingzi was successively president of the Board of Punishments (1664–66), the Board of War (1666–69), and the Board of Ceremonies (1669–73). The famed poet and literary critic Wang Shizhen served as police magistrate of Yangzhou in 1659 and became a frequent guest at Mao's nearby estate at Rugao during that period; he later became president of the Censorate and of the Board of Punishments.[6] Although the liaisons of such authors as Mao Xiang, Gong Dingzi, and Wu Weiye with the famed courtesans of the age have been much discussed, no scholar has yet examined the circulation of actors among them.[7]

This occlusion reflects in part the paucity of sources beyond the group of poems in tribute to Xu Ziyun. These poems are the most substantial surviving body of texts regarding any seventeenth-century actor, indeed any actor prior to the mid-Qing. Numerous poems in tribute to actors throughout the ages survive, and in the case of a more famous actor such as Gong Dingzi's traveling companion Wang Zijia 王紫稼 (1622–57), several sets of poems are still extant.[8] Mao's circle also wrote poems to three of Mao's other actors, Qinxiao 秦簫, Lingchu 靈雛, and Yangzhi 楊枝, commemorating birthdays and partings.[9] However, no other set of poems in tribute to an actor is comparable to the Ziyun corpus. Nor can such detailed documentation of the relationship between an actor and a literatus be found elsewhere.[10] In most poems in praise of actors from this period, the actors are identified only by surname, to which the suffix *lang* 郎 ("master" or "boy") is added; other than the troupe with which they might have performed, little is known about them.[11]

These poems in praise of Xu Ziyun, then, offer a rare opportunity to discuss the social significance of the circulation of actors among literati during the early Qing.[12] In elucidating the significance of these poems, I have employed two different approaches. First, I draw on the anthropological literature on the gift to speculate about the ways in which the circulation of the poems created or strengthened bonds among their authors and show how individual poets map themselves into these social relations by describing their passion for the boy. In the pages that follow, I not only examine Mao Xiang's gift of Xu Ziyun to Chen Weisong but also discuss the more abstract exchanges that take place as the body of the actor circulates implicitly through these poems. The extensive anthropological literature on the gift focuses largely on the ways in which the circulation of gifts creates networks of social connection that may be deployed instrumentally. But a less prominently developed path of argument has also illuminated the ways in which the circulation of gifts creates paths of emotional connection.[13] These poems of longing and desire allow us to examine how the exchange of poems as gifts establishes a topography of emotional indebtedness among the poets of Chen's circle. It is not only the implicit gift of the actor that creates such bonds; on a more immediate level, the poem is a material object whose exchange contributes to the instantiation of sociality. Given the governing assumptions of traditional Chinese poetics, the connection between poet and poem is so strong as to be metonymic. As the poems circulate among the members of this circle, the poets do as well, enchained by their inalienable relation to the poem as gift. These poems become, like the body of the actor, the site of concealed social relations; in them are inscribed the ties among their authors, Chen, and Ziyun.

Second, I examine the implications of these poets' claims to be "crazed with passion" (qing chi 情痴). As discussed below, qing is itself a paradoxical concept. The term itself eludes definition; it often functions metaphorically and seems to point to something else. In my analyses of the poems, I argue that this metaphorical operation of qing takes several forms: not only do the emotions professed by the speakers often index other emotions, but the speaker's emotions often exist only as analogue to those of Chen Weisong. The poets dramatize their own qing by likening it to that of Chen Weisong and write in empathic resonance with him. One consequence of qing's metaphorical operation is that it is difficult for us to say whether the desire expressed in these poems is homoerotic or, to use Eve Sedgwick's term, homosocial—that is, it is hard to determine which is more important, the expression of desire or the creation of social relations through the expression of shared desire.[14]

Although these texts are part of the seventeenth-century vogue for male love that scholars such as Vivien Ng, Bret Hinsch, and Giovanni Vitiello have discussed, the significance of the expression of homoerotic desire in this context needs to be carefully weighed.[15] Hinsch, Ng, and Vitiello view the new prevalence of texts that touch on male love as evidence of an increase in the prevalence and openness of such relations in the late Ming. However, there may be other reasons for the greater discursive visibility of male love. The ubiquity of qing as a theme in seventeenth-century literature and the strong interest in qi qing 奇情 (extraordinary qing) may in part account for the increased attention given to affective bonds between men in the literature of the period. Michel Foucault's "repressive hypothesis" (his suggestion that "the steady proliferation of discourses concerned with sex" that began in eighteenth-century Europe marked the onset of a degree of sexual repression previously unknown) counters the assumption that greater discursive exposure reflects a growth in actual practice.[16]

Moreover, it is difficult to ascertain the degree to which these poems attest to their author's desire for the actor, as opposed to the degree to which they fulfill the social obligation of flattering Chen's desire by echoing it. Did the authors of these poems act or intend to act on the desires expressed in them, or were they merely cultivating a shared bond with Chen Weisong? The poems furnished a kind of currency that was not necessarily tied to the gold standard of having experienced the actor's performance. Some of the poems were penned by intimates of Chen Weisong's who had a long acquaintance with the actor; others were probably written by men who had seen only the actor's portrait.

To what degree would these poems in tribute to Xu Ziyun have been considered transgressive? The answer depends largely on whose point of view we consult. The moralists who strewed warnings against liaisons with actors across the pages of notation books would certainly have condemned such declarations of desire for the actor.[17] Among the men who sojourned at Mao Xiang's estate in Rugao, however, connoisseurship of the theater—and of actors—was a mark of sophistication, even cultivation. In the paradoxical literary culture of the late Ming and early Qing, the transgression of boundaries of status and of conventional heteroerotic norms lent an extra cachet. To the degree that a form of desire was considered unconventional (*qi* 奇) and in opposition to traditional orthodoxies, it was thought authentic (*zhen* 真), and authentic passion (*zhen qing* 真情) was the most prized attribute in seventeenth-century literary culture.[18]

In these poems, Chen Weisong is frequently compared to the Tang poet Du Mu 杜牧 (803–52), who was often invoked during the late imperial period (and even during his own time) as the last of the romantics, a figure of disregard for social convention. The actor Xu Ziyun was himself named after the Tang courtesan Ziyun, with whom Du Mu was said to be smitten. According to the Tang dynasty author Meng Qi 孟棨, Du Mu's infatuation with Ziyun occasioned a legendary violation of social decorum. Du Mu was not invited to a banquet attended by the luminaries of Loyang society at which Ziyun was to perform. Because Du Mu's duty as a censor was to discipline other officials, the host had been afraid that his presence might dampen the party. But when Du Mu made it known that he wished to attend, the host had no choice but to include him. Du Mu did hinder the conviviality of the gathering, not so much because he imposed restraint on others as because he imposed none on himself. When he received the last-minute invitation, Du Mu was already drunk. Arriving at the party, he alienated the guests by simply staring at them. Du then asked the host to point out Ziyun, an act that enraged the other courtesans. Having offended everyone present, Du Mu got up and composed a poem commemorating his own discourteousness.[19]

In likening Chen to Du Mu, the men of Chen Weisong's coterie deftly legitimated the social impropriety of Chen's relationship with Xu Ziyun. Chen's eccentricity in engaging in a serious romance (as opposed to an evening's dalliance) with an actor was rendered socially acceptable by portraying him as "crazed with *qing*" (*qing chi*). The members of Mao's salon affirmed their common understanding not just through mutual appreciation of the boy's charms and the shared expression of desire for him but through a collective indulgence of Chen's passion for a servant. At the same time, the poets aspired to demonstrate that they, too, were fools for love (*qing chi*) by declaring their desire to enter into Chen and Ziyun's relationship.[20]

Theatricals at Mao Xiang's Estate

When Mao Xiang followed his father in refusing to serve the newly established Qing dynasty, they retired to a country estate, the Shuihui yuan 水繪園, northeast of Rugao and only a hundred miles from the capital in Nanjing. There Mao entertained the cultural magnates and political notables of the age. Since both Mao and his father claimed to be in reclusion, the Shuihui yuan was presented as a rustic retreat divorced from political concerns, a refuge from the vicissitudes of political life for the cosmopolitan libertines of Nanjing.[21] These poems about private theatricals make no reference to contemporary politics. Yet given the cast of characters who attended such entertainments, they could not by definition be so isolated. According to the contemporary observer Jiang Jingqi 蔣景祁 (1646–?), Mao Xiang and Chen Weisong's father, Zhenhui 陳貞慧 (1605–56), spent their entire family fortunes entertaining men of reputation (ming shi 名士).[22] This statement is no doubt an exaggeration, but it points to the importance of such entertainments in fostering political connections.

Mao's entertainment of prominent members of the political and cultural elite featured his prized troupe of actors. His descendant Mao Heting 冒鶴亭 (1873–1959) wrote:[23]

From all four directions, the guests arrived as though they were returning home, men such as the sons and brothers of friends from the Donglin 東林, Jishe 幾社, and Fushe 復社 parties. . . . Mao Xiang would earnestly detain his guests, bringing out his actors to entertain them.[24] The actors included Xu Ziyun, Yangzhi, Lingchu, and Qinxiao, but Yunlang's [Xu Ziyun's] artistry and looks were superior to those of his peers, and people today still praise the everlasting love that he shared with Chen Qinian 陳其年 [Weisong]. (QYLS, p. 958)

The Donglin party and its successors, the Jishe and Fushe, were loosely organized political coalitions, formed in part for the advancement of civil service examination candidates.[25] These political societies were repeatedly subjected to purges. Chen Weisong's grandfather, Yuting 陳于廷, an influential member of the Donglin, and his father, Zhenhui, a key member of the Fushe, were victims of such purges. His grandfather, a censor noted for his frank words against the government, lost his post after displeasing Ruan Dacheng 阮大鍼, the notorious henchman of the eunuch Wei Zhongxian 魏忠賢.[26] His father was thrown into prison after denouncing Ruan's corruption, and according to Mao Heting, Mao Xiang spent several thousand taels of gold to have him released (*QYLS*, p. 959).[27] In stating that adherents of the Donglin, Jishe, and Fushe were frequent guests in Rugao, Mao Heting was indicating that his ancestor had regaled all the men of note on the "right side" of the factional politics of the period—the side that initially suffered at the hands of the eunuch Wei Zhongxian but won in the courts of public opinion.

As Mao Heting suggests, the social and sexual circulation of actors in this world of private theatricals helped Mao Xiang affirm his connections with the members of these political societies. The Xu Ziyun poems owe their genesis in part to Mao Xiang and Chen Weisong's position at the center of the most rarified stratum of the mid-century elite, which made the men of the age anxious to establish social connections with them. Although these poems testify to the social pleasure of expressing desire for the actor, they testify even more to the pleasure of expressing membership in a community centered around Chen Weisong and, perhaps more important, his powerful patron Mao Xiang.

Chen Weisong was the son of one of the most privileged aristocrats of Jiangnan.[28] His father was known as one of Jiangnan's "Four Lords" (*si gongzi* 四公子). The "Four Lords"—the others were Mao Xiang, Fang Yizhi 方以智, and Hou Fangyu 侯方域—were distinguished not only for their aristocratic birth and literary talent but also for a combination of political loyalism and romantic dissipation unique to the last decades of the Ming.[29] Among the loyalists gathered in the southern capital of Nanjing, they were eminent and active within the Donglin party and set the tone in the pleasure quarters of Qinhuai, where they found sanctuary among the most famous courtesans and actors of the age.[30]

Chen Weisong was eminently poised for an illustrious literary career because of his father's friendships with such men as Mao Xiang and Wu Weiye. Wu Weiye tutored the young Weisong in poetry and did much to publicize his talent by proclaiming him one of the rising poets of the southeast.[31] When Chen Zhenhui died, Mao Xiang invited Chen Weisong to live at his estate while studying for the examinations.[32] The backing of this powerful patron positioned Chen among men of great influence. Yet despite Mao's patronage, Chen encountered great difficulty in obtaining a civil service position. Like his father before him, Chen passed only the *shengyuan* examinations, repeatedly failing subsequent attempts at the provincial level although he tried until the age of 52.[33] Until the age of 53, his only government employment was a post in Nanyang, provided for him in 1669 by Mao Xiang's friend Gong Dingzi.

In 1679, when Chen was 53 years old, he sat for the *boxue hongci* 博學鴻詞, a special set of examinations sponsored by the Kangxi emperor as a means of recruiting talented members of the Han Chinese literati and, in particular, of co-opting Southern intellectuals into the Qing government in Beijing.[34] Although a number of eminent scholars declined the opportunity to participate in these examinations out of continuing loyalty to the Ming, it was primarily the men of the older generation that resisted most strongly. The calligrapher Fu Shan 傅山 (1607–84), in his seventies at the time of the examination, journeyed to Beijing so as not to offend a powerful patron, yet once there, claimed to be too ill to sit for the exams.[35] Members of Chen's circle such as Deng Hanyi 鄧漢儀 (1617–89) and Sun Zhiwei 孫枝蔚 (1620–87), who were only somewhat younger, did participate.[36] Chen's generation could not ignore the fact that the examinations constituted a test of loyalism, but they were also enticed by the examination's prestige as a cultural event, for the *boxue hongci* drew scholars from all over the nation together to exchange ideas and provided an occasion for the first large-scale literary gathering and scholarly exchange since the Qing conquest.[37] Chen had not yet begun his career, and the examinations offered him an excellent opportunity. After passing the examinations, Chen began work on the compilation of the history of the Ming dynasty, a project that had stalled until successful candidates in the *boxue hongci* were assigned to the project. Chen died four years later, when his career as an official had just begun.

Chen's repeated failures in the examinations prior to the *boxue hongci* left him without means but with plenty of leisure, and he became a permanent house guest at Mao Xiang's estate at Rugao, spending years there preparing for the exams that he repeatedly failed. After each failure, not daring to venture home, he returned to Rugao, where he benefited from Mao's indulgence. The size of Chen's corpus of song-lyrics testifies not only to his talent but to a life spent at leisure in the world of private theatricals; he was one of the most prolific writers of song-lyrics during the late imperial period.[38]

More important for our story, Mao also gave Chen Weisong the actor Xu Ziyun as his personal servant during Chen's sojourns at Rugao. When he met Chen in 1658, Ziyun was in his teens, some fifteen years younger than Chen.[39] One of the most cherished performers in the acting troupe Mao kept to entertain his friends, Ziyun was famed for his singing and his playing of the flute. He was already an actor before he entered Mao's service, although it is not clear where he had performed. Nor is it known how Ziyun came to be in Mao's possession.

Chen did not own Ziyun, and the relationship was permitted to continue, it seems, only at Mao's pleasure. When in 1668 Chen and Ziyun left Rugao for Beijing without daring to inform Mao, the elopement caused a small scandal. On the way to Beijing, to make matters more awkward, the couple accidentally met Mao's son Danshu 冒丹書 (b. 1639). When the pair reached Beijing, Gong Dingzi, who was at the time president of the Board of War, wrote to Mao to intercede on their behalf:

Xu Ziyun followed Chen and they are very happy together, but he feels uneasy because he did not inform you when they left. On the way they met Qingruo 青若 [Danshu]; this news must have reached you. My old friend, I know that because of your capacity for deep feeling you have cared for others more deeply than for yourself your whole life long. You must care for (lian 憐) Qinian [Weisong] more than you care for Xu Ziyun, so you certainly will not want to punish him after the fact. (QYLS, p. 968)

This episode is often cited as proof of Mao's largesse toward Chen and Ziyun. Han Tan 韓菼 (1637–1709), a friend of Mao's who later became chancellor of the Hanlin Academy and president of the Board of Ceremonies, added in a note to his poem "Lamenting the Death of Zheng Jun 徵君 [Mao Xiang]" that Mao "had a servant whom he loved who was led away by a guest, but he never asked about it, and treated him even better afterwards" (QYLS, p. 969). Gong Dingzi's reasoning, "You must care for Qinian [Chen Weisong] more than you care for Xu Ziyun, so you certainly will not want to punish him after the fact" is especially striking. The implication seems to be that Chen is the guilty party and that Ziyun, since he was of base status—indeed, the property of the Mao household—was not responsible for the elopement. Yet Gong also speaks of Mao's affection for the actor in the same breath that he speaks of his affection for his best friend's son. Ziyun was not simply a plaything. He was a beloved member of the household.

Ziyun died in Yixing, Chen's ancestral home. Mao Heting suspects that he died at the beginning of the fourth month of 1675. Among the original drafts of Chen's poems, one mourning Ziyun, "Moved by Thoughts of the Past on Tomb-Sweeping Day" ("Qing ming gan jiu" 清明感舊), had a note attached to it in Chen's hand: "At this time Yun had recently passed away." Chen attached twenty poems by his friends on the subject of Yun's death.

The deletion by Chen's brother, the editor of the printed edition of Chen's works, of the note about Yun's death suggests that Chen's family was not as accepting of the relationship as were Chen's friends (*QYLS*, p. 971).

Although the actor married, the marriage seems to have had little impact on his relationship with Chen—at least to judge from the poems by Chen's friends. Chen took a concubine several years after his wife died. At the time, Chen was with Ziyun in Zhongzhou. The concubine gave birth to a son in 1676, but when the son died two years later, her relationship with Chen ended. In 1682 Chen died in the capital, mourned by Mao Xiang, who had buried Chen's father as well.

Touchable Untouchables: The Social Status of Actors

To understand the extraordinary nature of these poetic tributes to the affair between Chen and Ziyun, we must recall that the relationship between actors and literati was highly charged because of the gulf in social status between them. Members of a debased status group called the "music households" (*yue hu* 樂戶) that also included musicians, prostitutes, and other entertainers, actors were ranked as slaves, thought tantamount to prostitutes, and considered base people (*jian min*). As the historian Matthew Sommer has observed, the hereditary servile status of the *yue hu* incorporated an expectation of engagement in sex work.[40] Actors were not held to the norms of chastity and marriage expected of commoners, but neither were they accorded any of the privileges of commoners. Legal statutes prevented the participation of *yue hu* in the examination system and even sought to foreclose the social mobility of their descendants by forbidding their marriage to or their adoption by members of nonservile castes.[41] The repeated iterations of bans on the participation of actors in the examination system attests to the continual anxiety to maintain the distinctions between commoners and the members of debased status groups.

Although the low social status of actors troubled commentators on social mores, who warned against fraternization between literati and actors, it was precisely the servile status of actors that engendered the expectation that they were sexually available. As feminized men, actors were not women but in a class below them.[42] Matthew Sommer discusses a revealing case memorialized by the governor of Shaanxi in 1824 in which two male actors of female roles were gang-raped. Even though there was no evidence that the victims had previously been penetrated by other men, the governor argued that because they were actors of female roles they were inherently unchaste and could not be treated as "sons of good family" (*liang ren zidi* 良人子弟). The rapists' penalty was then reduced by one degree.[43]

The moralists who fretted over the association of literati with actors viewed actors as *femmes fatales* bent on social advancement. Intimacy between literati and actors was particularly threatening given the protean malleability of the actor's gender. It was feared that actors would first use their feminine wiles to ingratiate themselves with officials and then take advantage of these liaisons to enter the world of officialdom themselves, ultimately assuming a masculine and empowered position. Shen Defu 沈德符 (1578–1642), the author of the commonplace book *Wanli yehuo bian* 萬曆野獲編 (Unofficial harvest of the Wanli years), claimed that professional actors (*xiao chang* 小唱) worked for the government as spies, eavesdropping in order to gain information about confidential matters, and for this reason should be viewed with mistrust and apprehension. Shen assumed that any association between actors and literati would inevitably lead to sexual relations and that the goal of the actor in such a relationship was to gain an official position himself. Warning that these actors would desert their lovers once they had achieved their desired ends, Shen emphasized that they were professionally trained to simulate and deceive.[44] Of course, it was precisely the actor's ability to create illusion—his power over representation—that delighted the literati aficionado of the theater. The source of the literatus's pleasure was also the source of danger.

From the late Jiajing (1522–66) through the Wanli (1573–1620) periods, the practice of owning acting troupes and sponsoring performances at home became fashionable among members of the gentry.[45] The practice dates at least as far back as the Southern Song and, during the mid-Ming, had enjoyed some popularity among aficionados of the theater such as the dramatist Li Kaixian 李開先 (1502–68), but it was not until the late Jiajing that it became *de rigeur* to entertain one's guests with one's private troupe. As the theater historian Lu Eting has observed, when having one's own actors became the norm for the gentleman of means, many men of the gentry housed actors simply to fulfill a social obligation; ownership of a troupe no longer testified to a deep interest in the theater.[46] However, many of Mao's closest friends were true connoisseurs. Gong Dingzi had his own troupe. Hou Fangyu's family owned a famed troupe that his father had purchased in Wuchang and brought back to the ancestral home in Shangqiu in Henan. A renowned musician hired especially for the purpose trained Hou's troupe, but Hou's father also personally coached them.[47] Mao Xiang's troupe was much acclaimed. A musician named Chen Jiu, whose son was Ziyun's peer, trained Mao's actors, and Mao and Chen Weisong also instructed them (QYLS, pp. 961, 977).

Such privately owned acting troupes might be composed of musicians who were bought specifically for the purpose of forming a troupe and were then made to perform menial tasks within the household, or of servants who originally belonged to the household and were then trained to act.[48] A page who was trained as a musician would be an especially valued companion for a literatus away from home; he could function as a secretary, entertainer, or sexual partner. Chen Weisong's poems suggest that Xu Ziyun performed just such a range of functions.

At Mao Xiang's estate, celebrated courtesans and actors mingled with the highest-ranking statesmen and literary talents of the period. A most eminent stratum of the elite feigned ignorance of caste distinctions, displaying their social confidence as they privileged talent over social status. The extreme privilege of Mao Xiang's circle most likely helped to insulate its members from the social opprobrium that could be attached to the fraternization of literati and actors, an opprobrium to which the death of the actor Wang Zi-jia in 1657 at the hands of the censor Lin Senxian 林森先 (n.d.) attests.[49] In the empyrean realm of Chen's circle, the transgressive expression of desire for the actor—transgressive in that it violated boundaries of both gender and status—became in itself a form of social currency. As the historian Timothy Brook has remarked, "Public exposure was essential to the social purpose of homoeroticism in the late Ming. Like the buying of rare display-able artifacts, it marked off the truly rarefied at the pinnacle of elite status."[50] The libertines of Chen's coterie were so secure in their position that they could risk their social capital by consorting with actors. This ability to as-sume risk allowed them to leverage that social capital by making fraterniza-tion with those of low status a mark of distinction that signaled their mem-bership in a cosmopolitan stratum of the mid-seventeenth-century elite.

The transgression inherent in Chen's relationship with a servant was mitigated by the universal acknowledgment of Ziyun's talents as an actor. Yet even if the distinction in social status between Chen and Ziyun was not a cause of apprehension in Chen's circle, it was still not insignificant. It heightened Mao's largesse in permitting the relationship to take place, emphasized the extraordinary nature of Chen's passion and devotion, and gave Mao's and Chen's friends opportunity to display their liberality in applauding the relationship. In a quatrain from a series written in 1662 entitled *Chao chang ci* 怊悵詞 (Lyrics of sorrow in loss), Chen reveals his self-consciousness about the difference in his and Xu Ziyun's social status:

> When suddenly I saw him at the banquet, I immediately felt close
>   to him,
> All this life I will cherish our predestined love.
> Don't say that an actor is base from birth,
> He is [as talented as] Jiang Yan 江淹. (*QYLS*, p. 962)

In the first couplet, Chen justifies his flouting of social convention by stating that their affinity was ineluctable. Suggesting that talent, not birth, should determine social status, Chen compares Ziyun to the Southern Dynasties author Jiang Yan, said to be so gifted that flowers seemed to fall from his brush.[51] In another quatrain from the same collection, Chen writes of Ziyun:

> Though the aphrodisiac is about to run out, the wine is still
>   being poured,[52]
> How can I repay my soulmate (*zhi yin* 知音) in this life?
> I will smash my inkstick and slash the writing silk, saying no more.
> Please take care of yourself, for you have the heart of a man
>   of letters. (*QYLS*, p. 963)

Chen describes the actor as his soulmate (*zhi yin*), a gesture as dramatic as the destruction of the inkstick and the writing silk. The usage of this term is particularly striking, for the mutuality inscribed in the trope of the "ideal listener" also suggests a certain degree of interchangeability that is encapsulated in the ambiguity of the last phrase, "You have the heart of a man of letters." Given the elliptical quality of Chinese poetic language, it is unclear whether Chen speaks of himself as a man of letters who has given his heart to Yun, or whether he means that Xu Ziyun himself has a heart equal to that of a man of letters. The first reading both points to Chen's high status and politely lowers it by humbly phrasing his request. The second reading raises Ziyun's status, making him an honorary literatus. Both gestures simultaneously acknowledge and attempt to disavow the gulf in social status between Chen and Ziyun.

As the sensitivity to status in these two poems indicates, it was the dramatic distinction in social status between the two lovers that made their passion noteworthy. These poems may seem a celebration of Ziyun's gifts, but they also celebrate the extraordinary and singular quality of Chen's passion. Moreover, the poets document their own capacity for feeling as they echo Chen's presumed sentiments. Dramatizing themselves as enraptured spectators, the poets affect an ignorance of the gulf in social status between themselves and the actor. This ignorance amplifies their passion by making it seem as though it knows no social stricture.

Actors and Poems as Gifts

Many of the poems quoted in this chapter were written when Chen Weisong recruited his friends and acquaintances to pen poems as colophons for a portrait of Xu Ziyun (see Fig. 3.1). These poems were subsequently collected in a compilation entitled *Jiuqing tuyong* 九青圖詠 (Poems on the portrait of Jiuqing [Xu Ziyun]).[53] The collection features over 150 poems by seventy-odd poets, a veritable Who's Who of mid-century Jiangnan that included Du Jun 杜濬 (1611–87), You Tong 尤侗 (1618–1704), and Sun Zhiwei, as well as the poets discussed below: Mao Xiang, Mao's son Qingruo, Han Tan, Deng Hanyi, Wang Shizhen, Wang's brother Shilu 王士祿 (1626–73), Wu Zhaokuan 吳兆寬 (d. 1680), and Chen Hu 陳湖 (1613–75). The poets commemorated the great passion between Chen and Ziyun, flattering Chen as they expressed their envy and their desire to emulate him.

It is likely that many of these poets would have had no interest in praising Ziyun had it not been for his relation with Chen Weisong. If Ziyun was an addressee, Chen Weisong was the primary addressee. The two formed two points of a triangle, the author inscribing himself as the third point as the three sides of the triangle became vectors of desire. To elucidate this geometry, let us consider the primary example of the exchange of the actor between elite men: Mao Xiang's gift of the actor to Chen Weisong.

Mao Xiang supposedly detected the budding romance between Chen and Xu Ziyun when he spied them flirting beneath the plum trees of his gardens. Niu Xiu 鈕秀 (d. 1704), a friend of Chen's, described Mao's discovery of the affair:

Fig. 3.1 The title of the painting, "Chu yu tu" 出浴圖 (Portrait on leaving the baths), cross-dresses Ziyun as Yang Guifei, the consort of Tang Emperor Xuanzong. Despite the title, Xu Ziyun is not depicted as the curvaceous Yang Guifei emerging seductively from the baths of the Huaqing pools. He is, however, portrayed in a coy and seductive pose: dressed in an elaborately figured robe that falls open loosely at the neck, he sits with one hand on his chin, a bare leg extended. A flute is placed next to him.

Mao Xiang cherished (*ai* 愛) his [Chen Weisong's] talent, and invited him to come to his country villa amidst the plum blossoms. There was a servant named Xu Ziyun, who was fetching in looks and had an excellent voice, and Mao Xiang commanded him to serve Chen in his study. As soon as Chen Weisong saw him, his spirit was moved. At that time the plum trees at the villa were in full blossom, and Chen Weisong and Xu Ziyun strolled beneath the trees in their dusky fragrance and scattered shadows.

Mao Xiang saw them. He feigned anger, had Xu Ziyun bound and pretended that he would have him beaten. Chen Weisong was at a loss as to what to do, but then realized that a word from Mao Xiang's mother was all that was needed to release Ziyun. It was approaching dusk. He went and knelt for a long time outside her door. When her maid opened it, he said, "I have an urgent matter. I ask that your Ladyship utter one jade-like word. Unless her Ladyship agrees, I will not rise." . . . Then he related the matter of Ziyun.

After a while, a maid emerged and said, "You may rest now. Mao Xiang has received his mother's order, and has already agreed not to punish Ziyun. But he must receive 100 poems on the subject of the plum blossom from you, to be completed this night, and then he will send Ziyun to be your personal servant." Chen Weisong was greatly pleased and gathered his robes and returned to his quarters, where he lit a lamp and moistened his ink, and set to work chanting poems (*kuyin* 苦吟) until the dawn. When the 100 quatrains were finished, he sent them to Mao Xiang. Mao Xiang read them aloud, beating out the rhythm. Then he laughed and sent Ziyun to Chen Weisong.[54]

The possibility that Ziyun might be punished severely clearly frightened Chen Weisong, who immediately sought the aid of the one person in the household whose word Mao Xiang had to heed: his mother. Although Niu Xiu claimed that Mao merely feigned anger, we cannot know whether Mao pretended to be angry simply to obtain the forfeit of poems or whether this was a later interpretation intended to make light of the situation. Certainly, Mao's request that Chen compose 100 poems on the plum blossom was not innocent. The penalty required Chen to lyricize the scene of his transgression. Moreover, by demanding that Chen Weisong work through the night to send him the poems by dawn, Mao Xiang reminded him of the imbalance of power between patron and poet. Mao simultaneously assigned Chen a schoolboy's punishment and challenged him not to succumb to doggerel as he repeatedly revisited the same theme. At the same time, the forfeit of poems allowed Mao Xiang to make light of the gravity of his gift of the actor to Chen Weisong. It eased Chen's indebtedness elegantly, granting him dignity by allowing him to win the actor.

Mao's refined wit emerges not only in the supposed frivolity of his request but in the pretense of equivalence between actor and poems. The poems became an initiatory gift that allowed Mao to make a countergift. Chen's sending of the poems to Mao created a path for the circulation of the actor, who traveled back toward Chen in a direction counter to the poems. The potential exchange of the actor for a poem—that is, of the attentions of the actor for a poem—is a current that runs through all these poems. In this regard, the poems unwittingly echo the initiatory exchange between Chen and Mao.

Just as Chen won sexual rights to Xu Ziyun by submitting poems to Mao, the poets jestingly imply that they would like to borrow these rights in the poems they sent to Chen. These requests for Xu's favor were addressed to Chen, rather than Mao. However, it is difficult to ascertain the sense in which Xu belonged to Chen. Even though Mao had given Xu to Chen as his personal servant within the Mao household, he was not free, for example, to leave the estate without Mao's permission, as the uproar following Xu and Chen's elopement to Beijing attests.

If the poets of Chen's circle write in emulation of him, they also register sentiments of loss and longing in emulation of Mao Xiang in anticipation of the generous deferral of their own desire. Mao gave his beloved servant Xu Ziyun to one whom he believed needed him more. His subsequent poems to Chen articulate longing for both Chen and Xu. By granting Xu to Chen, he created a pair who functioned as a unit without him. In Mao's poems, he attempts to reinsert himself as the third corner in a triangle. Wittingly or not, the poets of this coterie empathically re-create this geometry, registering *their* sentiments of loss as they assert their desire to become Chen's rivals. The presumed sentiments of the two men on the exchange of the actor are conflated as the poets model themselves after both parties simultaneously.

In these poems, the experience of reading about the actor is often compared to that of meeting the actor himself. The poets repeatedly complain that literary representations of the actor stir their desire but do not satisfy it. The ensuing longing inspires poems in tribute to the actor—as though putting poems of desire into circulation might induce the actor to travel back toward the poet along the path traversed by the poems. If the experience of reading about the boy is not enough, neither is the experience of seeing the boy in person sufficient to satiate the poet's claimed desire. Both literary consumption and visual consumption fuel the circulation of more poems. If the poet could possess the actor, the actor would no longer need to circulate, and the poet would no longer be connected to the other poets through the reciprocal exchange of representations of the object of desire. At a more elemental level, if his desire could be satisfied, it would no longer be *qing*.

It was because Xu Ziyun was so cherished that Mao's gift of him to Chen established him as a channel for the flow of sentiment between Mao and Chen themselves.[55] Mao's sacrifice of his beloved actor not only testified to his love for Weisong but created a path along which future expressions of sentiment flowed. The other members of Mao's circle may have viewed Ziyun only as an object of connoisseurship. But given their empathic resonance with Mao's and Chen's sentiments for the actor, the actor became a channel of emotional connection among the men of this coterie as well.

The Materiality of Poems: The Metonymic
Circulation of People and Things

The community of poets defined by *Poems on the Portrait of Jiuqing* is delineated by the flow of poems as gifts, gifts that create networks of social relations. The poem, however, is not simply an object; it is an artifact of a person, an extension of the author that circulates in his or her stead. This metonymic relation between persons and poems accounts for the peculiar status of poems among other types of artistic production. The poem is an archetypal example of the distinction Bronislaw Malinowski made long ago between ordinary commodities and valuables that can be exchanged only for other valuables and in specifically encoded contexts.[56] We might consider for a moment the obvious and yet suggestive fact that individual poems were not meant to be sold.[57] Although there are indications that individual poems, like paintings, were sold for "brush-wetting silver" and then circulated as the compositions of the purchaser, the exchange of poems for money was certainly covert. Individual poems (as opposed to anthologies or collections) were primarily exchanged between individuals and exchanged only for other poems or, occasionally, for paintings.

These distinctive features of the poem as an object of exchange stem from the governing assumption of Chinese poetics: the poem is a spontaneous emanation of what is "intensely on the mind," an overflow of powerful emotion.[58] Not only the poem but also the landscape that the poet witnesses and inscribes in the poem are viewed as metonymic extensions of the poet; the poem is seen as a material artifact of the poet's state of mind. These suppositions may not describe the actual circumstances under which poems were composed, but they did govern traditional Chinese codes of reading, which assumed a metonymic relation between poet and poem that rendered the social circulation of poems equivalent to the social circulation of people.[59] It is not merely the body of the actor that implicitly travels the networks established by these poems; the poets themselves do. Poetry was central to the political and social life of the Chinese elite because poems could circulate socially in a person's stead; think, for example, of the tactics used by civil service examination candidates during the Tang to have their poems presented to examiners in advance of the exams.

Both actors and poems possess a singular sociability; neither is meant to be enjoyed by one man alone. The poem's relation to the poet is, in fact, analogous to the relation of the actor to his patron—although intimately attached to his patron, the actor by definition must circulate socially. Both the actor Xu Ziyun and the poems in tribute to him became channels for the flow of sentiment between Chen Weisong, Mao Xiang, and the other members of their literary community as they circulated. This flow of sentiment is expressed as an empathic resonance among the poets, a resonance that leads to the composition of more poems as a poet is moved to write about Chen and Xu Ziyun's relationship by the poems he reads about it. The representations of the actor become fruitful and multiply, as each poem acts as a magnet that draws more poems into the network. Mao's and Chen's sentiments ripple through the community in ever-widening circles. The poems of Mao's and Chen's friends send the sentiments of the principals back to the center, so that the expression of Mao's and Chen's longing for the actor is echoed by the poets in a kind of call and response. This empathic resonance between the principals' sentiments of loss and longing and those voiced by the poets underscores the sense of lack of fulfillment that is so central to the self-dramatizing expressions of *qing* in the literary culture of this period.[60]

Empathic Resonance: Fools for Love

There is a tantalizing lack of clarity as to the nature of Chen and Xu Ziyun's relationship. The sources employ highly allusive language. A glance at a description of the relationship written by a guest of Mao Xiang at Rugao, the renowned poet Jiang Pingjie 蔣平階 (n.d.), illustrates the difficulties for the modern reader of pinpointing its nature. The description below is drawn from Jiang's preface to Chen's *Lyrics of Sorrow in Loss*, written when Chen and Xu Ziyun were separated in 1662.

Their affair of "the shared peach" and "the rent sleeve" has lasted four years,[61] but although they have moved each other with subtle words, they have never gone astray.[62] In this way Weisong cast off previous lovers and shed no tears[63] and still loved Yunlang [Xu Ziyun] increasingly, even though he commandeered the duke's chariot.[64] This can truly be called a level of favor deeper than that given consorts and palace ladies or enjoyment greater than one has in a beautiful woman. (*QYLS*, 962)

    The multiple allusions Jiang employs seem to work at cross-purposes; some suggest physical consummation and others imply that the relationship was simply an emotional attachment. Such phrases as "the shared peach," "the rent sleeve," and "they cast off previous lovers and shed no tears" clearly filiate Chen and Ziyun to historical precedents that describe the love of emperors and aristocrats for male favorites. They suggest that Weisong abandoned all his previous favorites (whether male or female, we do not know) to engage in a monogamous relationship with Ziyun, that he ignored conventional boundaries of status in his consideration for him, and that even though Ziyun took advantage of Chen's besotted affection to demand greater and greater privileges, Chen only increased his devotion to the actor. Yet the phrase "they have never gone astray," an allusion to the Tang dynasty tale "The Story of Yingying" 鶯鶯傳, suggests that Chen and Ziyun, despite their love for each other, had never had sex. This seeming contradiction may or may not have posed a problem for the original readers of this text. It is easier for us as modern readers to know how such terms functioned in the original sources than what seventeenth-century authors meant when they deployed them as allusions.[65]

The elusive quality of the term *qing*, which seventeenth-century authors used to describe sentiments of desire, love, and affection, compounds the problem of how we ought to understand the relationship between Chen and Ziyun. The term *qing* seems omnipresent in the literature of the late Ming. The early seventeenth-century author Feng Menglong 馮夢龍 wrote in the preface to his massive compendium of tales about *qing, Qing shi leilüe* 情史類略 (A topical outline of the history of *qing*): "Would that all those who have *qing* could gather together to speak of its Dharma"; as Anthony Yu has quipped, the efflorescence of seventeenth-century literature about *qing* seems to have been written in answer to Feng's call.[66]

An enigmatic term, *qing* can be translated as lust, passion, desire, longing, love, emotion, affect, feeling, disposition, or sentiment.[67] There is something quintessentially metaphorical about *qing*; it always points to something else. This is true even of the range of emotions that the term incorporates. When *qing* seems to indicate love, it is quickly glossed as lust.[68] The way in which *qing* seems always to indicate absence in presence is also characteristic of *qing*'s relation to its object, for the object is often so undeserving as to seem a placeholder or a metaphor for something else. The expression of *qing* ultimately speaks not so much to the desirability of the object but to the passion of the desiring subject. One can be crazed with love (*qing chi*) or a fool for love (*qing zhong* 情□), but there is no syntactical way of using *qing* in conjunction with a direct object—one cannot *qing* someone or something else. This grammatical inflexibility points to the self-reflexive, self-consuming quality of *qing*. More than anything else, *qing* desires its own perpetuation, and so it remains perennially unsatisfied. The term speaks more to the feeling subject than to the object of desire or affection.

The capacity of *qing* to confer social distinction was in direct proportion to its elusiveness, and it became the most sought after quality among the seventeenth-century literary elite. In the context of these poems, the elusiveness of *qing* itself contributes to a sense of the elusiveness of the actor as the beloved. The poems pay tribute to Chen's relation with Ziyun by expressing desire for the actor, but at the same time, they acknowledge that the actor is bound to Chen and can never be theirs. The poets, then, are nostalgic for the lost object of desire even in advance of the articulation of desire for him.[69]

Maram Epstein, Martin Huang, Wong Siu-kit, Li Wai-yee, and Anthony Yu have all engaged in extensive historical overviews of the polyvalent significances of the term *qing*.[70] My intention in this chapter is to illuminate a quality of *qing* that is often noted but seldom explicitly discussed: empathy. Empathy is in fact at the heart of the self-proclaimed "historian of *qing*" Feng Menglong's own definition of the term. In his first preface to *The Anatomy of Qing*, Feng describes his own *qing* in terms of his capacity for empathy:

Since I was a young man, I have been burdened by being crazed with *qing* (*qing chi*). To my friends and acquaintances, I gave all I had. I would be concerned about them through times of good fortune and bad. If I heard that someone was unusually destitute or suffering grave injustice, even if I didn't know him, I would seek to provide for him. Sometimes my efforts would not be sufficient, and then I would sigh for days on end, tossing and turning in the middle of the night, unable to sleep.[71]

The gatha Feng cites in his first preface also points to the centrality of empathy in his understanding of *qing*: "With *qing*, the distant become intimate; without *qing*, the intimate become distant."[72]

The empathic quality of the Ziyun poems is brilliantly encapsulated in Jiang Pingjie's preface to Chen's *Lyrics of Sorrow in Loss*, quoted above. The poems describe Chen's despair on being parted from Xu Ziyun in 1662. Jiang depicts his own grief on reading them:

At this time the autumn waters were about to be moved by winter winds, and the cicadas of the New Year would soon begin to hum. So Chen quit the farewell banquet and said that he would return home. He left his seat and prepared to depart. The winds on the river blow for over a thousand miles. How could they [Chen and Xu Ziyun] be expected to meet again? Thus we have these poems on parting, tunes that exhaustively describe the feelings of troubled hearts about to part. How could I not respond with emotion—and how could one possibly overcome such emotions? My heart grieved as I read these poems, and there was no way to relieve my sorrow. I beat the rhythm of these poems and composed poems in response, but the poems I wrote only increased my sorrow. (*QYLS*, p. 962)

Jiang describes the relation between Chen's poems and his own as an empathic echoing. Moved by Chen's poems describing his despair at being parted from Ziyun, Jiang is inspired to write his own. In so doing, he amplifies Chen's sentiments. But although he composes poems as a means of catharsis, "to relieve his sorrow," in fact the poems only increase it.

Jiang dramatizes his own capacity to feel passion (*qing*) in part by suggesting that his passion has been evoked by Chen's own. The object of that passion, Xu Ziyun, is largely occluded. Given that many of the poets indicate that they had never met the actor, the sentiments of loss and longing that pervade these poems are striking. The poems often speak more to the poet's relationship with Chen than the poet's desire for the actor. The poet's desire echoes Chen's; his empathic resonance with Chen's desire is another instance of the metaphorical nature or operation of *qing*. Although the poems are ostensibly stimulated by desire for the actor, since they are generated in resonance with Chen's sentiments, the actor himself becomes insignificant. The primary emotional connection is not between author and actor, but between the author and the poets who have inspired him.

But if the poet's nostalgia regarding the loss of an actor he has never met is expressed in empathy with and emulation of Chen, it is also expressed in *rivalry* with him. This rivalry is in fact quite companionable. Its primary motivation seems to be to compliment Chen Weisong rather than truly to contest his place. The poems might be compared to those poems men wrote to their friends congratulating them on the purchase of a concubine or lamenting the death of one. They play with the confusion caused by the mixed sentiments of empathy and rivalry.

Mao and his friends tease Chen by attempting to enter his relationship with Xu Ziyun. Wang Shizhen, for example, wrote a poem to Xu Ziyun subtitled "Written as Qinian [Weisong] in Jest" ("Xi dai Qinian" 戲代其年). (The character for "in jest" [*xi*] here is also the character for "theater" and thus carries the association of role-playing.) Wang Shizhen also baited Chen by asking if he would lend Xu Ziyun to him "to hold his inkstand" (*QYLS*, 967). (The phrase implies that Ziyun would function as a "servant in the study," a well-known synonym for a sexual plaything.) Wang Shizhen's elder brother, Shilu, posed as Chen's rival as he reproached Chen for being unworthy of his primary claim on the actor:

> As my dream fades and I wake from a drunken night, I ache
> with longing,
> Yet what can I do but stand before his portrait in hopes of
> seeing him.
> On the day we parted at the banquet, I could not find him,
> I am surprised that even the censor Du was not as outrageous
> as you. (*QYLS*, pp. 965, 968)[73]

Wang Shilu indicates his chagrin at having to settle for a representation of the actor rather than the actor himself. Both the dream and the painting only add to his longing. At the moment of greatest promise, Wang claims, he could not find Ziyun at the banquet. He has inevitably been defeated in his rivalry with Chen—for Chen has not only inherited Du Mu's mantle but superseded him.

Wang Shilu and Chen Weisong participated in a poetry circle in Yang-zhou during the 1660s that included the editor Deng Hanyi. (Deng also lived at Mao Xiang's home in 1670 and served on Gong Dingzi's staff as a secretary from time to time.)[74] Like Wang Shilu, Deng represents the banquet as a site of contestation for the actor's favors. He, too, declines to compete with Chen, declaring that he dares not admit his desire for Ziyun in public:

> I listen to his clear song the whole night long,
> Dressed in red sleeves, he is even more pleasing.
> I've been beguiled by him since that time of confusion
> among the flowers in the mist,
> But dare not call to him at the banquet. (*QYLS*, p. 961)

Deng declares that although something happened at a previous enter-tainment between himself and "the flowers in the mist" (Ziyun and the other entertainers), he dare not signal Ziyun publicly. This lyric may function as a means of communication with Ziyun, the ultimate recipient of the collection. But more likely, the poem provided a means of flattering Chen, the compiler, as the author conceded his defeat in advance. Deng's admission of failure fashions a bond between himself and Chen. His admission of a desire that is doomed to unfulfillment and thus nostalgic even in advance of its expression is phrased as though it were private, but it is in fact a public and sociable act.

Friends of Chen's who had likely never seen Ziyun participated in this social circulation of polite admissions of unfulfilled desire. Wu Zhaokuan's poem, like Deng Hanyi's, registers a wistful longing for Ziyun. His longing is a longing doubly deferred, however, for he seems to know Ziyun only through his portrait and the lyrics in tribute to him:

> I love to light the lamp and read the songs about Jiuqing [Xu Ziyun].
> The sounds of his song ripple through the air, stirring the figured
>   gauze of his robe.
> Unfurling the painting in the spring breeze, I see his face for
>   the first time.
> What can I do when he is so far away, separated by the clouds of Chu.
> (QYLS, pp. 965, 984)

Wu's first line reveals that Chen circulated the painting and the previously submitted poems to Wu for his comment, a comment that took poetic form. Wu wryly registers the fulfillment of a social duty. The redundancy of the expressions of desire for Ziyun recorded in this collection indicates that they were polite concessions to social and poetic convention (although such politesse might not have precluded stronger emotions). Although Wu has never seen Ziyun in person, he constructs a ground of shared interest with Chen and Mao by posing as a rival; he forms a bond with them by envying their possession.[75] One belongs to this community by expressing longing for the actor, by voicing a desire that is inevitably already deferred.[76] Once again, we are reminded that the object of desire is secondary. What is primary is the empathic resonance between elite men.

Homosocial Homoerotics

If empathic resonance is the principle behind these poets' emulation of Chen, we ought to consider the ways in which desire infuses the act of emulation, in which desire *to be* another and desire *for* another may often become confused. Building on the arguments of Claude Lévi-Strauss and Gayle Rubin regarding the "traffic in women," feminist theorist Eve Sedgwick has argued that although the exchange of a woman between two men serves to instantiate sociality through the common expression of heteroerotic desire, the bonds between men created by this exchange also open channels for the expression of desire between the men themselves.[77] Under the aegis of the homophobia that Sedgwick sees as constitutive of modern patriarchy, this desire is viewed as social rather than sexual; for this reason, Sedgwick labels it "homosocial." The Ziyun poems provide an interesting contrast to Sedgwick's model, for in them homoerotic desire is not suppressed. Instead, the social sharing of these articulations of desire for the boy becomes potentially confused with the desire of one literatus for another. As René Girard has argued, a desire for the object of another's affection may in fact be a means of displacing desire for that person.[78] Such a desire will always be thwarted, for it is misdirected in rivalry. In these poems, the expression of desire for the actor facilitates the expression of longing among elite men. Although it is impossible to reconstruct the significance of these sentiments of longing, the triangulation of desire through the actor Xu Ziyun, who is inherently a sexualized figure, implicitly eroticizes and sexualizes the bonds between Chen and the poets.

These bonds are not formed simply out of the expression of mutual desire for the boy; rather, they arise through the communal indulgence of Chen's extraordinary passion for a servant. The flouting of conventional boundaries of status is as important as the transgression of heteroerotic norms in fashioning these homosocial bonds. The two gestures need not, of course, be defined as mutually exclusive; the transgression of boundaries of status may itself have been eroticized. The seeming ignorance of status boundaries in these poems also permits the longing for the actor to become confused with a longing for the literatus. Mao Xiang's poem "Missing Qinian [Weisong]" ("Huai Qinian" 懷其年), written when Chen Weisong took Xu Ziyun back to Chen's natal home of Yixing in 1666, seamlessly slides between longing for Chen and for Xu Ziyun:

> I think of you in my illness,
> And call repeatedly for Yunlang [Xu Ziyun].
> Although the person I cherish is far away, still I see him,
> Longing for you intensely, I believe that I hear your voice.
> (*QYLS*, p. 969)

The title of the poem is "Missing Qinian," and yet the poem speaks of Mao's longing for Xu Ziyun. There is a certain slippage between Chen and Xu Ziyun; Mao does not distinguish between the types of longing he feels for them. This slippage is noteworthy in that the types of sentiments that Mao would express toward Chen, his best friend's son, would ordinarily be quite different from those he would have for the servant Xu Ziyun. The confusing equivalence between Chen and Xu Ziyun makes it seem as though Mao has entered the relationship as a third party.

In the following sequence of poems, written by Mao to Chen, Mao reminds Chen of his love for him by recalling his gift of the actor to him. Now it is Ziyun who has become the third point of a triangle. His insertion into the relations between Mao and Chen alters the character of the bond between them:

> At night I sent the servant boy to accompany you as you studied,
> I cherished my guest more than the most beautiful jade.
> When for six years you departed, my feeling was vast as the sea,
> When you meet him in the painting, he will ask after me.
>   (QYLS, pp. 970, 993)

> Chen's rare talent makes riot of the classics,
> Chen's a fool in love, as much of a fool as Yunlang.
> There is none on earth who knows you as I do,
> I gave him to you instead of sending him away. (QYLS, p. 985)

Mao loved Chen and therefore sent him the beloved Ziyun, setting in motion a merry-go-round of displacement. Longing or desire is triangulated through the actor: "When you meet him in the painting, he will ask after me." Ziyun becomes an alternative route for a current of sentiment between Mao and Chen. But Chen could also be seen as the alternative route for a current between Mao and Ziyun. If the object of desire were Chen, we would assume that Mao's love was not eroticized; if it were Ziyun, we would assume that it might be.

In the second poem, Mao modifies the statement he made in the first, "At night I sent the servant boy to accompany you as you studied," declaring: "I gave him to you instead of sending him away." Ziyun was Mao's property; in this poem he reminds Chen that the transfer created bonds of obligation and shared interest. Mao's gift to Chen bound Chen closer to Mao, just as a wife's selection of a concubine for her husband might help cement a sense of partnership between husband and wife. The triangular vectors of relation between poet, actor, and Chen do not simply describe the paths the actor as gift might travel. The nostalgic longing that these poets express suggests that these social relations are also mapped within the poet himself.[79]

That the expression of desire for the actor in these poems was a particularly encoded discursive practice becomes clear when we contrast it to the types of sentiments for the actor registered in other genres. In their letters, Mao and his friends exchange news of the actors' families and health. In a letter to Gong Dingzi, for example, Mao wrote: "Qinxiao is ill-fated and is already useless. This past spring, his face was thin as a needle. He repeatedly lay down and could not get up" (*QYLS*, p. 976). We would never find such sentiments in a poem about an actor. The contrast suggests that the expression of emotions of desire and rivalry within the poems constituted a kind of literary game.

Mao's son Qingruo composed a poem to accompany Ziyun's portrait that can be read as a comment on that game:

> My passion (*qing*) dies and rises again, though I myself am unaware
> Occasionally this passion ties me to thoughts of you
> If you want to understand my sorrow without end
> Just look at that wisp of light cloud (*yun* 雲). (*QYLS*, p. 970)

The poet states that he himself is unaware (*bu zizhi* 不自知) of the rise and fall of his passion; it moves involuntarily. It seems as though his passion needs no object. Rather, it rises and ebbs with a rhythm of its own, alighting on the boy only casually. Qingruo blames the actor for his heartbreak, but in a sophisticated twist, his description of Ziyun (literally, "Purple Cloud") as a "wisp of light cloud" renders the actor trivial and insignificant in comparison to the "sorrow without end" that he has inspired.

The seventeenth-century cult of *qing* made the expression of intense feeling a literary necessity; excess became the norm. The expression of desire in these poems is clearly indebted to a discourse of connoisseurship anchored in poetic convention. Although these poems play games with the conflation and confusion of homosocial bonds and homoerotic desire, we cannot know how firmly articulated the connections between discourse and practice were. We can safely surmise only that these authors desired to identify themselves as members of a community by speaking in this mode.

We ought also to keep in mind that although these poets voice homoerotic sentiments, it is conceivable that they merely flirt with the possibility of winning the actor's favors. Chen's poems were written in compensation for a transgression. But the other poets of the circle simply flirt with the notion of transgression. This was not a community of men united by sexual congress with the actor or even a community of men linked by desire for the actor. It was a community defined by the shared expression of disappointment at *not* being able to consummate longing for the actor. Although these poets employ a discourse of homoeroticism, since their expressions of desire always inscribe the impossibility of their satisfaction, they may well rest comfortably in the knowledge of that impossibility.

Self-Dramatizing Spectators

The album *Poems on the Portrait of Jiuqing* gained more poems as it circulated and its readers submitted testimonies to the charms of Ziyun's portrait and to their own capacity for *qing*. In submitting these poems to the regard and consumption of the group, the poets allowed their *qing* to become an object of connoisseurship. As they did so, they themselves became actors on a public stage. Ironically, they signal their cognizance of this position by dramatizing themselves as spectators. In the following excerpt from a lyric subtitled "to show to Mao Xiang" (*shi Mao Pijiang* 示冒辟疆), Chen Hu cynically observed that they did so by emulating Chen Weisong himself:

> . . . Chaste master Xu, aged fifteen or sixteen,[80]
> Wisps of black hair falling over his forehead, face like jade.
> I'm afraid that the Ziyun of yore could not equal you,
> All in the audience (*man zuo* 滿座) model themselves after
>   Du Mu in their lack of restraint . . . (*QYLS*, p. 961)[81]

Chen Hu portrays Chen Weisong's rivals as engaged in a mass mimicry of Du Mu. But since Chen Weisong is frequently referred to as Du Mu in these poems, it is in fact he whom they seek to emulate. Chen, rather than Xu Ziyun, is the true focus of their attention. Chen's passion becomes the object of the spectators' connoisseurship and the focus of their desire: their desire is not to be with Chen, but to *be* him.

Chen Hu inscribes a chain of viewing pleasure: as the audience watches the boy, the poet watches the spectators. The first three lines are devoted to connoisseurship of the boy; the last subjects the spectators themselves to evaluation. If the spectator usually believes himself unseen, Chen lets the poets of this coterie know that they are seen. And indeed, they seem to crave a witness. It is the desire for a witness that leads them to draw attention to their lack of restraint.

Although these spectators desire to stand, like the actor, on a public stage, they mimic not the actor but the missing ideal spectator. As the film critic Miriam Hansen observes, mimesis is one of the spectatorial pleasures, for it allows the spectator to stand on his or her own stage.[82] Mimesis, then, is inherently histrionic. We have noted that many of these poems are written in emulation of Chen and in empathic resonance with his desire for the actor. Mimesis leads the poet to dramatize himself in his empathic response to Chen's Weisong's sentiments.[83] Jiang Pingjie's preface described how he began to beat the rhythm of Chen's poems and spontaneously chanted his own poems in response to Chen's. Dramatizing themselves as spectators, the poets of Chen's coterie simultaneously watch the performance of Xu Ziyun (and Chen) on the main stage and perform spectatorship on a side stage.

Chen Hu places these spectators in a double bind: they can measure up neither to the model of the past, the Tang dynasty Du Mu, nor to the present incarnation of Du Mu, Chen Weisong himself. In both cases, these spectators are caught in the paradox of studied spontaneity. All parties vie to be the primary spectator, the man of unbridled passion, or *zhen qing*. Once unbridled passion comes to function as a sign of distinction, however, it becomes impossible to express it without self-consciousness.[84]

This poem comments on the motivations that shape the entire collection. It is the desire to be seen (and to be seen as a member of a particular group) that emerges most clearly in these poems. That is why they yield so persuasively to an analysis that considers questions of social distinction. But ironically, one could say that to a certain degree these poets also desire to remain unseen, in that the self-inscription of these poets is highly generic and lacking in particularity. In modeling themselves after Chen Weisong, for example, the poets ensure that whatever might be unique or specific to themselves or their desire for the boy remains unknown. This is why we shall never be able to locate the desire expressed in them on the continuum between the homosocial and homoerotic; the importance of empathic resonance in the generation of these poems renders it impossible to isolate a single author's desire from that of the collective.

Xu Ziyun's Wedding

Ziyun married around 1675, when he likely would have been close to thirty years old. As a wedding gift for Ziyun, Chen wrote a song-lyric to the tune *Ho xinlang* 賀新郎 (Congratulating the bridegroom). Niu Xiu noted that at the time of its composition, "Ziyun had been betrothed, and a date had been set for the wedding; Chen was dazed, as though he had suffered a loss." Niu concluded with the statement: "This lyric circulated quickly from one mouth to another, and those who heard it were bowled over by it."[85]

> I sip a little wine.
> I am pleased that this morning,
> Hairpins gleam in the silhouette of your tresses,
> Bobbing before the lamp.
> On the other side of the screen, laughter and chatter,
> As they announce that the sparrow hairpins are about to appear.[86]
> Once again I stealthily cast,
> A glance at Pan Yue.[87]
> I can't tell whether you are cock or hen,
> But when the wind lifts your robes,
> I furtively measure your feet.
> I send you off,
> To raise the bridal curtain on the marriage bed.
>
> For six years, staying in lonely inns, you were my intimate companion.
> Hardest to forget,
> Are the red grasses beside the pillow,
> The tears like flowers that we gently shed.
> Today, you will be wed,
> Wife follows husband in sinuous chant.
> Try your best,
> To act the role of a good husband.
> It's just that my gauze quilt is cold as iron,
> As I clutch my bamboo mat (tao sheng 桃笙),[88]
> It is as though dawn will never come.
> On my account,
> You must grieve no more. (QYLS, p. 966)[89]

In this poem, Chen addressed the relation between role playing and intimacy. Opening with his sentiments on viewing Xu Ziyun dressed in his wedding finery, he genially adopts the detached voice of a benevolent patron calmly sipping his wine and looking with pleasure on the actor. A screen partitions Chen and Xu Ziyun from the bridal party. The bride and the feminine Xu Ziyun come to form mirror images of each other, their shadows simultaneously cast from opposite sides of the screen. A palimpsest of shadow plays forms on the single screen.

At first, the bridal party seems a histrionic space, and Chen's moment with Xu Ziyun on the other side of the screen an intimate space. In stating that the bride is about to appear, Chen in fact employs a phrase that could describe the entrance of an actor on a stage. But somehow, although Xu Ziyun's side of the screen is quiet, it is lacking in the kind of intimacy we would expect. The man whom we thought was Chen Weisong now seems a spectator in a theater, bedazzled by Xu Ziyun, the cross-dressed actor. The spectator's knowledge of Xu Ziyun is suddenly so limited that he cannot even discern whether he is man or woman. Moreover, his access to Xu Ziyun is so circumscribed that he can only cast glances at him stealthily: "I furtively measure your feet."[90] The imminent separation between Chen and Xu Ziyun is evoked by Chen's lack of recognition of Xu Ziyun. His comment "I can't tell whether you are cock or hen" is a phrase commonly used to praise an actor's ability to impersonate a woman. Chen reverses the normal usage of the phrase. Xu Ziyun today impersonates a man; originally Chen's bride, he now plays the role of groom. Duly inspected, Xu Ziyun is sent off by his patron to "raise the bridal curtains on the marriage bed," a phrase suggesting that the marriage bed is yet another theatrical space.

There is a quick turn in mood between the first and second stanzas, a shift much prized among connoisseurs of the song-lyric. The next stanza abruptly veers to the deep intimacy Chen and Xu Ziyun shared in days past. Chen's voice suddenly grows maudlin as he recalls how Xu Ziyun was his most intimate companion when they traveled far from home "staying in lonely inns." His vision quickly telescopes to the pillow he and Xu Ziyun shared; as he speaks of the "red grasses beside the pillow, / the tears like flowers that we gently shed," he leaves no doubt that theirs was a romantic intimacy. The declaration "Today, you will be wed" ruptures this moment. Unexpectedly, with the recollection that the wedding is at hand, we are back in the realm of the staged, as "wife follows husband in sinuous chant." Chen's admonition, "Try your best to act as a model husband" sounds as though he were merely coaching the actor in one more role. In Chen's final lines, he himself strikes a histrionic pose, depicting himself lying alone in bed, a martyr to his quixotic devotion to the actor.

Conclusion

Like dust or dreams or silk floss,
Who knows of my tacit affection?
I regret coming home so late,
No need to rattle the latch,

Just knock slowly upon the screen.
A shower of rain in the blue emptiness outside the window,
By the third watch you have long been gone.
In vain you left your beautiful lines,
Pale clustered flowers on the paper,
The phoenix-leg lamp aslant. (QYLS, p. 962)

This poem by Chen Weisong responded to a poem by Xu Ziyun that has long been lost. Ziyun paid a call upon Chen; not finding him in, he left a poem to that effect. Returning around midnight, Chen answered the poem, praising the actor's "beautiful lines" like "pale clustered flowers on the paper." This rather mundane poem—and the absence of the poem that inspired it—point to the tantalizing mysteries that trouble the reader of these occasional poems.

The regret regarding the actor's absence that Chen registers in this poem is emblematic of the absence of the actor in the collections of poems we have discussed. The poets complain of unsatisfied desire, speaking through a haze of longing even as they sit before the actor at a performance. Like Chen in the poem above, they have always "just missed" the actor. All that is left are traces of the actor as these authors wake from dreams of him or sit before his portrait lost in reverie.

In this chapter, I have examined the ways in which the circulation of poems as gifts instantiated a community centered on Chen Weisong and Ziyun. Analyzing the mode in which these poems facilitated the implicit exchange of the actor between elite men, I suggested that the bond so formed conflated the homoerotic and the homosocial. And lastly, I argued that the poets' longing for the actor became confused with his longing to be like Chen Weisong as these poems were generated by the principle of empathic resonance.

These analyses do not so much examine what it was like to be the object of exchange as investigate the concerns of the men who performed the exchanges. This is a problem endemic to the theoretical literature that has inspired my readings. Arguments regarding social distinction seldom explore what it is like to be the object that confers distinction. The literature on the gift seldom has opportunity to interrogate the sentiments or subjectivity of the gift itself. Arguments regarding the traffic in women, even Gayle Rubin's and Eve Sedgwick's feminist reformulations of them, give far less consideration to the women exchanged than to the quality of the bonds formed between the men who exchanged them. The empathic resonance I have set forth as the generating principal of the collection explains only the ways in which these poems resonate with the sentiments of Mao and Chen Weisong. They may resonate with Ziyun's sentiments as well; we cannot know, for his poems have not survived. Ziyun's poems might have told us what it was like to be the object that conferred distinction, the gift whose circulation reinforced networks of patronage and obligation. But we can only echo Chen Weisong's sentiments of regret at having arrived too late.

Notes

For comments and suggestions, I thank Bai Qianshen, Andrea Goldman, Patrick Hanan, Jonathan Hay, Donald Moore, Stephen Owen, Shang Wei, Sun Jingtao, Ann Waltner, Ellen Widmer, and Judith Zeitlin.

1. For example, one late Ming notation book notes that the *kunqu* enthusiast Pan Fangbo 潘方伯 (1525–1601) of Shanghai bought actors in Suzhou who were "quite elegant and beautiful" (see Fan Lian 范廉, *Yunjian jumu chao* 雲間據目鈔 [A record of things witnessed in Yunjian], Biji xiaoshuo daguan, vol. 13 [Yangzhou: Guanglin guji kanyinsuo, 1983], p. 111). The entry on actors appears between notes on the new fad for summer stockings and the excellence of Huating 華亭 wine, an indication that actors, even though they were often cherished for their abundance of affect (*qing*), were also considered objects of consumption.

2. Craig Clunas, *Superfluous Things: Material Culture and Social Status in Early Modern China* (Cambridge, Eng.: Polity Press, 1991), p. 36.

3. Many of these poems are found in a collection entitled *Jiuqing tuyong* 九青圖詠 (Poems on the portrait of Jiuqing), which consists of over 150 poems inscribed as colophons on a portrait of Ziyun. Poems in tribute to Ziyun by Chen Weisong's and Mao Xiang's contemporaries are also reprinted in an early Republican collection, *Yunlang xiaoshi* 雲郎小史 (A brief history of Yunlang), compiled by Mao Xiang's late nineteenth-century descendant Mao Heting 冒鶴亭. A noted bibliophile, Mao Heting collected the surviving works of his ancestors and published them under the title *Maoshi congshu* 冒氏叢書 between the years 1911 and 1917. *Yunlang xiaoshi* includes letters and prefaces by contemporaries of Mao Xiang as well as a number of poems written to commemorate Ziyun's performances, bid him farewell, and to mourn his death. Both collections are reprinted in Zhang Cixi 張次溪, *Qingdai Yandu liyuan shiliao* 清代燕都梨園史料 (Historical materials on the theater in Beijing during the Qing dynasty; hereafter cited as *QYLS*) (Beijing: Zhongguo xiju chubanshe, 1988), 2: 958–1001. Some of these poems also appear in *Xu ben shi shi* 續本事詩, edited by the seventeenth-century literatus Xu Qiu 徐釚 (1636–1708), a friend of Chen Weisong's and a colleague of Chen's in compiling the official Ming history (see Xu, *Ben shi shi* 本事詩 and *Xu ben shi shi* 續本事詩 [Shanghai: Shanghai guji chubanshe, 1981], pp. 245, 367, 370, inter alia).

4. Chen was the leader of the Yangxian 陽羨詞 school of song-lyrics (*ci*). One of the three dominant schools of the Qing, the Yangxian school took the "virile" (*hao fang* 豪放) lyrics of Su Shi 蘇軾 and Xin Qiji 辛棄疾 as its models (Chia-ying Yeh, "The Ch'ang-chou School of Tz'u Criticism," in James R. Hightower and Florence Chia-ying Yeh, *Studies in Chinese Poetry* [Cambridge, Mass.: Harvard University Asia Center, 1998], p. 439).

5. Susan Mann (*Precious Records: Women in China's Long Eighteenth Century* [Stanford: Stanford University Press, 1997], p. 38) describes the "base people" or "pariahs" (*jian min*) of Qing society as follows: "They included slaves, persons engaged in what were considered polluting or degrading occupations (butchers, yamen runners, actors), and certain local outcast groups. Though the criteria defining these groups varied, all were subject to the same constraints in the early Qing period under laws inherited from Ming times: first, no descendants in the male line could sit for the civil service examinations or purchase a degree; second, no pariah male could marry a 'respectable' (*liang* 良) woman."

6. On Wu Weiye, see Arthur Hummel, *Eminent Chinese of the Ch'ing Period* (Washington, D.C.: U.S. Government Printing Office, 1943), pp. 882–83, and Frederic Wakeman, Jr., *The Great Enterprise: The Manchu Reconstruction of Imperial Order in Seventeenth-Century China* (Berkeley: University of California Press, 1985), pp. 821–72; for Gong Dingzi, see Hummel, p. 431; for Wang Shizhen, see Hummel, pp. 831–32, and Wakeman, p. 1002.

7. Indeed, Mao Xiang, Gong Dingzi, Wu Weiye, and their circle were the architects of the courtesan cult of the late Ming and early Qing. Mao Xiang's biography of the former courtesan Dong Bai 董白, who became his concubine; Hou Fangyu's 侯方域 (1618–55) biography of the courtesan Li Xiangjun 李香君, with whom he was romantically involved; Gong Dingzi's poems in tribute to the courtesan Gu Mei 顧媚, whom he also married; and Wu Weiye's songs in tribute to the courtesan Bian Yujing 卞玉京, who once proposed to him, contributed to a literature that romanticized the courtesan as a figure of nostalgia and an emblem of loyalism (Kang-I Sun Chang, *The Late-Ming Poet Ch'en Tzu-lung: Crises of Love and Loyalism* [New Haven: Yale University Press, 1991]; and Wai-yee Li, "Heroic Women in Qing Literature," *Harvard Journal of Asiatic Studies* 59, no. 2 [1999]: 363–443). In the corpus of poems in tribute to Xu Ziyun, however, there is no mention of these courtesans, nor of Mao's concubines Cai Han 蔡含 and Jin Yue 金玥, who were, like Dong Bai, famed for their talent as painters (for more on the paintings of Mao Xiang's concubines, see Marsha Weidner, ed., *Views from Jade Terrace* [New York: Rizzoli, 1988], pp. 98–99, 112–17). When courtesans are mentioned, it is only in the abstract and only in service of the assertion that the charms of the actor are superior. A poem entitled "Quatrains by Qu Youzhong on Watching a Performance" describes the courtesans of Nanjing as "muck and shit" in comparison to the beautiful boys of Mao's theatricals:

> Qinxiao 秦簫 sings and Yangzhi 楊枝 dances,
> In their mist Ziyun is dangerously alluring.
> Hong'er 紅兒 and Xue'er 雪兒 are not worthy of being named
> And Taoye 桃葉 and Taogen 桃根 are like muck and shit. (*QYLS*, p. 961)

This seeming discrepancy between the disparagement or even occlusion of the courtesan in poems in tribute to actors and the romanticization of the courtesan in the other works of these poets can be explained if we place the poems in tribute to boy actors in the context of the literature on male love, in which arguments regarding the superior virtues of the love of boys play a strong role.

8. The same poets who celebrated Xu Ziyun also exchanged a number of poems written to or about the actor Wang Zijia. Wang, who was originally from Suzhou, is commemorated in Wu Weiye's "Wang lang qu" 王郎曲 (Song of Master Wang; in *Wu Meicun quanji* 吳梅村全集 [The complete poems of Wu Meicun (Wu Weiye)] [Shanghai: Shanghai guji chubanshe, 1990], pp. 283–85) as a wily trickster who mesmerizes a new generation of youths after the fall of the Ming and continues to perform as though the dynasty had not succumbed. Meng Sen 孟森 (*Xinshi congkan* 心史叢刊 [Shenyang: Liaoning jiaoyu chubanshe, 1988], p. 89) believes that Wu wrote "Wang lang qu" for Wang in 1656 as a poem on parting. Qian Qianyi 錢謙益 (1582–1664) also presented Wang with a set of fourteen quatrains to mark their parting when Wang traveled to Beijing in 1652. Three years later, when Wang left Beijing for the South, Gong Dingzi wrote a set of fourteen matching quatrains that rhymed with Qian Qianyi's. Gong also wrote twelve quatrains mourning Wang's untimely death at the hands of the censor Lin Senxian 林森先. These sources are collected in Meng, *Xinshi congkan*, pp. 85–98.

9. Xu Qiu 徐釚, *Ciyan congtan* 詞苑叢談 (A garden of lyrics: collected conversations), ed. Tang Guizhang 唐圭章 (Shanghai: Shanghai guji chubanshe, 1981), pp. 271, 320; *QYLS*, 958–59.

10. See Zhao Shanlin 趙山林, *Lidai yongju shige xuanzhu* 歷代詠劇詩歌選注 (Selected and annotated poems and songs on the theater through the ages) (Beijing: Shumu wenxian chubanshe, 1988), for a comprehensive collection of poems concerning the theater. Few actors are identified by more than their surname; that the given names of Wang Zijia and Xu Ziyun are used by their patrons tells us that they were both more respected and more intimate with the literati who wrote about them than the ordinary actor. However, that three different sets of characters are used to write Wang Zijia's given name suggests that his given name was seldom written and that he likely did not engage in poetic correspondence. In contrast, Xu Ziyun had a literary pseudonym (*hao*), Jiuqing 九青, and a style name (*zi*), Manshu 曼殊, in the manner of a literatus.

11. Portrayals of erotic liaisons between actors and literati in dramas are surprisingly scarce. I know of only one dramatic episode that directly discusses the erotic relations between actors and literati spectators, a one-act skit within Shen Jing's 沈景 (1553–1610) collection of skits *Bo xiao ji* 博笑記 (A world of jokes). Most fictional representations of the relations between actors and literati are far later in date than these poems. Only one set of stories may be roughly contemporaneous, a col-

lection of four stories in the classical language entitled *Bian er chai* 弁而釵 (Hairpins beneath a cap; see *Bian er chai* 弁而釵, ed. Chen Ch'ing-hao 陳慶浩 and Wong Chiu-kuei 王秋桂, Si wu xie hui bao, vol. 6 [Taipei: Taiwan Daying baike, 1995], p. 18). Their date of composition is in question; they were probably written and published during the Chongzhen reign period (1628–44).

12. We could create a portrait of the relations between actors and literati from fictional sources such as *Hairpins Beneath a Cap* or the nineteenth-century novel *Pinhua baojian* 品花寶鑑 (Ranking flowers in a precious mirror), but such texts are far from realistic. Fictional portrayals and anecdotes in notation books (*biji* 筆記) regarding the relations between actors and literati were motivated largely by a desire to warn against the promiscuity and unseemly social aspirations of actors (or to negate such stereotypes). On *Pinhua baojian*, see Chloe Starr, "Shifting Boundaries: Gender in *Pinhua Baojian*," *Nannü: Men, Women and Gender in Early and Imperial China* 1, no. 2 (1999): 268–302.

13. Yunxiang Yan, *The Flow of Gifts: Reciprocity and Social Networks in a Chinese Village* (Stanford: Stanford University Press, 1996), pp. 141–46.

14. Eve Kosofsky Sedgwick, *Between Men: English Literature and Male Homosocial Desire* (New York: Columbia University Press, 1985), pp. 1–5.

15. Vivien W. Ng ("Homosexuality and the State in Late-Imperial China," in *Hidden From History: Reclaiming the Gay and Lesbian Past*, ed. Martin Duberman, Martha Vicinus, and George Chauncey [New York: Penguin Books, 1989], p. 76) speaks of a "discursive explosion." Bret Hinsch (*Passions of the Cut Sleeve* [Berkeley: University of California Press, 1990], p. 119) notes a more intense awareness in the late Ming of a "homosexual tradition." On the proliferation of late Ming sources on male love, see also Giovanni Vitiello, "The Dragon's Whim: Ming and Qing Homoerotic Tales From *The Cut Sleeve*," *T'oung Pao* 78 (1992): 341–73. The new interest in male love was more apt to be expressed in classical and vernacular fiction than in drama or poetry. In the dramatic corpus, the only play that I know of that deals with male love is Wang Jide's 王驥德 *Nan wanghou* 男王后 (The male queen), written sometime between the end of the sixteenth century and Wang Jide's death in 1623; this may have been because affairs between actors and patrons were so prevalent in the theater that the subject of male love seemed obvious and distasteful. (Li Yu's 李漁 [1611–80] play *Lian xiang ban* 憐香伴 [Pitying the fragrant companion] does, however, treat the subject of same-sex love between women.) In the poetic canon, those poems concerning male love nearly always describe male actors and prostitutes.

16. Michel Foucault, *The History of Sexuality*, vol. 1, *An Introduction* (New York: Vintage Books, 1980), pp. 18–49.

17. See Lu Rong 陸容, *Shuyuan zaji* 菽園雜記 (Miscellaneous notes from the bean garden) (Beijing: Zhonghua shuju, 1985), p. 124; Shen Defu 沈德符, *Wanli yehuobian* 萬曆野獲編 (Unofficial harvest of the Wanli years) (Beijing: Zhonghua

shuju, 1980), 2: 621; Xie Zhaozhe 謝肇淛, *Wuzazu* 五雜俎 (A fivefold miscellany) (Shanghai: Tianyi chubanshe, 1935), p. 305; and Zhang Han 張翰, *Song chuang meng yu* 松窗夢語 (Dream discourses at the pine window) (Shanghai: Shanghai guji chubanshe, 1986), pp. 122–23.

18. Maram Epstein, *Competing Discourses: Orthodoxy, Authenticity and Engendered Meanings in Late Imperial Chinese Fiction* (Cambridge, Mass.: Harvard University Asia Center, 2001), p. 8.

19. Meng, *Xinshi congkan*, pp. 18–19.

20. As Vitiello ("The Dragon's Whim," p. 370) writes, "For a man of *qing* the common laws, the relative rules of society and of its pragmatic ethic, mean very little."

21. Mao Xiang left Nanjing and Suzhou to return to Rugao because of pressure to join literary cliques in those urban centers. Mao's family had lived in Rugao since the end of the Yuan. Both his father and his grandfather had been high officials, and he had considerable social advantages. He became, for example, a friend of the artist Dong Qichang 董其昌 at age fourteen. Although he never passed the provincial examinations, he was active in politics as a member of the Restoration Society (Fu she 復社). For more on Mao Xiang, see Wakeman, *The Great Enterprise*, p. 139.

22. "Chen Weisong was a guest at Rugao for ten years, where Mao Xiang was his host. At the end of the Ming, his father, Zhenhui, of Jialing, and Mao Xiang of Rugao, Hou Fangyu of Shangqiu, and Fang Yizhi of Tongcheng . . . spent their entire families' wealth in getting to know the famed men of the age, and they were universally known as the 'Four Lords'" (Jiang Jingqi 蔣景祈, "Jialing xiansheng waizhuan" 迦陵先生外傳 [An unofficial biography of Chen Weisong], quoted in *QYLS*, p. 959). Jiang Jingji (*zi* Jingqi 景祁) was a noted *ci* poet from Yixing in Jiangsu.

23. Although Mao Heting wrote during the late Qing, his scholarship of Mao Xiang's corpus as well as of the literary works of Mao's circle was formidable, and I see no reason to doubt his characterization.

24. As Mayfair Yang (*Gifts, Favors and Banquets: The Art of Social Relationships in China* [Ithaca, N.Y.: Cornell University Press, 1994], pp. 137–39) points out in a more contemporary context, the hosting of banquets is, like gift giving, important to fostering social connection (*guanxi* 關係). It was not uncommon for actors to perform at a banquet and then make themselves available for guests to fondle. We read about this practice, for example, in Chen Hongmo's 陳洪謨 notation book *Zhishi yuwen* (治世餘聞 [Sundry things I have heard about governing the realm] [Beijing: Zhonghua shuju, 1985], p. 53; cited in Brook, *The Confusions of Pleasure*, p. 231) and the anonymous late sixteenth-century novel *Jin Ping Mei* (see *Jin Ping Mei cihua* 金瓶梅詞話 [The golden lotus], ed. Dai Hongsen 戴鴻森 [Hong Kong: Joint Publishing Company, 1986], p. 454).

25. The Donglin, or Eastern Forest Party, had for its base an academy of the same name founded in Wuxi in 1604; see Frederic Wakeman, Jr., "The Price of Autonomy: Intellectuals in Ming and Ching Politics," *Daedalus* 101, no. 2 (1972): 35–70.

26. Hummel, *Eminent Chinese of the Ch'ing*, p. 82.

27. According to ibid., p. 82, Chen Zhenhui was released from prison through the intervention of Lian Guoshi 練國事, senior vice president of the Board of War.

28. The area referred to as Jiangnan (literally, south of the river) is a triangular region bordered by Hangzhou, Suzhou, and Nanjing.

29. Although numbered among the Four Lords of Jiangnan, Hou Fangyu was a native of Shangqiu in Henan.

30. Chen noted in a poem that his father and Mao Xiang were "brothers" in the Qinhuai pleasure quarters (*Qinhuai jiu xiongdi* 秦淮舊兄弟; see *QYLS*, p. 967).

31. In later life, Chen became close to the poets Nalan Xingde 納蘭性德 (1655–85) and Zhu Yizun 朱彝尊 (1629–1709) as well as to Cao Xueqin's grandfather Cao Yin 曹寅 (1658–1712), a confidant of the Kangxi emperor; see Jonathan Spence, *Ts'ao Yin and the K'ang-hsi Emperor: Bondservant and Master* (New Haven: Yale University Press, 1966), pp. 51–56.

32. According to Mao Heting (*QYLS*, p. 967), Chen Weisong required three taels of gold (*san jin* 三金) per month for his expenses at Rugao; Mao Xiang was surprised at his extravagance but permitted it because he cherished Chen's talent. Mao Heting gives no source.

33. Hummel, *Eminent Chinese of the Ch'ing*, p. 103.

34. One hundred and eighty-odd candidates were summoned to take the *boxue hongci* examinations on April 11, 1679. Of these, 36 declined, feigned ill health, or died before the exam took place, 102 failed, and 50 candidates passed (Lawrence Kessler, *K'ang-hsi and the Consolidation of Ch'ing Rule, 1661–1684* [Chicago: University of Chicago Press, 1976], p. 159).

35. Qianshen Bai, "Fu Shan and the Transformation of Chinese Calligraphy in the Seventeenth Century" (Ph.D. diss., Yale University, 1996), pp. 237–38.

36. Tobie Meyer-Fong, "Site and Sentiment: Building Culture in Seventeenth-Century Yangzhou" (Ph.D. diss., Stanford University, 1988), p. 135. Qianshen Bai ("Turning Point: Politics, Art and Intellectual Life During the *Boxue Hongci* Examination [1678–1679]," forthcoming) points out that the expectation of loyalism did not pertain to the sons of loyalists; five of Gu Yanwu's 顧炎武 nephews, for example, obtained *jinshi* degrees under the Qing.

37. Qianshen Bai ("Turning Point") notes that "large-scale gatherings like those held by one of the major societies, the Fu She, which had had as many as several thousand attendees and exerted tremendous influence nationwide" had not taken place since the fall of the Ming; the excitement that surrounded the *boxue hongci* was in part a response to the renewal of such opportunities.

38. Chen's collected works, the *Huhailou ji* 湖海樓集 (published in 1721), consists of six volumes of prose, ten volumes of parallel prose, eight volumes of *shi* poetry, and 30 volumes of song-lyrics. He was well known both for his parallel prose and for his song-lyrics. He published three collections of *ci* lyrics: the *Wusi ci* 烏絲詞, *Jialing ci* 迦陵詞, and the *Zhu Chen cun ci* 朱陳村詞, a collaboration with Zhu Yizun that made him nationally famous.

39. The date of Xu Ziyun's birth is unclear. Mao Heting gives it as 1644 because of a poem written by Chen Hu 陳湖 (1613–75) in 1658 that seems to commemorate a first meeting with Ziyun. It begins with the lines "A Yun at age fifteen / Stands charmingly beside the screen" (*QYLS*, p. 967). (If the poem accurately describes Xu Ziyun's age, he would have been fourteen by Western count.) The first line is a conventional opening for poems about entertainers; Chen Weisong uses it as well in a poem to an actor named Yuanlang (Master Yuan). For this reason, we cannot take it too literally. However, we might surmise that Ziyun was in his teens at the time the poem was written.

40. Matthew Sommer, *Sex, Law and Society in Late-Imperial China* (Stanford: Stanford University Press, 2000), pp. 212–13.

41. Actors were banned from taking the civil service examinations from the fourteenth century until the examination system was abolished in 1905. The Qing government seems to have been particularly strict about this. In 1652 the ban was reiterated, with the government adding a provision that anyone who had succeeded in bypassing the prohibition would be dismissed from his position. Literati legally adopted members of servile classes in order to circumvent that ban, but such adoptions were forbidden by a decree of 1770. See Colin Mackerras, *The Rise of the Peking Opera, 1770–1880* (Oxford: Clarendon Press, 1972), p. 43; and Wang Liqi 王利器, *Yuan Ming Qing sandai jinhui xiaoshuo xiqu shiliao* 元明清三代禁毀小說戲曲史料 (Historical materials on forbidden and destroyed novels and dramas of the Yuan, Ming and Qing dynasties) (Taipei: Heluo tushu chubanshe, 1980), pp. 6, 11. Matthew Sommer quotes the following statute from the Ming code: "Any official who marries an entertainer (*yue ren*) as wife or concubine shall receive 60 blows of the heavy bamboo, and [the couple] shall be divorced. If the son or grandson of an official marries one, his penalty shall be the same" (*Da Ming lü jijie* 大明律集解 6.30b; as cited in Sommer, *Sex, Law, and Society in Late-Imperial China*, p. 219).

42. Actors were considered feminine because of the common practice of crossdressing to play female roles. They were also feminized by their implied sexual availability and by their exchange as commodities and gifts. Writing with regard to the exchange of gifts in Melanesia, the anthropologist Marilyn Strathern (*The Gender of the Gift* [Berkeley: University of California Press, 1988], p. xi) has argued that the phrase "traffic in women" is a productive misnomer, for it is not the sex of the person exchanged, but his or her position in the network of exchange that genders that

person. Those who conduct the transaction are always gendered masculine; the object of exchange is feminized, whether the person exchanged be male or female. A son given to one's brother for adoption would be gendered feminine in the context of the exchange.

43. Sommer, *Sex, Law, and Society in Late-Imperial China*, p. 129.

44. Shen, *Wanli yehuobian*, 2: 621.

45. For information on private acting troupes, see Lu Eting 陸萼庭, *Kunqu yanchu shigao* 崑曲演出史稿 (A draft history of *kunqu* performance) (Shanghai: Shanghai wenyi chubanshe, 1980); Sun Chongtao 孫崇濤 and Xu Hongtu 徐宏圖, *Zhongguo youling shi* 中國優伶史 (A history of China's actors) (Beijing: Wenhua yishu chubanshe, 1995); and Wang Anqi 王安祈, *Mingdai chuanqi zhi juchang jiqi yishu* 明代傳奇之劇場及其藝術 (The stage of the Ming southern drama and its art of performance) (Taipei: Xuesheng shuju, 1986). One of the most renowned owners of such private troupes was Ruan Dacheng. Ruan became infamous as the adopted son of the eunuch Wei Zhongxian, but he was also much respected as a playwright, and his actors were known for their high levels of musicianship. Wu Weiye (*Wu Meicun quanji*, p. 773), in a piece written for Mao Xiang's fiftieth birthday, recalled that Mao, Chen Zhenhui, and Fang Yizhi were once drinking at the Crowing Cock Inn in Nanjing when they sent for Ruan's players and had them perform selections from Ruan's play *The Swallow Letter*. Ruan hoped that this was a signal that the three men no longer despised him, but his hopes were dashed when they lamented the immorality of the author even as they praised the opera's novel lyrics and scorned his efforts to redeem himself by offering his play. Kong Shangren 孔尚任 used this anecdote as the basis for scene four of his play *Taohua shan* 桃花扇 (Beijing: Renmin wenxue chubanshe, 1991), pp. 31–33.

46. Lu Eting, *Kunqu yanchu shigao*, p. 123.

47. Ibid., pp. 128–29.

48. The abundance of terms used to refer to these servants suggests the flexibility of their services. They were referred to as *jia yue* 家樂 (household musicians), *jia you* 家優 (household actors), *jia ling* 家伶 (household actors), *jia tong* 家童 (household servants), *sheng ji* 聲伎 (musical performers), and *si er* 伺兒 (servants). Literati households kept not only male but also female troupes; Zhang Dai's 張岱 family, for example, had five troupes, including one female troupe (see Zhang Dai, *Tao'an mengyi* 陶庵夢憶 [Dream recollections of Tao'an] and *Xihu mengxun* 西湖夢尋 [In search of dreams of West Lake] [Shanghai: Shanghai Zhangguji chubanshe, 1982]).

49. Lin was not only a friend of Gong Dingzi, who was Wang's patron, but himself also an admirer of the actor. However, the rumors swirling around the actor's corruption of officials and gentry women were such that he could not ignore them. Lin had Wang flogged and then forced him to stand in the cangue until he died (Meng Sen, *Xinshi congkan*, pp. 90–98). In another example of the censure of rela-

tions between literati and actors, Gong Dingzi's impeachment from his position as superintendent of the Northern Beijing Police in 1646 was in part due to his flagrantly conspicuous relations with actors and courtesans. The impeachment noted his affairs with cross-dressed male actors as well as his devotion to his concubine Gu Mei (a distinguished courtesan for whom he had paid 1,000 pieces of silver) to the neglect of his parents, wife, and children (Wakeman, *The Great Enterprise*, p. 871). As the simultaneous mention of actors and courtesans would suggest, it was likely that not only Gong's fraternization with actors but also the broader notion of dalliance during a period of mourning was found offensive. On the price Gong paid for Gu Mei, see Clunas, *Superfluous Things*, p. 118.

50. Timothy Brook, *The Confusions of Pleasure: Commerce and Culture in Ming China* (Berkeley: University of California Press, 1998), p. 232.

51. The instant and wordless recognition that Chen invokes often describes love matches in seventeenth-century sources, but it is also used to characterize the relation between the connoisseur and the object of his affection (see Judith T. Zeitlin, *Historian of the Strange* [Stanford: Stanford University Press, 1993], pp. 69–97).

52. Magpie's brain (*que nao* 鵲腦) was an aphrodisiac added to wine.

53. It is unclear whether the portrait was painted by Chen Weisong himself, or whether he commissioned an artist named Chen Gu 陳沽 to paint it. The subtitle of a poem by Mao Xiang informs us that "Qinian [Chen Weisong] painted (*hua* 畫) a small silhouette of Ziyun and sought lyrics to inscribe on it from everyone" (Xu, *Ciyan congtan*, p. 245). However, later sources say that the portrait was painted by a Chen Gu of Wulang 五郎. The last two inscriptions in *Jiuqing tuyong* are by mid-Qing owners of the portrait. Writing during the Yongzheng reign period (1723–36), Wu Qing 吳綮 states that he bought the portrait in a market and that Chen Gu of Wulang had painted it; this information is inscribed on the facsimile reproduction of the portrait (*QYLS*, p. 999). A copy of the portrait was made during the Qianlong (1736–96) period by Luo Liangfeng 羅兩峰. Mao Heting saw this copy in his youth (*QYLS*, p. 964).

54. Niu Xiu 鈕琇, *Gu sheng* 觚賸 (Leftover writing tablet) (Taibei: Wenhai chubanshe, 1982), pp. 40–41; also cited in *QYLS*, pp. 959–60. Niu Xiu's narrative seems to form the basis for later versions of this story. For a partial compilation of prose sources regarding Chen and Ziyun, see *Qing ci ji shi hui ping* 清詞紀事會評 (Accounts of events that inspired *ci* lyrics of the Qing dynasty, with joint commentary), ed. You Yiding 尤以丁 and You Zhenzhong 尤振中 (Hefei: Huangshan shushe, 1995), pp. 164–65. Ye Gongzhuo's 葉恭綽 (1881–?) version conforms most closely to the stereotypical story of the wily actor seducing the literatus, perhaps because it was written long after the others (see Ye Gongzhuo, *Qingdai xuezhe xiangzhuan heji* 清代學者象傳合集 [Portraits of Qing dynasty intellectuals] [Taibei: Wenhai shuju, 1969], p. 86).

55. Various anthropologists who have studied the gift have spoken of how transactions in persons—for example, the gift of one's child to a sister—allow the person who serves as the gift to become a channel for the flow of future gifts. Indeed, the person who is exchanged becomes a channel not only for the transport of goods but also for the flow of sentiment between donor and recipient. We could view Mao Xiang's gift of Xu Ziyun to Chen Weisong in this light. See, e.g., Marcel Mauss, *The Gift*, trans. Ian Cunnisan (London: Cohen and West, 1954), p. 7.

56. Bronislaw Malinowski, *Argonauts of the Western Pacific* (Prospect Heights, Ill.: Waveland Press, 1984 [1922]), p. 184.

57. A possible exception would be the sale of poems by women poets in order to support themselves. The woman poet Shen Shanbao (1808–62) mentions in her poems that she sold her own poems and paintings to eke out a living; it is unclear from the text whether she sold individual poems or a collection, although it would be more likely that she sold a collection (Grace S. Fong, "Writing Self and Writing Lives: Shen Shanbao's [1808–1862] Gender Auto/Biographical Practices," *Nan nü: Men, Women and Gender in Early and Imperial China* 2, no. 2 [2000]: 274–75). The seventeenth-century poet Huang Yuanjie also sold her own poems and paintings to support herself; Shen may have taken her as a model (ibid., p. 275). Another exception to the taboo on the sale of poems would be the sale of anthologies of poems, and it is a telling exception, for in an anthology, the poem is no longer a metonymic extension of an individual person but an example of the literary production of a group. The anthology then becomes a *thing*, which can be used instrumentally for educational or other purposes.

58. Traditional Chinese literary theory describes the poem as an unmediated, almost physical expression of emotion, like dancing or clapping. The poem is a pure reflection neither of the poet's interiority nor of the external scene; rather, it reveals the process of the external scene becoming part of the poet's interior emotional landscape and then becoming externalized again in the poem. See Stephen Owen, *Omen of the World: Traditional Chinese Poetry and Poetics* (Madison: University of Wisconsin, 1985), p. 58.

59. Ibid., pp. 39–40.

60. As Wai-yee Li has remarked, "the infinitude of *qing* is best expressed through unfulfillment, the representation of how the desires of the self find no place in the scheme of things" (*Enchantment and Disenchantment: Love and Illusion in Chinese Literature* [Princeton: Princeton University Press, 1993], p. 54). This empathic resonance (empathic rather than directly inspired by desire for Xu Ziyun) is characteristic of poems composed at parties and other gatherings. Poets would write poems in response to those composed at a party long after the party had taken place; the generating fiction behind the composition of these poems was this emphatic resonance.

61. "The shared peach" refers to the love of Duke Ling of Wei for his male favorite Mi Zixia 彌子瑕; the duke did not see it as a violation of etiquette when Mi Zixia offered him the remainder of a peach he had been eating, but viewed it as touching evidence of Mi Zixia's consideration for him (Han Feizi 韓非子, Han Feizi jishi 韓非子集釋, ed. Chen Qiyou 陳奇猷 [Shanghai: Shanghai renmin chubanshe, 1974], pp. 223–24). "The rent sleeve" refers to the tenderness of the Emperor Ai of the Han toward his male favorite Dongxian. When the emperor was called from an afternoon nap to attend court duties, he had the sleeve of his robe cut rather than disturb Dongxian 董賢, who was sleeping beside him (Ban Gu 班固, Han shu 漢書 [History of the Han] [Beijing: Zhonghua shuju, 1962], 93.3733).

62. In the Tang tale "Yingying zhuan" (The story of Yingying), the phrase "they have never gone astray" indicates that the two lovers have not yet had sex. It is unclear whether by this point in time the meaning of the phrase was still so narrowly defined.

63. This phrase refers to the story of Lord Longyang 龍陽 and the King of Wei. Lord Longyang, the king's current favorite, was fishing with the king when suddenly he began to cry. When the king inquired what was the matter, he replied that he had suddenly realized that as the king's current favorite, he was like a fish who would be cast back into the water once a bigger fish were caught (Liu Xiang 劉向, Zhanguo ce 戰國策 [Stratagems of the Warring States] [Shanghai: Shanghai guji chubanshe, 1998], p. 917).

64. This allusion refers to a violation of sumptuary laws by a male favorite and is taken from the same story as the phrase "the shared peach." Mi Zixia, the favorite of the ruler of Wei, forged an order from the ruler in order to use his chariot to see his sick mother. Instead of punishing him, the ruler praised his filiality, but after Mi Zixia lost favor, the ruler criticized him for having stolen his chariot (Han Feizi, pp. 223–24).

65. Contemporaries of Chen's used other allusions that described Ziyun as a sexual companion of Chen's; Deng Hanyi wrote in a poem after Ziyun's death that "Ziyun is already gone and Yangzhi has withered [a pun on the actor Yangzhi's name, "Willow branch"]; / Master Chen has buried Yingtao in the shallow earth" (QYLS, 976). An entertainer who became the male favorite of Shi Jilong 石季龍 of the Eastern Jin, Zheng Yingtao 鄭櫻桃 came to represent the stereotype of the actor with designs upon a lover; Shi Jilong supposedly murdered two wives at Zheng's behest.

66. Feng Menglong 馮夢龍, Qingshi leilüe 清史類略 (A topical outline of a history of qing), in Feng Menglong quan ji 馮夢龍全集, ed. Wei Tongxian 魏同賢, vols. 37 and 38 (Shanghai: Shanghai guji chubanshe, 1993), 20.2a; Anthony Yu, Rereading the Stone: Desire and the Making of Fiction in "Dream of the Red Chamber" (Princeton:

Princeton University Press, 1997), p. 109. For an extensive investigation of the Confucian discourse on *qing*, see Yu, pp. 53–109.

67. Maram Epstein (*Competing Discourses*, p. 61) observes that *qing*'s multiple meanings have led it to be used in contradictory ways, even by the same author.

68. Conversely, seventeenth-century authors who wished to elevate the term relied on its ambiguities and defined it as fellow feeling that forms the basis of social relations rather than as passion, which leads individuals to act in ways that are antisocial (Martin W. Huang, *Desire and Fictional Narrative in Late Imperial China* [Cambridge, Mass: Harvard University Asia Center, 2001], pp. 46–47).

69. Although possible translations for the term are legion, in translating and discussing these poems, I favor the term "desire" because it incorporates a sense of the insatiability of *qing*.

70. Epstein, *Competing Desires*, pp. 61–119; Huang, *Desire and Fictional Narrative in Late Imperial China*, pp. 23–56; Li, *Enchantment and Disenchantment*; Siu-kit Wong, "Ch'ing in Chinese Literature" (Ph.D. diss., Oxford University, 1967); Yu, *Rereading the Stone*, pp. 53–109.

71. Feng, *Qingshi leilüe* 20.1b–2a. For translations of and commentary upon this passage, see Li, *Enchantment and Disenchantment*, p. 91; and Epstein, *Competing Discourses*, pp. 114–15.

72. Feng, *Qingshi leilüe*, p. 7.

73. See also Xu, *Ciyan congtan*, p. 366.

74. Meyer-Fong, "Sight and Sentiment," pp. 147–53.

75. Wu's last line, "What can I do when he is so far away, separated by the clouds of Chu," may refer to Ziyun's sexual involvement with Chen Weisong. The phrase "the clouds of Chu" refers to the sensual pleasures of "clouds and rain" that, according to literary tradition, King Xiang of Chu 楚襄王 enjoyed with the goddess of Wu 巫 mountain. The line may also hint at Mao Xiang's proprietary rights to Ziyun, given the identity between the character "Xiang" in Mao Xiang's name and that of King Xiang of Chu. The *Shen nü fu* 神女賦 (Rhymeprose on the divine goddess) attributed to Song Yu describes the tryst of King Xiang of Chu with the goddess of Wu mountain (Xiao Tong 蕭統, comp. *Wenxuan* 文選 [Shanghai: Shanghai guji chubanshe, 1998], pp. 135–36).

76. On one level, this deference is simply polite. The temporal deferral of one's approach toward the object of desire is a form of deference to Chen's privileged relation to the actor. On another level, this deference emulates Mao's and Chen's own deferral of their desires. As we have noted, it was not only Chen's sentiments of loss as he gave Ziyun up to marriage but Mao's sense of bereavement after he gave his beloved actor to Chen that inspired these poets' empathic expression of loss and longing. Mao's poems repeatedly spiral back to the moment at which he gave Ziyun to Chen and speak of the pain inherent in his own largesse, the cost to himself of his

radical generosity. If these poets write in emulation of Mao's longing, they refer implicitly to their own largesse in allowing Chen to keep the actor. Their defeat in their rivalry with Chen, then, becomes re-encoded as an act of generosity.

77. Sedgwick, *Between Men*, pp. 21–27; see also Claude Lévi-Strauss, *The Elementary Structures of Kinship* (Boston: Beacon Press, 1969), pp. 61–68; and Gayle Rubin, "The Traffic in Women: Notes Toward a Political Economy of Sex," in *Toward an Anthropology of Women*, ed. Rayna Reiter, pp. 157–210 (New York: Monthly Review Press, 1975).

78. René Girard, *Deceit, Desire and the Novel* (Princeton: Princeton University Press, 1973), p. 17.

79. The incurable wistfulness of these poems recalls the endless mourning of Freud's melancholic subject, who is doomed to introject the lost object of affection and carry it within in an attempt to recuperate the loss. The occlusion that Mao feels on stumbling across Xu Ziyun and Chen resurfaces in the insistence of these poets on *inclusion*, in the fraught relationship between longing and belonging in these poems.

80. There is certainly an irony in Chen's vision of Xu Ziyun as "chaste." Not only was Ziyun, as an actor, inherently considered unchaste, but the term used here for "chaste" (*yaotiao* 窈窕) is drawn from the first poem of *The Classic of Poetry*, which, according to Han commentary, describes the courtship of the Duke of Zhou and his consort. (In fact, the term *yaotiao* did not have the connotation of "chaste" before the Mao commentary of the Han dynasty; this is an example of the power of commentary to change the significance of the terms it glosses.)

81. See also Xu, *Ciyan congtan*, p. 292.

82. Miriam Hansen, *Babel and Babylon: Spectatorship in American Silent Films* (Cambridge, Mass.: Harvard University Press, 1991), p. 26.

83. The social importance of dramatizing oneself as spontaneously impassioned helps explain the prevalence of empathic longing in these poems. For empathy is by definition spontaneous. Chen's friend Jiang Pingjie, for example, writes in the preface to Chen's *Lyrics of Sorrow in Loss*: "How could I not respond with emotion, and how could one overcome such emotions?" (*QYLS*, p. 962). Empathy allows the sidelined spectator to overcome the hurdle of self-consciousness, to gain a sense of belonging.

84. Jonathan Hay suggests that this self-consciousness was in part due to the incursion of mercantile values into literati culture: "Literati life was first made over into spectacle toward the end of the fifteenth century, when literati painters in Suzhou discovered that a socially exclusionary art form originally developed for a private culture of like minds was eminently marketable to the larger, moneyed public that was beginning to make its presence felt in Jiangnan life" (*Shitao: Painting and*

Modernity in Early Qing China [Cambridge, Eng.: Cambridge University Press, 2001], p. 53).

85. Niu, *Gu sheng*, p. 41. Xu Qiu's *Ciyan congtan* (p. 205) similarly states that "everyone was bowled over by it."

86. The sparrow hairpins refer to the bride's headdress.

87. Pan Yue was a famous male beauty of the Six Dynasties.

88. A *tao sheng* was a mat woven of a type of bamboo called "peachwood bamboo" (*tao zhi zhu* 桃之竹).

89. See also Chen Weisong 陳維崧, *Huhai lou ciji* 湖海樓詞集 (Collected song lyrics of the towers by lakes and seas), in *Qing ba da ming jia ci ji* 清八大名家詞集, ed. Qian Zhonglian 錢仲聯(Changsha: Yelu shushe, 1992) , pp. 327–28.

90. Actors never bound their feet; Chen is merely employing a common index of gender.

Works Cited

Bai, Qianshen. "Fu Shan and the Transformation of Chinese Calligraphy in the Seventeenth Century." Ph.D. diss., Yale University, 1996.

———. "Turning Point: Politics, Art and Intellectual Life During the *Boxue Hongci* Examination (1678–1679)." Forthcoming.

Ban Gu 班固. *Han shu* 漢書 (History of the Han). Beijing: Zhonghua shuju, 1962.

Bian er chai 弁而釵. Ed. Chen Ch'ing-hao 陳慶浩 and Wong Chiu-kuei 王秋桂. Si wu xie hui bao, vol. 6. Taipei: Taiwan Daying baike, 1995.

Brook, Timothy. *The Confusions of Pleasure: Commerce and Culture in Ming China.* Berkeley: University of California Press, 1998.

Chang, Kang-I Sun. *The Late-Ming Poet Ch'en Tzu-lung: Crises of Love and Loyalism.* New Haven: Yale University Press, 1991.

Chen Hongmo 陳洪謨. *Zhishi yuwen* 治世餘聞 (Sundry things I have heard about governing the realm). Beijing: Zhonghua shuju, 1985.

Chen Weisong 陳維崧. *Huhai lou ciji* 湖海樓詞集 (Collected song lyrics of the towers by lakes and seas). In *Qing ba da ming jia ci ji* 清八大名家詞集, ed. Qian Zhonglian 錢仲聯. Changsha: Yelu shushe, 1992.

Clunas, Craig. *Superfluous Things: Material Culture and Social Status in Early Modern China.* Cambridge, Eng.: Polity Press, 1991.

Da Ming lü jijie 大明律集解 (The Ming code with collected commentaries). Beijing: Zhonghua shuju, 1991.

Epstein, Maram. *Competing Discourses: Orthodoxy, Authenticity and Engendered Meanings in Late Imperial Chinese Fiction.* Cambridge, Mass.: Harvard University Asia Center, 2001.

Fan Lian 范廉. *Yunjian jumu chao* 雲間據目鈔 (A record of things witnessed in Yunjian). Biji xiaoshuo daguan, vol. 13. Yangzhou: Guanglin guji kanyinsuo, 1983.

Feng Menglong 馮夢龍. *Qingshi leilüe* 清史類略 (A topical outline of a history of *qing*). In *Feng Menglong quan ji* 馮夢龍全集, ed. Wei Tongxian 魏同賢, vols. 37 and 38. Shanghai: Shanghai guji chubanshe, 1993.

Fong, Grace S. "Writing Self and Writing Lives: Shen Shanbao's (1808–1862) Gender Auto/Biographical Practices." *Nan nü: Men, Women and Gender in Early and Imperial China* 2, no. 2 (2000): 259–303.

Foucault, Michel. *The History of Sexuality*, vol. 1, *An Introduction.* New York: Vintage Books, 1980.

Girard, René. *Deceit, Desire and the Novel.* Princeton: Princeton University Press, 1973.

Han Feizi 韓非子. *Han Feizi jishi* 韓非子集釋. Ed. Chen Qiyou 陳奇猷. Shanghai: Shanghai renmin chubanshe, 1974.

Hansen, Miriam. *Babel and Babylon: Spectatorship in American Silent Films.* Cambridge, Mass.: Harvard University Press, 1991.

Hay, Jonathan. *Shitao: Painting and Modernity in Early Qing China*. Cambridge, Eng.: Cambridge University Press, 2001.

Hinsch, Bret. *Passions of the Cut Sleeve*. Berkeley: University of California Press, 1990.

Huang, Martin W. *Desire and Fictional Narrative in Late Imperial China*. Cambridge, Mass: Harvard University Asia Center, 2001.

Hummel, Arthur. *Eminent Chinese of the Ch'ing Period*. 2 vols. Washington, D.C.: U.S. Government Printing Office, 1943.

Jin Ping Mei cihua 金瓶梅詞話 (The golden lotus). Ed. Dai Hongsen 戴鴻森. Hong Kong: Joint Publishing Company, 1986.

Kessler, Lawrence. *K'ang-hsi and the Consolidation of Ch'ing Rule, 1661–1684*. Chicago: University of Chicago Press, 1976.

Kong Shangren 孔尚任. *Taohua shan* 桃花扇 (The peach-blossom fan). Beijing: Renmin wenxue chubanshe, 1991.

Lévi-Strauss, Claude. *The Elementary Structures of Kinship*. Boston: Beacon Press, 1969.

Li, Wai-yee. "Heroic Women in Qing Literature." *Harvard Journal of Asiatic Studies* 59, no. 2 (1999): 363–443.

————. *Enchantment and Disenchantment: Love and Illusion in Chinese Literature*. Princeton: Princeton University Press, 1993.

Liu Xiang 劉向. *Zhanguo ce* 戰國策 (Stratagems of the Warring States). Shanghai: Shanghai guji chubanshe, 1998.

Lu Eting 陸萼庭. *Kunqu yanchu shigao* 昆曲演出史稿 (A draft history of *kunqu* performance). Shanghai: Shanghai wenyi chubanshe, 1980.

Lu Rong 陸容. *Shuyuan zaji* 菽園雜記 (Miscellaneous notes from the bean garden). Beijing: Zhonghua shuju, 1985.

Mackerras, Colin. *The Rise of the Peking Opera, 1770–1880*. Oxford: Clarendon Press, 1972.

Malinowski, Bronislaw. *Argonauts of the Western Pacific*. Prospect Heights, Ill.: Waveland Press, 1984.

Mann, Susan. *Precious Records: Women in China's Long Eighteenth Century*. Stanford: Stanford University Press, 1997.

Mauss, Marcel. *The Gift*. Trans. Ian Cunnisan. London: Cohen and West, 1954.

Meng Sen 孟森. *Xinshi congkan* 心史叢刊. Shenyang: Liaoning jiaoyu chubanshe, 1988.

Meyer-Fong, Tobie. "Site and Sentiment: Building Culture in Seventeenth-century Yangzhou." Ph.D. diss., Stanford University, 1988.

Ng, Vivien W. "Homosexuality and the State in Late-Imperial China." In *Hidden From History: Reclaiming the Gay and Lesbian Past*, ed. Martin Duberman, Martha Vicinus, and George Chauncey. New York: Penguin Books, 1989.

Niu Xiu 鈕琇. *Gu sheng* 觚賸 (Leftover writing tablet). Taibei: Wenhai chubanshe, 1982.

Owen, Stephen. *Omen of the World: Traditional Chinese Poetry and Poetics*. Madison: University of Wisconsin, 1985.

Qing ci ji shi hui ping 清詞紀事會評 (Accounts of events that inspired *ci* lyrics of the Qing dynasty, with joint commentary). Ed. You Yiding 尤以丁 and You Zhenzhong 尤振中. Hefei: Huangshan shushe, 1995.

QYLS, see Zhang Cixi.

Rubin, Gayle. "The Traffic in Women: Notes Toward a Political Economy of Sex." In *Toward an Anthropology of Women*, ed. Rayna Reiter. New York: Monthly Review Press, 1975, pp. 157–210.

Sedgwick, Eve Kosofsky. *Between Men: English Literature and Male Homosocial Desire*. New York: Columbia University Press, 1985.

Shen Defu 沈的符. *Wanli yehuobian* 萬歷野獲編 (Unofficial harvest of the Wanli years). Beijing: Zhonghua shuju, 1980.

Sommer, Matthew. *Sex, Law and Society in Late-Imperial China*. Stanford: Stanford University Press, 2000.

Spence, Jonathan. *Ts'ao Yin and the K'ang-hsi Emperor: Bondservant and Master*. New Haven: Yale University Press, 1966.

Starr, Chloe. "Shifting Boundaries: Gender in *Pinhua Baojian*." *Nannü: Men, Women and Gender in Early and Imperial China* 1, no. 2 (1999): 268–302.

Strathern, Marilyn. *The Gender of the Gift*. Berkeley: University of California Press, 1988.

Sun Chongtao 孫崇濤 and Xu Hongtu 徐宏圖. *Zhongguo youling shi* 中國優伶史 (A history of China's actors). Beijing: Wenhua yishu chubanshe, 1995.

Vitiello, Giovanni. "The Dragon's Whim: Ming and Qing Homoerotic Tales from *The Cut Sleeve*." *T'oung Pao* 78 (1992): 341–73.

Wakeman, Frederic, Jr. *The Great Enterprise: The Manchu Reconstruction of Imperial Order in Seventeenth-Century China*. Berkeley: University of California Press, 1985.

————. "The Price of Autonomy: Intellectuals in Ming and Ching Politics." *Daedalus* 101, no. 2 (1972): 35–70.

Wang Anqi 王安祈. *Mingdai chuanqi zhi juchang jiqi yishu* 明代傳奇之劇場及其藝術 (The stage of the Ming southern drama and its art of performance). Taipei: Xuesheng shuju, 1986.

Wang Liqi 王利器. *Yuan Ming Qing sandai jinhui xiaoshuo xiqu shiliao* 元明清三代禁毀小說戲曲史料 (Historical materials on forbidden and destroyed novels and dramas of the Yuan, Ming and Qing dynasties). Taipei: Heluo tushu chubanshe, 1980.

Weidner, Marsha, ed. *Views from Jade Terrace*. New York: Rizzoli, 1988.

Wong, Siu-kit. "*Ch'ing* in Chinese Literature." Ph.D. diss., Oxford University, 1967.

Wu Weiye 吳偉業. *Wu Meicun quanji* 吳梅村全集 (The complete poems of Wu Meicun [Wu Weiye]). Shanghai: Shanghai guji chubanshe, 1990.

Xiao Tong 蕭統, comp. *Wenxuan* 文選. Shanghai: Shanghai guji chubanshe, 1998.

Xie Zhaozhe 謝肇淛. *Wuzazu* 五雜俎 (A fivefold miscellany). Shanghai: Tianyi chubanshe, 1935.

Xu Qiu 徐釚. *Ciyan congtan* 詞苑叢談 (A garden of lyrics: collected conversations). Ed. Tang Guizhang 唐圭章. Shanghai: Shanghai guji chubanshe, 1981.

———. *Ben shi shi* 本事史 and *Xu ben shi shi* 續本事史. Shanghai: Shanghai guji chubanshe, 1981.

Yan, Yunxiang. *The Flow of Gifts: Reciprocity and Social Networks in a Chinese Village.* Stanford: Stanford University Press, 1996.

Yang, Mayfair. *Gifts, Favors and Banquets: The Art of Social Relationships in China.* Ithaca, N.Y.: Cornell University Press, 1994.

Ye Gongzhuo 葉恭綽. *Qingdai xuezhe xiangzhuan heji* 清代學者象傳合集 (Portraits of Qing dynasty intellectuals). Taibei: Wenhai shuju, 1969.

Yeh, Chia-ying. "The Ch'ang-chou School of Tz'u Criticism." In James R. Hightower and Florence Chia-ying Yeh, *Studies in Chinese Poetry.* Cambridge, Mass.: Harvard University Asia Center, 1998, pp. 439–61.

Yu, Anthony. *Rereading the Stone: Desire and the Making of Fiction in "Dream of the Red Chamber."* Princeton: Princeton University Press, 1997.

Zeitlin, Judith T. *Historian of the Strange.* Stanford: Stanford University Press, 1993.

Zhang Cixi 張次溪, ed. and comp. *Qingdai Yandu liyuan shiliao* 清代燕都梨園史料 (Historical materials on the theater in Beijing during the Qing dynasty). Beijing: Zhongguo xiju chubanshe, 1988.

Zhang Dai 張岱. *Tao'an mengyi* 陶庵夢憶 (Dream recollections of Tao'an) and *Xihu mengxun* 西湖夢尋 (In search of dreams of West Lake). Shanghai: Shanghai Zhangguji chubanshe, 1982.

Zhang Han 張翰. *Song chuang meng yu* 松窗夢語 (Dream discourses at the pine window). Shanghai: Shanghai guji chubanshe, 1986.

Zhao Shanlin 趙山林. *Lidai yongju shige xuanzhu* 歷代詠劇詩歌選注 (Selected and annotated poems and songs on the theater through the ages). Beijing: Shumu wenxian chubanshe, 1988.

Part II

Print Culture and Networks of Reading

'Jin Ping Mei' and Late Ming Print Culture

Shang Wei

Jin Ping Mei cihua 金瓶梅詞話 (hereafter, *Jin Ping Mei*), a late Ming novel about the rise and fall of the merchant Ximen, marks several important changes in the history of the Chinese novel.[1] First, it forged a new kind of narrative focused on a comprehensive range of quotidian experience, which had until then barely been treated on its own terms in the vernacular novel. Second, despite the novel's overall structural unity, the narrative often seems to take on the features of the experience it recounts, becoming just as detailed, kaleidoscopic, and fragmentary. Third, this narrative fragmentation is compounded by the mixing of a variety of literary modes, texts, and genres, such as popular songs, jokes, and plays adapted from an extremely wide range of sources. For instance, *Jin Ping Mei* quotes nearly 600 popular songs.[2] Since "these songs are merely copied into the novel," as C. T. Hsia pointed out, "the author often takes considerable pains to devise situations where the use of such songs is dramatically appropriate." Thus, "in a sense, the novel is almost a poetic anthology within a narrative framework."[3] Critics have long noted the patchwork quality of the narrative; indeed no earlier novel borrowed from such a broad range of texts and genres, and in such large quantity. *Jin Ping Mei* is such a hybrid that its generic identity itself became a question: What was a *cihua* 詞話? Was *Jin Ping Mei* a *cihua*—a traditional genre that combines prose narrative with various forms of poetry—or a unique work that tests the normative system of generic categorization?[4] For literary scholars, the question has been: How do these fragmented and unrelated materials work together to form a single, coherent narrative?[5]

If in *Jin Ping Mei* we see the rise of a new type of novel, the question we have to ask is How can we explain such a change? Indeed, as an abrupt departure from the tradition of earlier vernacular novels, *Jin Ping Mei* appears to be a great leap of artistic genius. But if we view the novel within the broad cultural context of its times, our perspective changes. Far from being an isolated phenomenon, it begins to emerge as an epitome of its age: with a new subject and a new mode of representation, it testifies to a larger cultural trend of the epoch, a trend that is manifested in other literary or nonliterary forms and in other related spheres of social and cultural practice.

This chapter examines the practice of print culture in the late Ming.[6] *Jin Ping Mei* was composed during an era in which commercial publishing played a more important role than ever before in shaping literary taste, sensibility, and imagination, as well as the concept and practice of literature itself. Although almost all earlier novels had stemmed from the tradition of professional storytelling, this was no longer the case with *Jin Ping Mei*. No evidence suggests that the main story of *Jin Ping Mei* had ever been rendered in the form of performing literature or that it underwent a long process of oral transmission and transformation before it was cast in manuscript and print form.[7] The earliest mention of *Jin Ping Mei* refers to it as being circulated in manuscript form around 1595–96.[8] More than two decades later it was published, and, according to Shen Defu's 沈德符 (1578–1642) account in his *Wanli yehuo bian* 萬曆野獲編, it quickly became a sensation in the literary marketplace, as the well-known compiler of fiction Feng Menglong 馮夢龍 (1574–1646) had predicted. Following contemporary practice, its publisher had it hung on the city gates to advertise it.[9]

Most important is that no earlier novel had depended as much on popular print materials. In fact, *Jin Ping Mei* would have taken an entirely different shape had it not borrowed from an extremely broad range of print texts: collections of popular songs, jest books, drama miscellanies, and all sorts of handbooks. There is no question that some of the source material—lyrics of popular songs and arias of operas—normally fall into the category of oral performing literature. But the argument that *Jin Ping Mei* developed from the tradition of oral literature is doubtful, because even in its depiction of the performance of the songs and plays, it often renders them exactly as they are found in collections of popular songs and drama. In other words, it not only copies the songs and plays from the print texts but also preserves the form in which they are presented in those texts. For example, the names of the matrixes for the songs quoted in *Jin Ping Mei* are often given parenthetically, just as they are in dramatic texts. David Rolston notes that "other conventional formulas used in printed texts to indicate the repetition of the previous song matrix (*qianqiang*, etc.), singing in harmony (*he*), and the insertions of refrains (*heqian*) all appear in the novel."[10] As I elaborate below, *Jin Ping Mei* constitutes part of the print culture of the day, and its relation to the oral sources of performing literature is mediated through the conventions of print media.

In another study, "The Making of the Everyday World: *Jin Ping Mei cihua* and Encyclopedias for Daily Use," I treat late Ming daily-life encyclopedias as a storehouse of common knowledge to be shared with the contemporary reading public, and I argue that these encyclopedias provide a knowledge system and a frame of reference for understanding *Jin Ping Mei*'s representation of the everyday.[11] This approach led me to see the novel itself as an "encyclopedic narrative." I use this term to describe the novel's extremely wide range of subject matter and its echoing of the system of categorization of daily-life encyclopedias, as well as its creation of characters as the living embodiment of the knowledge, skills, and verbal virtuosity presented in these compendiums as necessary to survival in the everyday world. Equivocal and complicated, this encyclopedic narrative of the everyday did not merely deviate from the convention of earlier novels. It presented a new prototype for the novel, one whose endless variations were to be displayed over the subsequent three centuries, as the vernacular novel became increasingly engaged in exploring the quotidian.

In this study, I use the term "encyclopedic narrative" in another sense, to refer to *Jin Ping Mei*'s creation of what amounts to a new narrative form in representing the everyday, a form that incorporates a broad spectrum of texts, genres, and literary modes drawn from multiple sources. To understand this hybrid form of multivocality, I first illuminate the editing mode of late Ming commercial publishing by examining how editors synthesized and organized texts and genres of different origins and sources. I also examine the format of late Ming print materials and its role in shaping the heterogeneous vision of the world these materials convey. It is in the print materials contemporary to *Jin Ping Mei* that we find not merely the textual sources of

Jin Ping Mei but also the recurring forms, genres, organizing patterns, and characteristic modes of discourse that helped shape the novel and the way it represents the world of the everyday.

I

Thanks to the efforts of many scholars, we can now see the new trends in the development of late Ming print culture. First, commercial publishing played a greater role than either private or official publishing in determining the overall orientation of print culture. Second, the late Ming witnessed a further growth in what is called "quantity printing."[12] With these changes, the power of editors relative to that of authors rose dramatically. Increasingly what figured prominently on the cover or title page of a book was the name of its editor, not that of its author. In the case of vernacular fiction, it was the commentator who adapted the fiction, gave it its final shape, and added the introduction and commentary to it to accommodate readers of different educational backgrounds and literacy levels. Similarly, the editor of a drama anthology often selected highlights from plays without even mentioning the names of the playwrights. Essential to the phenomenon of the rise of the editor was the emergence of a variety of compiled books, books in which the editors incorporated miscellaneous materials from multiple sources, especially from the best-sellers of the day, in order to meet and cultivate the needs of the market. As appropriation, adaptation, and incorporation became the norms of commercial publishing, a large repository of common references appeared. These in turn often served as the sources for other texts.

No books embody this practice better than the daily-life encyclopedias and literary miscellanies, which synthesize almost all the literary and nonliterary genres prevalent during the late Ming period. The encyclopedias include guidebooks on everyday practices and leisure entertainments such as the interpretation of dreams, divination, fortune-telling, geomancy, medicine, jokes, and chess, as well as verbal games to be played at parties and banquets. The literary miscellanies introduce a variety of popular genres (riddles, jokes, popular songs, essays, stories, and dramas) and thus could be read as encyclopedias of literature.[13] The editors of *Siku quanshu zongmu* 四庫全書總目, the imperial bibliography compiled under the aegis of the Qianlong emperor (r. 1736–95), had difficulty coping with the variety of Ming dynasty commercial printed materials and in the end placed them under the general rubric of *zajia* 雜家 (miscellanies).[14] Although the term "miscellany" captures the ba-

sic features of these books, here I use this term in a narrower sense to designate two types of popular reading materials: drama miscellanies, which are
composed of abridged dramatic texts or highlights from dramas, and miscellanies of a more comprehensive kind, which include almost all the existing
literary genres, as exemplified by *Guose tianxiang* 國色天香, *Yanju biji* 燕居
筆記, *Xiugu chunrong* 繡谷春容, and *Wanjin qinglin* 萬錦情林. Often seen
in both types is a cluster of literary or nonliterary genres such as jokes, riddles, popular songs, travel guides, manuals of composition, verses used in
drinking games, and slang used in brothels or in the marketplace.

In some essential aspects, the miscellanies resemble modern magazines,
which did not come into being in China until the early nineteenth century.[15]
Drawing from a wide range of contemporary popular print materials, they
constituted a late Ming version of the *Reader's Digest*, so to speak. Particularly
important in this regard is their adoption of a format similar to that used in
modern magazines and newspapers. Each page presents diverse and unrelated
materials in two or three parallel registers. Although not published as a series
or on a regular basis, these miscellanies were compiled in a way not unlike that
of modern magazines. As scholars have observed, in the editorial notes on the
cover or title page of literary miscellanies and guidebooks, the editors did exactly what their modern counterparts do. In the language familiar to the readers of modern magazines, they advertised their publications and, in the case of
guidebooks, asked readers to submit information.[16]

No one could have compiled such miscellanies without a large quantity of
contemporary printed texts to draw on. One illustration of how widely circulated texts contributed to the making of various kinds of late Ming miscellanies is the official gazette (*dibao* 邸報).[17] Throughout most of the Ming
and especially during the late Ming, *dibao* were published on a daily basis and
distributed through the official delivery system. Although *dibao* were usually
copied manually, in the Wanli reign attempts were made to bring out a
printed edition. These attempts culminated in the eleventh year of the
Chongzhen reign (1638), with the movable typesetting of *dibao*. In addition
to the texts of imperial edicts, memorials, and listings of official appoint-
ments, *dibao* covered a wide range of gossip and sensational news of crimes,
rebellions, assassinations, floods, and strange incidents that might be construed as omens.[18] The news reports transmitted through *dibao* found their
way into other reading materials of the day. Beyond the official realm, there
were nonofficial newspapers (*xiaobao* 小報 or *zabao* 雜報; literally, "miscel-

laneous gazettes"), which copied reports from *dibao* and supplemented it with more miscellaneous (*za*) and less significant (*xiao*) stories, as their names suggest. More important to this chapter is another practice: *dibao* news was frequently mentioned, quoted, and paraphrased in notation books (*biji* 筆記), jest books, miscellanies, officials' diaries, and official histories.[19] One such example can be found in two volumes of jokes and comic parodies—Feng Menglong's *Gujin tan'gai* 古今談概 and Tu Long's 屠隆 (1542–1605) *Kaijuan yixiao* 開卷一笑, which quote from *dibao* a report about the discovery of the bodies of two thieves in the drain of the imperial treasury and treat it as a story of folly.[20] At the late Ming moment of crisis, literati authors often turned to *dibao* for up-to-date information about ongoing political and military events. By combining the news presumably taken from *dibao* and other sources with their imagination, they created what I shall call "*dibao* fiction" (*dibao xiaoshuo* 邸報小說).[21]

Dibao news circulated rapidly through contemporary print materials, crossing the hierarchical boundaries of genres; it was separated from its original contexts, placed under a different rubric, incorporated into a new sequence of texts, and used to create a new narrative genre or transform an existing one. What is of interest to the concerns of this chapter is not *dibao* *per se* but the ways in which various types of discourse, genres, unrelated narratives, and texts from different sources encounter, coexist, and merge with one another. One example of the ways in which the editors of miscellanies appropriated, adapted, and incorporated texts from other sources is *Wanjin jiaoli* 萬錦嬌麗 (Ten thousand charms and beauties), an early Qing literary miscellany.[22] The upper register of pages 21 to 31 is the first chapter of *Rou putuan* 肉蒲團 (The carnal prayer mat), a seventeenth-century novel concerning the erotic adventures of a young libertine by Li Yu 李漁 (1611–80). This chapter is, however, isolated from its original context and presented as if it were an independent, self-contained essay. Yet, the immediate source might not have been Li Yu's *Rou putuan*; an early Qing novel called *Wutong ying* 梧桐影 (The shadow of wutong trees) begins with exactly the same chapter, which is transcribed from *Rou putuan*.[23] More interesting still, in the same register of *Wanjin jiaoli*, this chapter is juxtaposed with another two stories adapted in similar fashion from contemporary vernacular novels and short stories: one duplicates the prologue to a short story in Feng Menglong's *Jingshi tongyan* 警世通言 (*juan* 11) and the other the novella *Fengliu pei* 風流配 in *Renzhong hua* 人中畫, an early Qing collection of *caizi jiaren*

才子佳人 (talented scholar and beautiful lady) fiction.[24] In both cases, the texts are abridged and modified, and their titles revised. Nowhere are their authors and origins mentioned. Instead we find the names of editor and collator, who give these abridged, modified texts the general title *Newly Selected Chuanqi to Educate the World* (*Jingxuan xin quanshi chuanqi* 精選新勸世傳奇). Moreover, any reader of these unrelated fictional narratives on the upper register could hardly ignore the highlights of such southern plays as *Pipa ji* 琵琶記 and *Jingchai ji* 荊釵記 presented on the bottom register of the page. As I shall show, the two-register format plays a great part in the making of heterogeneous texts.

The important point is that the editor of *Wanjin jiaoli*, when adapting and compiling dramatic and fictional texts, was unconcerned about authorship or textual integrity and unity. He took a piece of text out of its context, imposed a fresh significance on it by incorporating it into a new sequence of texts, and thus ended up creating a hybrid book out of miscellaneous, fragmented pieces. Despite individual variations, the same can be said of the editors of literary miscellanies in general. Given the popularity of literary miscellanies during the late Ming, we might wonder how often contemporary readers read the "complete" versions of dramatic and fictional texts. To examine the form in which literature was presented to the readers of the time, we must, therefore, turn to late Ming literary miscellanies. What matters most here is not the way the editors adapt a specific text but their general attitude toward texts and the written word. In fact, there is almost no text or genre that they did not incorporate, at some point, into their miscellanies. And whatever they did to these texts—cutting, pasting, modifying, renaming, reassembling—they saw no need to justify their practices. This play with different types of texts, genres, languages, and discursive modes is one of the fundamental characteristics of the miscellanies, and it is manifested not merely in the overall design of miscellanies but in the inclusion of such components as jokes, riddles, *xiehouyu* 歇後語,[25] and verses used in drinking games (*jiuling* 酒令).

Let us consider the making of one specific genre. *Jiuling* are often juxtaposed with other fragments of verbal literature on the middle row of miscellanies. As demonstrated in *Yugu xinhuang* 玉谷新簧, a drama miscellany published in 1610, in composing a piece of *jiuling* one combines phrases, sentences, or lines from incompatible sources: one sentence might be taken from a popular collection of poems called *Qianjia shi* 千家詩 and the other from the Confucian *Four Books*, to produce a couplet in which the Confucian passage forms a kind of punch line.[26] In another instance, the rule requires the *jiuling* to be composed of one line from *Qianjia shi* and the other from *Xixiang ji* 西廂記, a romantic play; and the two lines must be connected by a plain, vulgar phrase or sentence (*suyu* 俗語).[27] During the late Ming period, about eight texts were widely used in such verbal games, including the *Four Books*, the *Qianjia shi*, and the popular primer *Qianzi wen* 千字文. In these games, appropriation is conventionalized, and the ironic fusion of incompatible texts becomes the norm of composition. The *jiuling*'s playful combination of discrete and contrasting languages and genres reflects the compositional principle of miscellanies in general: on each page of drama miscellanies, one row is often reserved for such vulgar forms as *jiuling, xiehouyu*, jokes, double entendres, and slang.[28] These low genres of common speech and verbal games are not, however, merely confined to their own register; they are often integrated into the dramatic texts and become part of the dialogue, as exemplified in the late Ming dramas *Mudan ting* 牡丹亭 and *Ge dai xiao* 歌代嘯.[29] In other words, these dramas accommodated all the fragmented comic texts and verbal genres displayed on the pages of miscellanies.

The way miscellanies organize and incorporate heterogeneous languages, texts, and genres constituted an indispensable prerequisite for the emergence of *Jin Ping Mei*. As I shall argue, in *Jin Ping Mei* the speech of characters, inserted genres (including *jiuling*, jokes, double entendres, riddles, and other verbal games), and borrowed texts are knitted together in evoking the multivocality of the novel. In stressing the concept of heteroglossia in my reading of *Jin Ping Mei*, I am indebted to Mikhail Bakhtin's theories of the novel, especially his study of novelistic discourse.[30] Yet, whereas Bakhtin focuses on the distinguishing feature of the stylistic of the novel as a genre, I am interested in the relation between *Jin Ping Mei* and the cultural trends of its time. I argue that as adaptation and incorporation became the norm of late Ming editing and publishing practices, the way in which a novel was composed changed as well. In the case of *Jin Ping Mei*, almost all the major categories of materials that make up contemporary miscellanies find their way into the novel. In the process, they leave traces in all its semantic layers, complicate its narrative discourse, and shape its entire stylistic profile. Thus, unlike any earlier novel, *Jin Ping Mei* becomes itself a sort of encyclopedia of all the types of languages and genres available in its time; its copied source texts, to quote Patrick Hanan, "represent the whole spectrum of Ming dynasty literature."[31]

Its motifs, patterns of narrative discourse, and characteristic modes of expression are often developed from a matrix of contemporary print materials. In this age of quantity printing, when diverse print materials came into circulation, *Jin Ping Mei* embodied an effort, it would seem, to absorb them into its narrative framework and to turn itself into a monumental text—a book of books.

A narrative work so composed challenges us to re-examine the concepts of author, fictional discourse, and literary unity. We know little about the person(s) responsible for the novel, despite all the scholarship on this subject. Although the novel may have been composed by an individual, as some scholars are inclined to believe, there is no reason to adopt an interpretative approach that views the novel as a manifestation of a single, predominant consciousness using a unitary language, consistent rhetorical devices and patterns, and a coherent form of narrative discourse. Following his predecessors in fiction commentary, Zhang Zhupo 張竹坡 (1670–98), a late seventeenth-century fiction commentator, developed what might be called a "poetics" of *Jin Ping Mei*.[32] He saw the novel as closely structured, consisting of scenes and incidents resonating with one another in a complex network of correspondences, contrasts, echoes, and foreshadowings. It follows that all the characters are placed in appropriate positions, according to some authorial design, and measured, explicitly or implicitly, by the author's value system, which dominates the novel and creates its unity. Despite his acute eye for the subtleties of the narrative, however, Zhang sees only one aspect of the novel. This is in part because he based his commentary on the Chongzhen edition of *Jin Ping Mei*, whose editor had substantially revised the text of the *cihua* edition by trimming a large portion of the popular songs and other borrowed texts and rewriting the introductory chapter. But even with the Chongzhen edition, Zhang from time to time overread the text, seeing patterns in places where they may not exist. In his opinion, every stroke of the writing serves some function within what he sees as the overall design of the novel; he even argues that the chronological discrepancies in the novel are part of a deliberate design to achieve specific narrative effects.[33] In all this, he neglected the complexity of the composition of the novel: since *Jin Ping Mei* embraces a multitude of the existing types of languages and genres, as well as a variety of borrowed texts, it raises issues about literary unity, narrative coherence, and integrity of fictional construction that need to be accounted for by new interpretive schemes.

In incorporating heterogeneous materials, the novelist always made adjustments to meet the needs of the specific scene or incident. More often than not, he used jokes, drinking verses, popular songs, and snippets from drama to predict forthcoming events or comment ironically on the characters and their situation. But these incorporated genres and texts are not always absorbed entirely into the narrative of the novel or subordinated to the narrator's voice. Instead, they bring with them their specific language forms, styles, tones, approaches, and modes of perception and representation. As they are introduced into the novel, they penetrate different levels of narrative discourse, becoming not merely part of the speech of individual characters but part of the narratorial discourse. Indeed, although heteroglossia is reflected primarily in the direct speech of characters in dialogue, inserted genres, and borrowed texts, a careful examination of narratorial discourse will show that it, too, often takes its style and tone from the languages of others (including those of the characters) and is sprinkled with quotations of common sayings, verses, doggerel, and every possible kind of maxim and aphorism that convey contrasting, if not conflicting, messages.

In Chapter 10 of the novel, as Ximen Qing's sworn brothers indulge themselves in a brothel, the narrator remarks:

> On the purple roads spring is at its height;
> In the red bowers the music is intoxicating.
> How long a span of life are we allotted?
> Not to enjoy it is to live in vain.[34]

By using the phrase zhengshi 正是 (truly) in introducing this verse, the narrator seems to affirm the hedonistic view of life that the verse expresses. But a closer look at the verse may lead us to see it more as an ironic summary of the characters' mind-set than as a statement of the novelist's unmediated intention. The narrator cites the verse as a quotation from some unknown source—an anonymous, collective voice or perhaps someone else's words. Thus, whatever points the verse makes, it is removed from the narrator's mouth, and its appearance in the form of quotation prevents it from signifying directly. The narrator's ability to distance himself from the material he quotes allows him to incorporate many different opinions into narratorial discourse. Thus, within the space of four or five chapters, the narrator shifts continually from one viewpoint to another, while commenting on the same behavior. At the beginning of Chapter 15, the narrator restates the recurring theme of hedonism that runs through the entire novel:

As the sun sinks amid the western hills,
the moon rises in the east;
Even the span of a hundred years
is like wind-blown tumbleweed.
Before one knows it, the red-cheeked lad one so admires,
in the twinkling of an eye turns into
a white-haired gentleman.
Do not waste the fullness of your youth
so quickly does it pass;
even Heaven-scaling wealth and success
are as evanescent as clouds.
One might as well seek to divert oneself
 among scarlet skirts;
hugging the turquoise and cuddling the red in houses of pleasure.
    (*JPM*: 15.1a; *Plume*, p. 298)

This attitude conflicts with the Confucian comment that the narrator makes at the beginning of Chapter 12, in which he charges Ximen and his sworn brothers with neglecting the "standards of decency and propriety" (*gangchang lishu* 綱常禮數) for their frequent visits to brothels (*JPM*, 12.1a; *Plum*, p. 224).

One could argue that a similar practice can be seen in the narratorial discourse of other novels and stories of the Ming and Qing periods, because fiction authors always model themselves on the conventional storyteller and speak in what might be called an anonymous voice. But *Jin Ping Mei* goes much further than other novels in incorporating multiple voices into its narratorial discourse, and it refers to so many conflicting views that it becomes almost impossible for us to accept any of them without critical reservations. Indeed, not only does the narrator shuttle between conflicting voices and views, but he often allows words of incompatible nature to be squeezed into one single sentence and ends up playing the same sort of verbal game found in *jiuling*.

As a case in point, consider how the novelist appropriates Confucius' phrase *bu yi le hu* 不亦樂乎 (Is it not delightful?) throughout *Jin Ping Mei*. No reader would have failed to recognize this phrase, which Confucius used in describing the enjoyment of learning and friendship. In the first paragraph of *The Analects*, Confucius says: "To learn and at due times to repeat what one has learnt, is that not after all a pleasure? That friends should come to one from afar, is this not after all delightful?"[35] Using a rhetorical question, he strikes home his message: it is beyond dispute that everyone should take

pleasure in learning and friendship. However, the author of *Jin Ping Mei* repeatedly used the same rhetorical question only to challenge its unquestionable assumptions about pleasure and enjoyment; he appropriated it to describe the reaction of a character to an act, usually sexual, that he or she
overhears or sees, and thus substituted for the pleasures of learning and
friendship those of voyeurism and eavesdropping.[36] He also used it at least
once to describe the pleasure that the wife of a servant of Ximen's enjoys in
an unexpected sexual encounter with Ximen Qing (*JPM*, 78.30a). The best
example of his ironic appropriation of the phrase can perhaps be seen in
Chapter 8. One hundred days after Ximen Qing and Pan Jinlian poison Wu
Da, Pan's husband, they ironically invite six Buddhist monks to perform a
"land and water" mass for his benefit. Following no religious observances,
they engage, instead, in coitus as the ritual is under way. Their lewd conversation is overheard by a monk, who is just as lascivious—if not more so.
"Who would have thought," the narrator writes, "that everything they said
to each other was overheard with such great delight by this baldy?" (*JPM*,
8.12a). To preserve the Confucian phrase in its original form of direct speech,
David Roy translates this passage as: "Who would have thought that everything they said to each other was so clearly overheard by that shaven-pated
rascal that he might well have ejaculated: 'Is it not delightful?'" (*Plum*, p. 167).

It is no accident that when the narrator goes on to depict the reaction of
the other monks as they discover what is happening inside the room, he once
again resorts to the blasphemous rhetoric of appropriation: "They are so
much enchanted [by the imagined scene] that, unconsciously, their hands
began to move and their feet to dance" (*JPM*, 8.12a).[37] Several sentences after
a passage that describes Pan Jinlian's "sighing, moaning, panting, and groan-
ing" in "a trembling voice and melting tones," this passage shows how these
entranced monks respond. The phrase "the hands began to move and the
feet to dance" is drawn from two Confucian texts describing the power of
the moral and artistic impulse that men and women feel deep inside and
manifest through bodily movement.[38] Here again, the words of sacred texts
are appropriated into an incompatible context and given an ironic distortion.
Although no single word is changed, the original subject of the passage is replaced altogether: the motivating force that drives the monks into a state of
ecstasy is irrepressible lust rather than the impulse that Confucians discern
in human nature.

This rhetoric of appropriation and replacement, so widely seen in the dramas, jokes, and other genres of the late Ming, has a special application to the *jiuling*. As mentioned earlier, the rules of the *jiuling* often require that Confucius' words be combined with language from other sources. To cite *Yugu xinhuang* again: "A *jiuling* requires that a line from *Qianjia shi* be combined with a sentence from the *Analects* to make sense." The examples *Yugu xinhuang* offers are: "That one's name should be put on the published list of successful candidates [for the civil official examinations], is this not delightful?" "As for a night spent in the nuptial chamber with painted candles, surely there is pleasure to be found in it (*le yi zai qizhong yi* 樂亦在其中矣)" (see Fig. 4.1).[39] The two *jiuling* are formed in a similar pattern: the first half quotes a popular poem and sets up the subject for a comment drawn from the *Analects*. Coincidentally, once again Confucius' phrase *bu yi le hu* is put to use as if it were part of a standard language exercise in which every reader is required to fill in a topic. Out of such a verbal game there developed the habit of playing with Confucian texts and constructing hybrid sentences, as witnessed by the narratorial discourse of *Jin Ping Mei*.[40]

In *Jin Ping Mei*, *jiuling* and other verbal games feature prominently in scenes of everyday life and leisure entertainment. In Chapter 21 of the novel, Ximen Qing, his wife, and concubines are portrayed as playing a drinking game in which each of them composes in turn a verse consisting of the title of a popular tune, the names of two domino combinations, and a line quoted from the arias of *Xixiang ji*, a romantic comedy of the Yuan dynasty. In another drinking game depicted in Chapter 60, Ximen Qing and his guests are required to link the name of a flower to a sentence from the *Four Books* (*JPM*, 60.5b). As Wu Yueniang, Ximen's wife, explains in Chapter 21, they play the game in accordance with the domino handbooks (*paipu* 牌譜), which we know were prevalent during the late Ming period (*JPM*, 21.15b).

For the purpose of this study, it is interesting to note that this verbal game, which occurs in a dialogue among the characters, is ironically recapitulated in narratorial discourse. Like his characters, the narrator rarely speaks in a homogeneous language or from a consistent viewpoint; he shares with them a similar predilection for organizing and incorporating the languages of incongruous styles, contents, and sources.

On a larger scale, the novelist employs various strategies in working texts and genres into the fabric of the narrative. He borrows a wide range of lyrics

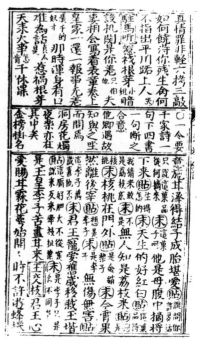

Fig. 4.1 *Yugu xinhuang* 玉谷新簧, a drama miscellany of the late Ming, pp. 116–17. The upper row includes excerpts from *Milan ji* 米欄記, and the bottom row from *Zhuanghe ji* 妝盒記. The middle row displays drinking verses under the rubric "Shixing gese jiuling" 時興各色 酒令 (A variety of popular drinking verses). The first subcategory of *jiuling* is "Sishu lei" 四書類 (The Four Books), which requires sentences from the Confucian *Four Books* to be combined with language from other sources; the second subcategory is "Qianjia shi lei" 千家 詩類 (Poems by a thousand poets), in which a *jiuling* is made of lines from *Qianjia shi*, a popular anthology of poetry.

from the collections of popular songs and puts them into the mouths of his characters. But so far as the self-expression of his characters is concerned, nothing seems more misleading than these borrowings, for they often project a romantic persona to which few characters measure up. Taking Pan Jinlian as an example, Katherine Carlitz and David Roy have argued that the novelist's constant portrayal of her appropriation of the lyrics of popular songs is an effective device for demonstrating her propensity for self-deception; it also exposes the inadequacy of these lyrics to convey the complexity and problematic qualities of human reality.[41] Although I concur with their argument, I would add that Pan's singing reveals at least a partial or temporary truth about her: as portrayed by these lyrics, she is indeed a helpless, lonely woman, overwhelmed by her longing for love during her prolonged wait for the return of her fickle lover and husband. In a more general sense, Pan's projection of her imagined self-image, deceptive as it may be, constitutes part of the reality of her complicated personality, which might otherwise be too elusive to capture. Thus, instead of postulating a contrast between Pan's self-expression or self-deception and her actions, I prefer to direct attention to what the novelist does with these quoted lyrics as he creates a novel of unprecedented complexity. It could be argued that he includes the lyrics of popular songs only in order to expose their limits in representing the characters he creates. In so doing, he may also present a context allowing these songs to modify what they are meant to express. But what is more important is that his strategy of including multiple genres and their characteristic modes of expression ultimately leads him to construct a narrative reality with a complexity beyond the reach of any single genre or mode of representation, including the novel. In so doing, he redefines what the vernacular novel or, in his own terminology, *cihua*, is and ought to be.

It is thus most relevant to see how the novelist adapts pre-existing stories and elements of earlier novels, especially *Shuihu zhuan* 水滸傳, the novel out of which he develops his novel and against which he defines it. Most revealing is an episode in Chapter 34, in which a shortened, revised version of a story drawn from an earlier collection of vernacular stories is put into the mouth of Ximen Qing, with all the stock phrases and expressions of conventional storytelling removed (*JPM*, 34.13a–14a).[42] Instead of representing the story from the perspective of a third-person, professional storyteller, the novelist allows Ximen Qing to project himself into the scenario of the story, to assume for himself the role of the judge in a case of manslaughter, and to tell the story from his own point of view. But what Ximen delivers is not so much a story as a court verdict: he spends the second half of his narration accounting for the court decision, and probably for this reason his narrative is more condensed, involving elements of the written language rarely seen in Ximen's everyday verbal communication.[43] In other words, here we are introduced to a different language zone, the register of such written forms of language as official memoranda, imperial edicts, court verdicts, *dibao*, and letters, as well as the diplomatic, formal language Ximen uses only in greeting civil officials and degree-holders.[44] Ximen often checks *dibao* for information on current official matters. In these episodes, the *dibao* contents are almost without exception presented verbatim. To make Ximen, a man of no formal education, a competent speaker or recipient of the official language, the novelist has to bring in several secretaries to help him deal with the exchange of letters and other forms of communication.

Nevertheless, for most readers, Ximen's command of so many forms of speech is far from convincing; despite his lack of education, Ximen speaks and comprehends the language of each of the circles he happens to associate with, and his vocabulary, which ranges from market slang to legal terminology to literary allusions, is contingent largely on circumstances.[45] Small wonder scholars of *Jin Ping Mei* have been unable to settle the issue of which local dialect is used for the characters' dialogue. The truth is that the novelist draws on the elements of different local dialects, not a single one, as some scholars would have us believe.[46] *Jin Ping Mei* is a complex structure containing multiple "languages," each with its own sphere of experience, its mode of expression, and its center of consciousness. At the level of the dialogue, we see how the novelist redisposes, redisperses, then reassembles these miscellaneous written and spoken languages into voices, and how he juxtaposes them in contrast, and forces them to conflict, negotiate, and communicate with one another. Fascinated by all existing forms of written language, as well as the accents, flavors, and nuances of dialogue, he allows himself to be led by languages, to be absorbed into their flow and matrix of rhetoric and meanings, to the point where he seems to be left with no privileged language of his own.

The author of *Jin Ping Mei* often seems more interested in showing what he is able to create from pre-existing texts than in creating his own narrative. He often, for example, draws on *Shuihu zhuan* to take apart and then repack its materials in the construction of his own novel. His narrative of Pan Jinlian in Chapter 8 of the novel is developed from *Shuihu zhuan*'s account of Pan Jinlian and Pan Qiaoyun combined, and ultimately from the larger matrix of similar narratives in late Ming literature.[47] In other words, it provides him with an occasion to rework the available topoi, metaphors, concepts, and motifs in stories of lewd monks and dissolute women. With sophisticated methods of adaptation and organizational skill, he knits them together to form an encyclopedic aggregate on the same subject.

In *Jin Ping Mei* these borrowed pieces are often brought in with no particular reason or carried further than the logic of the story of *Jin Ping Mei* would require. In some cases, they bring with them their own logic, which can hardly be integrated into the narrative of *Jin Ping Mei*. For instance, "Xinqiaoshi Han Wu mai chunqing" 新橋市韓五賣春情, a story based on earlier sources and included in Feng Menglong's *Gujin xiaoshuo* 古今小說 (Stories old and new), tells how a young man named Wu Shan is seduced by Han Jinnu, a prostitute in disguise, and then suffers the humiliating consequences.[48] In Chapters 98 and 99 of *Jin Ping Mei*, the novelist adapts this story in his account of Chen Jingji, Ximen's son-in-law, who, after Ximen's death in Chapter 79, seems to have stepped into the latter's shoes to become associated with all the women of the Ximen household. Two major scenes—Chen's encounter with Han Aijie, the daughter of Han Daoguo, the former manager of Ximen's silk goods store, and his subsequent lovemaking with her—are rendered in the manner of the Feng Menglong story.[49] Given the numerous discrepancies between the two narratives, the author of *Jin Ping Mei* had to take such pains to work the incidents and trivial details of the story into his novel that it would seem to have been, as Patrick Hanan puts it, simpler and quicker to invent them himself.[50] Here the novelist demonstrates that, like so many of his contemporaries, he is an editor at heart. But he is an editor of a different order, one of enormous ambition. And indeed, so ambitious is his attempt to absorb all types of texts and genres into his novel, to make them part of its narrative, that each of them has to redefine its own existence through its relation to the encyclopedic, all-encompassing *Jin Ping Mei*.[51]

In conclusion, *Jin Ping Mei* is connected to contemporary print culture in several aspects. It not only incorporates an extremely wide range of contemporary print materials but also recapitulates in narrative form the process through which they are circulated, accumulated, combined, proliferated, and corrupted. It participates in the reproduction of print culture through its perpetual recycling and reorganizing of the "ready-made," and its editing mode resembles the way in which those print materials were compiled. During the period when quantitative printing began to flourish, *Jin Ping Mei* signified the breakdown of the hierarchical order of social and linguistic registers. Its excessive fascination with such diverse print genres as *dibao*, contracts, and menus and its engagement in containing and combining all contemporary narrative motifs, modes, languages, and texts were closely linked to the particular historical experiences of cultural production and consumption its author witnessed during the late Ming.

II

As collections of discrete texts taken from multiple sources, literary miscellanies exhibited a distinctive page design, not to mention typography and other physical qualities. The format of the miscellanies allows unrelated, heterogeneous texts and genres to be presented on the same page and thus fundamentally shapes readers' perceptions and conceptualizations of the text world. The transfiguration of the text world was an integral part of the ongoing changes in late Ming cultural practice. It facilitated new writing and reading habits and evoked the multiplicity of voices, styles, and languages essential to the vision of the everyday represented in these print materials. Study of the issues of writing, reading, and the configuration of the text world will further contribute to our understanding of the composition of *Jin Ping Mei*.

In late Ming print materials, we see a general tendency toward a more and more sophisticated way of organizing the text world. One such method is to structure the texts of each page into several registers or rows. Although the division of pages into two rows of text dates to earlier times, it was not until the Wanli reign that the three-row format became popular, especially in drama miscellanies.[52] The format that divided each page into two or more rows of texts had at least two effects: it served as a means for ordering otherwise disorganized texts, and it also allowed unrelated texts to coexist on the same page.

Late Ming editors explored many possibilities within the two-row format (see Fig. 4.2). Besides the standard type, which has illustrations above and text below (*shangtu xiawen* 上圖下文), they experimented with various ways of combining two or more separate narrative texts: some books had abridged vernacular novels above and excerpted dramas below; some short classical tales above and vernacular fiction below; and some *Shuihu zhuan* above and *Sanguo yanyi* 三國演義 below.[53] In some cases, the upper row occupies two-thirds of the page, with the texts appearing in smaller characters than those in the lower row.[54] In still other cases, the upper row is reduced to one-fifth of the page and includes such short items as popular songs, jokes, riddles, slang, comments on courtesans, travel guides, and drinking verses to provide short amusements for readers of the extended narrative in the lower row.[55] In most cases, the texts of the two rows are unrelated to each other, as

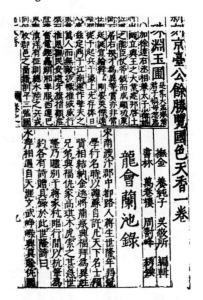

Fig. 4.2 *Guose tianxiang* 國色天香, a literary miscellany of the Wanli reign (preface dated 1587), p. 1. Included in the upper row are essays of earlier writers under the heading "Zhuyuan yupu" 朱淵玉圃 (Store-house of pearls and jades), which are in smaller type than the classical tale "Long hui Lanchi lu" 龍會蘭池錄 (Dragons meet in the Orchid Pond) in the bottom row.

exemplified in *Guose tianxiang*, a literary miscellany of the Wanli reign, in which the biography of a high-minded gentleman ("Xuanming gaoshi zhuan" 玄明高士傳) is followed by a comic allegory of sexual adventure ("Fengliu lequ" 風流樂趣), with romantic and erotic classical fiction unfolding in the row below.

The three-row format enabled the editors to include even more diverse texts. Normally, the entire middle row of the drama miscellanies is reserved for the short pieces described above.[56] Put together randomly, these pieces are related neither to one another nor to the dramatic texts in the top and bottom rows. One such example is *Da Ming tianxia chun* 大明天下春, a drama miscellany probably published in the early Wanli era. In *juan* 6 of the book the middle row has 108 satirical poems making fun of the physical defects of courtesans; the row above presents *chuanqi* 傳奇 plays on romantic themes; and the row below plays that describe the adventures of the heroes of *Sanguo yanyi* (see Fig. 4.3). In these examples, the special arrangement of the texts highlights the ironic contrast between high and low, refined and vulgar, serious and comic.

As late Ming editors squeezed unrelated and even incompatible texts on the same page, they also redefined the relation between text and picture. In the drama collections produced during the Chongzhen reign, the illustra-

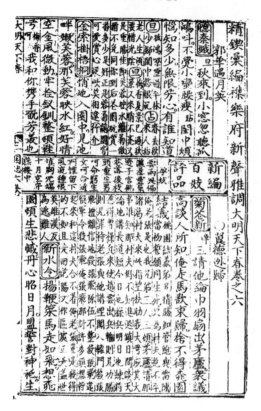

Fig. 4.3 *Da Ming tianxia chun* 大明天下春, another late Ming drama miscellany adopting the three-row format: the upper row features excerpts from *Yanzhi ji* 胭脂記; the bottom one, a scene from *Gucheng ji* 古城記; and the middle one, a collection of the comments on courtesans entitled "Xinbian baiji pingpin" 新編百妓評品 (Newly edited evaluations of the courtesans).

tions are sometimes not closely connected to the content of the text. As Ma Meng-ching notes, the illustration page usually has two sides. One still represents the scene of the play, but it focuses not so much on the characters as on the scenery (in fact, the characters are reduced to minimal size, and it becomes difficult even to identify them and see what they are doing). The other depicts landscape, flowers, birds, and other stock motifs of literati paintings that bear no relation to the play. Framed within a round circle, this second type of "illustration" seems to have been directly taken from contemporary printed painting albums (*huapu* 畫譜);[57] it is an independent painting transplanted into a book that has nothing to do with the subject of the illustration (see Fig. 4.4).

Related to this trend of reorganizing the text world is the unprecedentedly wide use of the commentary format in almost all types of late Ming print materials. Whether a medicine book or a collection of popular songs, at least one commentary accompanies the text, as if it would be incomplete

Fig. 4.4 Illustrations from *Xixiang ji* 西廂記 (Story of the western chamber) published by the Li Family of Shanyang 山陽 during the Chongzhen reign (1628–44). In Zhou Wu 周蕪, *Zhongguo banhuashi tulu* 中國版畫史圖錄 (Shanghai: Shanghai renmin meishu chubanshe, 1988), 2: 844–45.

without this bit of apparatus. Accordingly, it becomes impossible to read the text without reference to the commentary, which normally appears on the upper margin of the page, between the lines of the text, at the beginning and the end of each section of the book, or in various combinations of these places. Although the practice of including commentaries dates to earlier times, it was not until the late Ming that publishers, editors, and authors fully explored its potential for the development of irony and multivocality. Occasionally a novelist even composed the commentary for his own work, speaking in the guise of a commentator's voice. This use of the commentary form allowed an author to articulate points otherwise impossible for his narrator to make and thus to add another layer of discourse to his work.[58] In contrast, a commentator on a text composed by someone else seemed interested more in developing his own voice or point of view than in comprehending the text he claimed to be interpreting. The result is a page that bears the distinct voices of different people. In creating this polyglot text world, late Ming authors and editors had several strategies at their disposal. They could employ the multiple-row format to juxtapose the miscellaneous texts and voices or use the commentary format to generate a subtext written in the margins and between the lines of the main text.

Although commentary was usually printed in smaller type, it was often mistakenly incorporated into the main text when the work was reprinted. When this happened, the commentator's voice was internalized and became one of the voices to be heard throughout the novel; the line of demarcation between commentarial discourse and the narrator's or character's discourse became blurred, if not erased altogether. Out of this complicated process of textual incorporation comes a multilayered, heterogeneous text—a hybrid construction that combines texts of various types and sources, including those originally attached to it as comments.[59]

Late Ming experiments with the typography of books had an influence beyond the immediate sphere of the publishing industry. In an age of print culture, the format of printed books itself becomes a model for other domains of cultural practice. The pattern of organizing textual and pictorial space found in books is frequently seen, for example, in calligraphy and porcelain decoration during the late Ming and early Qing periods. Writing of late Ming innovations in calligraphy and the visual arts, Bai Qianshen shows how Fu Shan 傅山 (1607–84), a highly admired calligrapher of the time, explored multiple ways of accommodating the book format: excerpted texts of different sources were juxtaposed in a single piece of work, with interlinear comments rendered in smaller characters in precisely the fashion of printed books. During the seventeenth century, Chinese porcelains began to bear so many texts and pictures copied from contemporary books that some of them almost became, to borrow Bai's characterization, "porcelain books." The texts (sometimes nearly a thousand characters in length) often coexist on the same ceramic with unrelated pictures, a format similar to contemporary miscellanies.[60]

The change in book format was not merely a matter of innovative technique; it signifies a new mentality. What the multiple-row format introduces is not only a new principle of structuring the print world but also a new way of perceiving and organizing the world of experience; it suggests the mental ability to see and represent things in their simultaneous, separate existences. Interestingly enough, similar formats are widely used in present-day magazines and newspapers. And nowhere else can the organizing principle of juxtaposition be better demonstrated than in the pages of magazines and newspapers, where the most diverse, miscellaneous material is laid out side by side. There are no obvious connections between these materials and no reason why they should be so juxtaposed except for pure temporal coincidence. Commenting on the way multiple incidents are organized in modern newspapers, Benedict Anderson observes that these events "happen independently, without the actors being aware of each other or of what the others are up to. The arbitrariness of their inclusion and juxtaposition shows that the linkage between them is imagined." Thus, "reading a newspaper," as he puts it, "is like reading a novel whose author has abandoned any thought of a coherent plot."[61] From a slightly different angle and for a different purpose, Mikhail Bakhtin describes the newspaper page as "a living reflection of the contradictions of contemporary society in the cross-section of a single day." He then proceeds to argue that Dostoevsky, whose artistic vision of the world is indebted to the influence of newspapers, is inclined to "see everything as coexisting, to perceive and show all things side by side and simultaneous."[62]

A full study of the relationships between fiction and modern newspapers and their mutual interactions would not be possible until the late Qing period, when fiction writers were often also journalists or editors of newspapers and magazines. Here I emphasize only two points. First, as mentioned above, the rudiments of modern newspapers and magazines can be detected in the printed materials of the late Ming, if not earlier. Not only do the late Ming miscellanies resemble modern magazines to a large extent, several types of late Ming official gazettes (*dibao*) and tabloids (*xiaobao* and *zabao*), which were distributed in both print and handwritten forms, played an important role in transmitting news, gossip, and rumor. *Dibao*, *xiaobao*, and *zabao*—like contemporary miscellanies, daily-life encyclopedias, and notation books combining fragments of texts from other sources—are organized by juxtaposing disjunctive material. Since they covered current and ongoing events and were, in some cases, published on a regular basis, the date of publication explains why diverse and unrelated materials appear in the same issue. In this regard they do anticipate modern newspapers.[63] What is important here is that they introduce a mode of perceiving unrelated things as connected because they coexist in a single point in time. And accordingly, their coverage of contemporary events conjures up a new vision of the world, which cannot be reduced to existing modes of coherent narrative. Second, this new vision of the everyday world is, I would argue, often embedded in, and secured by, the design, format (both the multiple row and commentary formats), and other physical qualities of the page on which it is presented.[64] These factors are especially relevant to the emergence of the sometimes nonlinear narrative of *Jin Ping Mei*, which simultaneously represents multiple voices and incidents.

It is beyond the scope of this chapter to present a systematic analysis of the narrative mode adopted in *Jin Ping Mei* for its account of the everyday. Suffice it for now to reiterate the argument that *Jin Ping Mei* is a hybrid construction of texts taken from multiple genres and sources. As the novelist attempted to absorb these miscellaneous materials into his novel, he also allowed his novel to be shaped by their generic codes, narrative patterns, and modes of expression. In fact, in this encyclopedic novel these borrowed texts are far from being fully assimilated; they carry with them the specific approaches, forms of thinking, nuances, and accents characteristic of the given genres, and they remain as miscellaneous as their original sources. Occasionally they are even presented in the same format as in their sources and are thus set apart from the main text of the novel: they constitute an extra layer of text within the text. I shall now try to illustrate the way in which these miscellaneous materials contribute to the making of the multilayered, nonlinear narrative that fashions *Jin Ping Mei*'s representation of the everyday.

Consider the party scene in Chapter 52. As Li Guijie, Ximen's favorite prostitute (who claims to be his adopted daughter), presents a song sequence, Ying Bojue, a hopeless scoundrel otherwise known as Beggar Ying or Sponger Ying who lives by his wits, keeps interrupting her singing with comic remarks (*JPM*, 52.9b–11b). What is noteworthy is that his remarks appear in the fashion of commentaries on the Classics in smaller type in double lines within the column of type, immediately after the phrase(s) or the line(s) they refer to. In other words, they are rendered literally as "comments" on the songs, not as an integral part of the main text of the novel. Moreover, rather than elucidating the romantic love songs, these interlinear comments create a swirl of deliberate distortion, insulting vulgarity, grotesque erudition, and comic appropriation of jokes and popular songs that undercut the singing persona's self-absorbed voice. In the novel's depiction of the singing scene, an ironic tension and contrast arises both between singer and audience and between the song lyrics and the commentaries inscribed literally between their lines. To illustrate this point, I enclose the interlinear comments with square brackets (*JPM*, 52.9b–11a; see Fig. 4.5).[65]

Li Guijie slowly took her lute and put it across her knees. She opened her scarlet lips and showed the whiteness of her teeth. Then she sang the song called "Yizhou santai ling" 伊州三台令:...

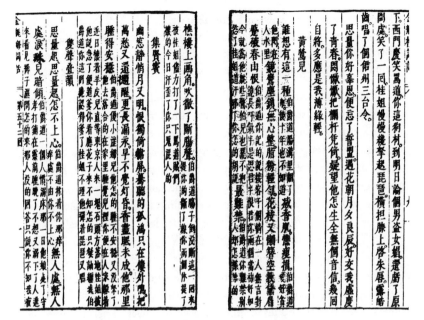

Fig. 4.5 *Jin Ping Mei cihua*, Chapter 52, pp. 9b, 10a.

"Huangyinger" 黃鶯兒:

Who would have dreamed that [Ying Bojue said: "How could you have expected that there would have been a shipwreck in the gutterway! You would not understand it even if I gave you ten more years to think about it."]

This so fragrant body could have been wasted

And brought low by suffering? [Ying Bojue said: "You may still love him, but he has dumped you anyway."]

My mirror is tarnished and I have no heart

To polish it.

I am too languid to adorn my face with powder,

Too languid to set flowers in my hair.

My brows are knit in bitterness. [Ying Bojue said: "Don't you remember the song that says 'Although I have entertained a thousand guests, I love only one person, and that is you. / Facing the mirror, with no words to say, I sigh deeply, I miss you as much as I hate you.' You used to like him, and thus no matter how much you are suffering now, you should not keep complaining about him." "You rascal," Li Guijie scolded, "what are you talking about?"]

Most hard to bear [Ying Bojue said: "How could you find it hard to take, if no one else makes a fuss about it?"]

Is the sound of the horn

Which the watchman blows on his tower of vigil.

It breaks my heart. [Ying Bojue said: "Your heart is not broken yet. But you and he have broken up. Don't mention the relationship anymore." Li Guijie hit him hard. "Damn you!" she shouted, "are you quite mad today that you mock me like this?"]

This passage is a perfect example of how the novelist turns a monologue into a dialogue. In it we see two irreconcilable voices and two different modes of discourse that are forced to confront and interact with each other. In commenting on the song Li Guijie is singing, Ying Bojue comes up with myriad ways of questioning the authenticity of the female speaker's voice. He insists on reading her self-indulgent lyrics from other angles and translating them into low and vulgar language. The most telling moment is when he comments on the lines from another song about love and betrayal: "Now I regret, / That I dealt with him so faithfully." Ying Bojue interjects, "You stupid whore. Why did you treat him faithfully? Nowadays, even a three-year-old kid can outfox you, to say nothing of the whoremasters." He then goes on to sing a song about the misery a prostitute suffers to remind us of Li Guijie's true identity and undermine what he perceives as her deceptive self-representation. To judge from the effect, his strategy works well: his comments drive Li to tears.

It is the novelist's use of the commentary format in this passage that creates this peculiar dialogue: the sentimental singing is punctuated, and at one point suspended, by the interpolated ridiculing remarks. In late Ming commentaries on popular songs, we can often hear a comic voice similar to Ying Bojue's.[66] But it is the author of *Jin Ping Mei* who gives that voice a speaker in Ying Bojue, who is portrayed as living on the margins of both society and text.

What we see in Ying's interpolations is not a written commentary on the lyrics of the songs but an oral response to the singing of the song, executed by a particular character at a particular moment. Within the context of *Jin Ping Mei*, the commentary format has an additional function: as the novelist conceives of distinct voices for his characters and drives them to encounter or quarrel with each other, he makes use of this format to help create the sense that these verbal interactions are taking place before the singing comes to an end. It is almost as if he is attempting to render visually comments that in the theater would be made by one actor while another actor was speaking. He places the interlinear comments after a specific phrase, line, or unit of lines, rather than at the end of one stanza or one song, suggesting that Ying Bojue's remarks occur during the singing, or while specific lines or phrases are sung. As shown at the beginning of the passage, Ying Bojue is so familiar with popular songs that he anticipates upcoming lyrics; he cuts in even before Li Guijie has finished the first line. Also included in the interpolations is a depiction of the physical interaction between Ying Bojue and Li Guijie.

As this farcical scene continues, Ximen Qing and Xie Xida intervene. In the next episode, Li Guijie resumes singing (*JPM*, 52.10b–11a; Egerton, *The Golden Lotus*, p. 359):

"Cuyulin" 簇御林:

    Men all say that he is noble and true . . . [Ying Bojue began to say something, but Xie Xida clapped a hand over his mouth, telling Li: "Please continue. Don't pay any attention to this guy."]

    But the rogue turns out to be a deceiver.

    His eyes are open wide, but lips and heart

    Speak different stories. [No sooner had Xie Xida taken his hand away from Ying Bojue's mouth than Ying began to speak again: "If they had spoken the same language, then how could you have gotten into such a plight?" . . . Ximen Qing and the others all laughed.]

As the singing continues, another story is unfolding in these interpolations, in the form of a double-lined commentary. Nor is this the only way that, in representing verbal and nonverbal acts, the author of *Jin Ping Mei* tried to generate a sense of simultaneity. His renderings of the characters' dialogue, for example, are constantly interrupted by seemingly irrelevant incidents; the same scenes are presented two or more times from the perspectives of different characters; or a seemingly uneventful, repetitive party scene may be depicted while something important is happening. Yet, this innovative use of the format of conventional commentary has a unique advantage: it adds another layer of text to the novel and tells a story that lurks between the lines of the main text, one quite at odds with that told in the main text.

This passage is more than just an illustration of the novelist's use of the commentary format to evoke multivocality and the sense of simultaneity in his narrative of everyday activities. It can also be read in the context of contemporary drama collections and miscellanies. Contemporary readers would have recognized the scene immediately, because in drama miscellanies (and sometimes in collections of popular songs) the lines of a song are often broken up by interpolated exclamations, monologues, and dialogues. David Rolston points out that when quoting from collections of popular songs and drama miscellanies, the author of *Jin Ping Mei* often preserves the orthographic convention of printing the interpolations in smaller characters in double lines within the column of print.[67] The best example of this can be found in Chapter 38, in which Pan Jinlian is portrayed singing a sequence of popular songs. Her singing is punctuated by her monologue, which is presented in the interpolations in small characters (*JPM*, 38.8b–9a, 10a–b). In another instance in Chapter 31, the novelist presents an ongoing *yuanben* 院本 farce (a comic skit about Wang Bo) drawn from the dramatic repertoire and includes in the interpolations the stage directions, using the technical term *ke* 科 to indicate the posture and action taken by the actors onstage (*JPM*, 31.13a–14b; see Fig. 4.6).[68] What we see here is not a realistic representation of a dramatic performance but a presentation of a dramatic text composed in the fashion of the drama miscellanies. The entire section is removed from the immediate context of the novel because it is rendered differently; its appearance in the format of drama miscellanies generates a distancing effect, and the inclusion of stage directions reminds us of its status as a written script that is yet to be enacted. Similarly, the Ying Bojue and Li Guijie passage is a farce, with Ying acting the part of the clown. As is normally the case in *yuanben* farce, this farcical scene begins with a verbal interaction between two comical characters and proceeds with one beating the other to provoke laughter. The passage is not only constructed in the farcical mode of *yuanben* but also presented in the printed form of the drama miscellanies. Accordingly we may read it as a dramatic text in the novel.

In examining the way in which *Jin Ping Mei* incorporates all the strata and forms of literary languages and genres, I have focused on the printed forms in which these genres and languages are presented. Granted, in *Jin Ping Mei* the borrowed texts are sometimes integrated into the novel with none of the visible formal marks that usually accompany them. But the examples given above show that the incorporated genres often carry with them not only their specific modes of expression and other generic and stylistic peculiarities but also their characteristic written and printed formats, which in turn determine the form of the novel in general. It is here that the study of late Ming print materials (especially literary miscellanies) and the way they organize the text world become relevant. By combining radically heterogeneous and traditionally incompatible forms, *Jin Ping Mei* created a special type of literary miscellany. It made little effort to absorb these distinct forms into it dominant prose narrative or to smooth the transition

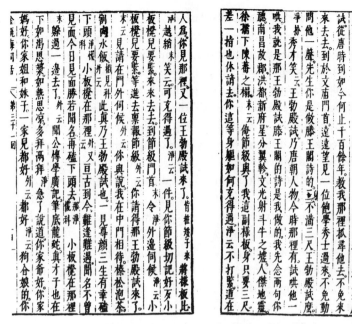

Fig. 4.6 *Jin Ping Mei cihua*, Chapter 31, pp. 13b, 14a.

from one form to another. In depicting singing, for example, it sometimes inserted a verse commenting on the content of the songs. Introducing the verse with the formulaic phrases of the conventional storytelling *you shi wei zheng* 有詩為證 (there is a poem to prove the point) or *zhengshi* (truly), it not only interrupts the flow of the singing but also creates an abrupt shift in narrative perspective.[69] Here as elsewhere, the juxtaposition of the commentary verse with the popular song contributes to the discontinuities and contradictions in the composition of the novel. Pushing this analogy with literary miscellanies further, one could argue that without adopting the multiple-row format, *Jin Ping Mei* still manages to internalize that format and turn it into a pattern of composition.

We should take into account the possible changes the format of miscellanies brought to contemporary modes of reading, for the response of the reader is most likely to be shaped by typography, page design, binding, and other features of the book as a physical object.[70] As Robert Hegel points out, the "string binding" (*xianzhuang* 線裝) format, which was commonly used in the Wanli era, permits fast or casual reading appropriate to such extended texts as plays and novels.[71] In a similar fashion, the way the editors of miscellanies organized the most diverse, incongruous materials within a single piece of work and their adoption of the multiple-row format may well have fostered new reading habits and changed the way people read books.

How would late Ming readers have read such a complicated novel as *Jin Ping Mei*, which deviated from the established model of vernacular novels, a novel that was composed of multiple genres and texts borrowed from other sources, shaped by the different formats of its components, and fraught with so many details and internal gaps? Assuming the voice of an authoritative guide for readers, Zhang Zhupo once advised them to read *Jin Ping Mei* as intensively as they had been trained to read the Confucian classics. Rather than gliding over the text paragraph by paragraph, they should read it word by word, and read it aloud, pointing at each of the characters.[72] One may wonder if anyone followed this advice when reading the novel, but it is clear that Zhang had his own agenda: devoted to promoting the status of the vernacular novel, he demanded that *Jin Ping Mei* be read closely, back and forth many times, and even recited as if it were a canonical text.

It is difficult, if not impossible, to reconstruct the way late Ming readers approached vernacular novels. But so far as *Jin Ping Mei* is concerned, intensive reading could be as frustrating as it was illuminating, for the novel has too many inconsistencies and too often slips into the habit of presenting uninterrupted sequences of songs, jokes, *jiuling*, and other verbal games of daily entertainment. For modern readers, there seems nothing in these sections of the novel to carry them along. And indeed, more often than not, these borrowed texts and genres occur in places where the narration becomes looser, such as the recurring party scenes, which may sometimes appear superfluous to the main story line of the novel. But by including these fragments borrowed from contemporary miscellanies, *Jin Ping Mei* might well have appealed to readers who shared this world of reference. For readers familiar with the popular print materials of the time, these sections of the novel would allow them to enjoy jokes, anecdotes, and popular songs that they already knew, and the novelist's frequent account of lantern riddles and *chaipai daozi* 拆白道字 (resolving characters into their basic components) would surely lure them into playing familiar verbal games and help to connect them to *Jin Ping Mei*'s recurring sense of leisure entertainment. In many instances, the novelist, as C. T. Hsia puts it, seems eager to "impress a special audience who will applaud his cleverness in offering other kinds of borrowed attractions."[73] And surely he deserves credit for his manifest talent in turning these familiar materials into the stuff of verbal exchange between his characters.

Since the novelist drew so heavily on contemporary miscellanies, to understand how the readers of the day read *Jin Ping Mei*, we would do well to begin by asking how they read miscellanies. With few exceptions, the editors of miscellanies adopted the multiple-row format; they presented readers with choices, allowing them to select what to read as they turned from page to page. As in the modern newspaper or magazine, the distinct discourses in different rows are the formal representation of "choice." Here we may once again compare the experience of reading miscellanies with that of watching a multiple-ring circus in the marketplace.[74] As we wander from one show to another, there is, indeed, no definitive route. In fact, the marketplace offers us such a variety of attractions that we are allowed, or even invited, to make our own choices. The mechanism of the markets is predicated on a theater of choice. The same is true of miscellanies, in which extremely diverse texts are placed side by side on the page for choice. In its depiction of the multiplicity of spheres in everyday life, *Jin Ping Mei* shares some of the features of the miscellany. But it is more than this. *Jin Ping Mei* is an elaborate drama about freedom of choice and its consequences, with economic and sexual choices being the dominant paradigm. It dramatizes not merely choice but the competition to be chosen. If the editors of miscellanies invite the reader to move from one item to another at will, in a similar way the variety of topics in *Jin Ping Mei* are organized according to Ximen Qing's whims. And interestingly enough, Ximen Qing is the first case of the consumer as protagonist in the Chinese novel.

How does the code of the marketplace, which is embedded in the format and narrative motifs and patterns of literary and nonliterary texts, regulate the way in which those texts are read? In the case of literary miscellanies, a reader following a drama on the bottom row from one page to the next might find it tempting to glance at the rows above for jokes, riddles, market slang, common sayings, and popular songs. These short pieces, which are usually included in the middle row, might be entertaining enough to lure the reader briefly away from the main story. Although they are not an integral part of the drama, in the actual reading experience the various elements on the page would become mixed up with one another; indeed, these side attractions threaten to interrupt at any moment and demand to be integrated into the actual reading process as one follows the drama in the row above or below. As a result of these distractions, the linear temporality of the reading process is constantly interrupted. As we read upwards and downwards simultaneously, crossing over three distinct rows, consciously or not, we develop a reading strategy to cope with fragmented materials on the page. That is to say, this format facilitates the development of random or casual reading habits. In a more general sense, this development is connected to the flourishing of late Ming commercial publishing, for the outpouring of a large quantity of books encouraged extensive rather than intensive reading.

As *Jin Ping Mei* creates a multilayered, variegated, nonlinear narrative in its account of the everyday, it conveys a new vision of the world, one that calls for new strategies of reading and comprehension. Daily-life encyclopedias and literary miscellanies represent a similar vision of the world in their incorporation of extremely rich and diverse materials on the same page. It is within this larger cultural context of perceiving and constructing the everyday that I discuss the issues of reading, writing, and the material forms in which the text world is presented. Obviously, the change in book format requires the acquisition of a new manner of reading and a new intellectual skill. Likewise, as readers developed an appetite for the consumption of large quantities of texts, publishers accordingly compiled and designed their books in such a way as to accommodate the need for fast, extensive, and random reading. The various miscellanies in wide circulation during the Wanli reign were produced in part to meet such a need. Wu Congxian 吳從先, a Suzhou literatus living in the late Ming period, once described his dissatisfaction with reading only one book at a time: "Generally speaking, when reading a short book, you will complain that it can be easily finished. Yet when reading a long book, you will complain that it is hard to finish it. Reading a book of resentment, your hair will bristle with anger; while reading a joyful book, you will beat your spittoon until it is broken."[75] Wu recommended striking a balance: "Whenever you read a book, you should have other books at hand as well." A miscellany is such a book. It combines texts of various lengths, tones, genres, styles, and contents into one single volume; it allows readers to read many books at once.

Readers familiar with the content and format of miscellanies would not find a novel like *Jin Ping Mei* an entirely new experience. Of course, late Ming readers would not read the novel in exactly the way they read miscellanies, for the novel and the miscellany are, after all, different species. But those practiced in what might be called random, non-linear reading when skimming through miscellanies, simultaneously covering two or more unrelated narratives in different rows, would almost certainly have had no serious problems coping with the fragmented narrative, inserted genres, and borrowed texts so often encountered in *Jin Ping Mei*. In this sense, *Jin Ping Mei* is indeed the product of late Ming print culture, and its composition is closely connected to the random reading habits conditioned by the format of contemporary print materials.

Notes

1. In this chapter, I cite a reprint of the edition in the Beijing Library: Lanling Xiaoxiao Sheng 蘭陵笑笑生, *Jin Ping Mei cihua* 金瓶梅詞話 (Hongkong: Taiping shuju, 1982).

2. For the dramatic and popular song materials in *Jin Ping Mei*, see Feng Yuanjun 馮沅君, "*Jin Ping Mei cihua* zhong de wenxue shiliao" 金瓶梅詞話中的文學史料, in *Guju shuohui* 古劇說匯 (Beijing: Zuojia chubanshe, 1956), pp. 48–57; and Patrick Hanan, "Sources of the *Chin P'ing Mei*," in *Asia Major* 10 (1963): 23–67.

3. C. T. Hsia, *The Classic Chinese Novel: A Critical Introduction* (New York: Columbia University Press, 1968), p. 169.

4. *Cihua* was one of the names used to designate the emerging novel during the sixteenth century. But *Jin Ping Mei* obviously outgrew the model provided by such earlier novels as *Shuihu zhuan* and *Sanguo yanyi* and became, so to speak, a genre of its own. A number of scholars who believe that *Jin Ping Mei* developed from the traditional *cihua* genre have done extensive research on the generic history of *cihua*, but it seems to me that none of them has convincingly explained how *Jin Ping Mei cihua* developed a sophisticated narrative form and episodic structure that obviously goes beyond the *cihua* genre. David Rolston ("Oral Performing Literature in Traditional Chinese Fiction: Nonrealistic Usages in the *Jin Ping Mei cihua* and Their Influence," *Chinoperl Papers* 17 [1994]: 34) argues that compared with the prosimetric texts printed in the Chenghua reign (1465–87) and found in a tomb near Shanghai and the late Ming work *Da Tang Qinwang cihua* 大唐秦王詞話 by Zhu Shenglin 諸聖鄰, *Jin Ping Mei* sets itself apart in the way it uses poetry (*shizan* 詩贊): "(1) while poetry (primarily *ci* and *qu*) is used to replace dialogue, in only one instance (86/8a) is narrative and dialogue mixed the way it is in the poetry of the other *cihua*, and (2) the material borrowed from oral performing literature is not used according to any one overriding convention but is experimental and largely unassimilated."

5. With Zhang Zhupo's 張竹坡 commentary on *Jin Ping Mei* as their guide, David Roy ("Introduction," in idem, trans., *The Plum in the Golden Vase or, Chin P'ing Mei* [Princeton: Princeton University Press, 1993], pp. xvii–xlviii) and Andrew Plaks (*The Four Masterworks of the Ming Novel* [Princeton: Princeton University Press, 1987], pp. 55–182) have tried to reveal the unifying structural patterns of the novel. In *The Rhetoric of "Chin P'ing mei"* (Bloomington: Indiana University Press, 1986), a study of the role of drama and popular song in the making of *Jin Ping Mei cihua*, Katherine Carlitz explored the ways the novelist manages to integrate multiple genres and sources into a coherent design for the novel. Other critics, inspired by Mikhail Bakhtin's theory about the novel, have pursued a different critical approach and made more theoretically complex statements about heteroglossia in *Jin Ping Mei ci-*

hua; see, e.g., Chaoyang Liao, "Three Readings in the *Jinpingmei cihua*," *Chinese Literature: Essays, Articles, and Reviews* 6 (1984): 77–99.

6. By "late Ming" I refer mainly to the period from the Wanli (1573–1620) through the Chongzhen reigns (1628–44), but in my discussion of print materials I occasionally include texts published in the Jiajing period (1522–66), which initiated the publishing development that culminated in the Wanli and Chongzhen reigns. I also touch on some publications of the early Qing period, because they were, to a certain degree, continuations of late Ming publishing trends, and some of them can only be tentatively dated to the period from the Chongzhen through the Shunzhi (1644–61) reigns.

7. In an article written in 1954, Pan Kaipei 潘開沛 ("*Jin Ping Mei de chansheng he zuozhe*" 金瓶梅的產生和作者, in idem, *Ming Qing xiaoshuo yanjiu lunwen ji* 明清小說研究論文集[Beijing: Renmin wenxue, 1959], pp. 173–80), argued that *Jin Ping Mei*, like other earlier novels, gradually took shape through the collective efforts of professional storytellers. This theory was refuted by Xu Mengxiang 徐夢湘 and other scholars, but reiterated most recently by Liu Hui 劉輝 and Xu Shuofang 徐朔方 (see Xu Mengxiang, "Guanyu *Jin Ping Mei* de zuozhe" 關於金瓶梅的作者, in *Ming Qing xiaoshuo yanjiu lunwen ji* 明清小說研究論文集, ed. Renmin wenxue chubanshe 人民文學出版社[Beijing: Renmin wenxue chubanshe, 1959], pp. 181–84; Liu Hui, "Cong cihua ben dao shuosan ben—*Jin Ping Mei* chengshu guocheng ji zuozhe wenti yanjiu" 從詞話本到說散本—金瓶梅成書過程及作者問題研究, in idem, *Jin Ping Mei lunwen ji* 金瓶梅論文集 [Taibei: Guanya wenhua shiye youxian gongsi, 1992], pp. 1–46; and Xu Shuofang, "*Jin Ping Mei* chengshu xintan" 金瓶梅成書新探, in "*Jin Ping Mei*" *pingzhu* 金瓶梅評注, ed. Cai Guoliang 蔡國梁[Guilin: Lijiang chubanshe, 1986], pp. 298–342). So far, however, the scholars in favor of this theory have not been able to produce any compelling evidence, and their basic argument—that *Jin Ping Mei* developed from the tradition of storytelling because its narrative is fraught with inconsistencies, repetitions, and a wide range of borrowed texts from popular songs and dramas—is questionable. As Andrew Plaks (*Four Masterworks*, pp. 69–70) observes, "There do exist a number of examples of popular treatment of episodes from the *Jin Ping Mei* in various folk genres (especially the *zidi shu*), the earliest evidence of which is mentioned in Zhang Dai's *Taoan mengyi*, but these all appear to be materials derived from the novel rather than the other way around."

8. See Yuan Hongdao's 袁宏道 (1568–1610) letter to Dong Qichang 董其昌 (1555–1636) in *Yuan Hongdao chidu quangao* 袁宏道尺牘全稿 (Shanghai: Shidai tushu, 1934), p. 46. For a detailed discussion of the letter, see Patrick Hanan, "The Text of the *Chin P'ing Mei*," *Asia Major* 9 (1962): 1–57.

9. See Shen Defu 沈德符, *Wanli yehuo bian* 萬曆野獲編 (Beijing: Zhonghua shuju, 1959), p. 652. It was presumably a common practice to hang books (or book

covers) on the city gates by way of advertisement. As Ellen Widmer ("The Huan-duzhai of Hangzhou and Suzhou: A Study in Seventeenth-Century Publishing," *Harvard Journal of Asiatic Studies* 56 [1996]: 93) notes, Wang Qi 汪淇 (1600?–1668?), the owner of Huanduzhai 還讀齋, a publishing house in the Jiangnan region, once described in the *fanli* 凡例 to his *Lichao jielu* 歷朝捷錄 that he did this to attract readers.

10. Rolston, "Oral Performing Literature in Traditional Chinese Fiction," p. 30.

11. In David Der-wei Wang and Shang Wei, eds., *Dynastic Decline and Cultural Innovation: From the Late Ming to the Late Qing* (Cambridge, Mass.: Harvard University Asia Center, forthcoming).

12. Here I base myself on Dorothy Ko's studies of trends in late Ming publishing; see her *Teachers of the Inner Chamber* (Stanford: Stanford University Press, 1994), pp. 34–41. But I am not suggesting that late Ming publishing underwent a transition from quality printing to quantity printing. In fact, it was during the late Ming that quality printing reached its zenith. For other studies of late Ming publishing business, see K. T. Wu, "Ming Printing and Printers," *Harvard Journal of Asiatic Studies* 7 (1943): 203–4; Tsien Tsuen-Hsuin, *Paper and Printing*, in Joseph Needham, ed., *Science and Civilization in China*, vol. 5, pt. 1 (Cambridge, Eng.: Cambridge University Press, 1985); Robert Hegel, *Reading Illustrated Fiction in Late Imperial China* (Stanford: Stanford University Press, 1998), pp. 127–63; Zhang Xiumin 張秀民, *Zhongguo yin-shua shi* 中國印刷史 (Shanghai: Shanghai renmin chubanshe, 1989), pp. 334–543; Li Zhizhong 李致忠, *Lidai keshu kaoshu* 歷代刻書考述 (Chengdu: Bashu shushe, 1990), pp. 217–44; Ye Shusheng 葉樹聲, "Mingdai Nanzhili Jiangnan diqu siren keshu gaishu" 明代南直隸江南地區私人刻書概述, *Wenxian* 文獻 32 (Feb. 1987): 213–29; Inoue Susumu 井上進, "Zōsho to dokusho" 藏書と讀書, *Tōhō ga-kuhō* 東方学 報 62 (Mar. 1990): 409–45; and Ōki Yasushi 大木康, "Minmatsu Kōnan ni okeru shuppan bunka no kenkyū" 明末江南における出版文化の研究, *Hiroshima daigaku bungakubu kiyō* 広島大学文学部紀要 50, special issue no. 1 (1991): 1–176.

13. Published mainly during the Wanli and Chongzhen periods by the commercial presses in Fujian, the encyclopedias for daily use left few traces in the bibliographies compiled by the official elite of the late Ming and the Qing periods. Thanks to the efforts of social historians and literary scholars during the past several decades, they have re-emerged and become an essential source for the studies of popular mentalities and social history. Several major encyclopedias are included in *Chūgoku nichiyō ruisho shusei* (Collection of Chinese encyclopedias for everyday use), published by Kyūko in 1998. For studies of late Ming encyclopedias for daily use and other related genres, see Sakai Tadao 酒井忠夫, "Mindai no nichiyō ruisho to shomin kyōiku" 明代の日用類書と庶民教育 (Encyclopedias for Daily Use and Popular Education in the Ming Dynasty), in *Kinsei Chūgoku kyōikushi kenkyū* 近世中国教育

史研究, ed. Hayashi Tomoharu 林友春(Tokyo: Kokudo, 1958), pp. 25–154; idem, "Confucianism and Popular Educational Works," in *Self and Society in Ming Thought*, ed. Wm. Theodore de Bary (New York: Columbia University Press, 1970), pp. 331–66; Niida Noboru 仁 井 田 陞, "Gen Min jidai no mura no kiyaku to kosaku shō-sho nado, nichiyō hyakka zensho no rui nijūshu no naka kara" 元明時代の村の規約と小作證書など、日用百科全書の類 二十種のなかから, in idem, *Chūgoku hōseishi kenkyū* 中国法制史研究 (Tokyo: Tobunken, 1962), pp. 741–829; Wang Ermin 王爾敏, "Chuantong Zhongguo shumin richang shenghuo qingjie" 傳統中國庶民日常生活情節, *Zhongyang yanjiuyuan, Jindaishi yanjiusuo jikan* 中央研究院近代史研究所季刊 21 (1992): 147–76; and Chen Xuewen 陳學文, *Ming Qing shiqi shangye shu ji shangren shu zhi yanjiu* 明清時期商業書及 商人書之研究 (Taibei: Hongye, 1997). On the relationships between the daily-life encyclopedias and late Ming vernacular novels, see Ogawa Yōichi 小川陽一, *Nichiyō ruisho ni yoru Min-Shin shōsetsu no kenkyū* 日用類書による明清小説の研究 (Tokyo: Kenbun, 1995); and Shang Wei, "The Making of the Everyday World: *Jin Ping Mei* and Encyclopedias for Daily Use," in *Dynastic Decline and Cultural Innovation: From the Late Ming to the Late Qing*, ed. David Der-wei Wang and Shang Wei (Cambridge, Mass.: Harvard University Asia Center, forthcoming). Late Ming literary miscellanies are often placed under different rubrics in traditional bibliographies and have only occasionally been treated as a genre. Scattered as they are, some of the miscellanies have been included in such series as *Guben xiaoshuo jicheng* 古本小說集成 (Shanghai: Shanghai guji chubanshe, 1990) and Wang Qiugui 王秋桂, ed., *Shanben xiqu cong-kan* 善本戲曲叢刊 (Taibei: Taiwan xuesheng shuju, 1984). On the novellas included in late Ming miscellanies, see Wang Gang 王崗, *Langman qinggan yu zongjiao jingshen: Wan Ming wenxue yu wenxue sichao* 浪漫情感與宗教精神—晚明文學與文學思潮 (Hongkong: Tiandi tushu, 1999), pp. 114–182. Encyclopedias and miscellanies are connected in many aspects. Yu Xiangdou 余象斗 (1560?–1637?), the editor of *Santai wanyong zhengzhong* 三台萬用正宗 (in *Chūgoku nichiyō ruisho shusei* 中國日用類書集成, vols. 3–5 [Tokyo: Kyūko, 1998]), purportedly one of the most comprehensive daily-life encyclopedias of the late Ming period, compiled *Wanjin qinglin*, a literary miscellany, which shares a large portion of its texts with *Santai wanyong zhengzhong*. Probably for this reason, Sun Kaidi 孫楷第 (*Riben Dongjing suojian xiaoshuo shumu* 日本東京所見小說書目 [Beijing: Renmin wenxue chubanshe, 1958], p. 127) and Hu Shiying 胡士瑩 (*Huaben xiaoshuo gailun* 話本小說概論 [Beijing: Zhonghua shuju, 1980], pp. 404–11) describe literary miscellanies as *tongsu leishu* 通俗類書.

14. See *Siku quanshu zongmu* 四庫全書總目 (Beijing: Zhonghua shuju, 1956), pp. 1106–40.

15. Several scholars have made such an observation in their studies of late Ming print materials. See Zheng Zhenduo 鄭振鐸, *Xidi shuhua* 西諦書話 (Beijing:

Sanlian chubanshe, 1983), pp. 147–48; Wang Zhongmin 王重民, *Zhongguo shanben-shu tiyao* 中國善本書提要 (Shanghai: Shanghai guji chubanshe, 1983), p. 383; Tan Zhengbi 譚正璧, *Guben xijian xiaoshuo huikao* 古本稀見小說匯考 (Hangzhou: Zhejiang wenyi chubanshe, 1984), pp. 26–28; and Hu Shiying, *Huaben xiaoshuo gailun*, pp. 410–11.

16. Patrick Hanan, *The Invention of Li Yu* (Cambridge, Mass.: Harvard University Press, 1988), pp. 24–25; see also Widmer, "The Huanduzhai of Hangzhou and Suzhou," pp. 93, 105.

17. A large number of *dibao* produced during the Wanli reign are included in *Wanli dichao* 萬曆邸鈔 (Yangzhou: Jiangsu Guangling guji keyinshe, 1991; Taiwan guoli zhongyang tushuguan, 1963). But these *dibao* have been edited by their compilers or transcribers and thus do not reveal the original shape in which they were presented. For a recent study of Ming *dibao*, see Yin Yungong 尹韵公, *Zhongguo Ming-dai xinwen chuanbo shi* 中國明代新聞傳播史 (Chongqing: Chongqing chubanshe, 1990). See also Liu Yongqiang 劉勇強, "Ming Qing dibao yu wenxue zhi guanxi" 明清邸報與文學之關系, *Xueren* 學人 3 (1992): 437–64; Wang Hongtai 王鴻泰, "Liudong yu hudong: you Ming Qing jian chengshi shenghuo de texing tance gong-gong changyu de kaizhan" 流動與互動—由明清間城市生活的特性探測公共場域的開展 (Ph.D. diss., Taiwan University, 1998), pp. 306–45; and Timothy Brook, *The Confusions of Pleasure* (Berkeley: University of California Press, 1998), pp. 171–72.

18. The term *xinwen* 新聞 was widely used in the late Ming to refer to news about current, sensational events; see Yin Yungong, *Zhongguo Mingdai xinwen chuan-bo shi*, pp. 15–16.

19. Ibid., pp. 165–73.

20. Feng Menglong, *Gujin tan'gai*, pp. 616–17. For Tu Long's *Kaijuan yixiao*, see Huang Lin 黃霖, "Jin Ping Mei zuozhe Tu Long kao" 金瓶梅作者屠隆考, in idem, *Jin Ping Mei kaolun* 金瓶梅考論 (Shenyang: Liaoning renmin chubanshe, 1988), pp. 199–217. See also Liu Yongqiang, "Ming Qing dibao yu wenxue zhi guanxi," p. 442.

21. One example of *dibao xiaoshuo* is a novel completed around 1630, *Jinbao congtan pinglu zhuan* 近報叢譚平虜傳 (Pacification and capture of the invaders, recent news and collected anecdotes; in *Guben xiaoshuo jicheng* 古本小說集成, vol. 22 [Shanghai: Shanghai guji chubanshe, 1990]). In this account of the Manchu invasion of the Ji (Hebei) area and Beijing, a contemporary event that would ultimately bring the Ming dynasty to an end, its author not only quotes numerous official documents but also indicates that the sources for each section of the novel are the official gazettes (*dibao*) or oral reports (*congtan*). For other novels in this category and their significance in the account of the current political and military "news," see Chen Dakang 陳大康, *Tongsu xiaoshuo de lishi guiji* 通俗小說的歷史軌迹 (Changsha:

Hunan chubanshe, 1993), pp. 126–33; Chen Dadao 陳大道, "Mingmo Qingchu shishi xiaoshuo de tese" 明末清初時事小說的特色, *Xiaoshuo xiqu yanjiu* 小說戲曲研究 3 (1988): 181–220; Ōki Yasushi, "Minmatsu Kōnan ni okeru shuppan bunka no kenkyū," pp. 135–38; and Hegel, *Reading Illustrated Fiction in Late Imperial China*, pp. 41–42.

22. See Wang Qiugui, *Shanben xiqu congkan*, vol. 21.

23. For the sources of *Wanjin jiaoli*, see Ji Guoping 季國平, "Xiqu zhaji erze" 戲曲札記二則, *Wenxue yichan* 文學遺產 6 (1990): 105–7; and Huang Qiang 黃强, "*Wanjin jiaoli* suoshou xiaoshuo dierzhong chuyu *Rouputuan*" 萬錦嬌麗所收小說第二種出於肉蒲團, *Wenxue yichan* 文學遺產 1 (1992): 122.

24. See Chen Liangduan 陳良端, "Yeshuo *Wanjin jiaoli* jiqi suoshou de sanzhong xiaoshuo" 也說萬錦嬌麗及其所收的三種小說, *Wenxue yichan* 文學遺產 3 (1990): 104–5.

25. Literally, "words that come after a pause." For a detailed explanation of the formation of *xiehouyu* and its use in *Jin Ping Mei*, see Roy, *Plum in the Golden Vase*, p. 488n28.

26. *Yugu xinhuang* 玉谷新簧, in *Shanben xiqu congkan* 善本戲曲叢刊, ed. Wang Qiugui 王秋桂 (Taibei: Taiwan xuesheng shuju, 1984), 2: 116.

27. Ibid., p. 139.

28. One such example can be seen in *juan* 8 of *Da Ming tianxia chun* 大明天下春, in *Haiwai guben wan Ming xiju xuanji sanzhong* 海外孤本晚明戲劇選集三種, ed. Li Fuqing 李福清 (Russian) and Li Ping 李平 (Chinese) (Shanghai: Shanghai guji chubanshe, 1993), pp. 579–644. See also "Jinling liuyuan shiyu" 金陵六院市語 in *Xiugu chunrong* 繡谷春容, in *Guben xiaoshuo jicheng* 古本小說集成 (Shanghai: Shanghai guji chubanshe, 1990), vols. 143–44, pp. 1070–73.

29. For instance, scene 17 of *Mudan ting* introduces Shi Daogu (Sister Stone), a Taoist nun, who describes her sexual experience by using the lines of *Qianzi wen*, a popular primer widely read in late imperial times; see Tang Xianzu 湯顯祖, *Mudan ting* 牡丹亭 (Beijing: Renmin wenxue chubanshe, 1997), pp. 83–86. In an even more dramatic fashion, *Ge dai xiao*, which is attributed to Xu Wei 徐渭 (1521–93), allows two Buddhist monks to appropriate the language of the Four Books in a lewd conversation about sexual intercourse; see *Xu Wei ji* 徐渭集 (Beijing: Zhonghua shuju, 1983), pp. 1135–36.

30. See Mikhail Bakhtin, *The Dialogic Imagination: Four Essays* (Austin: University of Texas Press, 1981). In his "Introduction" to *Plum in the Golden Vase*, David Roy (p. xliii) refers to Bakhtin's concept of "heteroglossia" and argues: "The text of the novel is replete with verbatim quotations from every level of traditional discourse as well as parodies of the generic characteristics of many of them. These discourses and genres speak in different voices and represent divergent or conflicting points of view, which result in apparent antinomies of every kind." But Roy does not fully explore

the thematic and narrative complexity of the novel from Bakhtinian perspectives; instead, he proceeds to argue that *Jin Ping Mei* is a Confucian novel, and its ideological or philosophical coherence is "provided by the particular brand of conservative orthodox Confucianism that is associated with the name of Xun Zi, the great Chinese philosopher of the third century B.C." (ibid., xviii–xix) without being aware that his Confucian reading of *Jin Ping Mei* is fundamentally irreconcilable with Bakhtin's concept of the novel. According to Bakhtin (*Dialogic Imagination*, p. 344), "Images of official-authoritative truth, images of virtue (of any sort: monastic, spiritual, bureaucratic, moral, etc.) have never been successful in the novel. It suffices to mention the hopeless attempts of Gogol and Dostoevsky in this regard. For this reason the authoritative text always remains, in the novel, a dead quotation, something that falls out of the artistic context (for example, the evangelical texts in Tolstoy at the end of *Resurrection*)."

31. Hanan, "Sources of the *Chin P'ing Mei*," p. 66.

32. See Zhu Yixuan 朱一玄 et al., eds., "*Jin Ping Mei*" *ziliao huibian* 金瓶梅資料匯編 (Tianjin: Nankai daxue chubanshe, 1985), pp. 198–354. For an introduction to Zhang Zhupo's comments on *Jin Ping Mei*, see David Rolston, *Traditional Chinese Fiction and Fiction Commentary: Reading and Writing Between the Lines* (Stanford: Stanford University Press, 1997), pp. 63–73, 196–251.

33. Zhu Yixuan et al., "*Jin Ping Mei*" *ziliao huibian*, p. 218.

34. *Jin Ping Mei* (hereafter JPM), 10.7b; Roy, *Plum in the Golden Vase* (hereafter, *Plum*), p. 201. Subsequent citations are given in the text. I use David Roy's translation of *Jin Ping Mei* with slight modifications.

35. See Authur Waley, trans., *The Analects of Confucius* (London: George Allen & Unwin, 1938), p. 83.

36. For instance, see *JMP*, 24.2b, 61.7a, 83.9a–b, and 99.8a. For the ironic use of the phrase *bu yi le hu* in *Jin Ping Mei*, see also Peter Rushton, *The "Jin Ping Mei" and the Nonlinear Dimensions of the Traditional Chinese Novel* (Lewiston, N.Y.: Mellen University Press, 1993), pp. 69–70.

37. This passage is borrowed from Chapter 44 of *Shuihu zhuan*.

38. The earliest source can be found in a passage in *Mencius*, 4A.27. In Legge's translation (*The Works of Mencius* [New York: Dover, 1970], pp. 313–14): "The richest fruit of benevolence is this,—the service of one's parents. The richest fruit of righteousness is this,—the obeying of one's elder brothers. . . . The richest fruit of music is this,—the rejoicing in those two things. When they are rejoiced in, they grow. Growing, how can they be repressed? When they come to this state that they cannot be repressed, then unconsciously the feet begin to dance and the hands to move." The author of the *Great Preface to the Book of Songs* used the last two sentences of the Mencian passage in a paragraph describing the joy of singing and dancing, which Legge (*The She King or The Book of Ancient History* [London: Trubner, 1876],

p. 34) translates as follows: "The feelings move inwardly, and are embodied in words. When words are insufficient for them, recourse is had to sighs and exclamations. When sighs and exclamations are not sufficient for them, recourse is had to the prolonged utterances of song. When those prolonged utterances of song are insufficient for them, unconsciously the hands begin to move and the feet to dance." For further information about this passage, see *Plum*, p. 501n43.

39. See *Yugu xinhuang*, pp. 116–17. The phrase *le yi zai qizhong yi* is quoted from Book 7 of the *Analects*: "The Master said: 'To eat coarse food, drink plain water, and pillow oneself on a bent arm—surely, there is pleasure to be found in these things.'"

40. Although such a phrase as *bu yi le hu* might have been just a cliché by this time, in these examples it is treated as a quotation from the Confucian *Analects*. For a use of the same phrase in the drinking games of the time, see also Yu Xiangdou, *Santai wanyong zhengzhong, juan* 19, "Drinking Games," pp. 1–2.

41. Carlitz, *Rhetoric of "Chin P'ing Mei,"* pp. 116–19; David Roy, "The Use of Songs as a Means of Self-Expression and Self-Characterization in the *Chin P'ing Mei*," *Chinese Literature: Essays, Articles, Reviews* 20 (1998): 101–26.

42. This story, entitled "Jiezhier ji" 戒指兒記, is taken from Hong Pian's 洪楩 *Qingping shantang huaben* 清平山堂話本 (Shanghai: Shanghai guji chubanshe, 1992), pp. 129–38. See Wu Xiaoling 吳曉鈴, review of the republished *Gujin xiaoshuo*, *Han-hiue* 2 (1947): 444–55.

43. For instance, in telling the story Ximen Qing frequently uses such adverbs as *sui* 遂 (therefore) and *guo* 果 (indeed, as expected) and verbal locutions such as *buqi* 不期 (not expecting).

44. For Ximen's use of formal language, see especially Chapter 36 of the novel, which gives a lengthy account of Ximen's conversation with two degree-holders.

45. See Chapter 36 of *Jin Ping Mei*. See also Chapter 21 in which Ximen is shown to quote arias from *Xixiang ji*.

46. Almost all existing studies of the authorship of *Jin Ping Mei* attempt, in one way or another, to identify the local dialects in the speech of characters in the novel. However, such studies seem to have helped little in locating the novelist in a specific dialect area; instead, they have shown that the composition of the novel involves a wide range of linguistic elements drawn from Mandarin and various dialects, mainly the Shandong and Wu dialects. For the recent debate on this issue, see Huang Lin 黃霖, "*Jin Ping Mei* zuozhe Tu Long kaoxu" 金瓶梅作者屠隆考續, in idem, *Jin Ping Mei kaolun* 金瓶梅考論 (Shenyang: Liaoning renmin chubanshe, 1988), pp. 218–31.

47. Chapter 2 of *Jin Ping Mei* contains a verse describing the beguiling look of Pan Jinlian from Ximen Qing's perspective (*JPM*, 2.5a). This verse is quoted from Chapter 44 of *Shuihu zhuan*, in which it portrays the appearance of Pan Qiaoyun, the unfaithful wife of Yang Xiong, who is eventually executed by her husband and

his sworn brother, Shi Xiu, whom she once attempted to seduce. Immediately after its account of Pan Qiaoyun's failed attempt in Chapter 44, *Shuihu zhuan* proceeds to tell of her affair with a Buddhist monk, Pei Ruhai. This episode consists of several parts, from the narrator's satirical comments on Buddhist monks as "sex-starved hungry ghosts," to his depiction of the reaction of the monks to the seductive appearance of Pan Qiaoyun as she attends a "land and water" mass for her deceased husband. Interestingly enough, these passages about Pan Qiaoyun are transposed to Chapter 8 of *Jin Ping Mei* and incorporated into the narration of Pan Jinlian's attendance at a similar mass for her husband and the monks' enchantment by her beauty, as mentioned earlier. For a systematic study of *Jin Ping Mei*'s indebtedness to *Shuihu zhuan*, see Huang Lin 黃霖, "Zhongyi shuihu zhuan yu Jin Ping Mei cihua" 忠義水滸傳與金瓶梅詞話, in idem, *Jin Ping Mei kaolun* 金瓶梅考論(Shen-yang: Liaoning renmin chubanshe, 1988), pp. 151–69. Moreover, the narrator's satirical comments on Buddhist monks in Chapter 8 of *Jin Ping Mei* (JPM, 8.11b) might share a common source with Feng Menglong's short story "Foyin Shi si tiao Qinniang" 佛印師四調琴娘 from *Xingshi hengyan* 醒世恒言 (in *Feng Menglong quanji* 馮夢龍全集, ed. Wei Tongxian 魏同賢[Shanghai: Shanghai guji chubanshe, 1993], 24: 626).

48. See *Feng Menglong quanji*, pp. 159–202.

49. See Hanan, "Sources of the *Chin P'ing Mei*."

50. Ibid., p. 65.

51. Since *Jin Ping Mei* absorbs into its narrative almost all the literary genres, narrative motifs, and modes of expression available in its time, it comes to embody the literary matrix from which any specific type of narrative could be derived. It is thus perhaps not a surprise that some modern scholars argue that it was Feng Menglong who copied *Jin Ping Mei*, rather than the other way around, despite the lack of supporting evidence (see Liu Hui 劉輝, "Jin Ping Mei yanjiu shinian" 金瓶梅研究十年, in idem, *Jin Ping Mei lunwen ji* 金瓶梅論文集 [Taibei: Guanya wenhua shiye youxian gongsi, 1992], p. 365). Xu Shuofang 徐朔方 argues that since Feng Menglong's *Gujin xiaoshuo* came out slightly later than *Jin Ping Mei*, it is hard to determine whether it is the *Gujin xiaoshuo* story that copied *Jin Ping Mei*, or the other way around; see Xu Shuofang and Liu Hui 劉輝, eds., "Jin Ping Mei" lunji 金瓶梅論集 (Beijing: Renmin wenxue chubanshe, 1986), pp. 69–75. But since Feng Menglong's collections of short stories were based on pre-existing narrative texts, some of which had already been in circulation in print or manuscript form, it is more likely that these texts provide the sources for *Jin Ping Mei*. Hanan ("Sources of the *Chin P'ing Mei*," p. 39) shows how much adjustment the novelist did to prepare for the adoption of the passages from his sourcework: "The account of how (Chen) Jingji was offered capital to set himself up in business is given just a few pages before this copied passage, and his purchase of the tavern immediately precedes it. It seems probable, since the tavern is not afterwards of any importance in the novel, that these episodes

have been created solely in order to accommodate the passages from the short story."

52. Pan Yuan-shih 潘元石 ("A Short History of the Art of Print-making in China" 中國版畫藝術發展史 [text in both English and Chinese], in *Zhonghua minguo chuantong banhua yishu* 中華民國傳統版畫藝術, ed. Huang Tsai-lang 黃才郎 [Taibei: Executive Yuan, Council for Cultural Planning and Development, 1986], pp. 117–29), argues that this illustration-above/text-below format can be dated to the Five Dynasties and was also used in the Song before it became popular during the Ming dynasty.

53. The volume that combines *Shuihu zhuan* and *Sanguo yanyi* is entitled *Yingxiong pu* 英雄譜 or *Han Song qishu* 漢宋奇書. In addition to the two novels, it also presents illustrations accompanied by poems attributed to famous literati authors. For more information on it, see Rolston, *Traditional Chinese Fiction and Fiction Commentary*, 18–19n51; see also Hegel, *Reading Illustrated Fiction*, pp. 40–41; Andrew Lo further explores this format in his Ph. D. dissertation, "San-kuo yen-i and Shui-hu chuan in the Context of Historiography" (Princeton University, 1981).

54. See *Wanjin jiaoli* 萬錦嬌麗, attributed to Tang Xianzu 湯顯祖, in *Shanben xiqu congkan* 善本戲曲叢刊, ed. Wang Qiugui 王秋桂, vol. 21 (Taibei: Taiwan xuesheng shuju, 1984).

55. See *Zhaijin qiyin* 摘錦奇音, attributed to Gong Zhengwo 龔正我 and published in 1611; in *Shanben xiqu congkan* 善本戲曲叢刊, ed. Wang Qiugui 王秋桂, vol. 3 (Taibei: Taiwan xuesheng shuju, 1984).

56. In some exceptional cases, the middle row presents illustrations for the dramas presented on the bottom row. For an example, see *Lijing ji* 荔鏡記, in *Mingben Chaozhou xiwen wuzhong* 明本潮州戲文五種, ed. Yang Yue 楊越 and Wang Guichen 王貴忱 (Guangzhou: Guangdong renmin chubanshe, 1985), pp. 469–581.

57. See Ma Meng-ching 馬孟晶, "Wan Ming Jinling Shizhuzhai shuhua pu Shizhuzhai jianpu yanjiu" 晚明金陵十竹齋書畫譜十竹齋箋譜研究 (M.A. thesis, Taiwan University, 1993), pp. 68–73.

58. Li Yu (1611–80) is one such example. See Patrick Hanan, trans., *The Carnal Prayer Mat* (Honolulu: University of Hawai'i Press, 1990), pp. v–xiv; for a further investigation of this phenomenon, see Rolston, *Traditional Chinese Fiction and Fiction Commentary*, pp. 269–83.

59. One such example can be seen in Cao Xueqin's 曹雪芹 (?–1763) *Honglou meng* 紅樓夢. As Wu Shih-Ch'ang (*On "The Red Chamber Dream": A Critical Study of Two Annotated Manuscripts of the XVIIIth Century* [Oxford: Oxford University Press, 1961], pp. 63–72) points out, the opening paragraph in Chapter 1 of the novel was originally a preface to the novel or to the introductory chapter of the novel, a preface that was probably written by Cao Tangchun 曹棠村, Cao Xueqin's younger brother. In the *jiaxu* 甲戌 text of the novel, this introductory paragraph was tran-

scribed two spaces lower than the rest of the text. But in later editions it was often taken as an integral part of the main text, as it is in most modern reprinted editions. According to Wu's studies, the novel begins, instead, with the paragraph that follows, with a question "Gentle reader, what, you may ask, was the origin of this book?"

60. Bai Qianshen 白謙慎, "Mingmo Qingchu shijue yishu zhong de linmo yu fuzhi xianxiang yanjiu" 明末清初視覺藝術中的臨摹與復制現象研究, unpublished paper.

61. Benedict Anderson, *Imagined Communities* (London: Verso, 1983; rev. and extended ed., 1991), p. 33n54.

62. See Mikhail Bakhtin, *Problems of Dostoevsky's Poetics* (Minneapolis: University of Minnesota Press, 1984), p. 30.

63. In the late Qing period, *jingbao* 京報, the Qing version of *dibao*, was reprinted on the front page of such major newspapers as *Shenbao* 申報.

64. As described above, on each page of drama miscellanies the dramatic text constitutes the central attraction, with jokes, drinking verses, songs, and other side attractions surrounding it. This, I suggest, is a verbal representation of the constellation of attractions one might find in the marketplace—storytelling, oral stunts, comic skits, and acrobatics and other sideshow attractions. In this sense, the multiple-row format of drama miscellanies can be regarded as the equivalent of the multiple-ring circus.

65. Here I have translated the *Jin Ping Mei cihua* text with reference to Clement Egerton's English translation of the novel, which is based on the abridged and revised "Chongzhen" edition of the novel. See Clement Egerton, trans., *The Golden Lotus* (London: Routledge & Kegan Paul, 1939), p. 357.

66. For instance, in his comments on his *Shan'ge* 山歌 and *Guazhier* song collections, Feng Menglong often quoted what is presumably his personal experience in commenting on the songs in question; he also gave alternative versions of the song and sometimes even engaged in an imagined dialogue with the female persona of the song; in these dialogues he revealed the unwitting irony in her self-representation, questioned the wisdom of her statements, and destabilized her monologic self-indulgences. When a speaker concluded her frustrated love song with the hypothesis that "even though you were a stone I would be able to warm you up," Feng commented in very much the way Ying Bojue does in *Jin Ping Mei*: "If he were indeed like a stone, then it would be absolutely no use warming him up" (Feng Menglong, *Guazhier* 掛枝兒, in *Feng Menglong quanji* 馮夢龍全集, ed. Wei Tongxian 魏同賢 [Shanghai: Shanghai guji chubanshe, 1993], 42: 160).

67. Rolston, "Oral Performing Literature in Traditional Chinese Fiction," pp. 30–31.

68. A similar phenomenon can be found in the description of the enactment of a scene from the southern version of *Xixiang ji* in Chapter 74 of the novel (*JPM*, 74: 8a–b); Katherine Carlitz, "The Role of Drama in the *Chin P'ing Mei*" (Ph.D. diss., University of Chicago, 1978), p. 258*n*.

69. In some other cases, narratorial comments are inserted into the song sequence without such introducing phrases, creating an even more abrupt shift in tone and perspective (see, e.g., *JPM*, 38.10b).

70. For recent scholarship on the history of reading and history of books, see Roger Chartier, *Forms and Meanings: Texts, Performances, and Audiences from Codex to Computer* (Philadelphia: University of Pennsylvania Press, 1995); and idem, "The Practical Impact of Writing," in *A History of Private Life*, vol. 3, *Passions of the Renaissance*, ed. Roger Chartier (Cambridge, Mass.: Harvard University Press, 1989), pp. 111–60.

71. Hegel, *Reading Illustrated Fiction in Late Imperial China*, pp. 73, 102–3.

72. Zhang Zhupo 張竹坡, "Piping diyi qishu *Jin Ping Mei* dufa huiping" 批評第一奇書金瓶梅讀法回評, in *"Jin Ping Mei" ziliao huibian* 金瓶梅資料匯編, ed. Zhu Yixuan 朱一玄 et al. (Tianjin: Nankai daxue chubanshe, 1985), p. 224. For an English translation of Zhang's above remarks, see David Roy in David Rolston, ed., *How to Read the Chinese Novel* (Princeton: Princeton University Press, 1990), p. 235. "Although I do not claim to have mastered anything," Zhang writes, "I am convinced that in reading a book one should not try to digest it in large chunks at a time. This is true not only of works in the literary language but even of novels like *Jin Ping Mei*." He is also wise enough to see the possible consequences of reading *Jin Ping Mei* in "a desultory fashion," because "if you read it that way you will only read the obscene passages" (ibid., p. 232).

73. Hsia, *The Classic Chinese Novel*, p. 170.

74. See note 64 to this chapter.

75. Wu Congxian 吳從先. "Shangxin leshi wuze" 賞心樂事五則, in *Mingren xiaopin ji* 明人小品集, ed. Liu Dajie 劉大杰 (Shanghai: Beixin shuju, 1934), pp. 37–38.

Works Cited

Anderson, Benedict. *Imagined Communities*. London: Verso, 1983. Rev. and extended ed., 1991.

Bai Qianshen 白謙慎. "Mingmo Qingchu shijue yishu zhong de linmo yu fuzhi xianxiang yanjiu" 明末清初視覺藝術中的臨摹與復制現象研究. Unpublished paper.

Bakhtin, Mikhail. *The Dialogic Imagination: Four Essays*. Austin: University of Texas Press, 1981.

———. *Problems of Dostoevsky's Poetics*. Minneapolis: University of Minnesota Press, 1984.

Brook, Timothy. *The Confusions of Pleasure*. Berkeley: University of California Press, 1998.

Carlitz, Katherine. *The Rhetoric of "Chin P'ing mei."* Bloomington: Indiana University Press, 1986.

———. "The Role of Drama in the *Chin P'ing Mei*." Ph.D. diss., University of Chicago, 1978.

Chartier, Roger. *Forms and Meanings: Texts, Performances, and Audiences from Codex to Computer*. Philadelphia: University of Pennsylvania Press, 1995.

———. "The Practical Impact of Writing." In idem, ed., *A History of Private Life*, vol. 3, *Passions of the Renaissance*. Cambridge, Mass.: Harvard University Press, 1989, pp. 111–60.

Chen Dadao 陳大道. "Mingmo Qingchu shishi xiaoshuo de tese" 明末清初時事小說的特色. *Xiaoshuo xiqu yanjiu* 小說戲曲研究 3 (1988): 181–220.

Chen Dakang 陳大康. *Tongsu xiaoshuo de lishi guiji* 通俗小說的歷史軌迹. Changsha: Hunan chubanshe, 1993.

Chen Liangduan 陳良端. "Yeshuo *Wanjin jiaoli* jiqi suoshou de sanzhong xiaoshuo" 也說萬錦嬌麗及其所收的三種小說. *Wenxue yichan* 文學遺產 3 (1990): 104–5.

Chen Xuewen 陳學文. *Ming Qing shiqi shangye shu ji shangren shu zhi yanjiu* 明清時期商業書及商人書之研究. Taibei: Hongye, 1997.

Da Ming tianxia chun 大明天下春. In *Haiwai guben wan Ming xiju xuanji sanzhong* 海外孤本晚明戲劇選集三種, ed. Li Fuqing 李福清 (Russian) and Li Ping 李平 (Chinese). Shanghai: Shanghai guji chubanshe, 1993, pp. 579–644.

Egerton, Clement, trans. *The Golden Lotus*. London: Routledge & Kegan Paul, 1939.

Feng Menglong 馮夢龍. "Foyin Shi si tiao Qinniang" 佛印師四調琴娘. *Xingshi hengyan* 醒世恒言. In *Feng Menglong quanji* 馮夢龍全集, ed. Wei Tongxian 魏同賢. Shanghai: Shanghai guji chubanshe, 1993, 24: 617–37.

———. *Guazhier* 掛枝兒. In *Feng Menglong quanji* 馮夢龍全集, ed. Wei Tongxian 魏同賢, vol. 42. Shanghai: Shanghai guji chubanshe, 1993.

————. *Gujin tan'gai* 古今談概. In *Feng Menglong quanji* 馮夢龍全集, ed. Wei Tongxian 魏同賢, vols. 39–40. Shanghai: Shanghai guji chubanshe, 1993.

————. "Xinqiaoshi Han Wu mai chunqing" 新橋市韓五賣春情. *Gujin xiaoshuo* 古今小說. In *Feng Menglong quanji* 馮夢龍全集, ed. Wei Tongxian 魏同賢. Shanghai: Shanghai guji chubanshe, 1993, 20: 159–99.

Feng Yuanjun 馮沅君. "*Jin Ping Mei cihua* zhong de wenxue shiliao" 金瓶梅詞話中的文學史料. In *Guju shuohui* 古劇說匯. Beijing: Zuojia chubanshe, 1956, pp. 48–57.

Guben xiaoshuo jicheng 古本小說集成. Shanghai: Shanghai guji chubanshe, 1990.

Guose tianxiang 國色天香. In *Guben xiaoshuo jicheng* 古本小說集成. Shanghai: Shanghai guji chubanshe, 1990, vols. 157–58, pp. 786–98.

Hanan, Patrick. *The Invention of Li Yu*. Cambridge, Mass.: Harvard University Press, 1988.

————. "Sources of the *Chin P'ing Mei*." *Asia Major* 10 (1963): 23–67.

————. "The Text of the *Chin P'ing Mei*." *Asia Major* 9 (1962): 1–57.

Hanan, Patrick, trans. *The Carnal Prayer Mat*. Honolulu: University of Hawai'i Press, 1990.

Hegel, Robert. *Reading Illustrated Fiction in Late Imperial China*. Stanford: Stanford University Press, 1998.

Hong Pian 洪楩. *Qingping shantang huaben* 清平山堂話本. Shanghai: Shanghai guji chubanshe, 1992.

Hsia, C. T. *The Classic Chinese Novel: A Critical Introduction*. New York: Columbia University Press, 1968.

Hu Shiying 胡士瑩. *Huaben xiaoshuo gailun* 話本小說概論. Beijing: Zhonghua shuju, 1980.

Huang Lin 黃霖. "*Jin Ping Mei* zuozhe Tu Long kao" 金瓶梅作者屠隆考. In idem, *Jin Ping Mei kaolun* 金瓶梅考論. Shenyang: Liaoning renmin chubanshe, 1988, pp. 199–217.

————. "*Jin Ping Mei* zuozhe Tu Long kaoxu" 金瓶梅作者屠隆考續. In idem, *Jin Ping Mei kaolun* 金瓶梅考論. Shenyang: Liaoning renmin chubanshe, 1988, pp. 218–231.

————. "*Zhongyi shuihu zhuan yu Jin Ping Mei cihua*" 忠義水滸傳與金瓶梅詞話. In idem, *Jin Ping Mei kaolun* 金瓶梅考論. Shenyang: Liaoning renmin chubanshe, 1988, pp. 151–69.

Huang Qiang 黃強. "*Wanjin jiaoli* suoshou xiaoshuo dierzhong chuyu *Rouputuan*" 萬錦嬌麗所收小說第二種出於肉蒲團. *Wenxue yichan* 文學遺產 1 (1992): 122.

Inoue Susumu 井上進. "Zōsho to dokusho" 藏書と讀書. *Tōhō gakuhō* 東方学報 62 (Mar. 1990): 409–45.

Ji Guoping 季國平. "Xiqu zhaji erze" 戲曲札記二則. *Wenxue yichan* 文學遺產 6 (1990): 105–7.

Jinbao congtan pinglu zhuan 近報叢譚平虜傳. In *Guben xiaoshuo jicheng* 古本小說 集成, vol. 22. Shanghai: Shanghai guji chubanshe, 1990.

Ko, Dorothy. *Teachers of the Inner Chamber.* Stanford: Stanford University Press, 1994.

Lanling Xiaoxiao Sheng 蘭陵笑笑生. *Jin Ping Mei cihua* 金瓶梅詞話. Hongkong: Taiping shuju, 1982. Reprint of the edition in the Beijing Library.

Legge, James, trans. *The She King or The Book of Ancient History.* London: Trubner, 1876.

————. *The Works of Mencius.* New York: Dover, 1970.

Li Yu 李漁. *Rou pu tuan* 肉蒲團. In Chen Qinghao 陳慶浩 and Wang Qiugui 王 秋桂, eds., *Si wu xie huibao* 思無邪彙寶. Taibei: Chengyi tushu, 1995, vol. 15.

Li Zhizhong 李致忠. *Lidai keshu kaoshu* 歷代刻書考述. Chengdu: Bashu shushe, 1990.

Liao, Chaoyang. "Three Readings in the *Jinpingmei cihua*." *Chinese Literature: Essays, Articles, and Reviews* 6 (1984): 77–99.

Lijing ji 荔鏡記. In *Mingben Chaozhou xiwen wuzhong* 明本潮州戲文五種, ed. Yang Yue 楊越 and Wang Guichen 王貴忱. Guangzhou: Guangdong renmin chubanshe, 1985, pp. 469–581.

Liu Hui 劉輝. "Cong cihua ben dao shuosan ben—*Jin Ping Mei* chengshu guocheng ji zuozhe wenti yanjiu" 從詞話本到說散本—金瓶梅成書過程及作者問 題研究. In idem, *Jin Ping Mei lunwen ji* 金瓶梅論文集. Taibei: Guanya wenhua shiye youxian gongsi, 1992, pp. 1–46.

————. "*Jin Ping Mei* yanjiu shinian" 金瓶梅研究十年. In idem, *Jin Ping Mei lunwen ji* 金瓶梅論文集. Taibei: Guanya wenhua shiye youxian gongsi, 1992, pp. 356–97.

Liu Yongqiang 劉勇强. "Ming Qing dibao yu wenxue zhi guanxi" 明清邸報與文 學之關系. *Xueren* 學人 3 (1992): 437–64.

Lo, Andrew. "*San-kuo yen-i* and *Shui-hu chuan* in the Context of Historiography: An Interpretative Study." Ph. D. diss., Princeton University, 1981.

Ma Meng-ching 馬孟晶. "Wan Ming Jinling Shizhuzhai shuhua pu Shizhuzhai jianpu yanjiu" 晚明金陵十竹齋書畫譜十竹齋箋譜研究. M.A. thesis, Taiwan University, 1993.

Niida Noboru 仁井田陞. "Gen Min jidai no mura no kiyaku to kosaku shōsho nado, nichiyō hyakka zensho no rui nijūshu no naka kara" 元明時代 の村の規約と小作證書など、日用百科全書の類二十種のなかから. In idem, *Chūgoku hōseishi kenkyū* 中国法制史研究. Tokyo: Tobunken, 1962, pp. 741–829.

Ogawa Yōichi 小川陽一. *Nichiyō ruisho ni yoru Min-Shin shōsetsu no kenkyū* 日用類書による明清小説の研究. Tokyo: Kenbun, 1995.

Ōki Yasushi 大木康. "Minmatsu Kōnan ni okeru shuppan bunka no kenkyū" 明末江南における出版文化の研究. *Hiroshima daigaku bungakubu kiyō* 広島大学文学部紀要 50, special issue no. 1 (1991): 1–176.

Pan Kaipei 潘開沛. "*Jin Ping Mei* de chansheng he zuozhe" 金瓶梅的產生和作者. In *Ming Qing xiaoshuo yanjiu lunwen ji* 明清小說研究論文集, ed. Renmin wenxue chubanshe 人民文學出版社. Beijing: Renmin wenxue, 1959, pp. 173–80.

Pan Yuan-shih 潘元石. "A Short History of the Art of Print-making in China" 中國版畫藝術發展史 (text in both English and Chinese). In *Zhonghua minguo chuantong banhua yishu* 中華民國傳統版畫藝術, ed. Huang Tsai-lang 黃才郎. Taibei: Executive Yuan, Council for Cultural Planning and Development, 1986, pp. 117–29.

Plaks, Andrew. *The Four Masterworks of the Ming Novel.* Princeton: Princeton University Press, 1987.

Rolston, David. "Oral Performing Literature in Traditional Chinese Fiction: Nonrealistic Usages in the *Jin Ping Mei cihua* and Their Influence." *Chinoperl Papers* 17 (1994): 1–110.

——. *Traditional Chinese Fiction and Fiction Commentary: Reading and Writing Between the Lines.* Stanford: Stanford University Press, 1997.

Rolston, David, ed., *How to Read the Chinese Novel.* Princeton: Princeton University Press, 1990.

Roy, David. "The Use of Songs as a Means of Self-Expression and Self-Characterization in the *Chin P'ing Mei.*" *Chinese Literature: Essays, Articles, Reviews* 20 (1998): 101–26.

Roy, David, trans. *The Plum in the Golden Vase or, Chin P'ing Mei.* Princeton: Princeton University Press, 1993.

Rushton, Peter. *The "Jin Ping Mei" and the Nonlinear Dimensions of the Traditional Chinese Novel.* Lewiston, N.Y.: Mellen University Press, 1993.

Sakai Tadao 酒井忠夫. "Confucianism and Popular Educational Works." In *Self and Society in Ming Thought*, ed. Wm. Theodore de Bary. New York: Columbia University Press, 1970, pp. 331–66.

——. "Mindai no nichiyō ruisho to shomin kyōiku" 明代の日用類書と庶民教育 (Encyclopedias for Daily Use and Popular Education in the Ming Dynasty). In *Kinsei Chūgoku kyōikushi kenkyū* 近世中国教育史研究, ed. Hayashi Tomoharu 林友春. Tokyo: Kokudo, 1984, pp. 25–154.

Sakai Tadao, ed., *Chūgoku nichiyō ruisho shusei* 中国日用類書集成. Tokyo: Kyūko, 1998– .

Shang Wei. "The Making of the Everyday World: *Jin Ping Mei* and Encyclopedias for Daily Use." In *Dynastic Decline and Cultural Innovation: From the Late Ming to the Late Qing*, ed. David Der-wei Wang and Shang Wei. Cambridge, Mass.: Harvard University Asia Center, forthcoming.

Shen Defu 沈德符. *Wanli yehuo bian* 萬曆野獲編. Beijing: Zhonghua shuju, 1959.

Siku quanshu zongmu 四庫全書總目. Beijing: Zhonghua shuju, 1956.

Sun Kaidi 孫楷第. *Riben Dongjing suojian xiaoshuo shumu* 日本東京所見小說書目. Beijing: Renmin wenxue chubanshe, 1958.

Tan Zhengbi 譚正璧. *Guben xijian xiaoshuo huikao* 古本稀見小說匯考. Hangzhou: Zhejiang wenyi chubanshe, 1984.

Tang Xianzu 湯顯祖. *Mudan ting* 牡丹亭. Beijing: Renmin wenxue chubanshe, 1997.

Tsien Tsuen-Hsuin. *Paper and Printing*. Joseph Needham, ed., *Science and Civilization in China*, vol. 5, pt. 1. Cambridge, Eng.: Cambridge University Press, 1985.

Waley, Authur, trans. *The Analects of Confucius*. London: George Allen & Unwin, 1938.

Wang, David Der-wei, and Shang Wei, eds. *Dynastic Decline and Cultural Innovation: From the Late Ming to the Late Qing*. Cambridge, Mass.: Harvard University Asia Center, forthcoming.

Wang Ermin 王爾敏. "Chuantong Zhongguo shumin richang shenghuo qingjie" 傳統中國庶民日常生活情節. *Zhongyang yanjiuyuan, Jindaishi yanjiusuo jikan* 中央研究院近代史研究所季刊 21 (1992): 147–76.

Wang Gang 王崗. *Langman qinggan yu zongjiao jingshen: Wan Ming wenxue yu wenxue sichao* 浪漫情感與宗教精神—晚明文學與文學思潮. Hongkong: Tiandi tushu, 1999.

Wang Hongtai 王鴻泰. "Liudong yu hudong: you Ming Qing jian chengshi shenghuo de texing tance gonggong changyu de kaizhan" 流動與互動—由明清間城市生活的特性探測公共場域的開展. Ph.D. diss., Taiwan University, 1998.

Wang Qiugui 王秋桂, ed. *Shanben xiqu congkan* 善本戲曲叢刊. Taibei: Taiwan xuesheng shuju, 1984.

Wang Zhongmin 王重民. *Zhongguo shanbenshu tiyao* 中國善本書提要. Shanghai: Shanghai guji chubanshe, 1983.

Wanjin jiaoli 萬錦嬌麗. Attributed to Tang Xianzu 湯顯祖. In *Shanben xiqu congkan* 善本戲曲叢刊, ed. Wang Qiugui 王秋桂, vol. 21. Taibei: Taiwan xuesheng shuju, 1984.

Wanli dichao 萬曆邸鈔. Yangzhou: Jiangsu Guangling guji keyinshe, 1991. Reprinted—Taiwan guoli zhongyang tushuguan, 1963.

Widmer, Ellen. "The Huanduzhai of Hangzhou and Suzhou: A Study in Seventeenth-Century Publishing." *Harvard Journal of Asiatic Studies* 56 (1996): 77–122.

Wu Congxian 吳從先. "Shangxin leshi wuze" 賞心樂事五則. In *Mingren xiaopin ji* 明人小品集, ed. Liu Dajie 劉大杰. Shanghai: Beixin shuju, 1934, pp. 37–38.

Wu, K. T. "Ming Printing and Printers." *Harvard Journal of Asiatic Studies* 7 (1943): 203–60.

Wu Shih-Ch'ang. *On "The Red Chamber Dream": A Critical Study of Two Annotated Manuscripts of the XVIIIth Century.* Oxford: Oxford University Press, 1961.

Wutong ying 梧桐影. Taipei: Taiwan daying baike, 1994.

Wu Xiaoling 吳曉鈴. Review of the republished *Gujin xiaoshuo*. *Han-hiue* 2 (1947): 444–55.

Xiugu chunrong 繡谷春容. In *Guben xiaoshuo jicheng* 古本小說集成 vols. 143–44. Shanghai: Shanghai guji chubanshe, 1990.

Xu Mengxiang 徐夢湘. "Guanyu *Jin Ping Mei* de zuozhe" 關於金瓶梅的作者. In *Ming Qing xiaoshuo yanjiu lunwen ji* 明清小說研究論文集, ed. Renmin wenxue chubanshe 人民文學出版社. Beijing: Renmin wenxue chubanshe, 1959, pp. 181–84.

Xu Shuofang 徐朔方. "*Jin Ping Mei* chengshu xintan" 金瓶梅成書新探. In *"Jin Ping Mei" pingzhu* 金瓶梅評注, ed. Cai Guoliang 蔡國梁. Guilin: Lijiang chubanshe, 1986, pp. 298–342.

Xu Shuofang 徐朔方 and Liu Hui 劉輝, eds. *"Jin Ping Mei" lunji* 金瓶梅論集. Beijing: Renmin wenxue chubanshe, 1986.

Xu Wei 徐渭. *Xu Wei ji* 徐渭集. Beijing: Zhonghua shuju, 1983.

Yanju biji 燕居筆記. In *Guben xiaoshuo jicheng* 古本小說集成, vols. 148–56. Shanghai: Shanghai guji chubanshe, 1990.

Ye Shusheng 葉樹聲. "Mingdai Nanzhili Jiangnan diqu siren keshu gaishu" 明代南直隸江南地區私人刻書概述. *Wenxian* 文獻 32 (Feb. 1987): 213–29.

Yin Yungong 尹韻公. *Zhongguo Mingdai xinwen chuanbo shi* 中國明代新聞傳播史. Chongqing: Chongqing chubanshe, 1990.

Yu Xiangdou 余象斗. *Santai wanyong zhengzong* 三台萬用正宗. In *Chūgoku nichiyō ruisho shusei* 中國日用類書集成, vols. 3–5. Tokyo: Kyūko, 1998.

Yuan Hongdao 袁宏道. *Yuan Hongdao chidu quangao* 袁宏道尺牘全稿. Shanghai: Shidai tushu, 1934.

Yugu xinhuang 玉谷新簧. In *Shanben xiqu congkan* 善本戲曲叢刊, ed. Wang Qiugui 王秋桂, vol. 2. Taibei: Taiwan xuesheng shuju, 1984.

Zhaijin qiyin 摘錦奇音. Attributed to Gong Zhengwo 龔正我 and published in 1611. In *Shanben xiqu congkan* 善本戲曲叢刊, ed. Wang Qiugui 王秋桂, vol. 3. Taibei: Taiwan xuesheng shuju, 1984.

Zhang Xiumin 張秀民. *Zhongguo yinshua shi* 中國印刷史. Shanghai: Shanghai renmin chubanshe, 1989.

Zhang Zhupo 張竹坡. "Piping diyi qishu *Jin Ping Mei* dufa huiping" 批評第一奇書金瓶梅讀法回評. In *"Jin Ping Mei "ziliao huibian* 金瓶梅資料匯編, ed. Zhu Yixuan 朱一玄 et al. Tianjin: Nankai daxue chubanshe, 1985, pp. 65–226.

Zheng Zhenduo 鄭振鐸. *Xidi shuhua* 西諦書話. Reprinted—Beijing: Sanlian chubanshe, 1983.

Zhou Wu 周蕪. *Zhongguo banhuashi tulu* 中國版畫史圖錄. Shanghai: Shanghai renmin meishu chubanshe, 1988.

Zhu Yixuan 朱一玄 et al., eds. *"Jin Ping Mei" ziliao huibian* 金瓶梅資料匯編. Tianjin: Nankai daxue chubanshe, 1985.

Duplicating the Strength of Feeling
The Circulation of Qingshu in the Late Ming

Kathryn Lowry

This chapter examines the emergence of the love letter (*qingshu* 情書) as a distinct literary genre in miscellanies, encyclopedias for daily use (*riyong leishu* 日用類書), and epistolary guides published in China during the late Ming, that is, in the late sixteenth and early seventeenth centuries. These publications were purportedly anthologies of selected examples of "genuine" *qingshu* from correspondence, model letters, random jottings (*biji* 筆記), and erotic fiction, presented as models or illustrations of how to express one's innermost feelings. *Qingshu* differ from the modern notion of a love letter in that they were written not only between lovers (actual or would-be) and spouses but also between friends and courtesans and their clients. The intermingling of literary genres and linguistic registers of "high" and "low" speech is perhaps the definitive formal feature of the *qingshu*. In this respect, *qingshu* differ from model letters for exchange between family members, which state the reciprocal obligations binding writer and recipient in conventionalized and abstract language, and from the correspondence preserved in the literary collections of individual authors (*bieji* 別集).[1]

The texts of *qingshu* incorporate a wide range of literary genres, such as *shi* 詩 poetry, quatrains, song-lyrics, and excerpts from dramas. The intermingling of genres and the rich array of styles represent an alternative to the highly formalized and impersonal forms prescribed in letter-writing manuals to codify and enforce social relationships. The tactic of quotation from different genres and the poetic compositions that writers append to letters serve as an antidote to the explosion of forms and phrases for letter writing in epistolary manuals. Rather than codifying verbal etiquette, *qingshu* experiment with language, seeking to convey the writer's sentiments across vast distances and to achieve an imaginary communion with the reader.

The *qingshu* redirect attention from the appropriate rhetoric for occasions in public life to the invention or "literary" depiction of the sentiments that arise in particular circumstances in the domestic and private realm. Moreover, the genre shifts the concern of writing away from social ritual to intimate relationships of a voluntary nature. The shift from epistolary language as a means to codify the emotions to the language of *qingshu*, which voice passion, melancholy, and, in many cases, illicit desire is achieved through a pastiche of genres. To put it differently, the *qingshu* depict sentiments from the inside out, revising or simply disregarding the learned conventions of letter writing. The tendency of *qingshu* to incorporate a wide range of genres highlights the tension between conventional forms of verbal etiquette and a range of genres that embody genius and passion, between orthodox social roles and individualism.[2]

The nature of *qingshu* as interpellated texts also highlights their ambiguous status as commodities and as reading material that contains symbolic, classificatory, and moral guidelines for the expression of feeling. As Arjun Appadurai writes, "things can move in and out of the commodity state" at varying speeds and effect a transfer that is "reversible or terminal, normative or deviant."[3] He defines the commodity not as an end product, a static artifact of manufacturing, but as the creation of discourses that define the exchangeability of things. His view of commoditization as a discursive process speaks directly to the concerns of this chapter with the love letter, duplication, and self-representation, although the issue here is the circulation of texts—not things. Epistolary guides are manufactured objects that the reader can consult for verbal etiquette to appropriate or enlist the learned forms to represent the self. *Qingshu* adapt the conventions of the epistolary manual to interpellate the writing subject and hail it into being. Generically, *qingshu* scrutinize the syntax and vocabulary that give rise to the expression of the subject.[4] In this respect, *qingshu* conceive the writing of passion and strong emotions as a social act, as knowledge elicited from print that is accessible to all. At the same time, the genre ironically highlights the processes of duplication and reproduction and, in doing so, underscores the distance between social conventions and the literary imagination of desire.

Duplication as a Trait of Late Ming Popular Reading Material

Qingshu enlist popular reading materials to conjure up *qing* 情, "feeling" or "desire." The language of desire is the result of a discursive process of reading. Yet it is manifested above all as a concern with the technical, visual, and physical means to order the *writing* of *reading*, as Judith Zeitlin and Lydia Liu note in the Introduction to this volume. Writing *qingshu*, in turn, entails the techniques of duplication, quotation, emendation, and, quite often, miscopying. The mechanisms of quoting and duplicating cast desire in a peculiar light. Desire, as the subject of the *qingshu*, creates demand, or transmuted desire, which engenders an unfaithful copy of itself. The process whereby copying engenders desire (or literature interpellates the self) defines the problematic of the *qingshu*.[5]

The numbers of printed epistolary works increased exponentially in the late Ming. There are at least eighty extant titles, in contrast to two or three letter-writing guides published and reprinted from the Yuan through the Ming, such as the early Ming *Hanmo daquan* (Complete reference [for writing] in pen and ink; see Appendix, no. 5) and *Qizha qingqian* (Forms of correspondence as good as ready cash; Appendix, no. 7). Household encyclopedias such as the *Wanbao quanshu* (A book of myriad treasures; Appendix, no. 11) included guides to letter writing as a standard feature, often in two chapters, one devoted to models for writing in public life, *wenhan men* 文翰門, and one giving detailed instructions for writing invitations and private correspondence, *shuqi men* 書啟門.

There is a high level of duplication and redundancy among the guides in encyclopedias for daily use, both because volumes went through several printings and because printers commonly reproduced model letters and vocabulary from previous works.[6] As Timothy Brook has observed, the rewriting, reprinting, and piracy of letter-writing guides not only indicate the popularity of such books but also attest to the circulation of letters among an expanding literate population and the increasing reliance on books for the conduct of daily life that came with literacy. Brook suggests that the manuals indicate that people were not able to compose a letter without consulting a primer.[7] However, the assumption that epistolary material in print was used as a how-to guide for writing letters overlooks the inertia of the genre. The stability of texts and conventions carried over from earlier works meant much of the epistolary literature ill suited the needs of less literate readers in the seventeenth century. The practices of duplicating material from different books and genres to compose a "new" work and of reprinting earlier epistolary guides are, rather, keys to the tensions between regulative and "literary" language and between the obligatory ties of kinship and the voluntary ties of desire that structure attitudes toward letter writing in the Ming.[8] This chapter seeks to unravel these tensions by examining the practice of duplication and the attitudes reflected in commentaries on the letters, which regard the act of copying or approximating phrases and images from the realm of print as testimony to the strength of feeling.

The format of the epistolary guide demands a sophisticated kind of reading skill. It is an intellectual endeavor: one adapts learned conventions to depict one's emotional state. The process is more than a matter of simple copying. Late Ming works on letter writing also presume the ability to cross-reference information in print, to personalize models, and to draw on vocabulary lists.[9] A growing number of seventeenth-century letter collections arrange letters by categories of emotion, in contrast to the common taxonomy indexed to occasions in daily life. This trend of valuing letter writing for its capacity to transmit powerful sentiments of passion, longing, and melancholy, along with the growing interest in the role of artifice in self-representation, matches the subtle reading skill required to change epistolary models to suit the needs of a given occasion.

The first part of this chapter draws on prefaces to miscellanies and epistolary works to illustrate the rhetorical tropes that treat writing, mediation, and self-representation. Preface writings emphasize the necessity of letter-writing guides for the conduct of daily life—not simply their utility in the context of mercantile activities or study for the civil service examination that might take a man away from his family for years. The prefaces present epistolary models as a means to simulate the voice, to fabricate the illusion of the writer's presence; the technique of copying or adapting the model letter is a way of creating a facsimile of the self. The modeling of emotion, in turn, is intended to spur a reader to respond in kind, by writing. The formats of late Ming letter-writing guides and their compass, which expanded to cover a growing list of topics and occasions in daily life, signal a growing awareness and acceptance of literary artifice and its use in daily life. The second half of this chapter examines *qingshu* for exchange between courtesans and clients and between spouses and demonstrates how the style of writing and the reading apparatus play upon the tensions between obligation and desire, between rules for composition and unrestrained expression of feeling. The *qingshu* takes as its generic concerns both the action of sending and the letter as something that is sent—marking a problematic relation among writing, the self, desire, and inheritance that Derrida has explored in his "sending," or *envois*, to *The Post Card*.[10] The letters, which freely quote from a range of genres that include poetry, rhapsody, and popular song, can be read as fiction of a peculiar kind that explores the central dilemmas experienced by contemporary readers. The *qingshu* is writing that questions the nature of writing.

I draw examples of *qingshu* primarily from two miscellanies compiled by the prolific editor and author of Taoist fiction Deng Zhimo 鄧志謨 (fl. 1596, pseudonym Baizhuo sheng 百拙生 [Master of ineptitude]). The first miscellany is titled *A Casual Reader* (*Sasa bian*, n.d.; Appendix, no. 9) and includes a chapter of *qingshu* among other writings having to do with romance. The second miscellany, entitled *The Gracious Love Letter* (*Fengyun qingshu*, preface dated 1618; Appendix, no. 4), prints *qingshu* in four chapters arranged by broad types of sentimental attachment (conjugal love, brotherhood, courtship, and courtesan-client liaisons), with an additional two chapters of love songs (*qingci* 情詞) and love poetry (*qingshi* 情詩). Each example of poetry and song lyric could constitute a letter in and of itself or might be incorporated in a letter.

The material in Deng Zhimo's two miscellanies on romance and the love letter was also duplicated in epistolary guides, to peculiar effect. For example, several dozen of the epistolary exchanges in *The Gracious Love Letter* are repackaged in the final chapter, also entitled "The Gracious Love Letter," of the epistolary guide *Plum Sprig Letters* (*Zhemei jian*; Appendix, no. 18). The letter-writing guide strips away marginal commentary but employs the same four categories of social relationship and prints a brief framing narrative to preface each exchange, rooting it in a specific locale and identifying its "real" authors. Such duplication is typical of late Ming reading materials, where it was common practice to expand and update books by drawing on works already in print. The *Plum Sprig Letters* (which is spuriously attributed to Feng Menglong 馮夢龍, 1574–1646) is itself a second or third printing of the printer-editor Yu Changgeng's 余長庚 epistolary guide *Phoenix from the Cinnabar Mountain* (*Danshan feng*; Appendix, no. 3), which adds a small number of new letters to the previous edition.[11] Although only one copy of each miscellany survives (in the Naikaku bunko), the wholesale reproduction and elaboration of themes found in the *Casual Reader* in the second miscellany, which is devoted solely to *qingshu*, suggest that a market existed for such books. In turn, the inclusion of *qingshu* in a small number of epistolary guides marks a trend in the seventeenth century to publish model letters that, like the casual essay (*xiaopin wen* 小品文), could be read for entertainment.[12]

Deng Zhimo's miscellanies were loosely based on the format of the letter-writing manual but expanded the scope of the commentary to teach readers how to read and appreciate the nature of writing that brings to light the "innermost feelings" (*youqing* 幽情). He did not suggest that the *qingshu* were intended as models for copying; rather, he counseled the reader to be mindful of the passion that compelled someone to write. The preface to *The Gracious Love Letter* describes the writer's state of mind as he "reveals his heart and spills forth his gratitude on a sheet of blank letter paper, spelling out his sincere feelings and affections so that they fill the reader's eyes with gracious words. The ease of these gracious words is truly like a butterfly's devotion to flowers or a fish's delight in water."[13] The preface argues that the writing of feeling in the *qingshu* is intuitive and as natural as the instinctive attraction creatures have to certain scents or colors. The appeal of this kind of reading material thus lies in the close rendering of the feelings and, in turn, in the chord a particular wording may strike in the letter's recipient. Further, the preface describes the capacity of *qingshu* to summon up the "graceful presence" of the writer before the reader's eyes, eliding the sense of *fengyun* both as gracious or "memorable" words and as a person's physical bearing.

The commentary touches on concerns ranging from social deportment to the mood and panache of the writer to vocabulary and allusions to exemplary character and literary skill. It thus appeals to a broad spectrum of readers of differing educational backgrounds. The reading apparatus in Deng Zhimo's *Gracious Love Letter* facilitates different modes of reading among an expanding literate audience, who might approach the book as a source of models for writing their own letters, as didactic literature, or as entertainment.[14] *The Gracious Love Letter* adds a narrative preface to each exchange that outlines the circumstances of writing (the cause for separation). It also features marginal commentary by one Tanran sheng 坦然生, the Master of Frankness, who singles out marvelous phrases and shows the reader how writing gives form to the emotions. Finally, a summary comment on each epistolary exchange, scrawled in an easy to read cursive script, states the lessons to be drawn both for social deportment and for understanding how writing can shape powerful emotions of passion and longing.

The genre's embrace of literary artifice makes it evident that the need to correspond through letters and to use appropriate wording to express the nuances of feeling had been internalized to a high degree. The broad acceptance of the importance of epistolary rhetoric for facilitating the conduct of affairs—and the evident need of an expanding literate population for guides to writing letters—bear witness to an outward turn in the *qingshu*. Collections of letters by their nature blur the line between the type and the particular and utilize verbal formulas and conventions to mediate communication, to make it seem as if one speaks directly to the reader. Like the epistolary guide, miscellanies such as *The Gracious Love Letter* annotate the *qingshu*. However, instead of offering these letters as specimens for copying, the marginal commentary and framing narratives help us to appreciate the technique of writing and to unravel the letters' meaning on the level of phrase, plot, character, and theme.

Letter Writing and Mediation

Letter writing was generally construed as a means to transcend spatial and temporal barriers. The standard figures for epistolary writing, the goose that can fly over the mountains and the carp (or paired carp) that swims through rivers bearing a letter in its stomach, denote the power to cross physical barriers in order to convey the writer's sentiments to a recipient. The epistolary guide *Phoenix from Cinnabar Mountain* (noted above as a conventional manual that tacked on a final chapter of *qingshu* and was reprinted as the *Plum Sprig Letters*) construes letter writing as a means to mediate communication. The printer-editor touts the manual as an aid to the writer of limited talent (or literacy): "To fulfill my desire [to gather with my friends and converse], I employ the brush as my tongue and paper as a substitute for a face-to-face meeting. I am, however, a man of limited talent, and my pen cannot naturally convey my thoughts; nor can the ink speak of its own accord. And so the warmth in my heart is unable to find ready expression." The brush and paper sublimate the writer's speech and physical presence.

The two titles *Phoenix from Cinnabar Mountain* and *Plum Sprig Letters* are figures for mediating communication. The former imagines the magnificent phoenix (instead of a goose, the standard metaphor for letter writing) who carries a letter that "can fill the belly of a poor man and enrich the man of learning";[15] the latter refers to the messenger who carries a sprig of plum as a sign of affection and as a stand-in for the writer.[16]

Letters fundamentally serve the function of representation, which is conceived as a substitution for the person's physical presence, ideally expressed in rhetoric so skillful that it seems to transmit the likeness and spirit of the person who is absent.[17] However, the Ming epistolary manual also conceives the letter as a supplement that can enrich a reader and would-be writer. Yu Changgeng's boast that the subtlety with which the letters in his book are worded will nourish the reader signals the commoditization of the discourse on the emotions and quotidian life. The model letters not only substitute for meeting face to face but also expand and enhance the means of self-representation.

The preface to the epistolary manual *New Forms for Letter Writing* (*Chidu xincai*; Appendix, no. 2), attributed to Chen Jiru 陳繼儒, looks more systematically at the letter's ability to mediate (*dai* 代), to embody the writer's physical presence. The author, Xu Guoqiu 許國球, first quotes the words of Su Shi 蘇軾, who is commonly invoked in epistolary prefaces as an authority on letter writing: "My friend, you use your eyes to hear, while my hand serves as my mouth" (*jun yi mu wei er, wu yi shou wei kou* 君以目為耳, 吾以手為口).[18] The preface likens the power of epistolary writing to conjure up the writer's presence to the illusionist capability of drama: "One can make it seem as if a person's voice and smile are directly before us, without having to don the actor's robe and hat." The preface emphasizes the importance of mastering rhetoric (*xiuci* 修辭) throughout as a means of naturalizing artifice in language. The requisite use of writing is to substitute for the physical body, and one achieves this by finding words to capture one's feelings. Letter writing "captures the meaning of one's speech, enabling people to join in spirit even if they are unable to meet face to face. One hears [the writer's] voice and longs for him."[19]

Some prefaces also describe letter writing as a technology for inscribing the writer's feelings in natural forms. Works like *Crane (Soaring) over the Forest* (*Shanglin hong*; Appendix, no. 10), attributed to Zhong Xing 鍾惺 (1574–1624), introduce a taxonomy that arranges letters according to emotions of longing, regret, intrigue, and so on. Lin Mei 林嵋, the author of the preface to this work, depicted writing with instruments that are as ephemeral as feeling itself: "Using a brush [fashioned of] frost to playfully render the scene. Setting wings of jade in motion by tracing [the form] of evening clouds" (*die shuangmao yi nong jing, zhen yuyu er lin xia* 疊霜毛以弄景， 振玉 羽而臨霞).[20] The attention in this work to allusions and stock phrases with which to express emotion is indicative of a trend in early seventeenth-century publications to approach letter writing as an aesthetic enterprise, not merely as a question of mediation and rhetorical mastery. Such guides unfold a canvas of literature on *qing*, feeling—in particular, emotions serving self-interest (*si* 私) rather than the interests of kin or other social networks. *Qingshu* exploit and manipulate the conventions established by epistolary guides, emulating their forms while larding the "real" love letters with quotations from popular literature and song.

Circulating qingshu *Between Courtesans and Clients: Transmuted Desire*

An examination of the language and themes of letters exchanged between courtesans and their clients will allow us to understand the way *qingshu* draw on materials in print. The miscellanies are organized by the four categories of social relationship rather than the occasion or topic for writing, and the four categories of *qingshu* tend to explore sentimental attachments in different and characteristic ways that reflect the literature and range of genres on which the writers draw. This arrangement of letters establishes a framework for reading the *qingshu* with reference to social role and the sentiments appropriate to a given kind of attachment. In turn, the commentary identifies allusions and quotations from various genres and restates the lesson conveyed by the exchange. Marginal comments highlight phrases that may delight and startle the reader. This tutelage in reading is ultimately the key to genres of literature that pertain to a given social role. Thus, the letters to and from courtesans show how the popular songs, card games, and the rules for composing drinking songs (*jiuling* 酒令) that circulated in the brothels provide the medium for a discourse on passionate desire. As I illustrate in the following section, *qingshu* written between husband and wife and letters exchange by courtesans and clients similarly represent two distinct treatments of sentiments based on a shared literature.

A number of the letters between courtesans and clients appear in letter-writing guides as well as in miscellanies. Epistolary manuals such as *As if Speaking Face to Face* (*Ru mian tan*; Appendix, no. 8) compiled by Zhong Xing printed a small number of *qingshu* for men who might need to refer to a model to write to a courtesan. The same texts also appear in miscellanies and in the final chapter, "The Gracious Love Letter," in *Plum Sprig Letters*, but there they are framed as contemporary writings, the products of local-ized exchange and a particular narrative context.

The exchange that appears in both contexts is a pair of letters written by linking tune names (italicized in the following), a practice that clearly reflects the context of courtesan-client relations. Music, popular songs, and verbal games were the staples of entertainment in the brothels. A Suzhou man, Su Shangmin 蘇商民 (possibly a generic name for a merchant), writes a letter to express his longing for a famous Nanjing courtesan, Fan Caiyun 范采雲, and fantasizes about the time when they will be reunited and he may "*Loosen*—my darling's—*Fragrant Sash* and *Take off Your Blouse*, fully *Taking Delight in the Three Pleasures* . . . until the *Fifth Watch Comes Around*." The let-ter is fabricated from song titles, with minimal additions of time words and an occasional pronoun. The courtesan responds in kind, using the same ma-terials to depict her longing: her *Broidered Sash* has grown loose as she pines for him. "I no longer *Sit Beside the Dressing Table* and am *Too Weary to Paint My Brow*."[21] The constraints on vocabulary for the composition limit the semantic content of the love letter. However, the preface to the exchange in *The Gracious Love Letter* (reprinted verbatim in *Plum Sprig Letters*) asserts that this kind of verbal game "makes it all the more evident how close they were" (*yi jian qinghao* 益見情好). The preface names the writer and recipient and creates the pretext of reflexivity—the courtesan's response to the pastiche of tune names in kind is a display of her trust.

The description of their longing is woven out of the fabric of the literature that circulated in the pleasure quarters. The ability to compose as well as to read the humor in this pair of letters relies on shared knowledge of popular songs. The exchange builds on this knowledge, using song titles, to conjure up the personae of the desiring male and the woman pining away in the absence of her lover. However, the desire evoked by this exchange of *qingshu* is a transmuted desire or demand. The form of the letter has a basic affinity with the drinking song, itself an object of consumption in the pleasure quarters. The song evokes passion and lovesickness in a strict compositional form; the exposition of longing is conducted in the spirit of a game. The letter made by joining tune names casts words of passion in the form of an object; that object, in turn, interrogates the recipient: Can you answer in kind?

As the letters are transferred from one reading context to another, the reader's attention shifts from the content to the style of the writing. These same *qingshu* were also printed as model letters on "parting from a beloved courtesan" (*bie qingji* 別情姬) in the epistolary manuals *As if Speaking Face to Face* and in *Paired Carp: Personal Correspondence* (*Chidu shuangyu*; Appendix, no. 1). They appear again with minor variations in *Letters on Gossamer Cloud* (*Yunjin shujian*; Appendix, no. 17).[22] The manual treats these ingenious compositions as writings that typify a client's liaison with a woman from the "blue tower" (courtesan house). Such verbal games that require composition based on a category of knowledge were doubtless familiar to readers of a particular class, since the rules for drinking songs composed along these lines are also a standard feature of miscellanies for those who fancied themselves *fengliu* 風流 (sophisticated men).

The letters to courtesans work within narrow constraints, such as linking tune names, to write a letter that "has a really intriguing zest" (*da you yizhong jiaqu* 大有一種佳趣).[23] The texts of many *qingshu* are composed by tacking together phrases from a single semantic field. *A Casual Reader* includes a series of letters whose sentences are variously formed by linking the names of medicines, card games, tune-types, or birds. The writer uses a pastiche of phrases to sketch a cursory narrative about parting or to imagine a reunion. One letter from the courtesan Liu Cuiqiong 劉翠瓊 threatens harsh consequences if her man is unfaithful; her ultimatum is composed by joining the names of card games.[24] The pastiche of names is almost unintelligible, but it makes sense in a different way, as a literary game that draws on one category of knowledge. It is both a message and a commodity, an object for aesthetic enjoyment comparable to the drinking songs that circulated in print and performance in the pleasure quarters.

Approaching *qingshu* as a verbal game is the logical extension of the practice of using writing manuals, which make it apparent that the writer's subjectivity is dependent on artifice and skill in rhetoric.[25] Another example from the miscellany *The Gracious Love Letter* illustrates the practice of copying material from one genre into another.

A man sends a letter whose text is a pastiche of the names of card games to the courtesan Peng Xixi 彭惜惜 in Jiangling (present-day Hubei).[26] Her reply uses the same form, and the formal correspondence and wit of their writings are judged to be "the most harmonious sort of love" (*qing zhi zui qia* 情之最洽). The letter modifies the practice of cross-referencing phrases of the sort that are listed in an epistolary guide. It crosses generic boundaries by transposing the rules for composing drinking songs to the genre of letter writing. In turn, their letters are written in a form that is comprehensible and appealing to readers of different social levels steeped in the culture of the pleasure quarters. This kind of literary game is similar to the drinking games and lantern riddles common in the pleasure houses. Print culture made these forms of composition accessible to readers in private homes in illustrated volumes of couplets arranged by topic and in miscellanies of current songs, drinking songs, and other genres.[27]

The Affinity of Genres in Print: Letters and Popular Song

Popular song texts in the miscellanies illustrate another dimension of the way in which the learned conventions of letter writing entered the literary imagination and could serve as an ingenious means to express feelings of longing or melancholy. A popular song text in the drama miscellany *Countless Arias for an Eternal Spring* (*Wanqu changchun*; Appendix, no. 12) conjures up the frustration of a woman parted from her lover by giving a first-person account of the process of opening a letter:

> Receiving your letter
> Teardrops fall on the wrapper.
> When I open it up, there is no more than half a sheet of paper.
> My love's cruel riddle is hard to fathom.
> There is not half a sentence, not one-half line of writing.
> You make me face a blank letter, longing in vain.[28]

The song reports the letter's form and appearance and materializes the woman's longing and frustration by dwelling on her efforts to decipher the writer's "cruel riddle" (*wumi* 謎謎) on the blank page. Other popular songs make similar attempts to describe longing, desire, and care through the inability to give them written form. As I discuss elsewhere, the close rendering of the process of writing a letter in popular song is the counterpart to the detailed guides and models for writing to the absent beloved that circulated in print. Popular song texts report how the woman words her letter and bargains for the reader's affection to illustrate how the writing of the emotions can bring them into being.[29]

In the assemblage of genres in miscellanies, late Ming publishers implicitly acknowledged the commonality of form among, on the one hand, letters of congratulation for birthdays, invitations, and good wishes with, on the other hand, drinking songs and couplets (*lianju* 聯句). In some cases publishers also explicitly addressed the formal and thematic continuities among popular literature and letter writing. The introduction (*fanli* 凡例) to the letter-writing guide *Letters on Gossamer Cloud* promises to elucidate the categories of knowledge on which the songs, couplets, and letters draw. It even celebrates the drinking song as a resource with references to the Classical canon, fruits, or card games, and so on that can furnish letter writers with all the nuances (*weimeng* 微蒙) found in the *Three Hundred Poems*.

Letter Writing and Fiction

Roger Chartier has suggested that the cumulative effect of reading model letters is similar to that of reading a sustained work of fiction. Letter-writing manuals assemble in rudimentary form all the essential features of fiction: the unfolding of a plot, the creation of a time-frame, and the sketching-in of characters. As a result, collected model letters can be read as part of a single exchange.[30] The reader's imagination supplies information about those involved and fills in the gaps in the plot between occasions for writing. Chartier's notion of the possibility of reading model love letters as fiction is interesting—precisely because it reveals what the seventeenth-century Chinese publications do *not* do. Rather than attempt to cast a narrative framework and consider how letter writing shapes a larger dynamic between writer and recipient, for example, the miscellany *The Gracious Love Letter* explores how different literary genres capture and condense the writer's feelings. The commentary on *qingshu* highlights the lyric mode, the ability of language to express or crystallize the writer's innermost feelings in discrete images.

The *qingshu* strike a peculiar balance between verbal formulas or clichés and passages of vivid and powerfully worded melancholy. The conventional phrases used in letters to household members, *jiashu* 家書, appear here as well.[31] For example, letters conclude with the phrase "the space of the letter [limits writing] all my feelings" (*jian duan qing chang* 箋短情長); "words cannot fully express my thoughts" (*ci bujin yi* 詞不盡意); "carelessly [drafting this], I will say no more" (*caocao bu xuan* 草草不宣).[32] Such set phrases are most common in model letters for exchange between husband and wife, which are hortatory in nature and detail both parties' interests in regulating the household and conducting business and warn each other not to neglect the household or to stray. *Qingshu* written between spouses incorporate such clichés and intersperse lines from the histories and famous poems. This interplay between lyric expression and the language of reciprocal obligation often creates a dissonance between linguistic styles and tone, which underscores the tension between duty and desire.

The language of the model letters published in conventional writing guides for exchange between husband and wife is terse and makes only a perfunctory attempt to express the melancholy and sorrow of being parted. In contrast, verbal formulas that mark the passage of time or, differently, indicate that emotion cannot be adequately expressed in the space of a letter appear relatively infrequently in the *qingshu* printed in Deng Zhimo's miscellanies. The paucity of set phrases can be explained in part by the fact that many of these letters omit the salutations and closing remarks. They are most evident in the chapter on conjugal sentiments. But in the *qingshu* (as opposed to conventional model letters) the emotional bond between husband and wife is the focal point of the letter and finds expression in a manner that is florid and sentimental and marked by vividly rendered scenes and gifts that attest to or contain feeling. Indeed, when the cliché of not being able to fully express one's feelings appears in the *qingshu* in the literary miscellany, it creates an interesting irony. The wives of merchants or officials threaten and cajole their husbands to return to them in language that is forceful and explicit. In such examples, stock phrases such as "words cannot fully express my thoughts" contrast with the eloquent statement of longing that precedes it. The stylistic irony of the closing phrase seems to promise a more concerted verbal assault should the recipient fail to respond to her queries or to meet the conditions detailed in her letter. The formula "the page is too small to express the extent of my thoughts" asserts that the act of writing has not quelled the writer's melancholy. The interplay between verbal formulas and stirring, descriptive passages that conjure up longing and the sorrow of separation (as well as notes in the commentary that single out particular phrases) highlights the artifice of the language describing the sentiments.

The language stipulating the mutual obligations of spouses or courtesans and their clients bears some resemblance to the contracts that also circulated in print, often in the same books that printed *qingshu*. A handful of epistolary guides and encyclopedias for daily use include *qingshu* in the same chapter as contracts and letters to family members. The makeup of a guide entitled *Five Cloud Letters* (*Wuyun shu*; Appendix, no. 14) even suggests a structural commonality: *qingshu* are appended to a chapter devoted to the "essentials of contracts" (*qiyue jiyao* 契約集要). In other works, they are printed following "letters to family members," *jiashu*.[33] The epistolary guides for letters to family members in household encyclopedias include contracts and writings that detail procedures for dividing inherited property. These letters share a common concern with maintaining the household and its goods.[34] Seen in this light, *qingshu*, contracts, and family correspondence are similar in nature; all are writings whose primary concern is to define the relation between persons and even to assert personhood in the public sphere. The few examples of *qingshu* printed in conventional epistolary guides are concerned with regulating the relations between courtesan and client. With the exception of the heavily annotated exchange between a student and a Nanjing courtesan that appears in *Crane Soaring over the Forest*, these models are fairly cut and dried. They are much like the models for writing invitations, requests to loan or procure objects, or notes to give or acknowledge gifts, which also address concerns within the public realm in that they define the obligations and favors contingent on social relationships.

Gracious Words for Conjugal Relations

Letters expressing "gracious words for conjugal relations" (*shijia fengyun* 室家丰韻) most commonly concern exemplary acts and conduct. For example, in one sequence in *Plum Sprig Letters*, a wife, Xu Yuzhen 許玉真, regrets that she is not able to "weave a fine palindrome" (*zhi huiwen zhi jin* 織迴文之錦) in order to persuade the emperor to allow her exiled husband to return.[35] An interlinear note identifies the reference to the story of Dou Tao 竇滔, "whose wife [Su Hui 蘇惠] presented a palindrome to the emperor to secure his return from exile."[36] This gloss on the historical allusion instructs the reader to view the exile's wife, who wishes to facilitate his return through her writings, as a virtuous wife. Her letter continues in the same vein, counseling her husband to cherish himself and look after his health for the sake of the state and family, and demonstrates that the wife's care for her husband reflects the nexus of the upright official, the family, and the empire.

Deng Chunren 鄧純仁, the exiled husband, responds by portraying his emotional state in imagery that can be interpreted both in the particular and in the categorical sense. Deng states his concern for the state, his longing for his family, and his fond memories of his wife in words "tender and delicate as a bird's song in the moonlight. His sobbing is like the goose's cry in the autumn wind. His melancholy is like water surging through a ravine." The Master of Frankness praises the acute sense of melancholy, which transcends his personal experience. At the close of his letter, Deng adapts the wording of Su Hui's palindrome, borrowing the imagery of the moon and clouds that she would become in order to catch a glimpse of her husband's face, to express his inner turmoil.[37] Deng Chunren himself reads the landscape as a reflection of a traveler's emotions: "A letter with news from home [stirs] myriad kinds of melancholy. The white clouds share my emotions as a traveler. The shining disk of the moon shares my regrets as one sojourning away from home."[38]

These images encapsulate the "myriad kinds of melancholy" (*wanduan chouxu* 萬端愁緒) that are stirred by the immediate event of getting a letter from home. However, Deng grounds these emotions in the experience of the traveler, *youzi* 遊子 and *jiren* 羈人. The Master of Frankness draws a link between the general depiction of the bitterness of an exile and the particular expression of Deng's sorrow and longing for his wife and home. He notes that the imagery of "white clouds and moonlight [allows us to] genuinely know Master Deng's emotions."

Such movement from the particular to the general level of description is characteristic of the language of *qingshu* and creates a peculiar resonance between story and model. As one reads, one can continually shift the frame of reference from the account of two individuals who are separated to the model for expressing emotions appropriate to a type of sentimental attachment and a social role. This same kind of tension is present in conventional letters in epistolary guides. However, the commentary in Deng Zhimo's miscellanies accentuates this tension and plays on the sometimes incompatible concerns with social convention, epistolary technique, and meaning of the genres on which they draw. The summary comment, *zongping* 總評, on the exchange between Xu Yuzhen and her exiled husband, for example, stresses the didactic intent of printing the letter and views the letters as testimony to the exemplary character of a loyal official and filial son and the actions of a devoted and filial wife. The marginal comment on this summary in *The Gracious Love Letter* boasts of "making this manifest" (*zai biao er chu zhi* 再表而出之) to the reader, and the marginal comments point out striking images and techniques of writing that demonstrate the character and feelings of the spouses throughout the exchange.

The most common forms of *qingshu* append poems or songs to convey the emotions. Such letters may open with a short explanation or series of questions, but the appended writing is the heart. For example, a wife sends three poems of her own composition on the theme "since you've been away" (*zi jun zhi chu yi* 自君之出矣) to her husband, who has resided in Nanjing for three years and has taken a concubine.[39] The melancholy of her poems causes the husband to weep without knowing it as he reads. He responds to her complaints with remorse and appends three compositions of his own on the topic "I shall return home" (*wo jiang guilai xi* 我將歸來兮) to capture the sadness (*bei* 悲) her writing stirred in him. The imagery of his compositions closely corresponds to her writings and replicates part of the scene she evoked as a promise to be a good companion to her in the future.

One unexpected outcome of the intertextuality of *qingshu* and the interest in encoding one's feelings in poetry or with reference to literary works is to efface the gender of the writer. There is little distinction between the male and the female voices, since both writer and recipient embroider on a shared literature and respond to the imagery and themes of the other's letter.[40] A letter from a wife by the name of Tao Yuying 陶瑜英 to her husband, Wu Chen 吳琛, a Zhejiang merchant who has been absent for three years, is an example in which the act of citation blurs gender roles. Invoking the literary prototypes of longing for the beloved in the *Chuci* 楚詞 (Songs of the South) and Song Yu's 宋玉 (ca. 290–223 BCE) *Gaotang fu* 高堂賦 (Rhapsody on Gaotang), she adopts the stance of a man of worth who is not recognized by his ruler. She speculates that the scenery of Chu has etched itself on his emotions and led him astray: "Surrounded by the lush foliage growing on the banks of the Xiang River, has someone turned your head and made you linger there? Or perhaps, since you are not far from Mount Wu, you fancy yourself able to drift like a cloud?"[41]

Tao Yuying is an exemplary wife, but it is her musical knowledge that makes her stand out among the wives whose letters are included in Deng Zhimo's miscellany. The ability "to stir [the listener] by playing the *qin* 琴

[Chinese zither]" (*seqin zhi gu* 瑟琴之鼓), noted in the preface to the exchange of letters, is manifested in the pointed allusions to the zither repertoire with which she berates her husband.[42] Tao first states the sadness that his absence has brought his elderly mother. Then, the tune title *Wu ye ti* 烏夜啼 (The crow cries at night) captures her longing, the mourning of a widow tending alone to her home. She names another *qin* melody, *Zhi chao fei* 雉朝飛 (The pheasant flies at dawn), to accuse him of neglect, and then launches into a string of vituperation. The marginal comment praises her for "using [the two tunes] to great effect" (*yong de qiahao* 用得恰好).[43] The husband's response similarly uses the conventional associations of works in the *qin* repertoire to state the regard he owes to his mother, his wife, and the household. The summary comment makes light of his change of heart and implies that the decision to abandon the solitary life of a traveler is ruled by sentiment: "Although the feeling between mother and son runs deep, that between husband and wife is still more weighty."

In these letters we also see the interplay between two types of language: discursive prose that imitates speech and poems that dilate on the meaning of return and its place in the psyche of the writer. The epistolary exchange bears witness to the starkly different aspirations of the man and woman. Tao Yuying belittles herself, as a mere woman who has shrouded herself in an "idle melancholy" (*xianchou* 閑愁). She articulates the difference between her wishes and the concerns that dominate a merchant's life (which are invoked no less in *qingshu* from a husband to his wife than in conventional model letters). "I'd as soon dispense with the reins [that drive one in pursuit] of fame and the fetters of profit . . . and do away with the impediments of melancholy."

The close relation between epistolary prose and poetry is a key element of *qingshu*. The wife's "vulgar poem" (*bishi* 鄙詩) is appended to her reproachful monologue and brings a shift into a purely affective register. She prefaces it by asking forgiveness for the boldness of her words. "You might fancy them a nightjar who appears weeping before you, having flown from the hills of spring":[44]

> Pearl-like tears drop swiftly into the inkwell,
> Sorrowfully I brace myself to write a poem on heartbreak.
> Since that time, long ago, when we parted hands,
> Up until this moment I have no interest in painting my brow.
> There is no medicine to cure the regret that fills the nights.

A wealthy man cannot buy the time of his youth.
The [elders in our] high hall now have hair white as snow.
Why has the wanderer not yet returned?

Although the composition is clumsy and does not introduce ideas not stated in the preceding letter, it embodies her sorrow in a form distinct from prose. The Master of Frankness notes this is "a letter in eight lines, a verse of *shi* poetry, one thousand kinds of longing [expressed] in a few traces of tears. My love, my love, could this fail to stir your sorrow?" He elucidates the features of the poem that should move the reader and makes it clear that the poem itself constitutes a letter. It is distinguished by its brevity, much as letters are, and by formal balance and the capacity to evoke longing and stir a reader.

The merchant's letter of response also appends a quatrain that gives "clear proof that her letter stirred his thoughts of returning home." However, the words with which he prefaces his poem are more interesting than the poem itself. Wu Chen reprises his wife's letter, rephrasing and restating her ideas, to state his longing to return: "The foliage growing along the Xiang River can enter my dreams, and yet the myriad tears of longing for my kin amid other mountains cannot fall on the hills of my home." He transforms the scene that she imagined might seduce him into striking images of absence and dislocation. To prove his isolation, he even offers a tally of "matters that went as I wished, numbering eighteen or nineteen, while there was not even two or three things I could utter to another person." His prelude to the quatrain composed for her draws on a song for the *qin* to find the core phrases and affect to express his intent to return: "Having left my little town behind, how could I forget the *Song of the Threshold*: 'I shall soon return. I shall soon return'?[45] My return is set for the time when the plums bloom on the grave mounds, but that shall be long before the nightjar cries up blood."

The last phrase recalls the image of the nightjar with which Tao Yuying prefaced her poem but invokes it to assure her of his swift return, long before spring when—in legend—the bird cries until it spits up blood. Wu Chen matches her quatrain with his own composition "to express his feelings of regret" (*wei xie yuanhuai* 為寫怨懷) and hopes she can "take solace in the [poetic] reflection of my feelings" (*wei qing qingzhao zhi xingxing* 惟卿情照之幸幸).

By incorporating poetry and alluding to other genres, the preceding examples of *qingshu* create an interplay between a narrative that details the

situation and names the obstacles that separate the writer and recipient, on
the one hand, and poetry that gives the emotions objective form, on the
other. The writer expresses his or her subjectivity by rehearsing incidents
from the histories, the *Shijing* 詩經 (Classic of poetry), or musical knowledge or amplifies the sentiments and gives them formal balance in a range of
poetic and song forms. In this respect, the "truth" of feeling, or the passionate self, draws on a framework of texts and practices of reading and duplication. Writers use a range of genres and hold up the texts as a mirror to life,
in an act of creative reading (or misreading). The reflexivity of the *qingshu*
also suggests the degree to which literacy (or in some case familiarity with
performance genres such as the *qin* repertoire or drama) determined the texture of daily life.

Letter Writing and Drama

The writers of *qingshu* draw on drama and a variety of other texts to re-enact
the sentiments discovered in literature. A letter from a wife to her husband,
whose father sent him away in a pique of anger after he failed the autumn
prefectural examinations, incorporates the passages her husband had under-
lined most heavily in his copy of the lover's bible, the *Xixiang ji* 西廂記
(Story of the western wing).[46] She writes out the lines: "Don't allow 'the yellow oriole to take away the majestic swan's ambition,' nor 'the lotus root
tendrils to restrict the flight of the giant *peng* 鵬 bird.' Nor let 'bawdy lyrics
sully your forceful dragon-and-snake script.'"[47] Her writing inverts the sequence of the printed text, and one could imagine her poring over the book,
randomly tracing her husband's reading marks to enact a sense of physical
proximity with him. She explains the intent behind copying the lines: "To
encourage my love, my love, to encourage [you], to encourage [you]." The
repetition of this pair of phrases at the close of her letter is redundant, but it
signals the importance of duplication in letter writing. By borrowing phrases
from the drama, she interpellates a persona that is solicitous and also implicitly desirous of the reader.

The opening passage of Dong Hui'e's 董蕙娥 letter, one of the most
memorable in the miscellany, recollects her husband's abrupt departure. Her
writing then conjures up the sights and sounds of autumn:

Moreover, the scenery this autumn is so lonely, what with the wind and falling
leaves. I worry that the rows of geese herald a cold winter and might add to your
melancholy. The autumn cricket and teardrops of dew might stir your sighs, and the

sound of rain on the banana leaves might cause your sighs to multiply. The cavalry that spurs the wind might cause you to grieve.

The commentator declares this "a parable for the desolate autumn scenery. This is a *Rhapsody on the Sounds of Autumn (Qiusheng fu)*," likening her flawed prose to the masterpiece by the renowned author and statesman Ouyang Xiu 歐陽修 (1007–52).[48] The *qingshu* broaches the subject of absence—a common problem—in an uncommon manner by beginning with his abrupt departure. Her scrutiny of the autumn scene and ability to evoke melancholy through a description of its sounds and sights is the focal point of the literary work. The wife reads the landscape and translates it into words that bring his mood (as well as her own) to life—an act of projection and a show of empathy for the absent husband. The commentary flatters her writing skill by likening it to the rhapsody, one of the most florid and eloquent of genres. Such an evocation of melancholy had special resonance for readers of the time, when prolonged separation was common both for members of the elite engaged in study for the civil service examinations or absent on official postings and for merchants in pursuit of profit. However, her letter is distinguished not by its basis in social fact but by its interest in entrusting the emotions to paper and "sending" them to create the ground for sentimental attachment.

The Event of Sending a Letter: Gifts and Borrowed Words

The "event" of the letter is the rationale it gives for choosing certain words to symbolize feelings of loneliness, melancholy, or desire that hover between writer and recipient. To state it differently, the event of the letter is the letter itself. *Qingshu* often accompany gifts and explain their symbolism, as an exhortation or emblem of the desired reunion between the writer and recipient. In a sense, the letter is also a present to the recipient. It is a gift of words that palpably embody the writer's desire.[49] The informality of the letter as a literary form, which may draw equally on classical and non-canonical texts, enables the writer to capture a complexity of feelings ranging from melancholy to joy. The *qingshu* take this malleable form in a somewhat different direction, since they render desire into text by borrowing other texts, objects, and images. The genre mines the significance of the act of sending, with its proprietary concerns to make desire known and to stake a claim to the reader's affection and also to trace the lineage of the message to the literature on romance. The status of the message is, thus, peculiarly rich: it not only states one's feelings and objectives but also has the quality of an artifact, an object in itself.

The pervasive logic in letters accompanying gifts is to use an object as an emblem of character and as a means to encode sentiments. This kind of writing on objects is the counterpart to the material practice of crafting a statement of intent from a range of literary texts. As discussed above, the letters exchanged by husband and wife often discourse on the same images, such as the nightjar that the husband, Tao Yuying, reproduces from his wife's letter. However, he recasts the figure of the legendary bird to make a promise to return before it cries at spring's arrival—a repetition that works to erase the sorrow that her reference to the bird evoked.

The gift is an emblem of what the writer wants the beloved to become. Numerous letters to courtesans on gifts elucidate the correspondence between objects and emotions, and their conventions are at times adapted in correspondence between husband and wife. For example, Liu Cong 劉聰 counsels his wife by sending objects that set forth his wishes for her conduct and says, emphatically, "I will not say they are without meaning" (fei yun wuyi 非云無意). He invites his wife to share his vision or wish (yuan 願), as he shares her wish that he will succeed in the examination, but he immediately questions whether there is a necessary relationship between what one wishes and what must happen (bi 必). The logic of the qingshu supplements the gift, delivering the sender's counsel and also implying the emotional hardship of the separation for both writer and recipient. The comment by the Master of Frankness on the explication of the gifts presses this point: "The three inanimate objects unambiguously utter words of passion" (fenming sanzhong wuqing wu, shuochu yiduan youqing hua 分明三種無情物, 說出一段有情話). The joke, of course, lies in viewing letters on conjugal sentiment in terms of the dialectic between objects that are inanimate or unfeeling (wuqing 無情) and words that are sentient or passionate (youqing 有情). The letter intermingles exhortations to act in an exemplary manner with writing on objects that confirm the conjugal bond.[50]

A number of letters to courtesans illustrate a similar logic concerning gifts. For example, a Hangzhou courtesan delivers a doggerel rhyme demanding five presents and names the five kinds of allure they will enhance in her and asserts they will please her client. The reply by the client, Tao Rugui 陶如圭, attaches a verse that he names "as extravagant and humorous as the gifts are cheap and trifling." Tao's response to the courtesan explains what—

and how—his gifts signify. He boasts of his "singular ability to use unfeeling objects to secure the affection of a beauty" (*du yi wuqing zhi wu, de jian lian yu meiren* 獨以無情之物得見憐于美人).[51] He also pays tribute to their shared "good fortune" (*xing* 幸)—not only of the objects that will adorn her but also of himself as giver of inexpensive trifles and the courtesan as the recipient of them. "It is the good fortune of the objects—and my good fortune as well. And fortunately, you may look on these with a smile and keep them." This logic links the three in a circle of reciprocity, which is distinguished by the fact that it is sealed with humor rather than by epistolary convention.

These two exchanges illustrate how the exchange of *qingshu* articulates the opposition and mutual correspondence between the inanimate and the sentient. The gifts may serve as the cement in a mutual regard between client and courtesan, but the exchange of verses and the willingness to converse, through *qingshu*, about the qualities they desire in one another forges a voluntary association. Further, the style of writing, which pastes together objects and explication, verse and prose, underscores the tension between, on the one hand, the conventional associations of the material objects and texts alike and, on the other, the individual writer's emotion.

The miscellany introduces the conventional associations of material goods, such as perfume, rouge, a round silk fan to symbolize reunion, jade hairpins or other objects that symbolize the body of the beloved, or spatial or natural forms such as the clouds that can follow and care for the beloved. As interpellated texts, the *qingshu* deploy different genres and images in a fashion intended to delight the reader. Much as the gifts in the letters just discussed delight the senses with the stimuli of fragrance and color and the poignant symbolism of jades, fans, and other love tokens, the writing is both inanimate and sentient. The materiality of the form and the density of allusions both to literature and to the sender's letter lend the genre of *qingshu* an ambiguity or duplicity, but they also confer on it the capacity to weave together moral, symbolic, and classificatory statements of the sentiments with great economy of means.

The practice of rewriting images like the nightjar that spits blood is fundamental to reading the *qingshu* and other informal genres of the late Ming, which transfer their meaning to the writing subject and shape an image of desire. The genre relies on habits of analogy, duplication, and variation that arise from the material practices of writing and publishing in the late

Ming. These habits are as fundamental to the reading of Chinese writing as the archetypal metaphor of the "voice of the shuttle," whose double metonymy signifies the link between cunning and craft, is to reading lyric poetry in the West.[52] The *qingshu* are affiliated with repetition, and recast the objects and clichés of romantic discourse to show the rootedness of feeling in material life.

Appendix: Annotated Bibliography of Sources of qingshu

1. *Chidu shuangyu* 尺牘雙魚 (Paired carp: personal correspondence). Full title: *Xinbian zengbu jiaozheng Yinji Xiong xiansheng Chidu shuangyu* 新編增補較正寅幾熊先生尺牘雙魚 (A new expanded edition of Mr. Yinji Xiong's *Paired Carp: Personal Correspondence*). 9 *juan*. Ed. Xiong Yinji 熊寅幾. Preface by Chen Jiru 陳繼儒. Printed by Ye Qiyuan 葉起元. Harvard-Yenching Library.

2. *Chidu xincai* 尺牘新裁 (New forms for letter writing). 10 *juan*. Attrib. Chen Jiru 陳繼儒. Preface by Xu Guoqiu 許國球. Baoren tang, late Qing. Harvard-Yenching Library.

3. *Danshan feng* 丹山鳳 (Phoenix from cinnabar mountain). Full title: *Xinke zhushi yasu bianyong yi zha san qi Danshan feng* 新刻註釋雅俗便用一札三奇丹山鳳 (A new annotated volume with three marvelous letters on any given topic for easy use by the refined and the common). 8 *juan*. Ed. Mei Fengting 梅鳳亭. Preface and printed by Yu Changgeng 余長庚. Naikaku bunko.

4. *Fengyun qingshu* 丰韻情書 (The gracious love letter). 6 *juan*. Ed. Deng Zhimo 鄧志謨. Preface by Tanran sheng 坦然生 (Master of Frankness), dated 1618. Commentary by Nanyang jushi 南陽居士. Naikaku bunko. Facsimile reprint in *Ming Qing shanben xiaoshuo congkan chubian* 明清善本小說叢刊初編, series 11 (Taiwan: Tianyi chubanshe, 1985).

5. *Hanmo daquan* 翰墨大全 (Complete reference [to writing] in pen and ink). Alternative title: *Xinbian shiwen leiju Hanmo daquan* 新編事文類聚翰墨大全, A new topically arranged complete reference [to writing] in pen and ink for social occasions). Ed. Liu Yingli 劉應李 (d. 1311). Reprinted several times from 1307 (preface by Xiong He 熊禾). Number of *juan* vary; the largest edition has 194 *juan*.

6. *Hanmo jun* 翰墨駿 (A fine mount for writing). Alternative titles: *Hanmo feihuang* 翰墨飛黃 (A flying brown [steed] for writing); *Xinbian simin bianyong zhujie Hanmo jun* 新編四民便用註解翰墨駿 (A fine mount for writing: a new, annotated compilation for easy use by the people of the four social classes). 5 *juan*. Printed by Yu Yinbo 余寅伯. Naikaku bunko.

7. *Qizha qingqian* 啟劄青錢 (Forms of correspondence as good as ready cash). Alternative title: *Xinbian shiwen leiju yao Qizha qingqian* 新編事文類聚要啟劄青錢 (New forms of correspondence as good as ready cash: topically arranged essentials of writing for social occasions). 2d ed., 1342. 51 *juan*. Printed by the Liu family Rixin tang 劉氏日新堂, in Jian'an (Fujian). Facsimile reprint, ed. Nagasawa Kikuya 長澤規矩 (Tokyo: Goten kenkyūkai, 1949).

8. *Ru mian tan* 如面譚 (As if speaking face to face). *18 juan*. Attrib. Zhong Xing 鍾惺. Annotated by Feng Menglong 馮夢龍. Number of *juan* and title vary. Modern typeset edition: *Minggong guifan chidu Ru miantan* 名公規範尺牘如面譚 (As if speaking face to face: epistolary models by renowned authors) (Shanghai: Zhongyang shuju, 1936).

9. *Sasa bian* 洒洒編 (A casual reader). *6 juan*. Ed. Deng Zhimo 鄧志謨. Comp. and preface by Wei Bangda 魏邦達 (Qufei juzhi 去非居士 [Master of Dispelling Dissent]). Naikaku bunko. Facsimile reprint in *Ming Qing shanben xiaoshuo congkan chubian*, series 11 (Taiwan: Tianyi chubanshe, 1985).

10. *Shanglin hong* 上林鴻 (Crane soaring over the forest). *4 juan*. Comp. Zhong Xing 鍾惺. Annotated by Chen Renxi 陳仁錫. Preface by Lin Mei 林嵋 (styled Xiaomei 小眉). Harvard-Yenching Library.

11. *Wanbao quanshu* 萬寶全書 (The book of myriad treasures) is a generic title for at least four related editions, such as the *Wanyong zhengzong* (see no. 13 below); *Wanbao souqi quanshu* 萬寶搜奇全書 (The book of gathered novelties and myriad treasures), University of California at Berkeley, East Asian Library; and the *Quanbu wenlin miaojin Wanbao quanshu* 全補文林妙錦萬寶全書 (Fully expanded marvelous tapestry of the realm of letters: a book of myriad treasures). Preface dated 1612. *38 juan*. Anzheng tang 安正堂 reprint by Liu Ziming 劉子明, Harvard-Yenching Library.

12. *Wanqu changchun* 萬曲長春 (Countless arias for an eternal spring). Full title: *Dingqie Hui Chi yadiao nanbei guanqiang yuefu dianban Quxiang da ming chun* 鼎鍥徽池雅調南北官腔樂府點板曲響大明春 (Arias echo in the bright spring: a fine edition of elegant melodies in the Hui[zhou] and Chi[zhou] regional styles, northern and southern official admonitions, and songs with phrase markings). Alternative title: 萬曲長春 (Countless arias for the bright spring). *5 juan*. Ed. Cheng Wanli 程萬里. Comp. Zhu Dingchen 朱鼎臣. Printed by Jin Kui 金魁 of the Gongtang 拱唐 printing establishment in Minjian. Sonkeikaku bunko. Facsimile reprint, ed. C. K. Wang 王秋桂, entitled *Da ming chun* 大明春, in *Shanben xiqu congkan* 善本戲曲叢刊, series 1, vol. 6 (Taiwan: Xuesheng shuju, 1984).

13. *Wanyong zhengzong* 萬用正宗 (The definitive text of manifold use). Full title: *Dingqin Chongwen ge huizuan shimin wanyong zhengzong bu qiu ren* 鼎鍥崇文閣彙纂士民萬用正宗不求人 (Seek no help from others: the definitive text, of manifold use to gentry and commoner, in a refined edition compiled by the Chongwen pavilion). Colophon dated 1607. *35 juan*. Comp. Long Yangzi 龍陽子. Printed by Yu Xiangdou 余象斗 (style name Wentai 文台). This edition and the 1599 *Leizhu Santai Wanyong zhengzong* 類聚三臺萬用正宗, *43 juan*, edited by Yu Xiangdou, which it duplicates, are in the Niida Collection, Tōyō bunka kenkyūjo.

14. *Wuyun shu* 五雲書 (Five cloud letters). Full title: *Dingjuan Mei gong Chen xiansheng bianji simin bianyong Wuyun shu* 鼎鐫眉公陳先生編集四民便用五雲書 (Five cloud letters: a fine edition compiled by Mr. Chen, Master Brow, for easy use by people of the four social classes). 4 *juan*. Ed. Chen Jiru 陳繼儒. Commentary by Chen Shilong 陳士龍. Printed by Yang Juli 楊居理 (Jianyang). Naikaku bunko.

15. *Xiatian jinzha* 霞天錦札 (Brocade letters from roseate clouds in the sky). Full title: *Dingjuan Zhang zhuangyuan huiji bianmin jiandu Xiatian jinzha* 鼎鐫張狀元彙輯便民柬牘霞天錦札 ([Selected] brocade letters from roseate clouds in the sky: a deluxe edition of letters for popular use compiled by the first-placed candidate Zhang). 5 *juan*. Comp. Zhang Yinghai 張瀛海. Annotated by Long Yangzi 龍陽子. Printed by Huang Taifu 黃台輔. Naikaku bunko.

16. *Yi zha san qi* 一札三奇 (Three marvelous models for each kind of letter). 8 *juan*. Comp. Deng Zhimo 鄧志謨. Annotated by Mao Shiqiao 毛士翹. Ming editions in Naikaku bunko and Harvard-Yenching Library. Facsimile reprint in *Ming Qing shanben xiaoshuo congkan chubian* 明清善本小說叢刊初編, series II (Taiwan: Tianyi chubanshe, 1985).

17. *Yunjin shujian* 雲錦書箋 (Letters on gossamer cloud). Full title: *Xinqin Lu Lin er xiansheng zuanji shimin bianyong Yunjin shujian* 新鋟陸林二先生纂輯士民便用雲錦書箋 (A new edition [of letters] compiled by Messrs. Lu and Lin for ready use by gentry and commoner). Ming ed. 6 *juan* with one appended *juan*. Ed. Lu Pei 陸培. Annotated by Lin Shidui 林時對. Naikaku bunko.

18. *Zhemei jian* 折梅箋 (Plum sprig letters). Late Ming. 8 *juan*. Attributed to Feng Menglong 馮夢龍. Printed by Yu Changgeng 余長庚. Facsimile reprint included in the *Feng Menglong quanji* 馮夢龍全集, ed. Wei Tongxian 魏同賢 (Shanghai guji chubanshe, 1993), vol. 43.

Notes

1. Roger Chartier notes a similar bifurcation between correspondence to family members and love letters that thematize a conflict of obligation and desire, in his "Introduction: An Ordinary Kind of Writing," in *Correspondence: Models of Letter Writing from the Middle Ages to the Nineteenth Century*, ed. idem, Alain Boreau, and Cecile Dauphin; trans. Christopher Woodall (Princeton: Princeton University Press, 1997), pp. 19–21.

2. Wm. Theodore de Bary's classic essay "Individualism and Humanitarianism in Late Ming Thought" explores the problem of individualism in early modern China. He notes the use of fiction, essays, letters, and other writings in the vernacular to repudiate traditional morality and shape a discourse on individualism and self-interest, with particular reference to Li Zhi 李贄 (1527–1602); see *Self and Society in Ming Thought*, ed. idem (New York: Columbia University Press, 1970), pp. 188–200.

3. Arjun Appadurai, ed., *The Social Life of Things: Commodities in Cultural Perspective* (Cambridge, Eng.: Cambridge University Press, 1986), pp. 13–14.

4. As Judith Butler puts it, the process of acquiring social meanings and values "initiates the individual into the subjected status of the subject"; see *Bodies That Matter: On the Discursive Limits of "Sex"* (New York: Routledge, 1993), p. 121.

5. Qianshen Bai has argued that copying and duplication are equally central to the mixture of writing styles that appear in calligraphy of the late Ming and early Qing; see "Mingmo Qingchu shijue yishu zhong linmo yu fuzhi xianxiang yanjiu" 明末清初視覺藝術中臨摹與復制現象研究 (The phenomenon of copying and duplication in late Ming and early Qing visual art), unpublished article.

6. Sakai Tadao argues that these works for daily use naturally reflect social change in the nature of their contents, which became more diverse in the Ming; see "Confucianism and Popular Educational Works," in *Self and Society in Ming Thought*, pp. 333–35; and idem, "*Mindai no nichiyō ruishu to shomin kyōiku*" 明代の日用類書と庶民教育 (Ming dynasty household encyclopedias and popular education), in *Kinsei Chūgoku kyōiku shi kenkyū* 近世中國 教育史研究 (Studies of the history of education in modern China), ed. Hayashi Tomoharu 林友春 (Tokyo: Kokudosha, 1958).

7. Timothy Brook, *The Confusions of Pleasure: Commerce and Culture in Ming China* (Berkeley: University of California Press, 1998), pp. 56–62. See also idem, "Communications and Commerce," in *The Cambridge History of China*, vol. 8, ed. Denis Twitchett and Frederick W. Mote (Cambridge, Eng.: Cambridge University Press, 1998), pp. 636, 639–40.

8. Roger Chartier ("Introduction: An Ordinary Kind of Writing," p. 21) explains how the inertia of material printed in letter collections shaped the approach of scholars studying the shifting practice of letter writing, necessitating comparison of

nineteenth-century model letter collections with manuals from the seventeenth century and earlier.

9. Chartier has argued that the growing practice of solitary reading played an important role in the privatization of life in early modern Europe; see "The Practical Impact of Writing," in *A History of Private Life: Passions of the Renaissance*, ed. idem, trans. Arthur Goldhammer (Cambridge, Mass.: Harvard University Press, 1989), pp. 111, 126. In "The Space of Reading" (unpublished article), I argue that *qingshu* conceptualize a space for emotions normally concealed but conceive it in active relation to learned conventions and orthodox social roles rather than as a private realm.

10. Jacques Derrida, "Envois," in idem, *The Post Card: From Socrates to Freud and Beyond*, trans. Alan Bass (Chicago: University of Chicago Press, 1987), esp. pp. 4, 37–38.

11. The copy of *Zhemei jian* in the Naikaku is a third edition of a work compiled by Mei Fengting 梅鳳亭, entitled *Danshan feng* (Phoenix from cinnabar mountain). It seems likely that the epistolary guide duplicates the *qingshu* printed in Deng Zhimo's miscellany, since it contains a number of corrupted characters.

12. The trend to publish anthologies of letters as *belles lettres* is attested by nearly twenty letter anthologies attributed to renowned authors that include Chen Jiru 陳繼儒, Xu Wei 徐渭, Tu Long 屠隆, Shen Jiayin 沈佳胤, Zhong Xing 鍾惺, and others.

13. Deng Zhimo, "Qingshu xiaoyin" 情書小引 (A prologue to the *qingshu*), in *Fengyun qingshu* (Appendix, no. 4), 2.

14. For a brief summary of the forms of commentary that facilitate reading the miscellanies as didactic literature and for entertainment and as a guide to writing, see my "Three Ways to Read a Love Letter in Late Ming," *Ming Studies* 44 (Fall 2000): 55–58.

15. Yu Changgeng, Introduction to *Danshan feng* (Appendix, no. 3).

16. The preface uses the phrase *yishi youdai*. The courier, *yishi*, is a figure for the plum, alluding to the story of Lu Kai, who sent a plum and a poem to his friend Fan Hua. See *Jingzhou ji*.

17. In this respect, the concept of letters in early modern China is similar to that in Europe of the Middle Ages, as *sermo absentium*, although at times the substance of the matter to be conveyed was reported by a messenger. See Giles Constable, *Letters and Letter Collections*, Typologie des sources du Moyen Age occidental, no. 17 (Belgium: Editions Brepols, 1976), pp. 13–14.

18. Su Shi is commonly cited in epistolary prefaces as an authority on letter writing. The quotation here is adapted from Su's account of his travels, in which he encounters a deaf man who was a remarkably skilled painter. See Bian Yongyu 卞永譽, comp., *Shigu tang shuhua huikao* 式古堂書畫彙考, 25.50a–b. SKCS, vol. 828.

19. Xu Guoqiu, Preface to *Chidu xincai* (Appendix, no. 2), 2b.

20. Lin Mei, Preface to *Shanglin hong* (Appendix, no. 10).

21. *Zhemei jian*, 8.20b, "Su Fan qinghao" 蘇范情好. For a translation of the exchange, see my "Personal Letters from Seventeenth-Century Epistolary Guides," in *Under Confucian Eyes: Writings on Gender in Chinese History*, ed. Susan Mann and Yu-Yin Cheng (Berkeley: University of California Press, 2001), pp. 164–65.

22. *Ru mian tan, juan* 8, "Liqing lei" 麗情類 ([Letters on] flowery sentiments), p. 242; *Chidu shuangyu*, 7.8b; *Yunjin shujian*, 6.17b–18a; the last omits some phrases.

23. *Fengyun qingshu*, 2.16b.

24. *Sasa bian*, 2.8a–9a.

25. The conscious attention to artifice in the miscellany bears striking similarities to publications of love letters in late sixteenth-century France and the fad for *Italianisme*, which was synonymous with artifice and disingenuousness. See Bernard Bray, *L'Art de la lettre amoureuse: des manuels aux roman (1550–1700)* (The Hague: Mouton, 1967), pp. 9–13.

26. *Zhemei jian*, 8.21a–b, "Lu Peng qinghao" 陸彭情好.

27. The method of composition by linking pre-existing phrases is termed *lian* 聯. Instructions for composing drinking songs, *jiuling*, by linking phrases from specific categories such as the *Classic of Poetry* for a given line or lines, are included in the late Ming miscellany *Boxiao zhuji* 博笑珠璣. Deng Zhimo himself published an illustrated volume of couplets for various occasions. The 1628 *Baijia Zhuzhi lian* 百家珠璣聯 (copy held in the Drama Research Institute, China Arts Research Institute) includes instructions for composing and reading such couplets, which are arranged by topic.

28. For this song text, see *Wanqu changchun*, 5.15a–b; it is number 16 in a series of "Dao Guazhi'er" 倒掛枝兒 in the middle register. Ibid., 4.20a–b, prints another song on trying to give form to feeling in painting.

29. Three sets of popular song texts in Feng Menglong's *Guazhi'er* 掛枝兒 concern efforts to capture emotions in writing or to decipher them in books or paintings. Song texts on these themes appear in clusters in three chapters: *juan* 3, entitled "Xiang" 想 (Longing); *juan* 6, "Yuan" 怨 (Resentment); *juan* 7, "Gan" 感 (Response) (modern reprint in *Ming Qing min'ge shidiao ji* 明清民歌時調集, vol. 1 [Shanghai: Shanghai guji chubanshe, 1987]). See my "Transmission of Popular Song in Late Ming" (Ph.D. diss., Harvard University, 1996), pp. 178–83.

30. Roger Chartier, *"Secretaires for the People,"* in *Correspondence*, p. 98.

31. For translations of model letters for exchange by husband and wife, see my "Personal Letters," pp. 160–63.

32. *Zhemei jian*, 8.2a–b (variation at close of 8.12), 8.1b; *Fengyun qingshu*, 1.3a–b, 7b, 8b.

33. *Wuyun shu*, 4.20b–23a. One exchange between a scholar and a courtesan is appended to specimens of "letters to family members" in *Hanmo jun*, 4.23b, and also in *Shanglin hong*, 1.22b–23.

34. See the discussion of epistolary writings and the public sphere in Elizabeth Heckendorn Cook, *Epistolary Bodies: Gender and Genre in the Eighteenth-Century Republic of Letters* (Stanford: Stanford University Press, 1996), chap. 1.

35. *Zhemei jian*, 8.2a–3a; *Fengyun qingshu*, 1.7ab. "Deng Xu qinghao" 鄧許情好 is the only exchange that is not contemporary. Deng Chunren is identified as a gentryman of good character, a native of Anhui who was exiled to Guangxi during the Southern Song.

36. Su Hui's story is recorded in the "Biographies of Virtuous Women" in the *Jin Records* (*Jin shu*, "Lienü zhuan"), *juan* 96, Biographies no. 66 (Beijing: Zhonghua, 1974), p. 2523. Her palindrome of 841 (29 x 29) characters expressed the depth of her melancholy and comforted her husband during his exile.

37. Su Hui's palindrome in 280 characters is printed in the chapter of love poetry (*qingshi*), as the first in a series of *qingci* (love lyrics), in *Fengyun qingshu*, 6.34b–35b.

38. *Fengyun qingshu*, 1.8b; *Zhemei jian*, 8.2a, preface details her intent in writing.

39. "Wu Tao qinghao" 吳陶情好, *Zhemei jian*, 8.3b–4b; *Fengyun qingshu*, 1.28–30b.

40. Roland Barthes writes that the man who utters (or writes of) the other's absence is "miraculously feminized." Barthes stresses that this is not because the roles have been inverted but because discourse on love is marked as feminine. It is Woman who gives shape to absence, spins and weaves descriptions of melancholy, and "elaborates its fiction" (*A Lover's Discourse: Fragments*, trans. Richard Howard [New York: Farrar, Straus and Giroux, 1978], p. 14). I thank Kang-i Sun Chang for bringing this passage to my attention.

41. "Wu Tao qinghao," *Zhemei jian*, 8.3b–4; *Fengyun qingshu*, 1.8b–11.

42. The value placed on musical knowledge also suggests their conjugal harmony, and the expression for her skill resembles the term for such a relation, *qinse tiaohe* 琴瑟調和. See *Xingshi yinyuan zhuan* 惺世姻緣傳 (Shanghai: Shanghai guji chubanshe, 1981), chap. 44, p. 638.

43. "Zhi chao fei" is a *qin* (Chinese zither) melody. The interlinear note identifies its author as Du Muzi 犢沐子, who was without a wife. Numerous marginal comments in the *Fengyun qingshu* single out a "perfect choice of phrase" (*yu qiahao* 語恰好), including clever comments on place-names (1.16a); an allusion to the *Classic of Poetry* (1.20b); and a phrase from the *Story of the Western Chamber* (2.35b).

44. The nightjar—or the cuckoo, as *fugui* is often translated—is said to be the transformation of a man who died of lovesickness.

45. The song "Baili xi ge" 百里奚歌 appears in (Yuan) Liu Lü's 劉履 *Fengya yi* 風雅翼, 9.9 (SKCS, vol. 1370). Said to be a composition by the wife of Xi Jingbo 奚井伯, who was reunited with her husband when she played the tune for him, it is also referred to as "Yanyi ge" 庱㞷 歌 (Song of the threshold).

46. *Zhemei jian*, 8.4b–5b; *Fengyun qingshu*, 1.13–15. On the use of *Western Wing* as a reference work on love, see the introduction by Stephen West and Wilt Idema to

270 ∞ KATHRYN LOWRY

Wang Shifu, *The Moon and the Zither: The Story of the Western Wing* (Berkeley: University of California Press, 1995), pp. 96–97.

47. *Xixiang ji* 西廂記, Book 3, Act 1 (Beijing: Renmin wenxue chubanshe, 1995), p. 127. I follow the translation in *The Story of the Western Wing*, trans. West and Idema, pp. 197ff.

48. *Ouyang Wenzhong gong quanji, juan* 15, pp. 139–40. See Arthur Waley, *Translations from the Chinese* (New York: Alfred A. Knopf, 1961), pp. 317–19.

49. For a note written by Su Shih describing the mood evoked in him by the winter scenery and the wish to send those complex feelings to a friend, see Ronald Egan, "Su Shih's 'Notes' as a Historical and Literary Source," *Harvard Journal of Asiatic Studies* 50, no. 2 (Dec. 1990): 585–86.

50. See "Zhou Dong qinghao" 周董情好, in *Fengyun qingshu*, 1.13–15; "Sun Du qinghao" 孫杜情好, in ibid., 1.25–28; and "Huang Shao qinghao" 黃邵情好, in ibid., 2.8–9.

51. "Taosheng fu Yunxian shu" 陶生復雲仙書, in *Fengyun qingshu*, 3.9b–11a. In "The Space of Reading," I discuss this pair of verses on the five gifts as rendering a representational space that the lovers can inhabit.

52. Geoffrey Hartman, "The Voice of the Shuttle: Language from the Point of View of Literature," in idem, *Beyond Formalism* (New Haven: Yale University Press, 1970), pp. 337–38.

Works Cited

Appadurai, Arjun, ed. *The Social Life of Things: Commodities in Cultural Perspective.* Cambridge, Eng.: Cambridge University Press, 1986.

Bai Qianshen 白謙慎. "Mingmo Qingchu shijue yishu zhong linmo yu fuzhi xianxiang yanjiu" 明末清初視覺藝術中臨摹與復制現象研究 (The phenomenon of copying and duplication in late Ming and early Qing visual art). Unpublished article.

Barthes, Roland. *A Lover's Discourse: Fragments.* Trans. Richard Howard. New York: Farrar, Straus and Giroux, 1978.

Bray, Bernard. *L'Art de la lettre amoreuse: des manuels aux roman (1550–1700).* The Hague: Mouton, 1967.

Brook, Timothy. "Communications and Commerce." In *The Cambridge History of China,* vol. 8, ed. Denis Twitchett and Frederick W. Mote. Cambridge, Eng.: Cambridge University Press, 1998, pp. 579–707.

————. *The Confusions of Pleasure: Commerce and Culture in Ming China.* Berkeley: University of California Press, 1998).

Butler, Judith. *Bodies That Matter: On the Discursive Limits of "Sex."* New York: Routledge, 1993.

Chartier, Roger. "Introduction: An Ordinary Kind of Writing." In *Correspondence: Models of Letter Writing from the Middle Ages to the Nineteenth Century,* ed. idem, Alain Boreau, and Cecile Dauphin, trans. Christopher Woodall. Princeton: Princeton University Press, 1997, pp. 1–23.

————. "The Practical Impact of Writing." In *A History of Private Life,* vol. 3, *Passions of the Renaissance,* ed. idem, trans. Arthur Goldhammer. Cambridge, Mass.: Harvard University Press, 1989, pp. 111–60.

Constable, Giles. *Letters and Letter Collections.* Typologie des sources du Moyen Age occidental, no. 17. Belgium: Editions Brepols, 1976.

Cook, Elizabeth Heckendorn. *Epistolary Bodies: Gender and Genre in the Eighteenth-Century Republic of Letters.* Stanford: Stanford University Press, 1996.

de Bary, Wm. Theodore. "Individualism and Humanitarianism in Late Ming Thought." In *Self and Society in Ming Thought,* ed. idem. New York: Columbia University Press, 1970, pp. 1–28.

Derrida, Jacques. *The Post Card: From Socrates to Freud and Beyond.* Trans. Alan Bass. Chicago: University of Chicago Press, 1987.

Egan, Ronald. "Su Shih's 'Notes' as a Historical and Literary Source." *Harvard Journal of Asiatic Studies* 50, no. 2 (Dec. 1990): 561–88.

Hartman, Geoffrey. *Beyond Formalism.* New Haven: Yale University Press, 1970.

Lowry, Kathryn. "Personal Letters from Seventeenth-Century Epistolary Guides." In *Under Confucian Eyes: Writings on Gender in Chinese History*, ed. Susan Mann and Yu-Yin Cheng. Berkeley: University of California Press, 2001, pp. 155–67.

————. "The Space of Reading." Unpublished article.

————. "Three Ways to Read a Love Letter in Late Ming." *Ming Studies* 44 (Fall 2000): 48–77.

————. "Transmission of Popular Song in Late Ming." Ph.D. diss., Harvard University, 1996.

Sakai Tadao 酒井忠夫. "Confucianism and Popular Educational Works." In *Self and Society in Ming Thought*, ed. Wm. Theodore de Bary. New York: Columbia University Press, 1970, pp. 331–64.

————. "*Mindai no nichiyō ruishu to shomin kyōiku*" 明代の日用類書と庶民教育 (Ming dynasty household encyclopedias and popular education). In *Kinsei Chūgoku kyōiku shi kenkyū* 近世中國 教育史研究 (Studies of the history of education in modern China), ed. Hayashi Tomoharu 林友春. Tokyo: Kokudosha, 1958, pp. 25–154.

Waley, Arthur. *Translations from the Chinese*. New York: Alfred A. Knopf, 1961.

Wang Shifu, *The Moon and the Zither: The Story of the Western Wing*. Ed. and trans. Stephen West and Wilt Idema. Berkeley: University of California Press, 1995.

Xingshi yinyuan zhuan 惺世姻緣傳. Shanghai: Shanghai guji chubanshe, 1981.

Considering a Coincidence

The 'Female Reading Public' Circa 1828

Ellen Widmer

The year 1828 saw the publication of two works of fiction that at first glance appear to inhabit different worlds. The first is *Zai zaotian* 再造天, a *tanci* 彈詞 (or prosimetric fictional narrative) by Hou Zhi 侯芝 (1764–1829), a woman editor, author, and poet. In contrast to some of her other output, *Zai zaotian* has not enjoyed much scholarly or readerly acclaim. This is in part because of its didacticism. The plot, which concerns a struggle over control of the throne during the Yuan dynasty, centers almost exclusively on the lessons to be learned from the good and bad qualities of the women who shape political events behind the scenes. The second is *Jinghua yuan* 鏡花緣, a *xiaoshuo* 小說, or novel, by Li Ruzhen 李汝珍 (1763–1830). It ranks in or near the top tier of novels in an artistic sense, and its plot is quite well known: a group of adventurers travel around the seas collecting talented young women from a variety of maritime kingdoms during the regime of Tang empress Wu Zetian 武則天. *Jinghua yuan*, too, is deeply concerned with women, at least in the sense that the vast majority of its characters are female. But far from preaching feminine orthodoxy, Li is at least willing to consider radical new possibilities in gender relationships, even though he seems to retract these as the novel ends. His apparent iconoclasm makes *Jinghua yuan* a foil to Hou's more orthodox line. The same is true of the novel's rhetorical open-endedness, which contrasts with Hou's often preachy articulation of right and wrong. Considering the differences in genre and artistic quality, the fact that both works were published in the same year might not seem worth pursuing. Nor do the rather striking parallels in the life spans of the two authors furnish a reason to conduct a deeper probe.

It is only a larger context, one that includes two other works of fiction as well as nonfictional publications by women, that lends meaning to the timing of their completion. By 1828, women were a force in literary production, not necessarily as consumers in the modern sense but as a presence on whose behalf publishers, fathers, brothers, husbands, and literate mothers worked to create a salutary literary climate, even as publishers sought to sell their works. In *Zai zaotian*, the book's direct address to women readers, as well as the author's autobiographical comments, produce a simulated context of conversation within the women's quarters. *Jinghua yuan*, in contrast, is aimed more at a male than a female audience, as is apparent from the fourteen endorsements in verse to the 1828 edition, of which four are by women. Such endorsements are more commonly found in collections of poetry or classical prose than in fiction. Here and in their more normal contexts, they are a succinct way of introducing or advertising the book to would-be readers through the social and intellectual standing of those who had already "signed on" to the work. Through these two types of evidence—narrative context and endorsements—we can show that women constituted a significant part of the intended audience for these two works.

The points of overlap in these works can sustain only limited speculation about the function of women as readers at the end of the first third of the nineteenth century, nearly a hundred years before the cultural upheaval of the May Fourth movement. By the early nineteenth century, women poets—and with them an implied community of women readers—inspired booksellers to supply them with "women's *tanci*" in printed form. These *tanci xiaoshuo* were apparently read rather than performed.[1] This same body of literate women also helps to account for the appeal to Li Ruzhen of women's issues and writings, including *tanci*, which were resources he utilized as he wrote his novel, however he may have reworked them for rhetorical effect.

The elite women of China had been reading and composing poetry since at least the end of the Ming dynasty, but fictional narrative in written form had only recently become important in their lives. The importance of the year 1828 has to be understood in relation to an earlier generation, which gave rise to two key narratives. The first of these is the *tanci Zaisheng yuan*

再生緣 by the woman author Chen Duansheng 陳端生, with a continuation by another woman, Liang Desheng 梁德繩 (1771–1847); the second is the world-famous *xiaoshuo Honglou meng* 紅樓夢, by the male literatus Cao Xueqin 曹雪芹 (1715?–63?). These works were written decades before they were published. The first edition of *Zaisheng yuan* came out in 1821, under the editorship of Hou Zhi; *Honglou meng* first appeared in print in 1791. The popularity of these two works among women is attested by the comments of the literatus Chen Wenshu 陳文述 (1775–1845), whose edited collection, *Xiling guiyong ji* 西泠閨詠集, is dated 1827,[2] just one year before the year on which this study focuses. Chen's remarks establish that *Zaisheng yuan* and *Honglou meng* were attracting great interest among women readers, and his evaluation sets *tanci* and *xiaoshuo* side by side. Against the trend of modern scholarship, which tends to separate these two generic categories, Chen implied that to women readers of the early nineteenth century, this divide was inconsequential. It is partly on this basis that my comparison of *Zai zaotian* and *Jinghua yuan* has little to say about genre.

What distinguishes the two predecessors from the two works lying at the heart of this study is their seminal quality. Arising seemingly out of nowhere, both *Zai shengyuan* and *Honglou meng* achieved canonical status in their respective genres.[3] In other words, neither *Zaisheng yuan* nor *Honglou meng* arose in response to readerly desire, since no one could have anticipated them, but *Zai zaotian* and *Jinghua yuan* gain added dimensions when considered in the light of the appetites engendered by these two masterworks. The relationship between original work and offshoot is almost opposite in the two cases, however. With the two *tanci*, *Zai zaotian* is an antidote to *Zaisheng yuan*'s disturbing questions about women who assume powerful political roles. As we shall see, despite Hou's role in publishing *Zaisheng yuan*, she seems to have intended to fight fire with fire, namely, to use the attractions of fiction to stamp out unorthodox aspirations to which *Zaisheng yuan* might have given rise. This dynamic is explored in more detail below.

As for the novels, *Jinghua yuan*'s demonstrable appeal to women readers lay in its continuation of a discussion launched by *Honglou meng*, one that raised new questions about the inevitability of the constraints and sacrifices to which women of talent could easily become resigned. Even if, as some believe, *Jinghua yuan* uses the issue of women allegorically and is basically a novel about philosophy,[4] the high proportion of women characters is one of its most striking features. Although not intended to be mimetic, these char-

acters at least succeed in capturing some of the frustrations of active and intelligent young women, whose real fates ruled out any individuated expression of talent and athleticism and subordinated ambition to family needs. As
will become apparent in the discussion below of the four endorsements by
women, *Jinghua yuan*'s overwhelmingly female cast of characters moved its female readers to reflect on such concerns. The date of Li's final edition also
meant that it could incorporate portraits of living women who reveled in their
talent. The point is not just that such women existed by 1828. This, too, had
been true for centuries. Rather, as readers of *Honglou meng* and *Zaisheng yuan*,
they had developed the habit of turning to fiction when contemplating the issues of talent and its suppression, matters of considerable concern.

Both *Zai zaotian* and *Jinghua yuan* are clearly products of an era in which
talented women sought to be taken seriously. Both works show sympathy
for the talented female, and both invoke the pathos of the quixotic female
who yearns for more freedom than the system allows. These common de-
nominators establish them as the products of a similar age. Simultaneously,
the differences between them—iconoclasm versus orthodoxy, in particular—speak to the potential for debate about the problems that *Honglou meng*
and *Zaisheng yuan* helped bring to the fore. These differences allow us to
conceptualize a "female reading public," not just as a large group of literate
women but also as a group monitored by would-be guardians, male or female. This body of fiction appears to have served as a forum in which debates over women's ambitions could emerge. Sometimes these debates took
place between successive fictions; sometimes they led to contradictions or
fault lines within a single work of fiction. Whether seeking to liberate
women or constrain them, works like *Zai zaotian* and *Jinghua yuan* can be
seen as part of a vast conversation about women's roles, conducted through
fiction, that would continue into the final days of the Qing.[5]

The discussion so far has concentrated on fiction, to the exclusion of
other categories of literature, in accounting for the new demand for works
by and for women. It has also concentrated on readers rather than writers.
Another perspective is gained when we introduce the anthologist Yun Zhu
惲珠 (1771–1833) into the discussion. Yun's *Guochao guixiu Zhengshi ji* 國朝
閨秀正始集 came out in 1831. An anthology of women poets with a
strongly moralistic bent, it gives another example of how female audiences
were conceptualized at this time. *Zhengshi ji* reached out well beyond the
Jiangnan area, even to non-Han enthnicities, with the aim of encouraging

women everywhere to join the ranks of the *guixiu* 閨秀 (gentlewoman). The anthologist put herself forward as an authority on virtue, which she propagated to women she could not have known personally. Although Yun many not have profited from this venture in a financial sense, her motives overlap with the ideological side of Hou Zhi's aim of bolstering morals through *tanci*. Her anthology could claim high cultural status in a way Hou Zhi's *tanci* could not, and it offers many other points of contrast, but its basic interest in improving women was the same. Yun's work can also be compared with Li Ruzhen's, especially in its vision of a pluralistic world.

The "female reading public" that is the subject of this chapter delineates the audience to whom fiction of two types—*tanci* and *xiaoshuo*—and poetry collections were directed. Women had been writing for other women for centuries. What is different about the early nineteenth century is the spread of audiences beyond the highest classes and beyond the boundaries of Jiangnan. With *guixiu* now just one element in a larger constituency of readers, literature written for women had more to say about *guixiu* status. At times, this literature tries to sell such status to people who may have hoped to acquire it through reading. At other times, it chips away at the assumptions and practices around which *guixiu* status was maintained. Whether the goal is to promote such status or to question it, authors and editors write assumptions about this audience into their publications. It is these assumptions that this chapter aims to explore.

Hou Zhi and Zai zaotian

Hu Shiying's biography provides a convenient point of departure from which to introduce Hou Zhi.[6] Hou was born in 1764, in Jiangning (southeast of Nanjing) and lived her whole life in the Nanjing area. Her father took an interest in her education when she was young. A successful official in the Canton area, he and his wife died before Hou reached maturity.[7] Her chief mentor and supporter was her brother (actually a cousin) Hou Yunjin 侯雲錦 (*juren* 1789), still known today as a painter. Another mainstay was her brother Hou Yunsong 侯雲松 (1774–1853), an official, painter, and writer.[8] Hou married Mei Chong 梅沖, a scholar whose family home was in Anhui but who resided in the Nanjing area. Mei was a disciple of Yuan Mei 袁枚 (1716–98).[9] Considering Hou's talents and Yuan's support for talented females, it is noteworthy that she kept her distance from Yuan. Hou's re-

278 CSELLEN WIDMER

serve is explained by her insistence on traditionally defined female propriety, an emphasis that put her at odds with Yuan's libertarian views.[10]

Hou had five children, the most famous of whom was Mei Zengliang 梅曾亮 (1786–1856), a disciple of the famous *kaozheng* scholar Yao Nai 姚鼐 (1732–1815). Another was a daughter named Shuyi 淑儀, who learned to read with Hou Yunjin's assistance and of whose poetic talents Hou was very proud.[11]

Mei Chong was quite impoverished and was often away from home. Hou's poems make it clear that she managed the household in her husband's absence. The family was sometimes so poor that Hou had to sell her clothes. In 1794, Hou became seriously ill and was bedridden for some time. It was at this point that she rediscovered her talent as a poet, which had not been fully employed since before her marriage. With the help of Hou Yunjin and Hou Yunsong, she made contact with other women writers in the vicinity and began exchanging verses with them, a practice that was deeply meaningful to her. Some of these women were quite well known, among them Wang Qiong 王瓊, the sister of Wang Yu 王豫 and with him co-editor of a collection entitled *Qunya ji* 群雅集. This collection came out in 1807 and 1811. Wang Qiong was also the editor of *Mingyuan shihua* 名媛詩話, a book of criticism that does not survive. Hou was fulfilled intellectually by her contacts with Wang and with other outstanding women for at least the next two decades.

Wang Qiong's biographical note on Hou appeared in the part of *Qunya ji* published in 1811 and gives an indication of Hou's reputation at this time. Pointing to Hou's unusually wide reading, it underscores the moral emphasis in her poetry, a point further emphasized by the prominent Mongol poet and critic Fa-shi-shan 法式善 (1753–1813), whose *Wumen shihua* 梧門詩話 was complete by 1813. In Fa-shi-shan's words:

[Few women poets write from a background of real knowledge. Those who do include] Hou Zhi of Jiangning, who has read widely in the Classics, and whose learning is informed by the idea of principle without corruption and plainness without decadence, drawn from Cheng-Zhu Confucianism. Chanting her poems infuses sincerity into what is customary and instructs in what is proper. Wang Qiong's *Mingyuan shihua* praises her as a model for other women.[12]

Fa-shi-shan's observation adds to the picture of domestic conscientiousness that emerges from sources closer to home.[13] Not only was Hou a good wife and mother, but she achieved wide recognition for her Confucian learning and was viewed as an outstanding poet by both men and women of her day.[14]

Around 1811, Hou began writing *tanci*, perhaps not giving up poetry altogether in the process but emphasizing *tanci* from this point on. In addition to *Zai zaotian*, Hou's other original *tanci* is *Jingui jie* 金閨傑 of 1824. Her edited *tanci* include *Jinshang hua* 錦上話 of 1813, *Zaisheng yuan* of 1821, and *Yuchuan yuan* 玉釧緣 of indeterminate date.[15] Hou may have abandoned poetry when she began her work on *tanci*, but she certainly had returned to it by the time of her death in 1829.[16] No collection of Hou's poems exists today, but a handful of anthologized pieces do survive.[17]

Hou had several distinct motives for focusing on *tanci*. The first is described in the 1821 preface to her edited version of *Zaisheng yuan*. As a genre, *tanci* are inferior to poetry, she argues, but when they are published they endure.[18] This view of *tanci* as inferior was based on their wide accessibility, their relatively popular language, and their closeness to oral performance. This same reasoning is again found in the opening autobiographical passage in chapter 13 of *Zai zaotian* (autobiographical prefaces and conclusions to chapters being a distinguishing feature of *tanci* by women):

> My studies progressed, I knew I learned a lot,
> But I would have to wait forever if I wanted to
>   transmit my writing through poetry.
> It was better to switch to *tanci*,
> In which case I might be praised as a good writer.[19]

On the basis of this and other passages, Hu Siao-chen sees Hou's conversion to *tanci* as motivated primarily by a yearning for renown.[20] Yet however Hou Zhi's venture into writing and publishing *tanci* may have affected her poetry, it did not cause her to break off all relations with her most prominent literary friends. Her first edited *tanci*, *Jinshang hua* of 1813, carries seven endorsements, one of which is by Wang Qiong. Others are by Luo Qilan 駱綺蘭 and Sun Yunfeng 孫雲鳳 (1764–1814), both disciples of Yuan Mei and acquaintances of Wang Qiong.[21]

A second important motive behind Hou's series of *tanci* was pressure from publishers. This is especially clear in the case of her work on *Zaisheng yuan*. *Zaisheng yuan*'s heroine, Meng Lijun, is famous to this day as a woman who defied traditional female roles. Disguised as a man, Meng becomes a prime minister of the Yuan dynasty. Chen Duansheng never completed this work, and the conclusion by Liang Desheng resolves the disruptive potential of Chen's fantasy by marrying Meng to Huangfu Shaohua, her longtime suitor. Hou benefited from this work's popularity, but she was offended by what she regarded as Meng's self-aggrandizing wish to become prime minister; still worse, she viewed her as unfilial.

Under the circumstances, one might well ask why Hou published an edition of *Zaisheng yuan*. The answer lies in the preface to *Jingui jie*. According to Hou, *Zaisheng yuan* had been snatched from her hands by eager publishers before she was ready to let it go: "I had not finished the editing when the bookseller wanted a preface. Since I do not like to refuse people's requests, I cobbled together a few words without expecting that the manuscript would be put into circulation."[22] This statement may say more about Hou's insecurities than what actually happened. In any case, it is clear that she was highly ambivalent about her association with *Zaisheng yuan*. The motive behind the writing of *Jingui jie* and *Zai zaotian* was apparently to compensate for her earlier "error" by rewriting and retroactively supplementing *Zaisheng yuan*, much to its detriment in the minds of critics.[23] Yet however incomplete or ambivalent they may have been, Hou's editorial efforts on behalf of *Zaisheng yuan* and other *tanci* and her original compositions in this medium add up to a seminal contribution to the genre.

The involvement of publishers in Hou's turn to *tanci* is confirmed at several other points in her writing, particularly in *Jingui jie*, which carries an unusually long autobiographical preface. Here Hou added new reasons for her involvement with *tanci*. The first is that it provided amusement for herself and her mother-in-law. Only later did booksellers (*fangzi* 坊梓) take an interest in them:

> I was not able to lavish food on my family
> But I entertained them with mere words instead of drink.
> This way I could get a smile from my mother-in-law,
> Never thinking that booksellers would haggle over them.
> Nowadays my manuscripts constantly drive up the price of paper.
> I have no time to spend money, I'm only a housewife.(?)
> But this vulgar business helps supply food for my blind mother.
> Moreover *tanci* allow me to point out right and wrong.

The evidence of this passage, added to the family's poverty, strongly suggests that economic factors were another important motive in Hou's decision to pursue this form. Economic need, amusement, and pressure from booksellers thus combined with Hou's moral mission to write respectable sellers thus combined with Hou's moral mission to write respectable fiction for her fellow *guixiu*.

A related question concerns how the booksellers learned of Hou's interest in the *tanci* she was churning out for her mother-in-law. Hou Yunjin and Hou Yunsong served as Hou's agents on other occasions,[24] and it is possible that they were the means through which her *tanci* made contact with the publishing world. Several of the first editions of her work carry the name of Xiangye ge 香葉閣, her own studio.[25] It is not clear whether Hou submitted drafts in the form of manuscripts or printed blocks, but it would presumably have been easy for commercial printers to acquire the texts from Hou, return to their establishments, and publish them under the names of their own firms. This kind of appropriation clearly took place with later editions of works edited by Hou, which enjoyed an extended life as reprints, no doubt in response to readerly demand.

Hou's relationship with commercial booksellers can be contrasted with the family-style presses through which most collections of women's poetry reached published form. Some of the bookstores that published Hou's *tanci* can be identified as long-standing establishments, although it is often difficult to assess what else they published.[26] Hou's reactions imply that their motives were different from those of family publishers, which functioned like vanity presses. The comment about *Zaisheng yuan* being snatched from her hands by eager booksellers and the poetical line about the commercial value of her writings support the view that booksellers viewed *tanci* as hot commodities, as potential best-sellers. Hou's observation in *Jingui jie* that "as long as many women read this, booksellers will certainly get it out in one day's time"[27] shows her awareness of the relationship between a work's popularity in the women's quarters and its commercial value.

Adumbrated in this comment and more clearly articulated elsewhere is a contrast between idealized *guixiu*, whose thoughts are never mercenary, and booksellers, who think about nothing but money. For example, Hou asked in the preface to *Jingui jie*, "Do you learned *guixiu* agree with my criticisms [of *Zaisheng yuan*]? It is not worthwhile discussing moral judgments with the publishers of this volume." In contrasts like these, she aligned herself with the *guixiu* camp, despite the likelihood that she herself was motivated by commercial gain. Another irony in this situation is the possibility that Hou's reputation for virtue may have been a selling point for her *tanci*. Publishers may have encouraged Hou's interest in writing and editing them precisely because they hoped that her unimpeachable reputation would help sell her work to well-educated women and girls.

Other aspects of Hou's relationship with her readers can be inferred from her writings. In the first place, she creates a narrative context that is inexorably slanted toward the feminine. This affects both her narrator and her vision of the reader. The *tanci* convention of autobiographical comments at the beginnings and ends of chapters was already in place with *Zaisheng yuan*. Hou merely continues this convention and, in the process, feminizes her narrator.[28] Another feminizing move, this time more original, is embedded in her terms of address to readers. Normally invoking them with the gender-neutral term *kan guan* 看官, she occasionally refers to them as "*guixiu kanjia*" 閨秀看管家, or "*guixiu* readers."[29] In addition, she counsels conservative behavior, with phrases such as "lack of knowledge is a virtue" and celebrations of "meekness" (*wenrou* 溫柔).[30] Another sign of outreach to women is her use of women as the chief means through which to observe the large matters of state around which the plot turns.

However, it would be a mistake to take Hou's conservative ethos at full face value. This is true both in her own life and in her fiction. As far as her life is concerned, her self-presentation as a *guixiu*, and as a filial daughter-in-law and good mother supporting her family, may have been used to obscure her interest in profit. Moreover, in the context of her apparent belief that "lack of talent in a woman is a virtue" (preface to *Zai zaotian*), her frank admission of a yearning for fame is startling. In reality, however, Hou appears to have taken this truism rather lightly. As she relates in the preface to a friend's poems, she was willing to sidestep family injunctions against female learning during her youth and take Hou Yunjin up on his offer to help her learn.[31] Later in life, again with the help of Hou Yunjin, she sought to educate her daughter, another sign of her less than complete adherence to orthodox norms.[32] When her *tanci* rehearse the view that lack of talent is a virtue or that "the creator" (*zaowu* 造物) dislikes talented women, this may have been her way of sugarcoating her own endeavor with positive qualities that her imagined readership would find palatable. The fact that her works reiterate traditional values surely made the more questionable aspects of her personal example easier to disguise.[33]

The plot of *Zai zaotian* shows other signs of sleight of hand. It revolves around a female villain, Huangfu Feilong, whose ambition to seize imperial power after the abdication of the Yuan emperor spells disaster for all concerned. Not too surprisingly, Feilong is a great fan of the Tang empress Wu Zetian. As she explains to horrified relatives:

In my opinion, if the Tang dynasty had not had Zetian in charge, if power had been held by the likes of Gaozong and Zhongzong, then the land would have split apart, as when Emperor Hui of the Jin allowed the five lakes region to be occupied. When Minghuang fled to Sichuan, the entire energy of the dynasty was dissipated. Zetian usurped the throne and returned things to normal. She executed and punished evildoers. She assessed talent and used it well. She clearly understood people. She is actually a great empress of her time. Among the rulers of the second half of the Tang, who can compare with her? (1: 6)

Feilong is also shown to be excessively active as a young woman—rushing about in the family garden, swinging, boating, watching dramas, playing the flute, practicing archery, teaching poetry to the servants, playing chess, pitching pennies, painting pictures, and drilling the servants in military maneuvers. Her combination of great beauty and vast talent is another reason for alarm.

Feilong's sad fate is construed as a lesson against the excessive ambition of her mother, Meng Lijun. Not only is Feilong marginalized by the author, but the other characters make disparaging remarks about female talent and ambition. These include Meng Lijun herself, who has to suffer through her daughter's execution once the abdicated emperor returns (1: 111). Yet too flat a dismissal of female talent would have discouraged Hou's women readers, who needed to be highly literate in order to read the book. A telling ambiguity hidden beneath the apparently transparent rhetoric appears to resolve this contradiction. This concerns Huangfu Changhua, wife of the abdicated emperor, a character who is always referred to as Taihou.

Taihou has the advantage of being right in every situation. Not only does she know from the beginning that Feilong should be kept from the inner circles of power, but she is also far wiser than her husband about his decisions to abdicate when he gets tired of ruling and to disappear from the capital and spend years in reclusion at Mount Wutai. Yet for a large part of the story, illness renders her powerless to stop the unfortunate developments that result in, and from, her husband's departure, especially once Feilong begins to appropriate power. Taihou sorrows over her husband's abdication because she knows that his son has little ability, and she wrings her hands when her husband flees the seat of power, prompting other characters to comment that he is as irresponsible as Sui Wendi (1: 98). Taihou is frequently praised by the other characters as, among other things, the "Yao and Shun of women" (*nüzhong Yao Shun* 女中堯舜; 2: 76), and a "heroic woman" (*yingxiong nü zhangfu* 英雄女丈夫; 1: 96), and it is clear the narrator shares her negative evaluation of Feilong. Eventually, Taihou recovers and helps to engineer the process by which order is restored. She is particularly instrumental in saving the life of her young grandson, whom Feilong had sought to destroy. When her husband is finally brought back to the capital and the dynasty is restored to power, she is duly modest about all that she has done.

Up to this point, readers have no difficulty inferring how the implied author thought a talented woman ought to behave. Despite its admonitions against talented females, *Zai zaotian* is not unsympathetic to women of talent; indeed it revolves around them. Still, the point is that talented women must put family obligations first. No matter how great her talent, a woman must accept the patriarchal "three submissions principle" (*sancong dao* 三從 道) that subordinates her to father, husband, and sons (2: 167). Like Hou Zhi herself, the ideal reader of the story would have acquired literacy at a young age and been willing to set reading and writing aside when she stepped into the roles of wife, mother, and daughter-in-law. Only when her children were grown, and then only in spare moments, would she have dared to resurrect her literary skills. The difference between Taihou, Lijun, and Feilong is not one of talent; rather, it is that Taihou has an unerring sense of how to keep hers under control.

This clear picture is complicated by the manipulations through which Hou Zhi's message is conveyed. It goes without saying that *Zai zaotian* benefits from Feilong's evil. Without it, Hou Zhi could not have set up the message she wants to convey. Yet other manipulations are required before Taihou can shine forth as a model. It is only because she is ill that Taihou fails to put a stop to Feilong's machinations in the first place. Illness thus allows Hou Zhi to present Taihou as innocent rather than negligent when she fails to intervene against Feilong at the beginning of her rise to power. At the same time, if the abdicated emperor had not disappeared to Mount Wutai and if it had not taken the other characters so long to find him, Taihou's talents might not have been needed to curb Feilong's noxious powers.

The interlude between Taihou's recovery and the emperor's return gives Hou a chance to present Taihou in what amounts to an imperial role. Even though she relies on male officials to carry out her initiatives and even though various of Lijun's sons play a large part in the restitution of the old emperor, it is Taihou alone whose wisdom is highlighted and whose presence turns the tables against the forces of evil. Thus, beneath *Zai zaotian*'s conventional manifest rhetoric lies a more subversive current. Clearly the situation has been manipulated to showcase Taihou's talents. Compared with Feilong, Taihou is much more passive, merely standing ready in case her efforts should be required. Yet she is every bit Feilong's equal in her readiness to take on major administrative roles. In this sense, *Zai zaotian*'s creator is as manipulative as Feilong in setting up the circumstances that propel Taihou to center stage.

Because she neither wants, seeks, nor accepts the limelight, Taihou is excused from the stigma of hubris that characterizes Feilong's use of talent and hovers around Meng Lijun in her reincarnation in *Zai zaotian*. Her posture could be compared with that of Hou Zhi herself, who ran a home for years in the absence of her husband yet modestly minimized her accomplishments. Lying beneath the surface of *Zai zaotian* is a latent respect for the woman who can handle the administration of a household, perhaps even a state, if duty called. This latent respect is Hou's compromise with the far bolder celebration of feminine talent and ambition in *Zaisheng yuan*.

A less startling but equally telling maneuver is found in the narrator's intertextual references. Every so often, works like *Shuihu* 水滸, *Shiji* 史記, and *Hou Hanshu* 後漢書 come up for comment, either directly or indirectly (2: 87, 116, 117). Although the references are brief and not essential to the story, they imply authorial reading of, and expectations of readerly acquaintance with, texts that goes well beyond the normal feminine canon of the day. They seem to contradict the ostensible narrator's comments about lack of talent as a virtue. Just as Hou's investment in Taihou undermines her manifest rhetoric about feminine ambition, so these occasional references undermine the call for feminine intellectual passivity on which her text seems to depend. Without claiming that they turn a didactic text into a subtle work of literature, one can still assert that they add to our sense of Hou as a more complicated author than might at first appear.

Such complications are of value both in understanding Hou Zhi as a person and in fathoming the female reading public for which her writings were designed. On the personal level, they make it easier to understand how someone as apparently straight-laced as Hou could have yearned for reputation even as she sought to downplay her vanity. They thus enable us to understand her preachiness not as pure conviction but, in part, as a cosmetic for her creative impulse. (Of course, a certain amount of her diffidence can be attributed to the normal protestations of authorial modesty common to both genders, with the difference that male writers did not make a point of discouraging writing by other males.) In terms of her readership, they encourage us to think in terms of a somewhat mixed constituency. As a "lower form of writing," *tanci* were directed at simple as well as subtle readers. Hou could, of course, design a text that put forth familiar homilies, here one that contradicted the "lessons" of *Zaisheng yuan*. At the same time, to write a *tanci* with intrinsic interest required considerable narrative powers. This meant intensive reading and a willingness to create seductive characters. Feilong's fascinating badness and Taihou's potentially troubling administrative skill were part of the arsenal of tricks Hou used to sustain readerly interest, even as her own manipulativeness as narrator, not to mention her personal search for fame and fortune, were obscured from view.

In sum, Hou Zhi's efforts with *tanci* constituted a major change of direction in her writing career. They also constituted a major change for *tanci*, which, with the exception of *Zaisheng yuan* and *Tianyu hua* 天雨花,[34] had not given rise to published writings by women until her time. The intercession of booksellers and the audiences they hoped to attract help account for these changes. Hou's disparagement of such forces, even when she stood to benefit financially from her writings, is one sign of the tension between profitability and gentility to which these new developments were giving rise. Another tension can be found in her conflicting impulse to entertain and to moralize. The idea that fiction could uplift even as it entertained was both her major contribution and the chief cause of contradiction in what she had to say.

Li Ruzhen *and* Jinghua yuan

Little is known of Li Ruzhen's life, and what is traditionally emphasized in his brief biography has nothing to do with women. Li was born in Daxing, Hebei (on the outskirts of present-day Beijing), but he made Banpu (outside Haizhou in northern Jiangsu) his home. He moved there as early as 1782, first in the company of his brother, Li Ruhuang 李汝璜, who was officially employed in the low-level job of salt receiver. After bonding with a famous teacher, Ling Tingkan 凌廷堪 (1757–1809), and making other friends in the Haizhou area, he stayed on in Banpu. Through his marriage, he became the brother-in-law of the Xu brothers, Xu Qiaolin 許喬林 and Xu Guilin 許桂林 (ca. 1778–1821), well-known local intellectuals.

Discussions about phonetics with Ling and the Xu brothers became the basis of one of Li's lifelong preoccupations and led him to write a book on the subject. The book has been praised for its innovative combination of northern and southern phoneticizations of Chinese.[35] Having passed only the first (*xiucai* 秀才) examination, Li could not pursue a grand official career, but beginning in 1801, he was employed in Henan over a period of about eight years as a consultant on river management. He returned at least once to the Haizhou area during his period of employment and settled there more or less permanently in about 1809, despite the fact that his brother had moved away.

Li's official career was modest, and his life is better defined by his writings: *Yin jian* 音鑑, the book on linguistics, completed in 1805 and published in 1810; *Shouzipu xuan* 受子譜選, a book on chess, published in 1817; and *Jinghua yuan*, which may have been initiated as early as the late 1790s and which existed in a published edition as early as 1817.[36] Almost all that is known about him derives from the prefaces to these publications and a handful of poems by friends. These sources relate that Li painted, carved seals, and was conversant with such fields as divination, astronomy, music, and mathematics, in addition to chess and linguistics.[37] The novel itself gives ample evidence of these areas of expertise. It further displays a knowledge of archery and river control.

Although skimpy, this biography has fueled contemporary interpretation of *Jinghua yuan* as a "scholar novel."[38] Its characters are almost all young women, but they are usually read as mouthpieces for the author's views on various subjects, such as the examination system, and their erudition is taken to represent the author's own. Hu Shi's 胡適 1923 study of the novel offered another, feminist interpretation, one that is often discounted in contemporary scholarship.[39] A fuller look at Li's friends and associates gives us reason to believe that some of Li's female characters were modeled on real women of his acquaintance. It also indicates that the intended readership included women as well as men.

Of the four female endorsers of the novel, two can be identified in more than name only. The first is Qian Shoupu 錢守璞. Qian appears in all the standard biographies of women writers. She was talented enough as an artist to have been taken on as a student by the painter Gai Qi 改琦 (1774–1829).

With her "companionate" husband Zhang Qi 張騏, Qian spent much of
her life in Yangzhou, where the couple sold paintings and poems to support
themselves.[40] A disciple of Chen Wenshu, Qian had links to other members
of Chen's expanded family, including his talented daughter-in-law, Wang
Duan 汪端 (1793–1839). Qian's ties to Chen and Wang meant, in turn, that
she was well connected to a wider network of women poets.

Another of Qian's acquaintances was the male official, scholar, and calligrapher Shi Yunyu 史韞玉(1756–1837), who wrote her biography. Shi is remembered today in conjunction with his celebrated employee Shen Fu 沈復
(1763–?), the author of Six Records of a Floating Life (Fusheng liuji 浮生六記),
a work praised for its sympathetic portrait of a woman.[41] Shi's biography of
Qian, "Lianyin zhuan" 蓮因傳, stands in sharp contrast to Qian's poems,
which tend to dwell on the poor fates of talented women, a complaint widely
current among literary women of the day. Shi focuses instead on Qian's unusual combination of talent, good fate, and good fortune. Underscoring her
exceptional privilege, he gives examples of women of talent who fell short in
the other two categories.[42] No doubt Shi's praise and Qian's self-effacement
were brought on by their respective rhetorical postures, and they may also
reflect authorial gender. More neutral indications are that, for a woman,
Qian had an unusually successful artistic and literary career.

The other identifiable woman is Jin Ruolan 金若蘭. Jin's endorsement
was printed next to that of her father, Jin Chong 金翀, with whom she was
closely identified throughout her writing career. Unlike Qian Shoupu, the
basis of whose acquaintance with Li remains a mystery, Jin and her family
are easily connected to Li Ruzhen. In 1801 Jin's father succeeded Li Ruzhen's
brother in the salt receiver job in Banpu and lived there until at least 1819.[43]
Jin's collection Yinhongge cichao 吟紅閣詞鈔 leaves no doubt that he knew
Li directly, for it contains a poem written for Li.[44] Li and the Jins also shared
other friends.[45] By tracing a line from the Jins to Wang Qiong and Wang
Yu, one can even link Li indirectly to Hou Zhi and her world.[46]

Jin Chong was his daughter's principal teacher, and he went on to promote her writings, which he published with his own, in two collections. The
first, which included his Yinhongge shichao 吟紅閣詩鈔, Yinhongge cichao, and
Yinhongge ci xuchao 吟紅閣詞續鈔, as well as her Huayu xuan shichao 花語
軒詩鈔, was published in 1810. The second, a simultaneously abridged and
expanded edition of these same sets of writings, came out a year later, in 1811.

According to Jin Ruolan's autobiography, appended as a colophon to *Yinhongge shichao*, she learned to write poetry at age 14 from her father. Eventually, after her father left for Banpu, her poems were edited by her uncle. Even after being tutored for over a decade, she still did not feel completely at ease when writing on her own. Jin Chong's work is not well known today, but he was rather famous in his own time, having won the praise of the celebrated Hong Liangji 洪亮吉 (1746–1809).[47] Like Li Ruzhen, Jin passed only the *xiucai* examination, but there is no doubt that he took himself seriously as a writer. Jin Ruolan was widowed early, one reason that she could visit her father in Banpu.[48]

The importance of these data is heightened by evidence of Li's demonstrable interest in *Tianyu hua* (preface dated 1651), the late Ming or early Qing *tanci* said to have been written by a woman.[49] The tale of a henpecked bandit and his shrewish wife in chapters 50 and 51 of *Jinghua yuan* are influenced by a similar scene in the first chapter of *Tianyu hua*.[50] If Li took an interest in one work of literature by a woman, is it not possible that he read and integrated others into *Jinghua yuan*?

The content of the Jins' poems supports the possibility that this particular father-daughter couple, if not others like it,[51] could have infused Li's imagination with ideas. The mutuality of their father-daughter relationship must have been striking in its day. In addition to copublishing with Ruolan, making her a member of his poetry society, and inviting her to edit one of his collections, Jin Chong frequently wrote linked verse with his daughter or matched poems on identical themes. Flowers are one of the most widely discussed subjects in their poetry and at times are presented in ways that recollect *Jinghua yuan*.[52] The very name of Ruolan's collection, *Huayu xuan shichao*, with its conceit of talking flowers, makes another possible bridge to *Jinghua yuan*. Another topic reminiscent of the novel in these writings is the imaginary and utopian island of Penglai. Like their poems endorsing *Jinghua yuan*, Jin Chong's and Jin Ruolan's poems about this island are linked in subject but different in meter.[53] The two also wrote about this utopia in other poems. The two Jins' collections of poems and Li's novel appear to be the products of very similar worlds. *Jinghua yuan* revolves in significant measure around the bond between Tang Ao and his daughter Tang Xiaoshan. Like Tang Ao, Tang Xiaoshan is very erudite, so much so that there is good reason to interpret her as a stand-in for educated men. Certainly Tang

Xiaoshan's superhuman accomplishments have no counterpart in the lives of living women. Yet on the issue of closeness to her father, she is highly reminiscent of Jin Ruolan.

Quite apart from the possibility that the plot of *Jinghua yuan* may have drawn on specific women's lives and writings, it is interesting to see how the female endorsers reacted to the novel. Qian's poem of endorsement reads as follows:

> Romantic poems are composed in the world of beauties.
> All are talented but endowed with different feeling.
> You name and record those women in Qihong ting [the spot in
>   chapter 49 where the fates of the characters are revealed].
> They tend to bad fates because of their great intelligence.
> The young women's writings are freshly transmitted on yellow silk.
> They are lucky to live in an auspicious time.
> I laugh [to see] they have not yet awakened from the *Red Chamber Dream*.
> They are still bound by the passions of ordinary youngsters.
> How could there be a little Penglai on this earth?
> Bright thoughts, strange ruminations, are brought to life by your pen.
> One hundred eight fates are drawn together by a single thread of Nirvana
> Not a word is tainted by dust.
> Now let me honor you, a banished immortal, with incense and a
>   solemn salute.
> In my last life I was an autumn lotus.
> I'd like to borrow your brush to convey my story.
> Please enter me into the flower roster of *Jinghua yuan*.

Qian's collected works contain a slightly abridged version of this poem under the title "A Prefatory Poem to Li Shaozi's *chuanqi Jinghua yuan*."[54] ("Shaozi" 少子 is the name Li uses to refer to himself in the novel.) This version omits the last two lines. Her *hao*, Lianyin 蓮因, which means "lotus fate," plays into her claim to have been an "autumn lotus" in a previous existence and thus to belong with the other female "flowers" whose lives are reviewed in *Jinghua yuan*.

Jin Ruolan's poem is rather similar to Qian's in its mood of sadness and withdrawal:.

> Don't go to Qihong ting;
> The dream of many flowers is already over.
> Plowing the mist you plant fairy grass,
> Dripping dew, you copy out your version of *Laozi*.

Wave after wave of blue for a thousand yards,
Hill after hill, all are dotted with green
Riding the wind, you enjoy going home
And leisurely watch the crane combing its feathers.

Jin appears to have been about 24 when she wrote this poem.[55]

Taken as a group, the four poems show that their female authors were struck more with *Jinghua yuan*'s sad than with its amusing side. Identifying strongly with the novel's doomed heroines, they found different ways of lamenting the fates of women whose talents could never be applied to real-life concerns. Identifying, as well, with the heroines of *Honglou meng*, who seldom found happiness, these women saw *Jinghua yuan* as its sequel and proclaimed themselves captivated by both works' fictional musings about what might have been.[56]

Looked at in light of this material, the various talents and accomplishments of *Jinghua yuan*'s many women are not merely decorative or comic. Lian Jinfeng's talent at underwater diving, Wei Ziying's ability at hunting, Tang Xiaoshan's brilliance in the examinations, Meng Zizhi's skill at chess—all are consonant with the dreams of young women of Li's acquaintance or with older women's remembered dreams. Even if in fact no "decent" young woman ever dove for pearls or hunted, characters like Lian and Wei might have been common in the fantasy life of women readers of Li's day. Li's attitude toward these characters can be contrasted with that of Hou Zhi toward the young Feilong. Hou expresses disapproval of Feilong for her activism; Li presents his active young heroines uncritically, even though he eventually turns them into proper wives. It is interesting, too, that no matter how wildly *Jinghua yuan*'s unmarried women transgress against the maidenly principles of composure, quietude, and seclusion, all are completely respectful toward parents and the older generation. If *Jinghua yuan*'s fantasy goes beyond what women were supposed to do and think, it does so in only limited ways. Judging in part from the reading skills necessary to understand *Jinghua yuan*, as well as from its constant emphasis on filial behavior, it is safe to conclude that the feminine part of this work's intended audience was not just any woman but women of considerable learning and proper socialization, in other words, *guixiu*.

Much of contemporary criticism focuses on unraveling the rhetoric of *Jinghua yuan*. The crux of the matter concerns Wu Zetian. In contrast to *Zai zaotian*, which simply dismisses Wu, *Jinghua yuan*'s position is puzzling. Does it support the reversal of the final chapters that dethrones Wu and in effect undoes her unusual encouragement of female talent? Or does it merely tack on this ending in order to camouflage its support for the more radical attitudes toward female talent and footbinding found in the earlier chapters? *Jinghua yuan* drew some of its ideas from *Shuihu zhuan*, especially the Jin Shengtan 金聖歎 edition, where similar ambiguities arise. I have argued elsewhere on this basis that whatever Li's views on Wu in particular and on learned women in general, he intended to create a rhetorical impasse at the end of *Jinghua yuan*. The impressive but ill-fated cast of female characters operates as a kind of paradox, with no clear resolution of where their ideal futures might lie and no clear resolution of the rhetorical position they are meant to occupy. In the end, it is impossible to prove that *Jinghua yuan*'s examinations for women are a covert call to change social mores or that footbinding was unacceptable to Li Ruzhen.[57]

The ironic self-portrait of the author within the text does nothing to resolve these questions. Unlike *Zai zaotian*, where authorial self-description is set apart from the main text, "Li Shaozi" now and then pops up within the story to explain how the manuscript fell into his hands. Inadequate though they may be at capturing the full complexity of her views toward her characters, Hou Zhi's self-portraits do at least help to pin down the woman-to-woman context in which her story is told. In contrast, Li Ruzhen's fleeting and ironic self-portraits afford no insight into where his sympathies lie.

Li's self-portrait is unlike Hou's in another way. Li provides no insight into his reasons for writing *Jinghua yuan*. Comments by male endorsers establish that he saw it as his magnum opus, and that—like Hou's work—it was significantly motivated by a yearning for renown. The novel's long gestation period (twenty years according to several of the preface writers) might at first seem to preclude the possibility of profit as a motive. The image of the "scholar-novelist" concocted in twentieth-century criticism might be another reason for questioning whether *Jinghua yuan* was created as a money-making venture. Yet it is not completely self-evident that the long gestation period was incompatible with mercenary aims. Certainly *Jinghua yuan*'s publishers were interested in profit, whatever Li's interest may have been. In contrast to Cao Xueqin and other visibly noncommercial authors, Li did at least see to his own work's publication—perhaps on three occasions[58]—even if he did not live long enough to realize much profit from sales. The work was a hit with publishers from the beginning, appearing in over a dozen different imprints from early on.[59] Such evidence tends to suggest a connection between *Jinghua yuan* and profitability, if only as far as publishers were concerned. If the work were indeed profit-driven, this could mean that Li's attention to women and their issues was partly motivated by what he (and booksellers) thought would attract women readers, even though it was clearly also inspired by other concerns.

To sum up, *Jinghua yuan*'s relationship to women readers has several dimensions. It draws on "women's *tanci*" for at least one of its plot segments, and its interest in accomplished women may be related to Li's circle of acquaintances. It also draws on *Honglou meng*, a fiction women held dear. Moreover, the large number of female characters may well have been designed to appeal to women readers and thus increase sales. Whatever the case on this last point, it is noteworthy that a magnum opus by an important writer should have paid so much attention to women and the fictions they enjoyed. Even though *Jinghua yuan* uses women allegorically, even though it can sustain readings that have nothing to do with feminism, it still bears traces of the female reading public of Li's day.

Enlarging the Context: Yun Zhu's Guochao guixiu Zhengshi ji *of 1831*

Zai zaotian and *Jinghua yuan* can also be seen as part of a larger series of developments in women's writing. The third decade of the nineteenth century was a time of increased production of private poetry collections by women, according to contemporary observers, after what may have been a slowdown in the eighteenth century.[60] This trend was accompanied by an increase in anthologies of women's poetry edited by women, a field of publishing that had lain dormant since the seventeenth century. One prominent example is Wang Qiong's *Mingyuan shihua*, mentioned above. Another woman writer, Wang Duan, took women's editing in a new direction with her *Ming sanshi jia shixuan* 明三十家詩選 of 1822, a collection of poems by famous male poets of the Ming. This may have been the first time that a woman edited the writings of male poets on such a large scale. The feminine provenance of this work is emphasized, not only through Wang's own contribution but also through the names of her many subeditors, all of whom were women (among them Wang Qiong and Sun Yunfeng). *Ming sanshi jia shixuan* is also remarkable for its strong ideological slant, which aimed to force a rethinking of canonical evaluations of Ming poetry. It attracted considerable attention, and it led some commentators to judge Wang the finest female critic of her day.[61]

Wang Duan's success as poet and critic had much to do with the help and support of Chen Wenshu, her father-in-law. Chen was well known for his interest in women writers, and his corpus of writing is itself quite innovative as far as gender conventions are concerned. Several of his edited collections focus on female poets, and at least one of his anthologies, *Xiling guiyong ji* (1827), employed prominent women poets as proofreaders. Like Wang Duan's *Ming sanshi jia shixuan*—like *Jinghua yuan* for that matter—Chen's *Xiling guiyong ji* invited a feminine readership, even as it reached out primarily to males.

Other signs of innovation in women's writings can be found outside the realm of poetry. The early nineteenth century was noteworthy for the interest of women editors in *Lienü zhuan* 列女傳, long staple reading fare for women, which had not had a woman editor since antiquity. Wang Zhaoyuan's 王照圓 *Lienü zhuan buzhu* 列女傳補注 was the first of the new crop. It was published in 1812. Liang Duan's 梁端 *Lienü zhuan jiaozhu duben* 列女傳校注讀本 was published in 1831 by a family related to Wang Duan and Liang Desheng.[62] At almost exactly the same time, Yun Zhu's *Langui baolu* 蘭閨寶錄 (1831) was published. Based on the idea of *Lienü zhuan*, it uses different female subjects and brings the list of exemplary women closer to Yun's day. The first two of these *Lienü*-related texts were originally published by the families of the editors and were later reissued in some cases by family members, in others by booksellers.[63] The third, *Langui baolu*, was initially published in a pocket edition and may have had a full-sized edition; the pocket edition in and of itself suggests that wide circulation was on the editor's mind.[64] These circumstances indicate a far greater attention to market demand than was normally the case with home-based publications. Seen against the background of such innovative publishing, Hou's venture into *tanci* is less remarkable than might at first appear.

This is certainly not to say that all the innovative writings by women during the first third of the nineteenth century can be linked to commercial publishers. Then as earlier, published collections of individual poetry (*bieji* 別集) were more likely to emerge in small, private editions, and some important and innovative writing by women, such as dramas, might circulate in manuscript, or via word-of-mouth or private performance, without ever being published.[65] Yet it would be a mistake to underestimate the role of commercial processes in fueling the increase in energy, quality, and complexity of women's writings at this time. In fact, the line between public and private ventures was often rather blurred. Although Wang Duan's, Chen Wenshu's, Wang Zhaoyuan's, and Liang Duan's publications were family productions in a technical sense, they show every sign of sensitivity to market demand. The blocks could be saved and reused or sold to commercial publishers. It is further likely, in at least some of these cases, that the print runs were rather large.[66] These data suggest that the private/public distinction is too crude to account for certain widely circulating but privately published works involving women at this time.

As we have seen, the female reading public can be distinguished from the general reading public in nineteenth-century China on the basis that commercially available reading materials intended for women were mostly preread by the guardians of female virtue, whether female or male. A second point of distinction now emerges: in contrast to women writers of, say, the seventeenth century, nineteenth-century women editors and writers aimed for a faceless female reader they could not have known personally or perhaps would not have associated with socially.[67] Even when nineteenth-century publications were not brokered by booksellers, the model of the bookseller was vestigially present when women sought to reach out broadly in geographical and social terms.

One of the most interesting examples of this process is provided by Yun Zhu's massive *Guochao guixiu Zhengshi ji*, which appeared in 1831, followed by a sequel (*xuji* 續集) in 1836.[68] Susan Mann's recent and thorough introduction of Yun's life and work allows us to confine ourselves to biographical highlights here.[69] Yun lived from 1771 to 1833. Her marriage to a Manchu and the success of her son Linqing 麟慶 (1791–1846), a high official, are two of the most salient features of her long life. Yun probably did not know Hou Zhi. None of Hou's poems appear in the collection, but a poem to Hou is there, along with a note identifying Hou.[70] As for Li Ruzhen, Linqing was a friend of Xu Qiaolin, Li Ruzhen's best friend and brother-in-law.[71] Yun was younger than Hou and Li by about eight years. *Zhengshi ji*'s implied readership helps to refine our understanding of the female reading public, and it complements our comparison of *Jinghua yuan* and *Zai zaotian*, whose publication it followed by just three years.

With 1,500 authors and 4,000 poems, *Zhengshi ji* was by far the largest anthology of women's poetry ever edited by a woman. The only female-edited anthology to compare with it in size was Wang Duanshu's 王端淑 (1621–ca. 1706) *Mingyuan shiwei* 名媛詩緯 of 1667, which had 1,000 authors and 2,000 poems. Yet in contrast to *Mingyuan shiwei*, *Zhengshi ji* is considerably more compact in size.[72] Like *Langui baolu*, it appears to have been designed for convenience of handling. Another contrast to *Mingyuan shiwei* is that *Zhengshi ji*'s primary purpose is didactic. Yun's opening preface talks of paying a carver "in order that it be broadly transmitted," and several of the accompanying prefaces and colophons mention wide circulation as one of its goals. Its main aims were not only to encourage women writers but also to limit their ambition by asking them to subordinate individual talent to more high-minded concerns. Yun was interested in female talent, but only when that talent was tempered by "meekness and gentleness" (*wenrou dunhou* 溫柔 敦厚). Yet her own deployment of talent as editor presents the same question that emerges from Hou Zhi's work; namely, Does Yun's self-presentation in *Zhengshi ji* live up to the standard of "meekness and gentleness" that she advocates for other women?

In compiling *Zhengshi ji*, Yun relied on Linqing's broad social contacts, on his and his brothers' fifteen years of foraging for texts, and on considerable expenditures of money.[73] Naturally, her distinguished lineage and high level of literary competence were indispensable aids to this same end. Profit may or may not have been one of Yun's incentives. If so, she was too ladylike to mention it. If not, the collection was motivated, rather, as a kind of charity or source of enlightenment for readers.[74]

Even in the rather unlikely event that *Zhengshi ji* was distributed free of charge, its large-scale distribution distinguishes it from more private forms of publishing. It thus counts as a work circulated to a "female reading public," along the model of *Zai Zaotian*, *Jinghua yuan*, and the several *Lienü zhuan*. Linqing's memoirs mention that *Zhengshi ji* did, in fact, circulate widely, and that many important women writers responded to it by sending endorsements or celebrating its publication in poetry, embroidery, and other forms.[75] Once again, there is no evidence of bookseller involvement, apart from professional printers, but the book's range of circulation was clearly large.

As with Hou Zhi's *tanci*, the way in which *Zhengshi ji* counsels good behavior to proper women implies an expanding audience of female readers. In part because of the switches in medium from *tanci* to edited collection and in language from vernacular to classical, Yun's strategies for reaching and increasing this growing band of women are a little different from Hou's. Hou uses a hectoring narrator as a way of keeping her audience on track, but Yun's method is to select authors wisely, and with them worthy poems, and she uses her comments about both to point readers in the right direction, morally speaking. Both Yun and Hou project a condescending attitude, on the idea that only someone of their level of virtue and education is qualified to make judgments about what women should read. Yun, however, articulates a much clearer and more consistent philosophy of educating readers. Some might think that "lack of talent in a woman" is a virtue, her argument runs, but she gives example after example to show that female literacy, when correctly applied to educating sons and helping husbands, is conducive to the smooth functioning of the home. In this way, Yun resolves the contradiction between virtue and talent that in Hou Zhi's work was unresolved. In Yun's words:

So if in recent times women have been studying poetry, what could be the harm in it? Only when the study of poetry neglects the Greater Odes (*Da ya*) does the teaching of the *Book of Odes* degenerate. Only then will the poet compete to [turn] the most seductive or sensual song or lyric into artful or frivolous habits. At worst her head may be turned by sexual attraction and carefree dalliance, and she will utterly neglect the dictates of meekness and gentleness (*wenrou dunhou*), but this is not the fault of poetry. It is actually the fault of not studying [proper] poetry.[76]

This logic paves the way for the image of the "good wife and wise mother" (*xianqi liangmu* 賢妻良母) that would come into its own at a somewhat later time.[77]

Despite these and other important differences, Yun's and Hou's texts are similar in their sense of audience. Although it has no built-in female recipient of narration, as *Zai zaotian* does, all of *Zhengshi ji*'s many prefaces, colophons, and postfaces are by women. This alone strongly implies that the book is directed primarily at female readers. *Zhengshi ji*'s readership can further be characterized through the collection's variegated nature. As the preface indicates, its authors are drawn from "Mongolian wives of imperial rank, talented Hami women, Tusi scholars, and seaside fishing wives,"[78] as well as from the women of Zhejiang and Jiangsu. This is not mere rhetoric. Women from each of these categories are represented in *Zhengshi ji*. The authors found in sections 16 through 20 in the first collection are particularly diverse in social composition, perhaps because these are the sections that deal with Yun's contemporaries. Linqing or his brothers were even able to obtain samples of poems by women whose writings had not been published.

Of course, such women were contributors to the volume and not necessarily its readers. But it is reasonable to assume that *Zhengshi ji* was meant to circulate to these individuals and their associates, as well as others. If this assumption is correct, *Zhengshi ji* reached outside the group of well-educated women that were Yun Zhu's immediate friends.[79] This assumption breaks down when it comes to *Zhengshi ji*'s handful of Korean poets, all of whom lived well before Yun's time. Yet the sense that Korea needed to be included is another point of resonance with Hou Zhi's *Zai zaotian*, one of whose plot lines takes place on Korean soil.

Zhengshi ji's heterogeneity is seen in two other areas, as well. The first is social class. The farmer's daughter He Shuangqing 賀雙卿 is included,[80] and some of the women from outlying areas are also social unknowns. These can be contrasted with the "*guixiu* from great houses" (*guixiu zhu dajia* 閨秀註大家) to whom the work was circulated for proofreading before publication and to whose social orbit Yun belonged.[81] Another source of diversity among its contributors and audience is age. The phenomenon of female geniuses learning to read and write when very young is familiar to students of women's poetry, and *Zhengshi ji* includes numerous examples of such precociousness, among them Wang Qiong and Wang Duan. Less familiar is the type represented by Zuo Muguang 左幕光, who learned to read in her fifties.[82] The point is that a woman of any age, class, or geographic location could become a *guixiu* if only she learned to write proper poetry and, in the process, learned the virtues that accompanied the role.

Still another kind of outreach is found in *Zhengshi ji*'s attitude toward male readers. In contrast to Hou, Yun and her various assistants make it clear that they welcome readers of both genders. Several of the preface writers report that the men of Yun Zhu's household, from Linqing on down, had read the collection and enjoyed it; the implication is, however, that they assessed the book for a feminine readership rather than reading it for their own enlightenment.[83] This is a contrast to Hou Zhi, whose works gave no overt sign of encouraging male readers, even though they surely were read by males.

In its hoped-for range of circulation, *Zhengshi ji* modifies some of the justification used by Hou to explain her interest in *tanci*, namely, that it was a lesser form of literature that would draw greater notice than a collection of individual poetry might do. To Yun, the poetical anthology was by no means a lesser form of literature, but she hoped that it would circulate broadly and did not shrink from exposing her book to many eyes. Yun's awareness of this visibility may be one reason behind her decision not to publish her own poems in *Zhengshi ji*. With few exceptions, the rest of her editorial staff (all family members) followed suit. Although Yun wrote poetry regularly throughout her life, her only surviving poems were collected and published by Linqing, ostensibly without her knowledge and well before the publication of *Zhengshi ji*.[84] It appears to have been embarrassment (real or rhetorical) over this event that led to Yun's interest in propagating the works of others. Again, there are signs that male authors of this era were constrained by similar inhibitions, but for a woman "marketing" virtue, it must have seemed especially important to keep her own works, and with it her vanity, from public view.

The feminine subject matter and hortatory tone of *Zhengshi ji* and *Zai zaotian* allow us to view them as the products of similar worlds. One important point of intersection between *Jinghua yuan* and *Zhengshi ji* lies in the area of cultural pluralism. Much of the action of *Jinghua yuan* takes place outside China, whereas in *Zhengshi ji*, the only true foreigners that appear are Koreans. Yet both these works project a sense that Han ethnicity is not the only one worth taking seriously. As long as foreigners (in *Jinghua yuan*'s case) or residents of outlying provinces (*Zhengshi ji*) learn the literature of China and behave in appropriate fashion, the fact that they began life outside Han culture does not matter. The foreign princess Yin Ruohua's acceptance of footbinding in *Jinghua yuan*'s chapter 46, when she was already an adolescent, may offend current sensibilities,[85] but it illustrates the point at hand. Similarly, Yun Zhu's poets of Hami or Tusi ethnicity mark her tolerance of other ethnicites, if only for the sake of recruiting them to Han values. Yun's marriage to a Manchu, most unusual in its time, may explain her interest in ethnicities beyond the pale.[86]

Li's interest in foreign lands, by contrast, derives in part from his wish to satirize China, but his study of phonetics gave him reason to view dialectical variations with interest and perhaps created tolerance at the same time. Li Ruzhen's embrace of diverse audiences overlaps with Yun's on a second point, as well. This is exemplified by his willingness to consider women in their fifties as educable, as exemplified in the case of the mother of the celebrated character Tingting. In chapter 53, Tingting's mother takes and passes the first examination, along with a group of girls.

Still another important common denominator lies in the various virtues practiced by that novel's female characters, both in their young and rambunctious days, when they are unfailingly filial, and later in life, when many of them lose their yearning for personal achievement and concentrate on serving their husbands. The young versions of these characters are far more active than Yun Zhu would have deemed appropriate, but the high level of activity of Li's young women is a function of their youth, as well as of the fact that many begin life outside China, where customs are not the same as Han customs. Like the young Han women in the story, most eventually accommodate themselves to a Chinese standard of behavior. By the time they marry, few if any violate the behavioral norms put forth in *Zhengshi ji*.

The final commonality between *Jinghua yuan* and *Zhengshi ji* is highly metaphorical. It concerns the ability of female leaders to transform the social equation that kept women in a state of ignorance. Li's Empress Wu provides the conceit that allows him to experiment with the idea of female high-achievers. Without this empress, none of the rest of what his "hundred flowers" accomplish (only to lose, in the end) would have been possible. In Yun Zhu's case, transformative female power is by no means a conceit. As we have seen, it is the result of intensely held personal convictions, very high social status, unusual literary talents, considerable expenditures of money, and Linqing's broad social networks. Yet Yun's reformulation of the convention that kept women illiterate or forced them to surrender all desire to read and write has something in common with Li's artistic rendering of Empress Wu's transformative reign. Yun Zhu would not have liked being compared to Empress Wu, but the breadth of *Zhengshi ji*'s vision, including its outreach to non-Han ethnicities and its reconciliation of the tension between talent and virtue, gave it a similar power to alter society.

Conclusion: The Female Reading Public in Early Nineteenth-Century China

The juxtaposition of *Jinghua yuan* and *Zai zaotian* allows us to posit a group of female readers that included but was larger than the elite literary circles of Jiangnan. These readers, or the implicit community thereof, affected the shape of *Zai zaotian* and *Jinghua yuan*.

Contoured in part by publishers, *Zai zaotian* is built around the idea of proselytizing among women readers. This is to say, it reaches outward and downward to a class of women Hou did not personally know or want to know. Superficially equating virtue and lack of talent, it uses female ambition as a weapon in the struggle to conscript and tame potential *guixiu*, whether these be overly active adolescents like Feilong or negligent mothers like Meng Lijun. Its aggressive propagation of what once had been class-based common knowledge is a good guide to the newly public face of *guixiu* culture and its new accessibility from below. As marketable commodities, published *tanci* sold a sense of how to negotiate issues such as female adventurousness and propriety. These works relied heavily on intermediaries for their circulation, most notably the fathers, husbands, and sons who had more direct access to the market than the women readers themselves. Published *tanci* thus had to contend with masculine views of what a proper woman was. At the same time, they had to appeal to women readers if they were to be read after they had been purchased.

With *Jinghua yuan*, the issue of women was more marginal. This is so in the literal sense that we gain access to it through prefatorial materials rather than through the story proper. It is also marginal in a figurative sense, inasmuch as Li Ruzhen clearly imagined male readers for his novel and granted them more importance in his mind. Yet the women's poems of endorsement leave little doubt that his text was meant to appeal to women, if only secondarily, and that it had a deep emotional appeal for such readers.

Zai zaotian and *Jinghua yuan* can also be viewed against the backdrop of evolving nonfictional avenues for feminine literary self-expression in nineteenth-century China. *Guochao guixiu Zhengshi ji* is merely one example of the broadening of possibilities as far as women's literary creativity is concerned. Despite its use of literary language, this anthology is no less ideological than *Zai zaotian*. Brushing aside the clichés about femininity and learning that Hou Zhi invoked only halfheartedly, it redefines *guixiu* culture as requiring, not just tolerating, literacy, and it sets down the terms under which that literacy should be deployed. Although hardly devoid of snobbery and class privilege, it conveys a sense that *guixiu* status could be acquired through reading and good behavior, not only through inheritance. As a work whose distribution may or may not have been profit-driven, *Zhengshi ji* complicates the picture of the ways authors reached out to unknown publics, but it again demonstrates the importance of those publics and the question of how to reach them as crucial issues for authors and booksellers of the time. *Jinghua yuan*'s point of intersection with *Zhengshi ji* is somewhat different, in that this novel does not proselytize; rather, it merely asks questions about the status quo. What it shares with *Zhengshi ji* is a sense that some aspects of the *guixiu* way of life can travel beyond Jiangnan, although it is more iconoclastic and hence more doubtful than Yun's anthology about the value of *guixiu* ideals. The new accessibility of *guixiu* culture was matched, on the producing side, by those who sought to take advantage of the developing market for social uplift and simple entertainment, whether these be booksellers anxious to sell books, women writers anxious for readers, or gentlemen of learning to whom gender mattered in more complicated ways.

Working backward from these observations, we arrive, finally, at the contours of the female reading public. Viewed through the lens of those who sought to engage it, it had to be handled with tact, as well as to be enticed with interesting reading. Female ambition could be used as bait to draw readers into a story, and feminine adventurers could be portrayed in positive terms, as long as they were young. But the ideological imperative called for modesty and self-effacement once a woman married and a willingness to subordinate personal ambition to family needs. Novels and *tanci* had to negotiate these complex rhetorical waters. A work like *Zai zaotian* could play to the ambitious side of its audience, but only if it reconciled ambition with submission, as in the story of Taihou. A work like *Jinghua yuan* could raise pointed questions about female talent, as long as it framed them with subjunctives and otherwise refrained from grappling too directly with prevailing norms. A work like *Zhengshi ji* could declare its version of a new millennium for women, but only with the proviso that the editors keep their own ambitions from public view. Eager to read but also easily offended, the female reading public mirrored in these writings conducts its give-and-take with the written word.

Notes

1. Hu Siao-chen, "Literary Tanci: A Women's Tradition of Narrative in Verse" (Ph.D. diss., Harvard University, 1994), pp. 112–13. On "women's *tanci*," see Zheng Zhenduo 鄭振鐸, *Zhongguo suwenxue shi* 中國俗文學史 (Beijing: Zuojia chuban-she, 1957), pp. 370–81. On the term *tanci xiaoshuo*, see, e.g., Hu Siao-chen 胡曉真, "Yuedu fanying yu tanci xiaoshuo de chuangzuo" 閱讀反應與彈詞小說的創作, *Zhongyang yanjiuyuan, Zhongguo wenzhe yanjiu jikan* 8 (Mar. 1996): 305–64. *Tanci* are normally considered part of oral performance literature, but they could also be pub-lished as literature to be read. Many of both kinds circulated in manuscript and were never published.

2. Chen Wenshu 陳文述, *Xiling guiyong ji* 西泠閨詠集 (Qiantang: Yidao tang, 1827; copy in Harvard-Yenching Library), 15.10 a–b. This comment is the reason we know that Chen Duansheng was the author of *Zaisheng yuan* and Liang Desheng was the author of the continuation. Chen's comments carry special weight because he was a relative of Chen Duansheng, and Liang Desheng was his daughter-in-law Wang Duan's surrogate mother. Wang was the editor of the section of *Xiling guiyong ji* in which these comments by Chen appear. This comment also mentions *Tianyu hua* 天雨花, another *tanci* popular among women readers. For perhaps as much as 150 years the only published *tanci* by a woman, *Tianyu hua* came out in a new edition in 1804. According to Chen, women used the slogan *nanhua beimeng* 南花北夢 to refer to *Tianyu hua* and *Honglou meng*, two classics they held dear.

3. For more on *Zaisheng yuan*'s canonical status, a plot summary, and a discussion of Chen's and Liang's differing postures as author/narrators, see Toyoko Yoshida Ch'en, "Women in Confucian Society—A Study of Three T'an-tz'u Narratives" (Ph.D. diss., Columbia University, 1974), pp. 178–257.

4. For an example of this approach, see Stephen J. Roddy, *Literati Identity and Its Fictional Representations in Late Imperial China* (Stanford: Stanford University Press, 1998), pp. 171–206.

5. For a later version of this conversation, see Patrick Hanan's introduction to Wu Lin and Wu Jianren, *The Sea of Regret: Two Turn-of-the-Century Chinese Romantic Novels*, trans. Patrick Hanan (Honolulu: University of Hawaii Press, 1995).

6. See Hu Shiying 胡士瑩, "Tanci nü zuojia Hou Zhi xiao zhuan" 彈詞女作家侯芝小傳, *Wenxian* 15 (1983): 87–93.

7. Guo Moruo 郭沫若, "*Zaisheng yuan* qian shiqi juan he tade zuozhe Chen Duan-sheng" 再生緣前十七卷和他的作者陳端生; reprinted in *Guo Moruo gudian wenxue lunwenji* 郭沫若古典文學論文集 (Shanghai: Guji chubanshe, 1985), p. 858.

8. For more on the two Hous, see Yu Jianhua 俞劍華, *Zhongguo meishujia ren-ming cidian* 中國美術家人名詞典 (Shanghai: Shanghai renmin yishu chubanshe, 1981), p. 568.

9. Mei Chong's status as Yuan's associate is confirmed by his inclusion in Yuan's "Xu tongrenji" 續同人集, in *Suiyuan quanji*,隨園全集, "yanji lei" 晏集類 (Shanghai: Wenming shuju, 1918), 3b–4a.

10. Fa-shi-shan 法式善, *Wumen shihua* 梧門詩話, ed. Shen Yunlong 沈雲龍, *Jindai Zhongguo shiliao congkan xuji* 近代中國史料叢刊續集 20 (Taibei: Wenhai chubanshe, 1975), p. 600. I have written more on this issue in "The Trouble with Talent: Hou Zhi (1764–1829) and Her Tanci *Zai zaotian* of 1828," CLEAR 21 (1999): 129–48.

11. Hou proudly refers to her daughter's talents in an autobiographical preface to *Jingui jie* 金閨傑 (Xiangye ge, 1822; copy in Tsinghua University Library). For more on this daughter, see Hu Wenkai 胡文楷, *Lidai funü zhuzuo kao* 歷代婦女著作考, rev. ed. (Shanghai: Guji chubanshe, 1985 [1957]), p. 547 (under Mei shi 梅氏).

12. Fa-shi-shan, *Wumen shihua*, pp. 598–99.

13. On domestic conscientiousness, see Hu Shiying, "Tanci nü zuojia Hou Zhi xiao zhuan," pp. 90–91.

14. Even Guo Moruo ("*Zaisheng yuan* qian shiqi juan he tade zuozhe Chen Duansheng," p. 857), who disliked Hou's *tanci*, found merit in her poetry.

15. Hu Wenkai, *Lidai funü zhuzuo kao*, p. 411.

16. Several sources set Hou's date of death in 1830. However, Hu Shiying ("Tanci nü zuojia Hou Zhi xiao zhuan," p. 92) is correct in his assertion that it was in 1829. Mei Zengliang, writing in 1832, mentioned that his mother's death had taken place three years earlier.

17. See Wang Yu 王豫, *Qunya ji* 群雅集 (1811; copy in Naikaku bunko), 2: 37.1a–3a.

18. Hu Siao-chen, "Literary *Tanci*," p. 107.

19. Ibid., p. 106. The translation is Hu Siao-chen's.

20. Ibid.

21. The name Biyun among these endorsements is that of Wang Qiong; see Hu Wenkai, *Lidai funü zhuzuo kao*, p. 256; Peixiang is Luo Qilan; see ibid., p. 761 and 939. On Sun Yunfeng, see Goyama Kiwamu 合山究, "En Bai to jodeshi tachi" 袁枚と女弟子たち, *Bungaku ronshū* 文學論集 31 (Aug. 1985): 115–16; and Hu Wenkai, p. 462. See also Hu Wenkai, pp. 411–12.

22. Preface to Hou Zhi, *Jingui jie*, 1822.

23. Guo Moruo, "*Zaisheng yuan* qian shiqi juan he tade zuozhe Chen Duansheng," pp. 855–58. See also Chen Yinke 陳寅恪, "Lun *Zaisheng yuan*" 論再生緣, in "*Zaisheng yuan*" yu Chen Yinke lun "*Zaisheng yuan*" 再生緣與陳寅恪論再生緣, ed. Yang Jialuo 揚家駱 (Taibei: Guoxue mingzhu zhenben huikan, 1975).

24. Hu Shiying's ("Tanci nü zuojia Hou Zhi xiao zhuan," p. 93) work shows several other points at which Hou Yunjin was helpful to his cousin, for he served as a

tutor to her children, in addition to turning out an edition of her poems when she was old and ill. Clearly, his devoted patronage of her literary efforts lasted her whole life. It could easily have been Yunjin who undertook the legwork that allowed her to make contact with commercial publishers while remaining cloistered at home. Hou's preface to Wang Qiong's 王瓊 *Ailanxuan shixuan* 愛蘭軒詩選 (1811; copy in Naikaku bunko) further notes that she received a copy of Wang Qiong's collected poems through Yunjin.

25. Evidence of Xiangye ge's involvement can be found for *Jingui jie*. The edition at Tsinghua University has "Xiangye ge xibi" 香葉閣戲筆 on the inside cover. This may or may not be the Huaigu tang 懷古堂 or Sanhua yuan 散花園 edition referred to in Hu Wenkai, *Lidai funü zhuzuo kao*, p. 411. Also, Xiangye ge is one of the publishers of *Zai zaotian*; see ibid., p. 411. According to Zheng Zhenduo (*Xidi shumu* 西諦書目 [Beijing: Wenwu, 1963], tanci, p. 66), a Xiangye ge edition of *Zai zaotian* came out in 1869. This is obviously a republication.

26. The publishers of *Yuchuan yuan* include Wencheng tang 文成堂 and Jingguan zhai 静觀齋; of *Jingui jie*, Sanhua yuan 散花園 and Huaigu tang 懷古堂; of *Zai zaotian*, Xiangye ge and Airi tang 愛日堂; and of *Jinshang hua*, Shancheng tang 善成堂, Baoshu tang 寶樹堂, and Xueyu tang 學餘堂: see Hu Wenkai, *Lidai funü zhuzuo kao*, pp. 411–12. Xiangye ge is Hou's own studio name. Airi tang may have been a publishing house of some duration; a firm of this name existed by the mid-eighteenth century; see ibid., p. 228, for an example of one work published by this house in 1751. Also, Hou Zhi's contemporary and apparent associate Sun Yunfeng published her poems with something called Airi xuan 愛日軒 of Hangzhou in 1814. According to Han Xiduo 韓錫鐸 and Wang Qingyuan 王清原, comps., *Xiaoshuo shufang lu* 小說書坊錄 (Shenyang: Chunfeng wenyi, 1987), an Airi tang in Yangzhou published novels dated 1853 and 1864 (p. 72); and a Wencheng tang published novels in 1885 and 1899 (p. 95). This source also reveals that several firms used the name Shancheng tang. One published a novel in 1852 (p. 25); it further establishes that Xueyu tang published only one novel, dated 1874 (p. 79). According to Guo Moruo ("*Zaisheng yuan* qian shiqi juan he tade zuozhe Chen Duansheng," p. 856), the publisher of the 1821 edition of *Zaisheng yuan* was Sanyi tang 三益堂. Cf. the catalogue of the Naikaku bunko, which lists the publisher of an 1822 edition as Baoren tang 寶仁堂. Both of these last two publishers also published novels, on which see Han and Wang.

27. Conclusion to chapter 8, *Jingui jie*.

28. Contrary to Mieke Bal's (*Narratology*, 2d ed. [Toronto: University of Toronto Press, 1997], p. 22) comments on the nongendered nature of narrators, Hou went out of her way to make the narrative context seem feminine.

29. For example, see the preface to *Zai zaotian* (Shanghai: Dada tushu gongyong-she, 1936), chap. 12: "I don't know whether any of my friends in the women's quarters have an interest in or talent for writing." See also note 22 to this chapter.

30. On fellow *guixiu*, see *Zai zaotian*, 2: 61. On lack of talent as a virtue and on meekness, see the opening poem to *Zai zaotian*.

31. Preface to Jiang Zhu 江珠, *Xiao Weimo shigao* 小維摩詩稿 (n.p., 1811; copy in Beijing Library).

32. Hu Shiying, "Tanci nü zuojia Hou Zhi xiao zhuan," p. 90.

33. On the relationship between moral uplift and publishing, see Anne E. Mc-Laren, *Chinese Popular Culture and Ming Chantefables* (Leiden: Brill, 1998), p. 285.

34. On *Tian yu hua*, see note 2 to this chapter and the discussion that follows.

35. Hu Shi 胡適, "*Jinghua yuan* de yinlun" 鏡花緣的引論, in Li Ruzhen 李汝珍, *Jinghua yuan* 鏡花緣 (Shanghai: Yadong tushuguan, 1923), pp. 14–16.

36. Sun Jiaxun 孫家汛, "*Jinghua yuan*" gong'an bianyi 鏡花緣公案辨疑 (Ji'nan: Jilu shushe, 1984), pp. 140–41. Sun believes *Jinghua yuan* was written over a period of twenty years, perhaps ending in 1815. Cf. Arthur Hummel, *Eminent Chinese of the Ch'ing Period* (Taibei: Chengwen, 1967 [1943]), pp. 472–73, which offers the more conventional opinion that it was written between 1810 and 1820. A partial copy of the 1817 edition of *Jinghua yuan* is held in the Tokyo University Library.

37. Hu Shi, "*Jinghua yuan* de yinlun," p. 17. See also Lu Xun, *A Brief History of Chinese Fiction* (Beijing: Foreign Languages Press, 1964), p. 329.

38. For example, C. T. Hsia, "The Scholar-Novelist and Chinese Culture: A Reappraisal of *Ching-hua yuan*," in *Chinese Narrative: Critical and Theoretical Essays*, ed. Andrew H. Plaks (Princeton: Princeton University Press, 1977), pp. 266–305; and Roddy, *Literati Identity and Its Fictional Representations in Late Imperial China*, pp. 171–206.

39. Hu Shi, "*Jinghua yuan* de yinlun." Cf. Frederick Brandauer, "Women in the *Ching-hua yuan*: Emancipation Toward a Confucian Ideal," *Journal of Asian Studies* 36, no. 4 (Aug. 1977): 646–60; and Maram Epstein, "Engendering Order: Structure, Gender, and Meaning in the Qing Novel *Jinghua yuan*," CLEAR 18 (1996): 101–27.

40. Yu Jianhua, *Zhongguo meishujia renming cidian*, pp. 1434, 884–85. See also Jiang Baoling 蔣寶齡, *Molin jinhua* 墨林今話 (Shanghai: Saoye shanfang, 1853), 17.5a–b.

41. Hummel, *Eminent Chinese of the Ch'ing Period*, pp. 658–59.

42. Shi Yunyu 史韞玉, *Duxuelu shiwengao* 獨學廬詩文稿 (1825; copy in National Taiwan University Library), 5:3.1.

43. On Jin's move to Banpu in 1797, see Jin Ruolan's autobiography, appended as a colophon to Jin Chong 金翀, *Yinhongge shichao* 吟紅閣詩鈔 (1810; copy in Library of Congress). On his term as salt receiver, see Wang Dingan 王定安, *Lianghuai yanfa zhi* 兩淮鹽法志 (Nanjing, 1895; copy in Harvard-Yenching Library), 135.14a–15a.

44. For the poem, see Jin Chong 金翀, *Yinhongge cichao* 吟紅閣詞鈔 (1810; copy in Library of Congress), 3.8a. Because this collection is not available in China, the poem has escaped the notice of Chinese scholarship on *Jinghua yuan*. It is a *ci* celebrating Li's painting of a fisherman.

45. Such as Sun Jichang 孫吉昌, the writer of a major preface to *Jinghua yuan*, who is also frequently the subject of poems by the two Jins.

46. The two Wangs were the publishers and editors of the two Jins' revised poetry collection of 1811, described below. As mentioned above, Wang Qiong and Hou Zhi were good friends.

47. Sun Jiaxun, *"Jinghua yuan" gong'an bianyi*, p. 25.

48. On her widowhood, see Wang Qiong's preface to the revised edition of Jin Ruolan 金若蘭, *Huayu xuan shichao* 花語軒詩鈔 (1810; copy in Library of Congress).

49. See note 2 to this chapter. *Tianyu hua* may have been written by a man, not a woman, and it is conceivable that the real publication date could be as late as 1804, the date of the second edition.

50. Tan Zhengbi 譚正璧, *Zhongguo nüxing wenxue shihua* 中國女性文學史話 (Tianjin: Baihua wenyi chubanshe, 1984), p. 382. For more on *Tianyu hua*, see note 2 to this chapter.

51. Tang Qingyu 唐清玉, daughter of Tang Guotai 唐國泰, is another example of a young woman from Li's world who died young. For more on Tang Qingyu, see Hu Wenkai, *Lidai funü zhuzuo kao*, p. 639. Tang's collection of poems is prefaced by Xu Qiaolin, Li Ruzhen's friend.

52. The theme of flowers is common in women's poetry, yet it is particularly common in the writings of both Jins. One poem by Jin Chong is about how various flowers open at different times (*Yinhongge cichao* 1:17). The reverse idea, that they all open at the same time, is one of the central conceits of *Jinghua yuan*.

53. Both are called "Penglai dao," and both are about Xu Shi's journey there with a boatload of boys and girls. For Jin Chong's, see *Yinhongge shichao*, 7.4a; for Jin Ruolan's, *Huayu xuan shichao*, 11a.

54. Qian Shoupu 錢守璞, *Xiufolou shigao* 繡佛樓詩稿 (1869; copy in Harvard-Yenching Library), 1.33b.

55. See the colophon to Jin Chong 金翀, *Yinhongge shixuan* 吟紅閣詩選 (1811; copy in Academy of Social Sciences Library, Literature Section, Beijing). I determined her age by adding fourteen, the age at which she started to write poetry, to the ten years of help that she says she has received with her writing. Jin's colophon is not dated, but it appears next to one that is dated 1809.

56. The two remaining poems are by Zhu Mei 朱玫 and Xu Yuru 徐玉如. The one by Zhu specifically mentions *Honglou meng*. The one by Xu is a lot like Qian Shoupu's in its emphasis on the sad fate of women as revealed at the Qihong

ting pavilion. I am grateful to Stephen Owen for help in translating these and related poems.

57. I make this argument in greater detail in my *"Jinghua yuan*: Where the Late Late Ming Meets the Early Late Qing," in *From the Late Ming to the Late Qing: Dynastic Decline and Cultural Innovation*, ed. David Wang and Wei Shang (Cambridge, Mass.: Harvard University Asia Center, forthcoming).

58. Sun Jiaxun, *"Jinghua yuan" gong'an bianyi*, p. 142.

59. Ōtsuka Hidetaka 大塚秀高, *Zōho Chūgoku tsūzoku shōsetsu shomoku* 増補中国通俗小説書目 (Tokyo: Kyūko shoin, 1987), pp. 152–55.

60. On the increase in published collections of women's poetry, see Fa-shi-shan, *Wumen shihua*, pp. 598–99. See also Chong Shuo's 崇碩 colophon to Yun Zhu 惲珠, *Hongxiang guan shicao* 紅香館詩草, in *Xiyongxuan congshu* 喜詠軒叢書, jiabian 甲編, ed. Tao Xiang 陶湘 (n.p.: Wujin Taoshi sheyuan, 1931).

61. Zhong Huiling and Andy S. L. Fung, "Wang Duan," entry in *Biographical Dictionary of Chinese Women: The Qing Period, 1644–1911*, ed. Clara Wing-chung Ho, p. 215 (Armonk, N.Y.: M. E. Sharpe, 1998).

62. Hu Wenkai, *Lidai funü zhuzuo kao*, pp. 243, 544. Liang Duan's work has a preface by Liang Desheng.

63. Some of this publishing history can be found in Hu Wenkai, *Lidai funü zhuzuo kao*, pp. 242–43, 544. See also Sun Dianqi 孫殿起, *Fanshu ouji* 販書偶記 (Shanghai: Guji chubanshe, 1982), p. 147. Wang Zhaoyuan's text includes the original edition, published by her husband's family (the Hao family Shaishu tang 郝氏曬書堂). According to the catalogue of the Harvard-Yenching Library, it was reissued by the Hao family in 1879, the Zhaoyang Cheng family 朝陽程氏 in 1917, and the Shangwu yinshuguan 商務印書館 in 1937. Liang Duan's text was originally published by her husband's family (the Wang family Zhenqi tang 汪氏振綺堂). It was reissued in 1874 with a postface by her nephew. According to the Harvard-Yenching Library catalogue, another edition came out in 1891, under the imprint of Zhao-Liu shi 趙劉氏 of Shanxi. A modern reprint appeared in 1933 under the imprint of the Shanghai Zhonghua shuju. I have not been able to see all these editions, and I cannot be sure which used the original blocks. No doubt the last editions in both these series were reprints, and some of the others may have been as well.

64. Hu Wenkai, *Lidai funü zhuzuo kao*, p. 636, refers to the pocket edition. This appears to be different from the full-sized edition found in the Tsinghua University Library. Both were published by Yun's own studio, Hongxiang guan 紅香館.

65. Hua Wei 華瑋, "Ming Qing funü xizuo zhong zhi 'ni nan' biaoxian yu xingbie wenti" 明清婦女戲作中之擬男表現與性別問題, in *Ming Qing xiqu guoji yantao hui lunwen ji* 明清戲曲國際研討會論文集 (Taibei: Zhongyang yanjiuyuan, Zhongguo wenzhe yanjiusuo, 1998), p. 615.

66. This is suggested by the rather great numbers of copies in existence today, including first-edition copies, and the number of reprints. Wang Zhaoyuan's and Liang Duan's texts were the subject of a discussion by Liang Qichao; see Hu Ying, *Tales of Translation: Composing the New Woman in China, 1899–1918* (Stanford: Stanford University Press, 2000), p. 8.

67. On conditions during the seventeenth century, see my "The Epistolary World of Female Talent in Seventeenth-Century China," *Late Imperial China* 10, no. 2 (Dec. 1989): 1–43. These questions are set in a broader context in Dorothy Ko's *Teachers of the Inner Chambers: Women and Culture in Seventeenth-Century China* (Stanford: Stanford University Press, 1994).

68. Hu Wenkai, *Lidai funü zhuzuo kao*, pp. 630–36.

69. Susan Mann, *Precious Records: Women in China's Long Eighteenth Century* (Stanford: Stanford University Press, 1997).

70. Yun Zhu 惲珠, *Guochao guixiu Zhengshi ji* 國朝閨秀正始集 (n.p.: Hongxiang guan, 1831), 16.23b. The poem is by Wang Naide 王迺德, a niece of Wang Qiong. The note gives Hou Zhi's name and identifies her as someone from Jinling.

71. See Linqing's preface to a collection edited by Xu Qiaolin 許喬林, *Haizhou wenxian lu* 海州文獻錄. This collection is dated 1829 and is held in the Beijing University Library.

72. *Mingyuan shiwei* measures approximately 10.5 × 6.75 × 3 inches. *Zhengshi ji* measures 7.5 × 5.25 × 4 inches. Copies of *Mingyuan shiwei* can be found in the National Central Library, Taibei, and the Peking University Library. *Zhengshi ji* is held in many libraries. For example, Harvard-Yenching Library has three copies.

73. Linqing describes his commitment in *Hongxue yinyuan tuji* 紅學因緣圖記 (Beijing: Guji chubanshe, 1984), 2 shang; on expenditures of money, see, e.g., Hu Wenkai, *Lidai funü zhuzuo kao*, p. 207.

74. It is unclear how much commercial publishers and publishing networks were involved in *Zhengshi ji*'s distribution. According to information printed in the texts, the printing was done commercially: the first (1831) collection was printed in Henan, at Biansheng Longwen zhai 汴省龍文齋, whereas the second, posthumously completed *Xuji* was printed in 1836 in Suzhou, at Gusu Wu Qingxia zhaiju 姑蘇吳清霞齋局. The format of the *Xuji* was identical to that of the first collection, and the two circulated as a set from 1836 on. Descendants of Linqing published a reprint from the original blocks in 1861. This one learns from a preface to the second printing by Jiang Zhongshen 蔣重中. Jiang was a niece of Cheng Mengmei 程孟梅, one of Linqing's wives. This means, as well, that she was a granddaughter of Yun Zhu. The 1861 printing took place at Jingdu liulichang changqiaonan Fuwen zhai 京都琉璃廠廠橋南富文齋. *Zhengshi ji*'s wide availability even today suggests that large numbers of copies were printed. Unfortunately, there is no way of knowing the exact number of copies or the price at which they sold.

75. Linqing, *Hongxue yinyuan tuji*, 2 shang, Zaizhi shixuan. Many of these endorsements are published in *Zhengshi ji*.

76. Yun Zhu, preface, *Guochao guixiu Zhengshi ji*, 1831, first preface, 1a. Translation is based on that of Susan Mann, *Precious Records*, pp. 116–17. For a simple biography of Yun, see the one by Li Yuning in Ho, *Biographical Dictionary of Chinese Women*, pp. 281–85.

77. See, e.g., Marjorie King, "Exporting Femininity, Not Feminism: Nineteenth-Century US Missionary Women's Efforts to Emancipate Chinese Women," in *Women's Work for Women: Missionaries and Social Change in Asia*, ed. Leslie A. Flemming (Boulder, Colo.: Westview Press, 1989), p. 124.

78. Yun Zhu, *Guochao guixiu Zhengshi ji*, "Liyan" 例言, 3b–4a. On the Tusi, see Hucker, *A Dictionary of Official Titles in Imperial China* (Stanford: Stanford University Press, 1985), p. 547.

79. The endorsements establish for certain that it reached women in Hunan and Anhui, and at least one Manchu woman saw a copy.

80. Yun Zhu, *Guochao guixiu Zhengshi ji*, 17.2a–b. For more on Shuangqing, see Paul S. Ropp, *Banished Immortal: Searching for Shuangqing, China's Peasant Woman Poet* (Ann Arbor: University of Michigan Press, 2001).

81. Colophon by Cheng Mengmei, first collection.

82. Yun Zhu, *Guochao guixiu Zhengshi ji*, 1.17.17b. See also Mann, *Precious Records*, p. 116.

83. See, e.g., the preface by Jiang Zhongshen to the reprint edition. It tells of her husband reading *Zhengshi ji* and deciding to reprint it.

84. Linqing, *Hongxue yinyuan tuji*, 2 shang, Zaizhi shixuan.

85. Hsia, "The Scholar-Novelist and Chinese Culture," pp. 301–2.

86. Ding Yizhuang 定宜庄, *Manzu de funü shenghuo yu hunyin zhidu yanjiu* 滿族的婦女生活與婚姻制度研究 (Beijing: Beijing daxue chubanshe, 1999), pp. 335–42. One could speculate that Yun's use of the term *guochao* in her title may point to the entire multiethnic Qing imperium rather than the part of it that was Han Chinese.

Works Cited

Bal, Mieke. *Narratology*. 2d ed. Toronto: University of Toronto Press, 1997.

Brandauer, Frederick. "Women in the *Ching-hua yuan*: Emancipation Toward a Confucian Ideal." *Journal of Asian Studies* 36, no. 4 (Aug. 1977): 646–60.

Cao Xueqin 曹雪芹. *Honglou meng* 紅樓夢. Beijing: Renmin wenxue chubanshe, 1972.

Chen Duansheng 陳端生 and Liang Desheng 梁德繩. *Zaisheng yuan* 再生緣. Ed. Zhao Jingshen 趙景深 and Liu Chongyi 劉崇義. Henan: Zhongzhou shuhua chubanshe, 1982.

Ch'en, Toyoko Yoshida. "Women in Confucian Society—A Study of Three T'an-tz'u Narratives." Ph.D. diss., Columbia University, 1974.

Chen Wenshu 陳文述. *Xiling guiyong ji* 西泠閨詠集. Qiantang: Yidao tang, 1827. Copy in Harvard-Yenching Library.

Chen Yinke 陳寅恪. "Lun *Zaisheng yuan*" 論再生緣. In *"Zaisheng yuan" yu Chen Yinke lun "Zaisheng yuan"* 再生緣與陳寅恪論再生緣. Ed. Yang Jialuo 揚家駱. Taibei: Guoxue mingzhu zhenben huikan, 1975.

Ding Yizhuang 定宜庄. *Manzu de funü shenghuo yu hunyin zhidu yanjiu* 滿族的婦女生活與婚姻制度研究. Beijing: Beijing daxue chubanshe, 1999.

Epstein, Maram. "Engendering Order: Structure, Gender, and Meaning in the Qing Novel *Jinghua yuan*." CLEAR 18 (1996): 101–27.

Fa-shi-shan 法式善. *Wumen shihua* 梧門詩話. Ed. Shen Yunlong 沈雲龍. *Jindai Zhongguo shiliao congkan xuji* 近代中國史料叢刊續集 20. Taibei: Wenhai chubanshe, 1975.

Goyama Kiwamu 合山究. "En Bai to jodeshi tachi" 袁枚と女弟子たち. *Bungaku ronshū* 31 (Aug. 1985): 113–45.

Guo Moruo 郭沫若. "*Zaisheng yuan* qian shiqi juan he tade zuozhe Chen Duansheng" 再生緣前十七卷和他的作者陳端生. Reprinted in *Guo Moruo gudian wenxue lunwenji* 郭沫若古典文學論文集. Shanghai: Guji chubanshe, 1985, pp. 854–81.

Han Xiduo 韓錫鐸 and Wang Qingyuan 王清原, comps. *Xiaoshuo shufang lu* 小說書坊錄. Shenyang: Chunfeng wenyi, 1987.

Ho, Clara Wing-chung. *Biographical Dictionary of Chinese Women: The Qing Period, 1644–1911*. Armonk, N.Y.: M. E. Sharpe, 1998.

Hou Zhi 侯芝. *Jingui jie* 金閨傑. Xiangye ge, 1822. Copy in Tsinghua University Library.

———. *Zai zaotian* 再造天. Shanghai: Dada tushu gongyongshe, 1936.

Hsia, C. T. "The Scholar-Novelist and Chinese Culture: A Reappraisal of *Ching-hua yuan*." In *Chinese Narrative: Critical and Theoretical Essays*, ed. Andrew H. Plaks. Princeton: Princeton University Press, 1977, pp. 266–305.

Hu Shi 胡適. "Jinghua yuan de yinlun" 鏡花緣的引論. In Li Ruzhen 李汝珍, Jinghua yuan 鏡花緣. Shanghai: Yadong tushuguan, 1923.

Hu Shiying 胡士瑩. "Tanci nü zuojia Hou Zhi xiao zhuan" 彈詞女作家侯芝小傳. Wenxian 15 (1983): 87–93.

Hu Siao-chen. "Literary Tanci: A Women's Tradition of Narrative in Verse." Ph.D. diss., Harvard University, 1994.

——— 胡曉真. "Yuedu fanying yu tanci xiaoshuo de chuangzuo" 閱讀反應與彈詞小說的創作. Zhongyang yanjiuyuan, Zhongguo wenzhe yanjiu jikan 8 (Mar. 1996): 305–64.

Hu Wenkai 胡文楷. Lidai funü zhuzuo kao 歷代婦女著作考. Rev. ed. Shanghai: Guji chubanshe, 1985 [1957].

Hu Ying. Tales of Translation: Composing the New Woman in China, 1899–1918. Stanford: Stanford University Press, 2000.

Hua Wei 華瑋. "Ming Qing funü xizuo zhong zhi 'ni nan' biaoxian yu xingbie wenti" 明清婦女戲作中之擬男表現與性別問題. In Ming Qing xiqu guoji yantao hui lunwen ji 明清戲曲國際研討會論文集. Taibei: Zhongyang yanjiuyuan, Zhongguo wenzhe yanjiusuo, 1998.

Hucker, Charles O. A Dictionary of Official Titles in Imperial China. Stanford: Stanford University Press, 1985.

Hummel, Arthur. Eminent Chinese of the Ch'ing Period. Taibei: Chengwen, 1967 [1943].

Jiang Baoling 蔣寶齡. Molin jinhua 墨林今話. Shanghai: Saoye shanfang, 1853.

Jiang Zhu 江珠. Xiao Weimo shigao 小維摩詩稿. N.p., 1811. Copy in Beijing Library.

Jin Chong 金翀. Yinhongge shichao 吟紅閣詩鈔, Yinhongge cichao 吟紅閣詞鈔, Yinhongge ci xuchao 吟紅閣詞續鈔. 1810. Copy in Library of Congress.

———. Yinhongge shixuan 吟紅閣詩選. 1811. Copy in Academy of Social Sciences Library, Literature Section, Beijing.

Jin Ruolan 金若蘭. Huayu xuan shichao 花語軒詩鈔. 1810. Copy in Library of Congress.

———. Huayu xuan shixuan 花語軒詩選. Copy in Academy of Social Sciences Library, Literature Section, Beijing.

King, Marjorie. "Exporting Femininity, Not Feminism: Nineteenth-Century US Missionary Women's Efforts to Emancipate Chinese Women." In Women's Work for Women: Missionaries and Social Change in Asia, ed. Leslie A. Flemming. Boulder, Colo.: Westview Press, 1989, pp. 117–36.

Ko, Dorothy. Teachers of the Inner Chambers: Women and Culture in Seventeenth-Century China. Stanford: Stanford University Press, 1994.

Li Ruzhen 李汝珍. Jinghua yuan 鏡花緣. Shanghai: Yadong tushuguan, 1923.

Linqing 麟慶. Hongxue yinyuan tuji 紅學因緣圖記. Beijing: Guji chubanshe, 1984.

Lu Xun. A Brief History of Chinese Fiction. Beijing: Foreign Languages Press, 1964.

Mann, Susan. *Precious Records: Women in China's Long Eighteenth Century.* Stanford: Stanford University Press, 1997.

McLaren, Anne E. *Chinese Popular Culture and Ming Chantefables.* Leiden: Brill, 1998.

Ōtsuka Hidetaka 大塚秀高. *Zōho Chūgoku tsūzoku shōsetsu shomoku* 増補中国通俗小説書目. Tokyo: Kyūko shoin, 1987.

Qian Shoupu 錢守璞. *Xiufolou shigao* 繡佛樓詩稿. 1869. Copy in Harvard-Yenching Library.

Roddy, Stephen J. *Literati Identity and Its Fictional Representations in Late Imperial China.* Stanford: Stanford University Press, 1998.

Ropp, Paul S. *Banished Immortal: Searching for Shuangqing, China's Peasant Woman Poet.* Ann Arbor: University of Michigan Press, 2001.

Shi Yunyu 史韞玉. *Duxuelu shiwengao* 獨學廬詩文稿. 1825. Copy in National Taiwan University Library.

Sun Dianqi 孫殿起. *Fanshu ouji* 販書偶記. Shanghai: Guji chubanshe, 1982.

Sun Jiaxun 孫家汛. *"Jinghua yuan" gong'an bianyi* 鏡花緣公案辨疑. Ji'nan: Jilu shushe, 1984.

Tan Zhengbi 譚正璧. *Zhongguo nüxing wenxue shihua* 中國女性文學史話. Tianjin: Baihua wenyi chubanshe, 1984.

Tao Zhenhuai 陶貞懷. *Tianyu hua* 天雨花. N.p: Xueku shanfang, 1891.

Wang Dingan 王定安. *Lianghuai yanfa zhi* 兩淮鹽法志. Nanjing, 1895. Copy in Harvard-Yenching Library.

Wang Duanshu 王端淑. *Mingyuan shiwei* 名媛詩緯. 1667. Copies in National Central Library, Taibei, and Peking University Library.

Wang Qiong 王瓊. *Ailanxuan shixuan* 愛蘭軒詩選. 1811. Copy in Naikaku bunko.

Wang Yu 王豫. *Qunya ji* 群雅集. 1811. Copy in Naikaku bunko.

Widmer, Ellen B. "The Epistolary World of Female Talent in Seventeenth-Century China." *Late Imperial China* 10, no. 2 (Dec. 1989): 1–43.

———. "*Jinghua yuan*: Where the Late Late Ming Meets the Early Late Qing." In *From the Late Ming to the Late Qing: Dynastic Decline and Cultural Innovation,* ed. David Wang and Wei Shang. Cambridge, Mass.: Harvard University Asia Center, forthcoming.

———. "The Trouble with Talent: Hou Zhi (1764–1829) and Her Tanci *Zai zaotian* of 1828." CLEAR 21 (1999): 129–48.

Wu Lin and Wu Jianren. *The Sea of Regret: Two Turn-of-the-Century Chinese Romantic Novels.* Trans. Patrick Hanan. Honolulu: University of Hawaii Press, 1995.

Xu Qiaolin 許喬林, ed. *Haizhou wenxian lu* 海州文獻錄. 1829. Copy in Peking University Library.

Yu Jianhua 俞劍華. *Zhongguo meishujia renming cidian* 中國美術家人名詞典. Shanghai: Shanghai renmin yishu chubanshe, 1981.

Yuan Mei 袁枚. "Xu tongrenji" 續同人集. In *Suiyuan quanji* 隨園全集, "yanji lei" 晏集類, 46. Shanghai: Wenming shuju, 1918.

Yun Zhu 惲珠. *Guochao guixiu Zhengshi ji* 國朝閨秀正始集. N.p.: Hongxiang guan, 1831. Xuji 續集, 1836.

———. *Hongxiang guan shicao* 紅香館詩草. In *Xiyongxuan congshu* 喜詠軒叢書, jiabian 甲編, ed. Tao Xiang 陶湘. N.p.: Wujin Taoshi sheyuan, 1931.

———. *Langui baolu* 蘭閨寶錄. N.p.: Hongxiang guan, 1831. Copy in Tsinghua University Library.

Zheng Zhenduo 鄭振鐸. *Xidi shumu* 西諦書目. Beijing: Wenwu, 1963.

———. *Zhongguo suwenxue shi* 中國俗文學史. Beijing: Zuojia chubanshe, 1957.

Part III

The Late Qing Periodical Press:
New Images, New Fiction

The New Novel Before the New Novel

John Fryer's Fiction Contest

Anonymous

The story of the modern Chinese novel, as it is usually told by literary historians, begins with Liang Qichao 梁啟超 (1873–1929), more specifically with his founding of the journal *Xin xiaoshuo* 新小說 (New fiction) in Yokohama in 1902. In his advertisement for that journal, Liang set forth the categories of subject matter that he commended, ranging from the historical and the political to the detective, romantic, and supernatural. Liang's own *Xin Zhongguo weilai ji* 新中國未來記 (The future of new China), published in installments in *New Fiction* in 1902 and 1903, is generally considered the first of the "new novels." Most of the famous novels of the late Qing period first appeared in serial publication in 1903, several of them in Liang's journal.

This story suffers from one major defect, however: it ignores an earlier "new novel," one that deserves to be considered in its own right as well as in terms of its contribution to late Qing fiction. The promoter of this earlier "new novel," which he labeled *shixin xiaoshuo* 時新小說,[1] was, strangely enough, a foreigner working in Shanghai. I believe that the full significance of his action has yet to be realized.

The promoter, John Fryer (1839–1928), was an Englishman who worked in China from 1861 until 1896, when he left to take up the Agassiz Professorship of Oriental Languages and Literature at the University of California. While in China he served for twenty-eight years, from 1868 to 1896, as head of the translation department of the Jiangnan Arsenal, where, working in tandem with Chinese colleagues,[2] he translated a prodigious number of works, mostly science and engineering textbooks. More than any other single person, he is credited with introducing nineteenth-century Western science to the Chinese.[3] Fryer also showed himself a tireless and gifted entrepreneur in sponsoring other ventures in scientific education: he was honorary secretary of the Chinese Polytechnic Institution in Shanghai from its inception in 1874; from 1877 he served as general editor of the School and Textbook Series Committee, which sponsored the publication of teaching materials for use in schools; in 1876 he founded his own journal of popular science, *Gezhi huibian* 格致匯編 (*The Chinese Scientific Magazine*, later renamed *The Chinese Scientific and Industrial Magazine*); and in 1884 he established his own science bookstore and publishing house in Shanghai, the Chinese Scientific Book Depot. (Branches were later set up in other cities.) One has only to read the minutes of the Chinese Polytechnic Institution or of the School and Textbook Series Committee to see the extent to which Fryer was the driving force behind both institutions.[4]

However, it was as owner of the bookstore that, improbably enough, he briefly involved himself in the development of Chinese fiction. In May 1895, seven years before the publication of Liang Qichao's *New Fiction*, he announced a public contest for new fiction and advertised it in the press.[5] The seven leading contestants were to receive prizes, and their work was to be considered for publication. Fryer also held out to prizewinners the possibility of long-term employment as writers of fiction. What he was seeking in the contest was fiction with a social purpose; it had to attack, as well as suggest remedies for, what he saw as the three great afflictions of Chinese society: opium, the examination essay, and foot-binding.

Let me wind up this particular story before going on to discuss the contest, its causes, background, and effects. In due course Fryer issued a report that listed the prizewinners and criticized various common faults in the other entries. Then in June 1896 he left his position at the Arsenal and moved to California. So far as is known, none of the entries was ever published; presumably all 162 manuscripts have been lost. (Had they survived, they would, by their sheer number, have dominated the fiction of that decade.) But Fryer's contest was not without its aftereffects. First, two novels survive that were clearly inspired by his contest, even though they were never entered in it. One of them, published at the end of 1895, ought, in my opinion, to be regarded as the earliest modern Chinese novel; the other, although written in June 1895, was published (in revised form) only in autumn 1897. Second, the kind of socially engaged or exposé fiction that Fryer was advocating may not have exerted a great influence on the thinking of Liang Qichao, who had different ideals in fiction, but it had a significant effect on the purpose and practice of fiction itself during the following decade.

Fryer, who had headed for China straight after graduating from a London normal college, evidently picked up much of his scientific knowledge from textbooks and manuals while working in China. (One of his earliest tasks at the Jiangnan Arsenal was to order scientific books and apparatus from London.) From at least the late 1860s, his consuming idea was that China's salvation lay in education, particularly in science and engineering; hence he strenuously objected to the examination system on the grounds that it channeled all education above the elementary level in another direction. In a talk entitled "Why Japan Has Developed Differently from China," he singled out "three great evils," opium, the literary examination essay, and foot-binding, and described the essay, whose "highest ambition was to reproduce the past," as an "insidious waste of time, thought and energy" that "has kept the brainy people . . . busily and harmoniously engaged."[6] In another context, he was quite capable of appreciating the essay for its own sake,[7] but in terms of its social effects he called it suicidal. He blamed it, and the educational system geared to it, for stifling inventive genius: the student "becomes a mere literary machine, with a prodigious memory, but with about as much original thought as a phonograph or a type-writer."[8] Fryer abominated opium use and foot-binding as much as anybody—he was involved in the formation of the Natural Feet Society (Tianzuhui 天足會) in Shanghai in April 1895[9]—but he saw the examination essay as the great institutional obstacle to progress. During the 1870s and 1880s, he tried to extend the scope of the examinations to include "Western learning," particularly science, but from 1895 he began calling for outright abolition of the traditional essay. He shared these and other ideas with Chinese reformers, on whom his scientific translations exerted a considerable influence.[10] In a talk delivered in California in 1900 he expanded on what the examination system was suppressing:

New opinions, new systems of philosophy, new forms of government, new theories to account for the existing state of things, new possibilities to which the nation ought to direct its energies. . . . In a nation almost always in fear of political agitation and jealous of innovation, any departure from the old paths and the well-known landmarks is at once deprecated and strongly opposed.[11]

The timing of his fiction contest was no accident. The terms of the Treaty of Shimonoseki, which concluded the disastrous war with Japan, provoked instant outrage, particularly among the examination candidates gathered in the capital. Before the treaty was even ratified, Kang Youwei 康有為 (1858–1927) had tried to present a mass memorial signed by the candidates. Such a furor among the elite was unprecedented in the nineteenth century, and foreign educators like Fryer were frankly elated, convinced that the long wished-for awakening was at hand. (Fryer writes of "the great burst of true patriotism that the war produced in all ranks of society.")[12] His advertisement, published a bare three weeks after the submission of the memorial, was designed to seize the mood of that particular moment; he meant, if possible, to turn that furor against the things that he most abominated in Chinese society.

It is harder to explain why Fryer left China so soon after the contest (and before any of the fiction was published). Jonathan Spence, who has given us an unduly depressing portrait of Fryer, believes that his departure for Berkeley was "an admission of defeat."[13] But at the time Fryer left, his ideas had triumphed, or seemed about to triumph. As an editor of the "Educational Department" of the *Chinese Recorder*, he wrote an article entitled "The Educational Outlook for 1896" that displays a positive euphoria:

The educational prospect for the year on which we have just entered is by far the most encouraging and satisfactory that has appeared in the entire history of foreign intercourse with China.

The war with Japan, with all its disasters and suffering, has not been without its educational lessons of immense benefit alike to the government and to the people of the "Middle Kingdom."[14]

He goes on to refer to "the literary and other societies that have recently been formed," including, presumably, the Qiangxuehui 强學會 (Society for the study of self-strengthening) formed by Kang Youwei and Liang Qichao, and asserts that "the national system of education, as well as the forms of religion and government, are already being weighed in the balance and found lamentably wanting." He looks forward, as joint editor of the "Educational Department," to having "a rapidly increasing series of advancements to announce in each monthly issue for 1896." The same euphoric note is echoed in his private correspondence.

The sales of translated books, which had been sluggish ever since the establishment of the translation department of the Jiangnan Arsenal, began to pick up.[15] In fact, the press could not even keep pace with the demand for some of the more popular items, and it was not long before Fryer found his own translations being pirated by the lithographic publishers.[16] If he had concluded at this point that his educational mission was a success and that he could simply declare victory and leave China, it would be understandable. He must surely have realized that the pioneer stage of introducing Western science was over, and that others were now available to carry on the task that he had begun. But although he did eventually turn his attention to other causes, such as the education of the Chinese blind, I know of no evidence to support that supposition. What caused him to move to Berkeley was a sense neither of defeat nor of victory, but something far more mundane: a domestic concern for his own family and finances.

Early in 1892 his second wife, Eliza Nelson, an American missionary whom he had met and married in Shanghai, moved to Oakland so that the children—Fryer had four surviving children by his deceased first wife—could complete their education. Unfortunately, the value of silver, which had been declining slowly for decades, took a sharp dip in 1892, followed by further dips in 1893 and 1894. Fryer, who was paid by the Arsenal in silver, now had to meet most of his expenses in dollars at a steeply reduced rate of exchange. In an August 26, 1892, letter to his brother George he describes himself as "half bankrupt" because of "the ruinous fall in silver."[17] (With his brother, who worked in a bank, he was always candid about such matters.) "My salary and savings are worth about two thirds of what they were, and every cent I send to America for the family costs nearly twice what it did years ago. Alas that I am tied to a silver country!" In another letter to his brother, written on March 31, 1894, he says he can no longer afford to keep his family in California and must bring them back to China.[18] Just at this juncture, however, he was approached about the Berkeley professorship, which had first been mentioned to him in 1893, when he visited the United States to report on the Chicago Exposition.[19] The negotiations and the appointment took a considerable time, and Fryer did not leave until the middle of 1896. Even then he did not sever all contact with China, but returned each summer to manage the affairs of his bookshop and to do more translations for the Arsenal.[20]

The organizational model for Fryer's fiction contest was a series of prize essay contests that he had conducted for the Polytechnic Institution since 1886. "The general object," he wrote in an 1887 report,

is to try and induce the Chinese literati to investigate the various departments of Western knowledge with the view to their application in the Middle Kingdom. . . . To popularize Western knowledge among the literati it is necessary to take advantage of all such existing national characteristics [as the institution of the examination essay]; and hence it was conceived that in essay writing there existed a most powerful means for inducing the better class of Chinese to read, think, and write on foreign subjects of practical utility.

The contest was but the "thin edge of the wedge."[21] Prize essay contests were nothing new in China—they had long been used by missionaries to stir up interest in their doctrines—but Fryer's contest was distinctive, not merely in its objective but also in its shrewd understanding of politics and the press.[22] His practice was to ask some high official of relatively enlightened views to propose a topic; Fryer would then advertise the contest in the newspapers. The official would judge the entries and also put up most, if not all, of the prize money; the newspapers were happy enough to print the winning entries. Contests were held each quarter, and the best entries for the year were published in book form, edited by the scholar Wang Tao 王韜. One reason for Fryer's speed on this occasion was the fact that he was sponsoring the fiction contest not from the Polytechnic Institution but from his own bookstore, under his own name, and at his own expense.

But what explains his choice of *fiction* as an instrument for his purpose? Since fiction had a low status in China, why did he go to the trouble of trying to elevate it? Fryer seldom refers to fiction in his writings.[23] His Berkeley lectures on Chinese literature mention only *Sanguo zhi tongsu yanyi* 三國志通俗演義, *Honglou meng* 紅樓夢, and *Liaozhai zhiyi* 聊齋志異, plus two well-known romances of the "brilliant and beautiful" type. His bookstore carried no fiction written after the eighteenth century.[24] Most Chinese narratives, he held, "are merely records of marvels, many of which are outside the limits of credibility, or are allied to the magical." His opinion of contemporary Chinese fiction, flourishing mightily in an era of cheap lithographic publishing, was distinctly low: "The country is flooded with trashy novels and stories which of course are professedly ignored by the literati though often if not chiefly read by them."[25]

More significant for his attitude to Chinese fiction is a statement in his 1900 talk: "The tendency of modern times is in the direction of a popular and easy Chinese style; and this has been necessitated by the demand for newspapers and general literature—which would have to be written in a manner easily understood by the majority of readers, so as to ensure an extensive and ready sale."[26] In addition to his attempt to appeal to the elite with his prize essays, Fryer had long shown a desire to interest a broader public, as in the case of his science magazine and school texts. The move to fiction was a far bolder step, however, and it may well have been inspired in part by the growth of newspapers and the power of journalism. In a paper written in 1901 he mentioned the demand for new newspapers, magazines, and periodicals and remarked on the "mighty power of the press."[27] His fiction contest was, in fact, an appeal to the elite; he hoped to enlist them in writing for a broad public that included women and children, and he was convinced that a certain kind of novel was the ideal medium for the purpose.

In planning the contest, he must have been advised by Chinese friends, perhaps including Wang Tao, although by the spring of the following year relations between Fryer and Wang seem to have become somewhat distant.[28] Zhan Xi 詹熙, author of *Hualiu shenqing zhuan* 花柳深情傳 (Love among the courtesans), one of the two surviving novels inspired by the contest, says that he checked with Wang Tao before deciding to have it published, which may at least indicate a belief that Wang was somehow involved in the contest.

Fryer makes it clear that, as we might expect, his idea derived largely from foreign fiction. In the July 1895 number of *The Chinese Recorder*, in the "Educational Department," there is a lengthy note, presumably by Fryer, explaining and justifying the contest:

The immense influence for good that a well written story can exert over the popular mind has often been exemplified, but perhaps never more fully than in the case of *Uncle Tom's Cabin* . . . in awakening people against slavery. . .

What China now wants, among many things, is a story or series of stories of the same thrilling description, true to the life, exposing the great evils that are everywhere rampant, and which the government is either unable or unwilling to counteract. Opium, foot-binding, and the literary examination system . . .

Nothing but the most thrilling sentiments, expressed through the most effective pictures that words can portray, will be likely with the Divine blessing to suffice for the purpose. There are doubtless well disposed Chinamen fully competent to write such books, if they can only be got hold of.[29]

He goes on to talk of fiction as affecting "the hearts and consciences of all classes of society in a way that has hardly yet been attempted" and declares his intention to "produce a series of books that may be of service in educational work." He was writing this for a missionary audience, but it seems highly likely that such works as *Uncle Tom's Cabin* indeed inspired Fryer's contest and, indirectly, the first modern Chinese novels.

His advertisement is headed "Qiu zhu shixin xiaoshuo qi" 求著時新 小說啟 (A call for the writing of new fiction) and appeared on five occasions in the *Shenbao* 申報, as well as in the *Wanguo gongbao* 萬國公報 (The review of the times).[30] The same advertisement appeared in the June number of the *Chinese Recorder*, among the advertisements at the back of the journal, together with an account in English. The Chinese advertisement reads:

I believe that there is nothing to equal fiction for moving people's hearts and minds and causing them to change their ways. With its wide and rapid circulation, fiction can, within a short period of time, become known to one and all, making it possible without difficulty to reform current practices. At present the most serious of China's age-old evil practices are three in number: opium, the examination essay, and foot-binding. Unless some means can be found of reforming these practices, there is no prospect of China's ever attaining wealth and power. I therefore invite all Chinese gentlemen who desire strength and prosperity for their country to write new and interesting fiction that will demonstrate the great harm done by these three practices and offer ingenious solutions for their elimination. The setting out of the case as well as its argument should be fully integrated into the work so as to form a coherent whole, with the result that readers' hearts and minds will be so moved that they will strive to eradicate the practices. It is vital that the language be clear and easily comprehensible, and essential that the import of the work be interesting and in good taste, so that even women and children will be able to read and understand. The events narrated must be current and near at hand. On no account should old formulas be followed. In terms of its conception, the work should not place any value on strangeness or peculiarity, and it should also avoid anything that would inspire shock or terror.

The deadline for submission is the end of the seventh month. The prizewinners will be selected after careful consideration. The first name on the list will receive 50 dollars, the second 30 dollars, the third 20 dollars, the fourth 16 dollars, the fifth 14 dollars, the sixth 12 dollars, and the seventh 8 dollars.

Any fine works capable of changing people's hearts and minds will be printed and published. It is also our intention to offer their authors regular employment to write similar works.

On completing your entry, wrap it up and seal it, taking care to write your name and address on the outside of the parcel, which should then be sent to the Chinese Scientific Book Depot on Third Avenue in Shanghai. An acknowledgment will be issued on receipt of your entry. The announcement of results and awards will be issued from the same address. Respectfully, John Fryer, British scholar

The fact that Fryer published the advertisement under his own name was no doubt to guarantee the validity of the contest in the mind of the public. The English account, under the heading of "Chinese Prize Stories," puts the matter a little differently, for a different audience:

The sum of $150, in seven prizes, is offered by the undersigned to Chinamen who produce the best moral stories, combining a graphic description of the evils of Opium, the Literary examinations, and Foot-binding, with practical methods by which they may be removed. It is hoped that students, teachers and pastors connected with the various missionary establishments in China will be shown the accompanying advertisement and encouraged to take part in the competition; so that some really interesting and valuable stories, in the easiest *Wen-li* may be produced, of a Christian rather than of a merely ethical tone, which will supply a long felt want and serve as popular reading books all over the Empire.

A receipt will be given for all sealed manuscripts, sent or delivered before the end of the seventh Chinese month to the *Chinese Scientific Book Depot,* 407 Hankow Road, or to

JOHN FRYER,
May 25, 1895   *Shanghai*

The chief difference between the two versions is that the Chinese says nothing about a Christian or even an ethical tone, whereas the English makes no appeal to patriotism (the attainment of wealth and power by China) and lays down no prescriptions with regard to subject matter. The Chinese emphasizes newness of approach and requires that the fiction deal with contemporary reality. It asks merely that the language be simple, not that it be in easy literary Chinese. In fact, most entries, following the example of the Chinese novel, would probably have been in the vernacular.

In the "Educational Department" of the July *Recorder* there appeared the piece, quoted above, about the example of *Uncle Tom's Cabin*. The October number contains a preliminary report noting that, by the close of the competition, about 155 manuscripts had been received, ranging "from a few modest pages written by the college student or village pedagogue up to the four or six volume sensational tale, bristling with poetry, which is the production of the expert novelist." Some of the manuscripts are in beautiful handwriting, tastefully bound, and even accompanied by illustrations. Several are "unmoral," and two "are positively immoral, and have been returned to their authors, who appear to know no better than they have written."

In March 1896 came the final report.[31] The prize money had been increased by $50, and the number of prizes increased to twenty. The names of the winners had been announced in the *Shenbao*, and the complete list of 162 names, plus an explanatory notice, had been sent to the *Wanguo gongbao* and the *Zhong Xi jiaohui bao* 中西教會報 (Missionary review).[32] At least half of the competitors were from mission schools and colleges. At the end of the report Fryer adopted the disdainful tone often affected by contributors to the *Recorder* and other foreign-language publications of the time:[33]

There is a great paucity of new ideas among the Chinese, and hence many of these attempts are merely old literary rubbish and poetry worked up in a new form under a new name with but little attempt at disguise. It is a common remark that the inventive powers of the Chinese are of a low order, and this fact is abundantly manifested in these stories. There is but little originality in them. . . . This experiment has, however, drawn out a few stories that really are worth publishing, and it is hoped that some of them will be issued before the end of the year, so as to supply the need that is felt for light reading of a healthful, moral tone and useful instructive character.

The tone of this report and the fact that he used the word "experiment" no doubt signaled his disappointment at the results of the contest. Although from our particular vantage point the contest seems to be one of his more notable contributions to the cause of reform in China, Fryer himself, who was not one to minimize his achievements, evidently set little store by it. It is not referred to again in his surviving writings, except in routine correspondence about the payment of prizes and the return of manuscripts.

The *Wanguo gongbao* and the *Missionary Review* printed only the list of prizewinners, together with the report. At least a third of the prizewinners opted to use pseudonyms—like the authors of the traditional novel—instead of their real names. In his report, entitled "Results of the Call for

New Fiction," Fryer took the opportunity to explain the principles behind the ranking—and incidentally to try to influence the direction of the new fiction. These opinions did not circulate as widely as the advertisement, but it seems worthwhile to give them in part:

This office issued a call for new fiction on the subject of the three evils of opium, the examination essay, and foot-binding. The exposition was to be integrated into the work in the manner of a novel (*zhanghui xiaoshuo* 章回小說) that would cohere from start to finish. The intention was to publish the fiction in order to move people's hearts and minds in such a way that they would understand the need for reform. Since even women and children should be able to read and be moved by this fiction, the writers' purpose must be to seek out matter that was interesting and in good taste. The events narrated should be plausible, and the description truthful and apt.

We received 162 manuscripts, all of them the product of study, from gentlemen near and far. It has taken us a hundred days to read through them. They all had the right intentions, but some were biased in their approach, giving too much weight to opium and too little to the examination essay; some contained strange arguments and implausible events; and others narrated fantastic things, often involving dreams. Still others used language that was coarse and shallow, including much local patois, and even went so far as to favor lewd expressions and to verge on the indecent; with their constant talk of brothels, concubines and maids they can be seen as belonging to the old category of the obscene novel, in direct violation of the requirement that the fiction be an encouragement to virtue. How can their novels possibly be read or listened to by women and children?

Fryer explained that two kinds of entry were disqualified as prose fiction: the ballad with its songs and verses (presumably he is referring to the *tanci* 彈詞 or *guci* 鼓詞), and the disquisition. As in his advertisement, he was concerned that the argument be fully dramatized.

The idea that fiction had a unique power to sway people's emotions did not originate with Fryer, although he may not have been aware of its history in China—it is found at least as early as the preface to Feng Menglong's 馮夢龍 *Gujin xiaoshuo* 古今小說 of about 1621. Nor did the principle that fiction should deal with the real rather than the fantastic originate with Fryer; it can be found as early as Ling Mengchu's 凌濛初 preface to his first collection of stories in 1628. But there is still a gulf between the way those ideas had been applied in fiction and the way Fryer proposed to apply them. He singled out three social practices, all of them well established, one of which, the examination essay, was the capstone of the educational and civil service system. Furthermore, he had linked them, in a way that had not been done before, to patriotic concerns, to China's prospects of attaining wealth and power. Fryer then asked the novel to perform a function it had scarcely been asked to perform in China—to treat and solve intractable problems of national concern. It was a conception of fiction that he must have known from the nineteenth-century English and American novel, but one that was probably unfamiliar to his Chinese audience.[34]

Of the two extant novels that constitute the most obvious legacy of his contest, *Xichao kuaishi* 熙朝快史 (Delightful history of a glorious age) is the earliest modern Chinese novel in two important senses: it concerns itself with the distinctively modern crisis of China's survival as a nation under the military, technological, and cultural onslaught of the West, and it adopts new methods of narration. At the same time, it resorts to traditional beliefs and tropes—karmic reincarnation, martial arts, court cases, and Daoistic withdrawal from public life. Although *Xichao kuaishi* is a well-written work that duly attacks the three evils, it is doubtful that it would have won a prize from Fryer; he would surely have objected to its use of prophetic dream and karmic rebirth.

All that we know of the authorship and date comes from the surviving edition in the library of Dongbei Normal University. It was published in Hong Kong with a preface by the Man of Leisure of Hangzhou (Xiling san-ren 西泠散人) dated the equivalent of December 23, 1895. Its editing is at-tributed to the Ambrosia-Sipping Layman (Yinxia jushi 飲霞居士), and its revision to the same Man of Leisure who wrote the preface. Surprisingly for a programmatic novel, the preface speaks mainly of the difficulties of fic-tional narrative and only secondarily of the three evils. The evils, it maintains, are the warp of the book, and the two main figures, Kang Jishi 康濟時 and Lin Menghua 林夢花, are the woof. The preface rebuts the suggestion that the author was afflicted with a sense of grievance and deliberately wrote in a jocular vein—that would be to ignore the great pains he took in writing this work. The fact that the preface mentions the author but says nothing more about him suggests that the Man of Leisure was in fact the author.

The novel has a notable opening. A provincial graduate from Hangzhou, a man of wide learning and uninhibited nature, is discussing the state of the nation with a few close friends. "Treating a nation is like treating a disease—you have to prescribe a remedy for it," he declares, before going on to diag-nose China as suffering from a chronic wasting disease, the remedy for which is to foster its vital energy. To his friends' amusement, he claims that if he held power in China, he would cure the national disease.

Climbing up Mount Ge by the West Lake, he and his friends come upon a pavilion called Guanriting (Pavilion for observing the sunrise). When they learn that a spectacular eclipse will occur the following day, they decide to stay, spending the night in a nearby temple. There the graduate dreams of an old man who is dispensing medicine to crowds of ailing people. His name is Jueshi 覺世 (Awaken the World), and he explains that China's three great afflictions are opium, the examination essay, and foot-binding; 70 percent of the population suffer from one or more of them. A brief argument ensues over foot-binding, which the graduate thinks may be pointless but is scarcely harmful to the nation. Jueshi stresses the pain and the physical enfeeblement that result from it and notes that none of the three afflictions has the sanction of ancient precedent—all are latter-day aberrations.

When the graduate professes a strong desire to save the nation, he is told that the time is not ripe for him. He himself is fated to die before long, but he will be reborn into the Kang family in Guiji of Shaoxing prefecture, and in his next life he will be able to fulfill the desire he has expressed—he will hold power and be in a position to cure the three evils.

The prophetic dream and the reincarnation belong to the traditional stuff of fiction, but the sunrise, or rather the eclipse, with its symbolic overtones, is a new development. This kind of symbolic opening becomes common enough in the fiction of the next decade; indeed, this opening forms a telling contrast—one that indicates the different moods prevailing in the two decades—with the scene at the beginning of *Lao Can youji* 老殘遊記 (Travels of Lao Can). The headings of Chapter 1 are as follows:

After discussing the ills of the time, he tours the hills and dreams a dream,
While writing a new book, [the author] embodies his ambitions in allegorical form.

The author is obviously identifying himself with the graduate whose ambitions are about to be fulfilled in the next generation.

Chapter 2 tells of the hero's father, Kang Fengji 康逢吉, who as a young man was about to compel a young girl to have sex with him when he looked up and "saw the red sun in the heavens" and promptly had a change of heart (2.459). Perhaps as a reward for his virtuous restraint, he fathers a son, Kang Jishi ("benefits the times"), a prodigy who reads widely in practical subjects as well as in the Classics, but who loathes the examination essay.

Kang Jishi's story is interwoven with that of Lin Menghua, a highly intelligent but weak-willed creature who serves as a handy foil. (The author has in effect added two extra evils to the prescribed three, fiscal corruption and official injustice, both exemplified by Lin.) Kang Jishi's ideas on modernization are clarified in his arguments with Lin Menghua (see especially 5.481–82). Lin had written a piece called *Xinxuelun* 新學論 (On the new learning), which Kang criticizes as glorifying Western learning at the expense of the Chinese. He claims that much Western learning is actually derived from the Chinese; hence the two cannot be considered separately. Even science and parliamentary government have Chinese antecedents. He draws up a twelve-point document listing the reforms that he favors, including the abolition of the three evils, and arranges to have the document presented as a memorial to the throne.

The second half of the novel deals mainly with Kang's suppression of a Moslem revolt in Gansu. A revolt did occur there in 1895, the first in over two decades, and the coincidence of dates is striking. The revolt broke out in August, and it was not until early December that the Chinese army gained its first victory. Since the preface of this novel is dated December 23, this seems to be an extreme case of the convergence of fiction and contemporary events that we frequently find in the next decade.

Kang's memorial is accepted, and the three evils are banned. He is appointed president of the Board of War and modernizes the army along Western lines with the aid of Western advisers. Like a latter-day Judge Bao, he also solves the case of a general who has abused his power.

At the very end of the novel, he meets a strange character who had earlier handed him a set of prophetic pictures. The man explains that Kang has already attained his life's ambition and that to continue in office would be superfluous. Kang departs to seek immortality.

We can only infer Fryer's influence on *Xichao kuaishi*, but in the case of the other novel, *Hualiu shenqing zhuan* 花柳深情傳 (Love among the courtesans), the fact is stated unambiguously in both preface and prologue. The author was an ardent reformer named Zhan Xi 詹熙 (1850–1927) from Quxian in Zhejiang, both of whose parents were published poets.[35] In the summer of 1895, he tells us in his prologue, referring to himself by his pen name, Lüyixuan zhuren 綠意軒主人 (Master of the Studio of the Green Impression), he was visiting Suzhou when he noticed Fryer's advertisement in the *Hubao* 滬報.[36] Impressed by the idea that fiction was the best means of changing people's hearts and minds, he thought of a notable family, the Weis, neighbors of his in Quxian, who would serve as an admirable example.

The subject of the novel's composition is taken up again in the second-to-last chapter. After many vicissitudes, the Weis have formed a modern community and are growing rich. They now seek some way of publicizing their achievement, so that they may serve as an example to others. A friend, Zheng Zhixin 鄭芝芯, who appears to be an alter ego of the author's,[37] recommends the Master as a chronicler of the family's descent and subsequent rise. The Master declines the commission, but six or seven years later, inspired by Fryer's advertisement, he recalls the case of the Weis. His employer (he is working as a tutor) encourages him to take his manuscript to Shanghai and visit Fryer. The employer also suggests a title for the manuscript, *Xing shi xinbian* 醒世新編 (A new tale to awaken the world)—*Hualiu shenqing zhuan*, which suggests a courtesan romance, is presumably a catchy title substituted by the publisher. The Master makes ready to leave. Then in a nightmare he is confronted by representatives of the three special interests he has attacked in his book. They argue that the opium trade is necessary because of the taxes it brings in, taxes that are more vital than ever now that China has to pay a huge indemnity to Japan; that officials all over the country owe their jobs to their skill at the very essay that he wants to abolish; and that small feet are the working capital of the courtesan. The book ends abruptly, with the author awakening from his nightmare.

His preface repeats the information about the advertisement and adds some detail. He wrote the novel in two weeks, he says, but instead of sending it to Fryer, he kept it with him as he traveled about the country doing various jobs. In the spring of 1897, when he was back in Shanghai making a living by his pen, he told Wang Tao about his manuscript and received his blessing to publish it. But immediately afterward he had to go north again— he was in demand as an art connoisseur—and had no time for revision. The seventh month found him back in Shanghai, where, after adding new material at the beginning and end of the novel, he had it published. He feels compelled to comment on the changes that have occurred in China since he wrote the first draft in 1895. Natural Feet societies have been established in Shanghai and Hubei; the examinations have been changed to include Western learning, and local societies have been set up to prohibit opium. He passes on a friend's formula for suppressing opium addiction. He also apologizes for his occasional humorous tone, explaining it away as a characteristic feature of the novel genre. The preface is dated the ninth of the ninth month of 1897 in Shanghai.

His revisions must have covered more than just the beginning and ending. In Chapter 14 (pp. 58–59), one character mentions reading a set of poems by the Master in that day's *Youxibao* 遊戲報 on the subject of *yeji* 野雞 (low-level prostitutes). The poems appeared in the *Youxibao* on the seventeenth of the eighth month, a scant three weeks before the date of the preface.[38] Other elements in the novel tie it closely to the author's life in Quxian as well as to the contemporary Shanghai scene.[39]

The novel conforms well enough to Fryer's prescriptions. The two eldest Wei sons are addicted to opium and obsessed with the examination essay, respectively, and the daughter suffers the pain and enfeeblement of foot-binding. The sons' pedantic tutor, Kong, illustrates the uselessness of the examination essay; Zheng Zhixin speaks for the author. The novel is set anachronistically amid the chaos of the Taiping rebellion, mostly in Quxian and its neighboring counties. The reforms it demonstrates stress practical learning, including technology. Books of modern science are mentioned, including some of those translated by Fryer. An engineer is brought in from Guangzhou to help open a silver mine, and a Chinese-speaking Westerner is hired to teach English. Little is said of either Chinese or Western values other than that of economic progress. The author's equation of himself with the narrator and his detailed account of the situation in which he comes to write are characteristic of novels written after 1895.

Beyond these two novels, Fryer's short-lived venture must have exerted a certain influence on modern Chinese fiction—even though the extent of that influence can only be a matter of conjecture. His was the first call for a specifically new kind of fiction, one that he defined in two ways: it had to engage social issues of immediate national concern, and it had to follow certain prescriptions that tended to distance it from traditional fiction. The engagement with social issues brought fiction close to journalism, but Fryer insisted that the dominant themes be fully dramatized, not merely stated. His prescriptions for new forms and methods, simple as they were, preceded those of other critics by a number of years.

His ideas had a certain influence on Liang Qichao as Liang took his cautious first steps toward recommending fiction as an instrument of reform. In one of Liang's essays on primary school education, which was published in *Shiwubao* 時務報 (no. 18, February 22, 1897), he recommended fiction as optional reading material during the last hour of the eight-hour school day. But students were not to read existing novels or stories, all of which were unsuitable; new fiction would have to be written for the purpose. Of the topics Liang recommends for fiction, the most important are the sages' teachings and the historical record, but he also suggests attacks on official corruption, the examinations, opium, and foot-binding. The last three topics are presumably the legacy of John Fryer. In November of that same year, also in *Shiwubao* (no. 44), Liang enthusiastically reviewed two new journals, *Mengxuebao* 蒙學報 and *Yanyibao* 演義報, edited by friends and a protégé, respectively. The uplifting fiction and other material that they evidently contained, intended for boys under fifteen, was surely what he was advocating. After his escape to Japan at the end of 1898, Liang began to promote the political novel, basing himself on Japanese examples[40]—the Japanese novelists had themselves been influenced by the work of Lytton and Disraeli—and had nothing more to say about the novel of social criticism. Even in 1902, when listing the types of fiction that his journal would publish, he ignored the social novel (*shehui xiaoshuo* 社會小說).[41] Only in the tenth issue was the omission rectified and the social novel included.

Needless to say, Liang Qichao's influence on many aspects of late Qing literature was infinitely greater than Fryer's. But Fryer's call for a new fiction came a good seven years before Liang's. And although Harriet Beecher Stowe (and perhaps also Charles Dickens and others) may seem remote from late Qing fiction, Fryer's conception of a novel that exposes, and seeks remedies for, current social ills is closer to the characteristic temper of late Qing fiction, with its frequent excoriation of social evils, than Liang's notion of the political novel. It is likely that Fryer's contest did in some degree affect the general direction of late Qing fiction. The story of the modern Chinese novel would not be complete without it.

Notes

I am grateful to Chen Jianhua and Shum Chun of Harvard University, Fred Dagenais of the Center for Chinese Studies at the University of California, and Laurie L. McFadden of Alfred University for providing me with material.

1. *Shixin*, "fresh, in season" or "fashionable," here evidently means "new."

2. The colleagues were true collaborators. According to Fryer's account, the foreigner would dictate an oral translation in Chinese sentence by sentence, and the writer would put it into easy literary Chinese. After any problems had been discussed, the writer would then revise it, normally without checking by the foreigner. See Fryer, "Science in China," pt. 2, *Nature* 24 (May 19, 1881): 55.

3. On the value of Fryer's scientific translations, see Xiong Yuezhi 熊月之, *Xixue dongjian yu wan Qing shehui* 西學東漸與晚清社會 (Late Qing society and the dissemination of Western learning) (Shanghai: Shanghai renmin, 1994), pp. 567–85.

4. For the minutes of the former, see, e.g., *Celestial Empire* 3, no. 3 (Jan. 21, 1875): 57–58. For the minutes of the latter, see the "Educational Department" section of the *Chinese Recorder* from 1893 to 1896.

5. The contest was briefly noticed by Wang Shuhuai 王樹槐, *Wairen yu wuxu bianfa* 外人與戊戌變法 (Foreigners and the 1898 reforms) (Nankang: Academia Sinica, 1965), p. 40. The first person to set out the main facts about the contest was Huang Jinzhu 黃錦珠, "Jiawu zhi yi yu wan Qing xiaoshuojie" 甲午之役與晚清小說界 (The Sino-Japanese War and the late Qing novelists), *Zhongguo wenxue yanjiu* 中國文學研究 (National Taiwan University), May 1991, pp. 3–7.

6. From an undated typescript in carton 1 of Fryer's "Correspondence and Papers," which are preserved in the Bancroft Library of the University of California at Berkeley. The Fryer material consists of one box of correspondence, including his bookshop correspondence from March 1896 to July 1901 ("Letter Journal"), plus six cartons of other papers, mostly in typescript. The contents of cartons 4–6 have not been classified and are unavailable to readers.

7. See "The Normal Chinese Essay" (in "Correspondence and Papers," carton 1). It was originally a talk delivered in California in 1902.

8. "Chinese Education—Past, Present and Future," pt. 1, *Chinese Recorder*, July 1897, p. 334. It was a talk delivered in California in 1896.

9. The subject of foot-binding reached a new level of prominence when Alicia (Mrs. Archibald) Little established the Natural Feet Society in Shanghai in April 1895, the month before Fryer's announcement of his contest. Fryer was evidently advising her. At the meeting of the Society on April 16, she brought up his suggestion that they should persuade the foreign ambassadors to appeal to the emperor to forbid any official to marry his son to a woman with bound feet (*Celestial Empire* of

Apr. 26, 1895, supp., p. 3). The suggestion was incorporated in a memorial the following year (see *Records of the Triennial Meeting of the Educational Association*, 1896 [Taipei: Ch'eng-wen, 1970], p. 286). A letter in the "Letter Journal" of Mar. 11, 1896, indicates that Fryer had conducted an essay contest for the society. Fryer may have been the first to designate this particular combination of evils. Other writers use the term *sanbi* 三弊 or 四弊 *sibi* (four evils), but with a different content; see, e.g., *Zilin Hubao* 字林滬報, Apr. 3, 1897. In his advertisement Fryer does not imply that *sanbi* is an accepted term; in his report on the contest, he does, however, imply it.

10. He first met Tan Sitong 譚嗣同 in 1893; see Wang Shuhuai, *Wairen yu wuxu bianfa*, pp. 103–4. Adrian Arthur Bennett (*John Fryer: The Introduction of Western Science and Technology into Nineteenth-Century China* [Cambridge, Mass.: Harvard University, East Asian Research Center, 1967], pp. 43–44) notes that a high proportion of the titles in Liang Qichao's list of important works of Western learning, *Xixue shumubiao* 西學書目表, were works translated by Fryer.

11. "The Literature of China," *University Chronicle* 4 (1901): 167.

12. "The War Between China and Japan" (in "Correspondence and Papers," carton 2), p. 31.

13. Jonathan Spence, *To Change China: Western Advisers in China, 1620–1960* (Boston: Little, Brown, 1969), pp. 156–57. Spence quotes a short passage by Fryer about the ardors of his job and comments, "his summation of his life's work makes bleak reading." But the passage is from Fryer's "Science in China," published in 1881, fifteen years before he left China. Actually it was first published in the *North-China Herald* of Jan. 29, 1880, only three months after his wife's death, which may account for the tone of weary dedication in this particular passage.

14. *Chinese Recorder*, Jan. 1896, pp. 36–39.

15. See a letter of June 7, 1897, in the "Letter Journal."

16. See *Chinese Recorder*, Aug. 1897, p. 383. Since the Japanese war "it has been impossible to reprint them fast enough." On pirating, see *Chinese Recorder*, Sept. 1897, p. 444. A June 23, 1897, letter to W. A. P. Martin in the "Letter Journal" also refers to heavy pirating.

17. In "Correspondence and Papers."

18. Ibid.

19. See Nellie Blessing Eyster, ed., *A Beautiful Life: Memoir of Mrs. Eliza Nelson Fryer, 1847–1910* (Berkeley, Calif.: privately published, 1912), p. 61.

20. Fryer did not regard the move to Berkeley as necessarily permanent; he left his colleagues in the Educational Association with the impression that he would be back before long (see *Records of the Triennial Meeting*, 1896, p. 19). Note that Timothy Richard recommended Fryer as W. A. P. Martin's successor in Beijing; see Richard, *Forty-Five Years in China* (New York: Frederick A. Stokes, 1919), p. 257.

21. See his report, "Chinese Prize Essays," in *The John Fryer Miscellany* (Bancroft Library, University of California), vol. 1. The report was evidently written in 1887. The essay contest is described in Wu Jianren's 吳趼人 novel *Ershinian mudu zhi guai xianzhuang* 二十年目睹之怪現狀 (Strange things witnessed during the past twenty years) (Nanchang: Jiangxi renmin, 1988), chap. 15.

22. Fryer served for eighteen months, until joining the Arsenal, as part-time editor of the *Shanghai xinbao* 上海新報 (Shanghai gazette). He even tried out briefly as sub-editor of the *North China Daily News*, but the job was too hectic for him; see his letter to his brother of Feb. 6, 1868 (misdated 1867).

23. There is an incomplete novel about the Jewish settlement in Kaifeng in carton 3 of "Correspondence and Papers."

24. See "Chinese Literature," pt. 2 (in "Correspondence and Papers," carton 1), p. 42. On the bookshop's holdings, see Bennett, *John Fryer*, pp. 112–15.

25. "Chinese Literature," pt. 2, p. 43.

26. "The Literature of China," pp. 165–66.

27. "The Chinese Problem" (in "Correspondence and Papers," carton 1), p. 34. This article, obviously written early in 1901, is Fryer's most forceful statement about the Chinese situation. The armies of "the chief nations of the world . . . have desolated and looted the Metropolis, and even the Imperial palace, committing atrocities equaling, if not surpassing, those of the Goths and Vandals at Rome *and at least vying with those perpetrated by the Chinese themselves.*" (The italicized passage was added afterward to the typescript by hand.) Fryer goes on to excoriate the missionaries for upsetting the existing religions, including ancestor worship, and then, "having sufficiently stirred up a hornets' nest," calling in the aid of their consuls (p. 10). Trade is equally to blame: "Bibles and opium have gone hand in hand all over the country" (p. 13).

28. This much is suggested by a letter of Mar. 23, 1896, in the "Letter Journal" from Fryer to Joseph Edkins. It refers to an article in the *Shenbao* on the prize essays that is "evidently from the hand of Mr. Wang Tao." That day's editorial argues that the sponsors of the essay contests should go beyond essays and promote scientific education in general. It seems strange that Wang had not been in touch with Fryer before publishing it.

29. Pp. 330–31.

30. See *Shenbao*, May 25, 28, 30, June 4, and June 8; and *Wanguo gongbao* 77: 31.

31. It was issued from the offices of his magazine, dated the middle of the tenth month of 1895. I do not know why it took so long to get published. The tone of the report reflects the rapid movement of opinion during 1895; it is much less tentative about reform than the advertisement.

32. See the Mar. 1896 numbers.

33. However, this is the only place in Fryer's writings I have noticed this tone.

34. Of course, some Chinese novels did satirize the examination system and even foot-binding, but their satire cannot be compared to the condemnation and remedy called for by Fryer. Note that at the time of the contest, Chinese readers still had little access to Western fiction. Edward Bulwer Lytton's *Night and Morning* was translated in *Shenbao* under the title of *Xinxi xiantan* 昕夕閒談 from 1873 to 1875. The Chinese translator's preface stresses the affective power of fiction, but in the cause of familiar virtues (see Hanan, "A Study in Acculturation: The First Novels Translated into Chinese," *Chinese Literature: Essays, Articles, Reviews* 23 [2001]: 55–80). A score of novels had also been composed or translated by Protestant missionaries, mainly to inculcate Christian doctrine; see Hanan, "The Missionary Novels of Nineteenth-Century China," *Harvard Journal of Asiatic Studies* 60, no. 2 (Dec. 2000): 413–43.

35. On Zhan Xi and his family, see *Quxian zhi* 衢縣志 (Gazetteer of Quxian) (Hangzhou: Zhejiang renmin, 1992), pp. 556–57.

36. Probably a mistake for the *Shenbao*.

37. His age, examination status, and opinions tally with those of the author. Moreover, it is he who tells the author about the Wei family.

38. The poems appeared on September 13. He was evidently working in Shanghai at the time. His advertisements of paintings for sale appeared on September 29, October 1 and 3, and his biography of a Shanghai courtesan on October 11. The editor of *Youxibao* at the time was Li Boyuan 李伯元, soon to become one of the best known novelists of the late Qing.

39. For example, Zheng Zhixin's extravagant praise of Puyang Zeng 濮陽增 and his family as benefactors in Chapter 21 (pp. 89–90). Puyang was a fellow artist in Quxian and presumably also a benefactor of Zhan Xi's; see *Quxian zhi*, p. 472. There is also a topical Shanghai reference to the aborted love affair between Zou Tao and the courtesan Su Yunlan 蘇韻蘭 in Chapter 14 (p. 57). The affair was the basis of Zou Tao's novel *Haishang chentianying*, of which the preface by Wang Tao is dated 1896 (see Zou Tao 鄒弢, *Haishang chentianying* 海上塵天影 [Shanghai shadows of the mortal world] [Nanchang: Baihuazhou wenyi, 1993]). At the very least, Chapter 14 of *Hualiu shenqing zhuan* must have been heavily revised in 1897 (see Zhan Xi 詹熙, *Hualiu shenqing zhuan* 花柳深情傳 [Love among the courtesans] [Beijing: Beijing shifan daxue, 1992]).

40. See Liang Qichao 梁起超, "Yiyin zhengzhi xiaoshuo xu" 譯印政治小說序 (Translation and printing of political novels), *Qingyi bao* 清議報, Dec. 23, 1898.

41. See the advertisement "Zhongguo weiyi zhi wenxuebao *Xin xiaoshuo*" 中國唯一之文學報新小說 (China's only literary journal *New Fiction*), *Xinmin congbao* 新民叢報 14 (Aug. 15, 1902). Yan Tingliang 顏廷亮 (*Wan-Qing xiaoshuo lilun* 晚清小說理論 [Late Qing fiction theory] [Beijing: Zhonghua, 1899], pp. 63–70) argues that the political novel, in the sense Liang gave to the term, was always central to his

thinking about fiction. On the categories of fiction, such as "political novel" and "social novel," see Ye Kaidi 葉凱蒂 (Catherine V. Yeh), "Guanyu wan Qing shidai de xiaoshuo leibie ji *Xin xiaoshuo* zazhi guanggao erze" 關於晚清時代的小說類別及 <新小說>雜誌廣告二則 (On the categories of late Qing fiction and two advertisements for the journal *New Fiction*), *Shinmatsu shōsetsu* 清末小說 (1989): 112–21.

Works Cited

Bennett, Adrian Arthur. *John Fryer: The Introduction of Western Science and Technology into Nineteenth-Century China*. Cambridge, Mass.: Harvard University, East Asian Research Center, 1967.

Eyster, Nellie Blessing, ed. *A Beautiful Life: Memoir of Mrs. Eliza Nelson Fryer, 1847–1910*. Berkeley, Calif.: Privately published, 1912.

Fryer, John. "Chinese Education—Past, Present and Future." Part 1. *Chinese Recorder*, July 1897, pp. 329–35.

———. "Chinese Literature." 2 pts. In idem, "Correspondence and Papers," carton 1.

———. "Chinese Prize Essays." In idem, *The John Fryer Miscellany*.

———. "The Chinese Problem." In idem, "Correspondence and Papers," carton 1.

———. "Correspondence and Papers." 1 box and 6 cartons. Bancroft Library, University of California.

———. *The John Fryer Miscellany*. Bancroft Library, University of California.

———. "The Literature of China." *University Chronicle* 4 (1901): 164–75.

———. "The Normal Chinese Essay." In idem, "Correspondence and Papers," carton 1.

———. "Science in China." 2 pts. *Nature* 24 (May 5, 1881): 9–11; (May 19, 1881): 54–57.

———. "The War Between China and Japan." In idem, "Correspondence and Papers," carton 2.

———. "Why Japan Has Developed Differently from China." In idem, "Correspondence and Papers," carton 1.

Hanan, Patrick. "The Missionary Novels of Nineteenth-Century China." *Harvard Journal of Asiatic Studies* 60, no. 2 (Dec. 2000): 413–43.

———. "A Study in Acculturation: The First Novels Translated into Chinese." *Chinese Literature: Essays, Articles, Reviews* 23 (2001): 55–80.

Huang Jinzhu 黃錦珠. "Jiawu zhi yi yu wan Qing xiaoshuojie" 甲午之役與晚清小說界 (The Sino-Japanese War and the late Qing novelists). *Zhongguo wenxue yanjiu* 中國文學研究 (National Taiwan University), May 1991, pp. 1–18.

Liang Qichao 梁起超. "Yiyin zhengzhi xiaoshuo xu" 譯印政治小說序 (Translation and printing of political novels). *Qingyi bao* 清議報, Dec. 23, 1898.

Little, Alicia. *Intimate China*. Philadelphia: Lippincott, 1899.

Quxian zhi 衢縣志 (Gazetteer of Quxian). Hangzhou: Zhejiang renmin, 1992.

Records of the Triennial Meeting of the Educational Association. Records of the 1893, 1896, and 1899 meetings. Reprinted—Taipei: Ch'eng-wen, 1970.

Richard, Timothy. *Forty-Five Years in China*. New York: Frederick A. Stokes, 1919.

Spence, Jonathan. *To Change China: Western Advisers in China, 1620–1960*. Boston: Little, Brown, 1969.

Wang Shuhuai 王樹槐. *Wairen yu wuxu bianfa* 外人與戊戌變法 (Foreigners and the 1898 reforms). Nankang: Academia Sinica, 1965.

Wu Jianren 吳趼人. *Ershinian mudu zhi guai xianzhuang* 二十年目睹之怪現狀 (Strange things witnessed during the past twenty years). Nanchang: Jiangxi renmin, 1988.

Xichao kuaishi 熙朝快史 (Delightful history of a glorious age). Hohhot: Nei Menggu renmin chubanshe, 1998.

Xiong Yuezhi 熊月之. *Xixue dongjian yu wan Qing shehui* 西學東漸與晚清社會 (Late Qing society and the dissemination of Western learning). Shanghai: Shanghai renmin, 1994.

Yan Tingliang 顏廷亮. *Wan Qing xiaoshuo lilun* 晚清小說理論 (Late Qing fiction theory). Beijing: Zhonghua, 1899.

Ye Kaidi 葉凱蒂 (Catherine V. Yeh). "Guanyu wan Qing shidai de xiaoshuo leibie ji *Xin xiaoshuo* zazhi guanggao erze" 關於晚清時代的小說類別及<新小說>雜誌廣告二則 (On the categories of late Qing fiction and two advertisements for the journal *New Fiction*). *Shinmatsu shōsetsu* 清末小說 (1989): 112-21.

Zhan Xi 詹熙. *Hualiu shenqing zhuan* 花柳深情專 (Love among the courtesans). Beijing: Beijing shifan daxue, 1992.

"Zhongguo weiyi zhi wenxuebao *Xin xiaoshuo*" 中國唯一之文學報新小說 (China's only literary journal, *New Fiction*). *Xinmin congbao* 新民叢報 14 (Aug. 15, 1902).

Zou Tao 鄒弢. *Haishang chentianying* 海上塵天影 (Shanghai shadows of the mortal world). Nanchang: Baihuazhou wenyi, 1993.

The Weird in the Newspaper

Rania Huntington

Alongside coverage of national and international politics, crime, and social events, late Qing periodicals recount stories of hauntings, monstrous births, and karmic retribution. Such stories suggest that the newspapers and pictorials were, among other things, a continuation of the *zhiguai* 志怪 (tales of the strange) genre. By studying the content, collection, and display of the strange in late Qing new media, this chapter examines the relationship between strangeness and the media in which it is produced and consumed. I contend that strangeness was central, not marginal, to late Qing periodical literature.

Strangeness is both a venerable part of the Chinese literary tradition and a crucial element in the periodical press in other times and places.[1] The *zhiguai*, brief anecdotes about weird happenings, first appeared in the Han and Six Dynasties and continued to appear in both specialized collections and miscellaneous notebooks through the late Qing.[2] In Qing writings, the strange is defined as "that which people have not yet seen or heard" or "that which is different from the norm."[3] On a practical level, I define the strange as, first, news items marked with the various words for strange—*guai* 怪, *qi* 奇, and *yi* 異—and second, subjects traditionally the topics of *zhiguai* collections.[4] As Judith Zeitlin has pointed out, strangeness is both a continuously evolving cultural construct and a psychological effect.[5] The question that this chapter strives to answer is how that construction and how the achievement of that effect change with the new media.

I examine two late Qing periodicals, both published in Shanghai and both the products of the same publishing house: the *Shenbao* 申報 and the *Dianshizhai huabao* 點石齋畫報. The *Shenbao*, founded by a pair of English brothers named Major, began publication in 1872. Later the Shenbao guan publishing house opened the first lithographic printing studio in China and in 1884 began to print the *Dianshizhai huabao*, China's first regularly appearing illustrated periodical. The Shenbao guan was also a prolific publisher of books of all sorts, including substantial amounts of both vernacular and classical fiction.[6] The following discussion is based on the complete run of *Dianshizhai huabao* from 1884 to 1896 and the *Shenbao* from 1872 to 1882, with spot checks of the period between 1882 and 1900.

Accounts of the strange are a recurring but not dominant presence in the *Shenbao*; they appear much more frequently in *Dianshizhai huabao*. The tastes for strangeness in the two periodicals differ. In the pictorial the preference for spectacle, reinforced by the new technology of the lithograph, is more pronounced. The *Dianshizhai huabao* is far more interested than the *Shenbao* in monstrous births and bizarre animals, whereas ghosts, shape-changing animals, and karmic retribution are shared territory.

The relatively small proportion of such material in the *Shenbao* seems to have resulted in nearly total scholarly neglect. Only Natascha Vittinghoff makes general observations; she notes that the Hong Kong newspaper *Xunhuan ribao* 循環日報 contains "mostly morally edifying stories, with the intention to enlighten, or critical satires in the tradition of the *Rulin waishi*, but the *Shenbao* places itself explicitly in the tradition of the entertaining *zhiguai xiaoshuo*."[7] The significance of the *zhiguai*-like content in the *Dianshizhai*, on the other hand, has been evaluated in various ways by scholars. In the 1950s Ge Gongzhen dismissed the periodical with the line, "Unfortunately its contents are similar to those of *Liaozhai* [*zhiyi*] 聊齋誌異 and do not relate to the contemporary situation."[8] More recently Wang Ermin rejected Ge's assessment on the grounds that material devoted to the supernatural material occupies only a tenth of the whole or a sixth if one uses a more generous definition of supernatural. Although Wang insists one should not use those fractions to judge the value of the periodical as a whole,[9] I contend that that is still too large a proportion to dismiss as unimportant. Nanny Kim has taken tales of the miraculous and monstrous seriously as indicative of the tastes and preferences of the pictorial's readership. I follow her lead but focus more on the details of the bizarre content.[10] Wu Meifeng discusses this material as a reflection of popular belief.[11] None of the authors who have noted the similarity of this material to earlier *zhiguai* has examined the relationship in depth.

With its two publications, the Shenbao guan offered not one but two new ways of consuming the strange. In both cases, the material conditions of publication changed the strange. In the daily newspaper, the strange was transformed by a multiplicity of successive textual voices. In the pictorial, the new visual format transformed the strange in the direction of carnival display. In both periodicals, the foreign emerged as both a source of marvels and a voice commenting on the strange.

Defining News and the Weird

Statements about the purposes of the *Shenbao* acknowledge a kinship between the newspaper and the tradition of weird anecdotes. One such statement in the introductory issue explained that in the past many events in China went unrecorded. Old books recorded only old events in language difficult to understand. "As for *xiaoshuo*, books have been transmitted from every dynasty, as when Zhang Hua 張華 [232–300] recorded curiosities, or Gan Bao 干寶 [fl. 320] recorded his search for the spirits, when Qixie 齊諧 made his book of *zhiguai*, or Yu Chu 虞初 selected essays. All of this type of text can be read in passing, but it is just that the events recorded therein are sometimes fabricated and unfounded, and their language is elegant and gorgeous. They can serve only as material for the pure conversation of the literati and cannot be enjoyed by common and elegant alike."[12] The works mentioned here include both legendary founders of *xiaoshuo*, Qi Xie and Yu Chu, and the historical authors of the best known of the Six Dynasties *zhiguai*, Zhang Hua's *Bo wu zhi* 博物志 and Gan Bao's *Sou shen ji* 搜神記. As records of events, they were evidently one of the possible rivals of the newspaper that had to be disparaged and dismissed.[13] The list of the desired contents of the newspaper includes, after national politics, the transformation of customs, Sino-foreign relations, and commerce, all "amazing and delightful matters" (可驚可喜之事).[14] In another statement about the role of the *Shenbao*, Ernest Major named "rare and strange matters" (稀奇怪異之事) as part of the desired content of the newspaper; each of these words for strange also figures prominently in titles of *zhiguai* collections.[15] *Xinwen* 新聞, "news," and *yiwen* 異聞, "strange tales," easily bleed into one another.

The *Dianshizhai huabao* is even more straightforward about the desire for strangeness: in a passage seeking submissions from people throughout the country, the editors regretted that some "strange events" from outside Shanghai had not made it into the newspaper. Anyone who knew of "amazing and delightful events" in his province should submit images, for which he would be paid.[16] In his preface to the first issue, Ernest Major described Western illustrated periodicals as "selecting the strange and novel items from the news of every publishing house; when a new device has been produced, or a rare thing seen, all of it will be illustrated in order to convince the readers." *Dianshizhai huabao* was meant to serve the same purpose for Chinese readers.[17] Yet in addition to that educational purpose, the end of the preface evokes an image of reading pleasure, more integral to the project of the pictorial than that of the text newspaper: "Opening these scrolls for amusement after wine and tea could also suffice to increase one's pleasure."

This presentation of marvels as both esoteric information and casual entertainment would have been familiar to readers of *zhiguai*. Boxue 博學, broad and esoteric learning, is one of the oldest justifications for recording *zhiguai* and continued to be evoked in the Qing.[18] Traditional *zhiguai* were also considered material for the idle conversation of those sated with tea and wine. Because of these similarities, Major's arguments for publishing coverage of hot air-balloons could easily be used to justify ghost stories. The line between edifying through tales of the marvelous and satisfying the taste for the strange is difficult to draw, since popular education was inextricably intertwined with delighting readers. *Dianshizhai huabao* thus shares in the combination of edification and entertainment that many scholars have noted in late Qing literature.[19]

Justifying the Strange in the Newspaper

On the level of individual anecdotes, the texts continue both traditional defensiveness about recording bizarre and dubious materials and traditional defenses. The excuses found in prefaces of earlier collections reappear in individual reports and captions, creating a series of miniature prefaces—one repeatedly enters the realm of the strange from adjacent stories. Some of these justifications are straightforward continuations of the *zhiguai* tradition; others reveal an awareness of the changed medium and changing times.

Claims that the strange could provide light entertainment or moral in-struction seem largely unchanged. "Speak recklessly, listen to it recklessly" (姑妄言之、姑妄聽之), a line from the *Zhuangzi* most famously used in a tale of Su Shi demanding to hear ghost stories,[20] is frequently evoked in both periodicals. Moral instruction is an equally conservative justification: even a story of dubious veracity can be recorded if it teaches a good moral.[21] One example is the tale of a virtuous woman who wards off the advances of an amorous ghost with filial thoughts of her mother-in-law.[22]

One of the most common justifications is to preserve anomalies, whether inexplicable or dubious, "so as to inquire of gentleman of broad learning" 存之以質博物君子,[23] recalling Zhang Hua's *Bo wu zhi*. Yet this is not simply an archaic defense: in a few cases in *Dianshizhai huabao*, the "gentle-man of broad learning" is replaced by the modern museum, *bowuguan* 博物館, and broad learning is expanded to include the possibility of scien-tific classification. When a monstrous child with no feet and the head of an animal is born, the commentator regrets it did not survive, for it could have been sent to a Westerner's museum to determine its species.[24] The gestures of invoking the man of broad learning and the museum are identical in that they shirk authorial responsibility for explanation or authentication and dis-place it to a higher authority, whose supposed presence serves to justify the tale. Yet to invoke the museum is to recognize a new institution rather than an individual and to offer the possibility of public display rather than private examination. This is an excellent example of how a new, translated term car-ries the baggage of the older phrase it incorporates; the institution is still marked as Western, but the term *bowu* promises Chinese access to the knowledge contained there.[25] By displaying the anomaly and posing the question, the pictorial itself plays the role of that museum.[26] Neverthe-less in the *Dianshizhai* pleas for later explanation seem an empty gesture, since explanations are almost never forthcoming. In the *Shenbao* the would-be Zhang Huas do submit possible interpretations, as we will see below. This one-way relationship with readers strengthens *Dianshizhai huabao*'s na-ture as display.

Another common justification, which dates back at least to Guo Pu's 郭璞 (276-324) preface to the *Shan hai jing* 山海經 (The classic of moun-tains and seas), states that since the world is larger and weirder than we can fathom, we should not doubt all marvels just because we have never seen

them.[27] On occasion this appeal to the world's vast variety is given a contemporary frame. A story about carnivorous plants overseas ends with the
affirmation that "in today's world" one cannot conclude things do not exist
just because one has not seen them personally, as these unplantlike plants
demonstrate.[28] The influx of information from the outside world, both the
West and the Qing's own colonial territories, undermines rather than
strengthens skepticism. The openness to novelty advocated by the periodicals could also encourage acceptance of more traditional objects of doubt.

The foreign was not the only new frontier of information: access to illustrated, well-printed Chinese texts continued to increase, thanks in no small
part to the efforts of the Shenbao guan. One story begins by stating that, according to another newspaper, an eyewitness who saw a beggar with a two-
headed pig drew a picture and pasted it up everywhere to transmit the story,
creating one of the informal publications that was a predecessor for *Dianshizhai huabao*. The narrator notes that in the past he had often doubted such
stories, since they were often fabricated by men fond of the strange and confirmed with contrived evidence from other lovers of hearsay. However, recently he had observed that the illustrations of the *Tushu jicheng* 圖書集成
portray items not found in the *Erya* 爾雅 and *Shan hai jing*. He closes: "If one
has seen little and is amazed by much, one can't help being mocked by the
erudite. I can't help but reverse Mencius' statement: if one does not believe
books, it is better not to have books."[29]

The rhetorical pose of the converted skeptic is common in earlier *zhiguai*,
but the textual context of credulity and incredulity has changed. The two-
headed pig story provides a survey of the late nineteenth-century textual
world: an informal, illustrated *xinwen zhi* 新聞紙, a primarily textual newspaper, the pictorial itself, and older illustrated texts that had recently been
republished all have a role to play. The central theme of the caption is
transmission, *chuan* 傳, which appears on three levels: the two-headed pig's
own complex line of transmission, the idea of fabrication and spurious oral
transmission of oddities, and the relation between published, illustrated
texts of varying degrees of antiquity. Both the second and the third level
serve as frames for the two-headed pig: the traditionally subversive force of
oral transmission of the strange and amusing casts doubt on the particular
example, and the more respectable forces of older but recently republished
books dispel that doubt. That the venerable *Shan hai jing* and *Erya* are
eclipsed by a Qing encyclopedia suggests the possibility of new knowledge

and discovery. This passage also serves as a "product placement" for one of the Shenbao guan's publications: a reprint of the *Gujin tushu jicheng* 古今圖書集成 was one of the larger book publishing projects of the Shenbao guan from 1885 to 1888, and Major had compared the *Dianshizhai huabao* to this work in his preface to the first issue.[30] In the end, the new trajectory of eyewitness to informal publication to newspaper to pictorial is affiliated with authoritative books rather than gossip. The final joke reversing a classical quotation suggests that one adopt a stance of absolute credulity in facing this burgeoning textual world, but this is not a serious conclusion. What matters is that the issue of doubt and belief is staged at all, for it is by framing the display of the marvel within this equivocating debate about truth and falsehood that this story is distinguished from the spreading of stories by lovers of the strange for their own pleasure. This story further establishes expectations that the new publishing culture will make anomaly widely accessible. It both indulges a taste for amazement and insists that the sophisticated reader will not be unduly amazed.

Visual and verbal transmission are intertwined in ways that seem to give the visual more credibility than the verbal alone. Of the three levels of transmission, only the least credible, the fabrications of lovers of the strange, has no visual element. Although Mencius' original quote referred to texts rather than illustrations, the gesture to credulity is made in the context of respectable, illustrated books. Nevertheless, because *Dianshizhai* gleaned this story from an unillustrated newspaper, the narrator does not claim a direct relationship between the illustration that accompanies his story and the eyewitnesses' sketch, in effect admitting this is a reconstruction based on a verbal description. The illustration in the pictorial does not suggest transmission, leaving that to the textual caption, but simply suggests profitable display: the piglet is in the foreground, with onlookers of various ages and both sexes arrayed behind it, the women leaning out of a doorway, and the beggar kneeling, gesturing toward his product.

Another story directly admits the impact of new technologies on the circulation of strange tales.

Since childhood I have heard the popular tales of wandering figures of the type known as the "iron abacus." It is said they can command ghosts to remove people's gold and silver without the victims' knowledge. I can't help doubting this story. Why in the forty years I've been in the world has no one been able to offer any proof? Some might say, "You inhabit one tiny corner, regarding the sea in a ladle, like a frog in a well; how could you know the expanses of the world?" But recently the telegraph cables have been connected everywhere, and a forest of newspaper articles stand, so that when a strange story occurs, it is known by the entire world. But if there really were such people, their followers should appear constantly, because what method of getting rich could be easier than this? What proof is there? When newspaper reports come, I still can't help being filled with doubts.[31]

Like the previous anecdote, this story links dubious oral narrative and the newspapers. The new technology, far from supplanting oddity and marvel, ensures its universal transmission.[32] This anecdote turns the assertion that one cannot judge the entire world based on one's own limited experience on its head: in a world of modern communications, no frog lives in a well. Following this skeptical opening, the narrator relates a tale of a gentry family who refuse to give alms to a pair of Daoists and later discover money and jewelry missing, arousing suspicion that the two were practitioners of the "iron abacus." The narrator expresses uncertainty about this interpretation. The illustration, as sometimes happens in *Dianshizhai*, shows two different narrative moments in the same image: the foreground portrays the Daoists' initial begging at the door, and the background, astonished family members opening an empty chest while two cloud-treading Daoists escape with the loot. The family's interpretation of events, questioned in the caption, is displayed on the same plane of reality as begging and the discovery that property is missing in the illustration. In contrast to the illustration of the piglet, in which the *Dianshizhai* reader shares in the same spectacle as the beggar's audience, the viewer of this illustration sees what the characters in the picture only imagine. (This common gap between skeptical text and credulous illustration is discussed below.) As in the previous anecdote, the impact of expanded communications on credulity and incredulity is ambiguous, but what the new world of media lacks in certainty it makes up for in quantity of the weird. The discrepancy between acceptance of a two-headed piglet and lingering doubt about a pair of sorcerers is explained by the fact that monstrous animals, in contrast to human sorcerers, do not pose a threat to the social order. The idea of the iron abacus is based on a fear of beggars and other transients who threaten to violate the boundaries of the household, and the narrator is interested in squelching both that fear and the hope of easy riches.

In the strange tales in both *Shenbao* and *Dianshizhai*, there is a conviction, continuing from the earlier *zhiguai* tradition, that writing about the weird needed to be justified, and that this could be done in terms of both knowledge and pleasure. Yet in *Dianshizhai* a few captions reveal an awareness of the changed terms of both knowledge and entertainment in the new world of mass media and communications. The *Shenbao* makes terser evocations of both knowledge and pleasure and does not seem to acknowledge changes self-consciously.

News Stories as zhiguai

Reading the anecdotes that appeared in these periodicals in the context of the *zhiguai* tradition is reasonable, because that is how they positioned themselves. Stories are deliberately affiliated with the written tradition about anomalies, with the names of *Liaozhai* or *Sou shen ji* often dropped in reference to ghosts and foxes, and the *Shan hai jing* invoked as the authority on weird animals.[33] The presence of a few of Ji Yun's 紀昀 (1724–1805) anecdotes in the main body of *Dianshizhai huabao* and of Wang Tao's 王韜 (1828–97) longer *chuanqi* 傳奇 tales in the supplements makes the relationship even more plain.[34]

Tales of the supernatural cannot be considered one of the principal topics of the *Shenbao*, but they are a recurring presence; in the years between 1872 and 1884, on the average one such story appeared roughly every five or six days.[35] Their number seems to grow gradually smaller over the course of the 1890s. The content is to a great extent comparable to earlier and contemporary *zhiguai*, including accounts of supernatural romances, haunting by snakes, ghost encounters, local cults, and poems received by planchette. The proportion of strange stories in *Dianshizhai* is higher and remains high throughout its run, save on those occasions when political news, often war reportage, monopolizes the pages of the pictorial.

Because *zhiguai* are presented as unembellished reportage of bizarre events, the stylistic similarities between journalistic accounts of the strange and the older genre are unsurprising. Like *zhiguai*, the basic format of the periodicals' stories is narration in relatively simple classical Chinese, often followed by a final comment. The *Shenbao* presents the strange in two ways that correspond loosely to the traditional generic divisions of *zhiguai* and *chuanqi*.[36] Stories in the first category are relatively simple incidents, and although they may mention the mundane details of daily life, they focus on content rather than style. On the other hand, longer, more elaborate tales are presented primarily as elegant entertainments, influenced perhaps by European models of serialized fiction. There is less generic variation in *Dianshizhai*, perhaps because of the relatively constant length of the stories.

The *Shenbao* does not seem to share the compulsion for interpretation evident in many Qing *zhiguai* collections. Many strange events are recorded without a moral or logical explanation of why or how such a thing should happen.[37] *Dianshizhai huabao* seems to have a stronger inclination toward explanation; if explanation is absent, that absence is emphasized. The pictorial provides incidents with more elaborate frames of introductory remarks and final judgments, whereas *Shenbao* is more likely to append only a terse assessment of the tale's credibility and perhaps its source. *Dianshizhai*'s introductory remarks often make general statements about the type of incident before moving on to the specific case, and it is these comments that contain the most references to other texts or traditions. The pictorial's more elaborate apparatus might be explained by either its nature as a second-generation publication, which often reprinted material that had appeared elsewhere, or its self-presentation as leisure reading rather than concentrated information. A more prosaic and material possibility is that the *Dianshizhai* captions are relatively uniform in length for visual reasons, whereas *Shenbao* stories could vary widely in length.

One striking difference from many earlier *zhiguai* is the anonymity of narratives in both periodicals, whether they involve strange encounters, family disputes, or crime. Although precise place-names are provided, often with urban street names, most of the protagonists are "so and so" 某 or at most "Wang So and so." Earlier *zhiguai* collections exhibit a broad range of specificity, from chronologically and geographically precise accounts told by named informants to anonymous third-person stories; the most dubious or allegorical stories are related with the vaguest provenances. Thus even more striking than the anonymity of the participants in newspaper stories is the anonymity of the informants, who in both periodicals are described simply as "friends" 友 and "guests" 客. Many of the most famous Qing collections named informants, most often members of the author's social circle. Why did more "modern" journalism lead to a movement away from precision? Rather than arguing that this anonymity protects the innocent or covers up for fabrication, I think it serves to preserve the outer circles of earlier *zhiguai*, by describing incidents among strangers of different social classes, while eliminating the inner circles of anecdotes relating the experiences of the author's family and friends. The anonymity of sources admits that such events are no longer limited to a single author's social circle and helps to establish a more distant, collective narratorial authority for the newspaper. A quasi-social relationship with those who submit stories, and by extension the readers, is still posited, but the smaller social circle is eliminated in favor of a larger one.

When the strange is presented in periodicals, we expect it to be contemporary as well as strange. In earlier *zhiguai*, the freshness of an incident in time was less important than its oddity. Nevertheless there were temporal limits. In the Qing the typical *zhiguai* collection's contents could include events that happened immediately before the author wrote them down, stories from his childhood, and stories from two or three previous generations. The cutoff point for the earliest stories for Qianlong-era authors, for example, seems to be the fall of the Ming; for Guangxu-era authors, the Qianlong.[38] In both periodicals, this time frame is shortened further, but not as much as one might expect. The two seem to have slightly different senses of time. As a daily paper, the *Shenbao* puts greater emphasis on the recent date of incidents or at least the recent reception of correspondence relating the incidents. Since *Dianshizhai* often reprises stories from other publications and had a longer gap (ten days) between issues, its sense of time is more vague and its immediacy diminished. Its stories are set in a general "recent" time more often than they are given exact dates, but events from many years ago are rarely presented. Often the recent event is deliberately framed in terms of historical or anecdotal precedents: "In books there are many tales of x."

Although on the printed page a strange story in the *Shenbao* does not appear very different from a tale in a *zhiguai* collection or *biji*, the tales in *Dianshizhai huabao* are transformed by illustration. Most earlier *zhiguai* had not been illustrated. The notable exception appears to have been the *Shan hai jing*, a text of disputed date, which introduces the bizarre creatures of distant places.[39] Early references to this work allude to illustrations, and some traditional critics thought the text had been composed as explications of pictures now lost, perhaps the legendary illustrations of strange beings of distant places that the sage-king Yu had ordered cast on the nine tripods.[40] The centrality of illustration to this text seems related to its nature as a storehouse of geographic, zoological, and botanical information rather than individual experience. Its chimerical creatures would be difficult to imagine without illustrations. From the late Ming through the early Qing, long and elaborate sagas of the supernatural, whether vernacular novels or, less frequently, *chuanqi* tales, were frequently illustrated, but the brief individual experience of the *zhiguai* ("Wang the Third from Qingzhou met a ghost one night"; "in Sichuan a calf with two heads was born") was not. Most *zhiguai* were preserved either in large anthologies (such as *Taiping guangji* 太平廣記) or individual author's *biji*, whose profusion of small narratives seemed to have discouraged illustration.[41] Even the most famous representative of the genre, *Liaozhai zhiyi*, was not illustrated until 1885, when a competitive publishing market and new technologies, such as lithography, caused previously unillustrated texts to be illustrated.[42] Thus the pictorial not only offers a new format of illustration but renders visual a class of narrative that had been exclusively textual.

The Many Voices of the Strange in the Shenbao

The most significant change a daily newspaper allows, in comparison to a personal collection or an anthology, is the multiplicity of voices that can be brought to bear on a single story over successive days. Stories can bring immediate response from readers, in the form of elaboration, contradiction, or explanation. The existence of this form of exchange proves that the *zhiguai* in the newspaper are not static vestigial remnants but evolving topics. This new polyphony affects even the most familiar of all *zhiguai* topics, karmic retribution. Rewards for the good and punishment for the wicked have been one of the mainstays of the *zhiguai* tradition since its foundation and were particularly popular in the Qing.[43] Successive accounts of a man allegedly slain by mice are a vivid example of an interchange that could not have been contained in earlier *zhiguai*. The initial account tells the story of a man who delighted in killing mice and is in consequence bitten to death by mice.[44] An expansion signed with a pseudonym follows almost a month later. Its author claims the victim was his friend, and his death was even crueler than the earlier story had suggested.[45] A week later a response, also signed with a pseudonym, is printed, claiming to come from a relative of the victim.[46] This third piece contends that the man's death was the result of a prolonged illness and that the tale of karmic revenge is a malicious slander.

Killing mice seems the most banal of crimes against life. This kind of punishment is more usually reserved for butchers or carnivorous gluttons, but the combination of pettiness and disproportionate response sets the mood for the entire exchange. Karmic interpretations, by their inherent structure, serve to make private vices public, but the nature of publicity is changed. This story is neither historically specific nor an anonymous illustration of the consequences of taking life: all the participants are identified only by surname or pseudonym, but the exchange of voices suggests that individual identities lurk below the surface. Although strange tales had been used in earlier periods to besmirch reputations (for example, the Tang tale of the white gibbon reputed to be someone's ancestor, *Bujiang zong baiyuan zhuan* 補江總白猿傳),[47] the potential for multiple voices and immediate response here is new. Since the meaning of karmic explanations resides in the link created between events, rather than in the events themselves, they are by their nature subject to interpretation and possible dispute but here their contested nature is dramatized. In this series karmic retribution is presented first as a simple fact and then as a grotesque display and ultimately revealed as a potentially powerful weapon in social interchange. Both supernatural revenge and its slanderous fabrication have become interesting reading topics. Although the dismissal of gory karmic revenge gets the last word, it does not erase the earlier story. Rather, it allows readers a range of choices. The paper's self-reference seems to assume a group of loyal, continuing readers who would be interested in all these choices.

A few years later, the old theme of karmic rewards for good behavior is transformed as it takes a specific, contemporary form, reward for charitable contributions (*zhuzhen* 助賑). The rise of this theme can be pinpointed with some historical accuracy: such stories are most common in the *Shenbao* around 1878 and recur for the next two decades. In both periodicals the message of karmic efficacy of charity is repeatedly hammered home in tales of supernatural intervention: an illness is miraculously cured; a man has a dream in which heavenly hosts tell him that active solicitation of charitable donations will move forward the year of his success in the examinations; the accumulated virtue of charitable donations makes it easier to exorcise a fox; a spirit descends to the planchette to urge the people attending the séance to make donations.[48] A current issue incorporates every possible variation of otherworldly response to human virtue. Moreover, the newspaper took a particularly active role in the promotion of this virtue by publishing lists of the people who made donations and noting how much they had given.[49] It became a crucial link in a new organization of karmic repayment. In one account a woman suffering from a chronic illness reads a newspaper report of cures brought about by charitable donations. She burns incense and vows to contribute a particular amount and is immediately cured.[50] This story resembles nothing so much as a testimonial in an advertisement. This story appeared in 1900, when the overall frequency of reports of supernatural incidents in the newspaper had diminished considerably, proving that karmic reward was among the most durable themes. A link between publication and karmic justice is not new—there are earlier accounts of men cured by particular deities printing and pasting up accounts of the divinity's efficacy in gratitude—but the newspaper's central role in organizing a specific form of virtue and reward is.

The new relationship between reader and author the newspaper makes possible is represented in the front-page article "Discussing Strange Matters." It relates three baffling cases of spontaneous human combustion: one heard recently from "people on the road," one from the author's own experience forty years earlier, and one from Yuan Mei's 袁枚 (1716–97) Zi bu yu 子不語 (Things of which the Master did not speak), a zhiguai collection from almost a century earlier. Forty years ago, when the author was celebrating the New Year at the home of an unnamed kinsman, an old married couple went to bed early. When the two failed to appear the next morning, the family went into their room to investigate and found the two dead, the woman lying on the floor and the man sitting at the edge of the bed, gripping a tobacco pipe. Their hands, mouths, and nostrils had been reduced to ashes, but there were no signs of damage to the tobacco pipe or other objects in the room. Ever since this inexplicable event, the author had been asking knowledgeable men for an explanation, but no one could help him. Now a recent story has jogged his memory, and he turns to the newspaper to answer a question unresolved by conventional means. "Since now in Shanghai there are many Chinese and Western gentlemen who are knowledgeable in gezhi 格致, I want to seek them all to instruct me to clear up decades of confusion."[51] Gezhi, a term found in the Great Learning, meaning "inquiring into and extending knowledge," became one of the possible translations for the European concept of science.[52] Recent hearsay, older personal experience, and textual reference could come together in a personal zhiguai collection as well, but here, on an added level, Shanghai is a special cultural space in which old mysteries can be solved through an active dialogue between the recorder and interpreters of the strange.

This essay in turn draws a front-page response, which replies to the stories of combustion with stories of human transformation into water and stone. Strikingly, the attribution of the story of transformation into stone to an American newspaper adds to the collage-like quality of the *Shenbao*'s contents. The respondent dismisses all these second- and third-hand stories as hearsay but considers the eyewitness account from the previous article worthy of investigation. He offers an entirely naturalistic explanation for the events. By invoking the petrified standing forms of Italian earthquake victims as evidence, the author suggests that strange events in China can be explicated in terms of an international context. He closes with a general dismissal of the supernatural: strange events that can be explained should not be considered strange.

The editors of the newspaper append a response, identifying the author of this submission, Jia Shancheng 嘉善程, as a man very fond of *gezhi*. After this flattering introduction, the editorial comment provides details that refute his theory and reiterate the desire for a Western perspective on this problem.[53] The editorial voice prefers to leave the strange unexplained rather than have the mystery solved; it especially prefers not to have all possible mysteries debunked. In this debate, *gezhi* still allows space for both Western and local ideas about the natural world.[54] In the editorial stance the *Shenbao* takes here, a Western perspective is seen as a valuable addition but not an overwhelming one, and not one that undermines interest in the bizarre.

These three examples—the victim of the mice, rewards for charitable donations, and debate over spontaneous human combustion—present three different subgeneric settings for the newspaper's polyphony: the incident in the center pages of the paper, the enumeration of donations at the end, and front-page editorials. These different placements in the paper help determine the effect of the idea of the vocal, active readership, whether it is gossip, self-promotion, or debate.

The Foreign and the Strange

The intersection between the foreign and the strange is one of the most obvious changes in the *zhiguai* in late Qing periodicals and reveals a fascinating contrast between the two publications. Curiosities of distant lands had been one of the categories of *zhiguai* since the *Shan hai jing*, but the supply of knowledge about them expanded exponentially in the late Qing. In the 1870s and 1880s, the foreign did not keep itself at the edges of the concentric circles of an ordered world, as it had in the *Shan hai jing*, but took up residence in the Chinese-yet-marvelous realm of Shanghai and, its extension, the Shanghai press. As a result the strangeness of the foreign became more nuanced, interwoven with other forms of strangeness.[55] Since the authors and editors had access to accounts of what foreigners themselves considered curiosities,[56] individual events, rather than general "odd customs," could be recorded. Rudolf Wagner describes this innovation as incorporating the Chinese into a "worldwide exchange on the level of the imaginary."[57]

This global exchange creates a new imagined geography in which anomaly can both link and distinguish the Chinese from the foreign, but with different results in the two periodicals. In the *Shenbao* the foreign is used primarily as a voice to comment on the Chinese supernatural, rather than displayed as oddity. In *Dianshizhai*, however, foreigners are both anomalies and the audience for anomalies; they are seldom presented, however, as an authoritative voice. In the *Shenbao* the geography of the strange is confined within the borders of China; in *Dianshizhai* weirdness is global. The greater prominence of the foreign in *Dianshizhai* is caused in part by its gleaning of notable oddities from other publications, both domestic and foreign. Kim lists examples of comparable dwarves, giants, half-humans, and monstrous births occurring in both China and various places overseas.[58] Nevertheless, the pictorial creates its own geography of anomaly. Monstrous births, crimes of passion, and natural disasters occur throughout the world, but foreign ghosts are rare.[59] Japan and Korea share fox spirits and some forms of black magic, which do not appear further afield.[60]

In *Dianshizhai huabao* a range of different relations between the foreign and the strange is possible. Foreignness can be an intermediate state between strange and normal. On the one hand, in some ways foreigners, by becoming a standard part of the pictorial's palette, are normalized, understandable given the Shanghai setting. A story about an earthquake, monstrous birth, or crime of passion set overseas focuses more on the violence or weirdness of the event than on ethnic identity. On the other hand, foreigners can add an extra degree of oddity, whether they are among the observers of a Chinese marvel or the marvels themselves, as when a giant is also a Westerner.[61] China and the rest of the world can be fit into a single matrix of strangeness, with both Chinese and foreigners staring in wonder at a strange creature. Alternatively, the strange can be an area of contention between Western and Chinese perceptions. Most important, both foreigners and Chinese are involved in a new economy of display of the anomaly for profit, whether overseas, in the Chinese provinces, or, most prominently, in Shanghai itself.

An anomalous early case in the *Shenbao* displays several layers of ideas about the foreign. "Tan ying xiaolu" 談瀛小錄 (A small record discussing foreign places) was serialized at considerable length over several consecutive days. This work is patently an abridged translation of the Lilliputian episode from *Gulliver's Travels*; it is foreign in both origin and content. But the traveler's origins are shifted to coastal China, and the text is introduced as an old, moldering manuscript submitted by a friend and surmised to have come from some literati family's library. Given the Shenbao guan's energetic commitment to seeking out and publishing rare manuscripts, this is not an implausible frame. The selections omit some of the satirical commentary on Lilliputian society in favor of the physical comedy resulting from the disparity in sizes.[62] In content it recalls accounts, printed elsewhere in the *Shenbao*, of experiences of Japanese or Okinawan merchants shipwrecked among the Taiwanese aborigines. The similarity of the content both to those shipwreck narratives and to *Jing hua yuan* 鏡花緣, as well as to other accounts of Chinese traveling in the larger world, may have ensured that this text did not feel entirely foreign and could easily be accepted as Chinese. After all, a Kingdom of Little People had already been recorded in the *Shan hai jing*.[63] A vision of the foreign from early in Europe's age of expansion is easily digestible to the Chinese in a century of Chinese wandering, made easier by parallels with traditional ideas of foreign strangeness.

This is an example of a tentative and experimental early age of translation, before the overwhelming success of Lin Shu's 林紓 (1852–1924) work.[64] The editor/translator apparently decided a double layer of foreignness, a European among the Lilliputians, would reduce the story's appeal. (It is interesting that the shipwreck experiences of non-Chinese Asians, in contrast, were presented as such.) A few days later, the story of Rip Van Winkle is also translated to Chinese soil, as the experience of a man named Wei who had always been fascinated by Daoist teachings.[65] It is striking that both of these early translations deal with the strange. In 1872 the content of an encounter with a strange, exotic people was of interest, but the text's identity as a foreign work was not. A decade later the editors and artists of *Dianshizhai* would make the opposite decision when Englishmen were shown confronting weird races in Africa or India. This could be explained by a change in genre or in historical moment. Copying images from foreign pictorials might be a fundamentally different relationship from translating a foreign text, or perhaps "double foreignness" was more successfully conveyed visually than verbally. Alternatively, perhaps the taste for foreignness had developed in the decade between 1872 and *Dianshizhai*'s printing in the 1880s.

In an example of the creation of a shared matrix of strangeness in *Dian-shizhai huabao*, two anecdotes about strange turtles, one foreign and one Chinese, are displayed side by side. The foreign turtle has a human head, whereas the Chinese one has the character for long life on its back and an inscription of astrological significance in smaller characters on its belly. There are textual references (from *Shiji* 史記 and *Shu yi ji* 述異記) explaining the inscribed turtle, but none for the human-headed turtle. The story closes, "As for these two turtles, one was born overseas, and the other was born in China, and now they are painted in the same issue and recorded in detail. That these two turtles, Chinese and foreign, are gathered together in the same category can also bring glory to the reptilian order."[66] Animals are territory where the foreign and the domestic strange, as well as the ancient textual tradition of the *Shan hai jing* and nineteenth-century biological science, can meet, yet the Chinese turtle, in contrast to its foreign counterpart, has a culturally specific, comprehensible content. The contrast is made stronger in the illustrations, with scholarly examination of the Chinese turtle (including clever use of a mirror so that the characters on both sides of the turtle are visible) contrasting with the Western fisherman's bewilderment. The self-conscious attention to the grouping of these anecdotes calls just as much attention to the separate cultural spheres as to the shared topic; a shared matrix of strangeness does not eliminate differences.

A more common means of constructing a single world of marvel is the routine links made between contemporary foreign oddities and classical texts: an account of a hot-air balloon closes, "One could even overtake Liezi walking on the clouds."[67] How seriously is the link between new technology and an ancient levitating immortal to be taken? Placing the foreign novelty in a Chinese context could be read as a humorous gesture, an explanation, or an attempt at containment.[68] As Wang Ermin notes, the allusions were not difficult for readers.[69] I would argue that they are light touches, with the gap between allusion and reference entertaining rather than jarring. The reader could at the same time be delighted with visual marvel and textual familiarity, demonstrating the strength and flexibility of clichés, which are not strained by such uses.[70] Both sides of these comparisons, novelty and the textual tradition, are marketable products for the Shenbao guan.

Fig. 8.1 "Xingtian zhi liu" 刑天之流, DSZ, *Ji* 己 (1.6) 9, 68, beginning of the second month, Guangxu 12, 3/6/1886. Drawn by Wu Youru 吳友如 (d. 1893).

The account of an Italian female convict's headless baby is an extreme example of the blending of strangeness from different sources. According to the first explanation provided, her fear that she would lose her own head deformed her fetus. But that explanation is overridden by identification of her child with one of the exotic species of the *Shan hai jing*, the *xingtian* 形天. After the *xingtian* had been beheaded for its crimes, it took its nipples as eyes and its navel as a mouth and danced with shield and spear.[71] The *xingtian* seems to have been a particular favorite to relocate at the edge of the world; a century earlier Ji Yun heard stories of them in the outer reaches of the Qing empire.[72] As the edge of the world is redrawn as the new exotic, older ideas of the exotic and an interest in monstrous births merge. The illustration itself is probably a pastiche, the figures of the mother and the astounded guards probably copied from a foreign periodical, and the image of the *xingtian* modeled on *Shan hai jing* illustrations[73] (Fig. 8.1). In the text, the *Shan hai jing* provides the answer for a case that baffled the foreigners. This kind of esoteric knowledge is one of the traditional justifications for strange texts, especially the Shan hai jing itself. This identification, with its air of smug satisfaction, rather than interpretation of the monstrous birth's meaning becomes the crucial point of the story.[74] The Shan hai jing's geography was discredited long ago, but it still acts as a useful bestiary; in later anecdotes it is habitually called on to classify chimeras and animals with excess limbs. The connection between current monstrous births and the old text adds significance to both.

Chinese Travelers Face the Foreign and the Strange

It was not only the gaze of the pictorial that roamed outside China, finding oddity. This was an era of Chinese travelers, whose experience, as recorded in Dianshizhai, compounds the foreign and the strange. An anecdote about a Japanese fox opens, "In the world seductive women are called foxes, because they are good at beguiling men. If a 'foxy' person can already beguile a man, how much more can a real fox, let alone a foreign fox?"[75] Foreignness is in the same category as foxiness—both have a capacity to beguile, and the two reinforce each other. A ravenous Chinese traveler lands on an unnamed Japanese island known for a high population of foxes. Substituting food for the more traditional lure of sex, a beautiful woman invites him to her place for a meal. He follows her eagerly until the sound of Western troops doing military exercises nearby alarms her. As she flees, she reveals her true form as a fox. Japan has its own fox lore, and the inclusion of these anecdotes could be a reflection of local beliefs; the presence of foxes is a sign that it is in a different category of foreign than the West.[76]

The danger of the foreign bewitching a Chinese youth links this story to an earlier account of a young merchant in Singapore seduced by a "black" (presumably Malay) woman. After he rebuffs her advances, she uses black magic to bewitch him. Only when his uncle hires an exorcist is he restored to his senses.[77] Both stories develop the image of the world overseas as a realm of temptation and danger for Chinese men, but it is danger they overcome.[78] Foreign beauty is flawed by ethnic or species markers. Just as the Malaysian woman's blackness discredits her claim on her lover's affections, the Japanese vixen is undermined by her tail. Although foxes in stories from earlier dynasties had had trouble concealing their tails, by the Qing most vixens never let them show.[79] The illustration accompanying this story

Fig. 8.2 "Yaohu xianmei"
妖狐獻媚, DSZ, Zi 子 (2.1)
7, 56, middle of the eighth
month, Guangxu 13,
9/27/1887. Drawn by
Jin Gui 金桂.

makes a visual link between the woman's obi and her tail, two marks of otherness; one suspects the tail is included purely for this reason. The man's long queue as he is seen from the back is in turn the unmistakable marker of his ethnic identity (Fig 8.2). The illustrations thus grant the reader additional immunity to foreign charms; in contrast, stories of domestic vixens and amorous ghosts often show them as glamorous humans with no hint of their true identities.[80] In the tale of the Japanese fox, Western soldiers' gunfire plays the role, usually reserved for hunting dogs, of exposing and expelling the fox; they are also given a place in the illustration, seen from the back on a distant ridge. An old story of attempted seduction and exorcism is performed by a multicultural cast. *Dianshizhai huabao* creates a geography full of stages for such encounters.[81]

Another story of exorcism with an international cast plays out in Vietnam. A merchant's son goes mad and babbles, "How bitter were our deaths! Just because we coveted momentary profit, we helped the French to attack the walls and moats. Blood and flesh flew through the air, and there was

Fig. 8.3 "Ming bing huantan" 名并桓檀, *DSZ, Wu* 午 (2.7) 8, 59, end of the eighth month, Guangxu 15, 9/15/1889. Drawn by Zhang Qi 張淇.

nowhere to bury our corpses. Now the French live in peace and pleasure, but we are starving souls, with nothing to rely on. Where can we vent our wrongs?" A translation reveals that these are the voices of African soldiers. When conventional means of exorcism fail, the possessing spirits are driven away by a group masquerading as the Chinese troops who had battled the French forces.[82] The illustration shows the moment of exorcism, with the sham army entering from the right, the patient, marked as Vietnamese by his headdress, reclining in the middle, and the black ghosts departing through the window on the left (Fig. 8.3). The reader sees the ghosts, who according to the narrative have been visible only to their victim. Recent history, which had been chronicled thoroughly in earlier issues of the pictorial, is retold as a ghost story, with a Chinese victory replayed.[83] This recapitulation is all the more necessary because the confrontation in Vietnam was actually humiliating for the Chinese. Traditionally, an exorcism is a validation of the exorcist and can also be a joke at the expense of the exorcised, whose weaknesses are revealed. Like Japan and Korea, Vietnam is culturally close enough to China for a comprehensible exorcism story to be played out, but the role of the ghost can be filled by a more alien foreigner. Ideas about the low status of the Africans are reinforced by their low status as ghosts, as the derogatory term "black devil" 黑鬼 and the conflation of all foreigners with ghosts hovers over the story. In the illustration, the ghosts' two kinds of strangeness reinforce each other: they are black, and they carry their severed heads in their hands. This story is a vivid dramatization of the colonial world, in which empires can bedevil the most distant regions with exotic ghosts, who torment the local people. The colonial rulers do not take part in these transactions. Different kinds of foreignness and different kinds of supernatural beings reinforce one another, making the seductive even more false and seductive, the despised and pathetic even more laughable.

The foreign and the marvelous blended in another way, creating a new territory, in the supplemental sections at the end of *Dianshizhai huabao*, where Wang Tao's *Songyin manlu* 淞隱漫錄 (also known as *Hou Liaozhai* 後聊齋) was printed in lavishly illustrated installments.[84] The presence of his tales, highly elaborate *chuanqi* on the model of *Liaozhai*, in the supplements illustrates both the kinship of such material to the rest of the pictorial and the difference between the two: they are printed under the same cover but in a distinct format. With one page of illustration separate from three pages of text, the image-text relationship is fundamentally different from the stories in the body of the pictorial. In one story, a grand tour of Europe is interwoven with a sojourn in Daoist fairyland. A man is swept off to Mount Emei by a mysterious Daoist, but once it is revealed that he has yet to overcome his carnal desires, he is sent plummeting to earth, more precisely, to Scotland. There he observes naval exercises, enjoys the company of two lovely European women, and sees all the sights, notably including the Crystal Palace, museums, and all the most prominent institutions of display. As the traveler wends his way from Switzerland to Berlin, the Daoist suddenly reappears, asks whether he has enjoyed his European trip, and flies away on a dragon.[85]

This ending is as ambiguous as it is abrupt. It plainly alludes to the "Zhenzhong ji" 枕中記 / "Nanke taishou zhuan" 南柯太守傳 tradition, in which a lifetime of wealth and glory is revealed as an illusion, but that conclusion is not made explicit. This sort of ending, bringing fantasy to an arbitrary end, is typical of this collection. One suspects that it is prompted by practical considerations rather than any necessity in the plot: almost all of these stories consist of three pages of text. The story may have ended when it filled up its allotted space, a dramatic illustration of the impact of material conditions on literature.[86] This story, save the ending, is a reworking of Wang Tao's journey, an account of which was reprinted and illustrated in the *Dianshizhai* supplements after *Songying manlu* and its sequel had been completed: actual and fantasy journeys occupy the same space. All the marvels of Western Europe are contained within a familiar Chinese genre and converted into the islands of Penglai. This seems possible only in the special space between journalism and entertainment fiction that Wang Tao commanded, perhaps the first of his kind in China.

The established patterns of supernatural seduction, marvelous dream, and exorcism are applied to the world outside China, adding the luster of the exotic to the familiar. *Dianshizhai huabao* promotes consumption of foreign anomaly in a way that the *Shenbao* does not. For its readers, the world was weird, but not all of it was weird in precisely the same way. Borrowing from other periodicals' collections of oddities results in a warping in the traditional center and periphery arrangement of the *zhiguai* collection: since European periodicals are important sources, Europe is both a center of another sphere and an exotic margin, and Africa becomes the margin of margins. In both periodicals, although others can be anomalies or consumers of anomalies, among foreigners only Westerners have a voice as judges of the strange.

Debating the Strange with the Foreigner

The strange could be used to define the difference between the Chinese and the foreign, not only by seeing foreigners as anomalies but also by constructing Westerners in particular as a group with peculiar and contradictory attitudes toward the strange. On the one hand, Westerners are linked to strangeness because they are perceived as particularly obsessed with the collection, display, and analysis of oddities, as shown in the institution of the museum discussed above. On the other hand, they are seen as intractable skeptics regarding the supernatural. In the former role Westerners appear in the pages of *Dianshizhai* as collectors and spectators; in the latter, a Western voice is deployed in arguments of truth and falsehood in both periodicals.

Tales of punitive lightning strikes are among the strange events recorded most frequently in both publications.[87] One such tale opens with a juxtaposition of the two views: "The Chinese say lightning is the anger of heaven, and those who are struck must have committed secret misdeeds; Westerners say when the electricity in the human body clashes with the lightning in the air, the person will die, but it is not necessarily the case that he has done good or evil deeds. Arguments about this are plentiful, and who will ask heaven to clear [the issue] up?" Although the tale opens with that voice of doubt, the answer it gives is clear: lightning strikes the tongue of a bawd and the ears of a male servant in a brothel, with the precise targeting underlining the point.[88] In another story the confrontation with the perceived Western view of lightning is personified in the servant of a Western minister traveling from Shandong to Tianjin by boat who is dramatically struck and engulfed in flame. The picture adds an additional element of vindication, with the amazed minister gazing from his boat at the blazing victim on land.[89] The narrator finds it implausible that this man was struck by chance. In this case a traveling Westerner confronts the strange on Chinese soil, but he himself is not the victim. In contrast, the *Shenbao* takes a more analytical approach. Rather than simply resolving the debate on lightning with an example, one article carefully distinguished between the meaning of lightning striking animate and inanimate objects.[90] Lightning was an especially contentious subject because it was both a form of electricity, relevant to the scientific and technical ideas being introduced into China, and the embodiment of the moral will of the universe, which must have seemed the most defensible form of the supernatural.[91]

In another example, a story in the *Shenbao* presents a confrontation between Western and Chinese attitudes toward the strange in oblique form, and a later version in *Dianshizhai* makes the confrontation more explicit and smug. The *Shenbao* article "Strange Creatures at Sea" opens:

The four seas are so large that there is no creature which does not exist there, and no beast that is not provided there, but men have seen little and so are easily amazed. Our paper earlier recounted the appearance of a giant snake among the islands at sea. All over Europe no one believed it, thinking that there are certainly no such giant creatures. Now we have seen the report of men who encountered a strange beast at sea and, fearing they would not be believed, went to the consulate and swore an oath. We translated their account in order to show that it [the snake we reported] was not unique and had a companion.[92]

There follows a translation of the ship captain's sworn deposition at the consulate. The huge turtle-like creature is described in great detail, and the measurements of its body, head, neck, and tail are given. It is noted that the creature was observed by both Chinese and Western passengers. The *Shenbao* confronts the skeptics with "their own" words, but this performance is really addressed to the predominately Chinese readership.

When a Western ship encounters a dragon, the unidentified, primarily zoological leviathan is replaced with the culturally specific. The account in *Dianshizhai* begins:

Accounts of dragons in old books heap up to the rafters and would make oxen sweat to move them. It is not certain that each and every one is an eyewitness account, yet still it is certain that they were not simply fabricated to deceive posterity. The Westerners are said to be good at empirical study, and they argue forcefully that these creatures do not exist. And Chinese, since dragons are seldom seen, agree with them. They listen to what they hear and imitate other people's faults.

Now, however, a Western newspaper has printed an account of an encounter off the coast of Africa with a mysterious, long-bodied, scaly creature. The story concludes:

But when Westerners conclude whether something does or does not exist, they depend on careful examination of the truth; this is called "not believing anything without proof." The Chinese know that dragons' transformations are unfathomable. Rising or descending at any moment, their bodies protected by clouds and wind, their greatness is displayed in thunder and lightning, how could one measure them in terms of ordinary, commonly seen things? One should use the Chinese to transform the barbarian, not be transformed by them.[93]

In contrast to the lightning example, the denial of dragons reveals not so much amorality as narrow-mindedness. Demonstrating the existence of a dragon is also a very different act from proving the existence of ghosts. Because of its grandeur as an unfathomable force of nature, the dragon is a compelling symbol of Chinese national pride, whereas ghosts are associated with fear and popular beliefs. The dragon lies between the realm of the "natural" anomalies more palatable to Western science and what the West would categorize as supernatural. Although the source might indeed be a foreign newspaper (in which the word "dragon" was likely never used), the image is unquestionably Chinese. The illustration, by the master Wu Youru 吳友如 (d. 1893), places the triumphant, vast body of the dragon in the foreground, dwarfing the boat with the small sailors on its deck in the background (Fig. 8.4). Thus the illustration offers us the perspective not of the

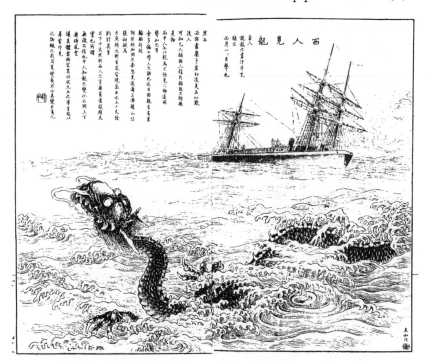

Fig. 8.4 "Xiren jian long" 西人見龍, *DSZ*, *Ji* (1.6) 12, 90, beginning of the third month, Guangxu 12, 4/4/1886. Drawn by Wu Youru.

Westerners but a Chinese gaze diametrically opposed to it, with the indisputable form of the dragon in the center. This contrasts with visions of dragons on Chinese soil, where they are nearly always seen in the distant clouds, with the Chinese observers in the foreground, closer to the viewer than the dragons.[94] This dramatic visual confrontation takes the place of the sworn testimony and technical details of the *Shenbao*. These two stories claim the seas as a realm of the strange open to both Chinese and Western observers.

The gap between Chinese and foreign perception of the strange can take on sinister significance. In a pair of stories, the lack of a belief in ghosts among Westerners seems to result in ghoulish treatment of corpses, because without ghosts disrespect is without consequences. One such anecdote recounts a special technique by which corpses can be shrunk "so that they can be placed in a wooden box and conveniently carried." The caption contrasts this alteration with Chinese sages' respect for the corpse and imagines the displaced ghosts, whose bodies are now too small to offer them shelter.[95] The Chinese respect for the body, linked with respect for ghosts, is contrasted with this uncanny skill and grisly "convenience." The other anecdote, which appeared more than a month later, depicts Westerners reprocessing corpses to make other products, the bodies into lime 鹼 and the bones into fertilizer.

[The Chinese] know that since the bodily soul of the dead desires peace, to keep a coffin unburied is a crime. They know that the cruelty of the greedy is far greater [than that of those who leave the dead unburied]; therefore those who open graves and rob coffins must be executed. At its most crude, it is a requirement; at its most refined, it is a policy for promoting benevolence. Recorded in the lawbooks, this is also a method of governing the country. These Westerners' science can also be extended to the government of the nation. If corpses are destroyed, then there will be no burials; there will be no graveyards, so there will be a broader expanse of tillable earth. If a family is poor and their parents die, then the corpse will be sold. Not only will the costs of burial be saved, but the profit could be kept. Those who sell [lime] can get a good price, and those who plow the earth would get good harvests. The nation would be rich, the people prosperous, and the way of government complete. This is Westerners' science.[96]

Here the Western pursuit of science is taken to extremes that horrify the Chinese reader, all in a grotesque parody of prudent statecraft. The captions in both these cases take on a satirical tone reminiscent of "A Modest Proposal," feigning admiration for this frightening efficiency and skill. The interest seems to be in the grotesque and shock value rather than xenophobia as such, but this time the periodical strayed into sensitive territory. This idea of foreigners' not properly respecting and containing the dead taints the entire culture with the stink of corpses; it stirred up fears of foreigners in general in a way in which technology or peculiar marriage customs did not.[97]

These stories are retracted, albeit after an interval of around five months. First a comment deploring their content is appended to a story relating a Westerner's achievement in educating the blind, deaf, and dumb. His school is a tourist attraction in the English concession. The text admires his efforts, but it also makes his students and their novel methods of communication a spectacle; in the illustration a crowd is staring at the door. The final laudatory comment states that foreign and Chinese are a single family, and the earlier stories about matters like shrinking corpses were clearly fabrications.[98] A display of unusual charity is used to diffuse the earlier ghoulish images. Here, too, the Westerner makes use of what might otherwise be thrown away, but this time it is in a positive sense.

A full-fledged retraction is given pride of place on the first page of the following issue. The special nature of this article is made plain by visual framing: the words are placed within the image, on a scroll in the hands of an astounded-looking reader. The periodicals from which *Dianshizhai huabao* gleans its stories are blamed, and the publishing house resolves to reform in the future. There is no discussion of why these particular inaccuracies should demand a strong response.[99] The pages following the retraction show no rejection of strange material—the ghost of a jealous wife figures prominently—but this issue restricts itself to domestic oddities. A retraction demands a different kind of conversation with the readers than captions questioning the accuracy of an individual anecdote, and these demands make the reader visible[100] and change the relationship between image and text. The foreign community who seem to have protested against the slander are absent in both text and illustration.

The absence of ghosts in the West is used to different effect in an essay in *Shenbao* discussing the belief that wronged ghosts seek substitutes. It was believed that those who died by certain violent and unjust means, such as drowning, hanging, poisoning, and the complications of childbirth, were condemned to remain as ghosts until they could incite another person to die by the same means and take their place. Psychologically this is a powerful and multivalent idea: the powerless, frequently women, who die wretched, often self-inflicted deaths are granted violent power. At the same time later disturbing deaths are explained: it is not the psychological distress of an individual but the historical residue of past violence that causes people to take their own lives. Yet this apparently eternal legacy of deadly, unpredictable resentment is troubling to those who would affirm a just and orderly universe in which each person receives individual justice. This essay opens boldly, "China and the outside world are a single world, with the same yin and yang, but overseas they do not believe in fate, and thus there are no ghosts and gods. In China all believe in it, and thus they gradually come to believe that such things really exist." Although all nations share one natural world, cultural differences create different supernatural worlds.[101] The idea that ghosts and gods are products of human belief does not render them powerless; precisely as such they can be extremely destructive. It shifts the onus of this destruction from the ghosts themselves to the human mind, particularly the minds of other classes. The argument that ghosts and the like have a psychological origin is of long standing in China and was particularly popular in the Qing. The introduction of a whole class of people who apparently neither believe in nor encounter ghosts merely confirms it.[102]

The essay goes on to point out logical flaws in the conception of these wronged dead. Why does one only hear of the ghosts of those who drowned in lakes, rivers, and wells, but never on the open seas? This discrepancy reveals a distinction between known and unmarked cultural landscapes. There must have been someone who drowned first to begin the chain of ghostly substitutions, but what explains that first death? Why does the person who dies of poisoning seek a substitute but the one who dies of medical malpractice take no revenge on the doctor? Similarly, when a woman dies in childbirth, she is believed to cause the death of childbearing women in her own family; why doesn't she seek out women in the incompetent midwife's family? In a revealing comment, the author contends if the god in charge of fate really demands that the wronged dead kill other innocents, it would be better if China, like foreign places, had no such god. It has already been implied that the Chinese have the power to decide this.

The author concludes that in China, in contrast to the West, one relies on heaven's justice more than on earthly law. The last cases, the unrepentant quack and midwife, cause the essay to take an unexpected turn to the practical, suggesting human order taking over where the divine order has apparently failed. Some unjust deaths at least could be avoided by better training of doctors and medical supervision of midwives. This, rather than their own ghastly revenge, is the way to deal with the problem of the wronged dead.[103] Insistence on justice and rationality in the other world turns to plans, on a much smaller scale, for justice in this one. There is an interesting disjunction between the two halves of this argument. The flaws of the idea of vengeful ghosts are pointed out, but the proposed solution addresses only the injustice that is most easily controlled. Some of the most frightening ghosts are still not exorcised. Mere existence is not the only issue in a multicultural debate about ghosts; rather, this debate turns on the benefits for society of both worldly and otherworldly institutions. This style of argument about the supernatural is highly reminiscent of Ji Yun, but to suggest changes in public policy based on such arguments is a departure. This use of the foreign as an impersonal voice and rhetorical tool, rather than as a spectator or spectacle, distinguishes the *Shenbao* from *Dianshizhai*.

Just as the strange helped to define the foreign, the disjunction between the Western fascination with biological specimens and freaks and Western skepticism toward Chinese popular beliefs redivides the strange. A distinction between the personified forces of ghosts, gods, and monsters on one side and birth defects, strange deaths, and "natural" disasters on the other was not new in the nineteenth century. Non-human sentient beings, especially ghosts, had been the target of skepticism at least since Wang Chong in the Han. In large part because of their relationships to popular belief, they have always been viewed with ambivalence by the elite. In these periodicals, however, the contrast between the Chinese and the foreign frames the contrast between these two kinds of strange in a new way: one kind of anomaly could be compared across borders, and the other was culturally specific.[104]

Illustration, Display, and the Carnival Trade

As noted above, the lavish illustration of *Dianshizhai huabao* was new to the *zhiguai*. In contrast to *Shenbao*, the polyphony of *Dianshizhai* tends to be between image and text rather than between multiple textual voices.

One striking aspect of the illustrations is the portrayal of mass spectacles: nearly every strange incident or creature is drawn surrounded by a mob of onlookers.[105] This feature becomes more obvious when one compares illustrations of monstrous births, such as the infant *xingtian* in Fig. 8.1, with the prodigies in early European broadsheets, which tended to feature the monster in isolation.[106] Onlookers were a common device in earlier illustrations of fiction, but *Dianshizhai huabao* shows a particularly strong preference for crowd scenes. These illustrations suggest not only a crowded urban milieu but also the necessity of the gaze of the crowd in making the marvel. In a period when Western circuses came to Shanghai, the new, imported aesthetic of the circus and sideshow was influential.[107] The circus was illustrated so many times that one later illustration had to justify why illustrating it once more was not redundant.[108] The mixed Chinese and Western crowd was a prominent feature of illustrations of the circus in Shanghai and was sometimes mentioned in the text as well.[109] The circus and sideshow, with their anomalies from all over the world surrounded by an audience, provide a model for *Dianshizhai huabao*'s own efforts.

Individual marvels also play a role in this culture of display. A leopard, the head of an American wild man, and an Italian dwarf are displayed as curiosities for profit in restaurants and teahouses. In all these stories, the location and name of the restaurant or other venue are given (in the case of the leopard twice, once in the caption and once in the restaurant's signboard in the illustration) a practice that contrasts sharply with the anonymity of people in most of the narratives. The foreign restaurant (番菜館) exhibiting the leopard evidently had a series of such attractions; at one point it had kept snakes.[110] These stories are narrated by an individual, first-person voice, an experienced guide to Shanghai, rather than the more distant third-person narrator of oddities from the provinces. The illustrations make *Dianshizhai huabao* part of this display, almost an advertising spectacle; the Shanghai reader could seek out the spectacles himself if he wished, and those in other places could be armchair travelers.[111]

The illustrations call continuous attention to the act of looking. The curiosities are surrounded by admiring crowds of all ages and both sexes, including children either being held up or demanding to be held up to see.[112] But the crowd and the spectacle are balanced in the case of the leopard and the wild man's head by a third element, the counter where admission fees are collected, which is surrounded by a second cluster of people (Fig. 8.5). In the case of the leopard the ticket counter comes first, and in the case of the wild man's head it is seen second, on the left, perhaps suggesting this case is more of an exposé. The verb in the title of the report on the wild man's head is "sell," and in the case of the leopard it is "see." The commodification of the spectacle is itself part of the display.

Both foreigners and Chinese were engaged in this commerce: the wild man's head pictured in Fig. 8.5 was displayed by an American merchant, who set up shop across from a well-known teahouse. According to Wang Ermin, this is the origin of the phrase "selling the wild man's head," an expression for chicanery still in use.[113] Both the image and the text mention all the flourishes of the show, such as the piano accompaniment and the ploy of having the head blow out a candle. The narrator concludes, "I knew in my heart it was a trick for earning money, with no mystery and not worth pondering; still, since it belongs to the category of news, why shouldn't it be drawn for those in the world who haven't seen it yet?" Showmanship and chicanery are news. The same argument could justify *Dianshizhai huabao*'s relaxed attitude toward accuracy; true or false, the pictures provide a good show. Even though it offers no explanation, the caption's skepticism allows the reader to feel he has seen through the trick; the illustration, in turn, takes part in the show.

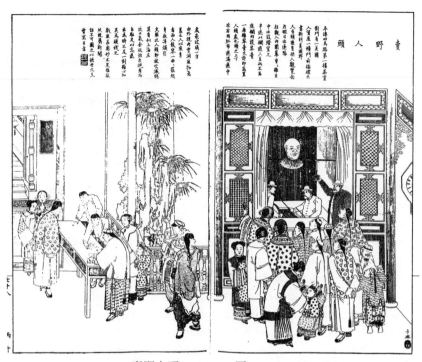

Fig. 8.5 "Mai yeren tou" 賣野人頭, *DSZ, Bing* 丙 10, 78, middle of the second month, Guangxu 11, 3/27/1885. Drawn by Tian Ying 田英.

Earlier *zhiguai* sometimes satisfied the same appetite. The display of human freaks was linked with the potentially threatening social forces of beggars and itinerant performers, but the narratives quickly move to emphasize control of this disorder. For example, *Liaozhai* describes a performing dwarf who is revealed to be a schoolboy kidnapped and magically stunted by a sorcerer. The investigating official kills the sorcerer but is unable to cure the boy.[114] *Dianshizhai* alludes to this tradition in the account of the Italian dwarf by speculating that foreigners had learned the technique of stunting children from Chinese beggars.[115] Even so, there is no attempt to control the show going on in the illustration.

The strange as commodity had not been contained in the text in the same way before. Older stories sometimes used the verbal formula "everyone was amazed," but here the viewer's amazement has become key to the spectacle. This change recalls the argument in other cultural contexts that it is commodification that changes a monster to a freak and converts horror to entertainment, although in earlier *zhiguai* horror was only one of many possible modes.[116] In the Six Dynasties a piglet with six legs or one resembling an ape would likely have been recorded as an omen, interpreted, and probably promptly butchered. In *Dianshizhai huabao* deformed livestock, rather than being seen as a bad omen, is regarded as a potential financial windfall: the owner of a donkey foal with two heads and five legs is determined to raise it carefully to make his fortune.[117]

Misshapen piglets are pictured surrounded by multiethnic spectators, and the circumstances of their display are narrated. There are relatively few attempts to explain what deformed livestock might mean; the story is concerned with display rather than explanation. The career of a piglet with two faces and eight ears reveals the role of the anomaly in urban space. When a Chinese man in Singapore lets others see this specimen, viewers block the street. The disturbance attracts the attention of the authorities, and his marvelous product is taken first to a doctor to be examined and then to the museum to await further investigation. The weird is a clearly public event and moves from being an uncontrolled to a contained spectacle. In the illustration a Western man and woman are looking on in wonder as the Chinese man displays his wares; he himself is looking at the spectators, not the marvel (Fig. 8.6). The woman is not mentioned in the text; one suspects she, with her elaborate skirts, is there for visual interest.[118] The final line of the caption reads, "One can see from this a bit of Westerners' respect for *gezhi*." This blending of *gezhi* and the passion for the strange helps define the authority the Western gaze is given in these illustrations. The weird is becoming a new form of urban entertainment, and the foreign gaze is an additional element in that entertainment.

Although the *Shenbao* does not take part in the culture of display in the same way, it records its textual traces. A pair of anecdotes about a five-legged calf in Sichuan and a three-armed man from Henan contain elaborate descriptions of the conditions of their display at temples and other tourist destinations and the crowds who go to see them there.[119] Even tales of karmic retribution show the marks of entertainment culture. When an unfilial daughter-in-law is turned into a dog-headed monster, the embarrassed family at first tries to keep her locked up at home. When too many people come to see her, they send her away to be kept at a Buddhist site for releasing life. She continues to be an attraction there, and the *Shenbao*'s correspondent in Hangzhou goes to see her himself.[120] The *zhiguai* convention of relating how the informant came to hear the story has become "I went to see the show."

Fig. 8.6 "Chuang jian yi zhu" 創見異豬, *DSZ*, *Wu* 戊 11, 87, end of the tenth month, Guangxu 11, 11/27/1885. Drawn by Tian Ying.

The international market for anomalies exists on the level not only of the imaginary but also of the actual carnival trade:[121] Chinese oddities traveled overseas, and Western anomalies were imported to China. One representative case is the Chinese giant Zhan Wu 詹五, originally from Anhui, who came to Shanghai to make a living and was discovered by a European circus. He traveled to Europe and eventually took a European wife.[122] In *Dianshizhai huabao* he is mentioned at least four times: once glimpsed on the streets of Shanghai, once compared with a Western giant who is indeed even taller, once compared with a dwarf who also has a successful career, and once performing overseas. His celebrity set the standard by which all other professional freaks are judged. Often he is first put in the context of great giants of the past. He seems rather diminished by the comparison; his only greatness is his size and appetite. Nonetheless foreigners think him amazing; one Frenchman explicitly says, "This marvelous piece of goods can be kept" 此奇貨可居.[123] There seems to be a slight contempt for foreigners' low threshold of amazement. There is also a class dimension to the overtone of disdain for Zhan: he was a peasant who had a glamorous overseas career through an accident of birth. When Zhan returns to Shanghai, he wears Western clothes, making him an oddity not merely for his stature but for his mixed cultural markers. In Europe, Zhan Wu's Chineseness was surely part of his exoticism, but in China his travels mark him as not quite Chinese. Since the carnival trade allows the strange and marginal figure to approach the foreign, anxieties about cultural loss and change are projected onto these figures.

The story of a talking ape,[124] another piece of goods in the carnival trade, dramatizes issues of the domestic, the foreign, and assimilation. When the ape was first captured by a hunter in Yunnan (itself a border region), it made sounds that resembled an unknown language, but gradually it learned human speech. The Chinese hunter took it overseas and sold it to a foreign merchant, who, fearing that the ape would not survive the change in environment, initially paid him 100 taels and promised to pay another hundred after a year if the ape survived. The vagueness of the geography in this story, with neither the foreign destination nor the ethnicity of the purchaser specified, makes it seem a parable. When the hunter came to collect, the ape clasped his hands to greet him but babbled incomprehensibly.

The hunter said, "After not seeing me for a year, how can you revert to your original face?"[125] When the ape heard his words, he realized something, and with a change of speech said, "What I was just speaking was Western language; also, I've long been apart from Chinese, and I've missed it." The hunter said, "I am originally Chinese, and you were also born in China. Even if you studied a few sentences of a Western language, why must you speak them to someone from your hometown?" The ape was deeply ashamed, but said, "I would not dare to show off vocal tricks in front of my old master, but with practice I became used to it, so I let it slip out without thinking."[126]

This could be read as a satire of Chinese who learned foreign languages, grew obsessed with the foreign, and thus came to seem like performing apes; this ape could also be modeled on the figure of the giant Zhan Wu, in his Western clothes on the streets of Shanghai. The hunter mistakes an unspecified Western language for the ape's native, inhuman language; becoming non-Chinese could mean reverting to the status of a beast. Even as parody, the ape's defense makes moving between cultural worlds seem natural and effortless. The ape first learns undifferentiated "human speech," with a stress on the distinction between men and beasts. Yet once it goes overseas and learns another human language, nationality becomes a distinction that even transcends species. The attempt to distinguish the ape's Chineseness as innate, as compared to the environmental influence of the foreign, is uneasy. Equally uneasily, the bond between the ape and the hunter is made to seem in retrospect one of loyalty rather than a lucrative transaction involving a hunter and his prey. The title itself, "An ape that can speak," which is half of the set phrase "An ape can speak, but it is still a beast," casts further doubt on assimilation. In the illustration the ape's cage is surrounded by a few Westerners and a single Chinese, the hunter, and the story emphasizes their different perspectives on the ape's words. Again, we have the theme of foreign and Chinese complicity in the exhibit of anomaly.

Alongside *Dianshizhai huabao*'s relish of the glamour of the carnival trade, there is acknowledgment of the complicated relationships it creates. These relationships do not fit a simple dichotomy of imperialists collecting colonial subjects for their menageries; everyone can play the roles of freak, carnival barker, and audience.[127] National origin and boundaries color these roles but do not dictate them. Everyone involved is marked by a combination of strangeness and money.

The impact of the idea of Westerners on the strange is ambiguous. On the one hand, they play the fascinating role of a group of absolute skeptics. Living without ghosts can seem enviable at some moments and horrifying at others. On the other hand, they are the most ardent consumers and merchants of the strange, as scientific curiosity easily blends into a more general *haoqi* 好奇, love of the strange.

From Freaks to Ghosts

In *Dianshizhai huabao* the culture of display also has an effect on the illustration of more intangible marvels. Unseen forces—immortals looking on in approval of good deeds, spirits possessing their victims, or private visions—are almost always portrayed in the illustration.[128] For a pictorial this may seem like an obvious decision, but it has consequences for the nature of the strange.

As in the account of the iron abacus, the illustration and text often express different levels of skepticism and credulity. An account of automatic writing begins with a moderately skeptical prologue: no matter whether the creature that descends to the planchette is an immortal, ghost, or god, it depends on the mental energy of living people to act. If those holding the planchette can write poetry, it can produce poetry; if they have good calligraphy, so will the spirit writing. Some of the prophecies are accurate; some are not. This is very close to Ji Yun's opinion of the planchette and was probably the commonsense, conservative view, which also resembles our explanation of how a ouija board works. In the Chinese tradition psychological and supernatural explanations are not mutually exclusive. Despite this cautious frame, in the illustration the figures summoned to the planchette, a man's late wife and a beheaded female convict, are visible above the two petitioners and the device, standing on a base of smoke that emerges from an incense burner (Fig. 8.7).[129] We are shown things that the participants of this story themselves do not see; in addition to the séance itself, the poems granted by the planchette are illustrated. The dynamics of looking are completely different from those in the illustrations of sideshow displays: the participants are focused on the planchette's brush, and the drama of the two spirits is reserved for external viewers. One suspects this anecdote has been selected for the sake of the visual contrast between the beautiful young wife and the ghoulish figure of the convict.

A second case provides a more drastic contrast between illustration and caption: the caption describes mediums who claim to be able to be possessed by the spirits of recently deceased relatives as charlatanism and deplores that even men have taken up this "art," but in the illustration the ghost is obviously present, albeit in the kind of balloon often used to indicate a dream.[130] In contrast, the 1885 illustrated version of *Liaozhai* illustrates a séance with a fox spirit by showing the human participants and incense but no image of the fox, since it was a disembodied voice in the narrative.[131] The *Liaozhai* illustrations are loyal to the texts, showing only the creatures the protagonists see; the relationship in *Dianshizhai* is more complex.

Tales of the strange are often ambivalent in framing the pleasure of the bizarre with moral meaning or explanation, but here the satisfaction of two appetites—having it both ways—is more clearly split between image and text. This thorough pandering to both appetites, even when the ticket booth is not visible, seems related to the strange as commodity developed in the culture of display.

Display dictates neither credulity nor incredulity. In both periodicals there is a particularly strong interest in exposing false ghosts, but in the illus-

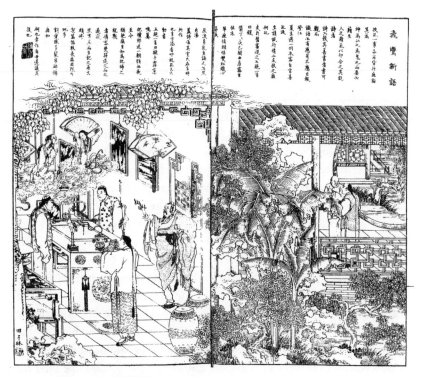

Fig. 8.7 "Feiluan xinyu" 飛鸞新語, *DSZ, Bing* 3, 22, beginning of the twelfth month, Guang-xu 10, 1/16/1885. Drawn by Tian Ying.

trations it is impossible to distinguish a false from a true spirit or ghost.[132] The show is what matters, whether it is true or false, and exposure of sham spectacle has its own appeal.

Conclusion

How does a society's way of talking about the strange change? In literary histories, late Qing *zhiguai* and more broadly all *wenyan xiaoshuo* are often considered a moribund tradition, spewing out derivative works and doomed to be supplanted by the new literature. It is not only the literary genre but also the ghosts they describe that are seen as about to be snuffed out, or at least recategorized as superstition, *mixin* 迷信, as in *Qingbai leichao* 清稗類抄 (A classified collection of Qing fiction; 1916). The presence of the strange in the periodicals not only compels revision of this literary-historical narrative but also is crucial to understanding the periodicals themselves. Looking at the strange is a way to begin to understand the periodicals' hybrid nature: *Shenbao* as a *biji* in increments and by committee, and *Dianshizhai huabao* as a *biji* of contending words and images.

The nature of collectors of the strange has altered. In the periodicals there is neither the single *bowu junzi* 博物君子 or raconteur whose voice or selection strategy unifies narrative fragment nor the framework of an encyclopedic anthology to reconcile divergent voices. Making up for some of this lack of personality in the collector are the distinct audiences for the collections. The two periodicals create two different possible audiences for the strange: a disparate, vocal circle that disputes the interpretation of anomaly and an audience of viewers gathered in groups to look. Both periodicals model how such audiences would act by recording discussions between readers or showing crowds of onlookers.

The display of ghosts and monstrous births has been interpreted as a sign of stability and reinforcement of existing moral standards or as a sign of instability and dread at a changing world.[133] I would argue that both are true. The strange offers a means of coping with change by combining older knowledge of the weird with new information. The anomalies in the periodicals reaffirm the value of this older knowledge and at the same time recognize that that knowledge and individual accounts of the weird are transmitted and consumed in new ways.

Notes

1. Mitchell Stephen, *A History of News* (New York: Viking Books, 1998), pp. 120–26; Bill Brown, *The Material Unconscious* (Cambridge, Mass.: Harvard University Press, 1996), p. 200.

2. For introductions to the genre, see Li Jianguo 李劍國, *Tangqian zhiguai xiaoshuo shi* 唐前志怪小說史 (Tianjin: Nankai daxue chubanshe, 1984); and Robert Campany, *Strange Writing: Anomaly Accounts in Early Medieval China* (Albany: State University of New York Press, 1996). For Qing *zhiguai*, see Allan Barr, "Pu Songling and *Liaozhai zhiyi*: A Study of Textual Transmission, Biographical Background, and Literary Antecedents" (Ph.D. diss., Oxford University, 1983); Judith Zeitlin, *Historian of the Strange: Pu Songling and the Chinese Classical Tale* (Stanford: Stanford University Press, 1993); and Leo Tak-Hong Chan, *The Discourse on Foxes and Ghosts: Ji Yun and Eighteenth Century Chinese Storytelling* (Honolulu: University of Hawai'i Press, 1999).

3. Li Jianguo, *Tangqian zhiguai xiaoshuo shi*, p. 11.

4. For a categorization of the content of *zhiguai* in a much earlier period, see Campany, *Strange Writing*, pp. 237–71. Although Wang Ermin 王爾敏 categorizes this material in order to exclude it from consideration, he provides a thorough list of the content of the strange in *Dianshizhai huabao*: "gods and immortals, shamans, ghosts, foxes, exorcisms, returns from death, retribution, prophetic dreams, and omens," as well as "the heavens raining grain, a dragon toying with a pearl," and all variety of human and animal deformities (see Wang Ermin, "Zhongguo jindai zhishi pujihua chuanbo zhi tushuo xingshi: *Dianshizhai huabao*" 中國近代知識普及化傳播之圖說形式—點石齋畫報 [The pictorial form of popular transmission of modern consciousness: *Dianshizhai huabao*], *Zhongyang yanjiuyuan, Jindai shi yanjiusuo jikan*, 19 [1990]: 169). On the difference between these three terms for strange, see Zeitlin, *Historian of the Strange*, pp. 5–6. This chapter deals more with the *yi* and the *guai* than the broader narrative space of the *qi*.

5. Zeitlin, *Historian of the Strange*, p. 6.

6. For an introduction to the *Shenbao* and the Shenbao guan, see Xu Ruifang 徐瑞芳 and Xu Zaiping 徐載平, *Qingmo sishi nian Shenbao shiliao* 清末四十年申報史料 (Beijing: Xinhua chubanshe, 1988); Rudolf Wagner, "Ernest Major's Shenbaoguan and the Formation of Late Qing Print Culture" (paper presented at the conference "Creating a Multiethnic Urban Culture: The Shanghai Concessions, 1850–1910," University of Heidelberg, June 1998); and Natascha Vittinghoff, "Freier Fluss: zur Kulturgeschichte des frühen chinesischen Journalismus" (Ph.D. diss., University of Heidelberg, 1997–98). For *Dianshizhai huabao*, see Wang Ermin, "Zhongguo jindai zhishi pujihua chuanbo zhi tushuo xingshi"; Xiaoqing Ye, "Popular Culture in Shanghai" (Ph.D. diss., Australian National University, 1993); and

Rudolf Wagner, "The Shanghai Illustrated Newspapers *Dianshizhai huabao* and *Feiyingge huabao*—An Introductory Survey" (unpublished MS).

7. Vittinghoff, *Freier Fluss*, p. 202. Translation from the German is my own.

8. Ge Gongzhen 戈公振, *Zhongguo baoxue shi* 中國報學史 (Beijing, 1955), pp. 248–49.

9. Wang Ermin, "Zhongguo jindai zhishi pujihua chuanbo zhi tushuo xingshi," p. 169. According to Wang, there are 443 tales of the supernatural, a tenth of the whole. In addition there are 304 accounts of weird but real events, and 31 illustrations of earlier *biji* 筆記.

10. Nanny Kim, "How to Read About Monsters and Miracles in an Illustrated Magazine from Late 19th Century Shanghai" (unpublished MS).

11. Wu Meifeng 吳美鳳, "Cong *Dianshizhai huabao* kan wan Qing shiqi de minjian xinyang yishi" 從點石齋畫報看晚清時期的民間信仰意識, *Lishi wenwu*, no. 91 (Feb. 2001): 33–57.

12. The passage then stresses the accessibility of the newspaper to all classes. The overlap of concern with fabrication and class issues is interesting. *Xiaoshuo* are often attributed to the easily deluded lower classes, but here they are instead read as exclusive and elite.

13. Julia Henningsmeier ("The Foreign Sources of *Dianshizhai huabao*, a Nineteenth-Century Shanghai Illustrated Magazine," *Ming Qing yanjiu* 1998: 78) notes that when adapting foreign materials, the *Dianshizhai huabao* did not distinguish between news articles and short stories, an attitude suggesting the two were seen as identical.

14. *Shenbao* (hereafter *SB*), twenty-first day of the third month, 1872, 1.1. References to the *Shenbao* are, for the period 1872–84, to the 40-volume *Zhongguo shixue congshu* 中國史學叢書 reprint edition (Taibei: Xuesheng shuju, 1965), and for later issues to the microfilm. After June 15, 1874, every issue gave the date in both the Chinese and the Western calendars; I cite both dates before that point and only the Western date after it.

15. Quoted in Xu Ruifang and Xu Zaiping, *Qingmo sishi nian Shenbao shiliao*, p. 5.

16. *SB*, 1884, sixth month; quoted in ibid., p. 336.

17. This chapter relies on the edition of *Dianshizhai huabao* reprinted in five volumes by Guangdong renmin chubanshe, 1983. Ernest Major's preface is reprinted in the first volume. See also Kim, "How to Read About Monsters and Miracles," p. 15. This kind of edifying illustration of animals and mechanical devices had also appeared in missionary publications that predate *Dianshizhai huabao*; see Jonathan Hay, "Painters and Publishing in Late Nineteenth-Century Shanghai," in *Art at the Close of China's Empire*, ed. Ju-hsi Chou (Tempe: Arizona State University, 1988), p. 136.

18. One commonly cited incident involves an official who is able to identify a strange bird because he had read the *Shan hai jing*. The incident is described in Liu

Xin's "Memorial Submitting the *Classic of Mountains and Seas*," translated in Campany, *Strange Writing*, pp. 134–36. See Chan, *The Discourse on Foxes and Ghosts*, pp. 22–23.

19. Among others, E. Perry Link, *Mandarin Ducks and Butterflies: Popular Fiction in Early Twentieth-Century Chinese Cities* (Berkeley: University of California Press, 1981).

20. Zhuangzi, "Qiwu lun" 齊物論; Ye Mengde 葉夢得, *Bishu luhua* 避暑錄話; *Hanyu da cidian* 漢語大辭典 (Shanghai: Hanyu da cidian chubanshe, 1990–93), 4.316. In the early 1880s, "guwang yanzhi" was occasionally used as a title for weird anecdotes in the *Shenbao*, a practice that foregrounds the pose of casual entertainment; see, e.g., "姑妄言之," *SB*, 12/14/1882, 37.24708.

21. Ji Yun 紀昀 makes the same rhetorical move; see, e.g., *Yuewei caotang biji yizhu* 閱微草堂筆記譯注 (Beijing: Zhongguo huaqiao chubanshe, 1994), 21. 1181, story 9.

22. The *Dianshizhai huabao*'s (hereafter *DSZ*) individual issues are not dated in the reprint. Rather, within each of the five volumes, the individual *ce* are labeled according to the heavenly stems, earthly branches, and other character lists. Below I cite them in the following form: character labeling *ce* (vol. number) issue number, page number. I have extrapolated approximate dates for individual issues based on the known starting dates and publishing interval. "Xiemou qianju" 邪謀潛沮, *DSZ*, Zi 子 (2.1) 11, 63, end of the ninth month, Guangxu 13, 11/6/1887.

23. "Bingzhong yitui" 病中易腿, *DSZ*, Jia 甲 (1.1) 4, 30, middle of the fifth month, Guangxu 10, 6/5/1884. Other examples include "Chunü chanwei" 處女產蝟, *DSZ*, Shen 申 (2.9) 10, 81, middle of the fourth month, Guangxu 16, 5/29/1890. The *Shenbao* also uses this justification, for example, in the tale of a rooster's egg among other miscellaneous anecdotes from Beijing; "Jingshi suowen" 京師瑣聞, *SB*, 5/8/1882, 34.22546.

24. "Jingfu yichan" 京婦異產, *DSZ*, Ren 壬 (1.9) 3, 17, beginning of the twelfth month, Guangxu 12, 12/25/1886. Other examples of creatures crying out for scientific classification are a strange fish, "Wangyu shuyi" 網魚述異, *DSZ*, Geng 庚 (1.7) 2, 11; end of the third month, Guangxu 12, 4/14/1886; and a corpse-eating monster, "Maoren haijian" 毛人駭見, *DSZ*, Geng 5, 35; end of the fourth month, Guangxu 12, 5/24/1886.

25. Lydia Liu (*Translingual Practice: Literature, National Culture, and Translated Modernity—China, 1900–1937* [Stanford: Stanford University Press, 1995], pp. 275, 292) includes the term *bowuyuan* in her appendix of neologisms from missionary Chinese, and *bowuguan* in her appendix of loanwords from Japanese. Wang Tao was particularly impressed by museums on his travels in Europe. Illustrated coverage of his travels, including the museums, were printed as an appendix to *Dianshizhai huabao*; see *Manyou suilu* 漫游隨錄 in *Dianshizhai huabao fulu* 點石齋畫報附錄 (copy in Shanghai library, n.d), 2.8a.

26. See the example given for "bowuyuan" in *Hanyu da cidian* (1: 910), from Sun Yirang 孫詒讓, "*Zhouli* zhengyao" 周禮正要, which presents it as a central place where people compete in displaying new inventions and strange objects, both for the sake of displaying oddity and their own fame and profit.

27. Actually Guo Pu's argument is more sophisticated than this; he argued that the strange lies not in the objects we consider strange but in our own minds (Campany, *Strange Writing*, pp. 150–51; see also Zeitlin, *Historian of the Strange*, pp. 18–19). For a straightforward use of this argument, see "Liang she hu dou" 兩蛇互鬥, DSZ, *Jia* (1.1) 11, 82, end of the sixth month, Guangxu 10, 8/21/48.

28. "Yangshu shuangqi" 洋樹雙奇, DSZ, *Ren* (1.9) 2, 16, end of the eleventh month, Guangxu 12, 12/16/1886.

29. "Liangtou zhu" 兩頭豬, DSZ, *Ren* 12, 89, beginning of the third month, Guangxu 13, 3/25/1887.

30. On the project of publishing the *Gujin tushu jicheng*, see Wagner, "Ernest Major's Shenbaoguan," pp. 64–67.

31. "Xieshu keyi" 邪術可疑, *Ding* 丁 (1.4) 3, 23, beginning of the fourth month, Guangxu 11, 5/14/1885.

32. Accounts of this practice can, in fact, be found in the *Shenbao*. One skeptical account concludes that the tales of the iron abacus are likely invented by people in the household who stole the goods themselves; see "Sutai zazhi" 蘇臺雜誌, SB, 5/29/1882, 34.22724. For another account, see, e.g., "Jianghu huanshu" 江湖幻術, SB, 3/5/1878, 22.14352.

33. *Dianshizhai huabao* refers to *Shan hai jing* more often than *Shenbao* does, probably because it is more interested in strange animals. For an exception, see "Wu ti niu" 五蹄牛, SB, 3/6/1876, 15.9340.

34. Stories from Ji Yun's *Yuewei caotang biji* include "Gebi xiehu" 戈壁蝎虎 DSZ, *Wu* 午 (2.7) 4, 25, middle of the seventh month, Guangxu 15, 8/7/1889; "Zhan gui wei cheng" 斬鬼謂成, DSZ, *Wu* 11, 84, end of the ninth month, Guangxu 15, 10/15/1889; "Huxie" 狐諧, DSZ, *Wu* 12, 89, beginning of the tenth month, Guangxu 15, 10/24/1889; "Hui bu ke zhui" 悔不可追, DSZ, *Yuan* 元 (5.2) 3, 24, beginning of the fourth month, Guangxu 22, 5/13/1896; "Zuling shi jie" 祖靈示戒, *Shen* (2.9) 3, 22, beginning of the second intercalendrical month, Guangxu 16/21/1890. The choice of *Yuewei caotang biji* as the collection to use in this way is interesting; perhaps Ji Yun's less embellished and highly interpretive style of *zhiguai* was closer to what was perceived as journalistic style. In "Chunyao hai shu" 春藥害鼠, one of his anecdotes is used in response to a contemporary situation; see DSZ, *Yuan* 2, 16, end of the third month, Guangxu 22, 5/3/1896. Yuan Mei's collections are also quoted a few times; there seems to be particular interest in the Qianlong generation.

35. I am indebted to my research assistant Huang Yanmei for her help in finding these stories.

36. For discussion of this generic division, see Zeitlin, *Historian of the Strange*, p. 4; and Li Jianguo 李劍國, *Tang Wudai zhiguai chuanqi xulu* 唐五代志怪傳奇敘錄 (Tianjin: Nankai daxue chubanshe, 1993), pp. 3–9.

37. See, e.g., the story of a dyemaker's encounter with a ghost, "Ranjiang yu gui" 染匠遇鬼, *SB*, 11/8/1880, 31.19920.

38. In *"Fengyue meng* and the Courtesan Novel" (*Harvard Journal of Asiatic Studies* 58, no. 2 [1998]: 345–72), on nineteenth-century vernacular fiction, Patrick Hanan raised the possibility of fiction becoming news, but I think the transition is somewhat more subtle for classical narrative than for vernacular fiction. Vernacular fiction before the late Qing would often be set in earlier dynasties, in contrast with the relatively contemporary nature of classical fiction. As for the temporal range of *zhiguai* and *biji*, Six Dynasties collections seem to feel free to go back as far as high antiquity, but later collections seem limited by the existence of earlier collections, which already should have recorded Song or Tang wonders. It would not seem plausible for a classical tale author to claim to have discovered previously unrecorded strange tales from an earlier period; only a collection framing itself as a collection of historical fragments from earlier texts would go further back.

39. Recent scholarship holds that some sections date to the Warring States Period and that later sections were written in the Han or Wei-Jin; see Campany, *Strange Writing*, pp. 34–35.

40. Ibid., pp. 102–4, 133–37; Li Jianguo, *Tangqian zhiguai xiaoshuo shi*, pp. 104–5. A Qing editor of the text, Hao Yixing 郝懿行, discusses the various references to illustrations of this text and concludes there have been several breaks in continuity of transmission; quoted in Yuan Ke 袁軻, *Shan hai jing xiaozhu* 山海經校注 (Chengdu: Bashu shushe, 1993), pp. 550–51.

41. The longer *chuanqi* tales in *Taiping guangji* were, however, illustrated when reprinted in smaller collections, such as *Yu chu zhi* 虞初志 or *Yanyi bian* 艷異編.

42. This illustrated edition, *Liaozhai zhiyi tuyong* 聊齋誌異圖詠, was advertised on the opening pages of *Dianshizhai huabao*. The advertisements were not included in the reprint. See *DSZ*, *Ren* 2, middle of the eleventh month, Guangxu 12, 12/16/1886.

43. Collections exclusively devoted to this topic include the early Qing *Guobao wenjian lu* 果報聞見錄 (ca. 1681) and *Xinzhenglu* 信徵錄 (preface dated 1701).

44. *SB*, ninth day of the seventh month, 1872.

45. "Xiangyan zhuo shu nie bao" 詳言捉鼠孽報, *SB*, fourth day of the eighth month, 1872, 2.873.

46. "Fulu bian shu nie Su mou laixin" 附錄辨鼠嚙蘇某來信, *SB*, eleventh day of the eighth month, 1872, 2.922.

47. Li Jianguo, *Tang Wudai zhiguai chuanqi xulu*, p. 120.

48. "Xiude huobao" 修德獲報 *DSZ*, *Chen* 辰 (2.5) 6, 25, beginning of the twelfth month, Guangxu 14, 1/2/1889; "Renshu qu xie" 仁術驅邪, *DSZ*, *Chen* 5, 21, end of

the eleventh month, Guangxu 14, 12/23/1888; "Xianren quan zhen" 仙人勸賑, *Mao yin* 卯 (2.4) 10, 40, middle of the tenth month, Guangxu 14, 10/15/1888.

49. See such lists in 1888, printed in the back with the advertisements.

50. "Ren'en yangyi" 仁恩洋溢, *SB*, 2/16/1900.

51. "Lun guai shi" 論怪事, *SB*, 10/3/1876, 17.10785.

52. On the changing understanding of *gezhi*, see Benjamin Elman, "From Pre-modern Chinese Natural Studies 格致學 to Modern Science 科學 in China" (paper presented at the conference "Translating Western Knowledge into Late Imperial China," University of Göttingen, 1999).

53. "Shu lun guai shi hou" 書論怪事後, *SB*, 10/14/1876. The debate continues with historical allusions to spontaneous human combustion in "Dubao louchen" 讀報陋陳, *SB*, 10/18/1876, 17.25.

54. For nineteenth-century use of the term *gezhi*, see Elman, "From Pre-modern Chinese Natural Studies 格致學 to Modern Science 科學 in China," pp. 22–26. This exchange of information is reminiscent of the amateur scientific discussions analyzed in Meng Yue, "The Forgotten Amateurs: Popular Scientists in the Creation of Shanghai, 1876–1917" (paper presented at the conference "Creating a Multiethnic Urban Culture: The Shanghai Concessions, 1850–1910," University of Heidelberg, June 1998). *Gezhi*, she argues, is a term that allows room for free exchange of information, regardless of its cultural origins, whereas the term for scientific knowledge that later replaces it, *xixue* 西學 "Western learning," assumes a Western monopoly on such knowledge.

55. Jonathan Hay ("Painters and Publishing in Late Nineteenth-Century Shanghai," p. 168) argues that observing the foreign residents of the city was one of the principal diversions Shanghai had to offer, part of "the discourse of *qi*, the fascinatingly strange."

56. Wang Tao tells some foreign stories in his classical tale collections; similar stories appear in other Guangxu-era *biji* and *zhiguai* collections, such as Baiyi jushi 百一居士 (pseud.), *Hutian lu* 壺天錄 (Taibei: Guangwen shuju, 1969). Many of the latter are likely to have been gleaned from the newspapers.

57. Wagner, "The Shanghai Illustrated Newspapers *Dianshizhai huabao* and *Feiyingge huabao*," p. 2.

58. Kim, "How to Read About Monsters and Miracles," p. 20.

59. The rarity of European and American ghosts cannot be explained simply by a lack of sources; this was at the height of the spiritualism movement and Victorian fascinations with fairies. The image of Western views of the strange is clearly selective, both in Westerners' self-presentations to the Chinese and in Chinese perceptions of the West. Both sides make rhetorical use of the idea of a culture without ghosts. An intriguing account of an English girl feigning poltergeist phenomena in the *North China Herald* of January 1884 makes for an interesting comparison. It also

indulges in literary allusions, comparing the creatures that caused chaos in her vicinity to Robin Goodfellow. The passage on the whole is very tongue in cheek, with the girl's fraud exposed at the end. The use of high culture references and the contempt for the gullibility of the common people is strikingly similar to the Chinese coverage of such phenomena.

60. In a tale of a Japanese woman tormenting a man by sticking needles in a doll, the narrator is amazed that this technique (from the borders of China) had spread so far; see "Chengkong yansheng" 呈控魘勝, DSZ, *Bing* 丙 (1.3) 4, 28, beginning of the twelfth month, Guangxu 10, 1/16/1885. A story of the ghost of a Korean concubine in the royal palace would seem culturally very familiar to Chinese readers; see "Wangfei xianling" 王妃顯靈, *Yuan* (5.2) 4, 26, middle of the fourth month, Guangxu 22, 5/23/1896.

61. For example, "Houlai jushang" 後來居上, DSZ, *Ren* (2.9) 4, 26, middle of the twelfth month, Guangxu 12, 1/4/1887.

62. "Tan ying xiaolu" 談瀛小錄, SB, fifteenth–eighteenth day of the fourth month, 1872, 1.130–31, 1.137–38, 1.146–47; 1.153–54.

63. In *Dahuang dongjing* 大荒東經; in Yuan Ke, *Shanhai jing xiaozhu*, p. 395.

64. On the history of translated fiction and fiction in periodicals, see Chen Pingyuan 陳平原, *Ershi shiji Zhongguo xiaoshuo shi* 二十世紀中國小說史 (Beijing: Beijing daxue chubanshe, 1997), pp. 30, 80.

65. "Yi shui qian nian" 一睡千年, SB, twenty-second day of the fourth month, 1872, 1.178.

66. "Yigui hezhi" 異龜合誌, DSZ, *Mao* (2.4) 5, 19, end of the seventh month, Guangxu 14, 8/28/1888.

67. "Xinyang qiqiu" 新樣氣球, DSZ, *Jia* (1.1) 1, 6, beginning of the fifth intercalary month, Guangxu 10, 6/23/1884.

68. There might be some parallel between this textual framing of foreign stories and Henningsmeier's ("The Foreign Sources of *Dianshizhai huabao*," p. 81) observation that in the illustrations, buildings and people are illustrated in a Western style whereas natural elements such as clouds and plants remain in a Chinese style.

69. Wang Ermin, "Zhongguo jindai zhishi pujihua chuanbo zhi tushuo xingzhi," p. 167.

70. In this I concur with Wagner's sense of the basic stability of *Dianshizhai huabao*'s world and Kim's presentation of the readership as delighting in both novelty and a stable worldview.

71. In *Haiwai xijing* 海外西經; in Yuan Ke, *Shan hai jing xiaozhu*, p. 259. "Xingtian zhi liu" 刑天之流, DSZ, *Ji* 己 (1.6) 9, 68, beginning of the second month, Guangxu 12, 3/6/1886. Another example of encountering a creature coming straight from the pages of the *Shan hai jing* at sea is "Lingyu chu hai" 陵魚出海, DSZ, *Tu* 土 (3.6) 8, 60, end of the second month, Guangxu 19, 4/7/1893. See also "Jushe tun

xiang" 巨蛇吞象, DSZ, *Mu* 木 (3.8) 1, 5, end of the ninth month, Guangxu 19, 10/30/1893.

72. Ji Yun, *Yuewei caotang biji*, 19.1105–6, story 3.

73. The recurrence of illustrations is also noted in Harold Kahn, *Dushi ou de: xue-shu yanjiang san pian* 讀史偶得: 學術演講三篇 (Taibei: Zhongyang yanjiuyuan, Jindaishi yanjiusuo, 1993), p. 79. Although he compares the recycling of that image to a French broadsheet's reuse of an image of a two-headed serpent, I think the use of the image of the *xingtian* here is more than a matter of convenience. Hen-ningsmeier ("The Foreign Sources of *Dianshizhai huabao*," p. 80) describes several ex-amples of DSZ's reworking of foreign visual sources. According to her argument, a pastiche like this was more typical of the 1890s than the 1880s.

74. Compare a story of a Chinese woman who has a headless baby as a result of viewing an execution: "Wutou xiaohai" 無頭小孩, *Ge* 革 (3.7) 10, 81, middle of the seventh month, Guangxu 19, 7/23/1893. In this story, the cultural world of the *Shan hai jing* is not evoked.

75. "Yaohu xianmei" 妖狐獻媚, DSZ, *Zi* 子 (2.1) 7, 56, middle of the eighth month, Guangxu 13, 9/27/1887.

76. In contrast, in *Yuewei caotang biji*, 6.263–64, story 264, Ji Yun commented that although there are foxes in Xinjiang, they do not become monsters and that there-fore foxes' attaining the ability to assume human form is dependent on Chinese cul-ture.

77. "Heifu mi ren" 黑婦迷人, DSZ, *Zi* (2.1) 6, 43, beginning of the eighth month, Guangxu 13, 9/17/1887.

78. The pictorial conveys the idea of the world outside China as a place of other kinds of adventure for Chinese travelers as well. One such story relates Chinese miners being rescued by "wild men" in America; see "Yeren baode" 野人報德, Jia (1.1) 10, 74, middle of the sixth month, Guangxu 10, 8/1/1884.

79. Appearances of a tell-tale tail in *Liaozhai* include "Gu'er" 賈兒 and "Dong sheng" 董生; see Pu Songling 蒲松齡, *Liaozhai zhiyi (huixiao huizhu huiping ben)* 聊齋誌異(會校會注會評本) (Shanghai: Shanghai guji, 1978), 1.125–29 and 2.133–36.

80. For example, "Chimei xi ren" 魑魅喜人, DSZ, *Bing* 3, 20, beginning of the twelfth month, Guangxu 10, 1/16/1885.

81. In another example of the Westerner taking up a role in a traditional fox story, in Korea, a Westerner investigating a hollow tree in which a fox dwells sets it on fire with his torch. People marveling at how a still living tree could be so easily ignited speculated that this was the catastrophe or conflagration (usually in the form of a lightning strike) that a fox must survive before it can become a *xian*. Heaven simply borrowed this man's fire for its own purposes. The illustration again makes the position of this story in multiethnic space clear with Korean onlookers, marked by their hats, in the background. See "Jiehuo yi hu" 劫火殪狐, DSZ, *Chou* 丑 (2.1) 3,

15, beginning of the eleventh month, Guangxu 13, 12/15/1887. In East Asia the foreigner becomes entangled in the local stories and categories of strange experience. For a story of a British hunter thwarted by a fox in a Guangxu collection, see Baiyi jushi, *Hutian lu*, 3.43b–44a.

82. "Ming bing huantan" 名并桓天, DSZ, Wu 午 (2.7) 8, 59, end of the eighth month, Guangxu 15, 9/15/1889.

83. For *Dianshizhai huabao*'s treatment of this conflict, see Wang Ermin, "Zhongguo jindai zhishi pujihua chuanbo zhi tushuo xingshi," pp. 145–46. Another recasting of historical events as ghost story is found in the tale of the ghost of a displaced Korean royal concubine; see "Wangfei xianling" 王妃顯靈, DSZ, Yuan (5.2) 4, 26, middle of the fourth month, Guangxu 22, 5/23/1896.

84. The reprint edition of *Dianshizhai huabao* I have been using does not include these sections. They can be found in *Dianshizhai huabao fulu* (in the Shanghai library).

85. "Haiwai zhuangyou" 海外狀游 (Ambitious journey overseas), in Wang Tao 王韜, *Songyin manlu* 淞隱漫錄 (Taibei: Guangwen shuju, 1976), 8.3. I am grateful to Lam Ling-hon of the University of Chicago for pointing out these stories, and Wang Tao's relevance.

86. Compare the abrupt ending of a fox romance with the intrusion of hunters in "Zheng zhixian" 鄭芷仙, in Wang Tao, *Songyin manlu*, 2.5. Given the autobiographical nature of the journeys, it is also possible that Wang Tao is presenting his own past experiences as dreams from which he has now awoken.

87. Among many examples is "Fenglei shi jing" 風雷示警, SB, 5/17/1877, 18.12290.

88. "Zhen ji kou er" 震及口耳, DSZ, Xin 辛 (1.8) 1, 1, middle of the seventh month, Guangxu 12, 8/10/1886. The illustration of this story is also interesting: the lightning is doubly personified, with figures in the clouds and an old, divine figure harrying the bawd at close hand. These figures are not mentioned in the text but add visual drama. As with the perception of Western ideas of ghosts, this perception of Western ideas of lightning is one-sided, ignoring earlier traditions which also identified lightning with divine wrath.

89. "Lei ji shizhe" 雷殛侍者, DSZ, Jia (1.1) 5, 34, end of the fifth month, Guangxu 10, 6/15/1884. Another interesting cultural contrast is found in a story of lightning striking a giant in Mexico illustrated with extravagantly Chinese spirits; see "Daniao fuzhu" 大鳥伏誅, DSZ, Yue 樂 (4.2) 11, 81, end of the seventh month, Guangxu 20, 8/21/1894.

90. "Lun lei ji long xian er shi" 論雷擊龍見二事, SB, 7/16/1877, 20.12705.

91. Westerners are not the only skeptics on this subject; some "foolish Confucians" also doubt moral interpretation of lightning, and they are similarly discredited; see "Lei ji ni zi" 雷殛逆子, DSZ, Si 巳 (2.6) 3, 21, beginning of the third month, Guangxu 15, 3/31/1889.

92. "Haizhong yiwu" 海中異物, SB, 10/13/1876, 17.10969.

93. "Xiren jian long" 西人見龍, DSZ, Ji (1.6) 12, 90, beginning of the third month, Guangxu 12, 4/4/1886.

94. See, e.g., "Huolong diexian"火龍叠見, Jin 金 (3.1) 4, 25, middle of the sixth month, Guangxu 17, 7/16/1891. I owe the observation about the dragons' perspective to a discussion group at the University of Chicago.

95. "Suoshi yishu" 縮尸異術, DSZ, Mao (2.4) 8, 32, end of the eighth month, Guangxu 14, 9/26/1888. A similar comment on Western lack of respect for the grave is found in a later entry on Egyptian mummies; "Bao shi bu bian" 保尸不變, Shu 書 (4.5) 2, 13, end of the fourth month, Guangxu 21, 5/14/1895.

96. "Gezhi yihai" 格致遺骸, Mao (2.4) 12, 49, beginning of the tenth month. Guangxu 14, 11/4/1888. A comparison of Western and Chinese views of eclipses in the Shenbao, although far less grotesque and controversial, also reaches the conclusion that the Western "scientific" view seems amoral: "Lun jiuhu rishi zhi fa zui gu" 論救護日食之法最古, SB, 5/21/1882, 34.22653.

97. Xenophobia in the service of the grotesque, as in this case, is to be contrasted with the grotesque in the service of xenophobia, which becomes very evident in the portrayal of the Japanese during the Sino-Japanese war. Comments on the sexual immorality of the Japanese are very pointed; see "Yi shen bao guo" 以身報國, DSZ, She 射 (4.3), 2, 14, end of the eighth month, Guangxu 20, 9/20/1894; and "Wo gui" 倭龜, DSZ, She 10, 76, middle of the eleventh month, Guangxu 20, 12/7/1894.

98. "Jinquan feiji" 矜全廢疾, DSZ, Si (2.6), 1, 2, middle of the second month, Guangxu 15, 3/12/1889.

99. "Huabao gengzheng" 畫報更正, DSZ, Si (2.6), 2, 7, end of the second month, Guangxu 15, 3/22/1889.

100. For a discussion of this as an image of Dianshizhai's ideal reader, see Kim, "How to Read About Monsters and Miracles," p. 5.

101. The effect of actual foreign geography on imagined geography is more straightforward in a tale of a Buddhist monk who correctly foretold the moment of his death. After an account of his demise, called in religious terms entering "the Western Heaven," the editorial voice mocks the belief. It points out that we know that India contains only human beings, and even if one goes further west, to England, Portugal, and France, there are only more human beings. Where are the Bodhisattvas? See "Laoseng zuohua" 老僧坐化, SB, 5/6/1882, 34.22528.

102. Compare a story of haunting by a snake spirit, in which the conclusion asks why no foreigners residing in China or overseas are ever troubled by such creatures. "It is evident that if one believes in them, they exist; if not, they don't" ("Bisui yiju" 避祟移居, SB, 12/27/1877, 22.13837). When an exceptional story of a ghost in America is recorded, it opens with the statement, "Westerners never believe in

ghosts." The poltergeist-type disturbances described would be very familiar to the Chinese reader; see "Xiren shuoguai" 西人說怪, *SB*, 1/5/1883, 37.24884.

103. "Lun shefa yi jiu wangsi" 論設法一救枉死, *SB*, 11/3/1876, 17.11001. The *Shenbao* itself frequently reports incidents of drowned or hung ghosts seeking substitutes; see, e.g., "Nigui taoti" 溺鬼討替, 3/1/1878, 22.14228.

104. In a few of his anecdotes, Ji Yun raised the question of the cultural specificity of the strange. He commented that foxes in Xinjiang do not become monsters, and elsewhere wonders why those who journey to the underworld encounter only Chinese ghosts. Does each nation have its own netherworld? See Ji Yun, *Yuewei caotang*, 6.263–64, story 264.

105. The largest exception is ghosts, which are still encountered in lonely places.

106. See the illustrations in Irene Ewinkel, *De Monstris: Deutung und Funktion von Wundergeburten auf Flugblättern im Deustchland des 16. Jahrhundert* (Tübingen: Niemeyer, 1995); or in Arnold I. Davidson, "The Horror of Monsters," in *The Boundaries of Humanity*, ed. James Sheehan and Morton Sosna (Berkeley: University of California Press, 1990), pp. 36–67.

107. For a discussion of this theme, see Wang Ermin, "Zhongguo jindai zhishi pujihua chuanbo zhi tushuo xingshi," p. 154. An example of a report on Chinese acrobatic acts is "Zou suo fan shen" 走索翻身, *DSZ*, *Bing* 11, 83, end of the second month, Guangxu 11, 4/6/1885. Other public amusements with a multiethnic audience include horseracing, "Saima zhisheng" 賽馬誌盛, *Jia* 2, 15, end of the fourth month, Guangxu 10, 5/5/1884; "Xiren paozhi" 西人跑紙, *Bing* 5, 35, end of the twelfth month, Guangxu 10, 2/5/1885; "Yijue buzhen" 一蹶不振, *Wu* 戊 10, 74, middle of the tenth month, Guangxu 11, 11/17/1885; a French display of lanterns for Bastille day, "Fajie xuan deng" 法界懸燈, *Ding* 10, 80, middle of the sixth month, Guangxu 11, 7/22/1885; and other contests among Westerners, such as an egg and spoon race, "Xiren saiji" 西人塞技, *Wu* 戊 10, 73, middle of the tenth month, Guangxu 11, 11/17/1885.

108. "Guan xixi shulüe" 觀西戲述略, *DSZ*, *Si* 11, 82, end of the fifth month, Guangxu 14, 6/20/1889.

109. "Xixi chonglai" 西戲重來, *DSZ*, *Geng* 6, 42, beginning of the fifth month, Guangxu 12, 6/2/1886.

110. "De kui quan bao" 得窺全豹, *DSZ*, *Bing* 5, 37, end of the twelfth month, Guangxu 10, 2/5/1885.

111. For a discussion of the term "armchair traveler," see Kim, "How to Read About Monsters and Miracles," p. 23.

112. I am grateful to Anne Burkus-Chasson for discussions of looking in the illustrations.

113. "Mai yeren tou" 賣野人頭, DSZ, Bing 10, 78, middle of the second month, Guangxu 11, 3/27/1885. Wang Ermin, "Zhongguo jindai zhishi pujihua chuanbo zhi tushuo xingshi," p. 155.

114. Pu Songling, Liaozhai zhiyi (huixiao huizhu huiping ben), 5.597. Another example is an account of a long-tongued old woman and a one-legged man in Zhang Jingyun 張景運, Qiuping xinyu 秋坪新語 (preface dated 1792), 3.3b. The story voices the suspicion that these people had been deliberately maimed for profit and urges that such practices be forbidden.

115. "Fujian zhuru" 復見侏儒, DSZ, Wu (1.6) 5, 37, end of the eighth month, Guangxu 11, 9/29/1885.

116. Brown, The Material Unconscious, p. 202. Davidson, "The Horror of Monsters," pp. 61–64.

117. "Luyi" 驢異, DSZ, Li 禮 (4.1) 1, 9, middle of the twelfth month, Guangxu 18, 1/17/1894.

118. "Chuang jian yi zhu" 創見異豬, Wu 戊 11, 87, end of the tenth month, Guangxu 11, 11/27/1885.

119. "Wu ti niu" 五蹄牛 and "San bi ren" 三臂人, SB, 3/6/1876, 15.9340. The paper records them side by side, noting that creation never produces a single freak, but always a pair.

120. SB, 10/8/1884, 11/18/1882, 24455.

121. On the American appetite for freaks imported from all over the world at approximately the same time, see Brown, The Material Unconscious, p. 202.

122. "Yu zhangren" 遇丈人, DSZ, Ren 2, 12, end of the eleventh month, Guangxu 12, 12/16/1886; "Houlai jushang" 後來居上, Ren 4, 26, middle of the twelfth month, Guangxu 12, 1/4/1887; "Xiaoren dezhi" 小人得志, Yin 寅 3, 16, beginning of the third month, Guangxu 14, 4/11/1888; "Yichang yiduan" 一長一短, Jin (3.1) 3, 21, beginning of the sixth month, Guangxu 17, 7/6/1891. See also Wang Ermin, "Zhongguo jindai zhishi pujihua chuanbo zhi tushuo xingshi," p. 150. He is also mentioned in the Shenbao; see "San bi ren" 三臂人, SB, 3/6/1876, 15.9340; as well as in a contemporary zhiguai collection; see "Changren" 長人, Xuan Ding 宣鼎, Yeyu qiudeng lu 夜雨秋燈録 (Harbin: Heilongjiang Renmin chubanshe, 1997), 4.136.

123. This phrase, which also appears as early as the Shiji, already uses the idiom of the merchant in reference to human talent, but I think that its use here has become more explicitly literal: the person has become the actual merchandise. A man from Suzhou also uses these words in response to a dwarf, "Xiaoren dezhi" 小人得志, Yin 3, 16, beginning of the third month, Guangxu 14, 4/11/1888. The phrase is also used in reference to the two-headed five-legged donkey in "Luyi" 驢異, DSZ, Li (4.1) 1, 9, middle of the twelfth month, Guangxu 18, 1/17/1894.

124. The term in the original is renxiong 人熊, which Hanyu dacidian (5: 43) defines as either a bear or a feifei 狒狒. In contemporary usage a feifei is a baboon, but

in traditional Chinese references it is a hairy, man-like creature, potentially confused with wild men or mountain demons.

125. This expression, to expose one's original form, is very suggestive of tales of animal transformation, in which a fox or other spirit who has been masquerading as human is finally exposed as an animal.

126. "Xingxing nengyan" 猩猩能言, DSZ, *Chou* 11, 77, end of the first month, Guangxu 14, 3/3/1888.

127. This is in marked contrast to the conflation of the freak and black men that Brown (*The Material Unconscious*, pp. 208–17) describes in the American context.

128. See, e.g., "Guize fuxin" 鬼責負心, DSZ, *Ren* 3, 19, beginning of the twelfth month, Guangxu 12, 12/25/1886.

129. "Feiluan xinyu" 飛鸞新語, DSZ, *Bing* 3, 22, beginning of the twelfth month, Guangxu 10, 1/16/1885. For another example of a visible ghost writer standing on incense smoke and using a planchette, see "Qinggui luanshu" 情鬼鸞書, *Yu* (4.4) 7, 54, middle of the second month, Guangxu 21, 3/7/1895.

130. "Yu yinguan wang" 遇陰關亡, DSZ, *Ding* 8, 65, end of the fifth month, Guangxu 11, 7/3/1885. Cf. the illustration of a sorcerous technique for kidnapping children. The illustration shows both the illusory tiger threatening a boy and the Daoist leading him to supposed safety. None of the watching crowd sees these things; their focus is on the confrontation between the child and his father, who is trying to hold him back. See "Mitu weiyuan" 迷途未遠, DSZ, *Shu* (4.5) 1, 4, middle of the fourth month, Guangxu 21, 5/5/1895. Although demons are routinely described as the products of the human mind, I have found only one case in which a man's interior horrors are banished from the illustration as well, the story of a retired soldier convinced the men he had slain were taking revenge on him. The editorial voice rejects this on the grounds that if this were true, all soldiers should die plagued by ghosts. The illustration shows the man confronting a blank wall in terror; see "Yixin shenggui" 疑心生鬼, DSZ, *Gui* 癸 1, middle of the third month, Guangxu 13, 4/4/1887.

131. Illustration of "Shang xian" 上仙, in Pu Songling 蒲松齡, *Xiangzhu Liaozhai zhiyi tuyong* 詳注聊齋誌異圖詠 (1886 ed.), 15.2a.

132. For an example of a fake fox spirit, see "Wunong qingchi" 侮弄情痴, DSZ, *Bing* 3, 17, beginning of the twelfth month, Guangxu 10, 1/16/1885. In the same issue is an illustration showing the beguiling surface of demonic illusion; see "Chimei xiren" 魑魅喜人, DSZ, *Bing* 3, 20.

133. For the former, see Wagner, "The Shanghai Illustrated Newspapers *Dianshizhai huabao* and *Feiyingge huanbao*," p. 23. For the monster as a sign of horror at a changing world, see Davidson, "The Horror of Monsters," pp. 37–38.

Works Cited

Baiyi jushi 百一居士 (pseud.). *Hutian lu* 壺天錄. Taibei: Guangwen shuju, 1969.

Barr, Allan. "Pu Songling and *Liaozhai zhiyi*: A Study of Textual Transmission, Biographical Background, and Literary Antecedents." Ph.D. diss., Oxford University, 1983.

Brown, Bill. *The Material Unconscious.* Cambridge, Mass.: Harvard University Press, 1996.

Campany, Robert. *Strange Writing: Anomaly Accounts in Early Medieval China.* Albany: State University of New York Press, 1996.

Chan, Tak-hung Leo. *The Discourse of Foxes and Ghosts: Ji Yun and Eighteenth Century Chinese Storytelling.* Honolulu: University of Hawai'i Press, 1999.

Chen Pingyuan 陳平原. *Ershi shiji Zhongguo xiaoshuo shi* 二十世紀中國小說史. Beijing: Beijing daxue chubanshe, 1997.

Davidson, Arnold I. "The Horror of Monsters." In *The Boundaries of Humanity,* ed. James Sheehan and Morton Sosna. Berkeley: University of California Press, 1990, pp. 36–67.

Dianshizhai huabao 點石齋畫報. Reprinted in 5 vols.—Guangzhou: Guangdong renmin chubanshe, 1983.

Dianshizhai huabao fulu 點石齋畫報附錄. Copy in Shanghai library, n.d.

Elman, Benjamin. "From Pre-modern Chinese Natural Studies 格致學 to Modern Science 科學 in China." Paper presented at the conference "Translating Western Knowledge into Late Imperial China," University of Göttingen, 1999.

Ewinkel, Irene. *De Monstris: Deutung und Funktion von Wundergeburten auf Flugblättern im Deustchland des 16. Jahrhundert.* Tübingen: Niemeyer, 1995.

Ge Gongzhen 戈公振. *Zhongguo baoxue shi* 中國報學史. Beijing, 1955.

Hanan, Patrick. "*Fengyue meng* and the Courtesan Novel." *Harvard Journal of Asiatic Studies* 58, no. 2 (1998): 345–72.

Hanyu da cidian 漢語大辭典. 12 vols. Shanghai: Hanyu da cidian chubanshe, 1990–93.

Hay, Jonathan. "Painters and Publishing in Late Nineteenth-Century Shanghai." In *Art at the Close of China's Empire,* ed. Ju-hsi Chou. Phoebus Occasional Papers in Art History, vol. 8. Tempe: Arizona State University, 1988, pp. 134–88.

Henningsmeier, Julia. "The Foreign Sources of *Dianshizhai huabao,* a Nineteenth-Century Shanghai Illustrated Magazine." *Ming Qing yanjiu* 1998: 59–91.

Ji Yun 紀昀. *Yuewei caotang biji yizhu* 閱微草堂筆記譯注. Beijing: Zhongguo huaqiao chubanshe, 1994.

Kahn, Harold. *Dushi ou de: xueshu yanjiang san pian* 讀史偶得: 學術演講三篇. Taibei: Zhongyang yanjiuyuan, Jindaishi yanjiusuo, 1993.

Kim, Nanny. "How to Read About Monsters and Miracles in an Illustrated Magazine from Late 19th Century Shanghai." Unpublished MS.

Li Jianguo 李劍國. *Tangqian zhiguai xiaoshuo shi* 唐前志怪小說史. Tianjin: Nankai daxue chubanshe, 1984.

———. *Tang Wudai zhiguai chuanqi xulu* 唐五代志怪傳奇敘錄. Tianjin: Nankai daxue chubanshe, 1993.

Link, E. Perry. *Mandarin Ducks and Butterflies: Popular Fiction in Early Twentieth-Century Chinese Cities.* Berkeley: University of California Press, 1981.

Liu, Lydia. *Translingual Practice: Literature, National Culture, and Translated Modernity—China, 1900–1937.* Stanford: Stanford University Press, 1995.

Meng Yue. "The Forgotten Amateurs: Popular Scientists in the Creation of Shanghai, 1876–1917." Paper presented at the conference "Creating a Multiethnic Urban Culture: The Shanghai Concessions, 1850–1910," University of Heidelberg, June 1998.

Pu Songling 蒲松齡. *Liaozhai zhiyi (huixiao huizhu huiping ben)* 聊齋誌異 (會校會注會評本). Shanghai: Shanghai guji, 1978.

———. *Xiangzhu Liaozhai zhiyi tuyong* 詳注聊齋誌異圖詠. 1886 ed.

Shenbao 申報, 1872–87 issues. Reprinted—Zhongguo shixue congshu 中國史學叢書. Taibei: Xuesheng shuju, 1965.

Stephen, Mitchell. *A History of News.* New York: Viking Books, 1998.

Vittinghoff, Natascha. "Freier Fluss: zur Kulturgeschichte des frühen chinesischen Journalismus." Ph.D. diss., University of Heidelberg, 1997–98.

Wagner, Rudolf. "Ernest Major's Shenbaoguan and the Formation of Late Qing Print Culture." Paper presented at the conference "Creating a Multiethnic Urban Culture: The Shanghai Concessions, 1850–1910," University of Heidelberg, June 1998.

———. "The Shanghai Illustrated Newspapers *Dianshizhai huabao* and *Feiyingge huabao*—An Introductory Survey." Unpublished MS.

Wang Ermin 王爾敏. "Zhongguo jindai zhishi pujihua chuanbo zhi tushuo xingshi: *Dianshizhai huabao*" 中國近代知識普及化傳播之圖說形式—點石齋畫報 (The pictorial form of popular transmission of modern consciousness: *Dianshizhai huabao*). *Zhongyang yanjiuyuan, Jindai shi yanjiusuo jikan*, 19 (1990): 135–72.

Wang Tao 王韜. *Hou Liaozhai zhiyi quanyi quanzhu* 後聊齋誌異全譯全注. Harbin: Heilongjiang renmin chubanshe, 1988.

———. *Songyin manlu* 淞隱漫錄. Reprinted—Taibei: Guangwen shuju, 1976.

Wu Meifeng 吳美鳳. "Cong *Dianshizhai huabao* kan wan Qing shiqi de minjian xinyang yishi" 從點石齋畫報看晚清時期的民間信仰意識. *Lishi wenwu*, no. 91 (Feb. 2001): 33–57.

Xu Ruifang 徐瑞芳 and Xu Zaiping 徐載平. *Qingmo sishi nian Shenbao shiliao* 清末四十年申報史料. Beijing: Xinhua chubanshe, 1988.

Xuan Ding 宣鼎. *Yeyu qiudeng lu*. 夜雨秋燈錄. Harbin: Heilongjiang Renmin chubanshe, 1997.

Ye, Xiaoqing. "Popular Culture in Shanghai." Ph.D. diss., Australian National University, 1993.

Yuan Ke 袁軻. *Shan hai jing xiaozhu* 山海經校注. Chengdu: Bashu shushe, 1993.

Zeitlin, Judith. *Historian of the Strange: Pu Songling and the Chinese Classical Tale*. Stanford: Stanford University Press, 1993.

Zhang Jingyun 張景運. *Qiuping xinyu* 秋坪新語. Preface dated 1792.

Creating the Urban Beauty

The Shanghai Courtesan in Late Qing Illustrations

Catherine Vance Yeh

During the late nineteenth century, a visual revolution began in the Chinese print industry. Spearheaded by Shanghai and its publishing houses and aided in part by new, foreign printing technologies such as copper engraving, lithography, and photography, new forms of visual publication started to have an impact on the marketplace.[1] As Western material culture in the form of imported goods made inroads into the daily life of Shanghai residents, new types of illustrated publications—magazines, urban and entertainment guides, and later newspapers—increasingly catered to this urban readership rather than to the traditional literati elite. At the center of this revolution was the image of the courtesan. Once the emblem of highest aesthetic refinement constructed by the literati and associated with their world order, the courtesan was transformed into the symbol of Shanghai's glamour and commercial might, as well as of its follies.

The transformation from the aesthetics of "exclusiveness" to the aesthetics of the "popular" brought a shift in the image of the courtesan from what might be called the "secluded, cultured beauty," a female depicted with no identifiable sign of belonging to a specific locale, to the "urban public beauty," a figure with identifiable local and urban characteristics. The break with the past was most pointedly made in the change of setting: the courtesan left the secluded and semi-private environment of the garden or boudoir and entered open urban space. Depicted as being in urban Shanghai, she was marketed by the Shanghai print industry as an object with the attractions of the new. These shifts from "secluded" to "public" and from "exclusiveness" to "popular" were the decisive first steps in the creation of the Shanghai "star culture," later typified by film stars.

A series of illustrated city guides published from the 1880s on helped establish the courtesan as a major component in the graphic narration of the city. As one of the most frequently illustrated figures, the courtesan dominated Shanghai illustrations and, like the city itself, captured the imagination of artists and viewers, both as idealized image and as the subject of satire. In publications such as *Dianshizhai Magazine* (*Dianshizhai huabao* 點石齋畫報), she became the subject matter of urban humor and entertainment.

During the 1890s, the illustrated figure of the Shanghai courtesan was so well established that it became a selling point in and of itself, and the image had a growing impact on public behavior, fashion trends, and the life-style of Shanghai women. By the end of the century, depictions of the Shanghai courtesan dominated the representation of leisure and entertainment. With the growth of the entertainment newspapers in the late 1890s, such as *Youxi bao* 遊戲報, *Caifeng bao* 采風報, and *Shijie fanhua bao* 世界繁華報, that featured the life and activities of the top-ranking Shanghai courtesans, their public persona was further enhanced.[2] As a star of the new mass media, the courtesan replaced the "beauty" of the past with her claims to refinement and to sophisticated as well as exclusive appreciation. These illustrations succeeded in refashioning the courtesan as the model for the new "urban beauty."

The depictions of the Shanghai courtesan were far from uniform. Between the late 1890s and early 1910s, when exploration of the commercial potential of her image was at its height, novels with a courtesan as the main protagonist began to appear.[3] In contrast to the glamorous image found in illustrations, the courtesans in these novels are mostly negative characters. This is rooted in the complex response of literati novelists to their social position in the Shanghai foreign settlements and their troubled identity in this city. Through the figure of the courtesan, they expressed their own ambivalence toward Shanghai's commercialism.

Created in the wake of the Opium War, the Shanghai foreign settlements quickly outgrew their original charter as a settlement for foreigners.

Shanghai became a place inhabited by people from different foreign countries and Chinese regions, governed by foreigners using Western administrative routines and legal concepts. With investment, immigration, and trade by foreigners and Chinese alike, and fairly secure because of its links with the West from the turmoils besetting the late Qing, the city thrived both financially and culturally.

The challenge posed, however, to traditional Chinese values by what might be called the evolving Shanghai Concession culture was formidable. One of the pivotal issues was the commercial spirit of the city, which put a premium on money and trade. As this increasingly undermined the value system and hierarchical order of traditional society not just in fact but also in articulation, the reaction, especially by the *wenren* 文人 class, who had the most to lose, was great. The transformation of the image of the Shanghai courtesan highlighted the conflict over the definition of the city's identity. As journalists and editors in newspapers and publishing houses, many *wenren* had a strong public voice. Traditionally the patrons of the courtesan, these literati confronted a new type of courtesan who made bold use of the protections afforded by the foreign concessions to recraft her public and private persona in a manner unparalleled in the rest of the Qing empire. The changes in the traditional social positions of both the literati and the courtesans in the Shanghai environment altered the status as well as the relationships of the two groups. The consequence was an image of the courtesan beset with contradictions. It reflects at once the aggrandizement of commercial success and the dubious morals associated with it; it stands for beauty and for the power to corrupt. Literati who desired to maintain control over the narrative of the courtesan had to deal with the demands and requirements of a developing print market as well as the opportunities afforded by it, not to mention the reshaping of the courtesan image under the impact of Western representational techniques, such as perspective, the development of new urban tastes, and self-confident moves by the top courtesans themselves.

After a brief look at courtesan illustrations from the late Ming and late Qing, this chapter sketches the modern transformation of the courtesan image and the complex historical message embedded in its construction. Given the substantial cultural capital associated with the courtesan's image and her central role in articulating the cultural identity of Shanghai, this transformation provides highly evocative material for studying the emergence of a new urban and commercial aesthetics. As the image of the courtesan changes from the traditional to the new and cosmopolitan, she is transformed from the emblem of an idealized world order in which her sexuality was intended to please and to support the power structure into the representative of Shanghai's aggrandizing and fascinating but also quite disturbing urban life-style. In the process, the role of the literati shifts from preferred patron, client, and potential lover and husband of the courtesan to that of a wage-earner making a living by writing on these rising stars while continuing to be part of their circle.

The Marker of Change: From Late Ming Secluded Beauty to Late Qing Urban Icon

The figure of the courtesan had by the Wanli period (1573–1620) of the Ming become a familiar subject of illustrations. She appeared in popular literary illustrations, as well as in the well-established genres of the illustrated album and the urban guide with biographies of courtesans.[4] Although greatly indebted to the tradition of the illustrated biographies of worthy women, lienü 烈女, and famous beauties, illustrated courtesan albums, known under the rubric of baimei tu 百美圖—"the illustrated one hundred beauties"—had by this time become a separate genre.[5] These albums reflect as much the flourishing of woodcarving art during the Wanli period as that of courtesan entertainment culture. The albums consist of records of different courtesan competitions and typically feature short biographies of the 100 courtesans who had been successful in these competitions, together with poetry dedicated to them. Each woman was matched with a particular kind of flower that symbolized her particular temperament and beauty. The top-ranking twenty or so courtesans were, in addition, the subjects of portraits, with their name, rank, and sometimes address given. In their depiction of individual courtesans and scenes from their private and professional life, these illustrations use set motifs.

The dominant features of the baimei tu follow the tradition of portraits of meiren 美人 (beautiful women) and the traditional caizi jiaren 才子佳人 (scholar and beauty) trope with their evocation of cultural refinement and desirability through the depiction of certain motifs or set scenes. The composition has much in common with that of female figures in literary illustrations: the woman is situated in a garden, tingyuan 庭園, nature, shanshui 山水, or her boudoir, shenyuan qushi 深院曲世, but never in what one

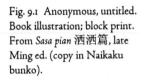

Fig. 9.1 Anonymous, untitled.
Book illustration; block print.
From *Sasa pian* 洒洒篇, late
Ming ed. (copy in Naikaku
bunko).

might call the "public realm" (Fig. 9.1). The mood and atmosphere conveyed
by these settings are those of a "dreamscape" rather than of a specific place
on earth (Fig. 9.2). The woman depicted in Fig. 9.1 exemplifies the motif of
"gazing into the distance" (*yuantiao* 遠眺), a well-established trope with romantic associations. The body gesture of one hand withdrawn into the
sleeve and one hand raised to the chin is described by Ellen Johnston Laing
as "a standard gesture of a lovelorn women." This interpretation is sup-
ported by the mildly erotic image of the banana plant, which "by virtue of
the melancholy sound of rain on its leaves, suggests the loneliness of the
abandoned, lovelorn woman."[6] The autumn season (a time of "desertion") is
suggested by the full moon and the Great Dipper in the night sky; they
evoke the sadness of lovers' separation where there should be reunion. The
sentiment is further accentuated by the catalpa (*wutong* 梧桐) tree, the Chinese name of which is a pun on the expression "we together" (*wutong* 吾同),
another standard trope in the romantic lament, in which the happiness of
nature is often contrasted with human grief.[7] In Fig. 9.2, the ornate
and elaborate style in which Huang Duanfu 黃端甫, one of the late Ming
master carvers of the Huang family of Huizhou, represented the world of
intimate relationship and the great attention to detail evoke the dreamlike

Fig. 9.2 Huang Duanfu 黃端甫 (active early 17th c.), untitled. Book illustration, block print. From *Qinglou yunyu* 青樓韻語 (Poetry from the green tower), Wanli period, 1: 12 (copy in Beijing tushuguan).

quality of the world of sensuous pleasures. The figure of the courtesan in these illustrations is thus both an embodiment of a culture of refinement and a symbol of an idealized social order.[8]

Beyond these elements, which they share with depictions of other women, the courtesan portraits also exhibit an overt eroticism (Fig. 9.3). The courtesan was a professional entertainer, and her figure allowed for a certain degree of freedom, expressed in illustrations of a playful manner in relationships with men. Even as these features set her apart from the depiction of women of good standing, they also give the artist greater leeway. In Fig. 9.3, "Elegant Banter," the courtesan is shown clasping a catalpa tree between her legs, evoking the notion and the image of "union"; this elicits a smile from the male figure on her left. The idea of a soft but transitory erotic encounter is subtly accentuated by the fan held in the courtesan's right hand. The fan, as Ellen Johnston Laing suggests in her study of *meiren* painting, evokes a woman's foreboding that love, like summer, will inevitably pass, and that she,

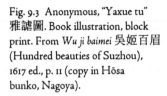

Fig. 9.3 Anonymous, "Yaxue tu" 雅謔圖. Book illustration, block print. From *Wu ji baimei* 吳姬百眉 (Hundred beauties of Suzhou), 1617 ed., p. 11 (copy in Hōsa bunko, Nagoya).

like the fan, will be cast aside.[9] The courtesan in "Elegant Banter" is shown as initiating sexual play, but the fan indicates her awareness of her role as a short-term lover.

Seen from the perspective of later developments, the Ming courtesan illustrations convey a quality of universality in their setting as well as in their beauty. The courtesans are routinely surrounded by trees, plants (especially banana), flowers (especially plum and lotus), garden rocks, mountains, and water, and at times they are accompanied by stars, clouds, and the moon; their world is one of harmony and tranquility. Their facial expressions and bodily postures suggest the highest degree of taste and cultivation. Although the *baimei tu* always depict local courtesans, a fact made clear through the inclusion of the place-name in their title, there is no sign of regional differentiation in terms of the environment depicted or of marked regional differences in figurative representation.

Of importance to this discussion of the emergence of the "urban beauty" is a change in the setting surrounding the *meiren* between the seventeenth and the eighteenth centuries. As James Cahill has pointed out, this was one of the most creative and dynamic periods in *meiren hua* 美人畫 (paintings of beautiful women). Of particular importance for the later developments is

Fig. 9.4 Jiao Bingzhen 焦秉貞 (fl. 1689–1726), "Lianzhou wanbo" 蓮舟晚泊 (Evening boating on the lotus pond). Ink and color on silk. National Palace Museum, Taipei. Source: Guoli gugong bowuyuan bianji weiyuanhui 國立故宮博物院編輯委員會, ed., *Shinü hua zhi mei* 仕女畫之美 (Paintings of beauties) (Taipei: Guoli gugong bowuyuan, 1988), pl. 72.

the transfer, at this time, of the beauty from the garden to the boudoir. As Fig. 9.4 from the late seventeenth or early eighteenth century demonstrates, the depiction of the interior was further enhanced by borrowings of Western illusionism, in particular perspective, to render the diagonal recession of architectural elements back into space learned from European prints.[10] The woman's figure was presented for the first time primarily in relationship to architectural structures.[11] This combination of architecture and the female figure was taken up in the late nineteenth-century Shanghai prints and developed into the depiction of the *meiren* as "urban beauty."

The harbinger of the radical break with the tradition of *meiren hua* was the founding of the Dianshizhai lithographic printing studio in Shanghai in 1879 by the Englishman Ernest Major (1842–1908) to introduce and popularize this printing technology. Major began his publishing career in China by founding one of the first, and certainly the most important, Chinese-language newspapers, the *Shenbao* 申報, in 1872; he played a decisive role in introducing the Western notions of the newspaper, journalism, and the illustrated journal into China.[12] Major and his company were instrumental in the visual revolution that ushered in the new urban beauty.[13]

Fig. 9.5 Wu Youru 吳友如, "Juhua shanxia xieji yinjiu" 菊花山下挾妓飲酒. Illustrated album leaf, lithography, from *Shenjiang shengjing tu* 申江勝景圖 (Illustrated grand scenes of Shanghai) (Shanghai: Dianshizhai, 1884), 2: 4.

In 1884, Major's company issued a lithograph album on Shanghai entitled *Illustrated Grand Scenes of Shanghai (Shenjiang shengjing tu* 申江勝景圖).[14] It was the first album published in China with illustrations printed by lithography. Its stunningly beautiful and finely executed illustrations were by Wu Youru 吳友如 (1846?-96?), who had started to work for the *Dianshizhai huabao* earlier that same year. As claimed in its introduction, the album departed from the traditional practice of depicting famous natural and man-made sights of a city and set out to "dazzle with the extraordinary and the foreign, and to boast with the outstanding and unusual" (*xuanyi jinqi* 炫異 矜奇). Shanghai was nothing short of "the epitome of human ingenuity that surpassed even the work of heaven" (*ren qiao ji er tian gong duo* 人巧極而天 工奪), and the album was intended to reflect that.[15] The Shanghai courtesan and courtesan entertainment life were part of these grand scenes of Shanghai (Figs. 9.5-6). The inclusion of these scenes in the album is highly

Fig. 9.6 Wu Youru 吳友如, "Nüshuchang" 女書場. Illustrated album leaf, lithograph. From *Shenjiang shengjing tu* 申江勝景圖 (Illustrated grand scenes of Shanghai) (Shanghai: Dianshizhai, 1884), 2: 30.

unusual. Although city guides and narratives previously had often mentioned courtesan entertainment, they had not been featured in the illustrations.[16] The unusual inclusion of the courtesan was part of the overall design of the album. Other depicted examples of the "extraordinary" are foreigners in a sack race, the Mixed Court with foreign and Chinese judges jointly presiding, a steamship, and the Shanghai clock tower. Together, these images weave a composite picture of the city as a place of exotic wonders.

The depiction of the Shanghai courtesan as part of Shanghai's uniqueness broke with tradition in two significant ways. First, it presented the courtesan in an urban setting as a public figure and as part of Shanghai's urban culture; although maintaining the high cultural stature implied in her portrait, it abandoned the exclusive setting traditionally used to convey this stature. Second, the locale of this urban setting was clearly rendered in a way that emphasized the activities of the courtesan as a unique local feature of the Shanghai foreign settlements rather than part of a generic environment.

The "Women's Story-Telling Hall" (Fig. 9.6) shows the "wonder" of the Shanghai courtesan publicly performing in a hall thronged with customers. The revolutionary aspect of this illustration lies in its image of the courtesan set in the public space, under the public gaze.[17] It highlights the unique conditions provided by the Shanghai foreign settlements, since public performances by women were strictly forbidden in the rest of the Qing empire. The illustration of patrons and courtesans celebrating under the "Mount of Chrysanthemums" (Fig. 9.5) depicts the semi-public place of an urban courtesan house and an entertainment ritual unique to Shanghai. The interior decoration with its distinctly Western components is very much Shanghai and signals at the same time the role of Shanghai courtesans as trendsetters. The most obvious signs are the kerosene lamps suspended in the middle of the halls, the Western-style pane-glass windows, and the lamppost in the garden, all of which had become symbols of the Western material culture unique to the city.

Although the "traditional beauty" was in fact depicted in other works of that period and even long after, the *Illustrated Grand Scenes of Shanghai* signaled a new approach to the theme. The public setting of the courtesan was part of a new exploration of the public space in Shanghai illustrations. This new exploration can be documented in other illustrations, but the existence of a strong and identifiable style of courtesan representation from the past allows us to highlight, by juxtaposition, the new approach projected in the *Illustrated Grand Scenes of Shanghai*.

The inclusion of the Shanghai courtesan in the *Illustrated Grand Scenes* was based on the high cultural status of the courtesan image in traditional illustrations. The courtesan figure carries the implicit message of prosperity and peace (*taiping shengshi* 太平盛世).[18] Her presence in depictions of Shanghai next to Western-style objects endowed the "foreign settlement" with the traditional emblems of prosperity and thus marked the cultural space within which these new material goods were to be perceived and appreciated. In this respect, the *Illustrated Grand Scenes* was a program piece. It set out to present the city as a "model settlement" of free and prosperous trade and of social, including ethnic, harmony.[19] The image of the courtesan was used to serve this larger design.

In the same year this album appeared, another remarkable illustrated city guide was published by the Guan ke shou Studio, the *Illustrations with Expla-*

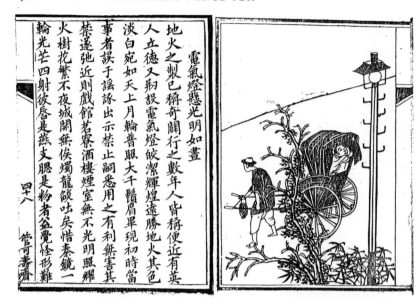

Fig. 9.7 Anonymous, "Dianqideng xuan guangming ruzhou" 電氣燈懸光明如畫. Illustrated album leaf, block print. From *Shenjiang mingsheng tushuo* 申江名勝圖說 (Illustrations with explanations of famous sights of Shanghai) (Shanghai: Guan ke shou zhai, 1884), p. 48.

nations of Famous Sights of Shanghai (Shenjiang mingsheng tushuo 申江名勝 圖說). A woodblock album, its orientation was in some ways quite different. Instead of parading grand scenes of the achievements of the foreign settlements, this album adopted a more critical stance. Although it also focused on the fantastic and the new, the "explanations" were not always favorable. Its representation of the Shanghai courtesan as part of the city's unique sights was more matter-of-fact and less idealized. The account of the fantastic powers of illumination of electrical lights (Fig. 9.7) and about the boost they gave to nighttime entertainment, including the entertainment offered by the courtesans, is a rather ironical introduction to this innovation. In the same manner, another account made lighthearted fun of an "outrage" to be found in Shanghai: courtesans and their clients taking a night drive through town (Fig. 9.8). Yet, perhaps because the foreign settlements were presented here with some ironical distance (unlike the *Shenjiang shengjing tu*, which closely identified with the city), the revolutionary transformation of the female figure from a secluded "private" setting to a public urban environment is executed here with seeming ease and little self-consciousness. The urban

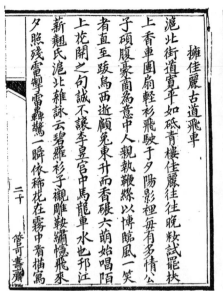

Fig. 9.8 Anonymous, "Yong jiali gudao feiche" 擁佳麗古道飛車. Illustrated album leaf, block print. From *Shenjiang mingsheng tushuo* 申江名勝圖說 (Illustrations with explanations of famous sights of Shanghai) (Shanghai: Guan ke shou zhai, 1884), p. 20.

landscape is represented simply by a streetlight with a female figure peering at it through the lifted blinds of a ricksha (Fig. 9.7) or by a courtesan and her client taking a ride in an open carriage under the moonlight (Fig. 9.8). In both illustrations, motifs from nature—trees and plants—dominate and have not yet been replaced by urban architecture. The attitude of the editors and illustrators of this album in depicting the "other" creates a distance between the city and the narration; this distance enabled the album to present the city's "grand scenes" with a certain bemusement.

The transposition of the image of the courtesan (and in general of the female image) from the ultimate cultural refinement of a secluded environment to the public arena was inspired in good part by the public behavior of Shanghai courtesans. As indicated in the illustrated guides to Shanghai, courtesans were moving freely through the city, from one entertainment establishment to the next—theaters, public parks, teahouses, restaurants, and the Zhang Gardens, where they had their own operatic performances, known as *Maoer xi* 貓兒戲.[20] The unusual sight of courtesans in full public view made them one of the most noted Shanghai phenomena. The

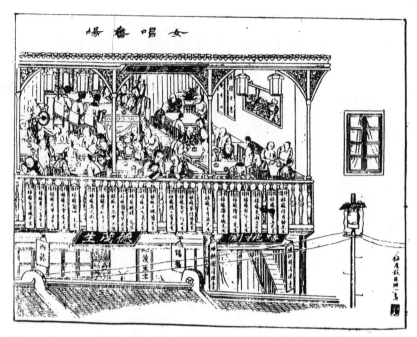

Fig. 9.9 Anonymous, "Nü changshu chang" 女唱書場. Illustrated album leaf, block print. From *Shenjiang shixia shengjing tushuo* 申江時下勝景圖說 (Illustrations with explanations of contemporary famous sights of Shanghai) (Shanghai, 1894), 2: 5.

increased presence of the courtesan in public entertainment and accompany-ing illustrations seems to have been a global phenomenon in the nineteenth century. Parallels can be seen in the different levels of public presence of gei-sha in the Gion and Pontochō districts in Kyoto.[21] The subject was also popular in illustrations and drawings by Parisian painters.[22] The high public profile of the Shanghai courtesan made her very much a subject for illustra-tion. The depiction of the female story-telling hall in still another lithograph album, the *Illustrations with Explanations of Contemporary Famous Sights of Shanghai (Shenjiang shixia shengjing tushuo* 申江時下勝景圖說), published in the 1890s (Fig. 9.9), emphasizes the open architecture of the hall and its loca-tion overlooking the street.[23] The public nature of the business activities of the Shanghai courtesan was the direct product of the openness and tolerance of the foreign settlements toward female entertainers. As the courtesans ex-tended their business from exclusive services offered to a select elite clientele to an ever-expanding public realm, they became a prominent "sight" in the illustrated narration of the city.

With Major's *Illustrated Grand Scenes* and the other illustrated Shanghai guides, an entirely new concept of the urban female figure was realized. In this revolution, the Western-style city environment replaced the idealized garden setting, and the extraordinary public persona of the Shanghai courtesan replaced the elegant secluded beauty. In the traditional definition, the courtesan had been synonymous with the "beautiful woman," *meiren*, as the generic painting album title *baimei tu* suggests. But what makes the courtesan figure revolutionary in these early Shanghai illustrated guides is her behavior in this new environment. Her public persona signals the new characteristics of the urban beauty.

The Beauty of the Street: A Double-Edged Image

The Shanghai courtesan was presented in the illustrated guides as the city's most glamorous icon. This still highly idealized image was challenged as its real-life counterpart became increasingly urbanized. Leading the way in an alternative depiction of the courtesan and, through her image, of the city, was the *Dianshizhai Illustrated Magazine*. Founded and managed by Ernest Major in 1884, the magazine was an illustrated journal in the style of the *London Illustrated News*, *Harpers*, *Frank Leslie's Illustrated Paper*, and *The Graphic*.[24] Designed to provide entertaining illustrations and leisure-time reading, the thrice-monthly magazine was immensely popular and successful in and beyond Shanghai; it ran for a total of fourteen years, from 1884 to 1898.[25] It focused on fantastic, outrageous, and generally newsworthy events in Shanghai, China, and the world. In all three respects of newsworthiness, the Shanghai courtesan loomed large as part of the sensations of Shanghai, and her depiction signals a different interpretation of the city.

The stature of the Shanghai courtesan as a newsworthy figure had been established by the *Shenbao* a decade earlier. From the very beginning of the paper in 1872, reports on the Shanghai courtesans were a regular feature. They were presented from different angles. The paper carried enthusiastic poems dedicated to courtesans, sentimental biographies, and sympathetic reports on their fate. At the same time, there were also reports on their arrogance, their lack of feeling, and their fickleness. Their newsworthiness was, however, demonstrated most vividly in reports on their public behavior. A good example is the detailed story of two top Shanghai courtesans coming to blows in a theater. It involved Hu Baoyu 胡寶玉 and Li Qiaoling 李巧玲, two of Shanghai's most legendary courtesans and the subject of several late

Qing novels.[26] Under the title "A Virago Robber," the newspaper reported
an incident that had occurred the previous evening when a famous Peking
opera singer performed at the Dangui xiyuan 丹桂戲園:

Last year Shanghai's top-ranking courtesan Li Qiaoling married and became the
wife of the opera singer Huang Yueshan 黃月山. After the Daguanyuan 大觀園
theater, in which Huang Yueshan has shares, had opened, Qiaoling went so far as to
assume what is commonly referred to as the role of the proprietress!

On the 6th of this month, when the opera singer Zhen Shisandan 真十三旦
was [performing] in the Dangui theater, so many people came that there was
scarcely any room left [in the theater]. Jiaoshu (校書 = highest-ranking courtesan)
Hu Baoyu, whose residence is in Xinggong lane, had reserved a box in the theater,
and to prevent others from taking it, she had sent a [woman] servant ahead of time
to guard it. [Li] Qiaoling went so far as to barge into this box, and when told by the
servant that it had been reserved by Baoyu, she flew into a fury and tried to box the
servant's ears. Terrified, the servant returned [home] and informed Baoyu. Upon
which Baoyu instantly went to the theater and demanded an explanation from the
manager how [the theater could tolerate] this behavior on the part of Qiaoling. The
manager replied insolently [to Baoyu], and in her anger Baoyu smashed a teacup
[that apparently had been prepared for Qiaoling]. Meanwhile, although Qiaoling
had come first [and got the box], she was displeased that she had not yet been
served tea. Upon hearing what Baoyu had said and that she had smashed the teacup,
she was even more angry than before. But after all there was not much she could do
in that situation.

On the evening of the 9th, Baoyu this time went to the Daguanyuan theater. In the
middle of the program she decided to leave and was seen by Qiaoling, who happened
to be standing by the hallway door leading to the boxes. Stopping Baoyu, Qiaoling
cursed her: "Don't be in such a hurry to leave. I ask you what did you mean by smash-
ing the teacup at the Dangui theater two [three?] nights ago? Baoyu answered: "Since I
did not smash a cup from your Daguanyuan, what business is this of yours?" Qiaoling
answered: "I presume that you wouldn't dare [to behave in the same manner here in
the Daguanyuan]." Baoyu replied: "Even if I did, what could you do about it?" Upon
hearing this, Qiaoling reached out to box the ears of Baoyu; at the same time she
grabbed the pearl ornament from Baoyu's hair. As Baoyu cried out for help, Qiaoling's
brother, the wife of the opera singer Zhao Xiangyu 趙湘玉, and some unidentified
persons burst onto the scene and robbed Baoyu of her gold watch, pearl earrings, and
all her jewelry. All this time, the guard of the theater was standing by. Not only did he
fail to help Baoyu, he actively prevented Baoyu's attendants from coming to her rescue.
Fortunately someone [respectable] whom Baoyu knew well came forth to mediate, so
that she could finally get down the stairs [and leave the theater].

Fig. 9.10 Anonymous, "Jingsan yuanyang" 驚散鴛鴦. Lithograph. From *Dianshizhai huabao*, *Yuan* 元 (1897), II: 87.

Hu Baoyu then went to the police and accused Li Qiaoling of robbing her of all her jewelry, which was worth 1,500 dollars. The article ends with the reporter exclaiming that "a theater is a public place where many people gather and is not like some desolate wilderness. Yet this person who has no regard for the law regards herself as the owner of the theater. To organize such a robbery is incredible indeed!"[27] This type of sensational reporting on courtesans shows that by the 1870s they were seen in Shanghai as newsworthy and familiar public figures and material for good urban human interest stories. Unwittingly, the article also reveals that by this early date the presence of women in theater audiences was quite common in Shanghai.

The behavior of the Shanghai courtesan in public became a favorite topic for *Dianshizhai huabao* illustrations. These reports give a lively and multifaceted profile of the courtesan. Her public persona was at the heart of the fascination she evoked. She is a source of titillating scandal. The illustration "The Startling Separation of the Mandarin Ducks" (Fig. 9.10) is based on

Fig. 9.11 Anonymous, "Yuanxiao xiongfei" 願效雄飛. Lithograph. From *Dianshizhai huabao*, *Le* 樂 (1894), 12: 95.

the report that Lin Daiyu 林黛玉, a prominent Shanghai courtesan, had been apprehended late at night by a Sikh policeman for breaking the law; she and one of her lovers had been making love while riding in her carriage on a secluded road. The illustration shows them kneeling before the Western magistrate begging to be let off. The courtesan was also fodder for sensational public outrage. In "The Desire to Imitate the Stride of the Male," a courtesan is caught walking on the street in men's clothes (Fig. 9.11). The courtesan also risks public ridicule. In "Fighting with Words in the Carriage" (Fig. 9.12), two courtesans stand in their carriages hurling insults at each other, with bystanders clapping and cheering them on. At the same time the courtesan is shown as capable of grand generosity. In "A Courtesan Eager to Perform Righteous Deeds" (Fig. 9.13), the courtesan Hong Wenlan 洪文蘭, whom the text describes as "valiant and heroic in bearing" and well-known for her "bold and generous character," is on an outing with a courtesan friend. When she sees a woman with a baby crying by the river, she stops her carriage and helps the woman with a generous donation.

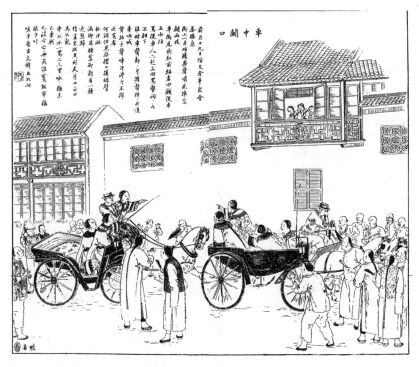

Fig. 9.12 Anonymous, "Chezhong doukou" 車中鬥口. Lithograph. From *Dianshizhai huabao*, *Yin* 寅 (1888), 12: 74.

These portraits are drawn in a realistic style and illustrate the public behavior of the Shanghai courtesan as a core ingredient in a new image of Shanghai. There is an unspoken reasoning of cause and effect. In "The Startling Separation of the Mandarin Ducks" (Fig. 9.10), Lin Daiyu is humiliated as she and her lover beg for clemency; by juxtaposing Lin and the foreign magistrate, the scene suggests that law and order as represented by the foreign official is necessitated by scandalous behavior. "The Desire to Imitate the Stride of the Male" (Fig. 9.11) seems to have the same message. The "misuse" of the public realm by the courtesan is highlighted in Figure 9.12 with its fighting courtesans in their luxurious open carriages dominating the street. Their Western-style carriages evoke the particular background of the Shanghai settlements and add to this scene of public disgrace. These illustrations subvert the image of Shanghai as the land of wonder conveyed by *Illustrated Grand Scenes of Shanghai* by recasting the wonders in a titillating and

Fig. 9.13 Anonymous, "Qinglou haoyi" 青樓好義. Lithograph. From *Dianshizhai huabao, Li* 利 (1898), II: 82.

even marginally outrageous real-life context. The glorious image is not fully negated, but a sense of ambivalence and urban irony is established.

As much as this portrait of the Shanghai courtesan reflects the nature of the news media and their hunger for scandal and sensation, it also highlights the ambivalent attitude toward the triumph of commercial culture under foreign domination. The vulgarization of the image of the courtesan reacts to the commercialization of Shanghai embodied by these women. Formerly, the image of the courtesan was built on the values and imagined world order of the literati; here is the portrait of its demise, with its onetime refinement replaced by materialism, Western-style urban accouterments, and moral corruption. These representations of the courtesans reflect the conflicting experiences of the city's commercial might and moral decadence. The triumph of commercialism is marked as an urban phenomenon, and it finds expression in scenes of vulgar behavior.

The illustrations and the texts accompanying them are careful to record the particular place where the event was observed. The unmistakable public landmarks of the Shanghai concession were emphasized in all these illustrations. The standard devices used to identify Shanghai in illustrations were kerosene lamps, Western-style carriages and the smooth roads on which they roll, Western-style buildings (at times recognizable by their pane-glass windows), the wood-plank streets in the *lilong* 里弄 quarters (a unique Shanghai architectural feature), and finally the uniforms of the carriage drivers with their characteristic straw boaters. The elegant open carriage signaled the Shanghai courtesans' extravagance and modern luxury, and it provided, in life and illustration, an elevated moving platform on which to stage themselves in public. With the carriage alone, the locale was identified and characterized as imbued with a Western presence. This new urban life-style includes unique and newsworthy, if occasionally scandalous, women as prominent parts of the public realm.

This transformation of the secluded beauty into the cosmopolitan beauty thus entailed a reinterpretation of cultural symbols. The traditional "dream-scape" was replaced by the sense of the "extraordinary" evoked by the foreign. Yet, depending on perspective, the Shanghai urban environment could have quite different implications. Unlike the presentation in the *Illustrated Grand Scenes*, the urban beauty of the *Dianshizhai Illustrated Magazine* inhabits crowd-filled streets and parks. The aggrandization of the city and its courtesans in the guides is here replaced by sensational reporting on events in crowded urban scenes. This representation fundamentally changes the cultural status of the "setting." The element of exclusiveness, one of the most important signs of high culture, was being erased. The public realm, although decorated with foreign things, remains the realm of the urban people in general. The image of the courtesan presented in this environment is an ironic reflection on the past of cultural refinement. As a newsworthy personality, she is read against the cultural assumption of what a "beauty" ought to be seen doing. By surrounding her with crowds and showing her behaving like a commoner, the *Dianshizhai* illustrations add a layer of irony to their depiction of this new Shanghai urban beauty. By treating her as a public personality, the *Dianshizhai* presents her with an ironical distance befitting a big city mentality and makes her into the occasional subject of general amusement. The "beauty" of the urban space, as portrayed in the *Dianshizhai*, thus combines the "extraordinary," *qi* 奇, with the new element of the "strange," *guai* 怪, which traditionally was not part of the *meiren* representation.

The Dialectics of Culture: Rebalancing the "High" and the "Low"

The unease revealed in the creation of the image of the urban beauty reflects
the mixed response by traditionalists to the ever more pronounced presence of
the Shanghai courtesan in the public limelight. The reluctance to accept this
new feature spawned a criticism of the moral degeneracy of the Shanghai foreign settlements. Beginning in the late 1890s, a series of novels appeared that
took the Shanghai courtesan as their central character. These serialized novels, such as *Haishang hua liezhuan* 海上花列傳 (Biographies of Shanghai
flowers; 1892–94) and *Haishang fanhua meng* 海上繁華夢 (Dreams of extravagance in Shanghai; 1903–8), portray Shanghai courtesans as cunning busi-
nesswomen and as symbols of the city's power to corrupt.[28]

As the Shanghai courtesan became a major literary and artistic topos, the
conflict in her representation became increasingly apparent. At stake was the
question how to represent Shanghai and its life-style. As much as some illustrated city guides used the image of the Shanghai courtesan to aggrandize
the city, the *Dianshizhai Illustrated Magazine*, a product of the same publishing
conglomerate, made fun of her, whereas novels and later cartoons used her
to denounce the place.

A reaction to this ambivalent linkage of the courtesan with the city can be
seen in another illustrated courtesan album, the *Jingying xiaosheng chuji* 鏡影
蕭聲初集 (Mirror reflections and flute sounds, first collection). Published
in 1887, this album with biographies and superb copper engravings of 50 distinguished Shanghai courtesans was written and drawn by a group of *wenren*
in Shanghai;[29] the engraving was done by Japanese artists in Tokyo.[30] The
most startling contrast between the representation of the Shanghai courtesans in this album and in the city guides or the *Dianshizhai* magazine is the
total absence of the city. Faithful to the tradition of the *Hundred Beauties Illustrated*, the courtesans are depicted as part of a universal order set in the
past. The depiction of the idealized dreamscape surrounding them goes back
to the topos of *shanshui huaniao tingtai* 山水花鳥亭臺—mountains and rivers (landscape), flowers and birds, pavilions and towers.[31] In the portrait of
Wang Zhexiang (Fig. 9.14), we see the familiar pose of the yearning *meiren*
with one hand under her chin, and the other holding a large fan and resting
on the banister. A pair of mandarin ducks with their connotation of enduring love is juxtaposed with the solitary *meiren* to evoke her sense of lonely

Fig. 9.14 Chengbei sheng 城北生, "Wang Zhexiang" 王者香. Illustrated album leaf, copper engraving. From *Jingying xiaosheng chuji* 鏡影簫聲初集 (Mirror reflections and flute sounds, first collection) (Tokyo, 1887), p. 35 (copy in Columbia University, East Asian Library).

separation. Standing on an elevated verandah, she looks straight at the viewer, not at the pair of ducks or into the distance (for her lover). A willow tree with its associations of beauty and eroticism frames her figure. The directness of communication between the viewer and the figure eliminates what might have been a scene of forlorn solitude. The focus is on emblems of exclusiveness and cultural sophistication. Universality has been reinstated, and no traces of a specific place are present. Shanghai is mentioned in the album's various introductions, but there is no reference to a locale in the title, although this had become a defining characteristic of this type of album. Since the album is clearly dedicated to the biographies of Shanghai courtesans, the omission of the locale seems deliberate. The issue of Shanghai and of urban identity seemed to be irritating to the compilers. The Preface explains that originally the title for the album was to have been *A Thousand Illustrated Beauties, Wanyan tu* 萬豔圖, but that it was changed due to the inspiring illustrations made by the artist, which captured so well the spirit of the courtesans' beauty and of their talents in the arts (referred to by the "mirror" and the "flute" in the new title).[32] This title was clearly intended to elevate its cultural status to compensate for the low cultural status of its urban content. The portrait of Hua Xiangyun 花湘雲 (Fig. 9.15) shows a

Fig. 9.15 Chengbei sheng 城北生, "Hua Xiangyun" 花湘雲. Illustrated album leaf, copper engraving. From *Jingying xiaosheng chuji* 鏡影簫聲初集 (Mirror reflections and flute sounds, first collection) (Tokyo, 1887), p. 13 (copy in Columbia University, East Asian Library).

dynamic female figure with one leg propped boldly on the bench, playing a flute, an overt erotic symbol. Flanked by a rock she is set against the background of a pair of catalpa trees and a banister. Again she looks straight at the viewer, full of self-confidence. Her upright torso leans slightly toward the left, giving the whole picture grace and energy. Without exception the illustrations in the album reveal the desire of the compilers to emphasize continuity with traditional *wenren* cultural values, which were at the time undergoing a rapid transformation.

In one respect, however, the album subtly betrayed its connection with Shanghai and that was in the use of copper engraving and of photographs of the individual courtesans as the models for the engravings. At the time, both were strongly identified with Western technology and with Shanghai. In fact the author of the album's colophon claimed that he had been collecting photographs of courtesans for years before he was able to find someone with the skills to reproduce their likenesses as book illustrations.[33] The album's prefaces are full of praise for the outcome of this "reproduction." If we compare the illustrations in this album with illustrations of courtesans in traditional *baimei tu*, the strong sense of individuality is distinctly modern and the result of photography. It is evoked through distinct physical and facial

Fig. 9.16 Gai Qi 改琦,
"Zijuan" 紫鵑. Block
print illustration. From
Honglou meng tu yong
紅樓夢圖詠 (Shanghai,
1879; reprinted—Taipei:
Yiwen yinshuguan, 1974).

features that defy standards current at the time as they may be seen in the
beauties in the album *Honglou meng tuyong* 紅樓夢圖詠 (Fig. 9.16) by Gai
Qi 改琦 produced in 1879. In contrast to Gai Qi's willowy bodies with their
disguised physicality and the amiable and vapid facial expressions, the
Shanghai courtesans in the *Jingying xiaosheng chuji* album are full-bodied
women with dynamic gestures; their facial expression engages the viewer
with their varied emotional and erotic charges.[34] As Richard Vinograd has
pointed out, in portraits by Shanghai artists the head began to "have a heavy
presence and precision of focus that suggest contact with photographic visualization."[35] When compared with portrait photographs of courtesans, the
illustrations of courtesans in *Jingying xiaosheng* show, in terms of the graphic
handling of the head, the straightforward looking gaze; the background setting of the scenes also strongly suggests a photographic counterpart (Fig.
9.17). Since Shanghai was the center of photography studios and the courtesans were among their most avid customers, this high-tech linkage makes
this modern city loom over all the "traditionalist" pages of the volume.[36]

The *Jingying xiaosheng* appears, however, to be the exception. Judging
from such contemporary titles as *Shanghai pinyan baihua tu* 上海品豔百
花圖, *Haishang baimei xinyong* 海上百美新詠, *Hushang xinhua baimei tu*

Fig. 9.17 "Zhang Shuyu shiqi sui shi ying" 張書玉十七歲時影 (Photograph of Zhang Shuyu at age seventeen). Zhang Shuyu was a top-ranking Shanghai courtesan in the late nineteenth century. Photograph from *Huaying jixuan* 花影集選 (A collection of courtesan photographs) (Shanghai, 1928), n.p.

滬上新畫百美圖, *Haishang qunfang pu* 海上群芳譜, and *Hujiang yanpu*, the explicit identification of the courtesan with Shanghai had become dominant by the 1880s.[37] The exact relationship, however, between the image of the courtesan and that of the city remained a point of contention. As seen from the *Jingying xiaosheng*, the critical issue was the cultural and artistic status of the urban environment. Since the city is traditionally associated with the common folk and the merchant, how could one avoid compromising the image of the urban courtesan? The other issue raised by the contrast between the *Jingying xiaosheng* and the other albums is the definition of the new personality of the Shanghai courtesan, who was in social fact increasingly becoming a public figure. To present the city as the suitable setting for the *meiren* meant upgrading the urban environment into a symbol of high culture. In the pages of Wu Youru's new *Feiyingge huabao* 飛影閣畫報 (Feiyingge illustrated magazine), which published works by Wu Youru and Zhou Muqiao 周慕橋 (1868–1922), a onetime colleague of Wu's on the *Dianshizhai*, we find a response to some of these questions.[38]

In 1890, the *Feiyingge huabao* serialized a new set of Shanghai beauties, later known as *Haishang baiyan tu* 海上百豔圖 (One hundred illustrated beauties of Shanghai).[39] The illustrations offered a new interpretation of the theme of urban beauty. The magazine, which at that time featured illustrations only by Wu Youru himself, is in many respects similar in style and content to the *Dianshizhai* magazine. In addition to reports on the "fantastic" in China and foreign lands, three new categories were added to this magazine: the *Baishou tu* 百獸圖 (The illustrated one hundred beasts), the *Shuo guiyan* 說閨豔 (Portraits of beautiful women; later known as *Gujin baimei tu* 古今百美圖, Illustrated one hundred beauties from the past to the present), and the *Huibian Huzhuang shinü* 彙編滬妝士女 (A compilation of ladies of fashion in Shanghai; later known as *Haishang baiyan tu*, One hundred illustrated beauties of Shanghai).[40] These introductions reflect Wu Youru's desire to explore traditional themes within this new type of illustrated publication. As he states in his introduction, however, the illustrated magazine, which originated in the West, is intended to "foster appreciation of (illustrate) the strange and mark the new (*lingyi biaoxin* 領異標新) so as to broaden [readers'] knowledge and help in warning and exhorting."[41] Under these headings, the Shanghai courtesan as the exemplar of urban fashion was included. The Shanghai courtesan is usually identified in these illustrations by the characteristic furnishings of her quarters, such as lamps suspended from the ceiling (Fig. 9.20) and large dressing mirrors in the background (Fig. 9.21) or by showing her riding in public in an open Western-style carriage (Fig. 9.18). She is at times identified by the fresh flowers covering her ear, feather fans, or musical instruments. Shanghai was evoked again through elements of urban infrastructure such as the electric street lamp, a tall building, pane-glass windows, a church tower, or a fire hydrant. In contrast to the *Huibian Huzhuang shinü*, the total absence of any reference to urban life-style or setting in *Shuo guiyan* with its illustrations of legendary women from the past makes it startlingly clear how singular the depiction of Shanghai within this genre must have appeared. Since these illustrations came from the same hand, the differences in the depiction of the historical beauties and the modern urban beauties are the result of a conscious decision that was fully aware of, and tried to reflect, the change that had occurred in the stature, life, and role of these women.

In the guides to Shanghai, the courtesan figured as one of the city's symbols of prosperity and high living; as we have seen, in *Dianshizhai* magazine the courtesan's depiction in the urban environment often came at the expense of her traditional cultural status. In contrast to both of these trends, the *Haishang baiyan tu* (1890–93) returns the courtesan to her traditional pedestal of high culture while at the same time elevating the status of the city. As part of this new interpretation, the courtesan is once again portrayed as the symbol of taste and refinement. This is evoked not only by her gestures,

Fig. 9.18 Wu Youru 吳友如, "Yibian canzhao" 一鞭殘照. Lithograph. From *Feiyingge hua-bao* 飛影閣畫報 (reprinted in *Shanghai baiyan tu* 上海百豔圖 [Changsha: Hunan meishu chubanshe, 1998], p. 52).

her mood, her luxurious clothing, and her accessories, but also, and most important, by the aura of exclusiveness with which she is presented. She is still represented as moving through the urban landscape in an open carriage, but the cityscape is now emptied of people. In Figure 9.18, "Yibian canzhao" 一鞭殘照 (Traveling at sunset), the Shanghai urban landscape is represented entirely through Western material culture: the building with its French windows and second-floor balcony, the cast iron (see-through) fence, the horse-drawn boat-shaped carriage. The figures in the illustration are parts of this urban space, not mere adjuncts to it. Both the chauffeur and the courtesans are at ease in the city. Even their personal accessories, the chauffeur's straw hat and the courtesan's tasseled umbrella, signal the easy personalization of this urban space through life-style. Such a scene of wonder and refinement could be realized only by altering the natural scene of a street. As

Fig. 9.19 Anonymous, "Hupan zhufeng tu" 湖畔竹風圖 (Wind in the bamboo grove by the lake; also known as "Yuanzhuang er meiren tu" 圓窗二美人圖, Two beauties and the round window). Suzhou New Year print, mid-Qing. From *Suzhou Taohuawu muban nianhua* (Nanjing: Jiangsu guji chubanshe, 1991), p. 139.

Figure 9.18 shows, there is no crowd even when the scene is directly situated within the cityscape, and the image of the courtesan comes with all the signs of glamour and exclusiveness. This representation of the *meiren* has much to do with the Suzhou school of woodblock New Year prints (Fig. 9.19), a craft with which Wu Youru was familiar. There, the *meiren* were depicted in a highly mannered style, and the atmospheric setting for the *meiren* was constructed with all the traditional tropes evoking the sense of a secluded paradise (*shiwai taoyuan* 世外桃源).[42] The mid-Qing example in Figure 9.19, "Hupan zhufeng tu" 湖畔竹風圖 (Wind in the bamboo grove by the lake; also known as "Yuanzhuang er meiren tu" 圓窗二美人圖 or Two beauties and the round window), shows two women in a palace garden with magnificent buildings in the background. The composition of the window to the "outer world," accentuated by landscape architecture, gives the beauties a sense of worldly liveliness and energy. This was later picked up by Wu Youru in his portrait of the urban beauty. But it was his invention to present the modern city as the suitable setting for the *meiren*.

In Wu Youru's reinterpretation of the Shanghai courtesan as *meiren*, the city not only does not disappear but is moved to the center of the illustration and becomes the courtesan's counterpart. In "Youmu chenghuai" 遊目騁懷

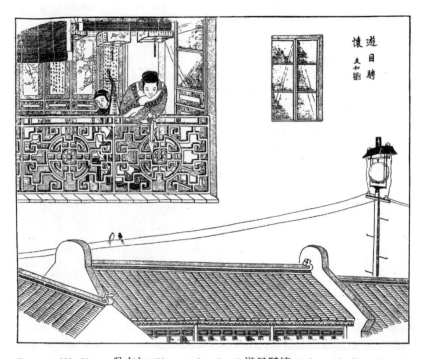

Fig. 9.20 Wu Youru 吳友如, "Youmu chenghuai" 遊目騁懷. Lithograph. From *Feiyingge huabao* 飛影閣畫報 (reprinted in *Shanghai baiyan tu* 上海百豔圖 [Changsha: Hunan meishu chubanshe, 1998], p. 32).

(Carried off by longing with wandering gaze; Fig. 9.20), the urban space is evoked through a fascinating combination of traditional *meiren* tropes and the newly established iconography of Shanghai. A realistically executed electric streetlamp on the right side dominates the scene. From its introduction in 1882, the streetlight had become the symbol of the city. Its relationship to the courtesan is established through a pair of swallows perched on the electrical wire. The courtesan adopts the traditional pose of the *meiren* leaning on the balcony gazing at the love birds, but her juxtaposition with the street lamp dominates the scene. The diagonal construction with the courtesan at the upper left and the lamp at the right evokes a mutual embodiment. The relationship, furthermore, is an active one. Unlike the traditional passive pose of the forlorn and sad *meiren*, the Shanghai courtesan here appears eager, even active, stretching her body over the banister. The "splendor" of the one interprets that of the other. The composition exhibits a new and modern sensibility.

Fig. 9.21 Zhou Muqiao 周慕橋, "Shiyuan weiming" 視遠惟明. Lithograph. From *Feiyingge huabao* 飛影閣畫報 (reprinted in *Shanghai baiyan tu* 上海百豔圖 [Changsha: Hunan mei-shu chubanshe, 1998], p. 80).

The assignment to urban space of a cultural status comparable to that of the natural landscape is a theme that runs through the album. The juxtaposition of beauty and city in "Shiyuan weiming" 視遠惟明 (Only when looking afar is there clarity; Fig. 9.21) evokes the element of the gorgeous. The city with its Western-style infrastructure and material culture has become the new symbol of high culture. The traditional trope of the beautiful woman standing on a tower and "looking into the distance" (*yuantiao*) is reformulated here with different emotional implications and composition. The feeling of loneliness and yearning for a long-missed lover that this motif is intended to evoke is replaced here by an overwhelming sense of fun and curiosity. With the help of a pair of binoculars, the courtesan intently scrutinizes the exotic scene of this Western-style urban landscape with Trinity Church in the distance. Here the traditional cultural status of the *meiren* and the newly established status of the Shanghai urban landscape combine in mutual reflection and change. The foreignness of Shanghai is essentialized into a new kind of dreamscape, a new iconographical myth. It is from this new interpretation of beauty and city, seen as integral parts of each other, that the essentialized and romanticized *meiren* of the city emerges.

Two aspects of Wu Youru's invention of the new urban beauty were significant and lasting: his creation of a new motif in which the city and the beauty were seen as an integral whole; and his essentialization of Western material culture into the new emblem of *fanhua* 繁華 suitable to the *meiren*. Both these features became defining elements in the genre.

The evolution of the new urban beauty highlights the vital role played by illustrated magazines. The illustrated magazine introduced by Ernest Major from the West and adapted by Wu Youru became the premier medium through which the new concept of the urban beauty was realized. Already with the *Shenjiang shengjing tu* the importance of the Western pictorial tradition was clear. It provided the conceptual model for the representation of the female in public space. The "foreignness" of the illustrated magazine became an asset in the articulation of the new. Standing outside Chinese tradition, it provided a unique opportunity to define the features of a new genre.

To what degree this medium opened up new possibilities of depiction becomes clear through a comparison of Wu Youru's illustrations and his own paintings. An illustration appearing in *Feiyingge magazine* entitled "Xunyang yuyun" 潯陽餘韻 (The reverberating rhythm of Xunyang; Fig. 9.22) depicts a courtesan in a long fur vest tuning a *pipa*; she is accompanied by another player and a maid. The title of the work identifies her as a courtesan by alluding to the courtesan in the famous Tang poem *Pipa xing* 琵琶行 by Bai Juyi 白居易. This is confirmed by the musical instrument itself, which is associated with courtesan entertainment, and by the flowers covering her ears.[43] As in other illustrations in the magazine the presence of Western objects in her surroundings, in this case the mirror on the back wall, the glass-covered table clock, and the more obvious cast-iron heating stove, marks the figure as a courtesan.

The same composition appears in one of Wu Youru's paintings (Fig. 9.23). The inscription at the top of the painting describes the scene as singing about the fate of Ming Fei 明妃 (Wang Zhaojun 王昭君), a song that leaves the singer in tears. The basic composition of the two works is the

Fig. 9.22 Wu Youru 吳友如, "Xunyang yuyun" 潯陽餘韻. From *Feiyingge huabao* 飛影閣
畫報 (reprinted in *Shanghai baiyan tu* 上海百豔圖, no. 11 [Dec. *zhong* 中, 1890]; reprinted in
Shanghai baiyan tu 上海百豔圖 [Changsha: Hunan meishu chubanshe, 1998], p. 210).

same, and so are the two female figures. But in the painting the long fur vest
is there to indicate winter; no heating stove is to be found. The Western objects surrounding the *meiren* or courtesan in the illustration and suggesting
urban comforts have a place only in the new genre of the magazine illustration but not in the painting. They have been replaced by books, flowers, a
stone, and trees. A wall shields the figure from public gaze. The viewer is
now the voyeur looking on a private scene. This setting corresponds to the
fixtures associated with the traditional *meiren* in the garden trope. Even a
Wu Youru felt bound by the restrictions of genre and made his innovations
in the generic no-man's land of the illustrated magazine.

The lithographic magazine illustration became the genre for developing
the new model of the urban beauty in the pictorial arts. The model of Wu
Youru's illustration on the subject spread through other types of illustrated
publications. Shanghai courtesan guides of the 1890s, for example, freely

Fig. 9.23 Wu Youru 吳友如, "Tancao shuangsheng tu" 檀槽雙聲圖. Hanging scroll; ink and color on paper, 19th century. From *Shanghai bowuguan cang Shanghai minghuajia jingpin ji* 上 海博物館藏上海名畫家精品集 (Masterworks of Shanghai school painters from the Shanghai Museum collection) (Hong Kong, 1991).

copied Wu Youru's illustrations from the *Shanghai baiyan tu*. One out-standing example is the illustrated Shanghai courtesan guide *Haishang qinglou tuji* 海上青樓圖記 (Illustrated record of Shanghai courtesan entertain-ment) published in 1891. The guide, which includes biographies of top-ranking Shanghai courtesans, is illustrated primarily with slightly altered copies of Wu Youru's illustrations.[44]

Conclusion: The Genre of the New "Baimei tu"

The image of the urban beauty was created in the context of the develop-ment of a mass market for urban leisure and entertainment. *Meiren* illustra-tions had always been a popular genre, subject to the taste not only of the literati but of a broader print market. The intrinsic flexibility of the *meiren* image made it easier to attach new cultural messages and cultural values to it.

The Shanghai courtesan with her public persona set into motion a new way of representing the public realm. The close connection between her and the Western material culture surrounding her in these illustrations was a reflection of the very condition that enabled her to expand her business activities into the public space. The freedom and leeway offered by the Shanghai foreign settlements made her a unique hallmark of the city. With her explorations of Shanghai as the new dreamscape, she became the transmitter of this new image of the city. Her traditional cultural capital gave her the wherewithal to substantiate the city's claim to culture and refinement and made her into one of the city's most powerful and attractive icons.

As we have seen from the *Dianshizhai Magazine*, the image is not without contradictions. As one of the extraordinary sights of Shanghai, the courtesan represented many aspects of late Qing Shanghai's cultural identity. Written into her image is both the triumph of Western material culture and Shanghai's commercial spirit as well as a critique and a certain ambivalence toward it. The cultural significance and function of her figure lie in the fact that she was the first female public personality; through her symbiotic relationship with urban space, Western material culture was transferred to the imaginary realm of prestige and glamour. Both these functions continued to be dominant traits in the image of the urban beauty throughout its evolution. It is easy to overlook the fact that the core of the visual revolution in the illustrations of *meiren* and urban space lies in the transformation not of the beauty but of her setting. The central driving force was the questionable status of urban space. In this context, the courtesan as *meiren* was used for a very specific purpose: to place her "alien" surroundings into the category of the "luxurious" and thus to make the unfamiliar acceptable and desirable. By the early twentieth century, her image was further transformed into the universal image of the "urban beauty" by shedding the particular attributes that had identified her as a courtesan. As a print product distributed nationwide, this image, however, continued to be coded as "Shanghai." "Universality" came only when Shanghai's urban sensibility was accepted by the country at large. The selling point of the later cigarette advertisements that feature the urban beauty is precisely their "Shanghai look," which was equated with fashion and glamour.

The commercial potential of the image of the urban beauty was quickly recognized by other commercial interests. In the early twentieth century, her attraction was first explored in advertisements of foreign and Chinese cigarette manufacturers. Her image became the vehicle for imagining urban space and life-style. Photographs also helped to spread the now individuated image of the beauty. As part of a world fashion, she became the cover image on literary magazines and the theme of photo albums. As the symbol of high fashion, her looks, dress, hair styles, and accessories all were portrayed as objects of admiration. She became, through her image, a potent symbol of desirability in the commercial culture of Shanghai, standing for taste, fashion, and a particular style of urban life. Later on, the type now called by the Chinese term "urban beauty," *dushi meiren* 都市美人, spread to other forms of print entertainment such as the illustrated newspapers and cigarette cards. She also became the central figure of the new *baimei tu*.

In the 1910s, following the further development of commercial illustration, a new group of *baimei tu* appeared. They were drawn by a new generation of illustrators, most of whom had become illustrators by working with advertisements. One important way for them to make their reputation was by drawing *baimei tu*. This seems to have become a Shanghai tradition after Gai Qi and Fei Danxu 費旦旭; the latter was famous both for his drawings and for his illustrations of the motif of the "one hundred beauties."[45] Among them were Dan Duyu 旦杜宇 (1896–1972), Ding Song 訂悚 (1891–1972), Shen Bocheng 沈伯誠 (1889–1920), and Qian Binghe 錢病鶴 (1879–1944).[46] Their works are marked by a sense of ease and maturity (Fig. 9.24), corresponding to the decline of the courtesan entertainment culture and the social prestige of the courtesan as a profession. In the urban beauties produced by this new generation of illustrators, the star quality of the late Qing courtesan was replaced by an emphasis on her urban origin and a cosmopolitanism evoked by an at times "naive simplicity."

Although the style and interpretation of the image of the urban beauty in their works were new in many respects, the fundamental structural elements in the depictions show a clear continuity with the late Qing. She is portrayed very much as part of the urban scene (Fig. 9.24). Her image is accentuated by the symbols of Western material culture. Public space is an integral part of her persona, and her image is closely connected with scenes of urban life. She moves with big city elegance and self-assuredness. The depiction of the urban setting largely follows the tradition set by Wu Youru: the city and the beautiful woman interact as counterpoints. The exclusiveness of the public space occupied by her signaled, together with her gestures and

Fig. 9.24 Dan Duyu 但杜宇, untitled. Lithograph. From *Duyu baimei tu xuji* 杜宇百美圖續集 (Shanghai, 1923), p. 18. (I thank David Faure for providing me with a copy of this album.)

attitude, high cultural status. The past, however, lingers on in the form of cultural memory. In Figure 9.25 the willow tree and the banana plant from the past peering over the high wall are elements from traditional *baimei tu*. Yet the street, the lamp post, the electric light, and the Western style

Fig. 9.25 Dan Duyu 但杜宇, untitled. Lithograph. From *Duyu baimei tu* 杜宇百美圖 (Shanghai, 1920s), p. 19.

Fig. 9.26 Dan Duyu
但杜宇, untitled.
Lithograph. From
Duyu baimei tu xuji
杜宇百美圖續集
(Shanghai, 1923), p. 19.

architecture are all unmistakably images that came to be associated with the urban beauty during the late Qing. In these new *baimei tu*, the city might not be part of the setting of the *meinü* 美女, but Shanghai as a specific locale is inscribed in, and evoked through, the Western-style furniture, the Western-style bound book, the room decorated with framed paintings and wallpaper, and even in the "gaze" and gestures of the beauty (Fig. 9.26). In these new *baimei tu*, there is no trace of ambivalence toward the city, the urban life-style, and Shanghai's commercial culture; here women are part of the cityscape and convey a sense of ease, affluence, and comfort. As the image of beautiful women came increasingly to be used to represent "Shanghai modern" in commercial advertisements, she in turn came to be associated with Shanghai's luxurious Western-style material culture.

The dominant role the illustrated magazine played in forging the new image of the urban beauty was continued by art illustrations in literary journals and photography magazines. Literary journals such as *Xiaoshuo huabao* 小說畫報 and *Libailiu* 禮拜六 carried high-quality illustrations drawn by the leading illustrators of the time. These magazines from the 1920s demonstrate the power of photography to define the new image of the urban beauty. Painters who were simultaneously working in commercial adver-

Fig. 9.27 Ding Song 丁悚, "Shanghai nüzi baitai (san)" 上海女子百態<三>. From *Xianshi leyuan ribao* 先施樂園 日報, Sept. 11, 1918, p. 2.

tisement and for entertainment newspapers introduced the genre of the urban beauty into these other media. A good example is Ding Song's *Shanghai nüzi baitai* 上海女子百態 (A hundred poses of Shanghai ladies; Fig. 9.27) published in the amusement park newspaper *Xianshi leyuan ribao* 先施樂園 報 in 1918.[47] Another example is Yu Shi's 余時 urban beauty in an advertisement for the Great World (Dashijie 大世界) amusement park (Fig. 9.28) also published in 1918.[48] As advertisements for Shanghai's allurements and representatives of urban fashion, urban mentality, and Western material culture, these beauties with their grace and physicality venture boldly forth. Although efforts were made in various illustrated journals to revive the traditional image of the *meiren*, the image of the new cosmopolitan beauty was clearly the dominant and the most popular image in the first half of the twentieth century.[49] Written into these images of the urban beauty was a silent revolution based on the union of the conflicting interests of art and commerce, of Chinese and Western aesthetics, and, most important, of different ways of ordering the world.

Fig. 9.28 "Pao bing: Dashijie jishi xingle tu" 跑冰: 大世界及時行樂圖. From *Dashijie* 大世界, Feb. 22, 1918, p. 2.

Notes

I thank James Cahill, Doris Croissant, and Ellen J. Laing for their careful readings and thoughtful comments on an earlier draft, which enabled me to make this paper much richer.

1. For an overview of late nineteenth-century publishing in Shanghai, see Jonathan Hay, "Painters and Publishing in Late Nineteenth-Century Shanghai," in *Art at the Close of China's Empire*, ed. Ju-hsi Chou (Tempe: Arizona State University, 1998), pp. 134–88.

2. On the entertainment newspaper and the creation of the Shanghai star culture, see Catherine V. Yeh, "Courtesan Stars and Entertainment Papers," in *City, Courtesan and Intellectual: The Rise of Shanghai Entertainment Culture, 1850–1910* (forthcoming); idem, "Li Boyuan and His Shanghai Entertainment Newspaper *Youxi bao*" and "Deciphering the Entertainment Press, 1896–1920: The *Youxi bao*, the *Shijie fanhua bao* and Their Descendants," both in *Joining the Global Public: Word, Image, and City in the Early Chinese Newspapers, 1870–1910*, ed. Rudolf G. Wagner (in press).

3. For these novels, see Lu Xun 魯迅, *Zhongguo xiaoshuo shilüe* 中國小說史略 (A brief history of Chinese fiction), in *Lu Xun quanji* 魯迅全集 (The complete works of Lu Xun) (Beijing: Renmin wenxue chubanshe, 1989), pp. 256–68; and David Der-wei Wang, *Fin-de-siècle Splendor: Repressed Modernities of Late Qing Fiction, 1848–1911* (Stanford: Stanford University Press, 1997).

4. One of the most outstanding examples is *Qinglou yunyu* 青樓韻語 by Zhu Yuanliang 朱元亮 and Zhang Mengzheng 張夢徵, a block print of the Wanli period (copy in the Zhongguo guojia tushuguan) illustrated by Zhang Mengzheng and carved by the famous Huang Yibin 黃一彬, Huang Duanfu 黃端甫, and Huang Guifang 黃桂芳 of the Wulin school; in Zhu Yuanliang 朱元亮 and Zhang Mengzheng 張夢徵, comps., *Qinglou yunyu* 青樓韻語 (Poetry from the green tower), 4 vols. (Wanli period; copy in Zhongguo guojia tushuguan; reprinted in *Zhongguo gudai banhua congkan erbian* 中國古代板畫叢刊二編 [Shanghai: Shanghai guji chubanshe, 1994], vol. 4; see also Zhou Wu 周蕪, *Zhongguo gudai banhua baitu* 中國古代板畫百圖 (One hundred Chinese woodblock prints from the classical period) (Beijing: Renmin meishu chubanshe, 1982), nos. 38 and 52; and Shi Gufeng 石古風, "*Qinglou yunyu ba*" 青樓韻語跋 (Postface to *Poetry from the Green Tower*), in *Zhongguo gudai banhua congkan erbian* 中國古代版畫叢刊二編 (Shanghai: Shanghai guji chubanshe, 1994), 4: 1–3.

5. Examples of this genre include Deng Zhimo 鄧志謨, *Sasa pian* 洒洒篇 (late Ming ed. in the Naikaku bunko); and Li Yunxiang 李雲翔, *Jinling baimei* 金陵百媚 (Hundred beauties of Nanjing) (preface dated 1618; copy in Naikaku bunko); and *Wuji baimei* 吳姬百媚 (Hundred beauties of Suzhou) (1617 ed.; copy in Hōsa bunko, Nagoya). I thank Patrick Hanan and Kathy Lowry for copies of these works. For a short analysis, see Patrick Hanan, *The Chinese Vernacular Story* (Cam-

bridge, Mass.: Harvard University Press, 1981), pp. 89–90. For an introduction to the evolution of the pictorial representation of women, see Søren Edgren, "The Ching-ying hsiao-sheng and Traditional Illustrated Biographies of Women," *Gest Library Journal* 5 (Nov. 1992): 161–73.

6. Ellen Johnston Laing, "Erotic Themes and Romantic Heroines Depicted by Ch'iu Ying," *Archives of Asian Art* 49 (1996): 68, 70.

7. Ibid., p. 77.

8. Although this representation of the Ming courtesan was true for the top courtesans and the cultural refinement they had achieved, it is by no means the whole picture. As in the Qing period, there was a whole range of courtesans from the well-trained and well-educated to the village prostitute. For discussions on the idealization of the late Ming courtesan, see Paul S. Ropp, "Ambiguous Images of Courtesan Culture in Late Imperial China," and Wai-yee Li, "The Late Ming Courtesan: Invention of a Cultural Ideal," both in *Writing Women in Late Imperial China*, ed. Ellen Widmer and Kang-I Sun Chang (Stanford: Stanford University Press, 1997), pp. 17–45 and 47–73, respectively.

9. Wai-yee Li, "The Late Ming Courtesan," p. 74.

10. Cahill, "Three Zhangs," *Orientations*, Oct. 1996, p. 59; idem, "The Emperor's Erotica (*Ching Yüan Chai so-shih* II)," *Kaikodo* (1999): 24–43.

11. In a discussion of *meiren* paintings, Lisa Claypool ("The Social Body: 'Beautiful Women' Imagery in Late Imperial China" [Master's thesis, University of Oregon, Department of Art History, 1994], pp. 24–26) insightfully points out the change that took place between the early and the mid-Qing in the setting of the *meiren*, but seems unfamilar with seventeenth-century illustrations of courtesans in gardens and garden architecture. She misidentifies the actual change and states that "before the Qing, *meiren* were never depicted in public spaces, or in landscapes with buildings"; moreover, the examples she gives cannot in any way be understood as depicting *meiren* in "public" since they are shown in gardens and boudoirs of the imperial palace.

12. On Ernest Major and the development of the Chinese newspaper and publishing enterprise, see Rudolf G. Wagner, "Ernest Major's *Shenbaoguan* and the Formation of Late Qing Print Culture," in *The Formation of a Multiethnic Identity: The Shanghai Concessions, 1850–1910*, ed. Catherine Yeh and Rudolf Wagner (in press).

13. See Rudolf G. Wagner, "Joining the Global Imaginaire: The Shanghai Illustrated Newspapers *Dianshizhai huabao* and *Feiyinggu huabao*—An Introductory Survey," in *Joining the Global Public: Word, Image, and City in the Early Chinese Newspapers, 1870–1910*, ed. R. Wagner (in press).

14. The circumstances leading to the publication of this first Shanghai illustrated guide are stated in the advertisement published in the *Shenbao* on January 3, 1885, which points to the important involvement of Ernest Major.

15. *Shenjiang shengjing tu* 申江勝景圖 (Illustrated grand scenes of Shanghai) (Shanghai: Dianshizhai, 1884), I: 1.

16. An example is the famous narrative guide *Yangzhou huafang lu* 揚州花舫錄 (The record of painted boats in Yangzhou) by the Qing writer Li Dou 李斗 (Nanjing: Jiangsu Guangling guji keyingshe, 1984); nothing of the entertainment mentioned in the text was the subject of its illustrations.

17. On the issue of Shanghai courtesans moving their business into the public realm, see Catherine V. Yeh, "Reinventing Ritual: Late Qing Handbooks or Proper Customer Behavior in Shanghai Courtesan Houses," *Late Imperial China* 19, no. 2 (Dec. 1998): 1–63.

18. For this meaning, see Miao Quansun 繆荃孫, "*Qinhuai guangji zixu*" 秦淮 廣紀自序 (Author's preface to *Encycloppeadia of Qinhuai*), in *Qinhuai guangji* 秦淮 廣紀 (Encycloppeadia of Qinhuai) (Shanghai: Shangwu yinshuguan, 1914), pp. 1–3.

19. The term "model settlement" was used to refer to Shanghai in the late nineteenth century; see, e.g., G. M. Dyce, *The Model Settlement: Personal Reminiscences of Thirty Years' Residence in the Model Settlement, Shanghai, 1870–1900* (London: Chapman and Hall, 1906).

20. *Maoer xi* became popular in the 1890s with top-ranking courtesan stars such as Lin Daiyu 林黛玉 taking the lead. They were performed in the first Chinese-owned public garden, the Zhangyuan 張園 and later in the Yuyuan 愚園, which featured many kinds of amusement; it was illustrated in entertainment guides such as *Haishang youxi tushuo* 海上游戲圖說 (Illustrations with explanations of Shanghai entertainment) (Shanghai, 1898), p. 8.

21. See Nishiyama Matsunosuke 西山松之助, *Yūjo* 遊女 (Prostitution) (Tokyo: Heibonsha, 1997), pp. 84–85; and Lisa Dalby, *Geisha* (New York: Vintage Books, 1985).

22. See, e.g., Constantin Guys's (1802–92) drawings of Paris courtesans, in Charles Baudelaire, *The Painter of Modern Life and Other Essays* (New York: Da Capo Press, 1986), figs. 9.17–19.

23. Meihua'an zhu 梅花盦主 (Li Ruiqing 李瑞清?), ed., *Shenjiang shixia shengjing tushuo* 申江時下勝景圖說 (Illustrations with explanations of contemporary famous sights of Shanghai) (Shanghai: Shanghai Jiangzuo shuling, 1894).

24. Rudolf G. Wagner, "The Role of the Foreign Community in the Chinese Public Sphere," *China Quarterly* 142 (June 1995): 423–43; Nanny Kim, "How to Read About Monsters and Miracles in the Illustrated Magazine from Late 19th Century Shanghai," in *Joining the Global Public: Text, Image, and City in the Early Shanghai Press*, ed. Rudolf Wagner (in press); Ye Xiaoqing, "Popular Culture in Shanghai, 1884–1898" (Ph.D. diss., Australian National University, 1991).

25. For a short history of the development of the Chinese illustrated magazine, see A Ying 阿英, "Zhongguo huabao fazhan zhi jingguo—wei *Liangyou* yibaiwushi

qi jinianhao zuo" 中國畫報發展之經過—為<良友>一百五十期紀念號作 (The processes by which the Chinese illustrated magazine developed, written for the celebration of the 150th issue of the *Liangyou*), in idem, *A Ying meishu lunwenji* 阿英美術論文集 (A Ying's collected essays on art) (Beijing: Renmin meishu chubanshe, 1982), pp. 75–83; for studies on the *Dianshizhai huabao* and Wu Youru, and the immense influence the journal had on the development of the Chinese illustrated magazines, see Yu Yueting 余月亭, "Woguo huabao de shizu—*Dianshizhai huabao* chutan" 我國畫報的始祖—點石齋畫報初探 (A preliminary analysis of the ancestor of the Chinese illustrated journals, the *Dianshizhai huabao*), *Xinwen yanjiu ziliao* 5 (1981): 149–81; and Wagner "The Shanghai Illustrated Newspapers *Dianshizhai huabao* and *Feiyinggu huabao*—An Introductory Survey."

26. Hu Baoyu appears in almost all the courtesan novels of the late Qing period. She was credited as a trendsetter in fashion and in female public behavior. Two works fictionalized her life: Lao Shanghai 老上海 (Wu Jianren 吳趼人?), *Hu Baoyu* 胡寶玉 (Shanghai: late 19th century; reprinted in *Shinmatsu shōsetsu* 14 [1991]: 90–156); and Menghuaguanzhu Jiang Yinxiang 夢花館主江陰香, *Jiuwei hu* 九尾狐 (The nine-tailed fox) (Shanghai: Shehui xiaoshuo she, 1908–10).

27. "Pofu qiangwu" 潑婦槍物 (A virago robber), *Shenbao*, Nov. 11, 1878, p. 2.

28. Han Ziyun 韓子雲, *Haishang hua liezhuan* 海上花列傳 (Biographies of Shanghai flowers) (Shanghai, 1892–94; reprinted—Beijing: Renmin wenxue chubanshe, 1985); Haishang shushi sheng 海上漱石生 (Sun Yusheng 孫玉聲), *Haishang fanhua meng* 海上繁華夢 (Dreams of extravagance in Shanghai) (Shanghai: 1903–5, 1906–8; reprinted—Nanchang: Jiangsu renmin chubanshe, 1988).

29. The first collection of the album features 50 courtesans, and the unpublished manuscript of the second collection has another 50 Shanghai courtesans (the manuscript is held by the Shanghai Municipal Library).

30. The publisher's colophon is printed on the back side of the first page. It states that the album was illustrated by Chengbei sheng 城北生, edited by Moli buguofen zhai zhuren 莫釐不過分齋主人 with poetry by Gumang sihua laoren 古莽司花老人, published by Lunhuaguan zhuren 掄花館主人, and engraved by Yokouchi Keizan 橫内桂山 in Tokyo.

31. Lunhuaguan zhuren, "Xu" 序, in *Jingying xiaosheng chuji* 鏡影簫聲初集 (Mirror reflections and flute sounds, first collection) (Tokyo, 1887; copy held at Columbia University, East Asian Library), p. 4.

32. Chubei hongzhou huazhu 楚北鴻洲花主, "Xu" 序, in *Jingying xiaosheng chuji*, p. 3.

33. Lunhuaguan zhuren, "Xu," in *Jingying xiaosheng chuji*, p. 4.

34. For a discussion of the stereotype of the *meiren* images produced during the middle of the nineteenth century, see James Cahill, "The Shanghai School in Later

Chinese Painting," in *Twentieth-Century Chinese Painting*, ed. Kao Mayching (New York: Oxford University Press, 1988), p. 71; and Claypool, *The Social Body*, pp. 44–48.

35. Richard Vinograd, *Boundaries of the Self: Chinese Portraits, 1600–1900* (Cambridge, Eng.: Cambridge University Press, 1992), pp. 141ff.

36. For a study on early photography in China, see Regine Thiriez, "Photography and Portraiture in Nineteenth-Century China," *East Asian History* 17/18 (June/Dec. 1999): 77–102.

37. On *Shanghai pinyan baihua tu, Haishang baimei xinyong, Hushang xinhua baimei tu,* see Shanghai tong she 上海通社, *Shanghai yanjiu ziliao* 上海研究資料 (Research materials on Shanghai) (Shanghai, 1935; reprinted—Shanghai: Shanghai shudian, 1985), pp. 583–86; Xiaolantian chanqing shizhe 小蘭田懺情侍者, ed., *Haishang qunfang pu* 海上群芳譜 (Biographies of Shanghai flowers) (woodblock print; Shanghai, 1886); Liangxi chilian jushi 梁溪池蓮居士, *Hujiang yanpu* 滬江豔譜 (The record of beauties in Shanghai) (Shanghai, 1883).

38. For a short introduction to Zhou Muqiao, see Chen Chaonan 陳超南 and Feng Yiyou 馮懿有, *Lao guanggao* 老廣告 (Old posters) (Shanghai: Shanghai renmin chubanshe, 1998), pp. 12–16.

39. The *Feiyingge huabao*, which was produced by lithographic printing and came out every ten days, was run very much along the same principles as the *Dianshizhai huabao*. For an introduction and study of this journal, see Yu Yueting 余月亭, "Guangxu nianjian de *Feiyingge huabao*" 光緒年間的飛影閣畫報 (The *Feiyinge huabao* of the Guangxu period), *Chuban shiliao* 1 (1987): 32–35; and Wagner, "The Shanghai Illustrated Newspapers *Dianshizhai huabao* and *Feiyingge huabao*."

40. See Wu Youru 吳友如, *Wu Youru huabao* 吳友如畫報 (Masterworks by Wu Youru) (Shanghai: Wenruilou, 1908; reprinted—Shanghai: Shanghai shudian, 1983).

41. Feiyingge zhuren 飛影閣主人 (Wu Youru), Introduction (untitled), *Feiyingge huabao* 飛影閣畫報 1890, no. 2, p. 1.

42. For examples of New Year prints from the Suzhou school on the *meiren* theme, see Jiangsu guji chubanshe 江蘇古籍出版社, ed., *Suzhou Taohuawu muban nianhua* 蘇州桃花塢木板年畫 (Taohuawu woodblock New Year prints, Suzhou) (Nanjing: Jiangsu guji chubanshe, 1991).

43. "Xunyang" 潯陽 refers to a line in Bai Juyi's poem on an aged courtesan, *Pipa xing*; see *Bai Juyi ji* 白居易集 (Anthology of Bai Juyi) (Beijing: Zhonghua shuju, 1979), I: 241.

44. Zizhu shanfang zhuren 紫竹山房主人, *Haishang qinglou tuji* 海上青樓圖記 (Illustrated record of Shanghai courtesan entertainment) (Shanghai, 1891). Unlike the original illustrations by Wu Youru, which intended to break new ground on the theme of *meiren hua*, these recycled illustrations operated on quite a different

cultural register. At times the original illustrations were truncated to create two illustrations from one. This illustrated guide also included works from *Jingying xiaosheng*, which, in their own way, carried the message of the glamour of Shanghai.

45. For example, see Fei Danxu 費丹旭, "Baimei tu" 百美圖 (One hundred beauties), scroll, ink on paper; reproduced in *Zhongguo xiandai huihua shi: Qingdai zhi bu—1840–1911* 中國現代繪畫史: 清代之部一八四零至一九一一 (History of modern Chinese painting: late Qing period, 1840–1911), ed. Li Zhujin 李鑄晉 and Wan Qingli 萬青力 (Taipei: Rock Publishing International, 1997), pp. 150–51; and *Fei Xiaolou baimei huapu* 費曉樓百美畫譜 (A book of model drawings on one hundred beauties by Fei Xiaolou) (reprint based on the 1926 edition—Beijing: Xuefan chubanshe, 2000). Fei Xiaolou is Fei Danxu.

46. For biographies of Dan Duyu, Ding Song, Shen Bocheng, and Qian Binghe, see Zheng Yimei 鄭逸梅, "Dui jiwei manhuajia de huiyi" 對幾位漫畫家的回憶 (Reminiscences on a few cartoonists), *Fengci yu youmo* 3 (1979): 2; and Bi Keguan 畢克官 and Huang Yuanlin 黃遠林, *Zhongguo manhua shi* 中國漫畫史 (History of Chinese cartoon drawing) (Beijing: Wenhua yishu chubanshe, 1986), pp. 37–40, 43–45, 56–61.

47. *Xianshi leyuan ribao* 先施樂園日報 (Shanghai, 1918–27).

48. *Dashijie* 大世界 (Shanghai, 1917–31).

49. Journals such as *Tuhua xunbao* 圖畫旬報 (1912), *Shangshi huabao* 尚時畫報 (1911), and *Shishi huabao* 時事畫報 (1907) published serialized versions of the traditional type of *beimei tu*.

Works Cited

A Ying 阿英. "Zhongguo huabao fazhan zhi jingguo—wei *Liangyou* yibaiwushi qi jinianhao zuo" 中國畫報發展之經過—為<良友>一百五十期紀念號作 (The processes by which the Chinese illustrated magazine developed, written for the celebration of the 150th issue of the *Liangyou*). In idem, *A Ying meishu lunwenji* 阿英美術論文集 (A Ying's collected essays on art). Beijing: Renmin meishu chubanshe, 1982, pp. 75–83.

Bai Juyi 白居易. "*Pipa xing*" 琵琶行 (The song of the pipa). In idem, *Bai Juyi ji* 白居易集 (Anthology of Bai Juyi). Beijing: Zhonghua shuju, 1979, 1: 241.

Baudelaire, Charles. *The Painter of Modern Life and Other Essays*. New York: Da Capo Press, 1986.

Bi Keguan 畢克官 and Huang Yuanlin 黃遠林. *Zhongguo manhua shi* 中國漫畫史 (History of Chinese cartoon drawing). Beijing: Wenhua yishu chubanshe, 1986.

Cahill, James. "The Emperor's Erotica (*Ching Yüan Chai so-shih* II)." *Kaikodo* (1999): 24–43.

———. "The Shanghai School in Later Chinese Painting." In *Twentieth-Century Chinese Painting*, ed. Kao Mayching. New York: Oxford University Press, 1988, pp. 54–77.

———. "Three Zhangs." *Orientations*, Oct. 1996, pp. 59–68.

Chen Chaonan 陳超南 and Feng Yiyou 馮懿有. *Lao guanggao* 老廣告 (Old posters). Shanghai: Shanghai renmin chubanshe, 1998.

Chou, Ju-hsi, ed. *Art at the Close of China's Empire*. Phoebus, Occasional Papers in Art History, 8. Tempe: Arizona State University, 1998.

Claypool, Lisa. "The Social Body: 'Beautiful Women' Imagery in Late Imperial China." Master's thesis, University of Oregon, Department of Art History, 1994.

Dalby, Lisa. *Geisha*. New York: Vintage Books, 1985.

Dashijie 大世界. Shanghai, 1917–31.

Deng Zhimo 鄧志謨. *Sasa pian* 洒洒篇. Late Ming ed. in the Naikaku bunko.

Dianshizhai huabao 點石齋畫報. Shanghai, 1884–94.

Dyce, G. M. *The Model Settlement: Personal Reminiscences of Thirty Years' Residence in the Model Settlement, Shanghai, 1870–1900*. London: Chapman and Hall, 1906.

Edgren, Søren. "The *Ching-ying hsiao-sheng* and Traditional Illustrated Biographies of Women." *Gest Library Journal* 5 (Nov. 1992): 161–73.

Fei Danxu 費丹旭. "*Baimei tu*" 百美圖 (One hundred beauties). Scroll, ink on paper. Reproduced in *Zhongguo xiandai huihua shi: Qingdai zhi bu—1840–1911* 中國現代繪畫史: 清代之部一八四零至一九一一 (History of modern Chinese painting: late Qing period, 1840–1911), ed. Li Zhujin 李鑄晉 and Wan Qingli 萬青力, pp. 150–51. Taipei: Rock Publishing International, 1997.

————. *Fei Xiaolou baimei huapu* 費曉樓百美畫譜 (A book of model drawings on one hundred beauties by Fei Xiaolou). Reprint based on the 1926 edition—Beijing: Xuefan chubanshe, 2000.

Feiyingge huabao 飛影閣畫報. Shanghai, 1890–93.

Gai Qi 改琦. *Honglou meng tu yong* 紅樓夢圖詠. Shanghai, 1879. Reprinted—Taipei: Yiwen yinshuguan, 1974.

Haishang shushi sheng 海上漱石生 (Sun Yusheng 孫玉聲). *Haishang fanhua meng* 海上繁華夢 (Dreams of extravagance in Shanghai). Shanghai: 1903–5, 1906–8. Reprinted—Nanchang: Jiangsu renmin chubanshe, 1988.

Haishang youxi tushuo 海上游戲圖說 (Illustrations with explanations of Shanghai entertainment). Shanghai, 1898.

Han Ziyun 韓子雲. *Haishang hua liezhuan* 海上花列傳 (Biographies of Shanghai flowers). Shanghai, 1892–94. Reprinted—Beijing: Renmin wenxue chubanshe, 1985.

Hanan, Patrick. *The Chinese Vernacular Story.* Cambridge, Mass.: Harvard University Press, 1981.

Hay, Jonathan. "Painters and Publishing in Late Nineteenth-Century Shanghai." In *Art at the Close of China's Empire,* ed. Ju-hsi Chou. Phoebus, Occasional Papers in Art History, 8. Tempe: Arizona State University, 1998, pp. 134–88.

Huaying jixuan 花影集選 (A collection of courtesan photographs). Shanghai: n.p., 1928.

Jiangsu guji chubanshe 江蘇古籍出版社, ed. *Suzhou Taohuawu muban nianhua* 蘇州桃花塢木板年畫 (Taohuawu woodblock New Year prints, Suzhou). Nanjing: Jiangsu guji chubanshe, 1991.

Jingying xiaosheng chuji 鏡影簫聲初集 (Mirror reflections and flute sounds, first collection). Tokyo, 1887. Copy held at Columbia University, East Asian Library.

Kim, Nanny. "How to Read About Monsters and Miracles in the Illustrated Magazine from Late 19th Century Shanghai." In *Joining the Global Public: Text, Image, and City in the Early Shanghai Press,* ed. Rudolf Wagner. In press.

Laing, Ellen Johnston. "Erotic Themes and Romantic Heroines Depicted by Ch'iu Ying." *Archives of Asian Art* 49 (1996): 68–91.

Lao Shanghai 老上海 (Wu Jianren 吳趼人?). *Hu Baoyu* 胡寶玉 (Hu Baoyu). Shanghai: late 19th century. Reprinted in *Shinmatsu shōsetsu* 14 (1991): 90–156.

Li Dou 李斗. *Yangzhou huafang lu* 揚州花舫錄 (The record of painted boats in Yangzhou). Nanjing: Jiangsu Guangling guji keyingshe, 1984.

Li, Wai-yee. "The Late Ming Courtesan: Invention of a Cultural Ideal." In *Writing Women in Late Imperial China,* ed. Ellen Widmer and Kang-I Sun Chang. Stanford: Stanford University Press, 1997, pp. 47–73.

Li Yunxiang 李雲翔. *Jinling baimei* 金陵百媚 (Hundred beauties of Nanjing). Preface dated 1618. Copy in Naikaku bunko.

Li Zhujin 李鑄晉 and Wan Qingli 萬青力, eds. *Zhongguo xiandai huihua shi: Qing-dai zhi bu—1840-1911* 中國現代繪畫史: 清代之部一八四零至一九一一 (History of modern Chinese painting: late Qing period, 1840-1911). Taipei: Rock Publishing International, 1997.

Liangxi chilian jushi 梁溪池蓮居士. *Hujiang yanpu* 滬江豔譜 (The record of beauties in Shanghai). Shanghai, 1883.

Liangyou huabao 良友畫報. Shanghai, 1926-41. Reprinted—Shanghai: Shanghai shudian, 1986.

Libailiu 禮拜六. 1914-16, 1921-23.

Lu Xun 魯迅. *Zhongguo xiaoshuo shilüe* 中國小說史略 (A brief history of Chinese fiction). In *Lu Xun quanji* 魯迅全集 (The complete works of Lu Xun). Beijing: Renmin wenxue chubanshe, 1989.

Meihua'an zhu 梅花盦主 (Li Ruiqing 李瑞清?), ed. *Shenjiang shixia shengjing tushuo* 申江時下勝景圖說 (Illustrations with explanations of contemporary famous sights of Shanghai). Shanghai: Shanghai Jiangzuo shuling, 1894.

Menghuaguanzhu Jiang Yinxiang 夢花館主江陰香. *Jiuwei hu* 九尾狐 (The nine-tailed fox). Shanghai: Shehui xiaoshuo she, 1908-10.

Miao Quansun 繆荃孫. "*Qinhuai guangji zixu*" 秦淮廣紀自序 (Author's preface to *Encyclopeadia of Qinhuai*). In *Qinhuai guangji* 秦淮廣紀 (Encyclopeadia of Qin-huai). Shanghai: Shangwu yinshuguan, 1914, pp. 1-3.

Nishiyama Matsunosuke 西山松之助. *Yūjo* 遊女 (Prostitution). Tokyo: Hei-bonsha, 1997.

"Pofu qiangwu" 潑婦槍物 (A virago robber). *Shenbao*, Nov. 11, 1878, p. 2.

Ropp, Paul S. "Ambiguous Images of Courtesan Culture in Late Imperial China." In *Writing Women in Late Imperial China*, ed. Ellen Widmer and Kang-I Sun Chang. Stanford: Stanford University Press, 1997, pp. 17-45.

Shanghai tong she 上海通社. *Shanghai yanjiu ziliao* 上海研究資料 (Research ma-terials on Shanghai). Shanghai, 1935. Reprinted—Shanghai: Shanghai shudian, 1985.

Shangshi huabao 尚時畫報. 1911.

Shenjiang mingsheng tushuo 申江名勝圖說 (Illustrations with explanations of fa-mous sights of Shanghai). Shanghai: Guan ke shou zhai, 1884.

Shenjiang shengjing tu 申江勝景圖 (Illustrated grand scenes of Shanghai). Litho-graph. Shanghai: Dianshizhai, 1884.

Shi Gufeng 石古風. "*Qinglou yunyu ba*" 青樓韻語跋 (Postface to *Poetry from the Green Tower*). In *Zhongguo gudai banhua congkan erbian* 中國古代版畫叢刊二編. Shanghai: Shanghai guji chubanshe, 1994, 4: 1-3.

Shijie fanhua bao 世界繁華報. 1901-10?

Shishi huabao 時事畫報. 1907.

Thiriez, Regine. "Photography and Portraiture in Nineteenth-Century China." *East Asian History* 17/18 (June/Dec. 1999): 77–102.

Tuhua xunbao 圖畫旬報. 1912.

Vinograd, Richard. *Boundaries of the Self: Chinese Portraits, 1600–1900.* Cambridge, Eng.: Cambridge University Press, 1992.

Wagner, Rudolf G. "Ernest Major's *Shenbaoguan* and the Formation of Late Qing Print Culture." In *The Formation of a Multiethnic Identity: The Shanghai Concessions, 1850–1910,* ed. Catherine Yeh and Rudolf Wagner. In press.

———. "Joining the Global Imaginaire: The Shanghai Illustrated Newspapers *Dianshizhai huabao* and *Feiyinggu huabao*—An Introductory Survey." In *Joining the Global Public: Word, Image, and City in the Early Chinese Newspapers, 1870–1910,* ed. R. Wagner. In press.

———. "The Role of the Foreign Community in the Chinese Public Sphere." *China Quarterly* 142 (June 1995): 423–43.

Wagner, Rudolf G., ed. *Joining the Global Public: Word, Image, and City in the Early Chinese Newspapers, 1870–1910.* In press.

Wang, David Der-wei. *Fin-de-siècle Splendor: Repressed Modernities of Late Qing Fiction, 1848–1911.* Stanford: Stanford University Press, 1997.

Wu Youru 吳友如. *Haishang baiyan tu* 海上百豔圖 (One hundred illustrated beauties of Shanghai). Changsha: Hunan meishu chubanshe, 1998.

———. *Wu Youru huabao* 吳友如畫報 (Masterworks by Wu Youru). Shanghai: Wenruilou, 1908. Reprinted—Shanghai: Shanghai shudian, 1983.

Wuji baimei 吳姬百媚 (Hundred beauties of Suzhou). 1617 ed. Copy in Hōsa bunko, Nagoya.

Xianshi leyuan ribao 先施樂園日報. Shanghai, 1919–27.

Xiaolantian chanqing shizhe 小蘭田懺情侍者, ed. *Haishang qunfang pu* 海上群芳譜 (Biographies of Shanghai flowers). Woodblock print. Shanghai, 1886.

Xiaoshuo huabao 小說畫報. Shanghai, 1917–20.

Ye Xiaoqing. "Popular Culture in Shanghai, 1884–1898." Ph.D. diss., Australian National University, 1991.

Yeh, Catherine V. "Courtesan Stars and Entertainment Papers." In *City, Courtesan and Intellectual: The Rise of Shanghai Entertainment Culture, 1850–1910.* Forthcoming.

———. "Deciphering the Entertainment Press, 1896–1920: The *Youxi bao,* the *Shijie fanhua bao* and Their Descendants." In *Joining the Global Public: Word, Image, and City in the Early Chinese Newspapers, 1870–1910,* ed. Rudolf G. Wagner. In press.

———. "Li Boyuan and His Shanghai Entertainment Newspaper *Youxi bao.*" In *Joining the Global Public: Word, Image, and City in the Early Chinese Newspapers, 1870–1910,* ed. Rudolf G. Wagner. In press.

———. "Reinventing Ritual: Late Qing Handbooks or Proper Customer Behavior in Shanghai Courtesan Houses." *Late Imperial China* 19, no. 2 (Dec. 1998): 1–63.

Youxi bao 遊戲報. Shanghai, 1897–1910?

Yu Yueting 余月亭. "Guangxu nianjian de *Feiyingge huabao*" 光緒年間的飛影閣畫報 (The *Feiyinge huabao* of the Guangxu period). *Chuban shiliao* 1 (1987): 32–35.

————. "Woguo huabao de shizu—*Dianshizhai huabao* chutan" 我國畫報的始祖—點石齋畫報初探 (A preliminary analysis of the ancestor of the Chinese illustrated journals, the *Dianshizhai huabao*). *Xinwen yanjiu ziliao* 5 (1981): 149–81.

Zheng Yimei 鄭逸梅. "Dui jiwei manhuajia de huiyi" 對幾位漫畫家的回憶 (Reminiscences on a few cartoonists). *Fengci yu youmo* 3 (1979): 2.

Zhou Wu 周蕪. *Zhongguo gudai banhua baitu* 中國古代板畫百圖 (One hundred Chinese woodblock prints from the classical period). Beijing: Renmin meishu chubanshe, 1982.

Zhu Yuanliang 朱元亮 and Zhang Mengzheng 張夢徵, comps. *Qinglou yunyu* 青樓韻語 (Poetry from the green tower). 4 vols. Wanli period; illustrated by Zhang Mengzheng and carved by Huang Yibin 黃一彬, Huang Duanfu 黃端甫, and Huang Guifang 黃桂芳. Copy in Zhongguo tushuguan. Reprinted in *Zhongguo gudai banhua congkan erbian* 中國古代板畫叢刊二編. Shanghai: Shanghai guji chubanshe, 1994, vol. 4.

Zizhu shanfang zhuren 紫竹山房主人. *Haishang qinglou tuji* 海上青樓圖記 (Illustrated record of Shanghai courtesan entertainment). Shanghai, 1891.

Part IV

Ethnography, Media, and Ideology

Texts on the Right and Pictures on the Left

Reading the Qing Record of Frontier Taiwan

Emma J. Teng

The ancients had histories on their right and maps (*tu* 圖) on their left, granting equal importance to visualizing and perusing (*guanlan* 觀覽). When Xiao He 蕭何 entered the passes, the first thing he did was to collect maps and written records. Without maps, one cannot have comprehensive knowledge of all the roads and their obstacles, of the terrain and its strategic passes.

—Xia Xianlun, *Taiwan yutu* (1879)

In the preface to a collection of maps of the Taiwan frontier, the nineteenth-century literatus Xia Xianlun 夏獻綸 set forth a claim for the importance of looking in addition to reading. He argued that comprehensive geographic knowledge cannot be gained without the aid of maps and implied that visual images allow for a way of comprehending space and place different from that afforded by words alone. Visual knowledge is a vital supplement to textual knowledge. The image of the literatus seated with texts on his right and *tu* (maps, pictures) on his left offers a vivid model of an idealized mode of late imperial geographic inquiry.

Visuality played a central role in late imperial practices of travel and geographic recording. The notion of "seeing for yourself" figured importantly in late imperial Chinese travel writing. The claims that "I have been there myself and seen with my own eyes" and "I am only recording that which I have seen with my own eyes" are standard clichés of travel literature. Another common move was to refute what one had heard about a place on the basis of one's firsthand experience of the place. As the Ming literatus Zhang Hong 張宏 explained after a journey to eastern Zhejiang in 1639, "About half [of the things I saw there] did not agree with what I had heard. So when I returned I got out some silk and used it to depict what I had seen, because relying on your ears is not as good as relying on your eyes."[1] In travel writing, the privileging of the eye as the most reliable sense is related to the privileging of experiential knowledge.[2] Whereas the ears are associated with hearsay—a type of knowledge many late imperial travel writers regarded as particularly suspect—the traveler's claim to have been an eyewitness to all that he records confers authority on the travel account.[3]

The importance of visuality in travel writing is further underscored by the common practice of late imperial readers of praising vivid description as *ruhua* 如畫, "like a painting," or *rutu* 如圖, "like a picture." Given the central place of visuality in travel, it is not surprising that travelers like Zhang Hong chose to record their experiences in pictorial as well as textual forms. Although art historians have written much on the association between domestic tourist travel and landscape painting (*shanshuihua* 山水畫), comparatively little has been written on the traveler's involvement with the class of visual materials known as *tu* (pictures, illustrations, maps, or diagrams). Yet many late imperial travelers produced *tu* as visual records of their observations in addition to the written accounts of their journeys.[4] Unfortunately, although much late imperial travel writing has been preserved in *bieji* 別集 or in Qing collectanea, due to the difficulties of reproduction, *tu* were generally not included in such publications. Wang Xiqi's 王錫祺 (1855–1913) mammoth travel anthology, *The Geographic Collectanea of the Xiaofanghu Studio* (*Xiaofanghuzhai yudi congchao* 小方壺齋輿地叢鈔; ca. 1877), which contains hundreds of accounts of exotic locales—everywhere from Taiwan to Turfan—includes no *tu*. Consequently, many *tu* have been lost or exist only in rare manuscript editions in museums or private collections. Sometimes our only clue to the existence of such *tu* is the colophon writer's lament that, "it is a pity that the *tu* have long been lost" (*xi qitu jiuyi* 惜其圖久佚). Thus, although text and *tu* originally circulated within the same milieu, the modern reader of Qing travel anthologies generally reads them as though texts existed in isolation from pictures—a practice reinforced by the academic distinction between literary studies and art history.[5] In this chapter, I will argue, however, that travel writing is best understood within a system of geographic representation that includes visual materials.[6]

Craig Clunas has recently argued for the importance of pictures and visuality in early modern China and demonstrated how pictures permeated virtually every aspect of life in this period.[7] Illustrated books of all kinds, including geographic works, were widely available. Readers were accustomed to looking at pictures in conjunction with texts. Robert Hegel has also greatly added to our understanding of the theory and practice of reading texts with pictures with his study of Ming and Qing illustrated fiction. Following the approach suggested by scholars like Clunas and Hegel, I seek to reinsert the reading of *tu* into the reading of travel literature, to read as Xia Xianlun would have us read.[8]

This chapter explores how *tu* worked in conjunction with texts to produce geographic knowledge of the Qing frontier of Taiwan, which was colonized by the Qing in 1683. Prior to the Qing conquest, few Chinese literati had traveled to the island, and firsthand accounts of Taiwan were rare. Following annexation of the island, however, Chinese literati began to travel to Taiwan in greater numbers. These travelers—colonial officials, military men, explorers, and private travelers—produced a significant corpus of literature on Taiwan. In addition to their writings, a number of travelers also produced various *tu*, both as personal mementos and as aids for the colonial administration. Although the surviving visual record of Qing Taiwan is far smaller than the textual record, it is no less significant. Like travel writing, *tu* are a highly mediated form of representation: *tu* thus reveal a great deal about how Qing travelers (often through the professional illustrators they hired) "saw" the frontier.[9] An examination of *tu* brings to the fore issues or perspectives that do not emerge from an examination of travel writing alone. Therefore, a more complete understanding of the cultural meanings that the frontier had for the Qing can be gained by reading *tu* in conjunction with texts such as travel accounts and gazetteers.

The Qing court recognized the importance of producing both visual and textual records of the frontiers. For the Qing, the visual representation of the frontiers, especially mapping, was bound up with the assertion of imperial power on both the practical and the symbolic levels.[10] As the Qing expanded its imperial possessions, the court commissioned a number of major projects to illustrate the empire. These projects included the Kangxi-Jesuit atlas, a comprehensive survey of the empire completed in 1717; the *Compre-*

hensive Gazetteer of the Great Qing Realm (*Da Qing yitongzhi* 大清一統志), completed in 1746; and the *Qing Imperial Tribute Illustrations* (*Huang Qing zhigongtu* 皇清職貢圖), commissioned in 1751.[11] The Qianlong emperor also commissioned a series of French copperplate engravings to commemorate conquests on the frontiers.[12] Such *tu* not only helped to visualize the extent of Qing imperial possessions but also to define, order, and celebrate these possessions.[13]

Picturing the Taiwan Frontier

One of the first tasks of Qing officials after the annexation of Taiwan was to map the island, for maps (*ditu* 地圖 or *shanchuantu* 山川圖) were considered crucial strategic and administrative aids.[14] The first official Qing map of Taiwan appeared as early as 1684, in the *Comprehensive Gazetteer of Fujian* (*Fujian tongzhi* 福建統志); many more followed soon after (see Figs. 10.1–4). A number of these maps were submitted to the imperial court, and others were employed by local officials. Private travelers, too, drew their own maps for inclusion in their travel accounts. Altogether, from 1684 until 1895 (the year the island was ceded to the Japanese), over 420 maps of Taiwan were produced.[15]

Travelers and colonial officials were also eager to collect information about the indigenous people of the island (known to the Chinese as "savages," *fan* 番) and their curious customs. Ethnographic description was prominent in travel writing, and the "record of customs" (*fengsuzhi* 風俗志) was an essential component of every gazetteer. Travelers and gazetteer compilers also commissioned ethnographic illustrations (*fengsutu* 風俗圖) to depict the local people and their customs. These illustrations focused on basic economic activities, such as deer hunting (see Fig. 10.5), farming, and fishing, as well as important rituals such as weddings and harvest festivals. Although we have no evidence concerning the numbers of such illustrations produced during the Qing, according to Du Zhengsheng's research on the subject, there are some ten kinds of ethnographic illustrations of Taiwan indigenes extant.[16] Officials stationed in Taiwan also submitted illustrations of the indigenous peoples for inclusion in the *Qing Imperial Tribute Illustrations* (see Figs. 10.6–9).

In addition to their ethnographic interests, travelers to Taiwan displayed a keen interest in the natural world. The documentation of local products

Fig. 10.1 Map of Taiwan from the *Taiwan County Gazetteer*, 1720 (section).

南像
崁阜
山南
見界

崇爻山

崇爻社

Fig. 10.2 Map of Taiwan's transmontane territory from the
Zhuluo County Gazetteer, 1717 (section).

(*fengwu* 風物, *wuchan* 物產, or *tuchan* 土產) in both travel writing and gaz-etteers was generally done with an eye to the economic potential or medici-nal value of local flora and fauna. But Chinese literati also evinced an interest in the sheer variety of the natural world. Travel writers, in particular, valued exotic flora and fauna purely for their strangeness (*qi* 奇). Travelers also commissioned illustrations of flora and fauna (*fengwutu* 風物圖) to docu-ment the specimens they found. As collections of unique local products, al-bums of flora and fauna helped to define and display what was different and special about the island.

The production of such *tu* was intimately bound up with the physical act of travel. A preface by the Manchu censor Liu-shi-qi 六十七, who served in Taiwan from 1744 to 1747, provides a picture of the context in which topo-graphical illustrations were created.

In the course of my duties I toured around and inquired after customs and strange products. I saw all kinds of unusual and weird things that have never been seen on the mainland. It was then that I began to believe that the world is so vast that there is nothing that it does not contain. In my spare time from official duties, I ordered a painter to make illustrations of those concrete things that I had seen and heard.[17]

As representations of perceived reality, *tu* were conventionally expected to be mimetic. Although verisimilitude was regarded as a lowly value in theo-ries of painting from the late Ming on,[18] "likeness in form" (*xingsi* 形似) was much prized in *tu*.[19] Statements made by a number of Qing travelers to Taiwan make it clear that an essential aim of *tu* was to convey likeness in form. Indeed, Qing travelers often turned to *tu* when they found something difficult to describe in words (*zhuang nan jinhua* 狀難盡話). As a direct rep-resentation of likeness in form, *tu* allowed for a nonverbal means of commu-nication.

Verisimilitude was particularly crucial when *tu* were to be used as a means of identifying people or objects. This does not mean that *tu* were nec-essarily drawn from life. Rather, they might be produced (by either a profes-sional painter or the traveler himself) based on the traveler's memory of what he had seen or perhaps samples of fruits and flowers that he had collected. Nonetheless, a foundation in firsthand observation was regarded as crucial, and Qing writers regularly criticized *tu* that were based on hearsay or fancy.

As such, the production of *tu* on the Taiwan frontier was no easy task, especially during the early Qing when much of the island had not as yet been

Fig. 10.3 Map of Taiwan from the *Taiwan Prefectural Gazetteer*, 1696 (section).

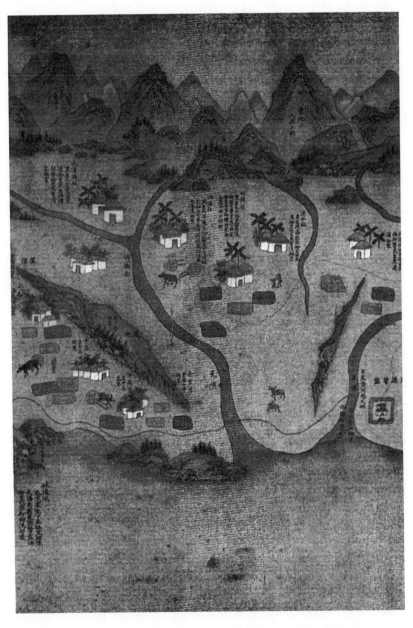

Fig. 10.4 Huang Shujing (attr.), *A Map of Taiwan's Savage Villages*
(*Taiwan fanshe tu*), Kangxi.

explored by Chinese. Zhou Zhongxuan 周鍾瑄, the editor of the first gazetteer of Taiwan's Zhuluo county, discussed the problems of mapping wilderness at length. He declared that it was nearly impossible to map the dense jungle and impenetrable mountain areas of the island accurately and lamented the difficulty of obtaining pictures of the "raw savages" of the island:[20]

Now as for the dark secluded areas deep within the lofty peaks of the inner mountains where the raw savages (*shengfan* 生番) live and the hobgoblins have their lairs, the Han Chinese have never gone there and gotten knowledge. Even the cooked savages (*shufan* 熟番) have no way of knowing about these areas. Thus, there is no means of making pictures.[21]

For Zhou, it was imperative that pictures be based on direct observation. Without a basis in empirical knowledge, he argued, pictures are no more than insubstantial images created from the imagination, no more than visual hearsay. Thus, he emphasized that "there is no means of making pictures" of those areas of the island that the Chinese were unable to penetrate. Travel and "seeing for yourself" are essential for good mapping and picturing.

In addition to the types of *tu* mentioned above, the range of subjects illustrated by Qing literati in Taiwan is enormous: there are architectural illustrations of civil, military, and religious structures; pictures of local Chinese industries; and *tu* commemorating events such as the annual review of troops on the island and the performance of Confucian rituals.[22] Such *tu* were often commissioned by the officials who had sponsored the building of particular structures or the performance of particular rituals. Aside from these commemorative *tu*, gazetteers might contain *tu* of the local government offices or of important local structures such as the Confucian school. In combination, these topographical *tu* provide a lively visual record of Qing Taiwan.

Tu *and Modes of Looking*

Tu enabled a variety of modes of visual comprehension, all of which can be correlated with different "ways of looking." The range of ways of looking in late imperial Chinese culture has been partially described by Craig Clunas in *Pictures and Visuality in Early Modern China*, where he takes up Roland Barthes's demand for a "history of looking." Focusing on the act of looking at paintings, Clunas analyzes *shangjian* 賞鑒 (to discriminate on the grounds of quality), *kan* 看 (to look), *guan* 觀 (to contemplate), and *du* 讀 (to read) as different ways of looking. When it comes to *tu*, especially topographical *tu*, yet other ways of looking become important.

LAN: SURVEYING

One mode of looking that is particularly privileged in travel is surveying (*lan* 覽). Travelers often climbed hilltops or towers in order to survey the landscape, a moment generally considered the climax of an excursion. *Tu* were similarly valued since they allowed the viewer to survey: maps, in particular, were associated with this way of looking. In surveying, the viewer is able to gain a quick grasp of the terrain, a general impression of the whole. As Tao Qian wrote in a poem about reading an illustrated version of the *Shan hai jing* 山海經: "I glance over the pictures [maps?] of mountains and seas. / In the space of a nod, I completely comprehend the universe."[23] As a means of viewing the overall layout of the terrain, maps were vital for both military strategy and local administration. As Chen Xiang 陳襄 (1017–80) wrote in *Essentials of Prefectural and County [Government]* (*Zhouxian tigang* 州縣提綱), with maps "the people, land configuration, mountains, forests, stream, and marshes [are] all in view; and whenever there are legal disputes, taxes and levies, droughts, and arrests, everything can be seen at a glance."[24] These various statements praising the ability to see at a glance reveal that *tu* were valued insofar as they enabled a different, more immediate, way of knowing than did verbal texts.

Indeed, word and image performed a complementary division of labor in late imperial geographic representation. Cordell Yee and others have demonstrated that gazetteer maps, for example, were intended primarily as illustrative accompaniments to the gazetteer text, which contained verbal descriptions of the geography. Maps provided a general idea of the topography and aided in understanding the spatial relations between landmarks. The text supplied such details as distances between locations and the names of villages, mountains, and other topographical features. Map and text thus assumed complementary functions, with maps allowing for qualitative understandings of the terrain and texts providing quantitative geographic information. This complementary relation was expressed in the idea that the "narration of events without maps is not clear, and maps without explanation are not intelligible."[25]

Fig. 10.5 Ethnographic illustration from the *Zhuluo County Gazetteer*, 1717.

If maps were valued primarily as they allowed a qualitative understanding of geography, this might in part explain why pictorial maps were so popular during the Qing, despite the existence of planimetric mapping techniques. Xia Liming's research has demonstrated that although Qing cartographers employed a variety of cartographic techniques, approximately 70 percent of all extant Qing maps of Taiwan are pictorial maps.[26]

This complementary relation between textual explanation and pictorial representation of likeness in form held true for other kinds of *tu* as well. As Zhou Zhongxuan explained in the *Zhuluo County Gazetteer*:

To the left [above] we have eleven landscape maps (*shanchuantu*), one picture of the county yamen, one picture of the Confucian school, and ten pictures of savage customs (*fansu* 番俗). . . . The detailed explanations are contained in "Borders" and can also be found scattered in the "Military Defense," and "Miscellaneous" sections. The *tu* simply provide a general impression of appearances. . . . For the customs of the cooked savages, see the "Record of Customs" ("Fengsu zhi"). We have illustrated their agricultural work, fishing and hunting, their dwellings, and a number of their seasonal feasts and song and dance festivals, in order to give the reader an idea of appearances through likeness in form (*xingsi*).[27]

Zhou instructed the reader to rely on *tu* only for a general impression of appearances and to turn to the appropriate sections of the text for detailed geographic information (see Figs. 10.2 and 10.5). The placement of *tu* in gazetteers—typically at the very front of the volume, preceding the body of the text—encourages a mode of reading consistent with the notion that *tu* provide a "general impression" to be seen "at a glance," whereas the text provides quantitative information. Thus, the reader first takes a quick look at the *tu*, visualizes the general appearances, and then turns to the text for explanations and more in-depth understanding.[28] *Tu* thereby serve as an important visual aid to reading.

CHENGLAN: IMPERIAL INSPECTION

Tu were particularly valued in the context of Qing expansionism since they enabled a privileged form of surveying—the imperial inspection (*chenglan* 呈覽). Qing officials who traveled to the frontiers submitted *tu*, both at imperial behest and of their own volition, in order that the emperor might visually inspect the terrain, people, flora and fauna, and architectural structures of his newly conquered territories. Imperial inspection enabled the emperor to view even the remotest corner of his empire without the need for travel, an expression of his power as the ultimate surveyor. Thus, the Kangxi emperor commissioned the Jesuit atlas of the empire so that he might "be able to view all parts of the empire at a glance."[29] Surveying is therefore linked to both immediate comprehension and the power of possession.

Maps, in particular, were associated with this symbolic power. The notion that the possession of maps signifies the possession of land dates back at least to the third century B.C. Maps and conquest became so closely associated that the presentation of maps to the ruler was conventionally known as the "presentation of rivers and mountains" (xian jiangshan 獻江山).[30] Taiwan travel writers and gazetteer compilers commonly used the term "entering the map" (ru bantu 入版圖) to denote the moment of Taiwan's incorporation into the Qing imperial domain.[31] The Newly Revised Taiwan Gazetteer (Chongxiu Taiwan fuzhi 重修台灣府志), for example, proclaimed: "Since antiquity, Taiwan has been a remote wilderness, a place beyond the reaches of civilization. Today, the emperor has been on the throne for twenty-one years, the vast seas are calm and clear, and there is peace throughout the land; even this wilderness has entered the map."[32] The addition of the island to the Qing Imperial Map (Da Qing bantu 大清版圖) carried great symbolic weight, signifying Qing dominion over the terrain.

The Qing Imperial Tribute Illustrations, commissioned by the Qianlong emperor in 1751, served a similar symbolic function. Taking approximately a decade to complete, the Tribute Illustrations is a massive compendium of pictures of various non-Han peoples within the Qing empire, as well as peoples from numerous Asian and European countries. Since illustrations of the former constitute some two-thirds of the work, the Tribute Illustrations is essentially a visual catalogue of the peoples of the empire. Although the final product was executed by the court painter Xie Sui, local officials from all corners of the empire participated in the project of compilation, at the command of the Qianlong emperor:

Our dynasty has unified the vast terrain that lies within the frontiers. The various barbarians, inner and outer, have submitted and turned toward civilization. Each of them has a different costume and appearance. We order the various officials of the coastal borders and frontiers to have illustrations made copying the likeness of the clothing and ornaments of the various tribespeople under their jurisdiction, as well as of the foreign barbarians and savages, and to submit these illustrations to the Privy Council, that they may be compiled and arranged for imperial inspection. Thereby will be displayed the abundance of the gathering of kings (wanghui 王會).[33]

The emperor might thus survey the peoples of his empire and his "tributary" states. The work also enabled the emperor to display his prestige as the ruler of an empire accepting tribute from all corners of the world. To survey and to display—both politically loaded visual activities—were thus the dual aims of the project.

The importance of the element of display is evident in the original scroll painted by Xie Sui: the brilliant colors of the figures and the fine and elaborate details of the costumes create a sense of pageantry. The visual impact goes beyond any possible impact that a textual cataloging could have. One of several projects of ethnographic collecting sponsored by the Qianlong emperor, the *Tribute Illustrations* provided a means not only of displaying the diversity and hence the great reach of the empire but also of classifying the peoples of the empire and thereby bringing order to this diversity.[34] Unlike textual compilations, the primary purpose of the *Tribute Illustrations* was to display *visual* difference—"the different costumes and appearances" of the various barbarians. The recording of customs was secondary and far from comprehensive.

SHI: VISUAL IDENTIFICATION

Tu were also a key instrument for the visual identification or classification of people and objects. The process of visually identifying an object involves a way of looking that is perhaps best described by the word *shi* 識, "to know" or "to recognize." This term is not usually thought of as a visual word in the same sense as *lan* or *kan*, but it connotes a process of visual identification, not unlike the English word "recognize." Qing writers frequently used this word to describe the visual apprehension of an object through *tu*. For example, Huang Shujing 黃叔璥, supervising censor of Taiwan in 1722, who commissioned two albums of Taiwan's fruits and flowers, described his motivation for producing such illustrations: "I sought to investigate (*kao* 考) the varieties and types [of flowers and fruits]. I distinguished their colors and fragrances/tastes (*wei* 味) in order to know (*shi*) them."[35] Since the act of distinguishing varieties of fruits and flowers was in large part a visual process for Huang, he used *tu* as a means of both collecting and classifying the strange specimens that he encountered during his travels.[36]

If illustrations of flora and fauna were to serve as visual aids for identifying plants and animals, then verisimilitude became crucial. The editors of a revised edition of Li Shizhen's 李時珍 (1518–93) *Classified Materia Medica* (*Bencao gangmu* 本草綱目) raised this issue in the introduction to the illustrations of the text. They criticized what they saw as a previous tendency to use illustrations primarily for decoration without "discriminating the likeness in form." As a result, they argued, "gentlemen with an interest in rare objects often possessed doubts concerning the distinction between the hawthorn and the pear, or the orange and the pomelo." In contrast, they claimed, the *Materia Medica*'s illustrations strove to "investigate in detail and collate items against one another" in order to assure the greatest accuracy. The objects pictured are classified by category—metals and stones, plants, fruits—and each individual specimen is displayed in a box and labeled with a name. By adhering to the likeness in form, it is implied, pictures could convey a clear and reliable distinction between the orange and the pomelo. "Therefore," the editors concluded, "any strange objects (*yiwu* 異物) can be looked up by referring to these pictures."[37] Overall, then, the pictures in the *Materia Medica* have an educational, and not a decorative, function; they are intended to help in the visual identification and classification of objects from the natural world. One viewer of Huang Shujing's pictures similarly asserted that the realism of his pictures, in addition to careful classification, enabled the viewer to learn about botanical items:

> With brilliant greens and cinnabar red,
> Imitating the real, the paintbrush is wielded.
> Attaching names and discriminating varieties,
> With reference to these pictures, all can be understood.[38]

A crucial part of this process of visual identification is the attachment of names to objects. The utility of *tu* as a means of learning the names of plants and animals or for identifying different ethnic groups was noted by a number of Qing writers. Pictures are unique in the respect that they allow for a direct correlation between an object's appearance and its name (when provided in a label). Pictures thus make possible a type of visual comprehension, a process whereby one can come to know either the appearance of an object through its name or the name of an object through its appearance, much as a child learns from an illustrated primer. Rather than comprehending an object through its description, then, one learns "what it is" through its likeness.

SHANG: LOOKING AS PLEASURE

The aesthetic dimension of *tu* cannot be overlooked, for in addition to their other functions, *tu* involved looking as visual pleasure, or *shang* 賞. *Tu* of all kinds had a decorative function: even maps, which were used primarily for strategic or administrative purposes, can be found adorning fans and other decorative objects. Illustrations of tropical flora and fauna, with their exotic colors and forms, had marked visual appeal.[39]

As aesthetic artifacts, illustrated albums were prized as souvenirs that could be shared with friends and colleagues—much as modern travelers share vacation photos with those back home. The importance of this activity is indicated in the writings of travelers. As Liu-shi-qi informed his readers, "I will keep [the album] in my travel trunk so that when I return I may present it to the learned and accomplished gentlemen at the capital and thereby expand their knowledge."[40] Huang Shujing also mentioned displaying his illustrations to his circle of friends. The acts of both presenting and displaying are essentially social activities. Likewise, the act of viewing such albums was an inherently social activity, involving *shang*, looking as appreciation. This type of looking required the viewer to praise the objects shown and often to write poems in commemoration of the occasion of viewing.

Certainly the pleasures of viewing were valued by readers, who praised illustrations for the "excitement to the senses" (*ermu wei yikuai* 耳目為一快).[41] One reader taken with the vivid colors of Huang Shujing's illustrations of tropical fruits and flowers declared that "all the exotic flavors could be tasted."[42] When illustrations had been lost, readers lamented that the enjoyment of reading had been diminished.

GUAN: LOOKING AND VICARIOUS TRAVEL

The notion that pictures could bring things to life made *tu* a favored medium for vicarious travel (*woyou* 卧遊).[43] Indeed, one viewer's final praise of Huang's pictures was that they allowed him to experience the thrills of the frontier vicariously. The idea that a painting could serve as a vehicle for vicarious travel can be found in early theories of the arts. Zong Bing 宗炳 (375–443), for example, argued that by meditating on a landscape painting, the viewer could feel as if nature were before him.[44] The image thus serves as a substitute for physical reality. The kind of looking that is involved in such acts of vicarious travel is *guan* 觀, looking as contemplation.

Of course, individual *tu* could be viewed in all these ways, allowing for multiple levels of visual understanding or pleasure. *Tu* thus served a wide range of practical, social, and aesthetic functions.

Images of an Island Wilderness

If *tu* conveyed a qualitative understanding of place and space, what kind of image of Taiwan did Qing pictures project? Qing pictorial maps of Taiwan depicted the island as seen from the perspective of the Qing conquerors. These maps typically showed only the western side of the island, as if Taiwan were viewed from mainland China. For most of the Qing colonial period, Chinese settlement was concentrated on the western plains of Taiwan, and the mountainous areas and the eastern half of the island were the domains of the indigenes. Until the nineteenth century, the eastern side of Taiwan was considered "beyond the pale," beyond Qing military and administrative control, and it was largely unexplored by Chinese. Thus, the conventional cartographic view of Taiwan was of the western plains with the central mountain range shown on the horizon in pictorial elevation. The imposing height of these mountains emphasizes the impenetrability of the terrain beyond them. On a number of maps, certain mountains are marked with the words "human footsteps have never entered here" (*renji weizhi* 人跡 未至) delineating the space that remained unexplored by Chinese.

Many Qing pictorial maps depict the visual iconography of Taiwan as a "wilderness beyond the seas." These maps commonly represent the island surrounded by gigantic, wildly exaggerated waves that stand in sharp contrast to the stylized fish-scale pattern waves conventionally depicted on Chinese maps. These waves emphasize both the isolation of the island and the difficulties of the crossing. Small ships tossed on these enormous waves further underscore the treacherous nature of the Taiwan Strait (see Fig. 10.1). Such imagery was consistent with the prevalent Chinese conception of Taiwan as an island "hanging alone outside the seas" (despite the fact that the strait is less than 100 miles wide).

Pictorial maps further convey images of "wilderness" through the representation of the island's landscape. On many maps, enormous, craggy mountains and dense, vigorous vegetation dominate the landscape, and human settlements are few and far between. A number of maps depict successive layers of mountains stretching off into the distance, emphasizing the impenetrability of the topography. Other maps show the mountains in outlandish, wild forms. In a rare map of Taiwan's eastern coast, the *Zhuluo County Gazetteer's* "map of the transmontane territory" (*shanhoutu* 山後圖), these features are even more exaggerated (see Fig. 10.2). This map shows craggy, forested mountain peaks. Giant waves pound the shores. Buildings are entirely absent, as if the terrain were uninhabited. The existence of indigenous settlements is marked only with text—"thirty-six villages of Gemalan"—without any specific location on the terrain. The vagueness of the map most likely reflects the lack of Chinese knowledge about this side of the island at the time the map was drawn (1717). Nonetheless, the map communicates a strong qualitative impression of "wilderness."

Qing maps generally tended to focus on important Chinese landmarks—county and prefectural cantonments, military outposts, forts, Chinese villages and ports, and so forth. Centered on these Chinese features, the typical map (see Fig. 10.3) provides a vivid image of the Qing presence on the island but downplays the indigenous presence. One notable exception to this pattern is a scroll-length map known as "Huang Shujing's map of the Savage Villages" (*Huang Shujing fanshe tu* 黃叔璥番社圖).[45] This map (Fig. 10.4) has long been attributed to Huang Shujing, who supposedly painted the map himself on completing his tour of inspection of the island and presented it to the Kangxi emperor. The map demonstrates extensive knowledge of the island's terrain and the indigenous population. The map is rendered in color and mounted on silk in the handscroll format, measuring 5,841 cm by 726 cm. Unlike other Qing maps, this map emphasizes the indigenous population rather than the Chinese population.[46] It thus conveys an understanding of the island qualitatively different from the typical Qing map.

The unique feature of this map is that it integrates both ethnographic and landscape illustrations. The map depicts the indigenous people of the island engaged in their daily occupations: farming, hunting, capturing oxen, driving oxcarts, carrying loads along the roads, and caring for children. Rice paddies and other fields are also depicted, as are wild deer, horses, buffalo, and other small animals. In many ways, the map is a visual travelogue and provides an experiential and subjective interpretation of the terrain. The map replicates the experience of moving through space, as the viewer unrolls the handscroll and moves his eye across the terrain. The viewer is able both to survey (*lan*) the terrain, to see the large picture at a glance, and to engage in a more detailed, slow visual reading (*du*) of the map's details. The map would have enabled the Kangxi emperor to gain a fairly comprehensive image of the island and its people.

Whereas pictorial maps of Taiwan largely represented the terrain as "wilderness," illustrations of Taiwan's flora and fauna represented the abundance of the island's natural products. The *Illustrations of Taiwan's Flora and Fauna* (*Taihai caifengtu* 台海采風圖), produced by Liu-shi-qi, for example, serves as a splendid visual display of the variety of Taiwan's wildlife. The album contains nine leaves, each picturing a selection of fruits, vegetables, flowers, bamboo, or small birds and animals. The items are rendered in vibrant, vivid hues of red, yellow, orange, green, and purple. Taken as a whole, the album offers potent visual evidence of the fecundity of Taiwan's soil.

Ethnographic illustrations, for their part, represented the island's indigenous people in terms of well-established Chinese images of "savagery." Pictures of the natives naked (or half-naked), tattooed, barefooted, or wearing animal skins fit into the visual iconography of savagery (see Fig. 10.5). Other details—the large earrings worn by men, the leg garters worn by women, or the nose flutes played by youths—were exotic and accentuated the otherness of these people. The customs depicted in such illustrations also confirmed the Chinese notion that the indigenes were uncivilized. Pictures of drinking parties, for example, that showed men and women drinking together played into Chinese ideas about native women's lack of modesty and sexual propriety. Thus, ethnographic illustrations served not only to give the reader an idea of the natives' appearance but also to produce ethnic difference through the display of strange customs and strange bodies.

Qing ethnographic illustrations accentuate the physical differences between the Han Chinese and the Taiwan indigenes. In color illustrations, the indigenes (especially the "raw savages" of the mountainous areas) are noticeably darker than the Chinese. Native women, however, are often shown as fair-skinned, highlighting their erotic appeal. Thus, both ethnic and gender difference are signified through the representation of skin color. Other visual signs of difference in these pictures include the indigenes' round eyes, large mouths, and lack of facial hair, features that Qing writers identified as distinguishing these people from the Han Chinese. Hairstyles also served as a marker of ethnic difference. Whereas the Han Chinese men wear the distinctive queue imposed on them by the Qing, the Taiwan indigenes sport rather different styles: the "cooked savages" of the plains areas are most often shown with their hair tied in two tufts on the sides of the head, or in a single topknot; the "raw savages" are shown with cropped hair or with long, loose hair (see Figs. 10.7 and 10.8).

Ethnic or racial distinctions are given even more explicit visual expression in the *Qing Imperial Tribute Illustrations* (see Figs. 10.6–8). In each of the thirteen illustrations devoted to the Taiwan indigenes, the differences between the savage body and the civilized body are emphasized. The strategy for representing savage bodies in this work, especially male bodies, is similar to Chinese pictorial conventions for representing what art historian Craig Clunas calls "the ugly bodies of the poor." Clunas writes that the bodies of the urban poor in works such as Zhou Chen's 周臣 (fl. 1472–1535) *Beggars and Street Characters* (1516) are "distinguished by their relative nudity and above all by their lack of verticality. The poor bend forward whether burdened by disease and want or stooped in toil over their tools, in contrast with figures who are both decently clothed and dominantly erect in posture [e.g., Chinese elites]."[47]

Similarly, the bodies of the Taiwan indigenes in the *Tribute Illustrations* are represented in varying degrees as underclothed, undisciplined, and coarse. Often, the figure is represented with legs spread apart and torso hunched over. Feet are bare, and heads uncovered. The muscles of the male savages are drawn in an exaggerated fashion, as are their facial lines—all to emphasize the grotesqueness of these figures. The strongly delineated muscles of the savage male are reminiscent of Chinese pictures of bandits or demons, figures whose musculature distinguishes them from the Chinese elites with their soft and languid limbs.[48]

That savagery is a matter of degree becomes clear when we compare the cooked savage of Fengshan county (Fig. 10.7) to the raw savage of the inner mountains of Zhanghua county (Fig. 10.8).[49] The cooked savage of Fengshan stands relatively erect, although he carries a burden over his shoulder. He is fully clothed except for the feet and head, and his hair is pulled back neatly in a bun. His facial expression is open and pleasing. His brightly colored costume is a combination of pale purple, blue, and brown, with a touch of red at his waist. Although his costume is exotic and he wears an earring, he does not appear to be too far removed from civilization.

In contrast, the raw savage of Zhanghua is the embodiment of the grotesque and the terrible. He is drawn in a demonlike stance, with one leg

Fig. 10.6 Picture of "cooked savage woman" from Danshui subprefecture,
Taiwan; from *Qing Imperial Tribute Illustrations*, ca. 1751.

Fig. 10.7 Picture of "cooked savage" from Fengshan county,
Taiwan; from *Qing Imperial Tribute Illustrations*, ca. 1751.

Fig. 10.8 Picture of "raw savage" from Zhanghua county,
Taiwan; from *Qing Imperial Tribute Illustrations*, ca. 1751.

raised, holding a spear in one hand as though ready to strike. This figure is depicted nearly naked, with bulging and rippling muscles. His hair is loose (a sign of wildness), and he sports a number of feathers in his headband. This figure presents quite a threatening mien, for he not only holds a sword but also carries two knives at his waist. The expression on his face is grotesque and contorted. Reinforcing the bellicose appearance of this figure, the scant costume he wears at his waist is a blazing, fiery red. Indeed, he strongly resembles the demon-queller, Zhong Kui 鍾馗, or the depictions of the *rakshas* in works such as the Ming *Illustrated Record of Strange Countries* (*Yiyu tuzhi* 異域圖志).

The visual representations of the cooked savage of Fengshan and the raw savage of Zhuanghua correspond to the textual descriptions of each group. The text describes the Fengshan subjects as "good at plowing and planting. They grow fragrant rice. The men cover their bodies with deer hide; some wear a blanket like a cape. The women wear blouses and skirts."[50] These people are thus associated with both agriculture and clothing, important indices of civilization for Chinese literati. In contrast, "the raw savages of the inner mountains live in the deep mountains and hidden valleys—places where human footsteps seldom reach. They dwell in nests and caves, eating fur and drinking blood. They are naked and fear neither the cold of winter nor the heat of summer. . . . When they meet mainland people, they immediately attack them with spears."[51] The artist's depiction of the physical appearances of the cooked savage and the raw savage thus correlates with their relative levels of civilization as described in the text. In particular, the grotesqueness of the raw savage is associated with both cultural backwardness and belligerence.

Racial difference as visualized in the *Tribute Illustrations* can be read as the embodiment of cultural difference; that is, the relative concepts of "civilized," and "barbaric" or "savage" are variously embodied in the human figures. At one end of the spectrum, we have the Korean gentleman (Fig. 10.9), the first figure in the collection.[52] Perhaps considered by the Qing to be the most "civilized" of all the barbarians, the Korean gentleman is not much different from the ideal Qing gentleman except for his lack of a queue. He is fully clothed, capped, and shod and stands erect with one hand to his bosom. He wears a placid expression on his face, which is painted a pallid white. At the other end of the spectrum, we have figures such as the raw savage of

朝鮮國夷官

Fig. 10.9 Picture of Korean gentleman from *Qing Imperial Tribute Illustrations*, ca. 1751.

Zhanghua (Fig. 10.8) whose difference from the civilized person is high-lighted in every possible way, figures that resemble demons more than men. In between, various figures embody relative degrees of barbarism.

If physical appearance can be read as the outward manifestation of cul-tural difference, it can also be read as the outward manifestation of a people's inborn nature (*xing* 性). The physical repulsiveness or ugliness (*e* 惡) of the raw savage of Zhanghua, for example, serves as an index of moral repulsive-ness, of an evil (*e* 惡) nature. In contrast, the *Tribute Illustrations* represents the tamed and submitted cooked savages as outwardly pliant and submissive in bearing. The depiction of countenance thus becomes a means of indexing a people's nature.[53]

Visual Knowledge Versus Textual Knowledge

These various images of the Taiwan indigenes reveal that *tu* did not simply function as a supplement to travel writing. Rather, sometimes text and *tu* do rather different things. If we compare ethnographic description and ethno-graphic illustration, for example, we find that whereas the physical difference of the other plays a relatively small role in Qing ethnographic discourse, in the realm of *tu*, "racial difference" is clearly visualized.[54]

In travel accounts of Taiwan, writers provided scant description of the physical appearance of the indigenous people. Travelers occasionally men-tioned in passing that the indigenous people had large eyes or dark skin or that the women were fair-skinned. But there are neither systematic descrip-tions of the physical characteristics of the indigenous people nor attempts to describe a physical typology. The reader is thus never given a clear picture of what the people look like. Gazetteers also display a similar lack of interest in physical appearance. I have only found one Taiwan gazetteer with an entry devoted to "appearance" (*zhuangmao* 狀貌), and this entry is placed under the "customs" section: most of the description in this entry is devoted to practices such as tattooing or ear-piercing. Even the textual descriptions in the *Tribute Illustrations* tend to focus on customs and only sporadically con-tain information about a people's physical characteristics. One gets the im-pression from reading such texts that Qing literati accorded far more impor-tance to cultural difference than physical difference in the construction of ethnicity.

In ethnographic illustration we find the bodies that are missing from Qing ethnographic discourse about the Taiwan indigenes. In these pictures, it is immediately clear in visual terms that the body of the savage is distinct from the body of the civilized Han Chinese. Physical differences are highlighted rather than downplayed. The existence of these illustrations is an indication that there were Qing literati who perceived the Taiwan indigenes to be markedly physically different from the Han Chinese. Thus, a certain tension exists between ethnographic texts, which foreground cultural difference as the determinant of ethnic alterity, and ethnographic illustrations, which highlight the physical difference of the other.

In the *Tribute Illustrations*, physical appearance, as well as ethnic costume, forms the basis for the classification of peoples: as the Qianlong emperor declared, "each of the [barbarians] has a different costume and appearance." In what ways does the picturing of non-Chinese bodies in this collection constitute the visualization of racial difference? First, the pictured figures in this collection represent particular ethnic "types," in the sense that physical characteristics are represented as group and not individual characteristics. Second, the physical differences pictured here can be understood as the embodiment of cultural difference. The Taiwan indigenes, for example, clearly display on their bodies the visual signs of savagery—nakedness, tattoos, piercings, bulging muscles, and belligerent postures. In contrast, the Korean gentleman is the embodiment of civilization—clothed, placid, and dominantly erect in posture. The cultural differences between the savage and the civilized are visualized in physical terms.[55] These visual differences are strikingly clear from a viewing of the two pictures. Physical appearance also serves as an index to inborn nature, for savagery and belligerence could be read through physiognomy: the moral qualities of good (*shan* 善) and evil (*e*) being revealed through a pleasant (*shan*) or ugly (*e*) aspect. Although texts might provide ample intellectual evidence for the cultural or moral inferiority of the savages, the sensory reaction that pictures elicit in the viewer makes for a more immediate apprehension of difference.

A more in-depth analysis of pictures of non-Chinese subjects is necessary for a fuller understanding of Qing concepts of race and ethnicity. Nonetheless, these illustrations form a corrective to the idea that the premodern Chinese orientation toward non-Chinese "others" was purely "culturalist," a notion that Frank Dikötter also disputes in his *The Discourse of Race in Modern China*. Qing ethnographic illustrations indicate that cultural, moral, and physical differences were intricately intertwined in Qing constructions of race and ethnicity. If we wish to understand historical Chinese conceptualizations of race and ethnicity, then, we must analyze the visual record in addition to the textual record.

This is simply one example of how an examination of the visual record can add to our understanding of Qing travel writing and other forms of geographic recording. As Joan M. Schwartz demonstrates in "*The Geography Lesson*: Photographs and the Construction of Imaginative Geographies," "imaginative geographies are the product of a variety of representations working in concert."[56] A reading of *tu* in conjunction with travel writing demonstrates the vital role of visual knowledge for Qing travelers and readers and also helps recover the material context in which Qing travel writing was produced and consumed.

Notes

EPIGRAPH: Xia Xianlun 夏獻綸, *Taiwan yutu* 台灣輿圖, Taiwan wenxian, vol. 45 (Taipei: Taiwan yinhang, 1959), p. 1.

1. James Cahill, *The Distant Mountains: Chinese Paintings of the Late Ming Dynasty, 1570–1644* (New York and Tokyo: Weatherhill, 1982), p. 39.

2. Travelers, including the famous Ming explorer Xu Xiake 徐霞客, frequently mention that they had been inspired to travel by a desire to prove that what they had heard about a particular place was either right or wrong. Moreover, travel writers often emphasize that they are recording only what they themselves have witnessed and excluding any material that could be considered hearsay. Thus, despite the fact that one subgenre of travel writing is called *wenjian lu* 聞見錄 (records of things heard and seen), I would argue that seeing is still the privileged term: that is, *wen* is no good without *jian*. Of course, not all late imperial literati considered the eye to be a reliable instrument of perception; see Anne Burkus-Chasson, "'Clouds and Mists That Emanate and Sink Away': Shitao's *Waterfall on Mount Lu* and Practices of Observation in the Seventeenth Century," *Art History* 19, no. 2 (1996): 169–90.

3. See Anthony Pagden, "*Ius et Factum*: Text and Experience in the Writings of Bartolome de Las Casas," in *New World Encounters*, ed. Stephen Greenblatt (Berkeley: University of California Press, 1993), pp. 85–100.

4. Unlike landscape paintings or other kinds of *hua*, which could stand on their own as objects of appreciation, these *tu* were generally produced and consumed in conjunction with written texts.

5. Nonetheless, due to the international effort of scholars, the visual record is slowly being reconstituted. Best known to Western collectors are the "Miao albums," brilliantly colored ethnographic illustrations of the people of southwest China produced from the eighteenth through twentieth centuries; see Laura Hostetler, *Qing Colonial Enterprise: Ethnography and Cartography in Early Modern China* (Chicago: University of Chicago Press, 2001).

6. Certainly, pictures (*tu*) had long been considered vital to geographic knowledge in China. Maps and other *tu* were a central component of local gazetteers, as well as the more comprehensive *Yitong zhi*. Cosmological diagrams and astronomical charts were produced with the hopes of making visible the "patterns of Heaven" (*tianwen* 天文). Emperors as far back as the Liang dynasty (502–57) commissioned the painting of tribute illustrations (*zhigongtu* 職貢圖) to record the appearance of foreign peoples. Illustrated versions of the *Shan hai jing* 山海經 were in circulation at least by Tao Qian's 陶潛 (365–427) time. Many of these *tu* have been analyzed by scholars of geography, cartography, and the history of science in China.

7. Craig Clunas, *Pictures and Visuality in Early Modern China* (Princeton: Princeton University Press, 1997).

8. The role of the visual in anthropology has also been a subject of renewed interest in recent years.

9. These *tu* are also informed by the conventions of a variety of Chinese painting genres, including *shanshuihua* 山水畫, *huaniaohua* 花鳥畫, *jiehua* 界畫, and *renwuhua* 人物畫.

10. Strategic maps, of course, greatly aided the Qing in the conquest of frontier lands.

11. The Qing tribute illustrations exist in two forms: a painted handscroll by the court painter Xie Sui 謝遂 and woodblock print reproductions based on this scroll.

12. Some of these were done by French engravers and some by Chinese engravers working in the European style. The representation of the frontiers in these engravings differs quite radically from the illustrations discussed here and is beyond the scope of this chapter.

13. There are parallels between these materials and the vast body of visual materials created by European colonizers during the same time period. See Hostetler, *Qing Colonial Enterprise*; James R. Ryan, *Picturing Empire: Photography and the Visualization of the British Empire* (Chicago: University of Chicago Press, 1997); Joan M. Schwartz, "The Geography Lesson: Photographs and the Construction of Imaginative Geographies," *Journal of Historical Geography* 22 (1996): 16–45; Christopher Pinney, "Classification and Fantasy in the Photographic Construction of Caste and Tribe," *Visual Anthropology* 3, no. 2–3 (1990): 259–88; and Elizabeth Edwards, "Photographic Types: The Pursuit of Method," *Visual Anthropology* 3 (1990): 235–58.

14. A small number of maps were drawn for private reasons, scholarly purposes, trade, or the settlement of land disputes. The existence of at least one set of maps drawn on a pair of fans indicates that maps could also be employed for decorative purposes. The aesthetic dimension of maps should not be ignored.

15. In his monograph on Qing maps of Taiwan, Xia Liming 夏黎明 (*Qingdai Taiwan ditu yanbianshi* 清代台灣地圖演變史 [Taipei: Zhishufang chubanshe, 1996]) demonstrates that although the exact number of maps produced during the period of Qing colonization (1683–1895) cannot be known, there are approximately 424 extant maps of the island. The majority of these maps appear in local gazetteers and books of maps. A smaller number of maps can be found in individual *wenji* 文集, alongside an author's travel writings, or in guidebooks. A handful of large-scale single scroll maps are also extant.

16. The majority of the extant illustrations take the form of painted albums, but there also exists a series of hanging scrolls. Although a number of these illustrations can be linked to travelers or local gazetteer compilers, some of the extant *tu* have obviously been copied from the earlier illustrations, probably by mainland Chinese painters who never saw Taiwan. There are extant in China and Taiwan at least five other sets of ethnographic illustrations, with probable dates ranging from the 1770s

to the 1870s. See Du Zhengsheng 杜正勝, "Pingpuzuqun fengsu tuxiang ziliaokao" 平埔族群風俗圖像資料考, in *Proceedings of the Symposium on Plains Aborigines and Taiwan History and Culture* (Taipei: Academia Sinica, Taiwan, 1998).

17. Liu-shi-qi 六十七, *Fanshe caifeng tukao* 番社采風圖考, Taiwan wenxian, vol. 90 (Taipei: Taiwan yinhang, 1961), p. 99.

18. Clunas, *Pictures and Visuality in Early Modern China*, p. 18.

19. This difference in attitude toward verisimilitude serves as one marker of the distinction between the pictorial and the painterly; see ibid., pp. 18–24.

20. The terms "raw savage" (*shengfan* 生番) and "cooked savage" (*shufan* 熟番) were used by Chinese to denote the unacculturated and often hostile "tribes" (*she* 社) of Taiwan and the partially acculturated tribes who had submitted to Qing rule, respectively. The Chinese terms *sheng* and *shu* express a host of binary concepts, not only raw and cooked, but also unripe and ripe, unworked and worked (as metal or stone), wild and tamed, unplowed and plowed, strange and familiar. These various shades of meaning are present in the concepts of raw and cooked peoples. All these concepts imply a process of transformation, from the raw to the cooked, from the unripe to the ripe, from the strange to the familiar. The agent of transformation might be fire or it might be culture. I have chosen "raw" and "cooked" to translate these terms since they are the most flexible in meaning and best able to convey the opposition between nature and culture. I use these terms in their metaphorical, and not literal, senses.

21. Zhou Zhongxuan 周鍾瑄, ed., *Zhuluo xianzhi* 諸羅縣志, Taiwan wenxian, vol. 141 (Taipei: Taiwan yinhang, 1962), p. 36.

22. Jiang Yuanshu 蔣元樞, who served as magistrate of Taiwan prefecture from 1776 to 1779 and as Taiwan circuit intendant for four months at the beginning of 1778, compiled an extensive volume of illustrations recording his achievements in public works. The original title of the illustrations is lost, but the album is now referred to as the *Pictures with Explanations of the Renovations of Various Architectural Structures in Taiwan* (*Chongxiu Taiwan ge jianzhu tushuo* 重修台灣各建築圖說, Taiwan wenxian, vol. 283 [Taipei: Taiwan yinhang, 1970]). The album contains 79 leaves. Some of these might be considered maps, but the majority are architectural drawings depicting yamens, military forts, temples, Confucian schools, bridges, and other government structures. Among the *tu* that might be considered maps, there are a number that document the location of military watchtowers on the island and one depicting the defensive barriers against hostile natives. The album also features one chart of Confucian ritual vessels, one chart of Confucian ritual instruments, and one chart of the implements and ritual actors used in the performance of a Confucian ritual. A number of local industries are also pictured. The *tu* were painted in color on paper, obviously by a professional painter (or group of painters) skilled in ruled-line painting (*jiehua*), the style used for architectural illustrations.

The explanations provide information about the buildings or activities pictured, their location, and Jiang's role in promoting these public works.

23. Cordell D. K. Yee, "Chinese Cartography Among the Arts: Objectivity, Subjectivity, Representation," in *The History of Cartography*, vol. 2, book 2, *Cartography in the Traditional East and Southeast Asian Societies*, ed. J. B. Hartley and David Woodward (Chicago: University of Chicago Press, 1994), p. 133.

24. Cordell D. K. Yee, "Chinese Maps in Political Culture," in *The History of Cartography*, vol. 2, book 2, *Cartography in the Traditional East and Southeast Asian Societies*, ed. J. B. Hartley and David Woodward (Chicago: University of Chicago Press, 1994), p. 91.

25. Ibid., p. 91.

26. This figure includes gazetteer maps, which frequently combined pictorial and planimetric modes of representation. That is, mountains, trees, and certain buildings were drawn in elevation, and the ground plane and streams were typically shown from a bird's-eye view.

27. Zhou Zhongxuan, *Zhuluo xianzhi*, p. 36.

28. Of course, the reader might flip back and forth as well.

29. Yee, "Chinese Cartography Among the Arts," p. 161.

30. See also Yee, *Chinese Maps in Political Culture*, p. 73.

31. Although the Ming loyalist Koxinga had arrived on the island decades before Qing troops, it was the Qing conquest that officially brought Taiwan onto the map.

32. Zhou Yuanwen 周元文, ed., *Chongxiu Taiwan fuzhi* 重修台灣府志, Taiwan wenxian, vol. 66 (Taipei: Taiwan yinhang, 1960), p. 3.

33. *Qing zhigongtu xuan* 清職貢圖選, Taiwan wenxian, vol. 180 (Taipei: Taiwan yinhang, 1963), p. 3

34. See Pamela Kyle Crossley, "*Manzhou yuanliu kao* and the Formalization of the Manchu Heritage," *Journal of Asian Studies* 46 (1987): 761–90; idem, "The Qianlong Retrospect of the Chinese-Martial (*Hanjun*) Banners," *Late Imperial China* 10, no. 1 (June 1989): 63–107; Hostetler, *Qing Colonial Enterprise*.

35. Huang Shujing 黃叔璥, *Taihai shicha lu* 台海使槎錄, Taiwan wenxian, vol. 4 (Taipei: Taiwan yinhang, 1957), p. 76.

36. As Huang (ibid.) explained in his travelogue, "Everywhere I went on my tour of inspection, whenever I would see a Taiwanese flower or fruit that does not exist on the mainland, I would order a painter to make some illustrations. I got more than twenty illustrations." Huang Shujing compiled two illustrated albums during his journey, *Illustrations of Savage Fruits* (*Fanguo tu* 番果圖) and *Illustrations of the Epiphyllum* (*Tanhua tu* 曇花圖).

37. Li Shizhen 李時珍, (*Jiaozheng*) *Bencao gangmu* (校正) 本草綱目 (Shanghai: Jinzhang tushuju, 1925), illustrations p. 1a.

38. Huang, *Taihai shicha lu*, p. 76.

39. Liu-shi-qi's *Taihai caifengtu*, for example, almost seems to be dominated by aesthetic considerations. The illustrations in this album are delicately painted in vibrant hues of red, yellow, green, and purple, such that each leaf is quite decorative. Unlike the *Bencao gangmu*, this album makes no (discernable) attempt to classify the plants and animals. Rather than being grouped according to category, the fruits, vegetables, and flowers seem to be grouped on an aesthetic basis, in the fashion of a still life. Two of the illustrations are nature studies: one a picture of bamboo with a snake and a lizard, the other a picture of two birds perched on a fruit-bearing branch. Overall, the album is quite stunning visually. Liu-shi-qi's illustrations thus resemble bird-and-flower paintings (*huaniaohua*) more closely than the botanical illustrations of the *Bencao gangmu*. The emphasis on aesthetics is perhaps consistent with Liu-shi-qi's stated interest in collecting exotica, rather than in documenting plants and animals with pharmaceutical or commercial values.

40. Liu-shi-qi, *Fanshe caifeng tukao*, p. 99.

41. Huang, *Taihai shicha lu*, p. 76.

42. Ibid.

43. Travel writing was, of course, also used for this purpose, but pictures allowed for a more immediate experience.

44. See Susan Bush and Hsio-yen Shih, *Early Chinese Texts on Painting* (Cambridge, Mass.: Harvard-Yenching Institute, 1985), pp. 36–39.

45. The map is currently held at the National Taiwan Museum. A late Qing copy can be found at the Taiwan Provincial Library. Although the map was long attributed to Huang Shujing, and there is evidence that Huang produced a *fanshetu* 番社圖 of some kind, there is no concrete evidence confirming his authorship of this map.

46. The map depicts major Chinese landmarks such as the Taiwan prefectural capital, the county seats, military posts, as well as villages (both Chinese and indigenous), and the old Dutch forts. The distances between these various sites are provided in Chinese characters next to each landmark.

47. Clunas, *Pictures and Visuality in Early Modern China*, p. 88.

48. Representations of the savage female in the *Tribute Illustrations* are comparatively less grotesque and less threatening. The women tend to be more fully clothed and less muscular than their male counterparts. Only one female figure in the set is depicted bare-breasted and bare-legged. The key signifier of the savage woman's ethnic difference is her bare feet, which form a sharp contrast with the small, bound feet of the ideal Han Chinese woman. Aside from this, the illustrators appear to have employed conventional notions of femininity in representing the savage women: they have demure facial expressions and are often fair-skinned, and a number of them are depicted with children. This gendered difference in the representation of the savage male and female is interesting in light of the fact that Qing travel writers

and gazetteer compilers made much of the supposedly dominant role of women among the indigenous Taiwanese. Qing writers frequently described what they saw as gender role reversal among the indigenous people. See Emma Jinhua Teng, "An Island of Women: The Discourse of Gender in Qing Travel Writing About Taiwan," *International History Review* 20, no. 2 (June 1998): 353–70.

49. Zhuang Jifa 莊吉發, ed., *Gugong Taiwan shiliao gaishu* 故宮台灣史料概述 (Taipei: Guoli gugong bowuyuan, 1995), pp. 252, 262.

50. *Qing zhigongtu xuan*, p. 16.

51. Ibid., p. 56.

52. See Zhuang Jifa 莊吉發, ed., *Xie Sui "Zhigongtu" Manwen tushuo jiaozhu* 謝遂《職貢圖》滿文圖說校注 (Taipei: Guoli gugong bowuyuan, 1989), p. 41.

53. Nineteenth-century European artists employed similar techniques to express character through physiognomy, particularly in representing racial others, the urban poor, as well as "criminal types"; see Mary C. Cowling, *The Artist as Anthropologist: The Representation of Type and Character in Victorian Art* (New York: Cambridge University Press, 1989).

54. In terms of local products, or flora and fauna, verbal descriptions tend to pay relatively little attention to appearance and relatively more to questions of nutritive or medicinal value and seasonality.

55. This notion of physical difference as the embodiment of cultural or intellectual difference is not unique to China; it can be found in nineteenth-century Western racial theories; see George W. Stocking, Jr., *Race, Culture, and Evolution: Essays in the History of Anthropology*, rev. ed. (Chicago: University of Chicago Press, 1982); and Robert Young, *Colonial Desire: Hybridity in Theory, Culture and Race* (New York: Routledge, 1995).

56. Schwartz, "*The Geography Lesson,*" p. 36.

Works Cited

Burkus-Chasson, Anne. "'Clouds and Mists That Emanate and Sink Away': Shi-tao's *Waterfall on Mount Lu* and Practices of Observation in the Seventeenth Century." *Art History* 19, no. 2 (1996): 169–90.

Bush, Susan, and Hsio-yen Shih. *Early Chinese Texts on Painting*. Cambridge, Mass.: Harvard-Yenching Institute, 1985.

Cahill, James. *The Distant Mountains: Chinese Paintings of the Late Ming Dynasty, 1570–1644*. New York and Tokyo: Weatherhill, 1982.

Clunas, Craig. *Pictures and Visuality in Early Modern China*. Princeton: Princeton University Press, 1997.

Cowling, Mary C. *The Artist as Anthropologist: The Representation of Type and Character in Victorian Art*. New York: Cambridge University Press, 1989.

Crossley, Pamela Kyle. "*Manzhou yuanliu kao* and the Formalization of the Manchu Heritage." *Journal of Asian Studies* 46 (1987): 761–90.

———. "The Qianlong Retrospect of the Chinese-Martial (*Hanjun*) Banners." *Late Imperial China* 10, no. 1 (June 1989): 63–107.

Dikötter, Frank. *The Discourse of Race in Modern China*. Stanford: Stanford University Press, 1992.

Du Zhengsheng 杜正勝. "Pingpuzuqun fengsu tuxiang ziliaokao" 平埔族群風俗圖像資料考. In *Proceedings of the Symposium on Plains Aborigines and Taiwan History and Culture*. Taipei: Academia Sinica, Taiwan, 1998.

Edwards, Elizabeth. "Photographic Types: The Pursuit of Method." *Visual Anthropology* 3 (1990): 235–58.

Hegel, Robert E. *Reading Illustrated Fiction in Late Imperial China*. Stanford: Stanford University Press, 1998.

Hostetler, Laura. *Qing Colonial Enterprise: Ethnography and Cartography in Early Modern China*. Chicago: University of Chicago Press, 2001.

Huang Shujing 黃叔璥. *Taihai shicha lu* 台海使槎錄. Taiwan wenxian, vol. 4. Taipei: Taiwan yinhang, 1957.

Jiang Yuanshu 蔣元樞. *Chongxiu Taiwan ge jianzhu tushuo* 重修台灣各建築圖說. Taiwan wenxian, vol. 283. Taipei: Taiwan yinhang, 1970.

Li Shizhen 李時珍. *(Jiaozheng) Bencao gangmu* (校正) 本草綱目. Shanghai: Jinzhang tushuju, 1925.

Liu-shi-qi 六十七. *Fanshe caifeng tukao* 番社采風圖考. Taiwan wenxian, vol. 90. Taipei: Taiwan yinhang, 1961.

Pagden, Anthony. "*Ius et Factum*: Text and Experience in the Writings of Bartolome de Las Casas." In *New World Encounters*, ed. Stephen Greenblatt. Berkeley: University of California Press, 1993, pp. 85–100.

Pinney, Christopher. "Classification and Fantasy in the Photographic Construction of Caste and Tribe." *Visual Anthropology* (Special Issue): Picturing Cultures: Historical Photographs in Anthropological Enquiry, ed. Joanna Scherer, 3, no. 2–3 (1990): 259–88.

Qing zhigongtu xuan 清職貢圖選. Taiwan wenxian, vol. 180. Taipei: Taiwan yinhang, 1963.

Ryan, James R. *Picturing Empire: Photography and the Visualization of the British Empire.* Chicago: University of Chicago Press, 1997.

Schwartz, Joan M. "The Geography Lesson: Photographs and the Construction of Imaginative Geographies." *Journal of Historical Geography* 22 (1996): 16–45.

Stocking, George W., Jr. *Race, Culture, and Evolution: Essays in the History of Anthropology.* Rev. ed. Chicago: University of Chicago Press, 1982.

Teng, Emma Jinhua. "An Island of Women: The Discourse of Gender in Qing Travel Writing About Taiwan." *International History Review* 20, no. 2 (June 1998): 353–70.

Xia Liming 夏黎明. *Qingdai Taiwan ditu yanbianshi* 清代台灣地圖演變史. Taipei: Zhishufang chubanshe, 1996.

Xia Xianlun 夏獻綸. *Taiwan yutu* 台灣輿圖. Taiwan wenxian, vol. 45. Taipei: Taiwan yinhang, 1959.

Yee, Cordell D. K. "Chinese Cartography Among the Arts: Objectivity, Subjectivity, Representation." In *The History of Cartography*, vol. 2, book 2, *Cartography in the Traditional East and Southeast Asian Societies*, ed. J. B. Hartley and David Woodward. Chicago: University of Chicago Press, 1994, pp. 128–69.

———. "Chinese Maps in Political Culture." In *The History of Cartography*, vol. 2, book 2, *Cartography in the Traditional East and Southeast Asian Societies*, ed. J. B. Hartley and David Woodward. Chicago: University of Chicago Press, 1994, pp. 71–95.

Young, Robert. *Colonial Desire: Hybridity in Theory, Culture and Race.* New York: Routledge, 1995.

Zhou Yuanwen 周元文, ed. *Chongxiu Taiwan fuzhi* 重修台灣府志. Taiwan wenxian, vol. 66. Taipei: Taiwan yinhang, 1960.

Zhou Zhongxuan 周鍾瑄, ed. *Zhuluo xianzhi* 諸羅縣志. Taiwan wenxian, vol. 141. Taipei: Taiwan yinhang, 1962.

Zhuang Jifa 莊吉發, ed. *Gugong Taiwan shiliao gaishu* 故宮台灣史料概述. Taipei: Guoli gugong bowuyuan, 1995.

———. *Xie Sui "Zhigongtu" Manwen tushuo jiaozhu* 謝遂《職貢圖》滿文圖說校注. Taipei: Guoli gugong bowuyuan, 1989.

Tope and Topos

The Leifeng Pagoda and the Discourse of the Demonic

Eugene Y. Wang

A site is often a *topos* in that it both marks a locus and serves as a topic. It is a common place that can be traversed or inhabited by a public and a rhetorical commonplace familiar to both its author and his audience.[1] Although there is no exact equivalent in Chinese to the Greek word *topos* that conveniently collapses the dual senses of locus and topic, the notion of *ji* 蹟 (site, trace, vestige) comes close. A *ji* is a site that emphasizes "vestiges" and "traces." It is a peculiar spatial-temporal construct. Spatially, a landmark, such as a tower, a terrace, a pavilion, or simply a stele, serves as its territorial signpost or perceptual cue, and it is perceived to be a terrain distinct from the humdrum environment. Temporally, this plot of ground resonates with the plot of some vanished cause or deed. A landmark alone, however, does not make a site. No site in China is without an overlay of writing. To make a site is to cite texts. Listed in local gazetteers and literary anthologies, each site (*ji*) gathers under its heading a body of writing by a succession of authors of the past. It is therefore as much a literary *topic* as it is a physical locus; it comes laden with a host of eulogies and contemplations.[2] A site is therefore textualized.[3] Once a locus congeals into a topic, its associated body of writing imbues it with a conceptual contour and an aura of distinction. A site is thereby perpetuated in the textual universe or by word of mouth, and conse-

Fig. 11.1 Huang Yanpei, *Leifeng Pagoda at Sunset*. Photograph. 1914. After *Zhongguo mingshen* (Scenic China), no. 4: *West Lake, Hangchow* [Hangzhou], ed. Huang Yanpei et al., 2: 19 (Shanghai: Commercial Press, 1915).

quently its topographic features and its landmarks become a secondary and tangential matter.[4] Cycles of decay and repair may render the landmark into something widely different from the original. That matters little. The only function of the landmark, after all, is to stand as a perceptual cue or synecdoche for the proverbial construct called a "site," a somewhat deceptive notion premised on the primacy of physical place, topographic features, and prominence of landmarks. In reality, a site is a topos etched in collective memory by its capacity to inspire writings on it and the topical thinking it provokes. To visit a site is to take up that topos. In China, few literarily inclined visitors can resist that urge. All they need is a prompt from a stele or a pavilion, landmarks that purport or pretend to have links to the vanished past that the site once witnessed.

A pagoda site (Fig. 11.1) is a curious anomaly. With its soaring height, the pagoda is easily the most prominent kind of landmark that stakes out a site. Yet it is not an easy topos. Other architectural types are more favored for the topoi they facilitate. A terrace often marks the location of a bygone imperial palace and hence a reminder of an unfulfilled cause that occasions posterity's sighs and lamentations. A tomb is an easy topos for mourning a historical figure whose martyrdom can be appropriated as a mirror for self-pity. A pavilion with its command of an open view stretching to the horizon, inspiring an outpouring of transcendental sentiments, is a commonplace of literary exercises. Not so for a pagoda with its dark overtones of numinous otherness. As a Buddhist monument that commemorates the Buddha Sakyamuni's sacred traces, it was adapted in China as a ritual signpost that facilitates the deceased's journey into the afterlife. A pagoda borders on the numinous realm and evokes dark supernatural forces that it seeks to pacify. Traditional Chinese literati were ill-disposed in their outings to note such unsettling matters. Moreover, the dearth of established discursive precedents make the pagoda less of a topos. One exception is the displacement of a pagoda into a tower or a pavilion on a height; it then became co-opted into the topoi surrounding pavilions, a topic about transcendental immortality in the Daoist imaginary.

Precisely because of its otherness, a pagoda presents itself as a potential alternative topos, one that engages the supernatural, the numinous, and the demonic. In traditional China, it was taken up by writers who explored folkloric sources as a reaction against an archaicizing orthodox taste. In modern times, it has engaged radical authors who tap the demonic other as a source of creative and subversive energy. To follow the perceptions and discursive use of a pagoda serves therefore not so much a purely architectural-historical interest as a literary one—it allows us to understand the role of physical signposts in generating a discourse. No other pagoda serves this purpose better than the Leifeng Pagoda 雷峰塔.

Tope and Texts: The Apocalyptic Prelude

To the west of the city of Hangzhou lies one of it most famous attractions, West Lake. Stepping out of the city and walking toward the lake, one sees on the left a hilly promontory jutting into the lake. The promontory is called Leifeng, Thunder Peak,[5] an extension of the South Screen Mountain that lies to its south (Fig. 11.2). The pagoda, which stood on the hill until it collapsed in 1924, was popularly known as the Leifeng Pagoda. It was built by Qian Hongchu 錢弘俶 (929–88) and his consorts in A.D. 976. Qian was the last ruler of Wu-Yue 吳越, a state struggling for survival when most of China had been unified by the Song in the north. Qian paid homage to the Song court and made sure that none of his symbolic trappings and protocols displayed separatist ambitions.

Fig. 11.2 Anonymous, *West Lake*. Ink on paper. Handscroll.
Southern Song (1127–1279) period. Shanghai Museum.

From the very beginning, the pagoda was deeply involved with writing
and texts. Its brick tiles were molded with engraved names or cryptic ideo-
graphs. A vast number of the hollow tiles had holes in which were inserted a
Buddhist *dhāraṇī-sūtra*,[6] prefaced with a votive inscription: "Qian Chu, Gen-
eralissimo of the Army of the World, King of Wu-Yue, has made 84,000
copies of this sūtra and interred them into the pagoda at the West Pass as
an eternal offering. Noted on a day of the Eighth Month of the Yihai Year."[7]
The content of the sūtra is strikingly congruent with the historical circumstances behind the construction of the pagoda and surprisingly prophetic of
its fate. At the request of a brāhman named Vimala Varaprabha, the sūtra
narrates, the Buddha leads his entourage to visit the brāhman's home to receive his offering. On his way, he passes a park with an ancient stupa in decay. "In decrepitude and shambles, the stupa was reduced to a mere earthen
mount, overgrown with brambles and hazel grass, with debris strewn
around." The Buddha circumambulates the stupa ruin for three rounds and
then takes off his robe to cover it. "Tears begin to stream down his cheeks,
mixed with blood. Having wept, he smiles. At that time, the Buddhas of
Ten Directions, all weeping, fix their gaze on the stupa. Their radiance illu-
minates the stupa." Asked why he weeps, the Buddha explains: the mount
used to be a seven-treasure stupa. Normally a structure enshrining a Buddha's "whole body" would have defied decay. But "in posterity that is overcome by the End of the Dharma when the multitude practice heresies, the
Wonderful Dharma ought to disappear. . . . It is this reason," says the Buddha, "that causes me to shed tears."[8]

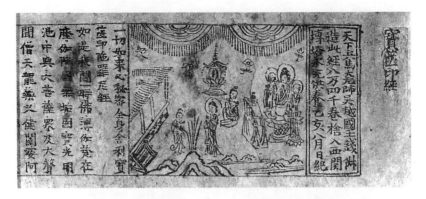

Fig. 11.3 Sutra frontispiece from the Leifeng Pagoda. 10th century.

A surviving copy contains an illustration of the passage cited above[9] that shows the Buddha present at the ruined mound and causing it to emit radiance. Behind the Buddha is the treasure stupa in its original form (Fig. 11.3). The graphic demonstration of the decaying of what initially is a splendid structure is a rather sobering visual parable.

The decision to place an illustrated version of this sūtra inside the Leifeng Pagoda was poignantly significant. Only three years after the construction of the pagoda, the prophecy of the "end of the Dharma" was fulfilled: the Wu-Yue kingdom was terminated.[10] Some five hundred years later, the pagoda itself was reduced to a ruin.

From the very outset, the pagoda was a breeding ground for fiction. Tradition has it that the pagoda was built for Qian's consort, Lady Huang 黃妃, and texts often refer to it as Consort Huang's Pagoda (Huangfeita 黃妃塔). In truth, there never was a Lady Huang.

A dedicatory inscription, written by Qian Hongchu and recovered from the pagoda, relates that the pagoda was built for pious reasons by a Buddhist layman, namely Qian himself, who "never stops reciting and poring over Buddhist sūtras in the little spare time between ten thousand administrative affairs." It identifies an "Inner Court" donor (a consort) who possessed a "lock of the Buddha's hair" and wished to have a pagoda built to enshrine it. Initially, she planned to build a thirteen-story affair. Financial strains made this impossible, and a seven-story tower was the compromise. Six hundred strings of cash were spent on the project.[11]

The identity of the "imperial consort" remains a mystery. According to a thirteenth-century copy of Qian's inscription, the pagoda was named after

Huangfei (Consort Huang). The standard history, which tends to be meticulous, if not entirely accurate, in documenting kings' and princes' consorts and family members, records that Qian had two consorts in succession, one named Sun and the other named Yu; neither of them was named Huang. The "Consort Huang" mentioned in the transcribed version of the inscription may well have resulted from a confusion between *wangfei* 王妃 (royal consort) and *huangfei* 黃妃 (Consort Huang), which in southern pronunciation are nearly identical. In the process of transcribing or typesetting the inscription, *wang* may have been rendered as *huang*.[12]

It is not clear which consort was the force behind the pagoda construction. Qian's wife Sun Taizhen 孫太真 accompanied her husband on his trip north to pay tribute to the Song court. Song Emperor Taizu made a controversial decision to confer the title "imperial consort of the Wu-Yue kingdom" on her, against opposition from his prime minister, who argued that a local prince's wife was not entitled to such an honor. Sun died in the first month of 977.[13] Qian's next wife was Lady Yu, who did not claim the title of "imperial consort." The near-coincidence between Sun's death and the date of the construction of the pagoda points to a connection with her, either during her sickness or her funeral, a standard practice in medieval China. In any event, a possible corrupt textual transmission may have spawned the fiction. Taking cues from the inscription, Wu Renchen 吳任臣, the Qing dynasty author of the *Spring and Autumn of the Ten Kingdoms* (*Shiguo chunqiu* 十國春秋), created a biography of this Consort Huang out of the profiles of Qian's two real consorts.[14] This he did in the spirit of writing history. In retrospect, the veiled association of the pagoda with a mystery woman is significant since women do figure prominently in the later popular tales that accumulated around the pagoda.[15]

Pagoda and Pavilion

In the first two centuries after its construction, the Leifeng Pagoda did not become much of a site. Following the Wu-Yue Kingdom, the Song ruled the Hangzhou area. The Thunder Peak Pagoda underwent a succession of notable renovations in the twelfth century.[16] Although its presence on the hilltop is unquestionable, there is no indication until the mid-thirteenth century that visitors to the site paid much attention to it. Su Shi 蘇軾 (1036–1101), who twice held an official post in Hangzhou, wrote profusely and enthusiastically about various scenes around the lake. As the temple gazetteer indicates, he visited the Jingci Monastery 淨慈寺, whose grounds included the Thunder Peak Pagoda, and bequeathed poems to the abbey. His poems fancifully conjure up the oneiric image of the "golden crucian carp" of the South Screen Mountain on which the Thunder Peak Pagoda stood (*JCSZ*, pp. 4020–21), but not the pagoda itself. In fact, nowhere in the huge number of works by Su Shi inspired by West Lake is the pagoda mentioned. Either the sight of the pagoda simply did not register with him, or it did not strike him as worthy of mention.[17] Lu You 陸游 (1125–1210) was another of the notable literary figures who visited South Screen Mountain. In his "Note on the South Garden," he mentioned that he did "look left and right" (*JCSZ*, pp. 4057–58). Still, the Thunder Peak Pagoda was simply not on his horizon. Likewise, Qisong 契嵩 (?–1071), an eminent monk of the Lingyin Monastery 靈隱寺 in the lake area, left a detailed description of an ascent of South Screen Mountain. Upon reaching the mountain top, with its sweeping view of the four quarters, he was overcome with lofty sentiments, but he spent not a drop of ink on the Thunder Peak Pagoda. Not that he was insensitive to landmarks. In fact, he took care to mark and punctuate his itinerary with pavilions. He began his trek with the Cloud-Clearing Pavilion and then passed by the Green-Gathering Pavilion, the Seclusion-Commencing Pavilion, and the White-Cloud Pavilion. He made a point of recording his trip "so that the future generation may admire [him] as a traveller."[18] In so doing, he also left a puzzle. One would imagine that unobtrusive pavilions are likely to be lost in the lush mountain forest. They simply do not compare in prominence with a pagoda on a hilltop. Why did Qisong pay meticulous attention to pavilions at the expense of the Thunder Peak Pagoda, which was no doubt in his visual field? His preference speaks volumes about the kind of values attached to these different architectural sites.

To a traditional Chinese writer, not all architectural sites make a topic. The monumental grandeur of the structure itself has almost nothing to do with this. Typically, the kinds of landmarks that serve as topics for a writer are towers, terraces, kiosks, and pavilions (*lou* 樓, *tai* 臺, *ting* 亭, *ge* 閣)— some for their nostalgic associations with imperial palaces or the vanished glories of remote or bygone eras; others for their open views of distant landscapes, which prompt transcendent aspirations.[19] In other words, landmarks and monuments are deemed worthy of remarking only when they accommodate two major topoi: contemplation of the vanished past (*huaigu* 懷古)

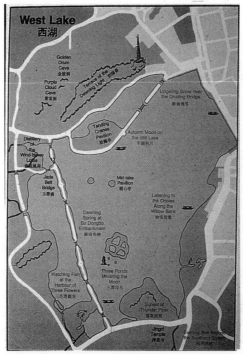

Fig. 11.4 Map of Ten Views of West Lake.

and journey to the lands of the immortals (*youxian* 遊仙), that is, immanent Confucian sentiment and transcendent Daoist yearning. The former may thus encompass a tomb of a martyr-minister or a chaste woman or the ruins of an imperial palace. Compared with these, Buddhist sites attract less profound discursive ruminations. The pagoda, the foremost example of Buddhist architecture, commands conspicuously less writing than a famous imperial consort's tomb. Whenever it does inspire writing, it is only because the pagoda is displaced in the mind of the writer and becomes a "cloud-scaling" tower (*lou*) good for immortal-aspiring thoughts. Even such an eminent monk as Qisong found little to say about the Thunder Peak Pagoda while leaving no stone unturned when it came to pavilions.[20]

The situation of the Leifeng Pagoda improved somewhat in thirteenth century. Some local dilettantes (*haoshizhe* 好事者; literally, "busybodies") divided the scenery of West Lake into ten topics known as "Ten Views of West Lake" (Fig. 11.4),[21] modeled after the popular imaginary topography of "Eight Views" of the Xiao and Xiang Rivers.[22] The "Fishing Village in

Fig. 11.5 Ye Xiaoyan, "Leifeng Pagoda at Sunset." Ink and color on silk. Album leaf from the set *Ten Views of West Lake*. 13th century. National Palace Museum, Taibei.

Evening Glow" from the Eight Views of Xiaoxiang became "Thunder Peak in Evening Glow" of West Lake. The Leifengta became the centerpiece of this view (Fig. 11.5) and consequently the topic for eulogies. The writings inspired by the pagoda were, however, rather generic, the kind engendered by any tower or pavilion.

Romancing the Pagoda: From "Ancient Site" to "Aberrant Site"

In the Jiajing era (1522–66) of the Ming dynasty, there emerged a discursive interest in taking a pagoda on its own terms instead of treating it as a displaced tower. Some time before 1547, a well-known publisher named Hong Pian 洪楩 printed *Stories by Sixty Authors* (*Liushijia xiaoshuo* 六十家小說),[23] a collection of tales drawn largely from the oral storytelling tradition. Included in the collection is "The Story of the Three Pagodas."

Set in West Lake, the story concerns Xi Xuanzan 奚宣贊, a young man of Lin'an, who rescues a young girl named Bai Maonu 白卯奴 who has lost her way and reunites the young girl with her family. Xi meets the young girl's mother, a sensuous woman dressed in white, and the girl's grandmother, who is attired in black. Xi becomes the lover of the woman in white, who customarily kills her previous lover when she takes a new one. The same misfortune would have befallen Xi had it not been for the intervention of the young girl. Eventually a Daoist exorciser exposes the true identity of the three women: the young girl turns out to be a black chicken; the woman in white, a white snake; and the woman in black, an otter. The exorciser raises funds to build three stone pagodas in West Lake. The three monsters are subjugated beneath them. Xi becomes a religious layman.[24] The tale of the Three Pagodas is the oldest surviving story of the White Snake woman involving a pagoda.[25]

The story of a young man's romantic involvement with a snake-turned-woman has a long tradition in Chinese literature.[26] The *Taiping guangji* 太平廣記, for instance, devotes four entire *juan* to narratives of human encounters with snakes. One story tells of a young man named Li Huang 李黄 whose erotic encounter with a white snake–turned–beauty ends in his horrible death in a deserted private garden.[27] In the same *juan* of *Taiping guangji*, a group of visitors to Mount Song gather under a pagoda. They kill a snake several *zhang* 丈 long encircling the inner pillar of the pagoda and in due time are struck down by thunder.[28]

For our purposes, what is remarkable about the story of the Three Pagodas is its interest in "ancient sites." It begins by noting the famous sites in the West Lake district: the Hall of Three Worthies, the Temple of Four Sages, the Vestige of Su Dongpo, and the Old Residence of Lin Bu, and so forth. It ends with the building of Three Pagodas to subjugate the three monsters. Moreover, it refers to the location of the Three Pagodas as "an ancient site that has survived up to this day."[29]

The author thus gives a bold new twist to the sense of an "ancient site." Technically, the Three Pagodas indeed qualified as "ancient sites" in the sixteenth century. Back in the late eleventh century, Su Shi, then prefect of Hangzhou, had built three pagodas on the lake, close to the islet near the south shore of West Lake, as territorial and boundary markers to control private farming activities on the lake. The site became one of the Ten Views

Fig. 11.6 Ye Xiaoyan, "Three Stupas Reflecting Moonlight." Ink
and color on silk. Album leaf from the set *Ten View of West Lake*.
13th century. National Palace Museum, Taibei.

of West Lake in the thirteenth century (Fig. 11.6). In the late fifteenth century, the greed and corruption of monks of the Buddhist monastery on the
nearby islet enraged Yin Zishu 陰子淑, a government inspector known for
his strict and bold administrative decisions. Yin ordered the monastery and
pagodas "instantly destroyed." So when "The Story of the Three Pagodas"
was published, the Three Pagodas were either nonexistent or in ruins, since
they were not rebuilt until 1611.[30] In either case, they were "ancient sites" (*guji*
古蹟).

Curiously, although any "traces" (*ji*) of Su Dongpo's activities are usually
diligently catalogued and often invented,[31] the site of the Three Pagodas,
which are unquestionably associated with him, was not accorded the prestigious designation "ancient site." For one thing, in the sixteenth century the
criteria for the "ancient" or "archaic" (*gu*) were quite strict. Nothing short of
Han prose and High Tang poetry qualified as "ancient." A site associated
with a Song figure, despite his fame, was consequently not "ancient."

The location, however, acquired the august appellation "ancient site" in conjunction with a high tale of the demonic. This odd association reflects an inner tension of the period. The archaicizing taste that put a premium on the literary standards of the Han and High Tang still dominated the first half of the sixteenth century. At the same time, a new interest in the contemporary "racy words from the streets," or folkloric ballads and tales, began to gather momentum. Open-minded scholars, such as Li Kaixian 李開先 (1502–68), were making a strong case for romance (*chuanqi* 傳奇) and other popular forms of folkloric literature.[32] Even Li Mengyang 李夢陽 (1473–1530), the most prominent proponent of archaism and a major force in shaping antiquarian taste, conceded late in his life that "nowadays, authentic poetry comes in fact from folkloric sources."[33] The association of the snake-woman story with a physical location labeled an "ancient site" therefore either reconciles the two competing impulses or legitimizes the burgeoning interest in folkloric literature.

Nor is it entirely surprising that a tale of the demonic such as the White Snake should be sited in a pagoda. In the mid-sixteenth century when the tale of the White Snake was taking shape in printed and stage versions, several pagodas were likely candidates to become the setting of the tale. Quite a few sites of pagodas in the lake area were associated with snake lore. The pagoda on the Southern Peak, also built under Qian Hongchu in the tenth century, stood close to Bowl Pond (Boyutan 鉢盂潭), a name that prompts an association with the bowl used by the monk Fahai 法海 to contain the white snake, as described in a story in Feng Menglong's 馮夢龍 (1574–1645) collection (see below). Beside the pond is White Dragon Cave. A huge boulder nearby is allegedly the altar where a Daoist once pacified a monster.[34] The Baoshu Pagoda 保叔塔 on the Northern Mountain across the lake was also built in the tenth century. Toward the end of fifteenth century, a thunderbolt killed three itinerant monks inside the pagoda together with a "huge snake which weighed fifty pounds. In its belly were ten or so white embryos." Soon after, the pagoda collapsed into ruins.[35]

At some point the ruins of the Three Pagodas and, across from them on the south shore, the Leifeng Pagoda became the setting of the story in printed versions. It appears that in the mid-sixteenth century, the story was not yet linked to a specific pagoda. In his topographic account of West Lake, Tian Rucheng 田汝成 (*jinshi* 1526) recorded a "popular saying" that the White Snake and Green Fish, two monsters from the lake, were imprisoned beneath the Leifeng Pagoda.[36] Elsewhere, he told a story of a young man named Xu Jingchun 徐景春 who has an amorous encounter on the lake with a beautiful woman attended by a maid. After a night of dalliance, the woman gives the man a "double-fish fan" as a souvenir. The man wakes up near the woman's grave.[37] The narrative resonates with the White Snake story in its cast and relationships, although it has no pagoda. Tian also noted, in a separate context, that the *taozhen* 陶真 performers of the lake area told stories set in the Southern Song (*taozhen* were a kind of *chantefable*, or "sing-speak," popular in the lower Yangzi region). Their repertoire included the tales of the Double-Fish Fan and the Leifeng Pagoda, which were treated as two separate stories. In the meantime, the White Snake lore was increasingly wedded to the Leifeng Pagoda. Surviving librettos of stage plays, with prefaces dated in the 1530s, include such titles as "Madame White Clasped Under the Leifeng Pagoda for Eternity."[38]

The Leifeng Pagoda had its share of snake lore, an association that may have prepared the way for its linkage with the White Snake story. During the late Northern Song, the pagoda was damaged in warfare between the imperial army and peasant insurgents. The affiliated monastery was destroyed, leaving the pagoda alone "standing dilapidated" amid brambles. Around 1130, a Southern Song construction force decided to pull down the pagoda to use its materials to fortify the city walls of Hangzhou against the northern Jurchen invaders. "Suddenly," according to a twelfth-century record, "a huge python appeared, encircling the foundation [of the pagoda]. . . . The numinous site (*lingji* 靈蹟) has thus manifested itself." The curious happening stopped the demolition and led to the restoration of the pagoda later in the twelfth century.[39]

An incident in the mid-sixteenth century may have strengthened the association between the Leifeng Pagoda and the White Snake. In 1553, pirates and bandits harassed the coastal region, including the lake district.[40] A rogue army of 3,000 troops turned the monastery into their barracks, sending monks in flight, "scurrying like rats." The soldiers ruined the landscape: "All the bamboos were razed" (*JCSZ*, 4042a). During this period of military chaos, a fire broke out in the pagoda. It burned away all the wooded eaves and interior stairways and left the pagoda an "empty shell," a colossal ruin with rampant plants growing from its brick eaves (Fig. 11.7).[41] Before the fire, the exquisite architectural structure had evoked, by virtue of its association

Fig. 11.7 Leifeng Pagoda in ruins. 1920s. After Tokiwa Daijo,
Shina bukkyō shiseki hyōkai (Buddhist monuments in China) (Tokyo: Bukkyō shiseki kenkyūkai, 1931), vol. 5, pl. 55.

with a Buddhist monastery, a kind of Chan tranquility that fulfilled people's
expectations of a landscape vista. The fire fundamentally changed the character of the pagoda and gave it a desolate mood. The ruin may have spawned
fantasies about the demonic and may have made its association with the
White Snake lore all the more compelling. In the Wanli years (1573–1620),
the tale circulated that "the Buddhist master contains the White Snake in a
bowl and clasps it under the Leifeng Pagoda. Tradition has it that underneath the Leifeng Pagoda are two snakes, one green and one white."[42]

Certainly by the early seventeenth century, the link between the White
Snake and the Leifeng Pagoda was cemented. Yu Chunxi 虞淳熙 (?–1621)
noted in the 1609 edition of the *Qiantang County Gazetteer*:

According to a popular saying, the Leifeng Pagoda serves to subjugate the monsters White Snake and Green Fish. People, old and young, keep telling the story to one another. During the Jiajing period, the pagoda belched smoke that spiraled up into the sky. They said it was the two monsters spouting venom. A closer look revealed that it was only swarms of insects. The romance (*chuanqi*) is indeed false.[43]

Yu also wrote a poem on the Leifeng Pagoda, which ends with the line "The serpentine monster traverses the stone blocks."[44]

The definitive touch comes from the short story "Madame White Eternally Subjugated Under the Leifeng Pagoda," which is included in Feng Menglong's *Jingshi tongyan* 警世通言 (1624). This narrative version is not only the earliest surviving comprehensive account of the subject,[45] but it also solidified the Leifeng Pagoda's position as the topographic locus for the story:

[Having turned Madame White and her maid into their original form of a snake and a fish], the venerable monk picked up the two tame creatures with his hand and dropped them into the begging bowl. He then tore off a length of his robe and sealed the top of the bowl with it. Carrying the bowl with him and depositing it on the ground before Thunder Peak Monastery, he ordered men to move bricks and stones so as to erect a pagoda to encase the bowl and keep it inviolate. Afterward Xu Xuan went about collecting subscriptions, and the pagoda eventually became a seven-tiered structure, so solid and enduring that, for thousands of years to come, the White Snake and Green Fish would be prevented from afflicting the world. When the venerable monk had subjugated these evil spirits and consigned them to the pagoda, he composed a chant of four lines:

> When the West Lake is drained of its water
> And rivers and ponds are dried up,
> When Thunder Peak Pagoda crumbles,
> The White Snake shall again roam the earth.[46]

All subsequent narrative versions and dramatic adaptations of the story end with this scene. The pagoda site thus truly becomes a topos, a common place (hence a commonplace) that admits a concentrated topical thinking and invention, a foundation or a scaffolding on which fiction and drama could be built.

This is indeed what happened later. One of the major theatrical adaptations after the seventeenth-century short story was Huang Tubi's 黃圖珌 1738 stage play *The Leifeng Pagoda*. In Huang's play, the construction of the Leifeng Pagoda becomes the structural framework: the play both begins and ends with it. In the opening scene, the Buddha anticipates the romance involving the White Snake and instructs Fahai to build a seven-story pagoda after the model the Buddha gives to him so that the "two monsters" can be subjugated under it for eternity. The play ends exactly as the opening anticipated.[47]

Nearly contemporary to Huang's adaptation is a script allegedly by a famous actor named Chen Jiayan 陳嘉言 and his daughter, a version that is staged more often. It survives in later copies and is still performed today.[48] In 1771, based on this version, Fang Chengpei 方成培 readapted the tale for the theater. Not only did Fang retain the title *The Leifeng Pagoda* and continue to use the pagoda construction as the structural framing device, but the pagoda looms even larger in his theatrical universe. Before the snake woman is subjugated and imprisoned under the pagoda, she gives birth to a child who grows up to succeed in the official examination system.[49] No longer is the final pagoda scene purely an act of subjugation. In an emotionally wrenching scene, the son pays a visit to his entombed mother and seeks her release. The pagoda, in fact, has become a prison. Obeying the traditional imperative of happy ending, the Buddha releases the snake woman and arranges for her and her husband to ascend to the Tushita Heaven.

By this point, the Leifeng Pagoda had become more than a mere setting and framing device; it is now truly a topos that can generate further narrative and dramatic possibilities. To intensify the emotional resonance of the play at its close, the playwright directs the audience's attention not to the characters in the play but to the pagoda itself. One of the Buddha's attendants suggests that the pagoda be destroyed. No, says the Buddha, it ought to be left for the posterity to look up to. The play thus ends first with the invitation: "Why not turn to West Lake and take a look at the soaring pagoda in evening glow?" This is followed by a poetic pastiche of eight lines, each taken from a Tang poet, celebrating the grandeur of the pagoda and the moral of the play. The pastiche thematizes the working of a topos: a pagoda is but a topic under which one can gather textual bits as building blocks to make a "soaring pagoda." To elaborate on the play is to build on the architectonic topos of the Leifeng Pagoda. It comes as no surprise that many subsequent playwrights seized on the pagoda scene to create dramatic situations. With the evocative pagoda as a locus and a cue, endless inventions and variations on the same theme become possible. In one Suzhou *tanci* 彈詞 (a storytelling performance to the accompaniment of string instruments), for instance, the snake woman gives birth to a child right inside the pagoda.[50] The pagoda is where the drama is.

The evocative power of the Leifeng Pagoda as a topos derives not so much from its architectural monumentality as from its efficacy as a haunted ruin that puts people in touch with the strange and the otherworldly. The generic associations of a ruin constitute a sufficient cue for writers to elaborate on the topos. The libretto of a popular storytelling performance (zidishu 子弟書) on the Leifeng Pagoda paints a chilling word picture:

The pagoda top soars into the sky. In the morning and evening views, it blocks out the sun and the moon. It metamorphoses into unpredictable moods with cloud and smoke, varying with the sun and rain. . . . The bleak sight is certainly saddening. The melancholy cloud hovers closely around the pagoda top. Dark vapors surround its base. Mournful winds from the four quarters rattle the bronze bells; drizzles chill the green tiles of the thirteen stories. Strange birds on top of the pagoda crow dolefully as if decrying an injustice. . . . And this is the sight of the Leifeng Pagoda at sunset. What a strange view![51]

Accuracy counts for little here; the Leifeng Pagoda has never been thirteen-story high, nor did it ever have green tiles. Either the writer had never seen the Leifeng Pagoda in person or he thought the empirical facts about the *real* Leifeng Pagoda irrelevant. For him and his audience, the Leifeng Pagoda was a topos to which one attaches words and situations. Whereas Huang Tubi, the author of the 1738 version of *Leifeng Pagoda*, was apologetic about the liberties he took with the Leifeng Pagoda and worried that they may have tarnished the reputation of the "thousand-year-old famous site," Fang Chengpei, the playwright of the 1771 version, was unrepentant about his project of "transforming the stinking decay into a miraculous wonder and alloying gold out of the debris of a ruin." In a preface to the play, Fang noted: "This pagoda, otherwise known as Huangfei Pagoda, was built by an imperial consort of the Wu-Yue kingdom. . . . It was ruined by fire during the Jiajing period. Whether the matter of the Buddhist master of Song subjugating the White Snake is true or not is simply irrelevant."[52] The pagoda is, as the closing lines of Huang's play would have it, "the site for visitors in the next thousand years to come to admire and sigh; it is what is left for the Buddhist community to perpetuate tales." Moreover, it is not just any ordinary topos, but one that allows posterity "to talk about sprites and spirits unlike humans, [a site where] a familiar situation may be transformed into an extraordinary scenario."[53] In other words, it is a topos for the supernatural and strange.

The *Story of the Three Pagodas*, the earliest surviving printed version of the White Snake story, is reticent about the demonic nature of the pagoda site where the subjugation of the monsters takes place. It chooses to veil it with the phrase "an ancient site and surviving trace" (*guji yizong* 古籍遺蹤).[54] By the seventeenth and eighteenth centuries, such reticence was no longer necessary. The site of the Leifeng Pagoda was recognized as the "aberrant site" (*guaiji* 怪蹟).[55] Mo Langzi 墨浪子, a southern writer of the Kangxi period (1662–1722), cast his stories in a purely topographic framework. Each of the sixteen stories published in his *Wonderful Tales of West Lake: Sites Ancient and Modern* (*Xihu jiahua gujin yiji* 西湖佳話古今遺跡) is attached to a specific "site" (*ji*). Moreover, each is characterized as a particular kind of site: an "immortal's site," an "administrative site," a "man of talent's site," a "poetic site," a "dream site," a "drunken site," a "laughing site," a "romantic site," an "imperial site," a "regretting site," and so on. The Leifeng Pagoda is the "aberrant site" (*guaiji*), and Mo made a point of defending the "aberrant":

I used to bear in mind Confucius' dictum that one ought not to speak of the aberrant. Hence I considered it trifling to bother with devious actions and matters that border on absurdity and would leave them aside. But, given the immensity of the universe, is there anything that does not happen? Absurdities are indeed not worth accounting for, but what if a matter can be traced [to its origin] and its site still survives? Take, for example, the Leifeng Pagoda prominent on West Lake. Researching its origin, one finds that it was built to subjugate monsters. It has survived up to this day. The Leifeng Pagoda in Evening Glow has become one of the Ten Views of West Lake. The aberrant has been normalized. The tombs of royal martyrs and hills of immortals have received detailed narration and provided pleasurable viewing for thousands of years. Why should the matters that are at once aberrant and normal be a taboo? Why can't they lend themselves to a delightful hearing?

He ends his story with the advice: "Those who admire the Leifeng [Pagoda] should visit the site and mull over the aberrant happenings (*guaishi*) associated with it."[56]

Here Mo Langzi takes on the Confucian bias against "the aberrant, the violent, the spiritual, and the strange." The traditional moral taxonomy underlying canonical "sites," such as Confucian virtues of loyalty and the Daoist ideal of immortality, is found to be wanting. New categories of "sites" are needed, such as the "aberrant sites," if only to revise our rigid classification system and expand our cognitive horizon, "given the immensity of the universe." Strategically, Mo Langzi tries to make his case by blurring the line between the aberrant and the normal. The force of his argument for the "aberrant sites" lies in its subversion of traditional value systems. It is not that the aberrant sites have virtues in themselves; rather, there is something fundamentally wrong with their banishment from the cultural and moral topography. Mo Langzi's sixteen kinds of sites are a new cognitive mapping that reconstitutes cultural topography; the "aberrant site" is one of the new features.

The recognition of the aberrant sites had been anticipated at the beginning of the seventeenth century. In 1609, Yang Erzeng 楊爾曾, also known as the Dream-Traveling Daoist of Qiantang (Qiantang woyou daoren 錢塘 臥遊道人), compiled and published the *Strange Views Within the [Four] Seas* (*Hainei qiguan* 海內奇觀). According to Yang, he was motivated by a desire to educate the armchair traveler: "There are metamorphoses of clouds, fogs, winds, and thunders under the blue sky and the bright sun; there are strange and weird people, creatures, and plants in the sandy region of the Ganges River. The mountains and rivers yonder are truly quaint and unpredictable....[I] have therefore marked them out to show what one's eyes and ears cannot reach."[57] The book includes a woodblock print of the "Leifeng Pagoda at Sunset," presumably as a specimen of "the truly quaint and unpredictable." Two young scholars, accompanied by an old rustic, stand at the foot of the pagoda and look up, apparently riveted by the spectacle of this ruined pagoda. Behind the scholars, two attendant boys are busy laying out inkstones and other instruments so that their masters can write down their thoughts on the spot (Fig. 11.8). The print visually makes a case for the pagoda as a topos: visit to the site occasions writing about it.

Yang Erzeng matches the print with a poem on the same subject by Mo Fan, 莫璠, a mid-Ming writer (Fig. 11.9):

> The setting sun bathes the ancient pagoda in ever-dimming red,
> The shadows of mulberries and elms half-shroud the houses along
>   the western shore.
> The reflection of the evening glow lingers on the waves like
>   washed brocade,
> This Buddhist kingdom amid a cloud of flowers is no mundane realm.
> Ten miles of pleasure boats nearly all beached on the shore,

Fig. 11.8 Chen Yiguan, "Leifeng Pagoda in Evening Glow." Carving by Wang Zhongxing of Xin'an. In *Strange Views of the World (Hainei qiguan)*, 1609, comp. Yang Erzeng. After *Zhongguo gudai banhua congkan erbian* (Shanghai: Shanghai guji chubanshe, 1994), 8: 269.

The lake reverberates with the chants of fishermen and water
    chestnut gatherers, a landscape apart.
In a lakeshore pavilion, a person waits for the moon to rise,
Red curtains rolled up, the railings await the return of the visitor.[58]

There is a glaring disjuncture between the print and the poem attached to it. The poem, written before the fire reduced the pagoda to a ruin, rhapsodizes about the celestial splendor of the edifice and the idyllic landscape surround-

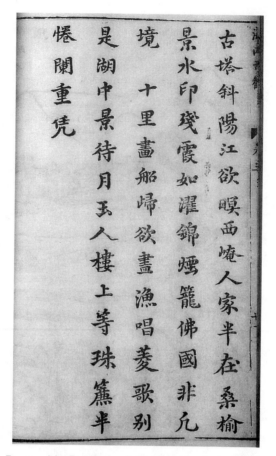

Fig. 11.9 Mo Fan (16th c.), "Leifeng Pagoda in Evening Glow." In *Strange Views of the World*, 1609, comp. Yang Erzeng. After *Zhongguo gudai banhua congkan erbian* (Shanghai: Shanghai guji chubanshe, 1994), 8: 269.

ing it; the print, made half a century after the fire, frankly presents the bizarre, fire-damaged pagoda as a curious sight. The print is more consistent with Yang's professed interest in the strange as articulated in his preface rather than the mellow poem anachronistically yoked to it. The disjuncture may have resulted from the compiler's intent to legitimize the newfound interest in the strange by a touch of elegance. It makes the indulgence in the strange sight as displayed in the print all the more an illicit pleasure.

An Alternative Topos: The Supernatural Naturalized

The strained yoking in *Strange Views* of the woodblock print of a strange sight with a poem praising serenity betrays an anxiety about the legitimacy of the strange.[59] The same kind of inner tension is also discernible in Huang Tubi's play. Once "a gigantic pagoda" is set on the stage, as we read from the script, the monk Fahai exclaims: "What a treasure pagoda!" He then sings:

> [I shall] embrace the white cloud and green hill and fill them in
>   the void of the pagoda.
> The spirits' craftsmanship and demons' axes make it a model of
>   extraordinary shape.
> They are indeed a splendor of gold and blue hues.
> From now on, among the Six Bridges and Ten Ponds,
> The Leifeng Pagoda ranks as the top one.
> It occasions poems with staying resonances.
> It spawns paintings of a vast serenity and cool mood.[60]

The otherwise demonic White Snake and Green Fish are poeticized into innocuous "white cloud and green hill." The unruly supernatural intimation of ghosts and spirits is displaced into a supernatural force harnessed for construction of the pagoda, a trope often deployed in praising an architectural splendor. Moreover, the poems and pictures generated from this architectural topos are just one of those landscape pieces.

The Leifeng Pagoda indeed constitutes a topos of the strange, yet its strangeness ranges from the eerily supernatural and darkly demonic to the blithely transcendent. At one end of the spectrum is the bleak vision of the pagoda shrouded in "dark vapors" and "melancholy clouds," with strange birds perched on its chilling "green tiles" "crowing dolefully" in the "mournful wind."[61] At the other end is the pastoral serenity of "white cloud and green hill," endowed with a touch of otherworldliness. Working with the same topos of the strange localized in the Leifeng Pagoda, dramatists and novelists, closer to folkloric culture, are more likely to toy with the dark force of the unruly monsters and spirits; the elite, on the other hand, tend to naturalize the supernatural, harmonize the disruptive, and use this topos, an intimation of the otherworldliness, to express eremitic aspirations.

Li Liufang 李流芳 (1575–1629), a literati-painter who frequented West Lake, is most responsible for propagating a transcendent topos out of the colossal ruin of the Leifeng Pagoda. In a colophon on his *Leifeng Pagoda in Twilight*, Li wrote:

My friend [Wen] Zijiang once said: "Of the two pagodas on the lake, the Leifeng Pagoda is like an old monk; the Baoshu Pagoda [across the lake] a female beauty." I really like this line. In 1611, while viewing lotus flowers in the pond with Fang Hui, I composed a poem: "The Leifeng Pagoda leans against the sky like a drunken old man." [Yan] Yinchi saw it and jumped to his feet, exclaiming that Zijiang's "old monk" is not as good as my "drunken old man" in capturing the mood and mannerism of the pagoda. I used to live in a pavilion on a hill overlooking the lake. Morning and evening, I faced the Leifeng [Pagoda]. There he is—a sagging old man hunched amid the mountains shrouded in twilight and violet vapor. The sight intoxicated me. I closed my poem with the line: "This old man is as poised and aloof like clouds and water." I did base myself on Zijiang's "old man" trope. Written after getting drunk in the Tenth Moon of 1613.[62]

Much of this mood is captured in his painting of an old monk (Fig. 11.10).

Li Liufang earned his *juren* degree in 1606. The failure of his subsequent attempts at the advanced degree crushed any hopes he may have had of an official career. Frustrated, he settled for earning a living by tutoring and selling his writings. He took to drink to escape from financial embarrassments, severe illness, and the bleak late Ming political landscape.[63] The images of the monk and a drunken old man he and his friend projected onto the Leifeng Pagoda are very much self-portraits: a convention-defying tipsy monk who rises above the world and plays his own games. Li curbed the mutinous energy of the image by qualifying the otherwise crazy monk with a mellowing old age and a "sensibility as placid as the mist and water," that is, anything but melodramatic, too old and exhausted to be swashbuckling despite inebriation. The Leifeng Pagoda plays right into Li's emotional needs. Decrepit and strange, it nevertheless stands still.

The characterization of the pagoda as a drooping old drunkard or a monk proved to be an infectious topos that attracted a massive following. Even a fiercely imaginative writer such as Zhang Dai 張岱 (1597–1679) seems never to have got enough of this topos. Four poems in his *Tracing West Lake in a Dream* are devoted to it:

> Master Wen portrays the Leifeng Pagoda—
> An old monk with his robe hanging there.
> He watches West Lake day and night,
> and never has enough of it in all his life.

Fig. 11.10 Li Liufang (1575–1629), "Monk Under a Tree." Ink on paper. Album leaf from *Landscapes and Flowers*. Shanghai Museum. After *Zhongguo meishu quanji huihuabian Mingdai huihua*, ed. Yang Han et al. (Shanghai: Shanghai renmin meishu chubanshe, 1988), 8: 99, pl. 92.4.

Fragrant breezes come, every now and then,
West Lake is a couch for drunkards.
There he is, standing upside down, the old drunken man,
In one breath, he gulps down the entire lake and all.[64]
The bleak and desolate Leifeng [Pagoda]
How can it stand the sunset at all?
Its body is all smoke and vapor,
Like an old man who lifts his long beards and howls.[65]

Elsewhere, he wrote about the "Leifeng Pagoda at Sunset" as one of the "Ten Views":

The crumbling pagoda borders on the lake shore,
A sagging drunken old fool.
Extraordinary sentiment resides in the rubble,
Why should the humans meddle with it at all?[66]

The trope of the Leifeng Pagoda as a drunken old monk is richly suggestive and apt for disgruntled literati. Its "strange" and freakish overtones serve as a canvas for the projections of their disenchantment with worldly affairs and their aloofness and withdrawal from them; at the same time, the image is mellow enough to keep them free of any suspicion of strident excess and dark and demonic riotousness, examples of bad taste and lack of elegance to be studiously avoided. Hence few of the literati who visited the Leifeng Pagoda were inclined to evoke the White Snake even though they were thoroughly familiar with the lore. The old drunkard or old monk suited their taste better. They could live with, and relate to, the sedate, sagging old-man-like pagoda ruins, but not the monstrosity, hailing from the theatrical universe, that haunts it.

This is best demonstrated by the Qianlong emperor's response to the pagoda site. Between 1751 and 1784, Qianlong made six tours of inspection to south China. Each time, the itinerary included West Lake, including the Leifeng Pagoda site. To entertain the emperor during his long boat trip, salt merchants recruited a group of celebrated actors and commissioned a new adaptation of the *Leifeng Pagoda*, which resulted in Fang Chengpei's *Romance of the Leifeng Pagoda* (1771). A stage was then constructed on two boats that preceded the emperor's boat, facing the emperor. Qianlong was thus able to watch the play on his way to its real site. He thoroughly enjoyed it.[67] His visits to the Leifeng Pagoda led to a total of eight poems, six on the view of the pagoda at sunset and two on the pagoda itself. The drama of the White Snake woman must have been fresh in his mind when he composed these poems. Yet none mentions it. Two themes run through his poems: a eulogy of the sunset view, and a lament over the "ancient site" that tells of the "rise and decline" of an imperial cause. In other words, Qianlong was just churning out poems that utilized two time-honored topoi associated with famous scenic sites and ruins. Had Qianlong written the poems in his study, he might have been under less pressure and turned out something better than these run-of-the-mill literary exercises. The palpable immediacy of the ruins must have made him realize the inadequacy of the topoi he used to measure up to the striking spectacle of the real. The supernatural riot conjured up on the stage, to which he had been freshly exposed, must have tempted him. Yet long ingrained in the traditional literati culture, Qianlong did not have the boldness to play with the themes provided by the dramatists. At one point, he nearly did: "[The pagoda site] demonstrates that all appearances (*se* 色) are emptiness (*kong* 空), such as this one."[68] The interplay between appearances and emptiness is a commonplace and is the refrain chanted as the moral at the close of the *Leifeng Pagoda*. The shadow of the snake woman apparently lurks behind the line, yet Qianlong reverted to the less disquieting images of "the pristine moonlight shadows" spreading up "lattice windows." The colossal ruin strained this old lyrical topos, and Qianlong resorted to conventions of the *huaigu* (contemplating the ancient), treating the ruin literally as an ancient site of the Wu-Yue imperial cause. This is a bungling effort nonetheless. It is generically unconventional to seize on a pagoda ruin as a vestige of an imperial cause,[69] and very few Chinese literati have considered the Leifeng site fitting for *huaigu*, for the inept Wu-Yue kingdom had never been seen as worthy of lamentation: one sighs only for those causes that follow periods of rise, those whose fall is all the more emotionally and cognitively unsettling.

The same site struck an Englishman in a different way. On November 14, 1794, Lord Macartney, the English ambassador to Qianlong's court, "travelled in a palaquin . . . in passing through the city" of Hangzhou. The entire West Lake struck him as "very beautiful," yet only one feature, one single landmark, leaped out and found its way onto his diary: the Leifeng Pagoda:

> On one side of the lake is a pagoda in ruins, which forms a remarkable fine object. It is octagonal, built of fine hewn stone, red and yellow, of four entire stories besides the top, which was moldering away from age. Very large trees were growing out of the cornices. It was about two hundred feet high. It is called the Tower of the Thundering Winds, to whom it would seem to have been dedicated, and is supposed to be two thousand five years old.[70]

It is no surprise that the pagoda ruin should appeal to the taste of the British Ambassador, whose sensibility had been finetuned by the contemporary English preoccupation with moss-grown ruins with their Gothic overtones.[71] The Chinese emperor, however, would not take the ruin on its own terms and see it as it is; he preferred what it once was. In his poems, he insisted that one should not let the present lamentable sight of the pagoda ruin tarnish its former splendor. This discomfort with the ruinous pagoda is reflected in a painting, originally by Giuseppe Castiglione (1688–1768) and then copied by Ji Ruinan 輯瑞南, depicting Qianlong's tour of the lake, with the Leifeng Pagoda in the background. Despite the documentary

Fig. 11.11 Ji Ruinan, *Emperor Qianlong's Tour of West Lake*. Ink and color on silk.
18th century. Copy after Giuseppe Castiglione (1688–1768). Private collection.

orientation of the painting, the painter restored the pagoda to its imagined
pre-fire condition (Fig. 11.11). Contemporary prints from the Suzhou area
betray a similar attitude toward the pagoda.[72] The compositions show a tendency to minimize the role of the Leifeng Pagoda in the sunset view. One,
entitled *Leifeng in Evening Glow* (Fig. 11.12), combines the picture with a poem,
inscribed above the composition. The poem was originally written by Yin
Tinggao 尹廷高, a thirteenth-century poet, who described the Leifeng Pagoda before the fire:

> The mist-shrouded mountains are blurred in the hazy light,
> The thousand-yard tall pagoda alone leans against the sky.
> The pleasure boats have all but turned ashore,
> Leaving the lonely hill to retain a piece of the sunset red.[73]

The choice of this poem as the inscription suggests a quixotic clinging to the
past. The print designer was probably embarrassed by the present state of
the pagoda. In the picture, the shabby pagoda is downscaled in the distance,
even though this runs the risk of undermining the inscribed poem that celebrates "the thousand-yard tall pagoda alone lean[ing] against the sky." The
central position usually occupied by the pagoda is here ceded to a bell tower,
premised perhaps on the idea that the reverberating bell in the evening air
may still retain the old mood of sunset-bathed Leifeng. The discrepancy

Fig. 11.12 Anonymous, *Leifeng in Evening Glow* [poem by Yin Tinggao (13th c.)]. 341 × 266. Woodblock print from Suzhou. 18th century. Tenri University Library, Japan. After Machida shiritsu kokusai hanga bijutsukan, comp., *Chūgoku no yōfūga ten: Minmatsu kara Shin jidai no kaiga, hanga, sashiebon* (Tokyo: Machida shiritsu kokusai hanga bijutsukan, 1995), p. 379, pl. 108.

between the thirteenth-century lyrical vision of the sunset pagoda and the pictorial diminishing of its eighteenth-century remnant demonstrates all too clearly a commonly shared sense of embarrassment, if not dismissal, toward this fire-ravaged monstrosity.

Another Suzhou print of identical style compresses six of the Ten Views into one coherent vista. Although the view of the Leifeng Hill in Evening Glow apparently occupies the high prominence, the print omits the pagoda altogether; in a stroke of visual ingenuity, there is instead an open pavilion sheltering a stele on which is inscribed "[*Lei*]*feng xizhao*," Leifeng in Evening

Fig. 11.13 *Leifeng in Evening Glow.* 344 × 523. Woodblock print from Suzhou. 18th century. Kyoto, private collection. After Machida shiritsu kokusai hanga bijutsukan, comp., *Chūgoku no yōfūga ten: Minmatsu kara Shin jidai no kaiga, hanga, sashiebon* (Tokyo: Machida shiritsu koku-sai hanga bijutsukan, 1995), p. 393, pl. 121.

Glow. Long shadows are cast over the water surface toward the east, thereby reinforcing the idea of a sunset view (Fig. 11.13). Every poem that eulogizes Leifeng in Evening Glow associates it with the pagoda. In fact, the pagoda is *the* view: "Each time the sun sets in the west," writes the author of the *West Lake Gazetteer*, "the soaring pagoda casts its long shadow; this view (*jing*) is unsurpassed."[74] Now, it can be dispensed with, only because it could be an embarrassment to those seeking the picture-perfect view, and their notion of what constitutes a perfect picture and a good view cannot accommodate a monstrosity. The pagoda in its fire-stripped decrepitude makes a mockery of all that is traditionally deemed lyrical, pictorial qualities that make a land-scape a "view."

To the eighteenth-century emperor and many of his contemporaries, the White Snake lore associated with the Leifeng Pagoda was a monstrosity to be confined to the world of make-believe on the stage; it was unthinkable in relation to the real physical colossus. Yet the stirring demonic matter that roils the stage cannot but cast its shadow over the eerie ruin and turn it into a monstrosity of sorts. Even freed from the association with the tale of the demonic, the pagoda ruin is itself a monstrosity in another sense: it strains the traditional literati's entrenched cognitive stock of tropes and topoi, none of which is adequate to this moldering colossus. That would have to await the arrival of a more modern age, able to take it up unflinchingly, completely on its own terms.

Xu Zhimo, Leifeng Pagoda, and the Modernist Topos

At 1:40 P.M. on September 25, 1924, the quiet of West Lake was disturbed by the sudden collapse of the Leifeng Pagoda, which raised a soaring dust column that "blocked out the sun" and sent clouds of crows and sparrows swarming the sky. It was quite a while before the dust settled. The seven-story edifice was reduced to a mammoth heap of rubble, and only one story remained standing. Soon, the site drew tens and thousands of spectators who combed the ruin for artifacts. Police were called in, and a protective wall was built to keep looters out. Half a month later, some soldiers, allegedly commissioned by a certain Mr. Ju in Beijing, broke in and took away copies of the sūtras inside brick tiles. That opened the floodgates. They were followed, some twenty or so days later, by a thousand soldiers who destroyed and plundered what remained. Local peasants followed suit. What was left of the Leifeng Pagoda was "a heap of yellow earth."[75]

The crumbling of the pagoda sent a shockwave throughout China and became an absorbing topic of conversations, inquiries, ruminations, and spasms of hand-wringing. For some, the collapse of the pagoda brought an epistemological crisis. It suddenly dawned on people that even the natural scheme of things was subjected to change and decline. For all its arbitrariness as a cultural construct, the Ten Views of West Lake—of which Leifeng in Evening Glow was one—had since the thirteenth century been fossilized into a natural given and presumed to be impervious to change and decay. Now with the tenfold vista suddenly incomplete, the "natural" landscape seemed to be dented. This realization "jolted many out of the slumber" that had sustained a dream of "completeness."[76] For others, the collapse of the pagoda was an academic topic, for it yielded unexpected archeological treasures. The number of sutras recovered from the ruin was second only to those discovered at Dunhuang two decades earlier. That these woodblock-printed sutras were produced only a century after the invention of woodblock printing highlighted the significance of the discovery.[77] The finding galvanized intense research by distinguished scholars such as Wang Guowei 王國維 and others.[78] To still others, not surprisingly, the collapse was a topic for elegy and spawned a renewed round of nostalgic outpouring in the form of poetry and painting. One painter-poet spoke of his heart "being pounded"; to his sensitive ears, the reverberating evening bell was "choking with tears."[79]

Radical intellectuals, however, reveled in the news of the collapse of the structure, for they saw a larger significance in it beyond the mere crumbling of the pagoda itself. The timing of the collapse was apocalyptically pointed: it occurred at the juncture when China was caught between an imperial past that had just recently ended and an uncertain future of possibilities. Awareness of the temporal disjuncture and anxiety about the transition from the old to the new intensified the perceptions of old buildings and ruins to which the weight of the past was attached. Zhou Zuoren 周作人, still a radical thinker at this time, argued in 1922 that nostalgia for the past was not a good reason for conserving ancient ruins. For him, ruins and historical sites should be landmarks that point to the future instead of the past. The modern travestying of ancient sites, such as Zhejiang cloth merchants' "vulgarizing" cosmetic touches to the Orchid Pavilion, repelled him. Zhou would rather see the "original fragmented vestige of dignity."[80]

Corresponding to the preoccupation with physical ruins were ruins as topoi in discourse. Metaphors of architecture and ruins often framed contentious arguments over the fate of Chinese culture, couched in the stark opposition between the old and the new, past and future, and oppression and liberation. In addressing the tension between traditional China and the modern West, Liang Shuming 梁漱溟 proposed a three-way scheme. He framed it by way of a central architectural metaphor: "a dilapidated house." The three major civilizations—China, India, and the West—he argues, would harbor different attitudes toward it. The Western response would be to demolish it and build a new one; the Chinese answer would be to repair it with care; and the Indian attitude, rooted in Buddhist quietism, would be to renounce the desire for housing altogether.[81] Embedded in this rhetoric is a preoccupation with the dialectics of destruction and construction.[82] The ruin topos played into this purpose with renewed relevance. The traditional Chinese meditation on ruins is an understated recollection in tranquility of a past event, at times traumatic. It is premised on a poignant resignation toward the leveling effect of the passage of time, which neutralizes and distances the drama of history, and on a recognition of the permanence of nature, which eclipses all dynasties and enterprises. A ruin is accepted as a larger historical fact; it rarely prompts visions either of willful destruction or of construction, even though a ruined site is perpetually caught in the cycle of decay and physical reconstruction. In the early twentieth century, the ruin topos underwent a change. It spawned visions of what Rose Macauley calls the "ruin-drama staged perpetually in the human imagination, half of whose whole desire is to build up, while the other half smashes and levels to the earth."[83]

Macauley's assertion that the "ruin is always over-stated" may not be always true with regard to traditional Chinese discourse; it certainly obtains with regard to two natives of Zhejiang: Xu Zhimo 徐志摩 (1896–1931) and Lu Xun 魯迅 (1881–1936), the most influential writers of 1920s China to harbor a radical vision. Both took up the Leifeng Pagoda topic and "over-stated" it in Macauley's sense.

Both savored a symbolic triumph in the collapse of the pagoda. On September 17, 1925, one year after the crumbling of the pagoda, Xu wrote the poem "The Leifeng Pagoda, No Longer to Be Seen." Seeing the pagoda reduced to "a deserted colossal grave," the speaker senses an urge to lament but quickly checks it with a self-interrogation: Why should I lament the "destruction by the passage of time," "the transfiguration that ought not to be"?

> What is it to lament about? This pagoda was oppression; this tomb is burial.
> It is better to have burial than oppression.
> It is better to have burial than oppression.
> Why lament? This pagoda was oppression; this tomb is burial.[84]

By "burial," Xu alluded to the White Snake imprisoned under the pagoda. It is easy for the romantic poet known for his defiance of conventional marriage and his passionate pursuit of free love to identify with Madame White. To him, the "affectionate spirit" suffers only because she took a "good-for-nothing" lover, and is thereby condemned to the base of the pagoda.[85] Xu was always sensitive to the symbolic overtones of tall structures. During the years of his study in the United States, he came to admire Voltaire and William Godwin—father of Mary Shelley—men who had the courage to "destroy many false images and to knock down many a tall building" in their times. He became enamored of the writings of Bertrand Russell, whose "gold shafts of light" had the power of bringing down the Woolworth Building, the imposing 58-story edifice towering over the city of New York, a symbol of the establishment and mighty structures in general.[86] The first time Xu visited the site of the pagoda in 1923, he was struck by its shaky condition: "The four big brick pillars inside the pagoda have been dismantled to the point where they stand as inverted cones. It looks extremely precarious." One wonders whether the pillars were not in fact displaced in a different context as organizing tropes for his polemic against conservatism:

Those who mentally embrace the few big pillars left over from ancient times, we call quasi-antiquarians. The posture itself is not laughable. We suspect he is firm in the conviction that the few pillars he clings to are not going to fall. We may surmise that there are indeed a few surviving ancient pillars that are infallible, whether you call them "cardinal guides" (*gang* 綱) or "norms" (*chang* 常), or rites (*li* 禮) or ethical tenets (*jiao* 教), or what have you. At the same time, in fact, the authentic is always mixed with the sham. Those reliable real pillars must be mingled with double their number of phantom pillars, rootless, unreliable, and sham. What if you hug the wrong pillars, taking the sham as the real?[87]

Lu Xun also resented the symbolic implication of the Leifeng Pagoda. He wrote two essays in response to its collapse. The first, "The Collapse of Leifeng Pagoda," appeared one month after the event. He had seen the pagoda before it collapsed: "a tottering structure standing out between the lake and the hills, with the setting sun gilding its surroundings." He was unimpressed.[88] As we have seen, traditional literati normally responded to it as the Leifeng Pagoda in Evening Glow, one of the Ten Views of West Lake, while ignoring the stormy dramatic romance of the White-Snake woman. Lu Xun, like his contemporary Xu Zhimo, saw the pagoda primarily in connection with the snake-woman romance—related to him by his grandmother—and hence, as a symbol of oppression.[89] "A monk should stick to chanting his sūtras. If the white snake chose to bewitch Xu Xuan, and Xu chose to marry a monster," observed Lu Xun, "what business was that of anyone else?" "Didn't it occur to him [the monk Fahai] that, when he built the pagoda, it was bound to collapse some day?" The "tottering structure" was an eyesore to Lu Xun whose "only wish . . . was for Leifeng Pagoda to collapse. . . . Now that it has collapsed at last, of course every one in the country should be happy."[90]

It may appear ironic that Xu and Lu should celebrate the collapse of the pagoda, for both were deeply attached to ruins. Their attraction to ruins, however, differed fundamentally from the *huaigu* topos of the traditional literati. The latter works more by way of *temporality* and *disjuncture*: I sigh over a ruin only because it evokes a past that is no more and that is separated from the present world by a gap to which the writer is resigned. To Chinese modernists, such as Xu and Lu, ruins signify primarily by way of *spatiality* and *subversion*. For them, ruins beckon not because they evoke a vanished past but because they embody imaginary realms and alternative modes of existence that threaten to take over and eclipse reality.

Xu may have resented the symbolic oppression signified by the Leifeng Pagoda; however, he found the eerie charm of the moonlit pagoda casting its shadow over the lake irresistible. Traditionally, the nearby site of the Three Pagodas was the primary *locus amoenus*, or "pleasant place," that attracted eulogies of moonlit scenes.[91] Xu Zhimo, however, made his dislike of "the so-called Reflections of the Three Pagodas" explicit. He was, instead, thoroughly enamored of the "utter serenity of the reflection of the moonlit Leifeng [Pagoda]." "For that," he vowed, "I would give my life."[92] After the collapse of the pagoda, he observed with a note of sadness: "It is rather regrettable that in our south, Leifeng Pagoda remains the only surviving ancient site (*guji*) *cum* art work. . . . Now the reflection of Leifeng Pagoda has eternally departed from the heart of the lake surface!"[93]

This observation comes out of a most unexpected context: his exposition of John Keats's "Ode to a Nightingale." A number of points of contact link Keats' poetic imaginaire to Xu's situation. To begin with, Keats's yearning to leave the world of "leaden-eyed despairs," of "weariness, the fever, and the fret / . . . where men sit and hear each other groan"[94] spoke directly to Xu Zhimo, who likewise felt the "pervasive pain and distress of our time." Keats listened to a nightingale singing and yearned to "fade away into the forest dim" in a moonlit night and to fly to some exalted, ethereal state of transcendence. In explicating the poem to his Chinese audience, Xu wrote of the "purist realm of imagination, the embalmed, enchanted, beautiful, and tranquil state."[95] In a similar mood, Xu could write about the moonlit Leifeng:

Leifeng Pagoda Under the Moon

I give you a reflection of Leifeng Pagoda,
The sky is dense with cloud dark and white;
I give you the top of Leifeng Pagoda,
The bright moon sheds its light on the bosom of the slumbering lake.

The deep dark night, the lonely pagoda reflection,
The speckled moonlit luminance, the delicate wave shimmerings,
Suppose you and I sail on an uncovered boat,
Suppose you and I create a complete dream world![96]

The relevance of Keats to Xu's world of Leifeng Pagoda does not stop here. In *Lamia*, Keats takes an ancient romance and reworks it into verse. Lycius, a young man of Corinth, encounters a beautiful woman named Lamia. They fall in a "swooning love" with each other. Their bliss is brought to an abrupt end by the arrival of Apollonius, an old philosopher, who sees through Lamia and proclaims her a "serpent," upon which, "with a frightful scream she vanished." Lycius dies in his marriage robe.[97] The story was first recorded in European literature by Philostratus. Resurfacing in the seventeenth century, it found its way into Robert Burton's *Anatomy of Melancholy*, which is the source Keats acknowledges. The Lamia story has striking parallels with the Chinese White Snake story.[98] Xu Zhimo was evidently familiar with both the Chinese tale and Keats's famous poem. There were even scholarly inquiries into the connection between the two in academic journals of his time.[99] The Western romantic treatment of a matter familiar to the Chinese inevitably had an impact on the sensibility of someone like Xu who was receptive to Western imagination. *Lamia* provides a new lens for viewing not only the White Snake romance but, more important for our purpose, the landscape of the Leifeng Pagoda that is the backdrop of the story. The new impulse is the demonic enchantment that suffuses an imaginary landscape with an oneiric quality and an eerie beauty. True, this poetic mood is not alien to Chinese tradition. Yet the long-lasting and ever-deepening Confucian wariness about the demonic has considerably tempered Chinese aesthetic taste over time. By Xu's time, the Chinese imaginary repertoire had been so sterilized and cleansed that the injection of the Keatsian demonic aesthetics had a refreshing impact.

The effect of the demonic enchantment on Xu Zhimo did not hinge entirely on his awareness of *Lamia*. Keats's poetry is shot through with it. In "Ode to a Nightingale," which Xu Zhimo knew by heart, the demonically charged landscape is just as striking. Enwrapped in the "embalmed darkness" of a bower, the speaker envisions "verdurous glooms and winding mossy ways" and "charm'd magic casements . . . in faery lands forlorn."[100] Nothing of this was lost on Xu Zhimo, who likened the experience of the ode as "a child descending into a cool basement, half-terrorized." In any event, it is apparent that Xu wholeheartedly embraced and internalized the eerie beauty of Keats's poetic world, a conflation of an ethereal transcendent otherness and a haunting demonic enchantment. It was thus inevitable that his poetic meditation on the Leifeng Pagoda departed from the traditional *huaigu* topos. The demonic specter that haunted the site in folkloric litera-ture and was largely banished from the literati discourse was welcomed back with a vengeance. Xu described the pagoda as the "ancient tomb of Madame White," "an affectionate demonic enchantress . . . [buried] deep in the wild grass" (1: 168).

> It has been thousand and one hundred years
> Since she was pitifully clasped under Leifeng Pagoda—
> A decaying old pagoda, forlorn, imposing,
> Standing alone in the evening bell of Mount South Screen. (1: 169)

Elsewhere, he saw the pagoda as a "desolate colossal grave, with entwining cypresses atop" and "one-time illusive dream and one-time love" buried un-derneath. In these poems, we can sense a resonance of Keats ("Forlorn! the very word is like a bell").[101]

The first time Xu visited the pagoda on October 21, 1923, he was struck by its "ineffably mysterious grandeur and beauty," which partly derived from its ruinous state. The paths leading to the pagoda were overgrown with brambles. The forlorn sight and site had repelled other visitors. A group of Xu's contemporaries climbed to the top of the Leifeng Hill in 1917 and saw the famed pagoda "standing in isolation": "So, this was what they call the Leifeng Pagoda! Underneath it, all the walls and fences were about to crum-ble. The broken tiles and fragmented bricks were everywhere, making it hard to tread through. The thistles and thorns of the undergrowth kept hooking our clothes. Disappointed, we all left."[102] Xu, however, was fascinated by the forlorn features of the site. His palanquin-carriers identified two bramble-overgrown tombs nearby the pagoda as those of Xu Xuan and the White Snake woman. Seven or eight mendicant monks in tattered robes, "with swan-like figures and turtledove-like faces . . . begged for money while recit-ing sūtras." A hawker claimed that a yard-long snake he was holding was the Little Green Snake, maid to Madame White, and offered to release it should anyone pay for it. Xu paid twenty cents and "saw the man tossing the snake into a lotus pond." He knew that before long "she would fall into his hands again." Others would have seen these events as pathetic and laughable. Xu, however, found the experience "rather poetic."

The pagoda ruin is indeed a historic site (*guji*) that dates to the Wu-Yue kingdom. Its association with the popular romance (*chuanqi*) of snake woman is largely confined to the realm of entertainment and make-believe. Few "serious" literati would transpose the romance to the *actual* pagoda site, preferring to leave it as a prop on stage. Xu, however, marries the romance with the physicality of the *real* pagoda. Early topographic descriptions distinguish between an "ancient site" (*guji*) and an "aberrant site" (*guaiji*) on the premise that a site cannot be both. Xu made the Leifeng Pagoda site both: it is at once a site heavy with historical memory and enlivened with romantic associations. "It has been thousand and one hundred years," he wrote longingly, "since she [White Snake] was pitifully clasped under Leifeng Pagoda." Not that he believes this to be an empirical fact, but, as a romantic, he insisted that the fiction of the White Snake take precedence over lackluster reality. "I would like to become a little demon," he wrote in his diary, "in the enchanting shadow of the Leifeng Pagoda, a demon who does not return to the shore, forever. I would! I would!"[103] This refusal to choose between dreaming and waking states characterizes Xu's perceptual mode. Thus in a memorial for Xu Zhimo, Lin Yutang observed: "Nothing that impinged on his eyes . . . was the contour of real things. It was invariably the shape of the fantastic constructs of his mind. This man loved to roam; and he saw spirits and demons. Once hearing an oriole, he was startled. He jumped to his feet, exclaiming: this is [Keats'] Nightingale!"[104]

Lu Xun's Visionary Worlds: Ruins Haunted by Serpentine Spirits

Lu Xun's loathing of the Leifeng Pagoda, fully articulated in his first essay on the collapse of the pagoda, is easily recognizable. What is less acknowledged is the role of the site in the making of his fiercely imaginary world. The contradiction between his resentment of the "tottering" pagoda and his attraction to ruins is in fact less self-evident than it first appears. The pagoda is no more than a locus and an analogue that allows him to string together often related thoughts into a coherent discursive ground. Both of his essays on the pagoda were written in the distinct genre of "miscellaneous writings" or "impromptu reflections." Such essays tend to respond to a current event or topic. The discussion usually extends beyond the immediate circumstances to their larger significance and, in the case of Lu Xun, the character of Chinese culture. Central to such an excursion is an organizing image or analogue. Foreigners' praise of a Chinese banquet provoked his reflections on the Chinese propensity to feast their conquerors and one another, reflections that brought him to his graphic claim that "China is in reality no more than a kitchen for preparing these feasts of human flesh." In this case, the banquet was the organizing motif.[105] The pagoda ruin is another such enabling analogue. It provided him with a platform to address two seemingly unrelated issues: the depressing cultural stasis of China and the dialectic between destruction and construction. Two attributes of the Leifeng Pagoda—that it is one of the Ten Views of West Lake and that it exists as a ruin—permit Lu Xun's reflection. He first took up the public regret over the collapse of the pagoda for destroying the wholeness of the Ten Views of West Lake. To Lu Xun, the dogmatic clinging to this arbitrary construct, with its falsifying wholeness, betrayed a cultural resistance to change. The Ten Views of West Lake embody a cultural landscape of stasis. Ruin, the second motif he extrapolated from the Leifeng Pagoda site, provoked thoughts on destruction and construction, first in the physical or material sense, then in the symbolic or metaphorical sense.

Men like Rousseau, Stirner, Nietzsche, Tolstoy or Ibsen are, in Brandes' words, "destroyers of old tracks." Actually they not only destroy but blaze a trail and lead a charge, sweeping aside all the old tracks, whether whole rails or fragments, that get in men's way, but making no attempt to pick up any scrap iron or ancient bricks to smuggle home in order to sell them later to second-hand dealers.[106]

The motif of symbolic destruction soon leads to the topic of drama and connects with the first motif of Ten Views of West Lake:

All the world is a stage: tragedy shows what is worthwhile in life is shattered, comedy shows how what is worthless is torn to pieces, and satire is a simplified form of comedy. Yet passion and humor alike are foes of this *ten-sight disease*, for both of them are destructive although they destroy different things. As long as China suffers from this disease, we shall have no madmen like Rousseau, and not a single great dramatist or satiric poet either. All China will have will be characters in a comedy, or in something which is neither comedy nor tragedy, a life spent among *the ten sights* which are modeled each on the other, in which everyone suffers from the ten-sight disease. (*Selected Works*, p. 97; italics added)

The theme of ruins allowed him to attack both the static traditionalism that resisted change and the pervasive pettiness of looting public properties. On the one hand, he envisioned China as a colossal ruin whose inhabitants are perennially given to mending the decaying structure rather than reconstructing a new state. Foreign invasions and internal unrest bring about "a brief commotion," only to be followed by the patching up of "the old traditions . . . amid the ruins." "What is distressing is not the ruins, but the fact that the old traditions are being patched up over the ruins. We want wreckers who will bring about reforms" (*Selected Works*, p. 99). The destruction Lu hailed is an overhauling of the entire old system, not the petty pilfering of public properties. To Lu, "the theft of bricks from the Leifeng Pagoda," which caused its collapse, was alarming not in and of itself, but because it betrayed a deeper social malaise that "simply leaves ruins behind; it has nothing to do with construction" (p. 99).

What Lu Xun got out of the Leifeng Pagoda as an analogue in the second essay demonstrates the workings of a topographic site as a topic. The locus generates arguments and brings out hidden relationships between domains of experiences that would otherwise remain unrelated to each other. As a consummate man of letters, Lu Xun worked on and through an imaginary ruin on which he launched his own symbolic destruction and construction all at once.

This is just part of the story. There is more to ruins and the Leifeng Pagoda than what Lu Xun articulated here. Granted, he identified Nietzsche and company as the forces of symbolic destruction much needed in China. But that remains a theoretical abstraction and program. It has yet to crystallize into visual images and tropes that are the stuff of Lu's mind and sustain the intensity of his thinking. The question then becomes: As he yearned for drama, what kind of symbolic drama did he envision?

The two essays on the Leifeng Pagoda themselves offer clues. The first celebrates the collapse of the pagoda as an oppressive symbol in the context of the White Snake; the second calls for a drama of destruction and construction. Is there a connection between the two? Is drama the thread that links the two essays and divulges Lu Xun's imaginary site? There appears to be more to the Leifeng Pagoda ruin in Lu Xun's mind than his essays spells out. We should not let Lu Xun's avowed aversion toward the Leifeng Pagoda beguile us into thinking that this is his attitude toward the site. That site, invigorated by the White Snake drama, is the imaginary stage on which Lu Xun's envisioned drama unfolds.

The paradigm is set up in his "From Hundred Plant Garden to Three Flavor Study," an account of his childhood. The essay is topographically structured; it turns on a binary opposition between the Hundred Plant Garden, the deserted backyard of his family estate, and the Three Flavor Study, the private school in which he was sent to study. The garden is an imaginary realm open to the wonders of nature and where fantasies about the supernatural could be sustained; the school is a confining place of rigid discipline and Confucian indoctrination where fantasies are banished. The garden is suffused with the imaginary presence of the "Beautiful Woman Snake—a creature with a human head and the body of a snake," who, as Lu is told by his nanny, once nearly seduced a young scholar, and would have succeeded had it not been for the intervention of an old monk, who detected "an evil influence on [the young man's] face." The young Lu Xun is therefore always in rapt anticipation, mindful of the "beautiful snake woman," when he "walks to the edge of the long grass in Hundred Plant Garden." In contrast, the Three Flavor Study is no place for the fantastic and the monstrous. The young Lu Xun, full of curiosity about the supernatural, visibly displeased his teacher when Lu asked about the nature of a legendary strange insect called "Strange Indeed" (*guaizai* 怪哉) associated with Dongfang Shuo 東方朔, an ancient magician.[107]

It is significant that Lu Xun mapped the White Snake story to his childhood memory of the deserted garden of his family home. A ruin haunted by a serpentine spirit was the symbolic topography on which many of Lu's imaginary scenarios unfolded. His fascination with the White Snake lore underlay his resentment of the Leifeng Pagoda, but the *imaginary* site of the pagoda, or a ruin, haunted by a serpentine spirit, is precisely the stage for his imaginary drama. In "Dead Fire," published in April 1925, the speaker envisions a surreal spectacle: "From my body wreathed a coil of black smoke, which reared up like a wire snake."[108] In "Stray Thoughts," which appeared in May 1925, three months after he wrote the second essay on the Leifeng Pagoda, Lu urged: "Whatever you love—food, the opposite sex, your country, the nation, mankind—you can only hope to win if you cling to it like a poisonous snake, seize hold of it like an avenging spirit."[109] In "The Good Hell That Was Lost," which came out in June 1925, the speaker "dreamed [he] was lying in bed in the wilderness beside hell. The deep yet orderly wailing of all the ghosts blended with the roar of flames, the seething of oil and the clashing of iron prongs to make one vast, intoxicating harmony, proclaiming to all three worlds the peace of the lower realm." He is then told that this "good hell" is lost to man who "wielded absolute power over hell ... reconstructed the ruins. ... At once the mandrake flowers withered."[110] In "Tomb Stele Inscription," also dating to June 1925, Lu Xun wrote:

I dreamed of myself standing in front of a tomb stela, reading the inscription. The tombstone seemed to have been made of a sandstone, moldering substantially, moss-grown, leaving only limited words— ... There was a wandering spirit, metamor-

phosed into a snake, with venomous teeth in its mouth. It does not bite human beings; instead, it gnawed into its own body until it perished. . . . Go away! . . . I circled
around the stela, and saw a forlorn tomb in barren ruins. From its opening, I saw a
corpse, its chest and back all deteriorating with no heart and liver in its body. . . . I
was about to leave. The corpse sat up, its lip unmoving, but said—

"When I turn into ashes, you shall see my smile."[111]

In "Regret for the Past," written in October 1925, Lu Xun envisioned a
glimmer of hope in a landscape of despair:

There are many ways open to me, and I must take one of them because I am still living. I still don't know, though, how to take the first step. Sometimes the road seems
like a great, grey serpent, writhing and darting at me. I wait and wait and watch it
approach, but it always disappears suddenly in the darkness.[112]

Lu Xun's dramatic vision of the spirit-haunted ruin was rooted in a memory
of the village opera he saw in his childhood in his native place, Shaoxing.
Foremost in the repertoire was the *Mulianxi* 目連戲, or *Dramatic Cycle of the
Tale of Mulian (Maudgalyayana)*. Based on a medieval Chinese Buddhist tale,
the play shows the descent of Mulian, one of the Buddha's disciples, into hell
to search and eventually rescue his mother who is condemned there for her
sins. The stage play as Lu Xun saw it as a child typically began at dusk and
ended at dawn of the next day.[113] The cycle opens with a ritual ceremony of
"Summoning of the Spirits," "those who had died unnatural deaths":

This ceremony signified that the manifold lonely ghosts and avenging spirits had
now come with the ghostly king and his ghostly soldiers to watch the performance
with the rest of us. There was no need to worry, though. These ghosts were on their
best behavior, and would not make the least trouble all this night. So the opera
started and slowly unfolded, the human beings interspersed with apparitions: the
ghost who died by fire, the ghost who was drowned, the one who expired in an examination cell, the one eaten by a tiger.[114]

This is followed first by a "Hanging Man Dance" and then a "Hanging
Woman Dance," which features a female ghost who complains about the
miserable life that led her to suicide. Now she seeks revenge. The female
ghost in particular fascinated Lu Xun. Many years later he recalled her terrible beauty with fondness.[115]

Two qualities in Lu Xun's memory of the village opera informed his
dramatic sensibility. First, it is inhabited by ghosts and spirits, in particular,

female ones. Second, it has a twilight or hazy mood. Not only was the "Summoning of the Spirits" enacted at the sunset, but the haziness exists in Lu Xun's mind in the form of *recollection*: "the hazy, moonlit outlines of a temporary stage erected on the empty strand between the village and the river . . . the faintly discernible abode of Daoist Immortals, bathed in a halo of torchlight that shrouded it like the sunset glow of evening."[116] These twin qualities—the twilight mood and the spectral energy—are precisely what the Leifeng Pagoda evoked: the view of the pagoda at sunset and the romance of the White Snake woman trapped under it. Indeed, Lu Xun was unimpressed with the sight of the "tottering structure standing out between the lake and the hills, with the setting sun gilding its surroundings," and he had no patience for the "Ten Views syndrome." What troubled him was the stale view of the "Pagoda at Sunset" divorced from the drama of the White Snake spirit. His two essays are attempts to restore drama, in its different senses, to the otherwise stagnant site. In other words, Lu Xun reconstituted the traditional Leifeng Pagoda in Evening Glow and refined it as a modernist topography.

A set of circumstances combined to intensify his vision. On April 8, 1924, five months before the Leifeng Pagoda collapsed and six months before he wrote his first essay on the subject, Lu Xun bought *Symbolism of Depression*, by Kuriyagawa Hakuson (1880–1923), a Japanese art critic. Five months later, he translated the book. The book apparently excited him, for it took him just 21 days to finish the project. He began translating another book by the same author, *Out of the Ivory Tower*, in late 1924 and finished it on February 18, 1925. Meanwhile, he was teaching at universities in Beijing, and he lectured on the *Symbolism of Depression* and made mimeographed copies of his galley proofs and distributed them as assigned reading.[117]

Kuriyagawa Hakuson was a prominent art critic in Japan in the early twentieth century. A graduate of Tokyo Imperial University, he continued his studies in the United States. He returned to Japan and taught at universities in Tokyo, Kyoto, and various places. He died in the 1923 Tokyo earthquake. The *Symbolism of Depression* was retrieved, as a friend recalled, "from the ruins of the master's residence."[118] Kuriyagawa was a follower of Bergson and Freud. His position, as spelled out in the two books that Lu Xun translated, is a rehash of Bergson and Freud: the ultimate motor driving artistic creation is the melancholy resulting from depression and oppression of the life force; art is capable of creating a world of individuality with total imaginative freedom; art can project mental images through concrete "symbols," and so forth.

Kuriyagawa's style is fierce, and his social criticisms scathing. From a radical stance, he relentlessly lampooned the problems that plagued Japanese society and the Japanese mentality. In this, he was not unlike Lu Xun. Kuriyagawa's appeal for Lu Xun should be obvious. From Kuriyagawa, Lu Xun acquired the Freudian calculus—the valorization of desire, the affirmation of the energy of the libido, and the awareness of its repression as the ultimate source of the eruptive "life force."[119] This new language gives his old sensibility—molded out of his rural upbringing—a new spin. It releases the demonic forces: the female ghost of the village opera, the spirits that populate the Buddhist hell, the demonic energy associated with the White Snake woman, and the monstrous union between a mortal being and a supernormal creature, and so on took on a new life in the theoretical light of modernism. The ruin of the Leifeng Pagoda lent itself as a primal site for Lu Xun to play out his modernist vision.

More specifically, Kuriyagawa was one of the first Asian scholars to introduce Keats's *Lamia* story to Asia and to note its similarity to the Chinese White Snake lore and its derivative treatment in Japan. Many of his works were translated into Chinese in the 1920s by several distinguished scholars, including Feng Zikai 豐子愷 and others.[120] As someone who consistently valorized sexual desire as the creative force, he was drawn to what he called "serpentine sexuality," and he praised the sympathetic treatment of snake lore by both Keats and Theophile Gautier, French romantic author of *La Morte amoreuse*. "Instead of loathing the demonic woman," he wrote, "they make one feel what is ineffably beautiful, a quality that can be characterized as chillingly bewitching." In comparison, he found the Japanese treatment of the matter wanting.[121] Kuriyagawa here reinforced a nearly forgotten traditional aesthetic category: "chillingly bewitching," *sai'en* 悽艷 (Ch. *qiyan*). It describes a curiously paradoxical effect, evocative at once of a chilly, mournful desolation and an irresistible enchantment—the twin qualities of the darkly suggestive landscape of the Leifeng Pagoda with its serpentine enchantress.

Lu Xun's life in the 1920s was deeply caught up with pagodas. From August 2, 1923, to May 25, 1924, he lived in a neighborhood in Beijing called "Brick Pagoda Alley." On April 17, 1924, on a lecture trip to Xi'an, he visited the Great Goose Pagoda of the Daci'en 大慈恩 Temple. The day before he wrote "On the Collapse of the Leifengta," he bought Kuriyagawa's book *Out of the Ivory Tower*, whose title contains the kanji-character *to* 塔 (*ta* in Chinese; "pagoda"). He was to live with this book for an extended period as he proceeded to translate it.[122] These circumstances may have cued his writing on the topic of pagodas.

Pagodas and women, unrelated to each other except in the Leifeng Pagoda lore, came to a head in the 1920s, a period that saw the surge of the women's liberation movement. Appointed to the faculty of Beijing Women's Normal College in July 1923, Lu Xun was actively involved in the women's cause. In April 1925, two months after Lu Xun wrote the second essay on the Leifeng pagoda, a heinous event rocked the country. Four female college students visiting an "ancient site," the Iron Pagoda at Kaifeng, were brutally raped by six soldiers. After this abominable act, the brutes ripped strips from each of the women's skirts as "souvenirs" and hung their clothes on the top of the pagoda. The women had to endure further humiliation at the hands of their school's administration. Fearful that the scandal might tarnish the school's reputation, they chose to silence the victims' voices and publicly denied the incident. The four women committed suicide. Zhao Yintang (1893–?), a lecturer in Chinese at Beijing Normal University, wrote on the event with anguished sarcasm:

Who asked them [the women] to visit the Iron Pagoda in that desolate place? The pagoda is indeed an extremely famous ancient ruin. Only the governor should be allowed to climb up and view the scenery; only celebrities and scholars should be allowed to inscribe their names there. Or to put it in a less dignified tone, only male students should be allowed to climb to the top to yell and scream. These women—what right did they have to visit [this site]? Unqualified with this right, they went anyway. Wasn't that indecorous? Shouldn't they die?[123]

The incident also enraged Lu Xun (*LXQJ*, 7: 274). Indeed, it occurred in the wake of Lu Xun's two essays on the Leifeng Pagoda, yet it epitomized an enduring social reality in which the weight of traditional values kept crushing innocent victims, particularly women. It dramatized the pagoda—a signpost of tradition in modern times—as the oppressive symbol and symbolized the social injustice women had to bear. The tragedy at the Iron Pagoda is almost an uncanny modern re-enactment of the Leifeng Pagoda and its subjugation of the White Snake woman. It testifies to the relevance of Lu

Fig. 11.14   Tao Yuanqing, cover design for Lu Xun,
trans., *Kumon no shōchō; Kumen de xiangzheng* (Symbolism of depression) by Kuriyagawa Hakuson
(1880–1923) (Shanghai: Weimingshe, 1924).

Xun's two essays and makes Lu Xun's loathing of the pagoda as an oppressive presence and his sympathy with the White Snake woman all the more
compelling.

Much as the landscape of the pagoda ruin served as a symbolic topography for modernist writers such as Lu Xun and Xu Zhimo and gave shape to
their discursive energy and imaginary universe, their work in turn inspired
visual constructs. Lu's vision found its visualizer in an able young artist
named Tao Yuanqing 陶元慶 (1892–1929), also a native of Shaoxing. Tao's
cover design for Lu Xun's translation of *Symbol of Depression* shows a nude
female figure imprisoned in a claustrophobic circle, wriggling among four
crimson patches of monsters threatening to gnaw into her. With her hands
seemingly entangled, the woman holds a trident with one foot, whose prongs

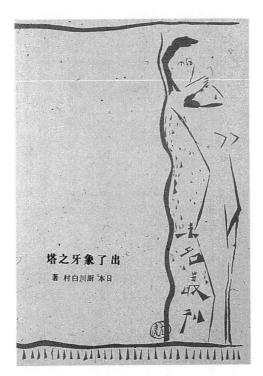

塔之牙象了出

著 村白川厨 本日

Fig. 11.15 Tao Yuanqing, cover design for Lu Xun,
trans., *Zōge no to o dete; Chule xiangya zhi ta* (Out of the
ivory tower) by Kuriyagawa Hakuson (1880–1923);
(Shanghai: Weimingshe, 1924).

touch her lifted chin (Fig. 11.14). Tao's design for the cover of *Out of the Ivory
Tower* again features a female nude, somewhat startled, standing against a
wavy and wriggling line (Fig. 11.15). It may be far-fetched to take the serpentine line in both cover designs as a coded visual allusion to the White Snake
woman, but the evocation of oppression, desire, and destruction in the first
design and the connection between woman and pagoda in the second are all
very suggestive. Lu Xun's dramatic vision of the Leifeng Pagoda is precisely
about these diverse impulses.

Lu Xun's imaginary ruins, haunted sites invigorated with supernatural
forces, became a topos widely shared by his contemporaries. It prompted a
group of young followers of Lu Xun in the 1920s and 1930s to cast their
mournful eyes to their own native places. They evoke ruins of the past and

Fig. 11.16 Li Jiqing, cover design for Tai Jingnong, *Jiantazhe* (Pagoda builder). 1928. (Beiping: Weiming she, 1930). After Tai Jingnong, *Jiantazhe* (Beijing: Renmin wen-xue chubanshe, 1984).

aspire toward the landmarks heralding the future. Among the group was Tai Jingnong 臺静農, whose short story "Pagoda Builder" relates the tale of an imprisoned young woman put to death by her oppressors. The thin narrative is premised on the conviction that "our pagoda is not built on soil and rocks, but on the foundation of our blood-congealed blocks."[124] The "Pagoda Builder" became the title for the author's collection of stories, published in 1928. Its cover, designed by Li Jiqing, shows a leftward-tilting grid of dark lines crossed by a red crescent band. An intersection generates a square in which a mason—apparently the "Pagoda Builder"—hammers a drill rod into a stone block. A tall tower soars above clouds, set against the sun. The more realistic scene inside the box thus thematically echoes the abstract coordinates outside it: illuminating the grid as a soaring structure in the making and the red band as a vague evocation of the sun, and by extension, a hopeful future. Consistent with the geometric mood, the characters of the book title are rendered in "art script" (*meishuzi* 美術字), as opposed to the traditional calligraphic scripts, to register a touch of modernism. In color scheme, the design thrives on a sharp contrast between red and black, set against a white background (Fig. 11.16). It is a modernist reworking of the Pagoda in Evening Glow: not only is the soaring structure, explicitly mentioned in the title as a *ta* (pagoda), envisioned as an obelisk with its foreign—hence, for the Chinese at the time, modernist—overtones, the sun—presumably anything but a setting sun—evokes blood, sacrifice, and passion, as evidenced in Tai's narrative. This futuristic-utopian pictorial construct brings this story of the Leifeng Pagoda to a close. The pagoda site, which began innocently as no more than a circumstantially rooted monument, ends up becoming an enduring signpost in the Chinese mental universe and a topos that generated an ever-increasing body of writing for centuries.

Notes

The following abbreviations are used in the Notes and Works Cited list:

JCSZ *Jingcisi zhi* (Gazetteer of the Jingci Monastery), comp. Ji Xiang (1805). In *WZC*, vol. 13.

LXQJ *Lu Xun quanji* (Complete works of Lu Xun). 16 vols. Beijing: Renmin wenxue chubanshe, 1981.

NJSZ Dahuo, *Nanping Jingcisi zhi* (Gazetteer of the Jingci Monastery of Nanping) (1616). In *Xuxiu siku quanshu*, vol. 719 (Shanghai: Shanghai guji chubanshe, 1995–99).

WZC *Wulin zhanggu congbian* (Compendium of local histories of Wulin), comp. Ding Bing (1888). 12 vols. Taibei: Tailian guofeng chubanshe, 1967.

YWSQ *Yingyin Wenyuange siku quanshu*. 1,500 vols. Taibei: Taiwan shangwu yinshuguan, 1983–86.

1. David Leatherbarrow, *The Roots of Architectural Invention: Site, Enclosure, Materials* (New York: Cambridge University Press, 1993), pp. 3–6.

2. See Stephen Owen, *Remembrances: The Experience of the Past in Classical Chinese Literature* (Cambridge, Mass.: Harvard University Press, 1986), p. 26.

3. Richard E. Strassberg, "Introduction," in *Inscribed Landscapes: Travel Writing from Imperial China* (Berkeley: University of California Press, 1994), pp. 6–7.

4. Stephen Owen (pers. comm.) first made this point to me. See also his commentary on the body of writing in connection with the Level Mountain Hall in Yangzhou, in his *An Anthology of Chinese Literature: Beginning to 1911* (New York: Norton, 1996), p. 634. Addressing the issue of visibility and the creation of place, Yi-Fu Tuan (*Space and Place: The Perspective of Experience* [Minneapolis: University of Minnesota Press, 1977], p. 178) also observes that "deeply-loved places are not necessarily visible. . . . Identity of place is achieved by dramatizing the aspirations, needs, and functional rhythms of personal and group life."

5. This commonly adopted translation may not be entirely adequate, for it ignores the origin of the character *lei*. *Lei* may have been a reference to a Daoist hermit named Xu Lizhi 徐立之, otherwise known as Mr. Huifeng 回峰, who once lived on the site. The name "Huifeng" may have changed into Leifeng over time. Another theory has it that a man named Leijiu 雷就 once lived on the site. Hence, the hill was named after him as Thunder Peak. See Qian Yueyou 潛說有, *Xianchun Lin'an zhi* 咸淳臨安志 (Xianchun [period] gazetteer of Lin'an), YWSQ, vol. 490, pp. 873–74; Tian Rucheng 田汝成, *Xihu youlan zhi* 西湖遊覽志 (Notes on touring West Lake) (Shanghai: Shanghai guji chubanshe, 1998), p. 33; and Chen Xingzhen 陳杏

珍, "Leifengta de mingcheng ji qita" 雷峰塔的名稱及其他 (The name of the Thunder Peak Pagoda and other issues), *Wenwu tiandi*, no. 6 (1977): 40–44.

6. The complete title is *Yiqie Rulai xin bimi quanshen sheli baoqieyin tuoluoni jing* 一切如來心秘密全身舍利寶篋印陀羅尼經 (Sanskrit: *Sarvatathāgata-adhistāna-hrdaya-guhya-dhātu-karandamudrā-dhāranī-sūtra*). It was first translated into Chinese by the Indian monk Amoghavajra (705–74), who went to China around 720, where he became a disciple of Vajrabodhi. The sūtra can also be found in Bunyiu Nanjio, *A Catalogue of the Chinese Translation of the Buddhist Tripitaka* (Oxford: Clarendon Press, 1883), no. 957. See also Sören Edgren, "The Printed Dhāranī-sūtra of A.D. 956," *Museum of Far Eastern Antiquities (Östasiatiska Museet)*, no. 44 (1972): 141; and Zhang Xiumin 張秀民, "Wudai Wu-Yue guo de yinshua" 五代吳越國的印刷 (The printing technology of the Wu-Yue kingdom of the Five Dynasties), *Wenwu* 1978, no. 12: 74–76.

7. See Yu Pingbo 俞平伯, "Ji Xihu Leifenta faxian de tazhuan yu cangjing" 記西湖雷峰塔發現的塔磚與藏經 (Note on the tiles and hoarded sutras inside the Leifeng Pagoda), in *Yu Pingbo sanwen zawen lunbian* 俞平伯散文雜文論編 (Prose and miscellaneous notes by Yu Pingbo) (Shanghai: Shanghai guji chubanshe, 1990), 123; Zhang Xiumin, "Wudai Wu-Yue guo de yinshua," p. 74.

8. Edgren, "The Printed Dhāranī-sūtra of A.D. 956," pl. 3.

9. See ibid., p. 141. For other copies, see Zhang Xiumin, "Wudai Wu-Yue guo de yinshua," p. 76.

10. Yu Pingbo ("Ji Xihu Leifengta faxian de tazhuan yu cangjing," p. 126) first noted the poignant circumstantial referentiality of the sūtra in the pagoda with regard to the fate of the pagoda itself.

11. The inscription is contained in Qian Yueyou, *Xianchun Lin'an zhi*, p. 874. The pagoda was most likely built in 976, based on the dated sutras and woodblock prints excavated from the pagoda. The *Baoqieying jing* retrieved from the pagoda is dated 975, which points to the date of the beginning of the construction. The woodblock print bearing a pagoda image retrieved from the hollow bricks is dated 976. Since Qian Hongchu's votive inscription records that the pagoda was built "within a moment of finger snap," and considering that the Wu-Yue Kingdom ended in 978, it is very likely that the construction was completed in 976 or shortly after, but not beyond 978. See Chen Xingzhen, "Leifengta," p. 42.

12. Chen Xingzhen ("Leifengta," p. 42) argues convincingly that the *huang* (yellow) is a misprint in the *Xianchun Lin'an zhi*; it should be *huang* 皇 (imperial) or *wang* 土. Similar observations were also made by Qing scholars; see Hu Jing 胡敬, comp., *Chunyou Lin'anzhi jiyi* 淳祐臨安志輯逸 (Chunyou gazetteer of Lin'an, with scattered fragments reconstituted), *WZC*, vol. 24.

13. Tuotuo 脫脫 (Toghto), *Songshi* 宋史 (Standard history of Song) (Beijing: Zhonghua shuju, 1977), 480.13900–901, 13909. *Wu Yue beishi buyi* 吳越備史補遺

gives the eleventh month of 976 as the date of her death; see Chen Xingzhen, "Leifengta," p. 43.

14. Wu Renchen 吳任臣, *Shiguo chunqiu* 吳越春秋 (Spring and autumn of the Ten Kingdoms), *YWSQ*, 466: 112.

15. The *Jingci sizhi* (4034a) records a popular saying that circulated widely in the region: tidal lappings on the Qiantang shore "produce imperial consorts." In particular, it mentions Qian Hongchu's consort, Sun Taizhen.

16. A fire during the war in the Xuanhe era (1119–25) razed everything around the pagoda to the ground, leaving the latter standing alone. The pagoda apparently sustained some damage. It was renovated in 1171 and 1199; see Qian Yueyou, *Xianchun Lin'an zhi*, p. 804.

17. Su Shi himself was not uptight about discussing outlandish matters. He is closely associated with the telling of ghost stories as a literati pastime. He also authored a *zhiguai* 志怪 collection titled *Dongpo zhilin* 東坡志林 (I thank Judith Zeitlin for alerting me to this fact). However, his response to the Leifengta site is still conditioned by the stock generic impulse; in any case, the pagoda site did not inspire him to poetry.

18. Qisong, "You Nanpingshan ji" 游南屏山記 (Touring South Screen Mountain), in *Xihu youji xuan* 西湖遊記選, ed. and annot. Cao Wenqu 曹文趣 et al. (Hangzhou: Zhejiang wenyi chubanshe, 1985), pp. 224–25.

19. For an excellent study of the literary association of these architectural types, see Ke Qingming [Ko Ching-Ming] 柯慶明, "Cong ting tai lou ge shuoqi: lun yizhong linglei de youguan meixue yu shengming xingcha" 從亭臺樓閣說起: 論一種另類的遊觀美學與生命省察 (Of kiosks, terraces, towers, and pavilions: notes on the aesthetics of excursions into otherness and existential introspection), in idem, *Zhongguo wenxue de meigan* 中國文學的美感 (Aesthetic modes of Chinese literature) (Taibei: Rye Field Publications, 2000), pp. 275–349.

20. The first source is Zhu Mu 祝穆, writing in 1240, according to whom the Ten Views are: (1) "Autumn Moon Above the Placid Lake," (2) "Spring Dawn at Su Dike," (3) "Remnant Snow on Broken Bridge," (4) "Thunder Peak Pagoda at Sunset," (5) "Evening Bell from Nanping Mountain," (6) "Lotus Breeze at Qu Winery," (7) "Watching Fish at Flower Cove," (8) "Listening to the Orioles by the Willow Ripples," (9) "Three Stupas and the Reflecting Moon," (10) "Twin Peaks Piercing the Clouds" (see Zhu Mu, *Fangyu shenglan* 方輿勝覽 [preface dated 1240], cited in *Xihu bicong* 西湖筆叢 [Compendium of writings on West Lake], ed. Lu Jiansan 陸鑒三 [Hangzhou: Zhejiang renmin chubanshe, 1981], p. 26). Half a century later, the same Ten Views were cited in Wu Zimu's 吳自牧 *Mengliang lu* 夢粱錄, although in a different order. The author attributes this tenfold landscape taxonomy to "recent painters who claim that the most remarkable of the four seasonal scenes come down to ten" (see Wu Zimu, *Mengliang lu* [Hangzhou: Zhejiang renmin chu-

banshe, 1980], pp. 103–6). For a good introduction to the subject, see Huishu Lee, "The Domain of Empress Yang (1162–1233): Art, Gender, and Politics at the Southern Song Court" (Ph.D. diss., Yale University, 1994), pp. 47–48.

21. See Zhai Hao 翟灝 et al., *Hushan bianlan* 湖山便覽 (Easy guide to the lake and mountains) (Shanghai: Shanghai guji, 1998), p. 27; Wu Zimu, *Mengliang lu*, pp. 103–6.

22. For studies of the pictorial representation of Xiaoxiang views, see A. Murck, "Eight Views of the Hsiao Hsiang by Wang Hung," in *Images of the Mind: Selections from the Edward L. Elliot Family and John B. Eliot Collection of Chinese Calligraphy and Painting*, ed. Wen Fong et al. (Princeton: Princeton University Press, 1984), p. 214; Richard Barnhart, "Shining Rivers: *Eight Views of the Hsiao Hsiang* in Sung Painting," in *Proceedings of the International Colloquium on Chinese Art History* (Taibei: National Palace Museum, 1992), 1: 45–95; and Valérie M. Ortiz, "The Poetic Structure of a Twelfth-Century Chinese Pictorial Dream Journey," *Art Bulletin* 76, no. 2 (1994): 257–78.

23. For the book, see Patrick Hanan, "The Early Chinese Short Story: A Critical Theory in Outline," 179n21.

24. Hong Pian 洪楩, ed., *Qingpingshantang huaben* 清平山堂話本 (Nanjing: Jiangsu guji chubanshe, 1989), pp. 25–36.

25. Most scholars agree that the story could date to the Southern Song. Many traits of the story (e.g., the place-names and official titles mentioned, the style of the prose) point to an early date. The story was in circulation at least by the Yuan dynasty (1279–1368). A catalogue of the Yuan *zaju* 雜劇 lists a play by the same title, now lost. See ibid., p. 25; and Huang Shang 黃裳, *Xixiangji yu Baishezhuan* 西廂記與白蛇傳 (*Romance of the West Chamber* and *Story of the White Snake*) (Shanghai: Pingming chubanshe, 1954), pp. 36–39.

26. The subject has spawned a huge scholarly literature. See, e.g., Nai-tung Ting, "The Holy and the Snake Woman: A Study of a Lamia Story in Asian and European Literature," *Fabula* 8 (1966): 145–91; Wu Pei-yi, "The White Snake: The Evolution of a Myth in China" (Ph.D. diss., Columbia University, 1969); Yen Yuan-shu, "Biography of the White Serpent: A Keatsian Interpretation," *Tamkang Review* 1, no. 2 (1970): 227–43; Hsu Erh-hung, "The Evolution of the Legend of the White Serpent," 2 pts., *Tamkang Review* 4, no. 1 (1973): 109–27, no. 2: 121–56; and Whalen Lai, "From Folklore to Literate Theater: Unpacking *Madame White Snake*," *Asian Folklore Studies*, 51 (1992): 51–66.

27. Li Fang 李昉 et al., comps., *Taiping guangji* 太平廣記 (Beijing: Zhonghua shuju, 1986), 10: 3752. *Juan* 456–59 (pp. 3720–62) are devoted to snakes.

28. Ibid., p. 3745.

29. Hong Pian, *Qingpingshantang huaben*, pp. 25–36.

30. Tian Rucheng, *Xihu youlan zhi*, 2.20; Zhai Hao et al., *Hushan bianlan*, p. 70.

31. Zhong Jingwen 鍾敬文, *Zhong Jingwen minjian wenxue lunji* 鍾敬文民間文學論集 (Essays on folkloric literature by Zhong Jingwen) (Shanghai: Shanghai wenyi chubanshe, 1985), 2: 85.

32. Li Kaixian 李開先, *Li Kaixian ji* 李開先集 (Complete works of Li Kaixian) (Shanghai: Zhonghua shuju, 1959), p. 6.

33. *Li Kongtong quanji* 李空同, juan 50; cited in Guo Shaoyu 郭紹虞 et al., eds., *Zhongguo lidai wenlun xuan* 中國歷代文論選 (Selected Chinese literary criticism of successive dynasties) (Shanghai: Guji chubanshe, 1980), 3: 55.

34. Tian Rucheng, *Xihu youlanzhi*, 3.38; Zhang Dai 張岱, *Xihu mengxun* 西湖夢尋 (A dream search for West Lake), in *Tao'an mengyi Xihu mengxun* 陶庵夢憶西湖夢尋 (Shanghai: Shanghai guji chubanshe, 1982), 4.67.

35. Tian Rucheng, *Xihu youlan zhi*, 8.86.

36. Ibid., 3.33.

37. Ibid., 26.481.

38. The earliest surviving libretto is titled *Yuhuatang zizhuan Leifengta chuanqi* 玉花堂自傳雷峰塔傳奇 (Romance of the Leifeng Pagoda composed by Yuhuatang [Jade Flower Hall]), with a preface dated 1530, in the collection of Dai Bufan 戴不凡. Another libretto known as *Nanxi yiyangqiang Jiajing shinian Jiguzhai keben Leifengta* 南戲弋陽腔嘉靖十年汲古齋刻本雷峰塔 (The Leifeng Pagoda in the Yiyang variety of Southern Drama from the Jigu Atelier, a woodblock print dated the tenth year of Jiajing), with a preface dated 1531, is in the collection of Wu Jingtang 吳敬塘. Since these two librettos have not been published, their content remains unknown. The connection made between the two monsters-turned-beauties and the pagoda is confirmed by another libretto, in print in 1532, titled *Bainiangzi yongzhen Leifengta chuanqi* 白娘子永鎮雷峰塔傳奇 (Madame White clasped under the Leifeng Pagoda for eternity, a romance). See Zhao Jingshen 趙景深 et al., "The Relationship Between the Romance of the White Snake and Folklore" (in Chinese), in *Baishezhuan lunwenji* 白蛇傳論文集 (Papers on the tale of White Snake), ed. Zhongguo minjian wenyi yanjiuhui, Zhejiang fenhui 中國民間文藝研究會浙江分會 (Hangzhou: Zhejiang guji chubanshe, 1986), p. 121.

39. Yang Kang 楊亢, "Record of Renovation" (dated 1199), in Hu Jing, *Chunyou Lin'an zhi jiyi*, 24: 7358.

40. Traditional sources identify the bandits as Japanese. Recent study shows that the mid-sixteenth-century coastal piracy involved ethnic Chinese just as well. See Richard von Glahn, *Fountain of Fortune: Money and Monetary Policy in China, 1000–1700* (Berkeley: University of California Press, 1996).

41. Lu Ciyun 陸次雲, *Huru zaji* 湖濡雜記, in WZC, 4:2087. Qing authors attributed the fire to the Japanese invaders who suspected an ambush inside the pagoda; see ibid.; and Liang Zhangju 梁章鉅, *Langji xutan* 浪蹟續談 (More trave-

logues), vol. 4 of *Biji xiaoshuo daguan xubian* 筆記小說大觀續編 (Collection of *biji* fiction: a sequel) (Taibei: Xinxing shuju, 1979), p. 4234.

42. Tian Rucheng, *Xihu youlan zhi*, 3.33. Wu Congxian 吳從先, *Xiaochuang riji* 小窗日記, cited by Xu Fengji, *Qingbo xiaozhi* (Shanghai: Shanghai guji, 1999), p. 77.

43. Yu Chunxi 虞淳熙, *Qiantang xianzhi* 錢塘縣志 (Gazetteer of the Qiantang county), reprint of 1893, "waiji," p. 33.

44. *NJSZ*, p. 407. The poem was written before 1616, since it was collected in Dahuo's 大壑 *Nanping Jingcisi zhi* 南屏淨慈寺志, published in 1616.

45. Feng Menglong 馮夢龍, comp., *Jingshi tongyan* 警世通言 (Beijing: Renmin wenxue chubanshe, 1984), pp. 435–64.

46. Ibid., p. 464; trans. from H. C. Chang, *Chinese Literature: Popular Fiction and Drama* (Edinburgh: Edinburgh University Press, 1973), p. 260.

47. Huang Tubi 黃圖珌, *Leifengta* 雷峰塔, in *Baishezhuan ji* 白蛇傳集 (A collection of White Snake stories), ed. Fu Xihua 傅惜華 (Shanghai: Shanghai chuban gongsi, 1955), pp. 282–338.

48. Fu Xihua, "Preface," in idem, ed., *Baishezhuan ji*, p. 5; Huang Shang, *Xixiangji yu Baishezhuan*, p. 43.

49. The invention of this plot is credited to actor Chen Jiayan and his daughter who adapted the White Snake materials for the stage, since Huang Tubi's version was considered not quite fitting for stage performance. Fang inherited Chen's plot. See A Ying 阿英, *Leifengta chuanqi xulu* 雷峰塔傳奇敘錄 (Introduction to the Romance of the Leifeng Pagoda) (Shanghai: Zhonghua shuju, 1960), p. 2.

50. *Baishe zhuan lunwen ji*, p. 161.

51. "Mourning in Front of the Pagoda," a print from the Guangxu era (1875–1908), in Fu Xihua, ed., *Baishezhuan ji*, pp. 110–11.

52. Fang Chengpei 方成培, "Preface to *The Leifeng Pagoda*," in *Zhongguo gudian xiqu xuba huibian* 中國古典戲曲序跋彙編 (Collection of prologues and postscripts to traditional Chinese drama), ed. Cai Yi 蔡毅 (Ji'nan: Qilu shushe, 1989), 3: 1941

53. Huang Tubi, *Leifengta*, p. 338.

54. Hong Pian, *Qingpingshantang*, p. 36.

55. Huang Tubi (*Leifengta*, p. 335), for example, explicitly refers to the Leifeng Pagoda as a "an aberrant site (*guaiji*) that bears viewing."

56. Mo Langzi 墨浪子, *Xihu jiahua* 西湖佳話, ed. and annot. Shao Dacheng 邵大成 (Hangzhou: Zhejiang wenyi chubanshe, 1985), pp. 266, 284.

57. Yang Erzeng 楊爾曾, *Hainei qiguan* 海內奇觀, in *Zhongguo gudai banhua congkan erbian* 中國古代版畫叢刊二編 (Compendium of traditional Chinese prints, 2d series) (Shanghai: Shanghai guji chubanshe, 1994), p. 26.

58. The compiler of the *Hainei qiguan* did not disclose the source of this poem. I have been able to identify Mo Fan, a mid-Ming poet, as the author of this poem; see

Zhejiang tongzhi 浙江通志 (Zhejiang gazetteer) (Shanghai: Shangwu yinshuguan, 1934), 4: 4867a.

59. For a survey of the historical trend in legitimizing the strange in the late seventeenth century, see Judith T. Zeitlin, *Historian of the Strange: Pu Songling and the Chinese Classical Tale* (Stanford: Stanford University Press, 1993), pp. 17–25.

60. Huang Tubi, *Leifengta*, p. 337.

61. "Mourning in Front of the Pagoda," in Fu Xihua, *Baishezhuan ji*, pp. 110–11.

62. Li Liufang 李流芳, *Tanyuanji* 檀園集 (Collection of the Sandalwood Garden), *YWSQ*, 1295: 394.

63. Waikam Ho, ed., *Century of Tung Ch'i-ch'ang* (Seattle: Nelson-Atkins Museum of Art and University of Washington Press, 1992), 2: 104.

64. The line alludes to a famous Chan-Buddhist motto. The lay Buddhist Pang Yun is reported to have asked Daoyi (709–88): "What kind of man is he who is not linked with all things?" To which Daoyi replied: "Wait until at one gulp you can drink up all the water in the West River, and I will tell you" (Fung Yu-lan, *A History of Chinese Philosophy*, trans. Derk Bodde [Princeton: Princeton University Press, 1953], 2: 393).

65. Zhang Dai, *Xihu mengxun*, p. 66.

66. Ibid., p. 4.

67. Xu Ke 徐珂, comp., *Qingbai leichao* 清稗類鈔 (Beijing: Zhonghua shuju, 1984), 1: 341.

68. *JCSZ*, p. 3702a.

69. There are, indeed, notable exceptions arising out of special historical circumstances. These include the pagoda at the Linggu Temple, next to the tomb of the Ming founder, and the so-called Porcelain Pagoda at the Bao'en Temple, built by the Yongle emperor; they were associated, after the fall of the Ming, by the loyalists with the Ming dynastic enterprise. I thank Jonathan Hay for bringing these to my attention.

70. J. L. Cranmer-Byng, ed., *An Embassy to China: Being the journal kept by Lord Macartney during his embassy to the Emperor Ch'ien-lung, 1793–1794* (Hamden, Conn.: Archon Books, 1963), p. 179. Macartney mistook "Leifengta" as 雷風塔, thereby translating it as "the Tower of the Thundering Winds."

71. See Kenneth Clark, *The Gothic Revival: An Essay in the History of Taste* (New York: Harper and Row, 1962), pp. 46–65.

72. Most Suzhou prints are undated. Based on a few dated prints of a similar style, these date to the Yongzheng (1723–35) and Qianlong (1736–95) reigns. One telltale sign in the prints is the phrase "Leifeng in Evening Glow" (*Leifeng xizhao* 雷鋒夕照) instead of the usual "The Leifeng Pagoda Bathed in West Sunset," a change in the wording made by the Kangxi emperor when he visited the site. Qianlong used Kangxi's phrase in his poem on the view in 1751. However, by 1757, he had

reverted to the pre-Kangxi phrase "Leifeng in Evening Glow." It is likely therefore that the Suzhou prints here, in following the old phrase, must have been dated to the second half of the eighteenth century. For the dating of the Suzhou prints in general, see *Chūgoku no yōfūga ten: Minmatsu kara Shin jidai no kaiga, hanga, sashiebon* (Exhibition of the Western-influenced style in Chinese painting, prints, and illustrated books from Ming to Qing dynasties) (Tokyo: Machida shiritsu kokusai hanga bijutsukan, 1995), p. 376.

73. The print does not reveal the source of the poem. I have been able to identify the late Song–early Yuan poet Yin Tinggao as its author; for the full text of the poem, see *JCSZ*, p. 3918a.

74. Li Wei 李衛 et al., comps., *Xihu zhi* 西湖志 (Gazetteer of West Lake) (1735 ed.), 3: 32–33.

75. Tong Danian 童大年, "Leifengta *Huayanjing* canshi zhenxing tiba" 雷峰塔〈華嚴經〉殘石真形題跋 (Comment on the fragmented stones with the *Flower Garland Sutra* from the Leifeng Pagoda); cited in Mei Zhong 梅重 et al., *Xihu tianxia jing* 西湖天下景 (West Lake: view of the world) (Hangzhou: Zhejiang sheying chubanshe, 1997), p. 86; Yu Pingbo, *Yu Pingbo sanwen zalun bian*, p. 116; and A. C. Moule, "The Lei Feng T'a," *Journal of the Royal Asiatic Society of Great Britain and Ireland* 1925: 287.

76. Shen Fengren, *Xihu gujin tan* (West Lake: past and present) (Shanghai: Dadong shuju, 1948), p. 3.

77. Yu Pingbo, *Yu Pingbo sanwen zalun bian*, pp. 121–22.

78. Wang Guowei 王國維, "Xiande kanben *Baoqieyin tuoluoni jing* ba" 顯德刊本寶篋印陀羅尼經 (Postscript to the *Baoqieyin Dharani sutra*), in idem, *Guantang jilin* 觀堂集林 (Shanghai: Shanghai shudian, 1992), 21.22.

79. Lou Xu 樓虛, "Song to the tune of Yu the Beauty," colophon to his painting *The Leifeng Pagoda*; cited in Pan Chenqing 潘臣青, *Xihu huaxun* 西湖畫尋 (In search of paintings of West Lake) (Hangzhou: Zhejiang renmin chubanshe, 1996), p. 149.

80. Zhou Zuoren 周作人, "Guanyu chongxiu Congtai de shi" 關於重修叢臺的事 (On rebuilding the Cong Terrace) (1922), in idem, *Tanhuji* 談虎集 (Speaking of tigers: essays) (Shanghai: Beixin shuju, 1928), 2: 463–66.

81. Guy Alitto, *The Last Confucian: Liang Shu-ming and the Chinese Dilemma of Modernity* (Berkeley: University of California Press, 1979), p. 83; Jonathan D. Spence, *The Gate of Heavenly Peace: The Chinese and Their Revolution, 1895–1980*, p. 208. Italics added.

82. See Spence, *Gate of Heavenly Peace*, p. 276.

83. Rose Macaulay, *Pleasure of Ruins* (London: Thames & Hudson, 1984), p. 100.

84. Xu Zhimo 徐志摩, *Xu Zhimo quanji* 徐志摩全集 (Complete works of Xu Zhimo) (Hong Kong: Shangwu yinshuguan, 1983), 1: 246.

85. Ibid., p. 169.

86. Spence, *Gate of Heavenly Peace*, p. 191.

87. Xu Zhimo, "Shoujiu yu 'wan'jiu" 守舊與"玩"舊 (Holding on to the old and "playing" with the old), in idem, *Xu Zhimo quanji*, 3: 2.

88. *Selected Works of Lu Hsun* (Beijing: Foreign Languages Press, 1957), 2: 82.

89. For a convincing demonstration of the impact of Freudian theory on Lu Xun with regard to Lu's perception of the Leifeng Pagoda, see Leo Ou-fan Lee, *Voices from the Iron House: A Study of Lu Xun* (Bloomington: Indiana University Press, 1987), pp. 119, 219n21.

90. Translation from *Selected Works of Lu Hsun*, 2: 82–84, with slight modifications.

91. On *locus amoenus*, see E. R. Curtius, *European Literature and the Latin Middle Ages*, trans. William R. Trask (New York: Pantheon Books, 1953), pp. 192–202; and Michael Leslie, "Gardens of Eloquence: Rhetoric, Landscape, and Literature in the English Renaissance," in *Toward a Definition of Topos: Approaches to Analogical Reasoning*, ed. Lynette Hunter (London: Macmillan, 1991), pp. 17–19.

92. Lu Xiaoman 陸小曼, ed., *Zhimo riji* 志摩日記 (Zhimo's diary) (Beijing: Shumu wenxian chubanshe, 1992), p. 24.

93. Xu Zhimo, *Xu Zhimo quanji*, 3: 65.

94. John Keats, *Complete Poems*, ed. Jack Stillinger (Cambridge, Mass.: Harvard University Press, 1982), p. 280.

95. Xu Zhimo, *Xu Zhimo quanji*, 3: 65.

96. Ibid., 1: 41–42.

97. Keats, *Complete Poems*, pp. 342–59.

98. Their similarity has spawned speculation about a distant and obscure common source, initially oral, not yet identified in Asiatic folklore. See G. R. S. Mead, *Apollonius of Tyana* (London, 1901), *passim*; Takeshiro Kurashi, "On the Metamorphosis of the Story of the White Snake," *Sino-Indian Studies*, 5 (1957): 138–46; and Charles I. Patterson, Jr., *The Daemonic in the Poetry of John Keats* (Urbana: University of Illinois Press, 1970), p. 185n3. Other scholars attribute the parallel to the workings of archetypes and assume the universal character underlying both narrative traditions; see, e.g., Henry Eckford, "The 'Lamia' of Keats," *Century Magazine*, n.s. 9 (Dec. 1885): 243–50; and E. G. Pettet, *On the Poetry of Keats* (Cambridge, Mass.: Harvard University Press, 1957), pp. 215, 229–31. For a most comprehensive study of both Asian and Western sources, see Ting, "The Holy and the Snake Woman," pp. 145–91.

99. For a discussion of Keats's *Lamia* in connection with the Chinese White Snake romance, see Qin Nü 秦女 and Ling Yun 凌雲, "Study of the Romance of White Snake" (in Chinese), *Zhong Fa daxue yuekan* 中法大學月刊 (*Revue de l'universite Franco-Chinoise*) 2, no. 3/4 (1932): 107–24.

100. Keats, *Complete Poems*, pp. 279–81.

101. The passage is a familiar one: "Forlorn! the very word is like a bell / To toll me back from thee to my sole self! / Adieu! the fancy cannot cheat so well / As she is fam'd to do, deceiving elf. / Adieu! adieu! thy plaintive anthem fades / Past the near meadows, over the still stream, / Upon the hill-side; and now 'tis buried deep / In the next valley-glades (Keats, *Complete Poems*, p. 281).

102. Fang Shaozhu 方紹耆, "Lüxing Hangxian Xihu ji" 旅行杭縣西湖記 (Journal written after a trip to West Lake of Hangxian), in *Xin youji huikan* 新遊記彙刊 (A collection of new travelogues) (Shanghai: Zhonghua shuju, 1920), 1.25.

103. Xu Zhimo, *Xu Zhimo quanji bubian* 徐志摩全集補編 (Complete works of Xu Zhimo: sequel) (Hong Kong: Shangwu yinshuguan, 1993), 4: 6.

104. Chen Congzhou 陳從周, *Xu Zhimo nianpu* 徐志摩年譜 (Xu Zhimo: a chronicle) (Shanghai: Shanghai shudian, 1981), p. 76. Lin Yutang here mistakenly attributed Keats's famous Nightingale to Shelley, who is better known for his skylark.

105. David E. Pollard, "Lu Xun's Zawen" in *Lu Xun and His Legacy*, ed. Leo Ou-fan Lee (Berkeley: University of California Press, 1985), p. 65. I adopt Pollard's suggestion of "analogue," which is particularly revealing about Lu Xun's discursive habits.

106. Lu Xun, "More Thoughts on the Collapse of Leifeng Pagoda," in *Selected Works of Lu Hsun*, p. 96.

107. Lu Xun, "From Hundred Plant Garden to Three Flavor Study," in *Selected Works*, 1: 387–93.

108. *Selected Works*, 1: 340.

109. *LXQJ*, 3: 49; trans. *Selected Works*, 2: 143–44.

110. *LXQJ*, 2: 199–200; trans. *Selected Works*, 1: 343–44.

111. *LXQJ*, 2: 202–3.

112. *LXQJ*, 2: 129; trans. *Selected Works*, 1:260

113. Zhou Zuoren, "On the Miracle Play of Mulian," in *Tanlongji* 談龍記 (Speaking of dragons: essays) (Shanghai: 1927), 140; Tsi-an Hsia, "Aspects of the Power of Darkness in Lu Hsün," in idem, *The Gate of Darkness: Studies on the Leftist Literary Movement in China* (Seattle: University of Washington Press, 1968), pp. 156–57.

114. Lu Xun, *Selected Works*, 1: 435.

115. Ibid., pp. 437–38

116. Lu Xun, "Village Opera," in William A. Lyell, trans., *Diary of a Madman and Other Stories* (Honolulu: University of Hawaii Press, 1990), pp. 210–12.

117. Feng Zhi, *Lu Xun huiyi lu* (Memoir of Lu Xun) (Shanghai: Wenyi chubanshe, 1978), 1: 84.

118. Lu Xun 魯迅, *Lu Xun quanji* 魯迅全集 (Complete works of Lu Xun) (Shanghai: Renmin wenxue chubanshe, 1973), 13: 129.

119. *LXQJ*, 10: 231–35.

120. Lu Xun was not the only translator of Kuriyagawa's *Symbolism of Depression*. Feng Zikai's translation appeared about the same time as Lu's, in March 1925. See

Feng Zikai 豐子愷, trans. *Kumen de xiangzheng* 苦悶的象征 (Symbolism of depression) (Shanghai: Shangwu yinshuguan, 1925).

121. Kuriyagawa Hakuson, "The Western Serpentine Sexuality," in Lü Jiao 綠蕉 and Liu Dajie [劉]大杰, trans., *Zouxiang shizi jietou* 走向十字街頭 (Walking toward the crossroads) (Shanghai: Qizhi shuju, 1928).

122. The translation was finished on Feb. 18, 1925.

123. *The Women's Weekly*, supplement of *Jingbao*, no. 21, May 6, 1925.

124. Tai Jingnong 臺靜農, *Jiantazhe* 建塔者 (Pagoda builder), 1st ed. 1928 (Beijing: Renmin wenxue chubanshe, 1984), pp. 121–25.

Works Cited

A Ying 阿英. *Leifengta chuanqi xulu* 雷峰塔傳奇敘錄 (Introduction to the *Romance of the Leifeng Pagoda*). Shanghai: Zhonghua shuju, 1960.

Alitto, Guy. *The Last Confucian: Liang Shu-ming and the Chinese Dilemma of Modernity.* Berkeley: University of California Press, 1979.

Barnhart, Richard. "Shining Rivers: *Eight Views of the Hsiao Hsiang* in Sung Painting." In *Proceedings of the International Colloquium on Chinese Art History.* Taibei: National Palace Museum, 1992, 1: 45–95.

Chang, H. C. *Chinese Literature: Popular Fiction and Drama.* Edinburgh: Edinburgh University Press, 1973.

Chen Congzhou 陳從周. *Xu Zhimo nianpu* 徐志摩年譜 (Xu Zhimo: a chronicle). Shanghai: Shanghai shudian, 1981.

Chen Xingzhen 陳杏珍. "Leifengta de mingcheng ji qita" 雷峰塔的名稱及其他 (The name of the Thunder Peak Pagoda and other issues). *Wenwu tiandi*, no. 6 (1977): 40–44.

Chūgoku no yōfūga ten: Minmatsu kara Shin jidai no kaiga, hanga, sashiebon (Exhibition of the Western-influenced style in Chinese painting, prints, and illustrated books from Ming to Qing dynasties). Tokyo: Machida shiritsu kokusai hanga bijutsukan, 1995.

Clark, Kenneth. *The Gothic Revival: An Essay in the History of Taste.* New York: Harper and Row, 1962.

Cranmer-Byng, J. L., ed. *An Embassy to China: Being the journal kept by Lord Macartney during his embassy to the Emperor Ch'ien-lung, 1793–1794.* Hamden, Conn.: Archon Books, 1963.

Curtius, E. R. *European Literature and the Latin Middle Ages.* Trans. William R. Trask. New York: Pantheon Books, 1953.

Eckford, Henry. "The 'Lamia' of Keats." *Century Magazine*, n.s. 9 (Dec. 1885): 243–50.

Edgren, Sören. "The Printed Dhāranī-sūtra of A.D. 956." *Museum of Far Eastern Antiquities (Östasiatiska Museet)*, no. 44 (1972): 141–46.

Fang Chengpei 方成培. "Preface to *The Leifeng Pagoda*." In *Zhongguo gudian xiqu xuba huibian* 中國古典戲曲序跋彙編 (Collection of prologues and postscripts to traditional Chinese drama), ed. Cai Yi 蔡毅, 3: 1941. Ji'nan: Qilu shushe, 1989.

Fang Shaozhu 方紹焘. "Lüxing Hangxian Xihu ji" 旅行杭縣西湖記 (Journal written after a trip to West Lake of Hangxian). In *Xin youji huikan* 新遊記匯刊 (A collection of new travelogues). Shanghai: Zhonghua shuju, 1920, 1.25.

Feng Menglong 馮夢龍, comp. *Jingshi tongyan* 警世通言. Beijing: Renmin wenxue chubanshe, 1984.

Feng Zhi 馮至. *Lu Xun huiyi lu* 魯迅回憶錄 (Memoir of Lu Xun). Shanghai: Wenyi chubanshe, 1978.

Fung Yu-lan. *A History of Chinese Philosophy*. Trans. Derk Bodde. 2 vols. Princeton: Princeton University Press, 1953.

Guo Shaoyu 郭紹虞 et al., eds. *Zhongguo lidai wenlun xuan* 中國歷代文論選 (Selected Chinese literary criticism of successive dynasties). Shanghai: Guji chubanshe, 1980.

Hanan, Patrick. "The Early Chinese Short Story: A Critical Theory in Outline." *Harvard Journal of Asiatic Studies* 27 (1967): 168–207.

Ho, Waikam, ed. *Century of Tung Ch'i-ch'ang*. Seattle: Nelson-Atkins Museum of Art and University of Washington Press, 1992.

Hong Pian 洪楩, ed. *Qingpingshantang huaben* 清平山堂話本. Nanjing: Jiangsu guji chubanshe, 1989.

Hsia, Tsi-an. *The Gate of Darkness: Studies on the Leftist Literary Movement in China.* Seattle: University of Washington Press, 1968.

Hsu Erh-hung. "The Evolution of the Legend of the White Serpent." 2 pts. *Tamkang Review* 4, no. 1 (1973): 109–27, no. 2: 121–56.

Hu Jing 胡敬, comp. *Chunyou Lin'anzhi jiyi* 淳祐臨安志輯逸 (Chunyou gazetteer of Lin'an, with scattered fragments reconstituted). WZC, vol. 24.

Huang Shang 黃裳. *Xixiangji yu Baishezhuan* 西廂記與白蛇傳 (*Romance of the West Chamber* and *Story of the White Snake*). Shanghai: Pingming chubanshe, 1954.

Huang Tubi 黃圖珌. *Leifengta* 雷峰塔. In *Baishezhuan ji* 白蛇傳集 (A collection of White Snake stories), ed. Fu Xihua 傅惜華, pp. 282–338. Shanghai: Shanghai chuban, 1955.

Ke Qingming [Ko Ching-Ming] 柯慶明. *Zhongguo wenxue de meigan* 中國文學的美感 (Aesthetic modes of Chinese literature). Taibei: Rye Field Publications, 2000.

Keats, John. *Complete Poems*. Ed. Jack Stillinger. Cambridge, Mass.: Harvard University Press, 1982.

Kurashi, Takeshiro. "On the Metamorphosis of the Story of the White Snake." *Sino-Indian Studies* 5 (1957): 138–46.

Kuriyagawa Hakuson. *Kumen de xiangzheng* 苦悶的象征 (Symbolism of depression). Trans. Feng Zikai 豐子愷. Shanghai: Shangwu yinshuguan, 1925.

———. *Zouxiang shizi jietou* 走向十字街頭 (Walking toward the crossroads). Trans. Lü Jiao 綠蕉 and Liu Dajie [劉]大杰. Shanghai: Qizhi shuju, 1928.

Lai, Whalen. "From Folklore to Literate Theater: Unpacking *Madame White Snake*." *Asian Folklore Studies*, 51 (1992): 51–66.

Leatherbarrow, David. *The Roots of Architectural Invention: Site, Enclosure, Materials.* New York: Cambridge University Press, 1993.

Lee, Huishu. "The Domain of Empress Yang (1162–1233): Art, Gender, and Politics at the Southern Song Court." Ph.D. diss., Yale University, 1994.

Lee, Leo Ou-fan. *Voices from the Iron House: A Study of Lu Xun*. Bloomington: Indiana University Press, 1987.

Leslie, Michael. "Gardens of Eloquence: Rhetoric, Landscape, and Literature in the English Renaissance." In *Toward a Definition of Topos: Approaches to Analogical Reasoning*, ed. Lynette Hunter. London: Macmillan, 1991.

Li Fang 李昉 et al., comps. *Taiping guangji* 太平廣記. Beijing: Zhonghua shuju, 1986.

Li Kaixian 李開先. *Li Kaixian ji* 李開先集 (Complete works of Li Kaixian). Shanghai: Zhonghua shuju, 1959.

Li Liufang 李流芳. *Tanyuanji* 檀園集 (Collection of the Sandalwood Garden). YWSQ.

Li Wei 李衛 et al., comps. *Xihu zhi* 西湖志 (Gazetteer of West Lake). 1735.

Liang Zhangju 梁章鉅. *Langji xutan* 浪蹟續談 (More travelogues). *Biji xiaoshuo daguan xubian* 筆記小說大觀續編 (Collection of *biji* fiction: a sequel), vol. 4. Taibei: Xinxing shuju, 1979.

Lu Ciyun 陸次雲. *Huru zaji* 湖濡雜記. In WZC.

Lu Jiansan 陸鑒三, ed. *Xihu bicong* 西湖筆叢 (Compendium of writings on West Lake). Hangzhou: Zhejiang renmin chubanshe, 1981.

Lu Xiaoman 陸小曼, ed. *Zhimo riji* 志摩日記 (Zhimo's diary). Beijing: Shumu wenxian chubanshe, 1992.

Lu Xun 魯迅. *Lu Xun quanji* 魯迅全集 (Complete works of Lu Xun). Shanghai: Renmin wenxue chubanshe, 1973.

———. *Selected Works of Lu Hsun*. Beijing: Foreign Languages Press, 1957.

Lyell, William A., trans. *Diary of a Madman and Other Stories*. Honolulu: University of Hawaii Press, 1990.

Macaulay, Rose. *Pleasure of Ruins*. London: Thames & Hudson, 1984.

Mead, G. R. S. *Apollonius of Tyana*. London, 1901.

Mei Zhong 梅重 et al. *Xihu tianxia jing* 西湖天下景 (West Lake: view of the world). Hangzhou: Zhejiang sheying chubanshe, 1997.

Mo Langzi 墨浪子. *Xihu jiahua* 西湖佳話. Ed. and annot. Shao Dacheng 邵大成. Hangzhou: Zhejiang wenyi chubanshe, 1985.

Moule, A. C. "The Lei Feng T'a." *Journal of the Royal Asiatic Society of Great Britain and Ireland* 1925: 287.

Murck, Alfreda. "Eight Views of the Hsiao Hsiang by Wang Hung." In *Images of the Mind: Selections from the Edward L. Elliot Family and John B. Eliot Collection of Chinese Calligraphy and Painting*, ed. Wen Fong et al. Princeton: Princeton University Press, 1984, pp. 213-35.

Nanjio, Bunyiu. *A Catalogue of the Chinese Translation of the Buddhist Tripitaka*. Oxford: Clarendon Press, 1883.

Ortiz, Valérie M. "The Poetic Structure of a Twelfth-Century Chinese Pictorial Dream Journey." *Art Bulletin* 76, no. 2 (1994): 257–78.

Owen, Stephen. *An Anthology of Chinese Literature: Beginning to 1911.* New York: Norton, 1996.

————. *Remembrances: The Experience of the Past in Classical Chinese Literature.* Cambridge, Mass.: Harvard University Press, 1986.

Pan Chenqing 潘臣青. *Xihu huaxun* 西湖畫尋 (In search of paintings of West Lake). Hangzhou: Zhejiang renmin chubanshe, 1996.

Patterson, Charles I., Jr. *The Daemonic in the Poetry of John Keats.* Urbana: University of Illinois Press, 1970.

Pettet, E. G. *On the Poetry of Keats.* Cambridge, Mass.: Harvard University Press, 1957.

Pollard, David E. "Lu Xun's Zawen." In *Lu Xun and His Legacy,* ed. Leo Ou-fan Lee. Berkeley: University of California Press, 1985.

Qian Yueyou 潛說有. *Xianchun Lin'an zhi* 咸淳臨安志 (Xianchun [period] gazetteer of Lin'an). YWSQ, vol. 490.

Qin Nü 秦女 and Ling Yun 凌雲. "Study of the Romance of White Snake" (in Chinese). *Zhong Fa daxue yuekan* 中法大學月刊 (*Revue de l'universite Franco-Chinoise*) 2, no. 3/4 (1932): 107–24.

Qisong, "You Nanpingshan ji" 游南屏山記 (Touring South Screen Mountain). In *Xihu youji xuan* 西湖遊記選, ed. and annot. Cao Wenqu 曹文趣 et al. Hangzhou: Zhejiang wenyi chubanshe, 1985, pp. 224–25.

Shen Fengren. *Xihu gujin tan* (West Lake: past and present). Shanghai: Dadong shuju, 1948.

Spence, Jonathan D. *The Gate of Heavenly Peace: The Chinese and Their Revolution, 1895–1980.* New York, Viking Press, 1981.

Strassberg, Richard E. *Inscribed Landscapes: Travel Writing from Imperial China.* Berkeley: University of California Press, 1994.

Tai Jingnong 臺靜農. *Jiantazhe* 建塔者 (Pagoda builder). Beijing: Renmin wenxue chubanshe, 1984 [1928].

Tian Rucheng 田汝成. *Xihu youlan zhi* 西湖遊覽志 (Notes on touring West Lake). Shanghai: Shanghai guji chubanshe, 1998.

Ting, Nai-tung. "The Holy and the Snake Woman: A Study of a Lamia Story in Asian and European Literature." *Fabula* 8 (1966): 145–91.

Tuan, Yi-Fu. *Space and Place: The Perspective of Experience.* Minneapolis: University of Minnesota Press, 1977.

Tuotuo 脫脫 (Toghto). *Songshi* 宋史 (Standard history of Song). Beijing: Zhonghua shuju, 1977.

von Glahn, Richard. *Fountain of Fortune: Money and Monetary Policy in China, 1000–1700.* Berkeley: University of California Press, 1996.

Wang Guowei 王國維. "Xiande kanben *Baoqieyin tuoluoni jing* ba" 顯德刊本寶篋印陀羅尼經 (Postscript to the *Baoqieyin Dharani sutra*). In idem, *Guantang jilin* 觀堂集林. Shanghai: Shanghai shudian, 1992, 21.22.

Wu Pei-yi. "The White Snake: The Evolution of a Myth in China." Ph.D. diss., Columbia University, 1969.

Wu Renchen 吳任臣. *Shiguo chunqiu* 吳越春秋 (Spring and autumn of the Ten Kingdoms). *YWSQ*, vol. 466.

Wu Zimu 吳自牧. *Mengliang lu* 夢粱錄. Hangzhou: Zhejiang renmin chubanshe, 1980.

Xu Fengji 徐逢吉. *Qingbo xiaozhi* 清波小志. Shanghai: Shanghai guji, 1999.

Xu Ke 徐珂, comp. *Qingbai leichao* 清稗類鈔. Beijing: Zhonghua shuju, 1984.

Xu Zhimo 徐志摩. *Xu Zhimo quanji* 徐志摩全集 (Complete works of Xu Zhimo). Hong Kong: Shangwu yinshuguan, 1983.

———. *Xu Zhimo quanji bubian* 徐志摩全集補編 (Complete works of Xu Zhimo: sequel). Hong Kong: Shangwu yinshuguan, 1993.

Yang Erzeng 楊爾曾. *Hainei qiguan* 海內奇觀. In *Zhongguo gudai banhua congkan erbian* 中國古代版畫叢刊二編 (Compendium of traditional Chinese prints, 2d series), 8: 1–677. Shanghai: Shanghai guji chubanshe, 1994.

Yen Yuan-shu. "Biography of the White Serpent: A Keatsian Interpretation." *Tamkang Review* 1, no. 2 (1970): 227–43.

Yu Chunxi 虞淳熙. *Qiantang xianzhi* 錢塘縣志 (Gazetteer of the Qiantang county). 1893.

Yu Pingbo 俞平伯. "Ji Xihu Leifenta faxian de tazhuan yu cangjing" 記西湖雷峰塔發現的塔磚與藏經 (Note on the tiles and hoarded sutras inside the Leifeng Pagoda). In *Yu Pingbo sanwen zawen lunbian* 俞平伯散文雜文論編 (Prose and miscellaneous notes by Yu Pingbo). Shanghai: Shanghai guji chubanshe, 1990, pp. 117–30.

Zeitlin, Judith T. *Historian of the Strange: Pu Songling and the Chinese Classical Tale.* Stanford: Stanford University Press, 1993.

Zhai Hao 翟灝 et al. *Hushan bianlan* 湖山便覽 (Easy guide to the lake and mountains). Shanghai: Shanghai guji, 1998.

Zhang Dai 張岱. *Xihu mengxun* 西湖夢尋 (A dream search for West Lake). In *Tao'an mengyi Xihu mengxun* 陶庵夢憶西湖夢尋. Shanghai: Shanghai guji chubanshe, 1982.

Zhang Xiumin 張秀民. "Wudai Wu-Yue guo de yinshua" 五代吳越國的印刷 (The printing technology of the Wu-Yue kingdom of the Five Dynasties). *Wenwu* 1978, no. 12: 74–76.

Zhao Jingshen 趙景深 et al. "The Relationship Between the Romance of the White Snake and Folklore" (in Chinese). In *Baishezhuan lunwenji* 白蛇傳論文集 (Papers on the tale of White Snake), ed. Zhongguo minjian wenyi yanjiuhui,

Zhejiang fenhui 中國民間文藝研究會浙江分會. Hangzhou: Zhejiang guji chubanshe, 1986, pp. 94-121.

Zhejiang tongzhi 浙江通志 (Zhejiang gazetteer). Shanghai: Shangwu yinshuguan, 1934.

Zhong Jingwen 鍾敬文. *Zhong Jingwen minjian wenxue lunji* 鍾敬文民間文學論集 (Essays on folkloric literature by Zhong Jingwen). Shanghai: Shanghai wenyi chubanshe, 1985.

Zhou Zuoren 周作人. "Guanyu chongxiu Congtai de shi" 關於重修叢臺的事 (On rebuilding the Cong Terrace). 1922. In idem, *Tanhuji* 談虎集 (Speaking of tigers: essays). Shanghai: Beixin shuju, 1928, 2: 463-66.

————. "On the Miracle Play of Mulian." In idem, *Tanlongji* 談龍記 (Speaking of dragons: essays). Shanghai, 1927.

A Folksong Immortal and Official Popular Culture in Twentieth-Century China

Lydia H. Liu

Five years after the new copyright laws and regulations protecting intellectual property rights went into effect in China in January 1991, a retroactive lawsuit over the violation of the copyrights in the film *Liu Sanjie* 劉三姐 was filed.[1] Released in 1961, this film had been adapted from a well-known musical drama written by a team of local writers from the Guangxi Zhuang Autonomous Region, which is dominated by the Zhuang 僮 nationality. In preparing the script, the writers had done extensive fieldwork among this minority group collecting folksongs, and on the basis of those materials, a local opera troupe produced a *caidiao* 彩調劇 opera and a musical drama called *Liu Sanjie* in 1959. The musical drama made a spectacular debut throughout the country after weeks of performance in Beijing and was copied and reproduced by professional and amateur theaters everywhere. The Changchun 長春 film studio promptly sent the scriptwriter Qiao Yu 喬羽—against whom the lawsuit would be brought decades later—to work with the local playwrights for the purpose of adapting the play to the screen. The film appeared in 1961 and became the number-one hit across the country.

I remember watching *Liu Sanjie* as a child. To me, the experience was primarily associated with the stage because my mother was cast as Liu Sanjie in one of the theatrical productions of the play. Night after night, I would sit in an out-of-the-way corner backstage watching her perform. To me and, I am sure, to the members of my generation, *Liu Sanjie* was the archetypal fairytale of the 1960s. Although its message of class struggle, which permeated all literary works at the time, would not have been lost on a mature audience, something about Liu Sanjie seemed to lift the work above official propaganda and made it appealing to both children and grownups. Few of us grew up watching or reading Snow White or Sleeping Beauty as part of our feminine upbringing. A maverick singer like Liu Sanjie who wielded the magic wand of mountain songs to protect her people against evil and oppression was absolutely enchanting. As popular entertainment, the story of Liu Sanjie entered our consciousness at an early age, not unlike the way the Disney production of *Fa Mulan* may have provided an alternative model of femininity to the children of the 1990s.

In recent years, a number of lawsuits have been filed against writers and publishers and, in theory—and one cannot afford to underestimate the power of theory in social practice—the copyright laws seem to offer an opportunity to those who take the laws seriously. It was in this context that the much publicized dispute over the copyrights to *Liu Sanjie* caught my attention and made me ponder the broad implications of this event for historical narrative, collective memory, and popular culture. In the course of working through these issues, my own childhood memories were being subjected to unexpected revisions and became entangled with the theoretical reflections. Soon, a question began to form in my mind: In what ways might the legacy of *Liu Sanjie* help illuminate the obscure truth of individual and collective memories to facilitate our understanding of the meaning of popular culture and folklore studies in the past and present? The desire to explore this and related questions at concrete levels led to the researching and writing of this chapter.

The notion of "official popular culture" may sound slightly paradoxical— How can literary and cultural productions be official and popular at the same time? Interestingly, the paradox provides us with a good starting point for re-examining some of the binaries prevalent in cultural studies, which often limit our ability to think beyond them.[2] For instance, one may well endorse folk production and spurn state-sponsored forms, but are the familiar concepts of "the people," "the folk" (*Volk*), "the masses," and "the popular" not the legacy of a global discursive history that has always served the purpose of state-building and reification of national identities? Should the legacy itself not be subjected to critical reflections? Harry Harootunian's study of folkism and its relationship to the rise of fascism in modern Japan sheds some interesting light on this problem. He shows that the work of Yanagita Kunio 柳田国男 and other Japanese folklorists looked to the figure of the folk and the unity and coherence of archaic community it embodied to pursue the colonial space of the Greater East Asia Co-Prosperity Sphere directed by imperial Japan. "Their privileging of the folk," Harootunian remarks, "could not help but supply fascism with its most powerful trope, an object of fantasy and political desire, and thus could not, itself, avoid complicity with the 'gathering' of fascism as it was increasingly articulated in promises to remove both unevenness and conflict and eliminate cultural abstraction in programs proclaiming the establishment of folkism."[3]

Yanagita Kunio, Takano Tatsuyuki 高野辰之, and the other Japanese folklorists studied by Harootunian were among those who inspired Lu Xun's brother Zhou Zuoren 周作人 and his fellow travelers to organize the first folksong campaign since the founding of the new republic. Moreover, through their translations of European folklore studies, the Japanese contributed the *Kanji* term *minzokugaku* 民俗學, or *minsuxue* in Mandarin, to the Chinese conceptualization of the discipline of modern folklore studies and, subsequently, to the ethnographic work surrounding the legendary folksong singer Liu Sanjie, who is the focus of this essay. The kinds of questions that these interesting circumstances bring to mind are How did modern folklore studies metamorphose as the discipline traveled from European colonial discourse through imperial Japanese expansionism to China? In what ways did a particular understanding of orality, ethnicity, and the folk legacy fashion the mainstream cultural imaginary of modern China? To what extent were modern folklore studies indebted to, or fundamentally different from, the long history of the official collection and imitation of folksongs in Chinese poetry that began with the *Book of Songs*?

Notwithstanding a professional commitment to oral literature and fieldwork, modern Chinese folklorists have not ruled out the use of extant *written records* from the dynastic era, a practice that raises interesting questions about the intersection of ethnography and textual scholarship in Chinese folklore studies.[4] The Appendix to this chapter highlights the main sources scholars used in the course of identifying and analyzing the Liu Sanjie legacy. The sources serve as a useful, preliminary context for our inquiry into the May Fourth rediscovery of Liu Sanjie and the subsequent ethnographical studies. In the first section, I re-examine the folklore movement spearheaded by Beijing University in 1918 that was continued by the faculty of the Zhong-

shan 中山 University in Guangzhou after 1927. The second section discusses the new folklore movement launched by Mao Zedong 毛澤東 in
1958, a nationwide campaign that drove teams of cultural workers into the
mountains and countryside to collect folksongs. This event soon led to the
making of the local *caidiao* opera and musical drama versions of *Liu Sanjie* in
1959 that I analyze and compare. In the final section, I take up the production of the film in 1961 and bring the discussion to a close by offering further
reflections on the post-Mao dispute over copyright issues.

The Ethnographic Turn: Liu Sanjie and Folklore Studies

The first generation of modern Chinese folklorists adopted the Japanese ne-
ologism *minsuxue* to name what they were attempting to do. The Japanese
had coined the term to translate "folklore studies" and were already conducting systematic ethnographic research in Japan and in its colonies when Zhou
Zuoren arrived there to study in 1906. Zhou developed a keen interest in the
work of the Japanese folklore scholars such as Yanagita Kunio and Takano
Tatsuyuki and, on his return to China, initiated a folksong campaign at Beijing University in 1918.[5] The folklorist Zhong Jingwen 鍾敬文 recalls that
the first appearance of the term *minsuxue* in China occurred in the inaugural
number of *Geyao zhoukan* 歌謠周刊 (Folksong weekly) in 1918.[6] The editor's
"Foreword" to this number placed the collecting and study of folksongs de-
finitively in the sphere of "folklore studies" and treated such studies as a central task in the rebuilding of a new Chinese national culture.[7] In 1927,
Zhongshan University (National Sun Yat-sen University) in Guangzhou
created a Folklore Studies Society and began to publish the seminal journal
Minsu 民俗 (Folklore weekly) and a folklore studies book series.[8] By this
time, *minsuxue* and its theory had become common subjects of discussion
and found their way into the mainstream discourse of the society.[9]

Gu Jiegang's 顧頡剛 well-known studies of Lady Meng Jiang 孟姜女
represented a high point in the early folksong movement.[10] Carried out at
about the same time as Gu's work, however, was the collecting of Liu Sanjie
legends that began with Liu Ceqi's 劉策奇 posting of a note entitled "Liu
Sanjie" in issue 82 of *Folksong Weekly*. The short text runs:

Legend has it that Liu Sanjie was a native of Chaomei 潮梅 in Guangdong. She had
a native talent for singing and traveled all over Guangxi and Guangdong, never finding her peer. Eventually she came to Liyufeng and encountered a farmer with whom
she matched songs. They sang continuously for three years and three months, until

Sanjie could carry on no longer. Her nervousness turned her suddenly into a stone statue. The farmer gazed at her, sighed, and departed in sorrow.[11]

After the demise of *Folksong Weekly* in June 1925, the new journal *Weekly Review*, of the Institute of National Learning at Peking University, published further research by Liu Ceqi on the legendary singer. This was followed by Zuo Tianxi's 左天錫 paper "The Story of Liu Sanmei and the *Folksongs of Guangxi*: A Sequel to the *Nine Songs* and the *Folksongs of Guangxi*" published in the *Monthly Journal of the Institute of National Learning*.[12] In 1928, *Folklore Weekly* brought out an interesting transcription by Yu Min 愚民 of an oral tale from a place called Wengyuan 翁源 that seemed to display marked difference from the written records or stories told in other locales.

Yu's tale conflates Liu Sanjie with the story of Luo Yin's 羅隱 ascension to the imperial throne (widespread among the Hakka). Luo Yin is said to have been a constellation in heaven. The Jade Emperor dispatched him to the human world to aid the afflicted and succor the people by acting as king and emperor. Luo Yin was able to speak and read as soon as he had issued from his mother's womb. But the Kitchen God misunderstood a remark made by his mother and reported it to the Jade Emperor. The Jade Emperor sent a servant to change one of Luo Yin's ribs, and because of this change, Luo Yin is not only unable to be emperor but cannot even pass the provincial examinations. He stays at home, disconsolate, and composes mountain songs, volume after volume, filling three large rooms. When he recites his songs to others, however, people dismiss them as too serious, too refined, and too obtuse. His sister urges him to write about women; Luo Yin agrees and begins to compose numerous books of mountain songs in praise of women and stores them all in his study. Then, Luo Yin becomes aware of Liu Sanmei's 劉三妹 (Sanjie) reputation, a woman of extraordinary talent who can recite verse and compose couplets and is especially adept at singing mountain songs. She can match songs with others for ten days or a fortnight without running out of verses and proudly asserts, "If anyone can match mountain songs with me and beat me, I'll marry him." And so Luo Yin brings three boatloads of his mountain songs to meet with her. As he draws close to Liu Sanmei's dwelling, he runs into a young woman doing laundry by the river. Luo Yin steps forward and says:

"Young lass! Do you know where Sanmei's dwelling might be found?"
"Why are you looking for her?"
"I want to match mountain songs with her and bring her home to be my wife."

"May I ask, sir, how many mountain songs you have?"

"Nine boatloads altogether; three boatloads at the provincial capital, three at Shaozhou 韶州, and three that I've already ferried to the riverbank."

"Then you'd better turn around; you're no match for Sanmei."

"What do you mean?"

"Get Lost," Sanmei burst into song.

"Washing clothes by the river is Liu Sanmei.
"Sing mountain songs with her, if you dare.
"Mountain songs come from the heart
"Who sends them over the water in a boat?"[13]

Luo Yin proves to be no match for Liu Sanmei and withdraws in defeat. In the recorded versions of these encounters, be it between Liu Sanmei and Luo Yin or some other "gentleman crammed with learning," these exchanges invariably celebrate the triumph of female peasant orality over literate male officialdom.[14]

Zhong Jingwen's *Collected Lectures on Folk Art* represents the first systematic treatment of the Liu Sanjie legend in what one might call the professional studies of Chinese folklore. Published in 1928, this short volume devotes an entire chapter to a detailed comparative analysis of the different versions of the folk legend known at the time. Table 12.1 makes the results clear at a glance. Zhong analyzed the similarities and discrepancies shown in the table and treated them as the quintessential features of oral literature: "The common folk are simpleminded and much given to embellishment; such is the reason for this development."[15] The legend of Liu Sanjie was a communal production of the people of Guangxi and Guangdong, and, accordingly, the question of whether she truly existed was unimportant.[16] To the scholar of folk literature, the more pressing question was to find out why and how the people created such stories. Zhong cites written evidence from Qu Dajun's 屈大均 *Guangdong xinyu* 廣東新語 (New account of Guangdong) to elaborate his point:

"[The people of] Yue are by custom skilled in singing, and whenever there is an auspicious occasion, they always sing in celebration. In ancient times, they would use song to compete for status; the most skilled would be rewarded and named *gebo* 歌伯 [song elder]. When seeking a bride and visiting the woman's family, the son-in-law would find a number of men of age and appearance similar to his own and of equal talent and intelligence, to serve as his 'groom companions.' The

Table 12.1

Versions of the Folk Legend of Liu Sanjie

Textual sources	Liu Sanjie's birthplace	Liu Sanjie's dates	Her opponent's name and birthplace	Place of competition	Place of worship
Guangdong xinyu 廣東新語	Xinxing, Guangdong 廣東新興	Tang dynasty (705–10)	Youth from Baihe 白鶴 village	Climbed a hill and sang	Flowery Stone Cliff at Yangchun 陽春
Yueshu 粵述	Xishan in Gui county, Guangxi 廣西貴縣 西山	Tang dynasty (705–10)	Zhang Weiwang 張偉望 from Baihe 白鶴 village, Langning 朗寧	White Stone Mountain	White Stone Mountain
Chibei outan 池北偶談	Shuinan village in Gui county, Guangxi 廣西貴縣 水南村	Tang dynasty (705–10)	Scholar from Baihe 白鶴 village, Yongzhou 邕州	Terrace in the Western Hills	
Dongxi xianzhi 峒谿纖志			Scholar from Baihe 白鶴 village	Seven Star Cliff in western Guangxi	Caves of the Miao and Yao peoples(?)
Liu Sanjie 劉三姐	Chaorei, Guangdong 廣東潮梅		Farmer	Standing Fish Peak in Liuzhou 柳州, Guangxi	Standing Fish Peak(?)

woman's family would block the gate with verses and songs; the son-in-law would *take a brush and write*, or have the groom-companions make drafts for him; some were refined and some unrefined, and in the end they would improvise, valuing the refined and elegant; [they continued] until the woman's family could not match them any longer, and then she would come forth."

The above shows that the custom among the people of Yue who love singing is an established fact, and we need not search through books or elsewhere for further evidence to prove this. We know that all human beings possess "a desire for knowledge." When children see beautiful things, they like to take them apart. Psychologists and educators attribute this behavior to an expression of desire for knowledge. The same can be said of natural savages whose behavior can be extremely naive—from their desire for knowledge originated all preposterous myths—especially the myth of genesis.[17] (Italics added)

Zhong observed that the Zhuang's communal love of singing was rarely found in more "civilized" areas. Since Guangxi and Guangdong lie in the distant south and removed from the influence of central dynastic culture, folk customs there retained the influence of primitive conditions. There is, however, a curious tension in Zhong's portrayal of the minority people as "oral" and "uncivilized," on the one hand, and the contradictory evidence he cited from the written sources, on the other, concerning the men's use of writing in courtship rituals. What is so primitive and uncivilized about the courtship customs described in *Guangdong xinyu?* By Zhong's own criteria of civilization, the folk customs are connected to the literati culture of the Han Chinese and the Zhuang's notion of courtship seems freer than that of the Han Chinese, or at least more in accord with the May Fourth notion of "free love." Why did Zhong eschew a reading that would have resonated with the contemporary fetishizing of "free love" and prefer instead to generalize about the ethnic group as "unrefined and uncivilized people"? According to Zhong, "The experiences and objects that served as the basis for their reasoning were infantile and crude; therefore, they created the fantastic tales based on customs familiar to them and steeped in their own absurdity."[18] Is this a typical case of Confucian condescension toward the illiterate and barbarians?

Stevan Harrell identifies a number of structural similarities in what he calls the successive civilizing projects of the past and present—namely, the Confucian project, the Christian project, and the Communist project—in his edited volume *Cultural Encounters on China's Ethnic Frontiers.* Each of the three projects is conceived of "as emanating from a particular center, as defining civilization (or the desired state) according to a certain set of philosophical principles, as separating groups according to some sort of criterion of 'ethnic identification,' and then giving these groups equal or unequal legal status, while scaling them according to one or another variable."[19] Harrell's threefold picture of the Confucian, the Christian, and the Communist projects is tantalizing but insufficient; an interrogation of the place that folklore studies and ethnology occupy in twentieth-century Chinese scholarship and popular entertainment may add a further dimension to it. For Confucianism, the Orientalist scholarship of missionaries such as Père Paul Vial or James R. Adam and Samuel Pollard, and the Communist theories and policies on ethnic minorities to *look similar* in retrospect, something more substantial than mentality or a vague set of "philosophical principles" must be at play.[20] In other words, a material linkage is required to explain how the Confucian or Christian project passed into the Communist project, if they did. What were the necessary steps of mediation during this time of rapid social changes?

It seems to me that the promotion of folklore studies and ethnography in early Republican China provides this link and can help illuminate our understanding of the modern concept of civilization and the reinvention of ethnicity and ethnic nationalism in China. What appears unchanging about the relations of domination between premodern and modern Chinese ethnic groups may turn out to be a less interesting question than what marks their paths of divergence. The characterization of the Zhuang people by the folklorist Zhong Jingwen, for example, calls for a genuinely historical explanation in place of Confucian condescension, for it reveals not only Zhong's mentality or personal bias but also a tension that has troubled folklore studies from the time the first architects of folksong studies at Beijing University began to imagine a new field of research and announced their goals in the "Foreword" to the inaugural issue of *Folksong Weekly*:

The aims of our society in collecting folksongs are twofold, academic and artistic. We believe that the study of folklore is very important in China today. Although we believe that no scholar has yet paid any serious attention to it, and little can be done by a limited number of devoted people, if each person could do his bit, we would at least be able to provide examples and arouse a certain interest. Folksongs are one of the major components of folklore. We intend to collect them for future research. This is our first objective. Because we believe that there is no such thing as obscenity or vulgarity in the academic field, it is not necessary for the contributors to weed out [such things] themselves. Send us what you have collected, and we shall select them on the basis of literary merit and compile them into a selected work on the voice of the folk. As Guido Vitale of Italy once said, "A new national poetry could perhaps spring up based on these rhythms and on the true feelings of the people." Therefore, this kind of work is not merely to bring to light things that have been hidden, but also to accelerate the speed of the development of a national poetry. This is our second objective.[21]

The creation of a new national poetry and an academic discipline traveled side by side, sometimes intersecting and sometimes diverging, with each constructing for itself a considerable set of mechanisms—mechanisms inextricably intertwined with the history of China's nation-building. Drafted with good intentions, this early document did not fully spell out what "the national" meant and where minorities figured in the big picture, but it did anticipate a new national literature and the coming of modern humanistic and social science disciplines in China. Within a matter of decades, the modern academic institution responsible for initiating folklore studies came to occupy the center stage of scientific rationality by virtue of its ability to define the "objective" relationship between the Han majority and the minority cultures in the name of the nation.[22] The figuring of the minorities in this manner, therefore, was less about the minorities and more about the subjectivity of the Han majority and its claims to power.[23] As Dru Gladney puts it convincingly, "The objectified portrayal of minorities as exoticized, and even eroticized, is essential to the construction of the Han Chinese majority, the very formulation of the Chinese 'nation' itself. In other words, the representation of the minorities in such colorful, romanticized fashion has more to do with constructing a majority discourse, than it does with the minorities themselves."[24] As if entering a Hegelian game of mutual recognition, the Han majority arrived at its self-consciousness by recognizing and being recognized by the other, each action mediated through the idea of the sovereign state.

One of the pivotal moments of self-consciousness in the scientific endeavors of folklore studies can be dated to March 1928 when the editors of the journal *Folk Literature and Art* of the Zhongshan University decided to adopt Gu Jiegang's proposal that the journal's name be changed to *Folklore Weekly*.[25] The change is indicative of a set of broader conceptual shifts from the folksong collecting of the previous decade to folklore studies; the emphasis was now on objectivity and social science approaches as a means of separating professional academic research from the arts or "applied folklore" (even if that division of labor was difficult to sustain in reality). The fledgling academic discipline accomplished its goal in part by stressing fieldwork and, no less important, by producing a full range of theoretical and technical apparatus justifying that work. It was at this time that the early Chinese folk-lorists began to take a serious interest in folklore theories and the proceedings of international folklore societies. Bronislaw Malinowski, Andrew Lang, Lucien Lévy-Bruhl, Franz Boas, and J. G. Frazer were among the first Western folklorists to be introduced to the Chinese audience. The book that found special favor among the Chinese folklorists was *The Handbook of Folklore*, written by the British folklorist Charlotte Sophia Burne, onetime president of the Folklore Society in London. Beginning with the first number of *Folklore Weekly*, the leading folklorist Yang Chengzhi 楊成志 translated and published the "Questionary" and "Terminology" sections of Burne's book in twelve continuous installments.[26] Burne's name also appeared in the early works of Zheng Zhenduo 鄭振鐸, Gu Jiegang, Zhong Jingwen, and Chen Xixiang 陳錫襄.

The theoretical position of *Folklore Weekly* was adumbrated by He Sijing 何思敬 in the inaugural essay published in issue no. 1 in 1928 and entitled "The Question of Folklore Studies." In it, the author singled out England for praise and emulation, "for just as France is the native home of sociology, so is England the home of folklore."[27] What inspirations did English folklore studies offer to its aspiring Chinese counterpart? Drawing on Burne's main line of argument, He Sijing stated that since the Industrial Revolution, the development of large-scale industry had led to the expansion of the metropolis and the enlargement of colonial territories. The extraordinarily rapid developments in these two spheres had produced discord in various areas—morality, belief, thought, emotion—between urbanites and nonurbanites in the home country and between the rulers and ruled in the colonies. Religions such as Christianity were no longer able to maintain their former authority. They were unable to reconcile the contradictions between city and country, between the old life and the new; nor had they proved capable of assimilating the thoughts of the natives of colonial areas and thus weakening their opposition. Folklore studies arose with the times, because understanding the thinking of the "vulgar," the country folk, the native inhabitants, and the uncivilized, grasping their psychology from their customs and legends, and assimilating this psychology in order to realize "political peace and stability, is a deeply felt administrative necessity." He Sijing continued: "The author of *The Handbook of Folklore*, 1894, Madame E. [*sic*] S. Burne, says that folklore studies cannot overestimate its contribution to the sum of human knowledge, yet one extremely useful result will come from studies of this sort; namely, that the governing nation can gain a more sort; namely, that the governing nation can gain a more effective means of controlling its subject peoples."[28] The English version of *The Handbook of Folklore* phrases this somewhat differently. In the introductory chapter, Burne remarked:

The conception of man's past history which has resulted from, and now directs, the study of folklore, has already made its impress on modern philosophical thought, and it would be difficult to over-estimate the additions to the sum of human knowledge which may be made in course of years by a continuance of the study on these lines. Meanwhile one very practical result should follow from it, namely, the improved treatment by governing nations of the subject-races under their sway. In the words of Sir Richard Temple, "We cannot understand the latter rightly unless we deeply study them, and it must be remembered that close acquaintance and a right understanding beget sympathy, and sympathy begets good government."[29]

He Sijing's desire to identify with the "governing nations" is palpable, but he neglected to consider where China stood on this map of colonial modernity. What was the subject-position of Chinese folklore studies in the Republican years? Who were the subject races as far as China was concerned?

Elizabeth Mary Wright's *Rustic Speech and Folk-Lore* (1913) proved to be helpful as He Sijing reflected on the peasants in "The Question of Folklore Studies," for the British folklorist was just as interested in the folk relics of her own culture as in the subject races of non-Western countries. He Sijing paraphrased Wright as follows: the secret for understanding the seemingly incomprehensible mentality of the rural people is to become thoroughly acquainted with their local dialect. "All of the country folk's inner secrets are connected with their traditional speech and rhythms. One has only to master the form of their speech; then the strings of their hearts will be in the palm of your hand."[30] Wright and the British folklorists regarded both the folk relics of the civilized world and the folkways of the colonies equally as raw materials for the study of human evolution.[31] Thus the subjects of comparative research in folklore studies came to be defined as the beliefs, customs, practices, stories, myths, legends, ballads, proverbs, riddles, nursery rhymes, children's songs, and so forth of uncivilized, semi-civilized, and uneducated peoples. Hermann Bausinger's study of German *Volkskunde* shows that the comparative and supranational scholarship in folklore studies that arose after its contact and confrontation with ethnology led to a generalized concept of *vulgus in populo* in the field, but the "idea of the nation" remained very much alive in the word *Volk*.[32] To the Chinese folklorist who was necessarily concerned with the idea of the nation, did the *Volk* of the civilized world unquestionably translate into minority peoples and the dialect groups within the Han Chinese?[33]

Indeed, what did all this mean in the larger picture of the social science research of the time? And how did folklore studies define its object of study and interject the criterion of objectivity into the requirements of scientific folklore collecting and presentation at the turn of the century? In a study of the American Folklore Society (founded in 1888) and the *Journal of American Folklore*, Regina Bendix examines the work of folklorist Otis Mason, who did not hesitate to draw a parallel between folklore specimens and the minerals or chemicals studied by the natural scientists. After comparing the folk "specimen" with the archaeologist's finds, the paleontologist's fossil, and the anatomist's rare animal, Mason concluded that the folk cabinet has a distinct advantage—namely, it is like the piles of enumerators' atlases in the Census Office, and the material is ever at hand to be considered.[34]

To what end? Mason's reference to the Census Office reminds us of Burne's concern with colonial rule and government considered above. The folklorist's aspirations to objectivity need not contradict the logic of governmentality in this specific historical framework, for objectivity and colonial governability together defined the scientific agendas of the modern empirical social science that came to maturity in the first decades of the twentieth century. The most successful and influential of the new social scientists was what has come to be called the "functionalist school" of anthropology in Britain, whose intellectual progenitor was the Polish émigré Bronislaw Malinowski.[35] Believing that African societies were too fragile, too fragmented, to accept rapid change, Malinowski saw the role of anthropology as that of instructing governments on how to make the best of these delicate social worlds and to coax them into the European-dominated future, without destroying them in the process. This he believed could be achieved only through understanding how their worlds operated and by working through native rules.[36]

In *Time and the Other: How Anthropology Makes Its Object*, cultural anthropologist Johannes Fabian argues that anthropology and folklore studies were erected on an ethnographic imagining of temporality that posits the "other" at the primitive end of the long march of history as opposed to the cultural superiority of the modern "us." In effecting temporal distancing from the other, anthropology has produced a "spatialization of time" that physically manifests itself in the trips anthropologists and folklorists undertake to engage in professional fieldwork outside their own society or community.[37] Since the objective situation of the other derives its meaning solely from its translatability or temporal convertibility, the rationale of doing fieldwork to study the other as the past of one's own humanity rules out the scholar's responsibility for attending to the present state of the other's material existence. That may explain the strange supposition that, after centuries of colonial experience and contact with the non-Western world and the global consequences of that contact, some observers still believe that the social structures of non-Western societies remain miraculously unchanged, as if the colonial encounter had never taken place.[38] The evolutionary spatialization of time is what establishes the cognitive basis of scholarly "objectivity" and gives cultural anthropology and folklore studies scientific credibility and authority in the eyes of the lay public. The collecting of black spirituals, to cite an example from Ronald Radano's study, enabled white Americans to extract the anonymous sounds of human transcendence from their real-life circumstances and thereby erase blackness in the name of preservation."[39] The possibility of what Fabian calls "co-evalness," or the likelihood of allowing the other to inhabit the same time and space as the anthropologist and enter into a real-life dialogue or disputation with their work, seems rather remote; to do so would contradict the logic of ethnographic research and threaten to abolish both the subjectivity and objectivity of the discipline. Indeed, scientific aspirations toward objectivity can hardly be separated out from the history of colonial rule and governmentality.[40]

Chinese folklorists seemed to have experienced a leap of faith as they went from translating and disseminating European theories of race and ethnicity to making China's minority groups *resemble*, by analogy, primitive tribes from "other parts of the world." But does this make sense? How can the relationship of colonial rulers and ruled be transposed onto a structure of domination between the Han majority and minority peoples when China itself was viewed as inferior and backward by the West? But that is precisely why the symbiosis of the structures of domination was deemed necessary. By turning their gaze on minorities, Han Chinese social scientists persuaded themselves that they could be the subject, not the object, of anthropology. Does this carry some echoes of centuries of ethnic tensions between the Han and the Manchus and other ethnic groups in the past? Yes, unmistakably.

Fig. 12.1 Tribal rituals
of mourning on a
Burmese island, an
illustration in *Folklore
Weekly*, no. 7 (1928).

But that is not the whole story. The reproduction of photographs in *Folklore Weekly* suggests that the Chinese folklorists had in mind a global picture rather than a narrow focus on minorities in China as they sought to emulate the British folklorists and reproduce some of their material. For example, pictures of native inhabitants and savages of the uncivilized "races" are printed inside the cover of issues 5 through 15/16. Apparently, the photographs were culled from European and American popular publications and reproduced without acknowledgment. The images are uniformly those of people of color; the absence of whites and Han Chinese (a dubious category of ethnicity to begin with) is notable. The photographs encompass the ethnic groups of India, Burma, Australia, New Zealand, the Philippines, the Melanesian Islands, northern Africa, southern Africa, Vietnam, Japan (tattooed figures), and Tibet.[41] Moreover, those pictures are placed side by side with the mountain songs that Chinese folklorists had collected from Guangxi and Guangdong, the ballads of Taiwanese aborigines, folksongs from Chaozhou 潮州, and so forth (Fig. 12.1–2).

In an essay on his recent fieldwork on the contemporary Han representation of Muslim Chinese, Dru Gladney makes a striking observation about

Fig. 12.2 Aborigines from central Australia and their totem figures, an illustration in *Folklore Weekly*, no. 7 (1928).

the meaning of similar juxtapositions today. A published poster from contemporary China bearing the caption "I Love the Great Wall" features men in Turkic and Hui Islamic hats, a veiled woman, and an African or black man. Gladney points out that the black man is shown on the wall with the Chinese minorities to demonstrate their ethnic solidarity and "to emphasize their corporate 'primitivity' (i.e., promoting the idea that China's minorities are like 'primitive' Africans), which is key to understanding the position of the minorities in the Marxist-Maoist evolutionary scheme."[42] Of course, as we have seen, such practice long predates the Marxist-Mao regime. It would be more accurate to say that the mimicking of colonial visuality marked the inauguration of Chinese folklore studies in the early twentieth century and has been perpetuated by the Marxist-Maoist evolutionary view of history and culture.

The cosmopolitan ambitions of *Folklore Weekly* suggest that the Chinese folklorists manufactured a subject-position for (educated) Han Chinese inasmuch as they are virtually *absent* from the space of representation as "natives." From the viewpoint of Chinese anthropology, the "natives" were not the Han majority but the primitive other and remnants of civilization.[43] The mission of the enlightened was thus to come to know the *Volk*, to educate them, and to liberate them from the burdens of the past. This was unequivocally spelled out by the folklorist and historian Gu Jiegang in a lecture he delivered to the students of Lingnan 嶺南 University in 1928:

The May Fourth movement of eight years ago is universally referred to as the New Culture movement. Yet it was the work of only a few instructors and students, namely the former literati class; and the movement can only be superficial. To this day, the New Culture movement has not really succeeded, and their outcry has long since died out. Our mission is to keep up the outcry and liberate the culture of the masses from the culture of the ancient sages. The liberation of the culture of the masses will lead to the realization of their own identity and give birth to a demand for the appreciation of their culture. Through a process of self-conscious reform, we will advance what was created unconsciously in the past and press ahead toward the objectives of the new life.[44]

Gu Jiegang may well have been speaking on behalf of those intellectuals who were genuinely concerned with the wellbeing of national culture, the vernacular language, and folk arts. Thanks to their work, the concepts of the "folk," the "masses," and the "popular culture" have continued to carry the distinct imprint of early folklore studies, even though they have long been appropriated by the mainstream political discourse in China.[45] The concepts themselves may be slippery, but the slippage is symptomatic of an evolving relationship among folklore scholarship, cultural production, and social movements in the Republican era. In its fluidity, "folk" sometimes refers to minority peoples and sometimes to the primitive "remnants" of the Han civilization or simply the Chinese peasantry. At no time was the "folk" simply conflated with the rural. On the contrary, the "folk" resided very much at the heart of the mass urban culture of Republican China that would later become the distinguishing feature of official popular culture I am going to analyze below.

The close ties between folklore research and social movements for enlightening the masses are of course embedded in the historical circumstances of that era. By participating in the education and liberation of the masses, scholars in the humanities and social sciences simultaneously fashioned their subjectivity as modern intellectuals. However, folklore studies could not monopolize the ideas of the "folk," the "masses," and "popular culture"; these also became the rallying cries of the revolutionary struggle and social reform.[46] The ironic twist in this power dynamic is that when the ruling party decided to act as the spokesperson for the masses and the nation, the intellectuals were cast aside and rejected as inauthentic voices. In that sense, folklore studies provide an important site for examining the changing relationship between the state, the Communist party, the masses, and the modern intelligentsia.

Chang-tai Hung tries to tackle some of these issues in his study of Chinese folklore studies by identifying a historical lineage between what he calls "folk populism" and the Maoist populism of the 1940s and after. In *Going to the People*, Hung shows that "the work initiated by folklorists and the momentum they generated no doubt made the Communist task much easier," but then a "direct link between the minority-culture study initiated by the folk-literature movement in the late 1920s and subsequent Communist interest in minorities is difficult to establish."[47] The continuous metamorphoses of Liu Sanjie in the subsequent decades not only points precisely to the existence of that link but also raises intriguing issues about the role of the media and mass audience in the birth of an official popular culture in the Mainland.

Liu Sanjie and Official Popular Culture

In *Yellow Music*, Andrew Jones examines the birth of the cultural industry in Shanghai and the ways in which the hybrid forms of popular music, be it "yellow (pornographic) music" or left-wing mass music, emerged. Jones draws our attention to the fact that these hybrids were "forged of the discursive, operational, and commercial interaction of new media technologies such as wireless broadcasting, sound cinema, and mass-circulation magazines in urban China." After jazzy "yellow music" was banned in Mainland China in the 1950s, "the producers and sing-song girls who had dominated the field (including Pathe-EMI Records and its stable of starlets) were banished to Taiwan and the British Crown Colony of Hong Kong. Throughout the 1950s and 1960s, Hong Kong became a sort of Shanghai manque—the epicenter of modern song and the Mandarin musical cinema."[48] On the Mainland itself, the state-owned technologies of wireless broadcasting, sound cinema, and mass-circulation magazines began to produce a different species of popular entertainment for the home audience.

The literary policies of the Chinese Communist Party exalted the forms of *minjian wenyi* 民間文藝 (folk literature and art) over and above other forms of popular entertainment, a practice that dated to Mao's Yan'an 延安

talks but was profoundly indebted to the work of the first generation of Chinese folklorists. The phenomenon of "official popular culture," however, did not come into its own until folk literature and arts were presented in mass-mediated forms. This aspect of popular entertainment seemed to translate particularly well across the actual and ideological borders. When the film *Liu Sanjie* was first shown in Hong Kong in the early 1960s, for example, the audience response was no less enthusiastic than in the Mainland; the soundtrack could be heard on the streets of Hong Kong for many months. Wai-Fong Loh informs us that the ultimate compliment came from the right-wing film producers of Hong Kong and Taiwan, who "imitated the music and songs of *Liu Sanjie* to produce a rightist version called *Shan'ge lian* 山歌戀 (Folksong love story). This movie was also a financial success and won a prize in Taipei."[49] That the film *Liu Sanjie* and its music should generate comparable enthusiasm across the divide of Cold War ideology is truly remarkable. Was it because the combination of folk materials and mass media gave rise to unintended meanings capable of rendering the official ideology irrelevant? What does it mean for a work like *Liu Sanjie* to become a hit in and outside of the Mainland?[50]

Mainland critic Li Tuo 李陀 sees "popular literature" as the basis for grasping the material condition of state ideology as well as for understanding the nature of literature produced in the post-Mao era. The popular *shanghen wenxue* 傷痕文學 (wounded literature) that mushroomed in the late 1970s, for example, should be viewed not, as is often claimed, as a radical departure from socialist realism but as a sentimental turn in (official) popular literature that sought to recenter the subjectivity of the intellectual elite as an important source of legitimacy for the reform government. In his seminal essay entitled "1985," Li Tuo reminds us of the popular *yangge* 秧歌 movement in Yan'an and its centrality in the subsequent unfolding of popular literary and artistic forms (including poetry, fiction, and theater) in the People's Republic. No matter how innovative or clichéd these works may appear to the critic, he argues, "the criteria for judging these works must register the fact that these works properly belong to the realm of the *popular* and should be evaluated and judged on that ground."[51] The material ground for Mao's popular literature was none other than the "folk" forms gathered and disseminated by the scholars of folklore studies in the Republican period. The work of Yan Yangchu 晏陽初, Li Jinghan 李景漢, and Zhang Shiwen 張世文 on the folksongs and *yangge* dances of Ding county 定縣 comes to mind, and, along with the scholarship of Gu Jiegang, Zhong Jingwen, and the others, these folk forms exerted a direct impact on the formation of Mao's concept of popular arts and literature in the 1940s.[52]

The collecting of folksongs among the Zhuang people of Guangxi got an official start during the "New Folksong movement" launched by Mao in 1958.[53] According to a somewhat inflated figure, the scriptwriting committee of the city of Liuzhou 柳州 gathered 20,000 folksongs, 200 volumes of folk-tales, several dozen musical tunes, and a great number of legends and stories about Liu Sanjie.[54] In the process of revising and rehearsing the script, the Liuzhou *caidiao* opera troupe also interviewed nearly a hundred folk singers. The Nanning Prefectural Cultural Troupe responsible for composing the musical score collected folk musical patterns from the various parts of Guangxi (the draft of the Nanning musical drama script is said to run to 300,000 characters). After numerous revisions, the third draft of the play, also known as the Third Liuzhou Draft, was adopted and printed in the September 1959 issue of *Juben* 劇本 (Drama script). It was entitled *Liu Sanjie in Caidiao.*

Publication of the script was greeted with enthusiasm, and drama troupes began to perform the play across the autonomous region. By the reckoning of those involved, 1,209 different organizations and nearly 58,000 profession-als and amateurs participated in stage productions of *Liu Sanjie.* In April 1960, the Communist party in Guangxi staged a mass performance of *Liu Sanjie* in the city of Nanning.[55] On the basis of these performances, the *caidiao* opera script underwent further revisions to become the musical drama script, which appeared in the August–September 1960 issue of *Juben*. In April 1961, China Theater Publishing House issued the first edition in book form, the first of many reprints.[56]

The definitive script of the musical drama *Liu Sanjie* consists of seven acts and an epilogue (or the eighth act). Beginning with the first act in which Liu Sanjie arrives to visit her relatives, the plot revolves around the conflicts be-tween the Zhuang people and the Han landlord Mo Hairen 莫海仁 (the characters are homophones for "Don't harm people"). Mo Hairen wishes to lay claim to the mountainside tea plantations owned in common by the mi-nority people. He closes off the mountain and forbids entry to the forest. Liu Sanjie, singing mountain songs, leads her kinfolk and neighbors to resist the landlord. Mo devises a bird-catching plot and sends a matchmaker to

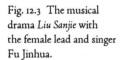

Fig. 12.3 The musical
drama *Liu Sanjie* with
the female lead and singer
Fu Jinhua.

seek Liu Sanjie's hand, meaning to take her as a concubine (a Han custom).
Sanjie responds with a counter-plot and proposes that "our Zhuang custom
is to have a singing contest before a marriage."[57] Master Mo promptly agrees
and invites three scholars, Tao, Li, and Luo, to match songs in his behalf. In
the climactic scene of "Song Matching," the three scholars bring boxloads of
songbooks but are unable to outwit Liu Sanjie. They leave in defeat. After
failing in the song competition, Master Mo asks the magistrate to issue a decree forbidding singing among the Zhuang people.[58] The magistrate proclaims that "the folk in this land disobey the ruler and sing subversive songs
to incite the people; so for the public good, I, the magistrate, forbid all singing henceforward." Sanjie responds by singing: "Big stars in heaven rule over
lesser stars, lions on earth rule over unicorns; the emperor rules over high officials, but who dares to rule over the singer of songs?"[59] Protected by her
community, Liu Sanjie successfully escapes the government pursuers; she
and Xiao Niu 小牛 (the peasant youth with whom she has plighted her
troth) bid farewell to their relatives and neighbors and set out to spread their
songs through the neighboring countryside (Fig. 12. 3–5).

Fig. 12.4 Young women
of the Zhuang nationality
pick tea leaves in Scene 2
of the musical drama *Liu
Sanjie.*

The early editions of the script handled the concluding scene in a number
of different ways. The present ending is drawn from the Yulin 玉林 and
Nanning 南寧 versions. In the original Liuzhou *caidiao* opera libretto, Liu
Sanjie "leaps from a cliff and becomes an immortal." But in the process of revision, the tragic ending was rejected "first, because the audiences generally
do not want Liu Sanjie to die, and secondly, in order to accord with the legend of Liu Sanjie spreading songs throughout the land."[60] Another, unstated
reason is that the aesthetics of the party would not accommodate an un-
happy ending.

In July 1960, the Guanxi Folk Musical Drama Troupe was invited to Beijing and spent two months giving performances to the public and performing for the leaders of the Communist party. After watching the drama, Mao
Zedong reportedly remarked: "*Liu Sanjie* opposes oppression. It is a revolutionary play."[61] Ye Jianying 葉劍英 wrote a poem praising Liu Sanjie's re-
bellious spirit against landlords.[62] The political interpretations given by the
heads of the nation did not, however, represent the views of the dramatists,
poets, critics, and audience of the time, who tended to view the work differently.[63] Playwright Ouyang Yuqian 歐陽予倩, for instance, published a review in which he commented: "The legend of Liu Sanjie has been around for
over a thousand years; likewise, mountain songs have enjoyed a long history.
In what sense do we regard them as novelties? The reason that the perfor-

mance of *Liu Sanjie* can move the hearts of today's audience is that it has carried on the tradition but weeded through the old to bring forth something new." Ouyang Yuqian criticized the scriptwriters' tampering with the folksongs and *caidiao* opera: "When written out, good mountain songs and *caidiao* make beautiful poems, but these songs are originally intended for singing, not for reading. Guanxi mountain songs and *caidiao* should be sung in accord with their original form; the people of Guangxi will then hear them with the warmth of recognition, and people from other provinces will hear them and feel something fresh and new."[64]

The musical drama *Liu Sanjie* took its place alongside *Ashima* 阿詩瑪 and *Dongfang hong* 東方紅 (The East is red) or popular musical drama that made minority songs and dances extremely popular in mainland theatre and film in the 1950s and 1960s. Some critics saw *Liu Sanjie* as the second milestone in the development of the new Chinese musical drama after *Baimao nü* 白毛女 (The white-haired girl).[65] But how are we to judge the popularity of such works? In a study of the operatic, cinematic, and balletic adaptations of *White-Haired Girl*, Meng Yue raises some good questions in this regard: Did the work owe its popularity to the dubious "folk form" or a "hybrid of indigenous and foreign forms"? If the state's ideological control was not complete, what kinds of dialogue, negotiation, or compromise occurred among

Fig. 12.5 Liu Sanjie matches songs with three scholars in Scene 5 of the musical drama *Liu Sanjie*.

the playwrights, filmmakers, choreographers, the audience, and the state in the reception of revolutionary works?[66] The making of *Liu Sanjie* provides us with further opportunity to examine the mechanisms of official popular culture and the entertainment sector of the society.

A distinguishing character of the musical drama *Liu Sanjie* is the Zhuang folksong. However, the use of orchestral accompaniment, vocal music, settings, props, and stage design vastly oversteps the artistic milieu and technical demands of folk performance. Like popular musicals in the West, the play relies for its dramatic effect on elaborate lighting, sets, and a professional stage furnished with double curtains. The tea-picking songs, "embroidered ball" songs, duets, choruses, and other scenes require a large performance space. As for the original folksongs of the Zhuang people, most of them were revised; others were invented. Take the Old Fisherman's song to Xiao Niu:

> The vine looks for a tree to entwine—
> How can a tree look for a vine?
> If the green vines do not cling to the tree,
> The spring will pass by in vain.[67]

This *carpe diem* verse was taken from the "Song of the Vine and the Tree" transcribed centuries earlier by the literati poet Wang Shizhen 王士禎 (see Appendix), but considerably altered for the worse. There are, in addition, a number of pieces that are part folksong and part fabrication. For instance, the lines "He washes his hands in a pond and the fish die; he walks the verdant hills and the trees wither" appeared in the original song as a satire against those who are ungrateful and unrighteous, vicious and deceitful, but the scriptwriters used them to berate the rich in a couple of jumbled lines:

> Don't boast of the landlord's wealth;
> His heart is more venomous than any snake;
> He washes his hands in a pond and the fish die;
> He walks the verdant hills and the trees wither.[68]

When the drama troupes from Liuzhou, Nanning, and elsewhere collected folksongs, they also gathered folksong melodies. On the basis of these melodies and the songs of *caidiao* opera, the composers adapted and created 62 tunes, effecting a synthesis of Guangxi *caidiao* operatic tunes with folk melodies and dance music. For orchestral accompaniment, native and Western notation forms were combined; the bass viol and the drums and gongs of

Peking and regional opera were employed. Although this approach may appear eclectic to the point of haphazardness, the composers did introduce a functional distinction between singing "songs" and singing "opera" in the work. In scenes such as "Song Matching" or "Banning Songs" that required a great number of songs, they employed the mountain songs of Liuzhou as well as folksongs from Nanning and other areas. In contrast, the music of Guangxi *caidiao* opera was used in the areas of narration, dialogue, and character portrayal.[69] The mixing of folk melodies, traditional opera, and modern drama undoubtedly weakened the authentic character of folk mountain songs, but it helped popularize the musical drama *Liu Sanjie* among different dialect groups and made it accessible across the vast areas of the mainland (Fig. 12.6). As Paul Clark has pointed out, the homogenization of the local and ethnic in the service of the nation characterizes all official appropriations of non-Han literary and artistic works of the period.[70] The costumes in *Liu Sanjie*, for example, are simply generic premodern Chinese costumes with little connection to what might be called the Zhuang's ethnic clothing.

Zheng Tianjian 鄭天健, one of the original scriptwriters, wrote a detailed account of how the *caidiao* opera version of *Liu Sanjie* was made and how the drama troupe set about adapting the Zhuang folk legends for modern theatre. Interestingly, since the scriptwriters classified the original materials of the folk legends in accord with the theory of class struggle, the issue of ethnicity did not figure prominently in the process.

There are numerous variations on the legends, accounts, oral tales, and relics relating to "Liu Sanjie." In some records, Liu Sanjie is portrayed as a girl prodigy, reading poetry at age seven and mastering the histories at age twelve, with no connection whatsoever with the working people. They praise "Sanjie, fabled in romantic tales, whose glamour shall linger for ten thousand generations." . . . This makes one look upon Liu Sanjie as no more than an extraordinary songwriter, a Song Immortal skilled at expressing romantic feelings. They say that Liu Sanjie matched songs with the scholar Bai He; they sang together for seven days and seven nights, joining both their voices and their hearts, until they became bound to one another as immortal lovers and ascended to heaven. Some legends use hackneyed phrases to describe Liu Sanjie as a female idler who never engaged in labor. Thus, "Singing songs one must sport and play; singing songs one sits upon the carp-fish crag." . . . All such accounts are obviously attempts by the ruling class of the past to slander and dishonor the image of the immortal, who came from among the people and was widely respected by the masses.[71]

Fig. 12.6 Lyrics and musical score from scene 2 of the musical drama of *Liu Sanjie*.

The rich ambiguities and polyvalence of the folk legends are thus reduced to a story of class struggle. If Liu Sanjie is a member of the laboring class, one must not allow her to be well versed in classical poetry or the histories, as some of the sources clearly suggest. Decisions as to which of the conflicting sources should be followed were made easier by the need to give Liu Sanjie a working-class background, which necessarily suppressed alternative interpretations. Zheng justified the selections in these terms:

Oral legends say that the Liu family had been peasants for generations. Liu Sanjie was originally an able worker, daughter of a poor peasant family, "taking her rest beneath a roof of thatch," "planting nine *tongs* of seedlings in the fields by the southern hills," "climbing the hills to chop firewood when there was no rice to cook in the pot." Some of her mountain songs extolled labor; others mocked the scholars or exposed the rich. . . . The oral accounts from the peasants of various regions and the handwritten manuscripts they have contributed all tell how Liu Sanjie solved difficulties for the working people, etc. There is also a story that Liu Sanjie was killed and that the murderer was none other than her own elder brother, Liu Er 劉二, because her brother resented her stirring up unnecessary trouble. Although this lurid and alarmist tale deceived more than a few people, the laboring people did not completely believe these lies. After more than a thousand years there were still some peasants who steadfastly remembered how Liu Sanjie was oppressed by the rich and wandered far and wide, and how in the end, while chopping firewood in the mountains, she was pushed off a cliff by a rich man. She clung to a vine to save herself, but the rich man cut the vine and sent her to her death.[72]

The story of Liu Sanjie's betrayal by her brother has long circulated among the Zhuang people. The passage from the *Yishan xianzhi* 宜山縣誌 included in the Appendix is one of the extant records of that tale. Dismissing it as unreliable, Zheng substitutes his own miraculous tale of the locals' long memories. Inasmuch as the vitality of folk legends lies in the openness of their signification and in the latitude they offer for reinvention and retelling, the positing of a single, correct version of the folktale contradicts the modality of folklore. For the same reason, we cannot lightly reject the opposition between Liu Sanjie's social status and that of the scholar in some other versions of the legend. The opposition evokes the struggle between the social classes, but it also points to the tensions between the Zhuang and the Han and between a woman and the patriarchal society. These remnants of the folk legend haunt the representation of class struggle and introduce an excess of meaning into the musical drama. As seen in the synopsis of the play given above, the drama of class struggle cannot but be a story of the Zhuang resistance to the Han and that of a Zhuang *woman's* resistance to the Han *patriarchal* oppression.[73]

Adapting Liu Sanjie *to the Screen*

A subversive reading of the musical drama Liu Sanjie is not something one can retroactively impose on the work. The screenplay writer Qiao Yu, for example, was quick to detect it and responded by eliminating traces of subversion in the film script. More important, Qiao strove to weaken the effect of the dramatized conflict between the Zhuang and the Han and that between Liu Sanjie and the patriarchal order. Where in the musical drama Liu Sanjie repeatedly uses the expression "we Zhuang" to challenge Han power, Qiao turns this central refrain into "we who sing songs." Revisions such as this bear witness to the fact that class struggle was staged in terms of ethnic and gender conflicts and that these were a principal mode of social struggle in the original musical.

In his preparatory notes for the film script, Qiao Yu envisioned Liu Sanjie as a revolutionary heroine and wrote in 1960:

She wields the dagger of mountain song so keenly and with such consummate skill as to carry all before her. This dashing air and this spirit of struggle stir the people's spirits, fascinate them, and make them both cheerful and impassioned. Our dramatic stage is not lacking in heroic characters who dare to resist, dare to struggle; yet the stirring appearance of this avatar of the working people, Liu Sanjie, indeed possesses an unparalleled vigor, an unparalleled splendor. It goes so far as to make people think that she does not merely walk on the stage in the ordinary manner, but storms into it, far beyond the imaginings of men. A portrait of class struggle formed around her as the main character must therefore possess a real plenitude of spirit.[74]

This image of Liu Sanjie echoes Mao's doctrine of class struggle and revolution by violent means. Qiao introduced a major change in the plot to obstruct a potential feminist reading of Liu Sanjie by playing up the romantic love scenes between Liu Sanjie and Xiao Niu and their *shared* class identity and consciousness. Huang Wanqiu 黃婉秋, the actress who played Liu Sanjie (sung by the singer Fu Jinhua 傅錦華) in the film, reproduces the affective energy of class struggle with her exaggerated performance. Glaring at the landlord with angry eyes and smiling tenderly at her own people, Huang's acting becomes almost a caricature of the revolutionary aesthetic with its emphasis on the ethical polarity of love and hatred.

As a visual spectacle, the film makes effective use of the legendary landscape of Guilin as the principal backdrop for the sentimental romantic comedy about Liu Sanjie and her lover. From love at first sight through the hero's rescue of the damsel in distress, their hand-in-hand flight, their swearing of everlasting fidelity, and their union as a happy couple—nearly all the scenes take place aboard a boat or at the water's edge. The towering peaks and oddly shaped stones (signifying masculinity) reflected in the yielding and tranquil surface of the lake (the feminine counterpart), the painterly landscape dotted with the fishermen's boats, and the strains of mountain songs drifting in from the distance serve as a commonplace, clichéd backdrop for the "boy meets girl" motif. (In contrast, the love story had a secondary role in the original musical drama). The incident of Liu Sanjie's imprisonment by the landlord Mo Hairen was added by the filmmaker. Besides foregrounding Liu Sanjie's fearlessness and purity, this incident serves to set the stage for her rescue by the hero. Xiao Niu inexplicably turns into a prince charming and arrives in time to help the distressed Liu Sanjie escape from the tiger's lair. Aided by peasants, the pair sets off down the river in a skiff and lives happily ever after (Fig. 12.7–9).

Commenting on the element of romance in *Liu Sanjie*, Wai-Fong Loh suggests that the theme of class struggle in the film overshadows the theme of romantic love.[75] But it seems to me that the film insists on the motif of romantic love as a necessary instantiation of class struggle. Love and hate are aestheticized as affective political moments. Loh's misreading of this important detail derives from a gender-blind interpretation of romantic love on the one hand and class struggle on the other. Without going into the polyvalent sources of the folk legend, a quick comparison with the stage version of the musical drama makes clear what Qiao Yu has accomplished in the film script: the independent and self-willed folksinger Liu Sanjie becomes a damsel in distress from a popular Hollywood film of the 1930s. This hackneyed romanticism is considerably different from the image of Liu Sanjie in the folk legends or even in the musical drama. The Liu Sanjie of the folk legends is a gifted female singer, fiercely competitive, and always eager to match her skills with men and literati scholars.

Fig. 12.7 The film star
Huang Wanqiu plays
Liu Sanjie in the film *Liu
Sanjie.*

The Changchun Studio completed the shooting of *Liu Sanjie* in 1961. The
director Su Li 蘇里 worked with the eminent composer Lei Zhenbang 雷
振邦 to incorporate 111 mountain songs into the film. Seventy-eight of them
were taken directly from the musical drama. Most of the songs were presented as part of the folksong competitions of the Zhuang locals but were
subjected to occasional alterations of lyrics. Take, for example, one of the
riddle verses in the opening scene in which Liu Sanjie matches songs with
the young men of her village. According to the field researchers, the original
folksong was:

> What has a mouth but cannot speak?
> What has no mouth but makes a din?
> What has feet but cannot walk?
> What travels far and wide with none?
>
> Bodhisattva has a mouth but cannot speak;
> A copper gong has none but makes a din;
> A stool has feet but cannot walk;
> A boat has none but travels far and wide.[76]

The scriptwriter modified the last two lines by replacing the objects (chair,
boat) with ideologically charged idioms:

What has a mouth but cannot speak?
What has no mouth but makes a din?
What has feet but cannot walk?
What travels far and wide with none?

Bodhisattva has a mouth but cannot speak;
A copper gong has none but makes a din;
A rich man has legs but won't walk.
His money has no legs but travels a lot.[77]

Such tampering with the folk composition is ingenious but hardly forgivable, even though the riddle-song competition survives the revisions.

Notably, the film's handling of scholars brings to mind the desperate social condition of the intellectuals at the time. Some of the mocking lines Qiao Yu puts in Liu Sanjie's mouth appear to have been lifted from Mao Zedong's "Talks at the Yan'an Forum on Literature and Art." Mao distrusted intellectuals and described them as "lazy bones" and "incapable of telling the five grains apart." These expressions found their way into the lyrics of Liu Sanjie's song competition with the scholars, and the audience was

Fig. 12.8 Liu Sanjie and her lover Xiao Niu.

Fig. 12.9 Liu Sanjie and the Zhuang people.

invited to join in this ritual of scapegoating (Fig. 12.10).[78] But there was no lack of outspoken critics following the release of the film in 1961. *Dazhong dianying* 大眾電影 (Popular cinema) first published a letter by A Yi 阿頤 (pen-name) who faulted the director and scriptwriter for modernizing the ancient folksinger and casting her in a realist mode. Liu Sanjie's behavior, manner, and style were "so distorted by the realist principle," he wrote, "that she no longer resembles the legendary Zhuang woman from ancient times and acts like a progressive woman from the land reform movement."[79] The critic Xu Jingguo 徐敬國 wrote a rebuttal to A Yi's criticism and maintained that the image of Liu Sanjie was true to life both historically and artistically and cited the Marxist principle of the dialectic of idealism and realism to prove the point.[80] Others such as Jia Ji 賈霽 disagreed and voiced their support for A Yi's charge of anachronism, citing examples to show that

Fig. 12.10 Liu Sanjie defeats the scholars in song matching, from an illustrated storybook, published in 1962, based on the film *Liu Sanjie*.

the film distorted the image of the folksinger to fit the revolutionary ideal and that the peasants in the film behaved in a manner too radical to be true; and the ideological consciousness of the ancients could not have reached this level of social progress.[81] One critic complained that he would rather see Liu Sanjie flying in the clouds like a true fairy.[82]

The conflict over the artistic merits and ideological soundness of *Liu Sanjie* suggest the ambivalence the critics felt about the film. This ambivalence eventually cost the film a major national award despite its popular success. The judges of the second official Hundred Flowers Film Awards held in Beijing on May 29, 1963, awarded *Liu Sanjie* fourth place in the contest for best feature film. In contrast, the 180,000 voters who participated in a film festival sponsored by *Popular Cinema* awarded *Liu Sanjie* three first prizes: best cinematography, best original composition, and best artistic design.

The Cultural Revolution brought yet another interesting twist to the *Liu Sanjie* story when Mao's wife, Jiang Qing 江青, openly voiced her contempt for kitschy folk plays. Jiang, a former film star in Shanghai, never liked folk-songs, found them native, vulgar, and low, and thought that they "cannot give expression to *modern life*." As a result, *Liu Sanjie* and other such popular works were barred from the stage to make room for the eight model plays masterminded by Jiang herself, who believed in the blending of the Peking opera with Western orchestral music and the mixing of folk dance material with Western ballet.[83] In the words of the novelist Wang Anyi 王安憶, the Cultural Revolution was a "mass movement of symphonic music," meaning literally the privileging of Western musical forms. Her remark opens a unique perspective for a reconsideration of artistic forms in the Cultural Revolution and their relationship to the mass media and popular culture.[84] The topic, however, requires a separate treatment.[85]

The lawsuit mentioned at the opening of this chapter was settled outside court after Qiao Yu publicly apologized to the *caidiao* scriptwriters. Interestingly, Huang Wanqiu, the actress who played Liu Sanjie in the film and now the president of the Cultural Bureau in Guilin, defended Qiao Yu. In an interview, she recalled:

In those days, people didn't think much about fame or self-interest. It was we, the Guangxi people, who invited Qiao Yu to come and help us adapt the story for the screen. After the completion of the film and the approval process, Qiao Yu's name was used as the screenplay writer and nobody raised an objection at that point. To my mind, no matter when and under what circumstances, one should not dismiss someone's work when that work bore the fruits of genuine efforts. Without Qiao Yu, the film *Liu Sanjie* could not have seen the light of the day. We the people of Guangxi must not forget the past and erase his contributions due to some unfortunate historical events while garnering fame from the film. Many of the lyrics were of Qiao's composition, such as Liu Sanjie's lyrics in the scene of song matching and the tea-picking lyric. Whatever you say after so many years, it was Qiao's film script that brought fame to Guangxi and made Liu Sanjie known to the nation and abroad. Legends about Liu Sanjie had existed for nearly a thousand years, but their true impact wasn't felt until the film entered the scene. Many of us, ordinary people as well as the cadres of Guangxi province, feel that it was wrong to sue Qiao Yu. Deep in their heart, people just couldn't swallow the idea. In terms of structure and plot, one could cite many differences between the third draft of *caidiao* opera and the film version. Even if similarities exist, plagiarism is not the word. After all, the material came from the folk in the first place.[86]

The *caidiao* scriptwriters who brought the case against Qiao Yu would not find Huang's defense palatable, especially since her own stardom in the 1960s depended on Qiao's work. But the argument about plagiarism, ownership, and intellectual property rights is just as dubious since it cannot but displace some of the important issues concerning the evolution of folklore studies and official popular culture that I have tried to bring to light in this essay. The anachronism of the lawsuit implies that the collective authorship of the script had been an original act of creation and ignores that fact that the Liuzhou writers had appropriated something collectively owned.

What the lawsuit leaves unquestioned ultimately is the ideological ground on which private ownership stands in the contemporary Chinese discourse of social transformation after Mao, a phenomenon I analyze elsewhere.[87] This is also the ground—namely, the postsocialist restructuring and liquidation of public and collective properties in the face of global capitalist challenges—on which the fantastic ownership of the Liu Sanjie script can be conjured and explained. The timing of the lawsuit coincided with a rapid succession of new government policies and legal institutional changes, both in China and in other former socialist countries, in which publicly and collectively owned properties have been transferred to or stolen by those in power and by the privileged few, all *in the name of* law, economic restructuring, and intellectual property rights.[88] The claiming of intellectual property rights at this juncture cannot but promote the ideology of private ownership even as it obscures the reality of massive migration of public property and public goods into private hands. Could an irony be more poignant? The lawsuit represents the newest phase of what one might call the ongoing political history of Liu Sanjie in modern China; the drama may continue in the future.[89]

Appendix: Primary Written Sources on Liu Sanjie from the Song Through the Qing Dynasties

The earliest extant written record that mentions Liu Sanjie is the entry "Sanmei shan" 三妹山 (Third sister mountain) in the *Yudi jisheng* 輿地紀勝 (Record of the landscape of the imperial domain) by Wang Xiangzhi 王象之 of the Southern Song. The brief text consists of fourteen characters: "Liu Sanmei was a native of Chunzhou 春州. She sat upon a stone cliff; hence its name."[90] This note was fleshed out by a late Ming–early Qing poet from Guangdong named Qu Dajun 屈大均 (1630–96):

Among the young women of Xinxing 新興 there was one Liu Sanmei; it is told that she was the first person to create songs. She was born during the reign of the Tang emperor Zhongzong 中宗 [705–7]. At the age of twelve *sui* 歲, she was thoroughly versed in the Classics and Histories and skilled in making songs. For a thousand *li* 里 around, those who heard of the fame of her songs came [to compete with her], but all found themselves, after one day or two or three, unable to match her verses and so departed. Sanmei knew musical composition and did wondrous things with it until she attained the Way. She roamed in the hills and along the rivers of Guangxi and Guangdong, where resided mostly uncultivated native people. She mastered the language of every place she came to, and when she encountered a certain place, she would make songs based on their language and match songs with them, and the people of this place would revere [her songs] as their model. Once she climbed a hill together with a youth from White Crane Village and sang [with him], which drew a large crowd of Yue, Yao 瑤, and Zhuang peoples. Men and women numbering in the thousands all took her to be an immortal. For seven days and nights the sound of singing continued unbroken until the singers turned into stone. Thereupon, the people of that locale worshipped her at Brocade Stone Cliff in Yangchun 陽春. The cliff is more than 30 *zhang* 丈 high, densely forested, with a thousand ancient camphor trees screening half of it from sight. At the mouth of the cliff there are stone steps, etched and embroidered with flowers of lichen, just like "bird-track" calligraphy. One stone is shaped like a curved table, large enough for a person to recline on; it gleams with a black luster, slick and shining, [and it is said to be] a relic of Sanmei. At the end of a month is often heard the sound of *sheng* 笙 pipes and of cranes, and in times of bountiful harvest it is almost as if someone mounts to the top of the cliff and sings. Sanmei is now called the "Song Immortal," and all those who make songs, whether people of Qi 齊 or the mountain folk of Lang 俍, Yao, Zhuang, and the like, upon completing their songs must first present a copy [to Sanmei's shrine]. The officiants keep it, and those who want the songs come and record them, leaving the originals there. They gradually accumulated several cases full [of verses]. Now, after the wars, the place is desolate.[91]

Over the past centuries, variants of this story have spread across the provinces of the south, especially in Guangxi and Guangdong. Some call the singer Liu Sanjie, and others Liu Sanmei, but all are unanimous in honoring her as the goddess of mountain song. For example, the Zhuang people's song festivals and singing competitions in the Lingnan region still preserve some of the related folk customs. Temples dedicated to her can be found throughout Guangxi and Guangdong, as well as sites such as the Sanmei Stone and the Terrace of the Song Immortal. [92]

The tremendous popularity of Liu Sanjie in the Qing dynasty is attested by the poet Wang Shizhen, who wrote in *Yuefeng xu jiu* 粤風續九 (Folksongs of Guangxi: a sequel to the Nine Songs):

The folkways of Guangxi are idle and licentious; as to folksongs in this region, there are Yao songs, Liang songs, Zhuang songs, Dan 蛋 songs, the fan songs of the Lang people, knife-play songs, the Zhuang people's "peach-leaf dance" songs, and many others. There is a great variety of them, but in general all the lyrics are of men and women flirting with one another. It is said that in the Shenlong 神龍 reign of the Tang [705–7] there was a certain Liu Sanmei who lived in Shuinan 水南 village in Gui 貴 county. She was skilled in song. She climbed a high terrace of the western hills with a scholar from Baihe 白鶴 in Yongzhou 邕州, and they sang for three days. The scholar sang a *zhifang* 芝房 melody, and Sanmei responded with a *zifeng* 紫鳳 song.[93] The scholar replied with "The Phoenix Tree Growing on the Southern Peak," and Sanmei matched it with "The Butterfly Skimming the Autumn Grasses." The scholar suddenly switched to a melody called "Flowers of Langling" 朗陵, with extremely mournful lyrics. Sanmei sang "White Stones on the Southern Mountain," which was even more tragic and moving, as if her voice could hardly continue. Everyone in the audience broke down and wept. Thus, they continued to match songs for seven whole days and nights, until both of them turned to stone; they stand upon Seven Star Cliff, with Seven Star Pond down below. Even today, on clear and moonlit nights, one still seems to hear the sound of singing there. My classmate Wu Jingqu 吳井渠 [Wu Qi 吳淇] of Suiyang 睢陽 held office in Xunzhou 潯州 and collected and recorded their songs to form the *Folksongs of Guangxi: A Sequel to the Nine Songs*. No doubt these are crude tunes, but at times they sound very much like the ancient poetry of the Music Bureau such as *Ziye* 子夜 songs. So I have included several examples herein.[94]

Among the songs that Wang Shizhen included for posterity is one called "Vine and Tree Song":

> Entering the mountains I espy a vine entwining a tree;
> Coming forth I see a tree entwined with a vine.
> When the tree dies, the vine dies clinging to the tree;
> When the vine dies, the tree dies entwined with the vine.[95]

This love song enjoyed a wide distribution from the Qing through the twentieth century. Different regions have produced different versions playing on the same images. For example, among the folksongs transcribed by a twentieth-century folklorist is this song:

> Entering the mountains I see a vine entwining a tree;
> Coming forth I see a tree entwined with the vine.
> When the tree dies, the vine dies entwining the tree;
> When the vine dies, the tree clings to the vine in death.[96]

Besides Wang Shizhen, Zhang Erhe 張爾翮 of the Qing also gave an elaborate account of the folkways of the Zhuang people in "Liu Sanmei gexian zhuan" 三妹歌仙傳 (Tale of the song immortal Liu Sanmei). His account, which is in the form of a travel diary, describes the strange events the narrator had heard and seen near the immortal's village. The narrator tells how, approaching a village on his trip to visit a friend in the western mountains, he heard some fantastic sounds floating toward him:

Above the layered peaks a sound echoed, now continuous and now broken, resounding within the forest. I looked around in all directions, but there was no one to be seen. Dark pinnacles filled my eyes, and far off I espied the mountain summit; there were only two stone figures sitting there side by side. I thought this rather uncanny. Ah, ah! No one in sight, and yet there was a sound, a sound in the empty firmament, drifting indistinctly among the clouds. Could it be the voice of the immortals? I bent my ear and listened closely; now it was hidden, and now it reemerged. Far off I espied three or four groups of human forms, singing together and answering one another. I heard only the sound of their voices; what tune they were singing I could not discern. What strange fantasy could equal this?[97]

The narrator goes on to describe a chance meeting with an old man, snowy-haired and baby-faced, who helps solve the riddle for him. What he had heard was the sound of the young village women singing back and forth and sporting with one another as they picked tea leaves. Their song was pleasant and moving because "of old in this place there was a song immortal, and, therefore, the young men and maidens born in the countryside are all skilled in song." The song immortal is Liu Sanmei, who was a descendant of Liu Chen of the Han, born in the first year of the Shenlong period under Emperor Zhongzong of the Tang. At the age of seven *sui* she was skilled with brush and ink, intelligent and perceptive, and her contemporaries called her the "girl prodigy." "At the age of twelve she was familiar with the scriptures and chronicles and skilled in fashioning songs. Her father and elders marveled at this; they would sometimes point to an object and ask for a song, whereupon she would promptly pour one out, complete and flawless in rhyme and meter."[98] The fame of Sanmei's skill in song making spread for several hundred *li*. Many came and matched songs with her, but no one could best Sanmei. And from this arose the name of "Song Immortal." It bears observing that Zhang's account of Liu Sanjie's origins makes specific mention of her "skill with brush and ink" and "familiar[ity] with the scriptures and chronicles," which reminds us of Qu Dajun's statement that Liu Sanjie "was thoroughly versed in the Classics."[99] However, the majority of the live *oral* accounts documented in the twentieth century portray her as a young woman of humble origins and a champion of the ordinary people.[100] It is the oral accounts, not the literati version, that became incorporated in the *caidiao* and musical drama versions of *Liu Sanjie*.

Local gazetteers of Guangxi and Guangdong provide another rich source of such literature.[101] Volume three of *Gazetteer of Yishan County*, for instance, contains a variant of the Liu Sanjie story centering on the cruelty of her elder brother, who hated her for singing and neglecting work for the family. One day, as they were climbing a steep cliff near the river to cut firewood, the brother pushed Liu Sanjie into the river by cutting the vine to which she was clinging. Liu Sanjie drowned and floated to Wuzhou 梧州. The people of [Wu]zhou pulled her body from the water, built a temple, and venerated her as their "Longmu" 龍母 (Dragon-mother). Her spirit is said to be extremely powerful.

The story of the brother's cruelty appears in several versions, but it is not universal. "Liu Sanniang" 劉三娘 in volume 18 of *Gazetteer of Cangwu County* 蒼梧縣誌 gives a totally different twist to the plot:

Liu Sanniang was a native of Xuluo 須羅 village in Cangwu 蒼梧, born in the Ming. On the third day of the third month, she was washing clothes in the stream, when wind and rain came up suddenly. All her brothers and sisters fled; alone, she encountered the spirits, and sat upon a stone, her clothes unsoaked. From then on she was able to sing, to write, and to tell others' secrets, all wondrously exact. When the makers of silk heard her songs, their silk was perfect; when those plowing the fields heard her songs, the harvest was bountiful. In times of drought she prayed for rain and was extraordinarily effective. One day she informed her family that she was leaving to become an immortal. She would return once each year on the third day of the third month. If anyone needed anything, they should go forth and sit upon the river stones and call her, and she would assuredly respond. Thereupon, she disappeared.

For several centuries, ceremonies and religious rituals of worship and sacrifice devoted to Liu Sanjie were solemnly observed among the Zhuang ethnic group. The *Gazetteer of Fuhuan County* describes an elaborate spectacle: on the first day of the first month every year, the thirteenth of the sixth month, the fifteenth of the eighth and so on, the people from a hundred *li* around would throng to the Huainan Temple to conduct a magnificent and spirited sacrificial ceremony. After the White Dew Festival, they would shoulder the goddess's palanquin for a procession, touring all the villages. Activities would continue for several fortnights, with no one begrudging expenses that ran into the tens of thousands.[102]

Notes

I am grateful to Theodore Huters, Haun Saussy, Joanna F. Handlin Smith, Judith Zeitlin, and Ellen Widmer for reading and commenting on earlier versions of this chapter and giving me valuable suggestions and to the anonymous readers who commented on it at various points in its gestation. I thank my research assistant Jami Proctor-Xu for her meticulous work and Ann McKnight for helping to verify the names of the Japanese folklorists. An earlier and very different Chinese version of this essay first appeared in Lydia Liu, *Yuji shuxie* 語際書寫 (Cross-writing: critical perspectives on narratives of modern intellectual history) (Hong Kong: Tiandi Publishing House, 1997). I thank Christopher Hamm for lending me a hand in translating a draft of the Chinese essay.

1. See Hu Tiege 胡鐵戈, *"Liu Sanjie* banquan shu shei?" 劉三姐版權屬誰 (Who has the rights to *Liu Sanjie*?), (*Meizhou*) *Wenhui zhoukan*, Jan. 20, 1996, section 3. See also Ren Xuelu 任學路, "Qunian, yingshi guansi buduan" 去年, 影視官司 不斷 (Endless film and television lawsuits in the last year), (*Meizhou*) *Wenhui zhoukan*, Mar. 16, 1996.

2. For an earlier attempt to question the elite/popular binary within the context of late imperial China, see David Johnson, "Communication, Class, and Consciousness in Late Imperial China," in *Popular Culture in Late Imperial China*, ed. David Johnson, Andrew Nathan, and Evelyn S. Rawski (Berkeley: University of California Press, 1985), pp. 34–72.

3. See Harry Harootunian, *Overcome by Modernity: History, Culture, and Community in Interwar Japan* (Princeton: Princeton University Press, 2000), p. 400.

4. I thank Theodore Huters for alerting me to this important connection.

5. Beijing University began collecting folksongs (*geyao* 歌謠) in the spring of 1918. A Bureau for Collecting Folksongs was set up with Liu Bannong 劉半農, Shen Yinmo 沈尹默, and Zhou Zuoren acting as principal editors, and Qian Xuantong 錢玄同 and Shen Jianshi 沈兼士 taking responsibility for researching local dialects. In the same year, Liu Bannong began a "Folksong Selections" column in *Beida rikan* 北大日刊 (Beijing university daily), publishing one ballad every day for a total of 148 items. During the May Fourth movement of the following year, the *Daily* stopped publication, and the "Folksong Selections" also temporarily halted. In the winter of 1920, Beijing University established the "Folkways Survey Society" with Shen Jianshi, Zhou Zuoren, Gu Jiegang, and others as the core, which continued to promote the work of folksong collecting and study. Within a few years, the Folkways Survey Society had compiled several thousand folksongs from some 22 provinces. On December 17, 1922, Zhou Zuoren and others launched the official publication of the Folkways Survey Society, the *Geyao zhoukan* 歌謠周刊 (Folksong weekly), to commemorate the university's twenty-fifth anniversary. The jour-

nal reissued guidelines for folksong research and made a concerted effort to promote the new studies and to attract the attention of the public at large. See Gu Jiegang 顧頡剛, "*Wuge jiaji zixu*" 吳歌甲集自序 (Author's preface to the *First Collection of the Songs of Wu*), *Geyao zhoukan*, June 28, 1925; and Rong Zhaozu 容肇祖, "Beida Geyao yanjiu hui ji Fengsu diaocha hui de jingguo" 北大歌謠研究會及風俗調查會的經過 (The history of Folksong Research Society and Folkways Survey Society at Peking University), *Minsu*, no. 15/16 (1928): 8. For a detailed study of *Geyao zhoukan* in English, see Chang-tai Hung, *Going to the People: Chinese Intellectuals and Folk Literature, 1918–1937* (Cambridge, Mass.: Harvard University Press, 1985), pp. 43–55. For a recent study of the circumstances of folklore studies and the rise of Japanese nationalism, see Mariko Asano Tamanoi, "Gender, Nationalism, and Japanese Native Ethnology," *positions: east asia cultures critique* 4, no. 1 (Spring 1996): 59–86; see also Uli Linke, "Folklore, Anthropology, and the Government of Social Life," *Comparative Studies in Society and History* 32, no. 1 (1990): 142.

6. See Rong, "Beida Geyao yanjiu hui ji Fengsu diaocha hui de jingguo," pt. 1, p. 1.

7. From December 1922 to June 1925, the *Folksong Weekly* published a total of 97 issues. The Folksong Research Society gathered about 13,000 folksongs. Besides the *Folksong Weekly*, its publications included *Geyao jinian zengkan* 歌謠紀念增刊 (Folksong memorial supplement), *Wuge jiaji* 吳歌甲集 (First collection of songs of Wu), *Meng Jiangnü gushi de gequ* 孟姜女故事的歌曲 (Songs and arias from the story of Lady Meng Jiang), *Kanjian ta* 看見她 (Seeing her), and other volumes. Gu Jiegang's studies of the story of Lady Meng Jiang are representative of the accomplishments of the last two years of the *Folksong Weekly*; see *Geyao zhoukan*, nos. 69–76 (1924–25).

8. In 1927, Zhongshan University established the Society for Folklore Studies (1927–43). *Folklore Weekly* became the society's principal regular publication, successively producing 123 issues, including the 1930s digest, *Jikan* (Quarterly), between 1927 and 1943. It made considerable contributions to the collecting of folksongs and the study of folk customs in China. The Society for Folklore Studies also published some 30-odd volumes of folklore collectanea, among which were Gu Jiegang's renowned studies *Meng Jiang nü gushi yanjiu ji* 孟姜女故事研究集 (Collected researches on the story of Lady Meng Jiang) and *Miaofengshan* 妙峰山; Zhong Jingwen's 鍾敬文 *Minjian wenyi conghua* 民間文藝叢話 (Collected lectures on folk art) (Guangzhou: Dongsheng yinwuju, 1928); Xie Yunsheng's 謝雲聲 *Taiwan qingge* 臺灣情歌 (Taiwanese love songs); Zhou Zhenhe's 周振鶴 *Yangzhou de gushi* 揚州的故事 (Stories of Yangzhou), and others. The Society for Folklore Studies organized numerous related activities in coordination with its publications, such as an exhibition hall for folk artifacts, a lecture series in folklore studies, and so forth; it cultivated a generation of folklore scholars.

9. Zhong Jingwen 鍾敬文, *Zhong Jingwen minjian wenxue lunji* 鍾敬文民間文學論集 (Essays on folk literature by Zhong Jingwen) (Shanghai: Shanghai wenyi chubanshe, 1982), 1: 174–75.

10. For an English-language study of Gu Jiegang, see Laurence A. Schneider, *Ku Chieh-kang and China's New History: Nationalism and the Quest for Alternative Traditions* (Berkeley: University of California Press, 1971), pp. 146–47.

11. As quoted in Zhong Jingwen, *Minjian wenxue lunji*, 1: 101.

12. See ibid., p. 91.

13. Yu Min 愚民, "Shan'ge yuanshi de chuanshuo ji qita" 山歌原始的傳說及其他 (The primitive origins of the mountain song and related matters), *Minsu*, no. 13/14 (1928): 44–45.

14. Legends also recount that the Zhuang people originally had no songs, but that songs immediately flourished in every region graced by Liu Sanjie's visit. Those places that she neglected to pass by consequently boast fewer people who can sing. See Tian Ying 天鷹, "Geju *Liu Sanjie* de renwu kehua ji qita" 歌劇劉三姐的人物刻畫及其它 (The portrayal of character in the musical drama *Liu Sanjie*), in *Liu Sanjie zhuanji* 劉三姐專集 (A special collection on *Liu Sanjie*) (Guilin: Guangxi shifan xueyuan, 1979), p. 108.

15. Zhong, *Minjian wenyi conghua*, 1: 95.

16. The author reiterated this viewpoint in his longer study of 1981, "Liu Sanjie chuanshuo shilun" 劉三姐傳說試論 (A tentative discussion of the legend of Liu Sanjie), in ibid., pp. 93–120.

17. Ibid., pp. 96–98.

18. Ibid., p. 98.

19. Stevan Harrell, ed., *Cultural Encounters on China's Ethnic Frontiers* (Seattle: University of Washington Press, 1995), p. 17.

20. On Père Paul Vial, see Margaret Byrne Swain's essay in ibid., pp. 140–85; on James R. Adam and Samuel Pollard, see Siu-woo Cheung's essay in the same volume, pp. 217–47.

21. See Rong Zhaozu, "Beida Geyao yanjiu hui ji Fengsu diaocha hui de jingguo," pt. 1, pp. 8–9. The translation is from Hung, *Going to the People*, p. 50. The Italian mentioned in the text is Baron Guido Amadeo Vitale (1872–1918), who lived in China for many years and served as translator at the Italian embassy in Beijing beginning in the 1890s. As early as 1896 and 1901, he had collected and published separate anthologies of Beijing folksongs and children's songs: *Pekingese Rhymes* (1896) and *Chinese Merry Tales* (1901). Twenty years prior to the founding of the Folkways Survey Society in Beijing, several studies of Chinese folklore by Westerners had been published, including Isaac Taylor Headland (1859–1942), *Chinese Mother Goose Rhymes* (1900) and *The Chinese Boy and Girl* (1901). The folklore scholar Zhao Jing-

shen 趙景深 (1902–85) confessed feeling ashamed that foreign scholars had taken the lead in these studies and believed that Chinese scholars must exert themselves to catch up. See Hung, *Going to the People*, p. 21.

22. For a critique of the institutional and discursive construction of modern Chinese nationhood, see Prasenjit Duara, *Rescuing History from the Nation: Questioning Narratives of Modern China* (Chicago: University of Chicago Press, 1995).

23. For a discussion of the Han majority as a recent phenomenon, see Dru Gladney, "Representing Nationality in China: Refiguring Majority/Minority Identities," *Journal of Asian Studies* 53, no. 1 (Feb. 1994): 98–99.

24. Ibid., p. 94. Whereas Gladney believes that this represents a new direction in contemporary China, it seems to me that the dialectic has been present from the early days of Chinese nationalism and Chinese folklore studies.

25. With the massive migration of Beijing intellectuals and scholars to the south after 1926, the center of folklore studies shifted. Gu Jiegang took up a professorship at the Zhongshan University in 1927 and on November 1 of that same year the university's *Folklore Weekly* made its appearance with Zhong Jingwen as the chief editor. This publication was originally titled *Minjian wenyi* 民間文藝 (Folk literature and art) and adopted the new name with the thirteenth issue in March 1928.

26. Yang Chengzhi's translations appeared in issues no. 1 through 15/16.

27. He Sijing 何思敬, "Minsuxue de wenti" 民俗學的問題 (Issues in the study of folkways), 2 pts., *Minsu*, nos. 1, 3 (1928).

28. Ibid., pp. 4–5.

29. Charlotte Sophia Burne, *The Handbook of Folklore* (London: Sidgwick & Jackson, 1914), pp. 3–4.

30. Ibid., p. 5.

31. For an informed analysis of the British elite's treatment of their own urban poor as "many savage tribes" in the empire, see Henry Mayhew, *London Labour and London Poor, 1851* (New York: Penguin, 1985).

32. Hermann Bausinger, *Folk Culture in a World of Technology*, trans. Elke Dettmer (Bloomington: Indiana University Press, 1990), p. 2.

33. This also led to the founding of the Dialect Survey Society at Beida on January 26, 1924. Hu Shi argued in 1918 that, in order to create a new "national-language literature" (*guoyu de wenxue* 國語的文學), one had to seek material from every possible source. Dialect literature was one such source because local dialects provided an inexhaustible supply of what he called "new blood" (*xin xuemai* 新血脈) for national-language literature. See *Hu Shi wencun*, 1: 154; as quoted in Hung, *Going to the People*, p. 63.

34. Regina Bendix, *In Search of Authenticity: The Formation of Folklore Studies* (Madison: University of Wisconsin Press, 1997), p. 127.

35. Malinowski trained the first generation of Chinese social scientists, such as Fei Xiaotong 費孝通.

36. John W. Cell, "Colonial Rule," in *The Oxford History of the British Empire*, vol. 4, *The Twentieth Century*, ed. Judith M. Brown and Wm. Roger Louis (Oxford: Oxford University Press, 1999), p. 246.

37. Johannes Fabian, *Time and the Other: How Anthropology Makes Its Object* (New York: Columbia University Press, 1983), pp. 71–104. For a similar critique, see John Comaroff and Jean Comaroff, *Ethnography and the Historical Imagination* (Boulder, Colo.: Westview Press, 1992).

38. Paul Rabinow was among the first to critique the field in his *Reflections on Fieldwork in Morocco* (Berkeley: University of California Press, 1977). For other influential critics, see also James Clifford and George Marcus, eds., *Writing Culture* (Berkeley: University of California Press, 1986).

39. Ronald Radano, "Denoting Difference: The Writing of Slave Spirituals," *Critical Inquiry* 22 (1996): 530.

40. Laura Hostetler (*Qing Colonial Empire: Ethnography and Cartography in Early Modern China* [Chicago: University of Chicago Press, 2001], pp. 25–30) makes a tantalizing analogy between European colonialism and Qing expansionism but does not address the issues of time, objectivity, scientific classification, and scientific racism that have been central to the former. European colonialism is not just about brute domination. It is also about producing objective knowledge in the disciplines of the social sciences that lead to a certain view of reality and power relations.

41. For the racial marking of photographs by European photographers, see Virginia-Lee Webb, "Manipulated Images: European Photographs of Pacific Peoples," in *Prehistories of the Future: The Primitivist Project and the Culture of Modernism*, ed. Elazar Barkan and Ronald Bush (Stanford: Stanford University Press, 1995), pp. 175–201.

42. Gladney, "Representing Nationality in China," p. 97.

43. Interestingly, mainland critic Chen Sihe 陳思和 (*Jiming fengyu* 雞鳴風語 [The cock crows, the wind blows] [Shanghai: Xuelin chubanshe, 1994], p. 30) uses the word "colonization" to characterize this relationship between the intellectuals and the folk.

44. Gu's lecture was entitled "Shengxian wenhua yu minjian wenhua" 聖賢文化與民間文化 (The culture of the sages and the culture of the people); as transcribed by Zhong Jingwen, it was printed in *Minsu*, nos. 5, 6 (1928).

45. For an interesting argument about the distinction of "folk literature," "urban literature," "popular literature," etc., see Wei Tongxian 魏同賢, "Minjian wenxue jieshuo" 民間文學界説 (Demarcating folk literature), in *Zhongguo minjian wenxue lunwen xuan, 1949–1979* 中國民間文學論文選 (Selected essays on Chinese folk literature, 1949–79) (Shanghai: Shanghai wenyi chubanshe, 1980), 1: 331–58.

46. From the 1920s to the 1930s, American-style social science as represented by Li Jinghan (Franklin Lee) and others continued to assimilate the problems of folklore studies into the general program of social reform. See Chiang Yung-Chen, *Social Engineering and the Social Sciences in China, 1919–1949* (Cambridge, Eng.: Cambridge University Press, 2001).

47. Hung, *Going to the People*, p. 175.

48. Andrew Jones, *Yellow Music: Media Culture and Colonial Modernity in the Chinese Jazz Age* (Durham: Duke University Press, 2001), pp. 17–18.

49. Wai-Fong Loh, "From Romantic Love to Class Struggle: Reflections on the Film *Liu Sanjie*," in *Popular Chinese Literature and Performing Arts in the People's Republic of China, 1949–1979*, ed. Bonnie S. McDougall (Berkeley: University of California Press, 1984), p. 174.

50. For a study of box-office performance in mainland cinema from the mid-1950s to the early 1960s that reflects the fast expansion of a national film audience in mainland China, see Paul Clark, *Chinese Cinema: Culture and Politics Since 1949* (Berkeley: University of California Press, 1987), pp. 61–62.

51. Li Tuo 李陀, "1985," *Jintian* 1991, no. 3/4: 64.

52. For a detailed study of the *yangge* and related folk plays, see David Holm, *Art and Ideology in Revolutionary China* (Oxford: Clarendon Press, 1990). See also Li Jinghan 李景漢 and Zhang Shiwen 張世文, eds., *Dingxian yangge xuan* 定縣秧歌選 (A selection of *yangge* of Ding county) (Shanghai: n.p., 1933); and the English translation by Sidney D. Gamble, *Chinese Village Plays from the Ting Hsien Region (Yang Ke Hsuan)* (Amsterdam: Philo Press, 1970). On the birth of social science in China in the twentieth century and its educational background in church schools and financial support by America's Rockefeller foundation, see Yung-Chen Chiang, *Social Engineering and the Social Sciences in China, 1919–1949*.

53. In the spring of 1958, Mao's call for the "collecting of folksongs" to imitate the ancient practice of *caifeng* 採風, or collecting folksongs, sparked an unprecedented "New Folksong movement" across the nation. But according to Zeng Zhaowen, author of the first draft of the *caidiao* opera *Liu Sanjie*, the collecting of mountain songs in the countryside began as early as 1951. In 1951, the Liuzhou Municipal Folk Chorus performed in the countryside and collected and recorded the local people's mountain songs, among which were those later selected for the *caidiao Liu Sanjie*. See Hu Tiege, "*Liu Sanjie* banquan shu shei." See also "Da guimo de shouji quanguo min'ge" 大規模地收集全國民歌 (Make a full-scale effort to collect folksongs nationwide), editorial in *Renmin wenxue*, Apr. 14, 1958; and Guo Moruo 郭沫若 and Zhou Yang 周揚, "Hongqi geyao bianzhe de hua" 紅旗歌謠編者的話 (Remarks by the editors of *Ballads of the Red Flag*), in *Zhongguo minjian wenxue lunwen xuan, 1949–1979* 中國民間文學論文選 (Selected articles on Chinese folk literature, 1949–79) (Shanghai: Shanghai wenyi chubanshe, 1980), 1: 47–49. See also the editorials in

Wenyibao, 1958, nos. 11 and 19. For a critical study, see Zhao Yiheng 趙毅衡, "Cunli de Guo Moruo: du *Hongqi geyao*" 村裏的郭沫若: 讀紅旗歌謠 (Guo Moruo in the village: Reading the *Ballads of the Red Flag*), *Jintian* 1992, no. 2: 190–200.

54. See Zheng Tianjian 鄭天健, "Guanyu *Liu Sanjie* de chuangzuo" 關於劉三姐的創作 (On the creation of *Liu Sanjie*), in *Liu Sanjie: bachang gewu ju* 劉三姐: 八場歌舞劇 (*Liu Sanjie*: a musical drama in eight acts) (Beijing: Zhongguo xiju chubanshe, 1961), p. 144.

55. See ibid., p. 5.

56. The People's Fine Arts Publishing House specially designed and published a comic book based on the musical drama for young readers; the artist himself was a member of the Zhuang ethnicity named Deng Erlong 鄧二龍. See Wu Jinnan 伍晉南, "Guanyu *Liu Sanjie* de chuangzuo" 關於劉三姐的創作 (On the creation of *Liu Sanjie*), in *Liu Sanjie zhuanji* 劉三姐專集, p. 10. In his article Wu Jinnan mentions that certain elegant and humorous folksongs in the scene of "Refusal to Marry" were the creation of an old singer from Heng county.

57. *Liu Sanjie: bachang gewu ju*, p. 32; the translation used is Yang Hsien-yi and Gladys Yang's *Third Sister Liu: An Opera in Eight Scenes* (Beijing: Foreign Languages Press, 1962), p. 31. I have made slight changes to their translation; subsequent references to the Yangs' text appear in brackets.

58. The ban on singing does not seem to be based on folk legend and was devised by the Liuzhou City drama troupe to highlight the confrontation; See Zheng, "Guanyu *Liu Sanjie* de chuangzuo," p. 147.

59. *Liu Sanjie*, p. 64 [p. 61].

60. Zheng, "Guanyu *Liu Sanjie* de chuangzuo," p. 158.

61. *Liu Sanjie zhuanji*, p. 28.

62. Ibid.

63. People enjoyed Liu Sanjie's cleverness, her ability to improvise a song, and her knack for producing lively and astonishing phrases; see Cai, "Lun *Liu Sanjie*," pp. 74–86.

64. Ouyang Yuqian 歐陽予倩, "You xin you mei de gewuju *Liu Sanjie*" 又新又美的歌舞劇劉三姐 (The lovely new musical drama *Liu Sanjie*), *Renmin ribao*, Sept. 8, 1960.

65. See Cai, "Lun *Liu Sanjie*," p. 83.

66. Meng Yue 孟悅, "*Baimao nü* yanbian de qishi: jian lun Yan'an wenyi de lishi duozhixing" 白毛女演變的啓示: 兼論延安文藝的歷史多質性 (The significance of the evolution of *The White-Haired Girl*: with a discussion of the historical polyvalence of Yan'an's literature and arts), in Tang Xiaobing 唐小兵, ed., *Zai jiedu* 再解讀 (Re-readings) (Hong Kong: Oxford University Press, 1993), pp. 68–69. See also Zhao, "Cunli de Guo Moru"; Huang Ziping 黃子平, "Wenxue zhuyuan ji" 文學住院記 (Literature being hospitalized), *Jintian* 1992, no. 4: 157–70; and Li Tuo

李陀, "Ding Ling bu jiandan: Mao tizhi xia zhishifenzi zai huayu shengchan zhong de fuza jiaose" 丁玲不簡單: 毛體制下知識分子在話語生產中的複雜角色 (Ding Ling is not so simple: the complex role of intellectuals in the production of discourse under the Maoist system), *Jintian* 1993, no. 3: 222–42.

67. *Liu Sanjie*, p. 24 [p. 23].

68. Zheng, "Guanyu *Liu Sanjie* de chuangzuo," p. 150. See Yang and Yang, *Third Sister Liu*, p. 47.

69. See Liu Jidian 劉吉典, "Xuexi *Liu Sanjie* de yinyue chuangzuo" 學習劉三姐的音樂創作 (Studying the musical creation of *Liu Sanjie*), *Renmin ribao*, Nov. 19, 1960.

70. See Clark, *Chinese Cinema*, pp. 108–9.

71. Zheng, "Guanyu *Liu Sanjie* de chuangzuo," pp. 145–46.

72. Ibid., pp. 146–47.

73. A feminist reading of the text of *Liu Sanjie* is almost certain. All the critical articles that I have seen, however, subsume gender questions under other topics, such as anti-feudalism, freedom of marriage, and the like. This is hardly surprising, because from the start folk culture and women's liberation have been tied up together and the call for women's liberation took the feudal household as its primary target in the May Fourth period. *Geyao zhoukan* collected a great number of old ballads on the hardships of women's lives and later published several special issues on the subject of marriage alone. As Liu Jing'an wrote in his article "Geyao yu funü" 歌謠与婦女 (Balladry and women) (subtitled "Funü de wenxue yu funü de wenti" 婦女的文學与婦女的問題 [Women's literature and the woman question]): "Some say that ballads concerning the women's question in China are nothing more than women's 'Jiating mingyuan lu' 家庭鳴冤錄 (Record of household grievances) and 'Rutong ji' 茹痛記 (Record of swallowing pain); and it seems to me that this statement is not unjustified" (quoted in Zhong Jingwen, *Minjian wenxue lunwen ji*, p. 364; see also Hung, *Going to the People*, pp. 69–72).

74. Qiao Yu 喬羽, "Ermu yi xin: tan geju *Liu Sanjie*" 耳目一新: 談歌劇劉三姐 (Novel to the eye and to the ear: remarks on the musical drama *Liu Sanjie*), in *Liu Sanjie: bachang gewu ju* 劉三姐: 八場歌舞劇 (*Liu Sanjie*: a musical drama in eight acts), p. 62.

75. See Loh, "From Romantic Love to Class Struggle: Reflections on the Film *Liu Sanjie*," p. 170.

76. *Liu Sanjie*, p. 12 [p. 11].

77. *Liu Sanjie* (film), as quoted in Loh, "From Romantic Love to Class Struggle: Reflections on the Film *Liu Sanjie*," p. 170.

78. Zhong Jingwen, the folklorist who collected and studied the legends of Liu Sanjie from the Republican era on, came under criticism in the late 1950s. Zhong Jingwen's fall from political favor has been attributed to an article he published in

1925 entitled "Fuhui de geyao" 附會的歌謠 (A misuse of folksong) to criticize the revolutionary martyr Peng Pai's 澎湃 appropriation of the Hailufeng 海陸豐 children's song "Red-Hearted Sister" to propagandize revolution. Zhong called Peng's effort "truly wretched and abominable." See Zhao, "Cunli de Guo Moruo," p. 195. For a discussion of Peng Pai's involvement in folksong collecting, see Isabel K. F. Wong, "*Geming geju*: Songs for the Education of the Masses," in *Popular Chinese Literature and Performing Arts in the People's Republic of China, 1949–1979*, ed. Bonnie S. McDougall (Berkeley: University of California Press, 1984), p. 121.

79. A Yi 阿頤, "'Lixiang' he 'xianshi'" "理想" 和 "真實" ("The ideal" and "the real"), *Dazhong dianying* 1961, no. 10 (Oct. 1961): 11.

80. Xu Jingguo 徐敬國, "Bingmeiyou ba Liu Sanjie xiandai hua" 並沒有把劉三姐現代化 (*Liu Sanjie* has not been modernized), *Dazhong dianying* 1962, no. 1 (Jan.): 11.

81. Jia Ji 賈霽, "Guanyu yingpian *Liu Sanjie* taolun de zagan" 關於影片劉三姐討論的雜感 (Miscellaneous thoughts on the comments about the film *Liu Sanjie*), *Dazhong dianying* 1962, no. 8 (Aug.): 20–23.

82. Wei Chunwu, "Yingpian *Liu Sanjie* de mei zhong buzu" (Imperfections in the film *Liu Sanjie*), *Dazhong dianying* 1962, no. 1 (Jan. 1962): 12.

83. See Jia Zhi 賈之, "Esha minjian wenxue shi 'Sirenbang' fan Makesi zhuyi de yichang fengkuang biaoyan" 扼殺民間文學是 "四人幫" 反馬克思主義的一場瘋狂表演 (What strangled folk literature was the Gang of Four's frenzied anti-Marxist performance), in *Zhongguo minjian wenxue lunwen xuan, 1949–1979* 中國民間文學論文選 (Selected essays on Chinese folk literature, 1949–79) (Shanghai: Shanghai wenyi chubanshe, 1980), 1: 246–70.

84. See Wang Anyi's 王安憶 novel *Gexing Riben lai* 歌星日本來 (A singer from Japan). Wang Anyi herself played violin in an ensemble during the 1970s. At that time, urban youths studied violin, accordion, or voice in order to stay and work in the city. The total number is probably on the same order as those who "took the plunge" in business in the 1990s. This shows the importance accorded it by the government and how prevalent Western-style music was in society. After the Cultural Revolution, a great number of talented musicians and singers emerged, all trained during the previous period of the all-out national pursuit of Western-style music.

85. For an English-language study of the subject in contemporary China, see Richard Kraus, *Pianos and Politics in China: Middle-Class Ambitions and the Struggle over Western Music* (New York: Oxford University Press, 1989).

86. Bo Qing 柏青, "'Liu Sanjie' Huang Wangqiu shuo: 'Liu Sanjie bu shi piaoqie zhi zuo'" "劉三姐" 黃婉秋說: "劉三姐不是剽竊之作" ("Liu Sanjie" Huang Wangqiu says: "The film *Liu Sanjie* was not a case of plagiarism"), *Qianjiang wanbao*, Apr. 23, 1996.

87. For a study of popular culture in the production of the postsocialist ideology of work, leisure, and transnational entrepreneurship, see my article "*Beijing Sojourners in New York*: Postsocialism and the Question of Ideology in Global Media Culture," *positions: east asia cultures critique* 7, no. 3 (Winter 1999): 763–97.

88. He Qinglian 何清漣 calls this process "the Enclosure movement of the 1990s" in her controversial book, *Xiandaihua de xianjing: Dangdai Zhongguo de jingji shehui wenti* 現代化的陷阱: 當代中國的經濟社會問題 (The traps of modernization: the socioeconomic problems of contemporary China) (Beijing: Jinri Zhongguo chubanshe, 1998). For an in-depth analysis of intellectual property rights and the patenting of bio-products in China and Third World countries by multinationals, see Shi Pengxiang 施鵬翔, Lu Sicheng 盧思騁, and Lin Yanmei 林燕梅, "Shengming zhuanli: Xin shiji de quandi yundong" 生命專利: 新世紀的圈地運動 (Patenting bio-products: the enclosure movement of the new millennium:), *Shijie*, no. 7 (Apr. 2002): 2–29.

89. At the time of the writing of this essay, the mainland filmmaker Zhang Yimo is said to be preparing to produce a new version of *Liu Sanjie* in the native place of the legendary singer. See Wang Yin 王寅, "He Xuntian: gaixie *Liu Sanjie*" 何訓田: 改寫劉三姐 (He Xuntian: rewriting *Liu Sanjie*), *Nanfang zhoumo*, Mar. 10, 2000.

90. Wang Xiangzhi 王象之, "Sanmei shan" 三妹山 (Third-sister mountain), in *Yudi jisheng* 輿地紀勝 (A record of the landscape of the imperial domain), *juan* 98 (Shenyingzhai ed., 1849).

91. See Qu Dajun 屈大均, *Guandong xinyu* 廣東新語 (New account of Guangdong) (Beijing: Zhonghua shuju, 1985), p. 261. See also Huang Zhigang 黃芝岡, "Yuefeng yu Liu Sanmei chuanshuo" 粵風与劉三妹傳説 (Traditions of the south and the legend of Liu Sanmei), *Zhongshan wenhua jiaoyu jikan* 4, no. 1 (1937): 763–82.

92. A widely circulated story says that in the Taiping army and the armies of various minority rebellions in the nineteenth century, some female commanders took "Liu Sanmei" as their sobriquet. See Xiao Zhuo 蕭拙, "Liu Sanmei yu Lingnan min'ge" 劉三妹與嶺南民歌 (Liu Sanmei and Lingnan folksongs), *Yangcheng wanbao*, Jan. 1, 1958. Among female poets of the past, Xi Peilan 席佩蘭 composed two lyrical poems to praise Liu Sanmei's extraordinary talent as a poet. See Zhong Jingwen 鍾敬文, "Ji ze guanyu Liu Sanmei gushi ziliao" 幾則關於劉三妹故事資料 (Several items concerning the story of Liu Sanmei), *Minsu zhoukan*, no. 19/20 (Aug. 1928): 28.

93. *Zhifang* means "house of divine plant," and *zifeng* means "divine bird"; both are titles of tunes.

94. Wang Shizhen 王士禎, "Yuefeng xu jiu" 粵風續九 (Folksongs of Guangxi: a sequel to the Nine Songs), in idem, *Chibei outan* 池北偶談 (Idle talks from the north of the pond), *juan* 16 (Shanghai: Wenming shuju, 1936). For a discussion of Wu Jingqi and his folksong collecting, see Hung, *Going to the People*, p. 23.

95. Wang Shizhen, "Yuefeng xu jiu."

96. See Xiao Zhuo, "Liu Sanmei yu Lingnan min'ge."

97. See Zhang Erhe 張爾翮, "Liu Sanmei gexian zhuan," recorded in *Gujin tushu jicheng: fangyu huibian zhifang dian* 古今圖書集成: 方輿彙編職方典 (Encyclopedia of ancient and contemporary works of geography) (Shanghai: Zhonghua shuju, 1934), vol. 144.

98. Ibid.

99. Written accounts of the legend of Liu Sanjie from the past are fragmentary and scattered among the *biji* type of literati writing. Besides those discussed above, Zhong Jingwen also mentions the following in *Zhong Jingwen minjian wenxue lunji* (pp. 93–120): Min Xu's 閔敘 *Yue shu* 粵述 (An account of Yue, *juan* 20); Chu Renhuo's 褚人獲 "Xitong geyao" 谿峒歌謠 (Ballads of the gullies and grottoes), in *Jianhu ji* 堅瓠集 (Books of firm gourd), *ji* 8, *juan* 4; Lu Ciyun's 陸次雲 "Shengge yuanshi" 聲歌原始 (The origins of song and music), in *Jiu xiaoshuo* 舊小說 (Old tales), *ce* 17; and Tan Jingzhao's 譚敬昭 "Youtong Zhenyan bingxu" 游通真岩并序 (Preface to the travels through Tongzhen cliff), in *Yangchun xian zhi* 陽春縣誌 (Gazetteer of Yangchun county), *juan* 14.

100. One of the few exceptions is a song from the Miao people that goes: "The one who reads is none other than Liu Sanmei" (Zhong, *Minjian wenyi conghua*, p. 94).

101. The often noted ones are: "Geyao" (Ballads) in *Guixian zhi* 貴縣誌 (Gazetteer of Gui county), *juan* 2; "Liu Santai" 劉三妹 in *Yishan xianzhi* 宜山縣誌 (Gazetteer of Yishan county), *juan* 3; "Liu Sanniang" in *Cangwu xianzhi* 蒼梧縣誌 (Gazetteer of Cangwu county), *juan* 18; "Liu Sanmei" in *Guangdong tongzhi* 廣東統志 (A complete Guangdong gazetteer), *juan* 3; "Liu nüxian shi" 劉女仙石 (The rock of goddess Liu), "Nüxian" 女仙 (Goddess), and "Liu xian zufu mu" 劉仙祖父墓 (Ancestral tomb of goddess Liu) recorded in *juan* 4, 11, and 12, respectively, of *Yangsuo xianzhi* 陽朔縣誌 (Gazetteer of Yangshuo county).

102. See "Guangdong tushen jianji: Liu Sanmei" 廣東土神簡輯: 劉三妹 (A brief introduction to the local gods of Guangdong: Liu Sanmei), *Guangxi ribao*, Mar. 4, 1949.

Works Cited

A Yi 阿頤. "'Lixiang' he 'xianshi'" "理想" 和 "真實" ("The ideal" and "the real"). *Dazhong dianying* 1961, no. 10 (Oct. 1961): 10–11.

Bausinger, Hermann. *Folk Culture in a World of Technology.* Trans. Elke Dettmer. Bloomington: Indiana University Press, 1990.

Bendix, Regina. *In Search of Authenticity: The Formation of Folklore Studies.* Madison: University of Wisconsin Press, 1997.

Bo Qing 柏青. "'Liu Sanjie' Huang Wangqiu shuo: 'Liu Sanjie bu shi piaoqie zhi zuo'" "劉三姐" 黃婉秋說: "劉三姐不是剽竊之作" ("Liu Sanjie" Huang Wangqiu says: "The film *Liu Sanjie* was not a case of plagiarism"). *Qianjiang wanbao,* Apr. 23, 1996.

Brown, Judith M., and Wm. Roger Louis, eds. *The Oxford History of the British Empire,* vol. 4, *The Twentieth Century.* Oxford: Oxford University Press, 1999.

Burne, Charlotte Sophia. *The Handbook of Folklore.* London: Sidgwick & Jackson, 1914.

Cai Yi 蔡儀. "Lun *Liu Sanjie*" 論劉三姐 (A discussion of *Liu Sanjie*). In *Liu Sanjie zhuanji* 劉三姐專集 (A special collection on *Liu Sanjie*). Guilin: Guangxi shifan xueyuan, 1979, pp. 74–86.

Chen Sihe 陳思和. *Jiming fengyu* 雞鳴風語 (The cock crows, the wind blows). Shanghai: Xuelin chubanshe, 1994.

Chiang Yung-Chen. *Social Engineering and the Social Sciences in China, 1919–1949.* Cambridge, Eng.: Cambridge University Press, 2001.

Clark, Paul. *Chinese Cinema: Culture and Politics Since 1949.* Berkeley: University of California Press, 1987.

Clifford, James, and George Marcus, eds. *Writing Culture.* Berkeley: University of California Press, 1986.

Comaroff, John, and Jean Comaroff. *Ethnography and the Historical Imagination.* Boulder, Colo.: Westview Press, 1992.

"Da guimo de shouji quanguo min'ge" 大規模地收集全國民歌 (Make a full-scale effort to collect folksongs nationwide). Editorial in *Renmin wenxue,* Apr. 14, 1958.

Duara, Prasenjit. *Rescuing History from the Nation: Questioning Narratives of Modern China.* Chicago: University of Chicago Press, 1995.

Fabian, Johannes. *Time and the Other: How Anthropology Makes Its Object.* New York: Columbia University Press, 1983.

Gamble, Sidney D. *Chinese Village Plays from the Ting Hsien Region (Yang Ke Hsuan).* Amsterdam: Philo Press, 1970.

Gladney, Dru. "Representing Nationality in China: Refiguring Majority/Minority Identities." *Journal of Asian Studies* 53, no. 1 (Feb. 1994): 92–123.

Gu Jiegang 顧頡剛. "Shengxian wenhua yu minjian wenhua" 聖賢文化與民間文化 (The culture of the sages and the culture of the people). Transcribed by Zhong Jingwen. *Minsu*, nos. 5, 6 (1928).

———. "Wuge jiaji zixu" 吳歌甲集自序 (Author's preface to the first collection of the songs of Wu). *Geyao zhoukan*, June 28, 1925.

"Guangdong tushen jianji: Liu Sanmei" 廣東土神簡輯: 劉三妹 (A brief introduction to the local gods of Guangdong: Liu Sanmei). *Guangxi ribao*, Mar. 4, 1949.

Gujin tushu jicheng: fangyu huibian zhifang dian 古今圖書集成: 方輿彙編職方典 (Encyclopedia of ancient and contemporary works of geography). Shanghai: Zhonghua shuju, 1934.

Guo Moruo 郭沫若 and Zhou Yang 周揚. "Hongqi geyao bianzhe de hua" 紅旗歌謠編者的話 (Remarks by the editors of *Ballads of the Red Flag*). In *Zhongguo minjian wenxue lunwen xuan, 1949–1979* 中國民間文學論文選 (Selected articles on Chinese folk literature, 1949–79). Shanghai: Shanghai wenyi chubanshe, 1980, 1: 47–49.

Harootunian, Harry. *Overcome by Modernity: History, Culture, and Community in Interwar Japan*. Princeton: Princeton University Press, 2000.

Harrell, Stevan, ed. *Cultural Encounters on China's Ethnic Frontiers*. Seattle: University of Washington Press, 1995.

He Qinglian 何清漣. *Xiandaihua de xianjing: Dangdai Zhongguo de jingji shehui wenti* 現代化的陷阱: 當代中國的經濟社會問題 (The traps of modernization: the socioeconomic problems of contemporary China). Beijing: Jinri Zhongguo chubanshe, 1998.

He Sijing 何思敬. "Minsuxue de wenti" 民俗學的問題 (Issues in the study of folkways). 2 pts. *Minsu*, nos. 1, 3 (1928).

Holm, David. *Art and Ideology in Revolutionary China*. Oxford: Clarendon Press, 1990.

Hostetler, Laura. *Qing Colonial Empire: Ethnography and Cartography in Early Modern China*. Chicago: University of Chicago Press, 2001.

Hu Tiege 胡鐵戈. "*Liu Sanjie* banquan shu shei?" 劉三姐版權屬誰 (Who has the rights to *Liu Sanjie*?). (*Meizhou*) *Wenhui zhoukan*, Jan. 20, 1996, section 3.

Huang Zhigang 黃芝岡. "Yuefeng yu Liu Sanmei chuanshuo" 粵風與劉三妹傳說 (Traditions of the south and the legend of Liu Sanmei). *Zhongshan wenhua jiaoyu jikan* 4, no. 1 (1937): 763–82.

Huang Ziping 黃子平. "Wenxue zhuyuan ji" 文學住院記 (Literature being hospitalized). *Jintian* 1992, no. 4: 157–70.

Hung, Chang-tai. *Going to the People: Chinese Intellectuals and Folk Literature, 1918–1937*. Cambridge, Mass.: Harvard University Press, 1985.

Jia Ji 賈霽. "Guanyu yingpian *Liu Sanjie* taolun de zagan" 關於影片劉三姐討論的雜感 (Miscellaneous thoughts on the comments about the film *Liu Sanjie*). *Dazhong dianying* 1962, no. 8 (Aug.): 20–23.

Jia Zhi 賈之. "Esha minjian wenxue shi 'Sirenbang' fan Makesi zhuyi de yichang fengkuang biaoyan" 扼殺民間文學是 "四人幫" 反馬克思主義的一場瘋狂表演 (What strangled folk literature was the Gang of Four's frenzied anti-Marxist performance). In *Zhongguo minjian wenxue lunwen xuan, 1949–1979* 中國民間文學論文選 (Selected essays on Chinese folk literature, 1949–79). Shanghai: Shanghai wenyi chubanshe, 1980, 1: 246–70.

Johnson, David. "Communication, Class, and Consciousness in Late Imperial China." In *Popular Culture in Late Imperial China*, ed. David Johnson, Andrew Nathan, and Evelyn S. Rawski. Berkeley: University of California Press, 1985, pp. 34–72.

Jones, Andrew. *Yellow Music: Media Culture and Colonial Modernity in the Chinese Jazz Age*. Durham: Duke University Press, 2001.

Kraus, Richard. *Pianos and Politics in China: Middle-Class Ambitions and the Struggle over Western Music*. New York: Oxford University Press, 1989.

Li Jinghan 李景漢 and Zhang Shiwen 張世文, eds. *Dingxian yangge xuan* 定縣秧歌選 (A selection of *yangge* of Ding county). Shanghai: n.p., 1933.

Li Tuo 李陀. "Ding Ling bu jiandan: Mao tizhi xia zhishifenzi zai huayu shengchan zhong de fuza jiaose" 丁玲不簡單: 毛體制下知識分子在話語生產中的複雜角色 (Ding Ling is not so simple: the complex role of intellectuals in the production of discourse under the Maoist system). *Jintian* 1993, no. 3: 222–42.

———. "1985." *Jintian* 1991, no. 3/4: 59–73.

Linke, Uli. "Folklore, Anthropology, and the Government of Social Life." *Comparative Studies in Society and History* 32, no. 1 (1990): 117–48.

Liu Jidian 劉吉典. "Xuexi *Liu Sanjie* de yinyue chuangzuo" 學習劉三姐的音樂創作 (Studying the musical creation of *Liu Sanjie*). *Renmin ribao*, Nov. 19, 1960.

Liu, Lydia H. "*Beijing Sojourners in New York*: Postsocialism and the Question of Ideology in Global Media Culture." *positions: east asia cultures critique* 7, no. 3 (Winter 1999): 763–97.

Liu Sanjie 劉三姐. Feature film. Director Su Li 蘇里. Changchun dianying zhipian chang, 1961.

Liu Sanjie: bachang gewu ju 劉三姐: 八場歌舞劇 (Liu Sanjia: a musical drama in eight acts). Beijing: Zhongguo xiju chubanshe, 1961. For English translation, see Yang Hsien-yi and Gladys Yang.

Liu Sanjie zhuanji 劉三姐專集 (A special collection on Liu Sanjie). Guilin: Guangxi shifan xueyuan, 1979.

Loh, Wai-Fong. "From Romantic Love to Class Struggle: Reflections on the Film *Liu Sanjie*." In *Popular Chinese Literature and Performing Arts in the People's Republic of China, 1949–1979*, ed. Bonnie S. McDougall. Berkeley: University of California Press, 1984, pp. 165–76.

Mayhew, Henry. *London Labour and London Poor, 1851*. New York: Penguin, 1985.

McDougall, Bonnie S., ed. *Popular Chinese Literature and Performing Arts in the People's Republic of China, 1949–1979*. Berkeley: University of California Press, 1984.

Meng Yue 孟悦. "*Baimao nü* yanbian de qishi: jian lun Yan'an wenyi de lishi duo-zhixing" 白毛女演變的啓示: 兼論延安文藝的歷史多質性 (The significance of the evolution of *The White-Haired Girl*: with a discussion of the historical polyvalence of Yan'an's literature and arts). In Tang Xiaobing 唐小兵, ed. *Zai jiedu* 再解讀 (Re-readings). Hong Kong: Oxford University Press, 1993, pp. 219–50.

Ouyang Yuqian 歐陽予倩. "You xin you mei de gewuju *Liu Sanjie*" 又新又美的歌舞劇劉三姐 (The lovely new musical drama *Liu Sanjie*). *Renmin ribao*, Sept. 8, 1960.

Qiao Yu 喬羽. "Ermu yi xin: tan geju *Liu Sanjie*" 耳目一新: 談歌劇劉三姐 (Novel to the eye and to the ear: remarks on the musical drama *Liu Sanjie*). In *Liu Sanjie: bachang gewu ju* 劉三姐: 八場歌舞劇 (*Liu Sanjie*: a musical drama in eight acts). Beijing: Zhongguo xiju chubanshe, 1961.

Qu Dajun 屈大均. *Guandong xinyu* 廣東新語 (New account of Guangdong). 2 vols. Beijing: Zhonghua shuju, 1985.

Rabinow, Paul. *Reflections on Fieldwork in Morocco*. Berkeley: University of California Press, 1977.

Radano, Ronald. "Denoting Difference: The Writing of Slave Spirituals." *Critical Inquiry* 22 (1996): 506–44.

Ren Xuelu 任學路. "Qunian, yingshi guansi buduan" 去年, 影視官司不斷 (Endless film and television lawsuits in the last year). (*Meizhou*) *Wenhui zhoukan*, Mar. 16, 1996.

Rong Zhaozu 容肇祖. "Beida Geyao yanjiu hui ji Fengsu diaocha hui de jingguo" 北大歌謠研究會及風俗調查會的經過 (The history of Folksong Research Society and Folkways Survey Society at Peking University). 2 pts. *Minsu*, no. 15/16 (1928): 1–10; no. 17/18 (1928): 14–31.

Schneider, Laurence A. *Ku Chieh-kang and China's New History: Nationalism and the Quest for Alternative Traditions*. Berkeley: University of California Press, 1971.

Shi Pengxiang 施鵬翔, Lu Sicheng 盧思騁, and Lin Yanmei 林燕梅. "Shengming zhuanli: Xin shiji de quandi yundong" 生命專利: 新世紀的圈地運動 (Patenting bio-products: the enclosure movement of the new millennium). *Shijie*, no. 7 (Apr. 2002): 2–29.

Tamanoi, Mariko Asano. "Gender, Nationalism, and Japanese Native Ethnology." *positions: east asia cultures critique* 4, no. 1 (Spring 1996): 59–86.

Tang Changfeng 唐長風 and Pan Boyu 潘伯羽, eds. *Liu Sanjie* 劉三姐. Illustrated by Deng Erlong 鄧二龍. Beijing: Renmin meishu chubanshe, 1962.

Tang Xiaobing 唐小兵, ed. *Zai jiedu* 再解讀 (Re-readings). Hong Kong: Oxford University Press, 1993.

Tian Ying 天鷹. "Geju *Liu Sanjie* de renwu kehua ji qita" 歌劇劉三姐的人物刻畫及其它 (The portrayal of character in the musical drama *Liu Sanjie*). In *Liu Sanjie zhuanji* 劉三姐專集 (A special collection on *Liu Sanjie*). Guilin: Guangxi shifan xueyuan, 1979, pp. 108–21.

Wang Shizhen 王士禎. "Yuefeng xu jiu" 粵風續九 (Folksongs of Guangxi: a sequel to the Nine Songs). In idem, *Chibei outan* 池北偶談 (Idle talks from the north of the pond), *juan* 16. Shanghai: Wenming shuju, 1936.

Wang Xiangzhi 王象之. "Sanmei shan" 三妹山 (Third-sister mountain). In *Yudi jisheng* 輿地紀勝 (A record of the landscape of the imperial domain), *juan* 98. Shenyingzhai ed., 1849.

Wang Yin 王寅. "He Xuntian: gaixie *Liu Sanjie*" 何訓田: 改寫劉三姐 (He Xuntian: rewriting *Liu Sanjie*). *Nanfang zhoumo*, Mar. 10, 2000.

Webb, Virginia-Lee. "Manipulated Images: European Photographs of Pacific Peoples." In *Prehistories of the Future: The Primitivist Project and the Culture of Modernism*, ed. Elazar Barkan and Ronald Bush. Stanford: Stanford University Press, 1995, pp. 175–201.

Wei Chunwu 韋純武. "Yingpian *Liu Sanjie* de mei zhong buzu" 影片劉三姐的美中不足 (Imperfections in the film *Liu Sanjie*). *Dazhong dianying* 1962, no. 1 (Jan.): 12.

Wei Tongxian 魏同賢. "Minjian wenxue jieshuo" 民間文學界說 (Demarcating folk literature). In *Zhongguo minjian wenxue lunwen xuan, 1949–1979* 中國民間文學論文選 (Selected essays on Chinese folk literature, 1949–79). Shanghai: Shanghai wenyi chubanshe, 1980, 1: 331–58.

Wong, Isabel K. F. "*Geming geju*: Songs for the Education of the Masses." In *Popular Chinese Literature and Performing Arts in the People's Republic of China, 1949–1979*, ed. Bonnie S. McDougall. Berkeley: University of California Press, 1984, pp. 112–43.

Wu Jinnan 伍晉南. "Guanyu *Liu Sanjie* de chuangzuo" 關於劉三姐的創作 (On the creation of *Liu Sanjie*). In *Liu Sanjie zhuanji* 劉三姐專集 (A special collection on *Liu Sanjie*). Guilin: Guangxi shifan xueyuan, 1979, pp. 4–12.

Xiao Zhuo 蕭拙. "Liu Sanmei yu Lingnan min'ge" 劉三妹與嶺南民歌 (Liu Sanmei and Lingnan folksongs). *Yangcheng wanbao*, Jan. 1, 1958.

Xu Jingguo 徐敬國. "Bingmeiyou ba *Liu Sanjie* xiandai hua" 並沒有把劉三姐現代化 (*Liu Sanjie* has not been modernized). *Dazhong dianying* 1962, no. 1 (Jan.): 11.

Yang Hsien-yi and Gladys Yang, trans. *Third Sister Liu: An Opera in Eight Scenes*. Beijing: Foreign Languages Press, 1962.

Yudi jisheng 輿地紀勝 (A record of the landscape of the imperial domain). Shenyingzhai ed., 1849.

Yu Min 愚民. "Shan'ge yuanshi de chuanshuo ji qita" 山歌原始的傳說及其他 (The primitive origins of the mountain song and related matters). *Minsu*, no. 13/14 (1928): 42–46.

Zhang Erhe 張爾翮. "Liu Sanmei gexian zhuan" 三妹歌仙傳 (Tale of the song immortal Liu Sanmei). In *Gujin tushu jicheng: fangyu huibian zhifang dian* 古今圖書集成: 方與彙編職方典 (Encyclopedia of ancient and contemporary works of geography). Shanghai: Zhonghua shuju, 1934, *juan* 144.

Zhao Yiheng 趙毅衡. "Cunli de Guo Moruo: du *Hongqi geyao*" 村裏的郭沫若: 讀紅旗歌謠 (Guo Moruo in the village: Reading the *Ballads of the Red Flag*). *Jintian* 1992, no. 2: 190–200.

Zheng Tianjian 鄭天健. "Guanyu *Liu Sanjie* de chuangzuo" 關於劉三姐的創作 (On the creation of *Liu Sanjie*). In *Liu Sanjie: bachang gewu ju* 劉三姐: 八場歌舞劇 (*Liu Sanjie*: a musical drama in eight acts). Beijing: Zhongguo xiju chubanshe, 1961.

Zhong Jingwen 鍾敬文. "Ji ze guanyu Liu Sanmei gushi ziliao" 幾則關於劉三妹故事資料 (Several items concerning the story of Liu Sanmei). *Minsu zhoukan*, no. 19/20 (Aug. 1928): 27–31.

———. *Minjian wenyi conghua* 民間文藝叢話 (Collected lectures on folk and art). Guangzhou: Dongsheng yinwuju, 1928.

———. *Zhong Jingwen minjian wenxue lunji* 鍾敬文民間文學論集 (Essays on folk literature by Zhong Jingwen). 2 vols. Shanghai: Shanghai wenyi chubanshe, 1982.

Reference Matter

Index

A Yi, 584

Actors: circulation among elite, 133, 139, 150–51; gifts of, 146–49, 151; poems in tribute to, 134, 168n8; private troupes, 133, 138, 140, 143–44, 173n48; relationships with elite, 137, 142–44, 168–69n11, 169n12, 173–74n49; seen as feminized, 142–43, 172–73n42; sex work expected of, 142; social status, 134, 142, 144; terms for, 173n48. See also Xu Ziyun

Adam, James R., 561

Advertisements, cigarette, 431–32

American Folklore Society, 565

Analects, 197–98, 199

Anderson, Benedict, 5, 18, 209

An Guo shrine, 73

Animals: accounts of strange, 349, 351, 358, 365–66, 374, 376–77; dragons, 366–67; foxes, 360–61. See also Flora and fauna; Snakes

Anthology of Ming Poetry (Liechao shiji; Qian Qianyi), 96

Anthropology, 565–66. See also Ethnography

Antiquarianism, 36–39, 41, 52, 58

Appadurai, Arjun, 240

As if Speaking Face to Face (Ru mian tan; Zhong Xing), 248, 249

Bai Juyi, 77–78, 428

Bai, Qianshen, 33, 105, 208

Baimao nü (The white-haired girl), 575

Baimei tu (illustrated albums of courtesans), 400–403, 411, 418–22, 432–34

Bakhtin, Mikhail, 194, 209

Banqiao zaji (Yu Huai), 102

Baoshu Pagoda, 499

Barr, Allan, 106

Barthes, Roland, 29–30, 66n31, 460

Bausinger, Hermann, 8–9, 564

Beauty: portraits of beautiful women (meiren), 400–404 passim, 418–19, 425, 426, 430, 435; urban beauty images, 404, 422, 429, 431–35

Beijing: Brick Pagoda Alley, 530; Palace Museum, 53, 58

Beijing University: folksong campaign, 556, 561–62, 593–94n5; Institute of National Learning, 557

Chen Wenshu, 275, 288, 294, 295

Chen Xiang, 461

Chen Xixiang, 563

Chen Yuting, 138

Chen Zhenhui, 138–39

Chenglan, see Imperial inspection

Chidu shuangyu, see Paired Carp: Correspondence

China Theater Publishing House, 572

Chinese Communist Party, 570–72. *See also* Communism

Chinese culture: Christianity and, 560–61; Communism and, 560–61; Lu Xun on, 525–26; tensions between tradition and Western culture, 518. *See also* Confucianism

Chinese Polytechnical Institution, 318, 322

Chinese Recorder, 320–21, 323–24, 326

Chinese Scientific Book Depot, 318, 322

Chongding xinshang pian (Recompiled texts on conoisseurship; Pan Zhiheng), 133

Chongxiu Taiwan fuzhi, see New Revised Taiwan Gazetteer

Christianity: in China, 560; missionaries, 7, 336n27, 561

Chuanqi (southern drama): ghost writing episodes, 82; illustrations, 352; included in miscellanies, 193; interest of literati in, 499; publication in *Dianshizhai huabao* supplements, 349, 363–64

Chuci (Songs of the south), 255

"Chunhua ge tie," 31–33, 63n6

Cigarette advertisements, 431–32

Cihua genre, 187–88, 220n4. *See also Jin Ping Mei cihua*

Circuses: comparison to miscellanies, 217; in Europe, 375; in Shanghai, 371

Civilizing projects, 560–61

Clark, Paul, 577

Classic Poetry by Renowned Women (*Mingyuan shiwei*; Wang Duanshu), 89–90, 98, 115n51, 119–20n85, 120–21n91, 296

Classified Materia Medica (*Bencao gangmu*; Li Shizhen), 466

Clunas, Craig, 7, 453, 460–61, 471

Collectanea of Contemporary Writings, A (*Zhaodai congshu guangbian*; Yang Fuji), 101, 107

Collection of Writings by and About Women, A, see Furenji

Colonialism, 564, 565, 566

Communism: civilizing project, 560–61; ethnic minorities and, 568, 570; folk populism, 570; literary policies, 570–72. *See also* Official popular culture

Comprehensive Gazetteer of the Great Qing Realm (*Da Qing yitongzhi*), 453–54

Confucianism: bias against the aberrant, 505; civilizing project, 560–61; classics engraved on steles, 36, 40; of Hou Zhi, 278–79; in *Jin Ping Mei cihua*, 197–98, 225–26n30; in verses used in drinking games, 194, 199

Consort Huang's Pagoda (Huangfeita), 492. *See also* Leifeng Pagoda

Contracts, 253

Conversations of Master Zhu, Topically Arranged (*Zhuzi yulei*), 81

Copyright: laws, 554; *Liu Sanjie* lawsuit, 553, 554, 586–87

Countless Arias for an Eternal Spring (*Wanqu changchun*), 250

Courtesans: competitions, 400; cult of, 167n7; decline of entertainment culture, 432; Du Mu and, 137; fictional

Vietnam, accounts of strange occur-
rences in, 361–63
Village operas, 528–29
Vimala Varaprabha, 491
Vinograd, Richard, 421
Vision, *see* Looking
Vitale, Guido, 561–62, 595*n*21
Vitiello, Giovanni, 136
Vittinghoff, Natascha, 342
Voltaire, 519

Wagner, Rudolf, 356
Walls, writing on, 11, 74, 85, 110*n*11. See
also *Tibishi* (poems written on
walls)
Wanbao quanshu (A book of myriad
treasures), 241
Wang Anyi, 586, 601*n*84
Wang Danian, 94, 96–97
Wang Duan, 288, 293–94, 295, 298
Wang Duanshu, *Classic Poetry by Re-
nowned Women* (*Mingyuan shiwei*),
89–90, 98, 115*n*51, 119–20*n*85, 120–
21*n*91, 296
Wang Ermin, 342, 358, 372
Wang Fu, 64*n*17
Wang Guowei, 517
Wang Mang, 38
Wang Qiong, 278, 279, 288, 293, 298
Wang Shilu: contributions to *Furenji*,
100, 107; *Lamp Oil Collection* (*Ranzhi
ji*), 99–100, 107, 108, 120–21*n*91;
poems in praise of Xu Ziyun, 146,
155; poems written on walls, 86, 87;
poetry circle, 155; on *tibishi*, 98–99
Wang Shizhen: career, 134; contributions to *Furenji*, 100; poems in praise
of Xu Ziyun, 133, 146, 154–55;
poems written on walls, 86, 87; poetry transcribed by, 576; *tibishi* dis-

covered by, 97, 98–99; *Yuefeng xu jiu*,
589–90
Wang Suyin, 98–99
Wang Tao, 322, 323, 331, 349, 363–64
Wang Wensun, 54
Wang Xiqi, 452
Wang Xizhi, 33
Wang Yu, 278, 288
Wang Yuanqi, 66*n*34
Wang Zhaoyuan, 294, 295
Wang Zhexiang, 418–19
Wang Zijia, 134, 144, 168*n*8, 173–74*n*49
Wanguo gongbao (The review of the
times), 324, 326
Wanjin jiaoli (Ten thousand charms
and beauties), 192–93
Wanjin qinglin, 191
Weekly Review, 557
Wei Yingwu, 78–79, 81
Wei Zhongxian, 138, 139
Westerners: attitudes toward strange-
ness, 364–71; educators, 368; skepti-
cism about supernatural, 364–65,
367–68, 371, 377; treatment of
corpses, 367–68. See also Foreigners;
Shanghai
Western Marchmount Hua Temple,
37, 41, 45. See also Stele of Mount
Hua
West Lake, 494, 496–97, 505–6. See
also Leifeng Pagoda; Ten Views of
West Lake
West Lake Gazetteer, 516
White Snake Woman: association
with Leifeng Pagoda, 499–504, 512,
516–29 passim; in dramas, 509; Lu
Xun's fascination with story, 527,
530, 532; similarities to Western
folklore, 522, 530; stories of, 496–97,
499, 502, 505

Harvard-Yenching Institute Monograph Series
(titles now in print)